Handyman
In~Your~Pocket

Compiled by
Richard A. Young
Thomas J. Glover

Sequoia Publishing, Inc.
Littleton, Colorado, U.S.A

This book belongs to:

_____

_____

_____

_____

_____

_____

Copyright 2001- 2002 by Thomas J. Glover and Sequoia Publishing Inc.

1st Edition, 5th Printing - September 2002

If you find errors or have suggestions about this book, please notify:

Sequoia Publishing, Inc.
Department 101
P.O. Box 620820
Littleton, Colorado 80162
(303) 932-1400
www.sequoiapublishing.com

Printed in the U.S.A.

Library of Congress Catalog Card Number 2001 131003

ISBN 1-885071-29-9

Publisher's Note

Sequoia Publishing has made a serious effort to provide accurate information in this book. However, the probability exists that there are errors and misprints, and that variations in data values may also occur depending on field conditions. Information included in this book should only be considered as a general guide and Sequoia Publishing, Inc. does not represent the information as being exact.

The publishers would appreciate being notified of any errors, omissions, or misprints which may occur in this book. Your suggestions for future editions would also be greatly appreciated. See Sequoia address and phone numbers on the copyright page.

The information in this manual was collected from numerous sources and if not properly acknowledged, Sequoia would like to express its appreciation for those contributions.

Errors and omissions which have been identified in any Sequoia publications have been compiled into an errata sheet. Errata sheets are available on Sequoia's web site at www.sequoiapublishing.com. (Once on the web site, click "site map" on the main menu bar and then look for "Errata sheets.")

Acknowledgments

The creation of a book is a very complex and time consuming process and it involves many more people than the authors. **Special thanks go to the following people for their monumental efforts in helping to make this book a reality:**

Mary Miller - Page Layout and Graphics Artist
Millie Young - Cover Art and Editing
Trish Glover - Graphics Artist
Mary Glover - Photographer
Jake Williams - Portrait Artist

Richard A. Young - Author
Thomas J. Glover - Author

About the Authors

Thomas J. Glover

Tom is the President of Sequoia Publishing, Inc. and founded the company in March 1989. He holds a bachelor of science degree from New Mexico State University, a Masters Degree in Geology from the University of Texas and is a registered AAPG Geologist. He has a broad background in engineering, computers and electronics and has been a small business entrepreneur since 1980. Tom is the author of Sequoia's best-selling, flagship product *Pocket Ref*, and has co-authored other books such as *Pocket PCRef*, *TechRef*, and *DeskRef*.

Richard A. Young

Richard is an author and civil engineer. He holds a bachelor of science degree from the University of Southwestern Louisiana (now University of Louisiana at Lafayette), a master of science degree from the University of California at Berkeley, and is a registered professional engineer. He worked as a civil engineer with the Corps of Engineers in New Orleans from 1968 to 1979 and as a civil engineer/research engineer with the Bureau of Reclamation in Denver from 1980 to 1994. Then he began work as an author/researcher/compiler for Blue Willow, Inc., co-authoring *Measure for Measure*, and subsequently Sequoia Publishing, co-authoring this book.

Table of Contents

Introduction (Publishers Note, Authors, Products)............2

Anchors..7

Belts, Pulleys, and Gears....................................41

Bolts and Threads...55

Carpentry and Construction 91

Drafting Symbols...185

Electrical 197

General Science 267

Glues, Paints and Solvent...281

Math...299

Nails, Spikes and Staples 357

Pipe and Fittings 385

Pumps and Tanks..519

Rope, Cable, and Chain..551

Screws..575

Sheet Metal, Plate and Wire 581

Tools 591

Water and Air 631

Welding 671

Weights and Properties of Materials 681

Conversion Factors...691

Index 747

More Sequoia Products

Shirt Pocket Reference Books

Bell's Guide
  A comprehensive, pocket-sized real estate handbook for everyone

How To Ski the Blues and Blacks (Without Getting Black and Blue) - Expert ski instruction + nationwide ski area directory

Pocket Ref - BEST SELLER! Everything you ever wanted to know - and then some!

Pocket Partner - Comprehensive law enforcement pocket reference

Pocket PCRef - Comprehensive PC computer reference

WinRef 98-95 In~Your~Pocket - A shirt pocket-sized guide to BOTH Windows 98 and 95!

Handbooks

DeskRef - The desktop version of PocketRef

Measure for Measure - THE conversion factor handbook!

Seldovia, Alaska - An historical portrait of Seldovia, Alaska

TechRef - Pocket PCRef and MORE in a desktop size!

Troubleshooting Your Contracting Business to Cause Success - Secrets for running a successful contracting business

Software

MegaRef, Version 2 - IBM/PC and compatibles software version of PocketRef.

Anchors

Photo Index of Anchors 8
Anchors for Concrete, Hollow Concrete Block, and Brick 10
Anchors for Gypsum Wallboard or Hollow Concrete Block 15
Anchors for Threaded Fasteners in Concrete 18
Epoxy Adhesive Anchors in Concrete 24
Low Velocity, Powder Actuated Fasteners....................................32
Torque-Controlled Self-Contained Anchors for Concrete..............34

Definitions used in the Anchors Chapter

Allowable tension load - The maximum safe load that can be applied before the anchor pulls out of the hole.

Anchor embedment - The minimum depth of the anchors drill hole. In solid concrete, the hole is deeper than the embedment by 50% of the diameter of the anchor. For example, for a ½" diameter anchor:
hole depth=anchor length(2")+½ anchor diameter (½ of .5")=2.25"

Pound-force per square inch - Commonly called "psi", this unit refers to the compressive strength of the concrete.

Anchors for Concrete, Hollow Concrete Block and Brick

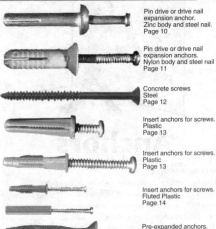

Pin drive or drive nail
expansion anchor.
Zinc body and steel nail.
Page 10

Pin drive or drive nail
expansion anchors.
Nylon body and steel nail
Page 11

Concrete screws
Steel
Page 12

Insert anchors for screws.
Plastic
Page 13

Insert anchors for screws.
Plastic
Page 13

Insert anchors for screws.
Fluted Plastic
Page 14

Pre-expanded anchors.
Steel
Page 14

Anchors for Gypsum Wallboard or Hollow Concrete Block

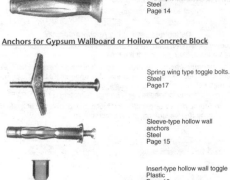

Spring wing type toggle bolts.
Steel
Page 17

Sleeve-type hollow wall
anchors
Steel
Page 15

Insert-type hollow wall toggle
Plastic
Page 16

Anchors for Gypsum Wallboard or Hollow Concrete Block (cont.)

Self-drilling gypsum wallboard anchors.
Zinc or plastic body
Page 17

Anchors for Threaded Fasteners in Concrete

Drop-in tool-set expansion sleeve anchor
Steel
Page 18

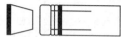

Drop-in bottom plug expansion sleeve anchor. Steel: Page 21

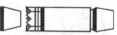

Self-drilling, bottom plug expansion sleeve anchor. Steel: Page 21

Drop-in single acting expansion sheild anchor. Steel: Page 19

Drop-in double acting expansion shield anchor. Steel: Page 20

Anchors for Lag Screws

Drop-in lag shield anchor
Zinc alloy body
Pages 22

Low Velocity Powder Actuated Fasteners for Concrete and Steel

Low velocity anchor driven into concrete
Plastic guide, steel nail
Page 32

Torque-Controlled, Self-Contained Anchors for Concrete

Expansion wedge anchor
Carbon steel
Page 34

Expansion sleeve anchor
Steel
Page 37

Anchors for Concrete, Hollow Concrete Block and Brick

Pin Drive or Drive Nail Expansion Anchors, ZINC Body and Steel Nail

Anchor Diameter (Inch)	Drill Hole Diameter (Inch)	Manufacturer[1]	Anchor Embedment In Drill Hole	Allowable Tension Loads in Pounds For Anchors Embedded In					
				Concrete with the Following Compressive Strengths in lb/in²				ASTM C-90 Hollow Block	Solid Red Brick
				2000	3000	4000	6000		
3/16	3/16	Star	1/2		125			225	
		Hilti	5/8					68	115
		Power F. (Rawl)	3/4			125	145		
1/4	1/4	M.K.T. (Gunnebo)	3/4	115	188				
			1		250				
			1-1/4		275				
			1-3/4		350				
		Hilti	3/4	169				318	223
			1	199				386	305
		Power F. (Rawl)	5/8	120		150	160		
			3/4	193		205	223		
			7/8	223		240	265		198
			1-1/8	245		288	308	120	205
			1-3/8	288		325	341	148	238
			1-1/2					200	254
			1-7/8					241	
		Star	3/4		150				
			1		188				
			1-1/4		240				
			1-1/2		275				
			2		288				

Pin Drive or Drive Nail Expansion Anchors, NYLON Body and Steel Nail

Anchor Diameter (inch)	Hole Diameter (inch)	Manufacturer[1]	Anchor Embedment in Drill Hole (inch)	Allowable Tension Loads[2] in Pounds For Anchors Embedded In					
				Concrete With the Following Compressive Strengths in Pound-force per Square Inch				ASTM C-90 Hollow Block	Solid Red Brick
				2000	3000	4000	6000		
3/16	3/16	M.K.T.(Gunnebo)	3/4	-	71	-	-	-	-
			1	-	93	-	-	-	-
			1-1/2	-	84	-	-	-	-
		Power F. (Rawl)	3/4	45	-	49	50	43	39
			1	50	-	55	58	45	43
		Star	3/4	-	50	-	-	-	-
			1	-	56	-	-	-	-
			1-1/2	-	66	-	-	-	-
1/4	1/4	M.K.T.(Gunnebo)	3/4	-	65	-	-	-	-
			1	-	80	-	-	-	-
			1-1/2	-	81	-	-	-	-
		Power F. (Rawl)	3/4	55	-	60	61	40	50
			1-1/4	58	-	63	65	43	55
			1-1/2	60	-	68	70	45	60
			2	64	-	71	75	50	63
		Star	3/4	-	50	-	-	-	-
			1	-	53	-	-	-	-
			1-1/2	-	63	-	-	-	-
			2	-	66	-	-	-	-

Concrete Screws, Steel

Anchor Diameter (inch)	Drill Hole Diameter (inch)	Manufacturer [1]	Anchor Embedment in Drill Hole (inch)	Allowable Tension Loads [2] in Pounds For Anchors Embedded In:					
				Concrete With the Following Compressive Strengths in Pound-force per Square Inch				ASTM C-90 Hollow Block	Solid Red Brick
				2000	3000	4000	6000		
3/16	5/32	Black & Decker	1	-	108	-	-	49	-
			1-1/4	-	189	-	-	95	-
			1-1/2	-	210	-	-	146	-
			1-3/4	-	279	-	-	190	-
		ITW Ramset	1	-	85	-	-	52	-
			1-1/4	-	145	-	-	89	-
			1-1/2	-	216	-	-	117	-
			1-3/4	-	265	-	-	137	-
		Power F. (Rawl)	1	165	-	183	255	160	155
			1-1/4	218	-	265	313	190	268
			1-1/2	260	-	303	398	248	305
			1-3/4	330	-	380	490	303	333
		Star	1-1/4	-	-	278	-	105	-
1/4	3/16	Black & Decker	1	-	224	-	-	95	-
			1-1/4	-	271	-	-	160	-
			1-1/2	-	455	-	-	179	-
			1-3/4	-	562	-	-	296	-
		ITW Ramset	1	-	195	-	-	102	-
			1-1/4	-	285	-	-	154	-
			1-1/2	-	384	-	-	213	-
			1-3/4	-	465	-	-	246	-
		Power F. (Rawl)	1	190	-	233	285	180	235

Concrete Screws, Steel (cont.)

Anchor Diameter (inch)	Drill Hole Diameter (inch)	Manufacturer[1]	Anchor Embedment in Drill Hole (inch)	Allowable Tension Loads[2] in Pounds For Anchors Embedded In:					
				Concrete With the Following Compressive Strengths in lbf/in[2]				ASTM C-90 Hollow Block	Solid Red Brick
				2000	3000	4000	6000		
1/4	3/16	Rawl	1-1/4	273	-	385	423	220	290
			1-1/2	380	-	463	553	273	330
			1-3/4	488	-	583	685	323	355
		Star	1-1/4	-	-	419	-	140	-

Insert Anchors For Screws, Plastic

Anchor Size (inch)	Drill Hole Diameter (inch)	Manufacturer[1]	Anchor Embedment in Drill Hole (inch)	Allowable Tension Loads[2] in Pounds For Anchors Embedded In:					
				Concrete With the Following Compressive Strengths in lbf/in[2]				ASTM C-90 Hollow Block	Solid Red Brick
				2000	4000	4500	6000		
#6 - #8 x 3/4	3/16	Power F. (Rawl)	3/4	46	53	-	56	45	25
		Star		-	-	-	-	118	-
#8 - #10 x 7/8	3/16	Power F. (Rawl)	7/8	75	110	-	130	73	40
		Star		-	-	-	-	132	-
#8 x 1	3/16	Hilti	1	-	-	23	-	-	-
#10 x 1	3/16	Hilti	1	-	-	49	-	-	-
#10 - #12 x 1	1/4	Power F. (Rawl)	1	88	138	-	160	88	70
		Star		-	-	-	-	294	-
#14 x 1-1/2	5/16	Hilti	1-1/2	-	-	101	-	-	-
#14 x #16 x 1-1/2	5/16	Power F. (Rawl)	1-1/2	210	210	-	225	210	220
		Star		-	-	-	-	323	-

Insert Anchors for Screws, Fluted Plastic

Anchor Size (inch)	Drill Hole Diameter (inch)	Manufacturer[1]	Anchor Embedment in Drill Hole (inch)	Allowable Tension Loads [2] in Pounds For Anchors Embedded In Concrete With the Following Compressive Strengths in pound-force per square inch		
				2000	4000	6000
#4-#6	3/16		3/4	30	35	40
#7-#9	7/32		7/8	55	59	63
#10-#12	1/4		1	110	123	135
		Power F. (Rawl)	1-1/4	123	135	148
			1-1/2	130	153	170
			1	130	143	155
#14	5/16		1-1/2	135	154	173

Pre-Expanded Anchors, Steel

Anchor Size (inch)	Drill Hole Diameter (inch)	Manufacturer[1]	Anchor Embedment in Drill Hole (inch)	Allowable Tension Loads [2] in Pounds For Anchors Embedded In Concrete With the Following Compressive Strengths in pound-force per square inch		
				2000	3000	4000	6000
3/16	3/16	Power F. (Rawl)	7/8	219	-	338	338
1/4	1/4	Power F. (Rawl)	1-1/8	413	-	550	550
		M.K.T.(Gunnebo)			503		
5/16	5/16	Power F. (Rawl)	1-3/8	640	-	975	975
3/8	3/8	Power F. (Rawl)	1-7/8	710	-	1,325	1,325
1/2	1/2	Power F. (Rawl)	2-58	800	-	1,550	1,550

(1) Manufacturers: M.K.Y (Gunnebo Fastening Corp), Lonoke, AR; ITW Ramset/Red Head, Wood Dale, IL; Hilti Inc., Tulsa, OK; Power Fasteners (Rawl), New York, New Rochelle, NY; Star Fasteners, Mountainville, NY

(2) A factor of safety of 4 has been applied to obtain Allowable Tension Loads. While these loads are typical for these anchors, they should be used only as a guide to the true capacity of a given anchor. Check manufacturer literature for additional information.

Anchors for Gypsum Wallboard or Hollow Concrete Block

Sleeve-Type Hollow Wall Anchors, Steel

Manufacturer[1]	Anchor Size Body Diameter (inch)	Body Length	Drill Hole (inch)	Allowable Tension Loads[2] (pound-force) Gypsum Wallboard — Thickness (inch)									ASTM C-90 Hollow Concrete Block
				1/4	3/8	1/2	5/8	3/4	1	1-1/8	1-1/4	1-3/4	1-1/2
Power F. (Rawl)	1/8		5/16	-	20	38	40	43	-	-	-	-	40
	3/16		3/8	-	23	44	48	53	-	-	-	-	48
	1/4		7/16	-	24	50	55	61	-	-	-	-	55
M.K.T.(Gunnebo)	1/8	short	5/16	-	-	30	-	-	-	-	-	-	-
		long	5/16	-	-	-	43	-	-	-	-	-	-
		extra long	5/16	-	-	-	-	-	-	-	87	-	-
	3/16	short	3/8	-	-	-	45	-	-	-	-	-	-
		long	3/8	-	-	-	-	-	-	87	-	-	-
		extra long	3/8	-	-	-	-	-	-	-	100	-	-
	1/4	short	1/2	-	-	-	47	-	-	-	-	-	-
		long	1/2	-	-	-	-	-	-	55	-	-	-
		extra long	1/2	-	-	-	-	-	-	-	67	-	-
Star	1/8	extra short	1/4	10	-	-	-	-	-	-	-	-	-
		short	1/4	-	18	18	-	-	-	-	-	-	-
		long	1/4	-	-	-	19	16	15	-	-	-	-
		extra long	1/4	-	-	-	-	-	-	-	-	16	-
	3/16	short	5/16	-	24	24	-	-	-	-	-	-	-
		long	3/8	-	-	-	21	17	17	-	-	-	-
		extra long	3/8	-	-	-	-	-	-	-	20	16	-
	1/4	short	7/16	-	12	12	16	15	13	-	-	-	-
		long	7/16	-	-	-	17	15	-	-	15	16	-
		extra long	1/2	-	-	-	-	-	-	-	15	10	-

Insert-Type Hollow Wall Toggle, Plastic

Manufacturer [1]	Drill Hole Diameter (inch)	Recommended Screw Size	Anchor Size	Allowable Tension Loads [2] (pound-force)						
				Gypsum Wallboard — Thickness (inch)						ASTM C-90 Hollow Concrete Block
				1/8	3/8	1/2	5/8	3/4	1	1-1/2
Power F. (Rawl)	5/16	# 6 to 12	mini	30	-	-	-	-	-	55
			short	-	34	-	-	-	-	70
			medium	-	-	-	-	-	-	88
			long	-	-	38	-	-	-	100
			extra long	-	-	-	43	45	-	113
			super long	-	-	-	-	-	55	40
Hilti	3/8	# 8 to 10	2	-	-	20	-	-	-	40
			3	-	-	25	-	-	-	50
			3	-	-	-	35	-	-	-
			4	-	-	-	-	-	-	70
Star	5/16	# 8	short	-	42	-	-	-	-	-
	5/16	# 8	long	-	-	30	-	-	-	-
		# 10	extra long	-	-	58	-	-	-	-
		# 8	extra long	-	-	-	50	-	-	-
		# 10	extra long	-	-	-	79	-	-	-
		# 14	extra long	-	-	-	83	-	-	-

(1) Manufacturers: M.K.Y. (Gunnebo Fastening Corp) Lonoke, AR; ITW Ramset/Red Head, Wood Dale, IL; Hilti Inc., Tulsa, OK; Power Fasteners (Rawl), New York, New Rochelle, NY; Star Fasteners, Mountainville, NY

(2) A factor of safety of 4 has been applied to obtain Allowable Tension Loads. These loads are typical for these anchors and should be used only as guides to the true capacity of a given anchor. Check manufacturer literature for additional information.

Self-Drilling Gypsum Wallboard Anchors, Zinc or Plastic

Manufacturer[1]	Material in Anchor Body	Anchor Size	Screw Size	Allowable Tension Loads[2] (pound-force) Gypsum Wallboard Thickness (inch)			
				3/8	1/2	5/8	3/4
Power F. (Rawl)	Plastic	Regular	# 6 to # 8	13	16	20	21
	Plastic	Junior	# 6 to # 8	11	14	18	19
M.K.T.(Gunnebo)	Zinc	Regular	# 6 to # 8	13	16	20	21
	Plastic	Regular	# 8 to # 10	17	22	31	-
Hilti	Zinc	Regular	# 8 to # 10	15	15	31	-
	Zinc	Regular	# 6 to # 8	15	15	20	-
Star	Plastic	Regular	# 6 to # 8	6	10	21	-
	Plastic	Regular	# 8	6	10	21	-
	Zinc	Regular	# 8	6	10	21	-

Spring Wing Type Toggle Bolts, Steel (* below = Factor of safety not stated by manufacturer.)

Manufacturer[1]	Anchor Diameter (inch)	Drill Hole Diameter (inch)	Wing Diameter (inch)	Allowable Tension Loads[2] (pound-force) Gypsum Wallboard Thickness (inch)				ASTM C-90 Hollow Concrete Block
				3/8	1/2	5/8	3/4	1-1/2
Power F. (Rawl)	1/8	3/8	1-1/16	38	50	63	73	78
	3/16	1/2	1-3/8	43	61	79	96	108
	1/4	5/8	1-1/2	71	78	88	105	208
	5/16	7/8	2-1/8	80	83	91	106	268
	3/8	7/8	2-1/8	81	85	96	113	346
	1/2	1-1/4	3	85	109	130	139	638
M.K.T.(Gunnebo)	1/8	3/8	1-1/16	-	109 *	-	-	-
	3/16	1/2	1-3/8	-	135 *	-	-	-
	1/4	5/8	1-1/2	-	145 *	-	-	-
	5/16	7/8	2-1/8	-	160 *	-	-	-
	3/8	7/8	2-1/8	-	160 *	-	-	-
	1/2	1-1/4	3	-	185 *	-	-	-

Anchors for Threaded Fasteners in Concrete

Part 1: For Bolts and Screws

Drop-In Tool-Set Expansion SLEEVE Anchor, Steel

Anchor Size (inch)	Bolt Size (inch)	Drill Hole Diameter (inch)	Embedment Depth (inch)	Manufacturer[1]	Allowable Tension Loads[2] in Pound-force For Anchors Embedded in Concrete With the Following Compressive Strengths in Pound-force per Square Inch		
					2000	4000	6000
1/4	1/4	3/8	1	M.K.T.(Gunnebo)	513	526	-
				Hilti	-	563	-
				ITW Ramset	-	801	-
				Star	-	575	-
3/8	3/8	1/2	1-1/4	Power F. (Rawl)	488	850	970
			1-9/16	M.K.T.(Gunnebo)	989	1,206	-
				Hilti	-	1,236	-
			1-5/8	Star	-	1,025	-
			1-7/8	ITW Ramset	-	1,588	-
				Power F. (Rawl)	808	1,600	1,435
1/2	1/2	5/8	2	M.K.T.(Gunnebo)	1,328	1,850	-
				Hilti	-	1,688	-
				ITW Ramset	-	2,136	-
				Star	-	1,500	-
5/8	5/8	27/32	2-3/8	Power F. (Rawl)	1,025	2,250	2,665
			2-9/16	Hilti	-	2,424	-
		7/8	2-1/2	M.K.T.(Gunnebo)	1,850	1,992	-
				ITW Ramset	-	3,805	-
				Star	-	2,075	-
			3	Power F. (Rawl)	1,418	2,615	2,808

Drop-In Tool-Set Expansion SLEEVE Anchor, Steel (cont.)

Anchor Size (inch)	Bolt Size (inch)	Drill Hole Diameter (inch)	Embedment Depth (inch)	Manufacturer[1]	Allowable Tension Loads[2] in Pound-force For Anchors Embedded in Concrete With the Following Compressive Strengths in lbf/in²			
					2000	3000	4000	6000
3/4	3/4	1	3-3/16	M.K.T.(Gunnebo)	3,075		4,005	-
				Hilti	-		4,009	-
				ITW Ramset	-		4,314	-
				Star	-		3,400	-
			3-1/2	Power F. (Rawl)	2,233		3,950	4,095

Drop-In Single-Acting Expansion SHIELD Anchor, Steel

Anchor Size (inch)	Bolt Size (inch)	Drill Hole Diameter (inch)	Embedment Depth (inch)	Manufacturer[1]	2,000	3,000	4,000	6,000
1/4	1/4	1/2	1-1/4	M.K.T.(Gunnebo)	-	580	-	-
			1-3/8	M.K.T.(Gunnebo)	-	750	-	-
				Power F. (Rawl)	263	-	593	685
				Star	-	588	-	-
5/16	5/16	9/16	1-1/2	M.K.T.(Gunnebo)	-	650	-	-
		5/8	1-3/8	M.K.T.(Gunnebo)	-	825	-	-
				Power F. (Rawl)	418	-	635	745
3/8	3/8	11/16	1-3/4	M.K.T.(Gunnebo)	-	910	-	-
		3/4		Power F. (Rawl)	495	-	865	1,005
			2-3/8	M.K.T.(Gunnebo)	-	1,500	-	-
1/2	1/2	7/8	2-1/16	M.K.T.(Gunnebo)	-	1,275	-	-
			2-1/4	M.K.T.(Gunnebo)	-	2,375	-	-
				M.K.T.(Gunnebo)	-	3,375	-	-
				Star	-	-	-	-
				Power F. (Rawl)	891	-	1,460	1,520
5/8	5/8	1	2-5/8	M.K.T.(Gunnebo)	-	1,455	-	-
				Power F. (Rawl)	1,473	-	2,438	2,625
3/4	3/4	1-1/8	2-3/4	M.K.T.(Gunnebo)	-	3,750	-	-
		1-1/4	3	M.K.T.(Gunnebo)	-	3,375	-	-
				Power F. (Rawl)	1,895	-	3,130	3,260

Drop-In Double-Acting Expansion SHIELD Anchor, Steel

Anchor Size (inch)	Bolt Size (inch)	Drill Hole Diameter (inch)	Embedment Depth (inch)	Manufacturer[1]	Allowable Tension Loads[2] in Pound-force For Anchors Embedded in Concrete With the Following Compressive Strengths in lbf/in²				
					2000	3000	4000	5000	6000
1/4	1/4	1/2	1-3/8	Power F. (Raw)	458	-	-	-	788
			1-1/2	M.K.T. (Gunnebo)	-	875	585	-	-
			1-5/8	Star	-	-	-	556	-
5/16	5/16	5/8	1-5/8	Power F. (Raw)	543	-	-	-	855
			1-7/8	M.K.T. (Gunnebo)	-	925	740	-	-
		3/4	2-1/8	Star	-	-	-	700	-
3/8	3/8	3/4	2	Power F. (Raw)	810	-	-	-	1,465
			2-1/8	M.K.T. (Gunnebo)	-	1,875	1,245	-	-
			2-1/2	Star	-	-	-	1,025	-
1/2	1/2	7/8	2-1/8	Power F. (Raw)	1,643	-	-	-	2,313
			2-1/2	M.K.T. (Gunnebo)	-	2,875	2,266	-	-
			2-5/8	Star	-	-	-	1,275	-
5/8	5/8	1	2-3/4	Power F. (Raw)	1,965	-	-	-	3,720
			3	M.K.T. (Gunnebo)	-	3,750	3,400	-	-
			3-1/8	Star	-	-	-	1,625	-
3/4	3/4	1-1/4	3-1/2	M.K.T. (Gunnebo)	-	4,500	4,250	-	-
			3-15/16	Power F. (Raw)	3,038	-	-	-	4,660
			4	Star	-	-	-	1,725	-
7/8	7/8	1-5/8	4-7/8	Star	-	-	-	2,175	-
1	1	1-5/8	4-7/8	Star	-	-	-	2,625	-

Drop-In Bottom Plug Expansion SLEEVE Stud Anchor, Steel

Anchor Size (inch)	Bolt Size (inch)	Drill Hole Diameter (inch)	Embedment Depth (inch)	Manufacturer[1]	Allowable Tension Loads[2] in Pound-force For Anchors Embedded in Concrete With the Following Compressive Strengths in lbf/in[2]				
					2000	3000	4000	5000	6000
1/4	1/4	1/4	1-3/8	Power F. (Rawl)	539		905		1,088
				ITW Ramset			477		
3/8	3/8	3/8	1-5/8	Power F. (Rawl)	1,223		1,658		1,805
				ITW Ramset			582		
1/2	1/2	1/2	1-7/8	Power F. (Rawl)	1,685		2,310		2,468
				ITW Ramset			1,457		
5/8	5/8	5/8	2-3/8	ITW Ramset			1,926		
3/4	3/4	3/4	2-7/8	ITW Ramset			2,399		

Self-Drilling Bottom Plug Expansion SLEEVE Anchor, Steel

Anchor Size (inch)	Bolt Size (inch)	Drill Hole Diameter (inch)	Embedment Depth (inch)	Manufacturer[1]	Allowable Tension Loads[2] in Pound-force For Anchors Embedded in Concrete With the Following Compressive Strengths in lbf/in[2]				
					2000	3000	4000	5000	6000
1/4	1/4	7/16	1-3/32	M.K.T. (Gunnebo)		915		678	
				ITW Ramset	510				
5/16	5/16	15/32	1-1/4	Power F. (Rawl)	625		750		975
			1-9/32	M.K.T. (Gunnebo)		1,010	540		840
3/8	3/8	9/16	1-5/16	Power F. (Rawl)	800		1,135		1,370
			1-17/32	M.K.T. (Gunnebo)		1,570			
1/2	1/2	11/16	2-1/32	Power F. (Rawl)	1,370	1,570	1,750	1,050	1,910
				M.K.T. (Gunnebo)		2,280			
5/8	5/8	27/32	2-15/32	Power F. (Rawl)	1,830	2,800	2,570	1,838	2,890
				M.K.T. (Gunnebo)					
3/4	3/4	1	3-1/4	Power F. (Rawl)	2,500	4,400	3,320	2,563	3,640
				M.K.T. (Gunnebo)			3,488		
7/8	7/8	1-1/8	3-17/64	Power F. (Rawl)	3,290	4,400	4,460	3,488	5,610
			3-11/16						

Part 2: Anchors For Lag Screws

Drop-In SHORT Lag Shield Anchor, Zinc Alloy

Screw Diameter (inch)	Screw Diameter (inch)	Drill Hole Diameter (inch)	Embedment Depth (inch)	Manufacturer[1]	Allowable Tension Loads [2] in Pound-force For Anchors Embedded in Concrete With the Following Compressive Strengths in Pound-force per Square Inch			
					2000	3000	4000	6000
1/4	1/4	1/2	1	M.K.T.(Gunnebo)	-	250	-	-
				Power F. (Raw)	94	-	135	-
				Star	-	-	-	180
5/16	5/16	1/2	1-1/4	M.K.T.(Gunnebo)	-	100	-	-
				Power F. (Raw)	-	500	-	-
				Star	-	200	-	-
		5/8	1-1/2	Power F. (Rawl)	150	-	243	-
3/8	3/8	5/8	1-3/4	M.K.T.(Gunnebo)	-	825	-	290
				Power F. (Rawl)	245	-	355	390
				Star	-	325	-	-
1/2	1/2	3/4	2	M.K.T.(Gunnebo)	-	1,375	-	-
				Power F. (Rawl)	290	-	685	730
				Star	-	525	-	-
5/8	5/8	7/8	2	Power F. (Rawl)	365	-	710	780
				Star	-	850	-	-
3/4	3/4	1	2	Power F. (Rawl)	545	-	905	965
				Star	-	1,250	-	-

Drop-In LONG Lag Shield Anchor, Zinc Alloy

Anchor Size (inch)	Bolt Size (inch)	Drill Hole Diameter (inch)	Embedment Depth (inch)	Manufacturer[1]	Allowable Tension Loads[2] For Anchors Embedded in Concrete With the Following Compressive Strengths in Pound-force per Square Inch			
					2000	3000	4000	6000
1/4	1/4	1/2	1-1/2	M.K.T.(Gunnebo)	-	313	-	-
				Power F. (Raw)	120	-	175	208
				Star	-	125	-	-
5/16	5/16	1/2	1-3/4	M.K.T.(Gunnebo)	-	625	-	-
				Power F. (Raw)	235	-	345	360
				Star	-	250	-	-
3/8	3/8	5/8	2-1/2	M.K.T.(Gunnebo)	-	1,025	-	-
				Power F. (Raw)	295	-	608	723
				Star	-	400	-	-
1/2	1/2	3/4	3	M.K.T.(Gunnebo)	-	1,700	-	-
				Power F. (Raw)	580	-	920	1,035
				Star	-	700	-	-
5/8	5/8	7/8	3-1/2	Power F. (Raw)	621	-	955	1,073
				Star	-	1,100	-	-
3/4	3/4	1	3-1/2	Power F. (Raw)	815	-	1,115	1,170

Epoxy Adhesive Anchors in Concrete

Threaded Rod Anchors, Steel

Anchor Rod Diam. (inch)	Hole Diam. (inch)	Anchor Embedment (inch)	Manufacturer [1]	Trade Name	Allowable Tension Loads [2] (in pounds) For Anchors In Concrete With The Following Compressive Strengths							
					2000	2500	3000	3500	4000	4500	5000	6000
1/4	5/16	1	Power F. (Rawl)	Chem-Fast	300	-	-	-	354	-	-	354
			Power F. (Rawl)	Foil-Fast	350	-	-	-	400	-	-	553
			ITW Ramset	Epcon Ceramic 6	-	-	-	413	-	-	-	-
		2	Power F. (Rawl)	Chem-Fast	506	-	-	-	594	-	-	594
			Power F. (Rawl)	Foil-Fast	593	-	-	-	738	-	-	1,105
		2-1/4	ITW Ramset	Epcon Ceramic 5	-	-	-	698	-	-	-	-
		3	Power F. (Rawl)	Chem-Fast	711	-	-	-	834	-	-	834
			ITW Ramset	Epcon Ceramic 6	-	-	-	705	-	-	-	-
3/8	7/16	1-1/2	Power F. (Rawl)	Chem-Fast	965	-	-	-	1,118	-	-	1,560
			Power F. (Rawl)	Foil-Fast	683	-	-	-	710	-	-	710
			ITW Ramset	Epcon Ceramic 6	-	-	-	900	-	-	-	-
		2-1/4	Power F. (Rawl)	Foil-Fast	753	-	-	-	1,195	-	-	1,390
		2-1/2	Power F. (Rawl)	Foil-Fast	1,129	-	-	-	1,674	-	-	1,960
		3-3/8	Power F. (Rawl)	Foil-Fast	1,324	-	-	-	1,553	-	-	1,553
			ITW Ramset	Epcon Ceramic 5	-	-	-	2,099	-	-	-	-
			ITW Ramset	Epcon Ceramic 6	-	-	-	2,142	-	-	-	-
			Power F. (Rawl)	Foil-Fast	1,665	-	-	-	2,271	-	-	2,655
		3-1/2	Power F. (Rawl)	Foil-Fast	1,943	-	-	-	-	-	-	2,815
			M.K.T.(Gunnebo)	Liquid Roc 300 Capsule	-	-	1,420	-	-	-	1,782	-
			M.K.T.(Gunnebo)	Liquid Roc 300 Pouch	-	-	1,731	-	-	-	2,002	-
			ITW Ramset	Epcon Ceramic 6	-	-	-	857	-	-	-	-

3/8	7/16	3-1/2	Power F. (Rawl)	Chem-Stud	1785	-	-	1955	-	-	2418
			Power F. (Rawl)	Hammer-Capsule	1830	-	-	2295	-	-	2440
			Power F. (Rawl)	Chem-Fast	1965	-	-	2395	-	-	2395
		4-1/2	ITW Ramset	Epcon Ceramic 6	-	-	2651	-	-	-	-
			Power F. (Rawl)	Foil-Fast	2333	-	-	2835	-	-	3420
		5-1/4	Power F. (Rawl)	Chem-Stud	2678	-	-	2931	-	-	3626
		7	Power F. (Rawl)	Chem-Stud	3569	-	-	3909	-	-	4835
			Power F. (Rawl)	Hammer-Capsule	3660	-	-	4590	-	-	4880
	15/32	3-1/2	Hilti	HAS	-	-	-	1170	-	-	-
	1/2	3-1/2	M.K.T.(Gunnebo)	Liquid Roc 300 & 400 Pump	1180	-	-	-	1480	-	-
		3-1/2	M.K.T.(Gunnebo)	Liquid Roc 500 Fast Set	1550	-	-	1622	-	-	-
		3-1/2	M.K.T.(Gunnebo)	Liquid Roc 500 Low Odor	-	2222	-	-	2,896	-	-
1/2	9/16	2	Power F. (Rawl)	Chem-Fast	973	-	-	1015	-	-	1015
			Power F. (Rawl)	Foil-Fast	1280	-	-	1971	-	-	2189
			ITW Ramset	Epcon Ceramic 6	-	-	1525	-	-	-	-
		3	Power F. (Rawl)	Chem-Fast	1745	-	-	1839	-	-	1839
			Power F. (Rawl)	Foil-Fast	1920	-	-	2841	-	-	3158
			Hilti	HAS	-	-	-	2130	-	-	-
		4-1/4	Power F. (Rawl)	Hammer-Capsule	2325	-	-	3225	-	-	3450
			Power F. (Rawl)	Chem-Stud	2338	-	-	3359	-	-	3749
			Power F. (Rawl)	Chem-Fast	2713	-	-	2868	-	-	2868
			Power F. (Rawl)	Foil-Fast	2879	-	-	4359	-	-	4615
		4-1/2	M.K.T.(Gunnebo)	Liquid Roc 300 Capsule	-	2,480	-	-	3623	-	-
			M.K.T.(Gunnebo)	Liquid Roc Pouch	-	2,663	-	-	2830	-	-
			ITW Ramset	Epcon Ceramic 5	-	-	3516	-	-	-	-
			ITW Ramset	Epcon Ceramic 6	2827	-	3625	-	-	-	3476

Threaded Rod Anchors, Steel (cont.)

Anchor Rod Diam. (inch)	Hole Diam. (inch)	Anchor Embedment (inch)	Manufacturer [1]	Trade Name	Allowable Tension Loads [2] (in pounds) For Anchors In Concrete With The Following Compressive Strengths							
					2000	2500	3000	3500	4000	4500	5000	6000
1/2	9/16	6	ITW Ramset	Epcon Ceramic 6	3884	-	-	4353	4925	-	-	5816
		6-3/8	Power F. (Rawl)	Foil-Fast	3506	-	-	-	5039	-	-	5624
			Power F. (Rawl)	Chem-Stud	4650	-	-	-	6450	-	-	6900
		8-1/2	Power F. (Rawl)	Hammer-Capsule	-	-	-	-	-	-	-	-
			Power F. (Rawl)	Chem-Stud	4675	-	-	-	6718	-	-	7498
5/8		4-1/4	M.K.T. (Gunnebo)	Liquid Roc 500 Low Odor	-	2596	-	-	-	4312	-	-
		4-1/2	M.K.T. (Gunnebo)	Liquid Roc 500 Fast Set	2703	-	-	-	2719	-	-	-
		4-1/2	M.K.T. (Gunnebo)	Liquid Roc 300 & 400 Pump	2267	-	-	-	-	-	2267	-
5/8	11/16	5	Hilti	HAS	-	-	-	-	3390	-	-	5400
			Power F. (Rawl)	Hammer-Capsule	3475	-	-	-	4675	-	-	5640
			Power F. (Rawl)	Chem-Stud	3663	-	-	-	5146	-	-	8243
		7-1/2	Power F. (Rawl)	Chem-Stud	5494	-	-	-	7720	-	-	10800
		10	Power F. (Rawl)	Hammer-Capsule	6950	-	-	-	9350	-	-	-
			Power F. (Rawl)	Chem-Stud	7325	-	-	-	10293	-	-	10990
			Power F. (Rawl)	Chem-Fast	1455	-	-	-	1485	-	-	1485
5/8	3/4	2-1/2	ITW Ramset	Epcon Ceramic 6	-	-	-	2194	2490	-	-	-
			Power F. (Rawl)	Foil-Fast	2130	-	-	-	2651	-	-	3228
		3-1/2	Power F. (Rawl)	Chem-Fast	2349	-	-	-	2651	-	-	2651
		3-3/4	Power F. (Rawl)	Foil-Fast	3195	-	-	-	3961	-	-	4840
		5	Power F. (Rawl)	Chem-Fast	3690	-	-	-	4401	-	-	4401

			Manufacturer	Product								
5/8	3/4	5	M.K.T.(Gunnebo)	Liquid Roc 500 Fast Set	4013	-	-	4867	-	-	-	-
			M.K.T.(Gunnebo)	Liquid Roc 500 Low Odor	-	4379	-	-	6172	-	-	-
		5-1/2	M.K.T.(Gunnebo)	Liquid Roc 300 & 400 Pump	2847	-	-	-	-	3607	-	-
			M.K.T.(Gunnebo)	Liquid Roc 300 Pouch	-	4806	-	-	-	5031	-	-
		5-5/8	M.K.T.(Gunnebo)	Liquid Roc 300 Capsule	-	3870	-	-	-	5987	-	-
			ITW Ramset	Epcon Ceramic 5	-	-	5166	-	-	-	-	6049
			ITW Ramset	Epcon Ceramic 6	4193	-	5720	-	-	-	-	8010
			Rawl	Foil-Fast	4793	-	-	-	-	-	-	-
		7-1/2	ITW Ramset	Epcon Ceramic 6	-	7544	7364	-	-	-	-	-
			ITW Ramset	Foil-Fast	-	7901	-	-	-	-	-	-
3/4	7/8	3	Power F. (Rawl)	Foil-Fast	6390	-	-	-	-	-	-	9680
			Power F. (Rawl)	Foil-Fast	1863	-	-	1955	-	-	-	1955
			Power F. (Rawl)	Foil-Fast	2478	-	-	2586	-	-	-	353/3
			ITW Ramset	Epcon Ceramic 6	-	-	3156	-	-	-	-	-
		4-1/2	Power F. (Rawl)	Chem-Fast	3094	-	3424	3424	-	-	-	3424
			Power F. (Rawl)	Foil-Fast	4465	-	4638	4638	-	-	-	6168
		6	Power F. (Rawl)	Chem-Fast	4325	-	4891	4891	-	-	-	4891
			Power F. (Rawl)	Hammer-Capsule	4925	-	6543	6543	-	-	-	8350
		6-1/2	M.K.T.(Gunnebo)	Liquid Roc 300 & 400 Pump	4553	-	-	-	-	4993	-	-
			M.K.T.(Gunnebo)	Liquid Roc 300 Pouch	-	5244	-	-	-	5485	-	-
			M.K.T.(Gunnebo)	Liquid Roc 300 Capsule	-	6070	-	-	-	6769	-	-
		6-3/4	M.K.T.(Gunnebo)	Liquid Roc 500 Fast Set	7222	-	-	7040	-	-	-	-

Threaded Rod Anchors, Steel (cont.)

Anch or/Rod Diam. (inch)	Hole Diam. (inch)	Anchor Embedment (inch)	Manufacturer[1]	Trade Name	Allowable Tension Loads[2] (in pounds) For Anchors In Concrete With The Following Compressive Strengths							
					2000	2500	3000	3500	4000	4500	5000	6000
3/4	7/8	6-3/4	M.K.T.(Gunnebo)	Liquid Roc 500 Low Odor	-	6974	-	-	-	8197	-	-
		6-3/4	Power F. (Raw)	Foil-Fast	6698	-	-	-	9734	-	-	10148
		6-3/4	ITW Ramset	Epcon Ceramic 6	-	-	-	8133	-	-	-	8440
		6-3/4	ITW Ramset	Epcon Ceramic 6	7417	-	-	8215	-	-	-	-
		6-5/8	Hilti	HAS	5438	-	-	-	5010	-	-	8910
		9	Power F. (Raw)	Chem-Stud	8930	-	-	-	6850	-	-	13033
		9	ITW Ramset	Epcon Ceramic 6	-	-	-	9716	-	-	-	-
		10	Power F. (Raw)	Foil-Fast	8208	-	-	-	11119	-	-	13449
		12	Power F. (Raw)	Chem-Stud	9850	-	-	-	10275	-	-	16700
		12	Power F. (Raw)	Hammer-Capsule	-	-	-	-	13085	-	-	-
		13-1/4	Power F. (Raw)	Chem-Stud	10875	-	-	-	13700	-	-	17820
7/8	1	3	ITW Ramset	Epcon Ceramic 6	-	-	-	4663	-	-	-	-
		3	Power F. (Raw)	Chem-Fast	1965	-	-	-	2169	-	-	2169
		3-1/2	Power F. (Raw)	Foil-Fast	3965	-	-	-	4733	-	-	5583
		5	Power F. (Raw)	Foil-Fast	3330	-	-	-	-	-	-	3588
		5-1/4	Power F. (Raw)	Foil-Fast	5941	-	-	-	8503	-	-	9003
		6-5/8	Hilti	HAS	-	-	-	-	6930	-	-	-
		7	Power F. (Raw)	Chem-Fast	4625	-	-	-	5005	-	-	5005
		7	Power F. (Raw)	Hammer-Capsule	6200	-	-	-	8615	-	-	9700
		7	Power F. (Raw)	Chem-Stud	6468	-	-	-	8773	-	-	9863
		7-1/2	M.K.T.(Gunnebo)	Liquid Roc 300 & 400 Pump	6027	-	-	-	-	-	6627	-
		7-1/2	M.K.T.(Gunnebo)	Liquid Roc 300 Pouch	-	-	6325	-	-	-	7789	-

Rotated table (product anchor reference chart):

Dia		Size	Manufacturer	Product								
7/8	1	7-1/2	M.K.T.(Gunnebo)	Liquid Roc 300 Capsule							9266	-
			M.K.T.(Gunnebo)	Liquid Roc 500 Low Odor		8008					10643	-
			M.K.T.(Gunnebo)	Liquid Roc 500 Fast Set	8276				9269			-
		7-7/8	ITW Ramset	Epcon Ceramic 6	8814		9429		9269			10256
			Power F. (Rawl)	Foil-Fast	8913				10596			13008
			Power F. (Rawl)	Chem-Stud	9701				13159			14794
		10-1/4	ITW Ramset	Epcon Ceramic 6			12803					-
		10-1/2	Power F. (Rawl)	Foil-Fast	11883				15890			17973
		14	Power F. (Rawl)	Hammer-Capsule	12400				17230			19400
		14	Power F. (Rawl)	Chem-Stud	12395				17545			19725
		4	Power F. (Rawl)	Chem-Fast	2230				2324			2324
1-1/8	1	4	ITW Ramset	Epcon Ceramic 6	5114		6259		6374			7748
		6	Power F. (Rawl)	Chem-Fast	3675				4188			4188
		6	Power F. (Rawl)	Foil-Fast	7658				9628			10638
		7	Power F. (Rawl)	Chem-Fast	4858				5120			5120
		8-1/4	Hilti	HAS					9090			-
1		8-1/4	M.K.T.(Gunnebo)	Liquid Roc 500 Fast Set	8875				9485			-
			M.K.T.(Gunnebo)	Liquid Roc 500 Low Odor		10453					12400	-
			Power F. (Rawl)	Hammer-Capsule	8850				11060			13350
			Power F. (Rawl)	Chem-Stud	8978				11950			13968
		8-1/2	M.K.T.(Gunnebo)	Liquid Roc 300 & 400 Pump	6200						7693	
			M.K.T.(Gunnebo)	Liquid Roc 300 Pouch		6606					7864	-

Threaded Rod Anchors, Steel (cont.)

Anchor Rod Diam. (inch)	Hole Diam. (inch)	Anchor Embedment (inch)	Manufacturer[1]	Trade Name	Allowable Tension Loads[2] (in pounds) For Anchors In Concrete With The Following Compressive Strengths							
					2000	2500	3000	3500	4000	4500	5000	6000
1	1-1/8	9	ITW Ramset	Epcon Ceramic 6	10827	-	-	11402	-	-	-	11209
			Power F. (Rawl)	Foil-Fast	11506	-	-	-	14889	-	-	16858
		12	ITW Ramset	Epcon Ceramic 6	-	-	-	15763	-	-	-	23244
			Power F. (Rawl)	Foil-Fast	15341	-	-	-	20151	-	-	20951
		12-3/8	Power F. (Rawl)	Chem-Stud	13463	-	-	-	17925	-	-	26700
		16-1/2	Power F. (Rawl)	Hammer-Capsule	17695	-	-	-	22120	-	-	27935
			Power F. (Rawl)	Chem-Stud	17950	-	-	-	23900	-	-	-
			Power F. (Rawl)	Chem-Fast	3913	-	-	-	4465	-	-	4610
1-1/4	1-3/8	5	ITW Ramset	Epcon Ceramic 6	-	-	-	9275	-	-	-	-
		7-1/2	Power F. (Rawl)	Foil-Fast	7753	-	-	-	10196	-	-	11745
			Power F. (Rawl)	Chem-Fast	11628	-	-	-	15295	-	-	17619
		8	Power F. (Rawl)	Chem-Fast	5805	-	-	-	7143	-	-	7443
		11-1/4	ITW Ramset	Epcon Ceramic 6	-	-	-	13250	-	-	-	26428
		15	Power F. (Rawl)	Foil-Fast	23256	-	-	-	30589	-	-	35238
		10-1/4	Power F. (Rawl)	Chem-Stud	14935	-	-	-	17443	-	-	22941
		12	Hilti	HAS	14535	-	-	-	17525	-	-	23100
1-3/8	1-1/2	15	ITW Ramset	Epcon Ceramic 6	-	-	-	16231	-	-	-	31250
		20-1/2	Power F. (Rawl)	Chem-Stud	21856	-	-	-	25646	-	-	-
			Power F. (Rawl)	Chem-Stud	29870	-	-	-	35050	-	-	37250
		5-1/2	Power F. (Rawl)	Foil-Fast	9275	-	-	-	12000	-	-	14054
		8-1/4	Power F. (Rawl)	Foil-Fast	13913	-	-	-	18300	-	-	21080
		12-3/8	Power F. (Rawl)	Foil-Fast	20870	-	-	-	27450	-	-	31620
		16-1/2	Power F. (Rawl)	Foil-Fast	27825	-	-	-	36599	-	-	42160

Threaded Rod Anchors, Steel (cont.)

1-3/8	10-1/4	Power F. (Rawl)	Chem-Stud	15750	-	-	-	18500	-	-	23750
	15	Power F. (Rawl)	Chem-Stud	23056	-	-	-	27021	-	-	31250
	20-1/2	Power F. (Rawl)	Chem-Stud	31510	-	-	-	35625	-	-	37250
1-1/2	6	Power F. (Rawl)	Foil-Fast	10935	-	-	-	14383	-	-	16568
	9	Power F. (Rawl)	Foil-Fast	16401	-	-	-	21574	-	-	24851
	13-1/2	Power F. (Rawl)	Foil-Fast	24603	-	-	-	32360	-	-	37276
	18	Power F. (Rawl)	Foil-Fast	32804	-	-	-	43146	-	-	45703
1-3/4	10-1/4	Power F. (Rawl)	Chem-Stud	16750	-	-	-	19500	-	-	24500
	15	Power F. (Rawl)	Chem-Stud	25115	-	-	-	29249	-	-	34350
	20-1/2	Power F. (Rawl)	Chem-Stud	33500	-	-	-	36250	-	-	37250

Low Velocity Powder Actuated Fasteners

Fasteners Driven Into Concrete

Shank Diameter Nominal	Shank Diameter Actual	Manufacturer [1]	Embedment Depth (inch)	Allowable Tension Loads [2] (in pounds) For Anchors In Concrete of the Following Compressive Strengths (in psi)					
				2000	2500	3000	3500	4000	5000
1/8	0.125	M.K.T.(Gunnebo)	1/2	-	125	-	130	-	210
			3/4	-	275	-	305	-	410
			1	-	350	-	360	-	660
			1-1/4	-	670	-	725	-	810
	0.130	ITW Ramset	3/4	44	-	49	-	55	-
			1	62	-	87	-	112	-
			1-1/4	68	-	134	-	200	-
	0.140	ITW Ramset	3/4	45	-	70	-	90	-
			1-1/4	110	-	175	-	235	-
			1-1/4	130	-	180	-	230	-
			1-1/2	187	-	227	-	268	-
9/64	0.143	M.K.T.(Gunnebo)	1/2	-	150	-	145	-	250
			3/4	-	320	-	315	-	460
			1-1/4	-	380	-	390	-	680
			1-1/4	-	700	-	775	-	860
5/32	0.152	ITW Ramset	1-1/4	105	-	150	-	197	-
	0.170	ITW Ramset	1-1/4	115	-	162	-	220	-
			1-1/4	165	-	185	-	210	-
			1-1/2	220	-	225	-	225	-
11/64	0.172	M.K.T.(Gunnebo)	1/2	-	160	-	150	-	260
			3/4	-	340	-	325	-	510
			1	-	410	-	415	-	860
			1-1/4	-	710	-	810	-	900
			1-1/2	-	810	-	890	-	1,200

13/64	0.205	ITW Ramset	13/16	80	90	-	-	105
			1-1/16	115	150	-	-	190
			1-1/4	165	230	-	-	295
			1-1/2	300	310	-	-	320
			1-7/8	385	370	-	-	350

Fasteners Driven Into Structural Steel

Shank Diameter		Manufacturer[1]	Allowable Tension Loads [2] (in pounds) For Anchors In Structural Steel of the Following Thicknesses: (in inch)				
nominal	actual		1/8	3/16	1/4	5/16	3/8
1/8	0.125	M.K.T.(Gunnebo)	350	860	1,030	1,370	1,725
9/64	0.140	ITW Ramset	-	130	270	-	370
5/32	0.143	M.K.T.(Gunnebo)	510	1,200	1,500	1,810	1,950
5/32	0.152	ITW Ramset	-	137	133	-	132
11/64	0.170	ITW Ramset	-	85	180	-	330
11/64	0.172	M.K.T.(Gunnebo)	510	1,200	1,500	1,810	1,950
19/64	0.205	ITW Ramset	-	480	-	-	550

(1) Manufactured by: ITW Ramset/Red Head, 1300 North Michael Drive, Wood Dale, IL 60191. M.K.T. (Gunnebo Fastening Corporation), 1 Gunnebo Drive, Lonoke, AR 72086

(2))Factors of safety between 8 to 10 have been applied to obtain Allowable Tension Loads for the ITW Ramset fasteners. Factors of safety for the Gunnebo fasteners are not stated in the manufacturer's literature. These loads are typical for these anchors and should be used only as a guide to the true capacity of a given anchor. Check manufacturer literature for additional information.

Torque-Controlled, Self-Contained Anchors for Concrete

Expansion WEDGE Anchors, Carbon Steel

Anchor and Hole Diam. (inch)	Manufacturer[1]	Installation Torque (ft lb-force)	Anchor Embedment in Drill Hole (inch)	Allowable Tension Loads[2] (in pounds) For Anchors Embedded in Concrete of the Following Compressive Strengths (in psi)			
				2000	3000	4000	6000
1/4	Hilti	7	1-1/8	250	308	358	438
			2	525	556	588	625
			3-3/4	625	625	625	625
	ITW Ramset	8	1-1/8	-	-	390	-
			1-15/16	-	-	750	-
			2-3/4	-	-	763	-
	Power F. (Rawl)	8	1-1/8	418	-	595	595
			1-1/2	530	-	640	646
			2	681	-	731	763
			2-3/4	763	-	763	763
	Star	10	1-1/8	-	-	410	-
	Star	15	1-5/8	-	-	760	-
3/8	ITW Ramset	25	1-1/2	-	-	805	-
			3	-	-	1,420	-
			4-1/2	-	-	1,484	-
	Hilti	25	1-5/8	500	613	706	800
			2-1/2	1,125	1,206	1,288	1,450
			4-1/4	1,250	1,300	1,350	1,450
	Power F. (Rawl)	28	1-5/8	891	-	1,031	1,038
			2	975	-	1,078	1,100
			3	1,200	-	1,485	1,505
			4-1/4	1,200	-	1,505	1,505
	Star	20	2-1/4	-	-	1,075	-
			2-1/4	-	-	1,346	-
1/2	ITW Ramset	55	4-1/8	-	-	1,833	-

Anchor and Hole Diam. (inch)	Manufacturer[1]	Installation Torque (ft lb-force)	Anchor Embedment in Drill Hole (inch)	Allowable Tension Loads[2] (in pounds) For Anchors Embedded In Concrete of the Following Compressive Strengths (in psi)			
				2000	3000	4000	6000
1/2	ITW Ramset	55	6	–	–	2,251	–
	Power F. (Rawl)	60	2-1/4	1,631	–	1,656	1,656
			3	1,784	–	2,013	2,188
			4	1,986	–	2,486	2,486
			6	1,986	–	2,573	2,573
	Hilti	65	2-1/4	1,100	1,231	1,363	1,625
			3-1/2	1,750	2,000	2,250	2,625
			6	1,950	2,163	2,375	2,625
5/8	Star	25	2-3/4	–	–	1,505	–
	ITW Ramset	90	5-1/8	–	–	2,545	–
			7-1/2	–	–	3,113	–
	Power F. (Rawl)	90	4	2,344	–	3,075	3,634
			5	2,753	–	3,178	4,103
			7	2,950	–	3,500	4,103
	Hilti	110	2-3/4	1,500	1,750	2,000	2,500
			4	2,250	2,668	3,088	3,925
			7	3,000	3,250	3,500	3,925
3/4	Star	40	3-1/4	–	–	2,155	–
	ITW Ramset	175	3-1/4	–	–	2,480	–
			6-5/8	–	–	4,122	–
			10	–	–	4,988	–
	Power F. (Rawl)	175	3-7/8	2,686	–	2,686	3,881
			4-1/2	3,714	–	4,405	4,845
			5-3/4	4,346	–	4,686	5,439
			8	–	–	5,439	–
	Hilti	235	3-1/4	1,850	2,175	2,500	3,000
			4-3/4	2,750	3,875	4,500	5,500

Expansion WEDGE Anchors, Carbon Steel (cont.)

Anchor and Hole Diam. (inch)	Manufacturer[1]	Installation Torque (ft-lb-force)	Anchor Embedment in Drill Hole (inch)	Allowable Tension Loads[2] (in pounds) For Anchors Embedded in Concrete of the Following Compressive Strengths (in psi)			
				2000	3000	4000	6000
7/8	Star	45	4	--	--	3,000	--
	ITW Ramset	250	6-1/4	--	--	3,418	--
			8-3/4	--	--	5,007	--
	Power F. (Rawl)	250	3-7/8	3,083	--	3,955	4,819
			4-1/2	3,575	--	4,405	5,249
			5-3/4	4,561	--	5,306	6,110
			8	4,561	--	6,125	7,795
1	Star	50	4-1/2	--	--	4,250	--
	ITW Ramset	300	4-1/2	--	--	5,218	--
			7-3/8	--	--	7,653	--
			10-1/4	--	--	9,455	--
	Power F. (Rawl)	300	4-1/2	3,470	--	4,998	6,843
			5-1/2	4,656	--	5,883	7,495
			6-1/2	5,843	--	6,833	8,104
			9	6,110	--	8,350	11,054
	Hilti	450	4-1/2	3,125	3,800	4,375	4,750
			6	4,625	5,625	6,625	7,875
			5-5/8	6,250	7,188	8,125	10,000
1-1/4	Power F. (Rawl)	450	10	5,365	--	6,830	9,050
			7	6,096	--	8,405	10,575
				8,290	--	13,069	15,800
	ITW Ramset	500	5-1/2	--	--	6,792	--
			8	--	--	13,315	--
			10-1/2	--	--	15,104	15,800

Expansion SLEEVE Anchors, Steel

Anchor and Hole Diameter (inch)	Manufacturer [1]	Installation Torque (lbf)	Anchor Embedment in Drill Hole (inch)	Allowable Tension Loads [2] (in pounds) for Anchors Embedded in Concrete of the Following Compressive Strengths (in psi)					
				2000	3000	3500	4000	5000	6000
1/4	ITW Ramset	3.5	1/2	-	-	-	125	-	-
	Power F. (Raw)	4	1-1/8	298	-	-	403	-	433
	Star	-	1-1/8	-	-	-	360	-	-
	M.K.T. (Gunnebo)	5 to 8	1	339	-	350	-	281	-
	Hilti	5	1	275	-	-	-	410	326
5/16	ITW Ramset	-	1-1/4	-	-	-	607	-	-
	Power F. (Raw)	8	1-1/2	398	-	-	438	-	528
	Star	-	-	-	-	-	380	-	-
	M.K.T. (Gunnebo)	18 to 22	1-1/8	460	-	475	-	413	-
	Hilti	5	1-1/2	275	-	-	-	510	414
3/8	ITW Ramset	15	1-1/4	-	-	-	649	-	-
	Power F. (Raw)	16	1-5/8	550	-	-	675	-	825
	Star	-	1-1/4	-	-	-	579	-	-
	M.K.T. (Gunnebo)	22 to 26	1-1/4	710	-	740	-	750	-
	Hilti	10	1-1/4	425	-	-	-	814	589
1/2	ITW Ramset	25	1-7/8	-	-	-	1,346	-	-
	Power F. (Raw)	28	2-1/4	875	-	-	1,254	-	1,319
	Star	-	1-1/2	-	-	-	753	-	-
	M.K.T. (Gunnebo)	34 to 38	1-1/2	1,166	-	1,215	-	1,000	-
	Hilti	30	1-1/2	820	-	-	-	1,336	766
9/16	Hilti	20	2-9/16	1,115	1,291	-	1,468	1,636	1,805
	Hilti	40	3	1,518	1,821	-	2,125	2,425	2,725

Expansion SLEEVE Anchors, Steel (cont.)

Anchor and Hole Diameter (inch)	Manufacturer[1]	Installation Torque (lbf)	Anchor Embedment in Drill Hole (inch)	Allowable Tension Loads[2] (in pounds) For Anchors Embedded in Concrete of the Following Compressive Strengths (in psi)					
				2000	3000	3500	4000	5000	6000
5/8	ITW Ramset	55	2	-	-	-	1,427	-	-
	Power F. (Rawl)	60	2-3/4	1,015	-	-	1,586	-	2,181
	Star	-	2	-	-	-	851	1,288	-
	M.K.T.(Gunnebo)	52 to 75	2	1,627	-	1,695	-	1,864	-
	Hilti	30	2	956	-	-	-	-	1,138
11/16	Hilti	60	3-3/16	1,970	2,390	-	2,810	3,230	3,650
3/4	ITW Ramset	90	2-1/4	-	-	-	1,618	-	-
	Power F. (Rawl)	90	3-3/8	1,383	-	-	2,284	-	2,975
	Star	-	2	-	-	-	1,265	1,663	-
	M.K.T.(Gunnebo)	90 to 110	2	2,107	-	2,195	-	2,414	-
	Hilti	30	2	1,266	-	-	-	-	1,533
1	Hilti	150	4-1/8	3,675	4,363	-	5,051	5,740	6,428
1-1/8	Hilti	300	5-1/8	5,150	5,763	-	6,375	6,994	7,613
1-1/4	Hilti	525	6-1/8	5,875	7,236	-	8,598	9,959	11,320

(1) Manufactured by: ITW Ramset/Red Head, 1300 North Michael Drive, Wood Dale, IL 60191.; Power Fasteners (Rawl) New York, 2 Powers Square, New Rochelle, NY 10802; Star Fasteners, 20 Industry Drive, Mountainville, NY 10953; Hilti Inc., 5400 South 122nd East Ave., Tulsa, OK 74146; Gunnebo Fastening Corporation, 1 Gunnebo Drive, Lonoke, AR 72086

(2) A factor of safety of 4 has been applied to obtain Allowable Tension Loads. These loads are typical for these anchors and should be used only as a guide to the true capacity of a given anchor. Check manufacturer literature for additional information.

Undercut Expansion SLEEVE Anchors, Steel

Anchor and Hole Diameter (inch)	Manufacturer [1]	Installation Torque (foot pound-force)	Anchor Embedment in Drill Hole (inch)	Allowable Tension Loads[2] (in pounds) For Anchors Embedded In Concrete of the Following Compressive Strengths (in psi)				
				2000	3000	4000	5000	6000
1/4	Power F. (Rawl)	7	7/8	319	-	361	-	413
			1-1/4	528	-	595	-	613
			2	558	-	595	-	613
	M.K.T.(Gunnebo)	8 to 10	1-5/8	572	-	592	-	-
			3-3/8	889	-	1,301	-	-
3/8	Power F. (Rawl)	35	2	1,004	-	1,210	-	1,328
			2-1/2	1,300	-	1,398	-	1,568
			3-1/2	1,396	-	1,538	-	1,888
	M.K.T.(Gunnebo)	15 to 30	1-5/8	572	-	592	-	-
			3-3/8	889	-	1,301	-	-
1/2	Power F. (Rawl)	60	2-1/2	1,484	-	1,854	-	1,871
			3	1,831	-	2,445	-	2,636
			5	2,015	-	2,714	-	2,865
	M.K.T.(Gunnebo)	25 to 50	2-1/4	1,030	-	1,267	-	-
			4-1/2	1,152	-	1,443	-	-
5/8	Power F. (Rawl)	100	2-3/4	2,018	-	2,110	-	2,313
			3	2,154	-	2,476	-	2,784
			4	2,613	-	3,171	-	3,915
			6	2,814	-	3,768	-	4,511

Undercut Expansion SLEEVE Anchors, Steel (cont.)

Anchor and Hole Diameter (inch)	Manufacturer [1]	Installation Torque (foot pound-force)	Anchor Embedment in Drill Hole (inch)	Allowable Tension Loads [2] (in pounds)For Anchors Embedded In Concrete of the Following Compressive Strengths (in psi)				
				2000	3000	4000	5000	6000
5/8	M.K.T.(Gunebo)	40 to 75	2-3/4	1,372	-	1,389	-	-
			5-5/8	1,739	-	2,324	-	2,794
3/4	Power F. (Rawl)	120	3	2,615	-	2,619	-	3,501
			4	2,886	-	3,086	-	-
			5	3,153	-	3,925	-	4,513
			7	3,543	-	4,553	-	6,018
	M.K.T.(Gunebo)	100 to 200	3-3/8	2,317	-	2,994	-	-
			6-3/4	3,320	-	4,050	-	-
7/8	M.K.T.(Gunebo)	125 to 225	4	2,437	-	3,476	-	-
			8	3,595	-	5,072	-	-
1	M.K.T.(Gunebo)	150 to 250	4-1/2	2,557	-	3,957	-	-
			9	3,870	-	6,094	-	-
	Hilti	60	5	-	4,384	4,384	4,384	4,384
1-1/4	M.K.T.(Gunebo)	200 to 350	6-1/2	3,680	-	5,773	-	-
	Hilti	150	6-3/4	-	8,205	8,205	8,205	8,205
1-5/8	Hilti	220	8-5/8	-	10,566	10,566	10,566	10,566

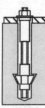

(1) Manufactured by:
ITW Ramset/Red Head, 1300 North Michael Drive, Wood Dale, IL 60191.
Power Fasteners (Rawl), New York, 2 Powers Square, New Rochelle, NY 10802
Star Fasteners, 20 Industry Drive, Mountainville, NY 10953
Hilti Inc., 5400 South 122nd East Ave., Tulsa, OK 74146
M.K.T.(Gunebo Fastening Corporation, 1 Gunnebo Drive, Lonoke, AR 72086)

(2) A factor of safety of 4 has been applied to obtain Allowable Tension Loads. These loads are typical for these anchors and should be used only as a guide to the true capacity of a given anchor. Check manufacturer literature for additional information.

Belts, Pulleys and Gears

Belts - Introduction 42

Belt and Gear Formulas 42

Belt Speed for Various Pulleys and Sheaves................................46

Pulley (Sheave) Selection Tables 48

Belts

Belts are used to transfer power through rotational motion from one shaft to another shaft. Two belt types are common:

- *friction belts*, such as automotive fan belts,
- *synchronous belts*, such as automotive timing belts.

Friction belts transfer power through friction between the belt and the pulley or sheave. Synchronous belts transfer power through mechanical linkage between teeth on the belt and grooves in the pulley. Synchronous belts work in a manner similar to spur gears.

Modern drive belts are engineered, laminated, composite units. The belt core can be natural rubber or synthetic rubber compounds such as polyurethane, neoprene, or styrene-butadiene. Most belts are tension reinforced with imbedded cords or strands of cotton, glass fiber, rayon, polyester, aramid, kevlar, or steel. Belts are often wrapped in woven cotton or nylon fabric to increase resistance to abrasion. Modern belts are heat-resistant, ozone-resistant, oil-resistant, and non-static- conducting.

The most common belt is the V-belt which can be solid or notched (also called "cogged") on the inside surface. For the same cross-section, a solid belt is stronger, but a notched belt is more flexible and dissipates heat better.

Belt and pulley drive systems using cast iron sheaves and static balancing should not be operated at belt speeds over 5,000 feet per minute. Cast iron sheaves and dynamic balancing should be used between 5,000 and 6,500 feet per minute. Ductile iron sheaves, dynamic balancing, and steel or kevlar reinforced belts should be used between 6,500 and 10,000 feet per minute.

Belt and Gear Formulas

Belt Speed:

To find BELT SPEED (feet per minute), multiply the PULLEY PITCH DIAMETER, D_p (inch), by REVOLUTIONS PER MINUTE, R, of the pulley by π and divide by 12.

$$\text{Belt Speed} = \frac{D_p \times R \times \pi}{12}$$

Belt Length:

The approximate BELT LENGTH (inch) is equal to the sum of the following: (1) the product of the DIAMETER, D_s (inch), of the small pulley times π divided by 2; (2) the product of the DIAMETER, D_l (inch), of the large pulley times π divided by 2; and (3) the product of the DISTANCE BETWEEN THE SHAFTS, L (inch), times 2.

$$\text{Belt Length} = (D_s \times \tfrac{\pi}{2}) + (D_l \times \tfrac{\pi}{2}) + (L \times 2)$$

A more exact BELT LENGTH (inch) can be calculated as follows:

$$\text{Belt Length} = (D_s \times \tfrac{\pi}{2}) + (D_l \times \tfrac{\pi}{2}) + (L \times 2) + \left[\tfrac{(D_l - D_s)^2}{L \times 4} \right]$$

Transmission Formulas for Belt and Pulleys or Gears:

The relationship between a drive shaft and a driven shaft connected by a belt and pulley system or by a gear system is based on the rotational speed of the shafts and either the diameters of the pulleys or the number of teeth on the gears.

For single transmission systems the following formulas apply:

<u>Belt and Pulleys:</u> REVOLUTIONS PER MINUTE, R_D, of the drive shaft times the DIAMETER, D_D, of the drive pulley equals the REVOLUTIONS PER MINUTE, R_d, of the driven shaft times the DIAMETER, D_d, of the driven pulley.

$$R_D \times D_D = R_d \times D_d$$

or

$$R_d = \frac{R_D \times D_D}{D_d}$$

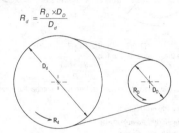

<u>Gears:</u> REVOLUTIONS PER MINUTE, R_D, of the drive shaft times the NUMBER OF TEETH, T_D, of the drive gear equals the REVOLUTIONS PER MINUTE, R_d, of the driven shaft times the NUMBER OF TEETH, T_d, on the driven gear.

$$R_D \times T_D = R_d \times T_d$$

or

$$R_d = \frac{R_D \times T_D}{T_d}$$

For multiple transmission systems the following formulas apply:

<u>Belts and Pulleys:</u> For a system of three shafts and four pulleys, number the components as follows:

- pulley #1 is on shaft #1,
- pulleys #2 and #3 are on shaft #2,
- and pulley #4 is on shaft #3.

Shaft #1 is the drive shaft and shafts #2 and #3 are driven shafts. The REVOLUTIONS PER MINUTE of the shafts are labeled R_1, R_2, and R_3 and the DIAMETERS of the pulleys are labeled D_1, D_2, D_3, and D_4.

The REVOLUTIONS PER MINUTE, R_1, of the drive shaft and the DIAMETERS of the pulleys are known and the REVOLUTIONS PER MINUTE, R_3, of the final driven shaft is required. Use the following equations:

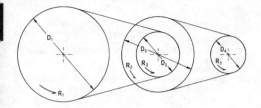

$$D_1 \times R_1 = D_2 \times R_2; \quad D_3 \times R_2 = D_4 \times R_3$$

Combine these equations to find:

$$R_3 = \frac{R_1 \times (D_1 \times D_3)}{(D_2 \times D_4)}$$

<u>Gears:</u> For a system of four shafts and six gears, number the components as follows:

- gear #1 is on shaft #1,
- gears #2 and #3 are on shaft #2,
- gears #4 and #5 are on shaft #3,
- and gear #6 is on shaft #4.

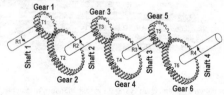

Shaft #1 is the drive shaft, and shafts #2, #3, and #4 are driven shafts. The REVOLUTIONS PER MINUTE of the shafts are labeled R_1, R_2, R_3, and R_4 and the NUMBER OF TEETH on the gears are labeled T_1, T_2, T_3, T_4, T_5, and T_6. The REVOLUTIONS PER MINUTE, R_1, of the drive shaft and the NUMBER OF TEETH on the gears are known and the REVOLUTIONS PER MINUTE, R_4, of the final driven shaft is required. Use the following equations:

$$T_1 \times R_1 = T_2 \times R_2; \quad T_3 \times R_2 = T_4 \times R_3 \ ; \ T_5 \times R_3 = T_6 \times R_4$$

Combine these equations to find:

$$R_4 = \frac{R_1 \times (T_1 \times T_3 \times T_5)}{(T_2 \times T_4 \times T_6)}$$

Design Horsepower:

To find DESIGN HORSEPOWER, multiply the MOTOR HORSEPOWER by the appropriate SERVICE FACTOR.

Design hp = Motor hp X Service Factor

Horsepower:

To find HORSEPOWER, multiply EFFECTIVE TENSION, *Te* (pound-force) by BELT SPEED (feet per minute) and divide by 33,000.

$$HORSEPOWER = \frac{Te \times BELTSPEED}{33,000}$$

To find HORSEPOWER, multiply TORQUE (pound-force) by REVOLUTIONS PER MINUTE, *R*, and divide by 63,000.

$$HORSEPOWER = \frac{TORQUE \times R}{63,000}$$

Speed Ratio:

To find the SPEED RATIO, divide the REVOLUTIONS PER MINUTE, *Rf*, of the faster machine by the REVOLUTIONS PER MINUTE, *Rs*, of the slower machine.

$$Speed\ Ratio = \frac{Rf}{Rs}$$

Belt Speeds for Pulleys and Sheaves

Pitch Diam. of Pulley	Values in Table are Belt Speed in Feet per Minute (fpm)						
	Revolutions per Minute (rpm) of Pulley						
(inch)	850	1,050	1,075	1,140	1,550	1,725	3,450
1.0	223	275	281	298	406	452	903
1.2	267	330	338	358	487	542	1,084
1.4	312	385	394	418	568	632	1,264
1.6	356	440	450	478	649	723	1,445
1.8	401	495	507	537	730	813	1,626
2.0	445	550	563	597	812	903	1,806
2.2	490	605	619	657	893	994	1,987
2.4	534	660	675	716	974	1,084	2,168
2.6	579	715	732	776	1,055	1,174	2,348
2.8	623	770	788	836	1,136	1,264	2,529
3.0	668	825	844	895	1,217	1,355	2,710
3.2	712	880	901	955	1,299	1,445	2,890
3.4	757	935	957	1,015	1,380	1,535	3,071
3.6	801	990	1,013	1,074	1,461	1,626	3,252
3.8	846	1,045	1,069	1,134	1,542	1,716	3,432
4.0	890	1,100	1,126	1,194	1,623	1,806	3,613
4.2	935	1,155	1,182	1,253	1,704	1,897	3,793
4.4	979	1,210	1,238	1,313	1,785	1,987	3,974
4.6	1,024	1,264	1,295	1,373	1,867	2,077	4,155
4.8	1,068	1,319	1,351	1,433	1,948	2,168	4,335
5.0	1,113	1,374	1,407	1,492	2,029	2,258	4,516
5.2	1,157	1,429	1,463	1,552	2,110	2,348	4,697
5.4	1,202	1,484	1,520	1,612	2,191	2,439	4,877
5.6	1,246	1,539	1,576	1,671	2,272	2,529	5,058
5.8	1,291	1,594	1,632	1,731	2,354	2,619	5,239
6.0	1,335	1,649	1,689	1,791	2,435	2,710	5,419
6.2	1,380	1,704	1,745	1,850	2,516	2,800	5,600
6.4	1,424	1,759	1,801	1,910	2,597	2,890	5,781
6.6	1,469	1,814	1,857	1,970	2,678	2,981	5,961
6.8	1,513	1,869	1,914	2,029	2,759	3,071	6,142
7.0	1,558	1,924	1,970	2,089	2,841	3,161	6,322
7.2	1,602	1,979	2,026	2,149	2,922	3,252	6,503

Belt Speeds for Pulleys and Sheaves (cont.)

Pitch Diam. of Pulley (inch)	Values in Table are Belt Speed in Feet per Minute (fpm)						
	Revolutions per Minute (rpm) of Pulley						
	850	1,050	1,075	1,140	1,550	1,725	3,450
7.4	1,647	2,034	2,083	2,209	3,003	3,342	6,684
7.6	1,691	2,089	2,139	2,268	3,084	3,432	6,864
7.8	1,736	2,144	2,195	2,328	3,165	3,523	7,045
8.0	1,780	2,199	2,251	2,388	3,246	3,613	7,226
8.2	1,825	2,254	2,308	2,447	3,327	3,703	7,406
8.4	1,869	2,309	2,364	2,507	3,409	3,793	7,587
8.6	1,914	2,364	2,420	2,567	3,490	3,884	7,768
8.8	1,958	2,419	2,477	2,626	3,571	3,974	7,948
9.0	2,003	2,474	2,533	2,686	3,652	4,064	8,129
9.2	2,047	2,529	2,589	2,746	3,733	4,155	8,310
9.4	2,092	2,584	2,645	2,805	3,814	4,245	8,490
9.6	2,136	2,639	2,702	2,865	3,896	4,335	8,671
9.8	2,181	2,694	2,758	2,925	3,977	4,426	8,851
10.0	2,225	2,749	2,814	2,985	4,058	4,516	9,032

Pulleys: Outside Diameter vs. Pitch Diameter

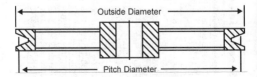

Pitch Diameter is the diameter at which the tension cord of the belt will run in the sheave groove.

Pulley (Sheave) Selection Tables - 850 rpm motor

Equipment Speed in revolutions per minute (rpm) for motors turning 850 rpm

Outside Diameter of Pulley on Motor	Outside Diameter of Pulley on Equipment														
	1.50	2.00	2.25	2.50	2.75	3.00	350	4.00	4.50	5.00	6.00	7.00	8.00	9.00	10.00
1.50	850	638	567	510	464	425	364	319	283	255	213	182	159	142	128
2.00	1133	850	756	680	618	567	486	425	378	340	283	243	213	189	170
2.25	1275	956	850	765	695	638	546	478	425	383	319	273	239	213	191
2.50	1417	1063	944	850	773	708	607	531	472	425	354	304	266	236	213
2.75	1558	1169	1039	935	850	779	668	584	519	468	390	334	292	260	234
3.00	1700	1275	1133	1020	927	850	729	638	567	510	425	364	319	283	255
3.50	1983	1488	1322	1190	1082	992	850	744	661	595	496	425	372	331	298
4.00	2267	1700	1511	1360	1236	1133	971	850	756	680	567	486	425	378	340
4.50	2550	1913	1700	1530	1391	1275	1093	956	850	765	638	546	478	425	383
5.00	2833	2125	1889	1700	1545	1417	1214	1063	944	850	708	607	531	472	425
6.00	3400	2550	2267	2040	1855	1700	1457	1275	1133	1020	850	729	638	567	510
7.00	3967	2975	2644	2380	2164	1983	1700	1488	1322	1190	992	850	744	661	595
8.00	4533	3000	3022	2720	2473	2267	1943	1700	1511	1360	1133	971	850	756	680
9.00	5100	3825	3400	3060	2782	2550	2186	1913	1700	1530	1275	1093	956	850	765
10.00	5667	4250	3778	3400	3091	2833	2429	2125	1889	1700	1417	1214	1063	944	850

Pulley (Sheave) Selection Tables - 1050 rpm motor

Equipment Speed in revolutions per minute (rpm) for motors turning 1050 rpm

Outside Diameter of Pulley on Motor	Outside Diameter of Pulley on Equipment														
	1.50	2.00	2.25	2.50	2.75	3.00	3.50	4.00	4.50	5.00	6.00	7.00	8.00	9.00	10.00
1.50	1050	788	700	630	573	525	450	394	350	315	263	225	197	---	---
2.00	1400	1050	933	840	764	700	600	525	467	420	350	300	263	233	---
2.25	1575	1181	1050	945	859	788	675	591	525	473	394	338	295	263	236
2.50	1750	1313	1167	1050	955	875	750	656	583	525	438	375	328	292	263
2.75	1925	1444	1283	1155	1050	963	825	722	642	578	481	413	361	321	289
3.00	2100	1575	1400	1260	1145	1050	900	788	700	630	525	450	394	350	315
3.50	2450	1838	1633	1470	1336	1225	1050	919	817	735	613	525	459	408	368
4.00	2800	2100	1867	1680	1527	1400	1200	1050	933	840	700	600	525	467	420
4.50	3150	2363	2100	1890	1718	1575	1350	1181	1050	945	788	675	591	525	473
5.00	3500	2625	2333	2100	1909	1750	1500	1313	1167	1050	875	750	656	583	525
6.00	4200	3150	2800	2520	2291	2100	1800	1575	1400	1260	1050	900	788	700	630
7.00	4900	3675	3267	2940	2673	2450	2100	1838	1633	1470	1225	1050	919	817	735
8.00	5600	4200	3733	3360	3055	2800	2400	2100	1867	1680	1400	1200	1050	933	840
9.00	6300	4725	4200	3780	3436	3150	2700	2363	2100	1890	1575	1350	1181	1050	945
10.00	7000	5250	4667	4200	3818	3500	3000	2625	2333	2100	1750	1500	1313	1167	1050

Pulley (Sheave) Selection Tables - 1075 rpm motor

Equipment Speed in revolutions per minute (rpm) for motors turning 1075 rpm

Outside Diameter of Pulley on Motor	Outside Diameter of Pulley on Equipment														
	1.50	2.00	2.25	2.50	2.75	3.00	350	4.00	4.50	5.00	6.00	7.00	8.00	9.00	10.00
1.50	1075	806	717	645	586	538	461	403	358	323	269	230	202	179	161
2.00	1433	1075	956	860	782	717	614	538	478	430	358	307	269	239	215
2.25	1613	1209	1075	968	880	806	691	605	538	484	403	346	302	269	242
2.50	1792	1344	1194	1075	977	896	768	672	597	538	448	384	336	299	269
2.75	1971	1478	1314	1183	1075	985	845	739	657	591	493	422	370	328	296
3.00	2150	1613	1433	1290	1173	1075	921	806	717	645	538	461	403	358	323
3.50	2508	1881	1672	1505	1368	1254	1075	941	836	753	627	538	470	418	376
4.00	2867	2150	1911	1720	1564	1433	1229	1075	956	860	717	614	538	478	430
4.50	3225	2419	2150	1935	1759	1613	1382	1209	1075	968	806	691	605	538	484
5.00	3583	2688	2389	2150	1955	1792	1536	1344	1194	1075	896	768	672	597	538
6.00	4300	3225	2867	2580	2345	2150	1843	1613	1433	1290	1075	921	806	717	645
7.00	5017	3763	3344	3010	2736	2508	2150	1881	1672	1505	1254	1075	941	836	753
8.00	5733	4300	3822	3440	3127	2867	2457	2150	1911	1720	1433	1229	1075	956	860
9.00	6450	4838	4300	3870	3518	3225	2764	2419	2150	1935	1613	1382	1209	1075	968
10.00	7167	5375	4778	4300	3909	3583	3071	2688	2389	2150	1792	1536	1344	1194	1075

Pulley (Sheave) Selection Tables - 1140 rpm motor

Equipment Speed in revolutions per minute (rpm) for motors turning 1140 rpm

Outside Diameter of Pulley on Motor	Outside Diameter of Pulley on Equipment														
	1.50	2.00	2.25	2.50	2.75	3.00	350	4.00	4.50	5.00	6.00	7.00	8.00	9.00	10.00
1.50	1140	855	760	684	622	570	489	428	380	342	285	244	214	190	171
2.00	1520	1140	1013	912	829	760	651	570	507	456	380	326	285	253	228
2.25	1710	1283	1140	1026	933	855	733	641	570	513	428	366	321	285	257
2.50	1900	1425	1267	1140	1036	950	814	713	633	570	475	407	356	317	285
2.75	2090	1568	1393	1254	1140	1045	896	784	697	627	523	448	392	348	314
3.00	2280	1710	1520	1368	1244	1140	977	855	760	684	570	489	428	380	342
3.50	2660	1995	1773	1596	1451	1330	1140	998	887	798	665	570	499	443	399
4.00	3040	2280	2027	1824	1658	1520	1303	1140	1013	912	760	651	570	507	456
4.50	3420	2565	2280	2052	1865	1710	1466	1283	1140	1026	855	733	641	570	513
5.00	3800	2850	2533	2280	2073	1900	1629	1425	1267	1140	950	814	713	633	570
6.00	4560	3420	3040	2736	2487	2280	1954	1710	1520	1368	1140	977	855	760	684
7.00	5320	3990	3547	3192	2902	2660	2280	1995	1773	1596	1330	1140	1140	887	798
8.00	6080	4560	4053	3648	3316	3040	2606	2280	2027	1824	1520	1303	1140	1013	912
9.00	6840	5130	4560	4104	3731	3420	2931	2565	2280	2052	1710	1466	1283	1140	1026
10.00	7600	5700	5067	4560	4145	3800	3257	2850	2533	2280	1900	1629	1425	1267	1140

Pulley (Sheave) Selection Tables - 1550 rpm motor

Equipment Speed in revolutions per minute (rpm) for motors turning 1550 rpm

Outside Diameter of Pulley on Equipment

Outside Diameter of Pulley on Motor	1.50	2.00	2.25	2.50	2.75	3.00	3.50	4.00	4.50	5.00	6.00	7.00	8.00	9.00	10.00
1.50	1550	1163	1033	930	845	775	664	581	517	465	388	332	291	258	233
2.00	2067	1550	1378	1240	1127	1033	886	775	689	620	517	443	388	344	310
2.25	2325	1744	1550	1395	1268	1163	996	872	775	698	581	498	436	388	349
2.50	2583	1938	1722	1550	1409	1292	1107	969	861	775	646	554	484	431	388
2.75	2842	2131	1894	1705	1550	1421	1218	1066	947	853	710	609	533	474	426
3.00	3100	2325	2067	1860	1691	1550	1329	1163	1033	930	775	664	581	517	465
3.50	3617	2713	2411	2170	1973	1808	1550	1356	1206	1085	904	775	678	603	543
4.00	4133	3100	2756	2480	2255	2067	1771	1550	1378	1240	1033	886	775	689	620
4.50	4650	3488	3100	2790	2536	2325	1993	1744	1550	1395	1163	996	872	775	698
5.00	5167	3875	3444	3100	2818	2583	2214	1938	1722	1550	1292	1107	969	861	775
6.00	6200	4650	4133	3720	3382	3100	2657	2325	2067	1860	1550	1329	1163	1033	930
7.00	7233	5425	4822	4340	3945	3617	3100	2713	2411	2170	1808	1550	1356	1206	1085
8.00	8267	6200	5511	4960	4509	4133	3543	3100	2756	2480	2067	1771	1550	1378	1240
9.00	9300	6975	6200	5580	5073	4650	3986	3488	3100	2790	2325	1993	1744	1550	1395
10.00	10333	7750	6889	6200	5636	5167	4429	3875	3444	3100	2583	2214	1938	1722	1550

Pulley (Sheave) Selection Tables - 1725 rpm motor

Equipment Speed in revolutions per minute (rpm) for motors turning 1725 rpm

Outside Diameter of Pulley on Motor	Outside Diameter of Pulley on Equipment														
	1.50	2.00	2.25	2.50	2.75	3.00	3.50	4.00	4.50	5.00	6.00	7.00	8.00	9.00	10.00
1.50	1725	1294	1150	1035	941	863	739	647	575	518	431	370	323	288	259
2.00	2300	1725	1533	1380	1255	1150	986	863	767	690	575	493	431	383	345
2.25	2588	1941	1725	1553	1411	1294	1109	970	863	776	647	554	485	431	388
2.50	2875	2156	1917	1725	1568	1438	1232	1078	958	863	719	616	539	479	431
2.75	3163	2372	2108	1898	1725	1581	1355	1186	1054	949	791	678	593	527	474
3.00	3450	2588	2300	2070	1882	1725	1479	1294	1150	1035	863	739	647	575	518
3.50	4025	3019	2683	2415	2195	2013	1725	1509	1342	1208	1006	863	755	671	604
4.00	4600	3450	3067	2760	2509	2300	1971	1725	1533	1380	1150	986	863	767	690
4.50	5175	3881	3450	3105	2823	2588	2218	1941	1725	1553	1294	1109	970	863	776
5.00	5750	4313	3833	3450	3136	2875	2464	2156	1917	1725	1438	1232	1078	958	863
6.00	6900	5175	4600	4140	3764	3450	2957	2588	2300	2070	1725	1479	1294	1150	1035
7.00	8050	6038	5367	4830	4391	4025	3450	3019	2683	2415	2013	1725	1509	1342	1208
8.00	9200	6900	6133	5520	5018	4600	3943	3450	3067	2760	2300	1971	1725	1533	1380
9.00	10350	7763	6900	6210	5645	5175	4436	3881	3450	3105	2588	2218	1941	1725	1553
10.00	11500	8625	7667	6900	6273	5750	4929	4313	3833	3450	2875	2464	2156	1917	1725

Pulley (Sheave) Selection Tables - 3450 rpm motor

Equipment Speed in revolutions per minute (rpm) for motors turning 3450 rpm

Outside Diameter of Pulley on Equipment	Outside Diameter of Pulley on Motor														
	1.50	2.00	2.25	2.50	2.75	3.00	350	4.00	4.50	5.00	6.00	7.00	8.00	9.00	10.00
1.50	3450	4600	5175	5750	6325	6900	8050	9200	10350	11500	13800	16100	18400	20700	23000
2.00	2588	3450	3881	4313	4744	5175	6038	6900	7763	8625	10350	12075	13800	15525	17250
2.25	2300	3067	3450	3833	4217	4600	5367	6133	6900	7667	9200	10733	12267	13800	15333
2.50	2070	2760	3105	3450	3795	4140	4830	5520	6210	6900	8280	9660	11040	12420	13800
2.75	1882	2509	2823	3136	3450	3764	4391	5018	5645	6273	7527	8782	10036	11291	12545
3.00	1725	2300	2588	2875	3163	3450	4025	4600	5175	5750	6900	8050	9200	10350	11500
3.50	1479	1971	2218	2464	2711	2957	3450	3943	4436	4929	5914	6900	7886	8871	9857
4.00	1294	1725	1941	2156	2372	2588	3019	3450	3881	4313	5175	6038	6900	7763	8625
4.50	1150	1533	1725	1917	2108	2300	2683	3067	3450	3833	4600	5367	6133	6900	7667
5.00	1035	1380	1553	1725	1898	2070	2415	2760	3105	3450	4140	4830	5520	6210	6900
6.00	863	1150	1294	1438	1581	1725	2013	2300	2588	2875	3450	4025	4600	5175	5750
7.00	739	986	1109	1232	1355	1479	1725	1971	2218	2464	2957	3450	3943	4436	4929
8.00	647	863	970	1078	1186	1294	1509	1725	1941	2156	2588	3019	3450	3881	4313
9.00	575	767	863	958	1054	1150	1342	1533	1725	1917	2300	2683	3067	3450	3833
10.00	518	690	776	863	949	1035	1208	1380	1553	1725	2070	2415	2760	3105	3450

Bolts and Threads

Steel Bolt and Screw Grades, Types and Classes.........................56

Notes on Clamping Force and Bolt Torque 61

Clamping Force and Bolt Torque - Carbon Steel Bolts
Coarse Inch Threads...63
Fine Inch Threads 68
Metric Threads 73

Effect of Anti-Seize Compounds, Lubricants, Platings,
Coatings, Torque Coeffficients, and Stress Levels on
Torque for Carbon Steel Bolts..78

Standard Dry Torque for Coarse-Threaded, Non-Ferrous
and Stainless Steel Bolts
Nylon 6/6...81
Aluminum 81
Yellow Brass 81
Silicone Bronze 82
18-8 Stainless Steel 83
316 Stainless Steel 83
Monel 84

Unified Inch Screw Threads - Standard Screw Thread Series 85

Clearance Holes for Bolts and Screws - Inch Series 87

Clearance Holes for Bolts and Screws - Metric Series 88

Bolt Head Styles Chart 90

Steel Bolt & Screw Grades, Types & Classes

INCH Series - SAE Standards		
Grades	**ID Mark**	**Types & Sizes (MTS=Min Tensile Stress)**
Grade 60M (SAE J82)		Machine Screws - #4 to 3/4" Carbon steel MTS 60,000 psi Proof Stress - none
Grade 120M (SAE J82)		Machine Screws - #4 to 3/4" Carbon steel, quenched & tempered MTS 120,000 psi Proof Stress - none
Grade 1 (SAE J429)		Bolts, screws, studs - 1/4"-1-1/2" Low or medium carbon steel MTS 60,000psi Proof Stress - 33,000psi
Grade 2 (SAE J429)		Bolts, screws, studs - 1/4"-1-1/2" Low or medium carbon steel MTS 74,000psi: 1/4"- 3/4" MTS 60,000psi: 7/8"- 1-1/2" Proof Stress - 55,000psi: 1/4"- 3/4" Proof Stress - 33,000psi: 7/8"- 1-1/2"
Grade 5 (SAE J429)		Bolts, screws, studs - 1/4"-1-1/2" Med carbon steel, quenched & tempered MTS 120,000psi: 1/4"- 1" MTS 105,000psi: 1-1/8"- 1-1/2" Proof Stress - 85,000psi: 1/4"- 1" Proof Stress - 74,000psi: 1-1/8"- 1-1/2"
Grade 5.1 (SAE J429)		Bolts, screws, studs - #6-5/8" Med carbon steel, quenched & tempered MTS 120,000psi Proof Stress - 85,000psi
Grade 5.2 (SAE J429)		Bolts, screws, studs - 1/4"-1" Low carbon martensite steel, quenched & tempered MTS 120,000psi Proof Stress - 85,000psi
Grade 7 (SAE J429)		Bolts, screws, studs - 1/4"-1-1/2" Med carbon alloy steel, quenched & tempered MTS 133,000psi Proof Stress - 105,000psi
Grade 8 (SAE J429)		Bolts, screws, studs - 1/4"-1-1/2" Med carbon alloy steel, quenched & tempered MTS 150,000psi Proof Stress - 120,000psi
Grade 8.2 (SAE J429)		Bolts, screws, studs - 1/4"-1" Low carbon martensite steel, quenched & tempered MTS 150,000psi Proof Stress - 120,000psi

INCH Series - ASTM Standards		
Grades	**ID Mark**	**Types & Sizes (MTS=Min Tensile Stress)**
A307 Grade A	307A	Bolts & studs, 1/4"-4" Low or medium carbon steel MTS 60,000psi Proof Stress - none
A307 Grade B	307B	Bolts & studs, 1/4"-4" Low or medium carbon steel MTS 60,000psi Proof Stress - none
A325 Type 1	A325	Structural & anchor bolts, 1/2"-1-1/2" Medium carbon, carbon-boron, or medium carbon alloy steel MTS - 120,000psi: 1/2"-1" MTS - 105,000psi: 1-1/8"-1-1/2" Proof Stress - 85,000psi: 1/2"-1" Proof Stress - 74,000psi: 1-1/8"-1-1/2"
A325 Type 3	A325	Structural & anchor bolts, 1/2"-1-1/2" Atmospheric corrosion resistant steel, quenched & tempered MTS - 120,000psi Proof Stress - 85,000psi
A354 Grade BC	BC	Bolts & studs, 1/4"-4" Medium carbon alloy steel, quenched & tempered MTS - 125,000psi: 1/4" - 2-1/2" MTS - 115,000psi: 2-5/8"-4" Proof Stress - 105,000psi: 1/4"-2-1/2" Proof Stress - 95,000psi: 2-5/8"-4"
A354 Grade BD	BD	Bolts & studs, 1/4"-4" Medium carbon alloy steel, quenched & tempered MTS - 150,000psi: 1/4" - 2-1/2" MTS - 140,000psi: 2-5/8"-4" Proof Stress - 120,000psi: 1/4"-2-1/2" Proof Stress - 105,000psi: 2-5/8"-4"
A449 Type 1		Bolts & studs, 1/4"-4" Medium carbon steel, quenched & tempered MTS - 120,000psi: 1/4" - 1" MTS - 105,000psi: 1-1/8"-1-1/2" MTS - 90,000psi: 1-3/4"-3" Proof Stress - 85,000psi: 1/4"-1" Proof Stress - 74,000psi: 1-1/8"-1-1/2" Proof Stress - 55,000psi: 1-3/4"-3"
A449 Type 2		Bolts & studs, 1/4"-1" Low or medium carbon martensite steel, quenched & tempered MTS - 120,000psi Proof Stress - 85,000psi
A490 Type 1	A490	Structural bolts, 1/2"-1-1/2" Medium carbon alloy steel, quenched & tempered MTS - 150,000psi Proof Stress 120,000psi

INCH Series - ASTM Standards (cont.)

Grades	ID Mark	Types & Sizes (MTS=Min Tensile Stress)
A490 Type 2	A490	Structural bolts, 1/2"-1" Low carbon martensite steel, quenched & tempered MTS - 150,000psi Proof Stress 120,000psi
A490 Type 3	A490	Structural bolts, 1/2"-1-1/2" Atmospheric corrosion resistant steel, quenched & tempered MTS - 150,000psi Proof Stress - 120,000psi
A574		Hexagon socket-head cap screws #0 - 4" Carbon alloy steel, quenched & tempered MTS - 180,000psi: #0 - 1/2" MTS - 170,000psi: 5/8" - 4" Proof Stress - 140,000psi: #0 - 1/2" Proof Stress - 135,000psi: 5/8" - 4"

METRIC Series - SAE Standards

Grades	ID Mark	Types & Sizes (MTS=Min Tensile Stress)
Class 4.6 SAE J1199	4.6	Bolts, screws, & studs, 5mm-36mm Low or medium carbon steel MTS - 400 Mpa Proof Stress - 225 MPa
Class 4.8 SAE J1199	4.8	Bolts, screws, & studs, 1.6mm-16mm Low-medium carbon steel, stress relieved MTS - 420 MPa Proof Stress - 310 MPa
Class 5.8 SAE J1199	5.8	Bolts, screws, & studs, 5mm-24mm Low-medium carbon steel, stress relieved MTS - 520 MPa Proof Stress - 380 MPa
Class 8.8 SAE J1199	8.8	Bolts, screws, & studs, 17mm-36mm Medium carbon steel, medium carbon alloy steel, low carbon alloy steel, or medium carbon boron steel, quenched & tempered MTS - 830 MPa Proof Stress - 600 MPa
Class 9.8 SAE J1199	9.8	Bolts, screws, & studs, 1.6mm-16mm Medium carbon steel, low carbon martensite steel, or medium carbon boron steel, quenched & tempered MTS - 900 MPa Proof Stress - 650 MPa
Class 10.9 SAE J1199	10.9	Bolts, screws, & studs, 6mm-36mm Carbon steel, medium carbon alloy steel, low carbon martensite steel, or medium carbon boron steel, quenched & tempered MTS - 1,040 MPa Proof Stress - 830 MPa

METRIC Series - ASTM Standards		
Grades	ID Mark	Types & Sizes (MTS=Min Tensile Stress)
Class 4.6 ASTM F568	4.6	Bolts, screws, & studs, 5mm-100mm Low or medium carbon steel MTS - 400 MPa Proof Stress - 225 MPa
Class 4.8 ASTM F568	4.8	Bolts, screws, & studs, 1.6mm-16mm Low or medium carbon steel, partially or fully annealed MTS - 420 MPa Proof Stress - 310 MPa
Class 5.8 ASTM F568	5.8	Bolts, screws, & studs, 5mm-24mm Low or medium carbon steel, cold worked MTS - 520 MPa Proof Stress - 380 MPa
Class 8.8 ASTM F568	8.8	Bolts, screws, & studs, 16mm-72mm Low or medium carbon steel, quenched & tempered MTS - 830 MPa Proof Stress - 600 MPa
Class 8.8.3 ASTM F568	8.8.3	Bolts, screws, & studs, 16mm-36mm Low carbon martensite steel, quenched & tempered MTS - 830 MPa Proof Stress - 600 MPa
Class 9.8 ASTM F568	9.8	Bolts, screws, & studs, 1.6mm-16mm Medium carbon steel or low carbon martensite steel, quenched & tempered MTS - 900 MPa Proof Stress - 650 MPa
Class 10.9 ASTM F568	10.9	Bolts, screws, & studs, 5mm-100mm Medium carbon, steel, medium carbon alloy steel, or atmospheric corrosion resistant steel, quenched & tempered MTS - 1,040 MPa Proof Stress - 830 MPa
Class 10.9.3 ASTM F568	10.9.3	Bolts, screws, & studs, 16mm-36mm Medium carbon alloy steel, quenched & tempered MTS - 1,040 MPa Proof Stress - 830 MPa
Class 12.9 ASTM F568	12.9	Bolts, screws, & studs, 1.6mm-100mm Alloy steel, quenched & tempered MTS - 1,220 MPa Proof Stress - 970 MPa

METRIC Series - ISO Standards		
Grades	ID Mark	Types & Sizes (MTS=Min Tensile Stress)
Class 3.6 ISO 898-1	3.6	Bolts, screws, & studs, 1mm-300mm Carbon steel MTS - 330 MPa Proof Stress - none
Class 4.6 ISO 898-1	4.6	Bolts, screws, & studs, 1mm-300mm Carbon steel MTS - 400 MPa Proof Stress - none
Class 4.8 ISO 898-1	4.8	Bolts, screws, & studs, 1mm-300mm Carbon steel MTS - 420 MPa Proof Stress - none
Class 5.6 ISO 898-1	5.6	Bolts, screws, & studs, 1mm-300mm Carbon steel MTS - 500 MPa Proof Stress - none
Class 5.8 ISO 898-1	5.8	Bolts, screws, & studs, 1mm-300mm Carbon steel MTS - 520 MPa Proof Stress - none
Class 6.8 ISO 898-1	6.8	Bolts, screws, & studs, 1mm-300mm Carbon steel MTS - 600 MPa Proof Stress - none
Class 8.8 ISO 898-1	8.8	Bolts, screws, & studs, 1mm-300mm Carbon steel, quenched & tempered MTS - 800 MPa: 1mm-16mm MTS - 830 MPa: 16mm-300mm Proof Stress - 640 MPa: 1mm-16mm Proof Stress - 660 MPa: 16mm-300mm
Class 9.8 ISO 898-1	9.8	Bolts, screws, & studs, 1mm-300mm Carbon steel, quenched & tempered MTS - 900 MPa Proof Stress - 720 MPa
Class 10.9 ISO 898-1	10.9	Bolts, screws, & studs, 1mm-300mm Carbon alloy steel, quenched & tempered MTS - 1,040 MPa Proof Stress - 940 MPa
Class 12.9 ISO 898-1	12.9	Bolts, screws, & studs, 1mm-300mm Alloy steel, quenched & tempered MTS - 1,220 MPa Proof Stress - 1,100 MPa

Note:
Abbreviations and symbols:
" = inch, mm = millimeter
psi = pound-force per square inch, MPa = megapascal
ASTM = American Society For Testing And Materials
ISO = International Organization For Standarization,
SAE = Society Of Automotive Engineers

Notes on Clamping Force and Bolt Torque

1. The tables which follow present Clamping Force and Standard Dry Torque for a variety of threaded fasteners. The tables cover a wide variety of material properties and fastener sizes.

2. It should be noted that some combinations of bolt size and proof strength or minimum tensile strength shown in the tables may not be available. Fastener standards written by ANSI, ASME, ASTM, IFI, ISO, and/or SAE can either overlap each other or leave gaps in either material properties or fastener sizes. These overlaps and gaps in information generally occur because each organization is addressing a different aspect of fastener technology. For instance, ASTM deals with the materials used in fastener manufacture and the testing of those materials for acceptability while ANSI/ASME deals with the dimensions of the manufactured fastener.

3. Clamping force and standard dry torque for <u>carbon steel bolts</u> were calculated for clean, dry, non-plated carbon steel with a torque coefficient (also called a friction factor or a nut factor) of 0.20. The clamping force and standard dry torque were calculated to produce a tensile stress in the fastener equal to 70% of the minimum tensile strength or 75% of the proof strength.

4. Standard dry torques for <u>stainless steel and non-ferrous bolts</u> were compiled from test data on fasteners as published by bolt manufacturers, in trade publications, and in fastener textbooks.

5. Clamping force and standard dry torque presented in these tables should be considered approximate because both values are sensitive to many factors which can vary from bolt to bolt. Some of these factors include nominal bolt diameter, material strength, tensile stress area, coefficient of friction at the bearing faces and thread contact surfaces, effective radius of action of frictional forces on the bearing faces and thread contact surfaces, thread half-angle, and helix angle of the thread.

6. Lubricants and Coatings: Lubricants reduce the torque required to produce a given tensile stress or clamping force while coatings (platings or oxidizes) can either increase or decrease the required torque. The table on page 78 presents factors which can be used to approximate the effect of various lubricants and coatings on the torque for <u>carbon steel</u> fasteners only. Lubricants and coatings may have the same effects on <u>stainless steel</u> and <u>non-ferrous</u> fasteners but the authors could not confirm this assumption. Note that lubrication applied to only the external threads is as effective as lubrication being applied to both external and internal threads.

7. Torque Coefficients and Tensile Stress Levels: As stated above, clamping force and standard dry torque presented in the following tables were calculated for a torque coefficient equal to 0.20 and a tensile stress level equal to either 70% of the minimum tensile strength or 75% of the proof strength. The table on page 78 also presents factors that can be used to approximate the effect of lowering the torque coefficient to between 0.20 and 0.15 and changing tensile stress level to between 50% and 80% of the proof strength.

8. Bolts with tensile strengths higher than 150,000 psi are not common except in aircraft applications. A few of these special fasteners are:

- NAS 144; 160,000 psi; high carbon alloy steel, quenched and tempered.
- MS2000; 160,000 psi; high carbon alloy steel, quenched and tempered.
- ASTM A574 - Socket Head Cap Screws; #0 to 1/2 " - 170,000 psi; 9/16" to 4" - 180,000 psi; high carbon alloy steel, quenched and tempered.
- NAS 623; 180,000 psi; high carbon alloy steel, quenched and tempered.
- Supertanium®; 180,000 psi; 8 points on head; special steel alloy, quenched and tempered.
- AAS; 200,000 psi; high carbon alloy steel, quenched and tempered.

Clamping forces and standard dry torques for all special alloy bolts should be obtained from the manufacturer.

9. Abbreviations:

AAS	- Aircraft Assigned Steel
ANSI	- American National Standards Institute
ASME	- American Society of Mechanical Engineers
ASTM	- American Society for Testing and Materials
IFI	- Industrial Fastener Institute
ISO	- International Organization for Standardization
MS	- Military Standard
NAS	- National Aircraft Standard
psi	- pound-force per square inch
SAE	- Society of Automotive Engineers

Clamping Force and Standard Dry Torque

Coarse <u>INCH-THREADED</u> Carbon Steel Bolts

Grades and Types: SAE J429 - Grade 1

Grade 1 (1/4" to 1-1/2")
Proof Strength = 33,000 pound-force/square inch (lbf/in²)

Bolt Size (inch)	Threads/ Inch	Clamping Force		Standard Dry Torque	
		pound-force (lbf)	kilonewton (kN)	foot pound-force(ft lbf)	newton meter (N m)
1/4	20	787	3.50	3.28	4.45
5/16	18	1,297	5.77	6.75	9.16
3/8	16	1,918	8.53	12.0	16.3
7/16	14	2,631	11.7	19.2	26.0
1/2	13	3,512	15.6	29.3	39.7
9/16	12	4,505	20.0	42.2	57.3
5/8	11	5,594	24.9	58.3	79.0
3/4	10	8,267	36.8	103	140
7/8	9	11,435	50.9	167	226
1	8	14,999	66.7	250	339
1-1/8	7	18,884	84.0	354	480
1-1/4	7	23,983	107	500	677
1-3/8	6	28,586	127	655	888
1-1/2	6	34,774	155	869	1179

Grades and Types: SAE J429- Grade 2

Grade 2 - (1/4" to 3/4")
Proof Strength = 55,000 pound-force/square inch (lbf/in²)

Grade 2 - (7/8" to 1-1/2")
Proof Strength = 33,000 pound-force/square inch (lbf/in²)

Bolt Size (inch)	Threads/ Inch	Clamping Force		Standard Dry Torque	
		pound-force (lbf)	kilonewton (kN)	foot pound-force (ft lbf)	newton meter (Nm)
1/4	20	1,312	5.83	5.47	7.41
5/16	18	2,162	9.61	11.3	15.3
3/8	16	3,197	14.2	20.0	27.1
7/16	14	4,385	19.5	32.0	43.3
1/2	13	5,853	26.0	48.8	66.1
9/16	12	7,508	33.4	70.4	95.4
5/8	11	9,323	41.5	97.1	132
3/4	10	13,778	61.3	172	233
7/8	9	11,435	50.9	167	226
1	8	14,999	66.7	250	339
1-1/8	7	18,884	84.0	354	480
1-1/4	7	23,983	107	500	677
1-3/8	6	28,586	127	655	888
1-1/2	6	34,774	155	869	1,179

Grades and Types: SAE J429 - Grades 5, 5.1, & 5.2

Grade 5 - (1/4" to 1"), Grade 5.1 - (#6 to 5/8"), and Grade 5.2 - (1/4" to 1")
Proof Strength = 85,000 pound-force/square inch (lbf/in²)

Grade 5 - (1-1/8" to 1-1/2")
Proof Strength = 74,000 pound-force/square inch (lbf/in²)

Bolt Size (# or inch)	Threads/ Inch	Clamping Force		Standard Dry Torque	
		pound-force (lbf)	kilonewton (kN)	foot pound-force(ft lbf)	newton meter (Nm)
6	32	579	2.58	1.33	1.81

8	32	893	3.97	2.44	3.31
10	24	1,116	4.96	3.53	4.79
12	24	1,543	6.86	5.55	7.53
1/4	20	2,027	9.02	8.45	11.5
5/16	18	3,341	14.9	17.4	23.6
3/8	16	4,941	22.0	30.9	41.9
7/16	14	6,777	30.1	49.4	67.0
1/2	13	9,046	40.2	75.4	102
9/16	12	11,603	51.6	109	147
5/8	11	14,408	64.1	150	203
3/4	10	21,293	94.7	266	361
7/8	9	29,453	131	430	582
1	8	38,633	172	644	873
1-1/8	7	42,347	188	794	1,077
1-1/4	7	53,780	239	1,120	1,519
1-3/8	6	64,103	285	1,469	1,992
1-1/2	6	77,978	347	1,949	2,643

Grades and Types: SAE J429-Grade 7

Grade 7 - (1/4" to 1-1/2")
Proof Strength = 105,000 pound-force/square inch (lbf/in^2)

Bolt Size (inch)	Threads/ Inch	Clamping Force		Standard Dry Torque	
		pound-force (lbf)	kilonewton (kN)	foot pound-force(ft lbf)	newton meter (Nm)
1/4	20	2504	11.1	10.4	14.1
5/16	18	4127	18.4	21.5	29.1
3/8	16	6103	27.1	38.1	51.7
7/16	14	8371	37.2	61.0	82.8
1/2	13	11,175	49.7	93.1	126
9/16	12	14,333	63.8	134	182
5/8	11	17,798	79.2	185	251
3/4	10	26,303	117	329	446
7/8	9	36,383	162	531	719
1	8	47,723	212	795	1,078
1-1/8	7	60,086	267	1,127	1,527
1-1/4	7	76,309	339	1,590	2155
1-3/8	6	90,956	405	2,084	2826
1-1/2	6	110,644	492	2,766	3,750

Grades and Types: SAE J429 - Grades 8 & 8.2

Grade 8 (1/4" to 1-1/2") and Grade 8.2 (1/4" to 1")
Proof Strength = 120,000 pound-force/square inch (lbf/in^2)

Bolt Size (inch)	Threads/ Inch	Clamping Force		Standard Dry Torque	
		pound- force (lbf)	kilonewton (kN)	foot pound-force(ft lbf)	newton meter (Nm)
1/4	20	2,862	12.7	11.9	16.2
5/16	18	4,716	21.0	24.6	33.3
3/8	16	6,975	31.0	43.6	59.1
7/16	14	9,567	42.6	69.8	94.6
1/2	13	12,771	56.8	106	144
9/16	12	16,380	72.9	154	208
5/8	11	20,340	90.5	212	287
3/4	10	30,060	134	376	509
7/8	9	41,580	185	606	822
1	8	54,540	243	909	1,232
1-1/8	7	68,670	305	1,288	1,746
1-1/4	7	87,210	388	1,817	2,463
1-3/8	6	103,950	462	2,382	3,230
1-1/2	6	126,450	562	3,161	4,286

Grades and Types: ASTM A307 - Grades A & B

Grades A & B (1/4" to 2")
Minimum Tensile Strength = 60,000 pound-force/square inch (lbf/in²)

Bolt Size (inch)	Threads/ Inch	Clamping Force		Standard Dry Torque	
		pound-force (lbf)	kilonewton (kN)	foot pound-force (ft lbf)	newton meter (N m)
1/4	20	1,336	5.94	5.57	7.55
5/16	18	2,201	9.79	11.5	15.5
3/8	16	3,255	14.5	20.3	27.6
7/16	14	4,465	19.9	32.6	44.1
1/2	13	5,960	26.5	49.7	67.3
9/16	12	7,644	34.0	71.7	97.2
5/8	11	9,492	42.2	98.9	134
3/4	10	14,030	62.4	175	234
7/8	9	19,400	86.3	283	384
1	8	25,450	113	424	575
1-1/8	7	32,050	143	601	815
1-1/4	7	40,700	181	848	1,150
1-3/8	6	48,510	216	1,112	1,507
1-1/2	6	59,010	263	1,475	2,000
1-3/4	5	79,800	355	2,328	3,156
2	4-1/2	105,000	467	3,500	4,745

Grades and Types: ASTM A325 - Types 1 & 3

Types 1 & 3 (1/2" to 1")
Proof Strength = 85,000 pound-force/square inch (lbf/in²)

Type 1 (1-1/8" to 1-1/2")
Proof Strength = 74,000 pound-force/square inch (lbf/in²)

Bolt Size (inch)	Threads/ Inch	Clamping Force		Standard Dry Torque	
		pound-force (lbf)	kilonewton (kN)	foot pound-force (ft lbf)	newton meter (N m)
1/2	13	9,046	40.2	75.4	102
9/16	12	11,603	51.6	109	147
5/8	11	14,408	64.1	150	203
3/4	10	21,293	94.7	266	361
7/8	9	29,453	131	430	582
1	8	38,633	172	644	873
1-1/8	7	42,347	188	794	1,077
1-1/4	7	53,780	239	1,120	1,519
1-3/8	6	64,103	285	1,469	1,992
1-1/2	6	77,978	347	1,949	2,643

Grades and Types: ASTM A354 - Grade BC

Grade BC (1/4" to 2")
Proof Strength = 105,000 pound-force/square inch (lbf/in²)

Bolt Size (inch)	Threads/ Inch	Clamping Force		Standard Dry Torque	
		pound-force (lbf)	kilonewton (kN)	foot pound-force (ft lbf)	newton meter (N m)
1/4	20	2,504	11.1	10.4	14.1
5/16	18	4,127	18.4	21.5	29.1
3/8	16	6,103	27.1	38.1	51.7
7/16	14	8,371	37.2	61.0	82.8
1/2	13	11,175	49.7	93.1	126
9/16	12	14,333	63.8	134	182
5/8	11	17,798	79.2	185	251
3/4	10	26,303	117	329	446
7/8	9	36,383	162	531	719
1	8	47,723	212	795	1,078

1-1/8	7	60,086	267	1,127	1,527
1-1/4	7	76,309	339	1,590	2,155
1-3/8	6	90,956	405	2,084	2,826
1-1/2	6	110,644	492	2,766	3,750
1-3/4	5	149,625	666	4,364	5,917
2	4-1/2	196,875	876	6,563	8,898

Grades and Types: ASTM A354 - Grade BD

Grade BD (1/4" to 2")
Proof Strength = 120,000 pound-force/square inch (lbf/in²)

Bolt Size (inch)	Threads/ Inch	Clamping Force		Standard Dry Torque	
		pound-force (lbf)	kilonewton (kN)	foot pound-force(ft lbf)	newton meter (Nm)
1/4	20	2,862	12.7	11.9	16.2
5/16	18	4,716	21.0	24.6	33.3
3/8	16	6,975	31.0	43.6	59.1
7/16	14	9,567	42.6	69.8	94.6
1/2	13	12,771	56.8	106	144
9/16	12	16,380	72.9	154	208
5/8	11	20,340	90.5	212	287
3/4	10	30,060	134	376	509
7/8	9	41,580	185	606	822
1	8	54,540	243	909	1,232
1-1/8	7	68,670	305	1,288	1,746
1-1/4	7	87,210	388	1,817	2,463
1-3/8	6	103,950	462	2,382	3,230
1-1/2	6	126,450	562	3,161	4,286
1-3/4	5	171,000	761	4,988	6,762
2	4-1/2	225,000	1,001	7,500	10,169

Grades and Types: ASTM A449 - Types 1 & 2

Types 1 & 2 (1/4" to 1")
Proof Strength = 85,000 pound-force/square inch (lbf/in²)

Type 1 (1-1/8"to 1-1/2")
Proof Strength = 74,000 pound-force/square inch (lbf/in²)

Type 1 (1-3/4"to 2")
Proof Strength = 55,000 pound-force/square inch (lbf/in²)

Bolt Size (inch)	Threads/ Inch	Clamping Force		Standard Dry Torque	
		pound-force (lbf)	kilonewton (kN)	foot pound-force(ft lbf)	newton meter (Nm)
1/4	20	2,027	9.2	8.45	11.5
5/16	18	3,341	14.9	17.4	23.6
3/8	16	4,941	22.0	30.9	41.9
7/16	14	6,777	30.1	49.4	67.0
1/2	13	9,046	40.2	75.4	102
9/16	12	11,603	51.6	109	147
5/8	11	14,408	64.1	150	203
3/4	10	21,293	94.7	266	361
7/8	9	29,453	131	430	582
1	8	38,633	172	644	873
1-1/8	7	42,347	188	794	1,077
1-1/4	7	53,780	239	1,120	1,519
1-3/8	6	64,103	285	1,469	1,992
1-1/2	6	77,978	347	1,949	2,643
1-3/4	5	78,375	349	2,286	3,099
2	4-1/2	103,125	459	3,438	4,661

Grades and Types: ASTM A490 - Types 1,2 & 3

Types 1 & 3 (1/2" to 1-1/2") & Type 2 (1/2" to 1")
Proof Strength = 120,000 pound-force/square inch (lbf/in²)

Bolt Size (inch)	Threads/ Inch	Clamping Force		Standard Dry Torque	
		pound-force (lbf)	kilonewton (kN)	foot pound-force (ft lbf)	newton meter (Nm)
1/2	13	12,771	56.8	106	144
9/16	12	16,380	72.9	154	208
5/8	11	20,340	90.5	212	287
3/4	10	30,060	134	376	509
7/8	9	41,580	185	606	822
1	8	54,540	243	909	1,232
1-1/8	7	68,670	305	1,288	1,746
1-1/4	7	87,210	388	1,817	2,463
1-3/8	6	103,950	462	2,382	3,230
1-1/2	6	126,450	562	3,161	4,286

Grades and Types: ASTM A574

(#1 to 1/2")
Proof Strength = 140,000 pound-force/square inch (lbf/in²)

(9/16" to 2")
Proof Strength = 135,000 pound-force/square inch (lbf/in²)

Bolt Size (# or inch)	Threads/ Inch	Clamping Force		Standard Dry Torque	
		pound-force (lbf)	kilonewton (kN)	foot pound-force (ft lbf)	newton meter (Nm)
1	64	276	1.23	0.336	0.456
2	56	389	1.73	0.557	0.755
3	48	510	2.27	0.842	1.14
4	40	633	2.82	1.18	1.60
5	40	836	3.72	1.74	2.36
6	32	954	4.25	2.20	2.98
8	32	1,470	6.54	4.02	5.45
10	24	1,838	8.17	5.82	7.89
12	24	2,541	11.3	9.15	12.4
1/4	20	3,339	14.9	13.9	18.9
5/16	18	5,502	24.5	28.7	38.9
3/8	16	8,138	36.2	50.9	69.0
7/16	14	11,162	49.6	81.4	110
1/2	13	14,900	66.3	124	168
9/16	12	18,428	82.0	173	234
5/8	11	22,883	102	238	323
3/4	10	33,818	150	423	573
7/8	9	46,778	208	682	925
1	8	61,358	273	1,023	1,386
1-1/8	7	77,254	344	1,449	1,964
1-1/4	7	98,111	436	2,044	2,771
1-3/8	6	116,944	520	2,680	3,634
1-1/2	6	142,256	633	3,556	4,822
1-3/4	5	192,375	856	5,611	7,607
2	4-1/2	253,125	1,126	8,438	11,440

Fine INCH-THREADED Carbon Steel Bolts

Grades and Types: SAE J429 - Grade 1

Grade 1 (1/4" to 1-1/2")
Proof Strength = 33,000 pound-force/square inch (lbf/in²)

Bolt Size (inch)	Threads/ Inch	Clamping Force		Standard Dry Torque	
		pound-force (lbf)	kilonewton (kN)	foot pound-force(ft lbf)	newton meter (N m)
1/4	28	901	4.01	3.75	5.09
5/16	24	1,438	6.40	7.49	10.2
3/8	24	2,173	9.67	13.6	18.4
7/16	20	2,938	13.1	21.4	29.0
1/2	20	3,960	17.6	33.0	44.7
9/16	18	5,024	22.3	47.1	63.9
5/8	18	6,336	28.2	66.0	89.5
3/4	16	9,232	41.1	115	156
7/8	14	12,598	56.0	184	249
1	12	16,409	73.0	273	371
1-1/8	12	21,186	94.2	397	539
1-1/4	12	26,557	118	553	750
1-3/8	12	32,546	145	746	1,011
1-1/2	12	39,130	174	978	1,326

Grades and Types: SAE J429 - Grade 2

Grade 2 - (1/4" to 3/4")
Proof Strength = 55,000 pound-force/square inch (lbf/in²)

Grade 2 - (7/8" to 1-1/2")
Proof Strength = 33,000 pound-force/square inch (lbf/in²)

Bolt Size (inch)	Threads/ Inch	Clamping Force		Standard Dry Torque	
		pound-force (lbf)	kilonewton (kN)	foot pound-force (ft lbf)	newton meter (Nm)
1/4	28	1,502	6.68	6.26	8.48
5/16	24	2,397	10.7	12.5	16.9
3/8	24	3,622	16.1	22.6	30.7
7/16	20	4,896	21.8	35.7	48.4
1/2	20	6,600	29.4	55.0	74.6
9/16	18	8,374	37.2	78.5	106
5/8	18	10,560	47.0	110	149
3/4	16	15,366	68.4	192	261
7/8	14	12,598	56.0	184	249
1	12	16,409	73.0	273	371
1-1/8	12	21,186	94.2	397	539
1-1/4	12	26,557	118	553	750
1-3/8	12	32,546	145	746	1,011
1-1/2	12	39,130	174	978	1,326

Grades and Types: SAE J429 - Grades 5, 5.1, & 5.2

Grade 5 - (1/4" to 1"), Grade 5.1 - (#6 to 5/8"), and Grade 5.2 - (1/4" to 1")
Proof Strength = 85,000 pound-force/square inch (lbf/in²)

Grade 5 - (1-1/8" to 1-1/2")
Proof Strength = 74,000 pound-force/square inch (lbf/in²)

Bolt Size (# or inch)	Threads/ Inch	Clamping Force		Standard Dry Torque	
		pound-force (lbf)	kilonewton (kN)	foot pound-force(ft lbf)	newton meter (Nm)
6	40	646	2.88	1.49	2.02
8	36	939	4.18	2.57	3.48
10	32	1,275	5.67	4.04	5.47
12	28	1,645	7.32	5.92	8.03

Bolt Size (inch)	Threads/Inch	pound-force (lbf)	kilonewton (kN)	foot pound-force (ft lbf)	newton meter (Nm)
1/4	28	2,321	10.3	9.67	13.1
5/16	24	3,704	16.5	19.3	26.2
3/8	24	5,597	24.9	35.0	47.4
7/16	20	7,567	33.7	55.2	74.8
1/2	20	10,200	45.4	85.0	115
9/16	18	12,941	57.6	121	164
5/8	18	16,320	72.6	170	230
3/4	16	23,779	106	297	403
7/8	14	32,449	144	473	642
1	12	42,266	188	704	955
1-1/8	12	47,508	211	891	1,208
1-1/4	12	59,552	265	1,241	1,682
1-3/8	12	72,983	325	1,673	2,268
1-1/2	12	87,746	390	2,194	2,974

Grades and Types: SAE J429-Grade 7

Grade 7 - (1/4" to 1-1/2")
Proof Strength = 105,000 pound-force/square inch (lbf/in^2)

Bolt Size (inch)	Threads/Inch	Clamping Force		Standard Dry Torque	
		pound-force (lbf)	kilonewton (kN)	foot pound-force (ft lbf)	newton meter (Nm)
1/4	28	2,867	12.8	11.9	16.2
5/16	24	4,575	20.4	23.8	32.3
3/8	24	6,914	30.8	43.2	58.6
7/16	20	9,348	41.6	68.2	92.4
1/2	20	12,600	56.0	105	142
9/16	18	15,986	71.1	150	203
5/8	18	20,160	89.7	210	285
3/4	16	29,374	131	367	498
7/8	14	40,084	178	585	793
1	12	52,211	232	870	1,180
1-1/8	12	67,410	300	1,264	1,714
1-1/4	12	84,499	376	1,760	2,387
1-3/8	12	103,556	461	2,373	3,218
1-1/2	12	124,504	554	3,113	4,220

Grades and Types: SAE J429 - Grades 8 & 8.2

Grade 8 (1/4" to 1-1/2") and Grade 8.2 (1/4" to 1")
Proof Strength = 120,000 pound-force/square inch (lbf/in^2)

Bolt Size (inch)	Threads/Inch	Clamping Force		Standard Dry Torque	
		pound-force (lbf)	kilonewton (kN)	foot pound-force (ft lbf)	newton meter (Nm)
1/4	28	3,276	14.6	13.7	18.5
5/16	24	5,229	23.3	27.2	36.9
3/8	24	7,902	35.1	49.4	67.0
7/16	20	10,683	47.5	77.9	106
1/2	20	14,400	64.1	120	163
9/16	18	18,270	81.3	171	232
5/8	18	23,040	102	240	325
3/4	16	33,570	149	420	569
7/8	14	45,810	204	668	906
1	12	59,670	265	995	1,348
1-1/8	12	77,040	343	1,445	1,958
1-1/4	12	96,570	430	2,012	2,728
1-3/8	12	118,350	526	2,712	3,677
1-1/2	12	142,290	633	3,557	4,823

Grades and Types: ASTM A307 - Grades A & B

Grades A & B (1/4" to 1-1/2")
Minimum Tensile Strength = 60,000 pound-force/square inch (lbf/in²)

Bolt Size (inch)	Threads/ Inch	Clamping Force		Standard Dry Torque	
		pound-force (lbf)	kilonewton (kN)	foot pound-force(ft lbf)	newton meter (N m)
1/4	28	1,529	6.80	6.37	8.64
5/16	24	2,440	10.9	12.7	17.2
3/8	24	3,688	16.4	23.1	31.3
7/16	20	4,985	22.2	36.4	49.3
1/2	20	6,720	29.9	56.0	75.9
9/16	18	8,526	37.9	79.9	108
5/8	18	10,750	47.8	112	152
3/4	16	15,670	69.7	196	266
7/8	14	21,380	95.1	312	423
1	12	27,850	124	464	629
1-1/8	12	35,950	160	674	914
1-1/4	12	45,070	201	939	1,273
1-3/8	12	55,230	246	1,266	1,716
1-1/2	12	66,400	295	1,660	2,251

Grades and Types: ASTM A325 - Types 1 & 3

Types 1 & 3 (1/2" to 1")
Proof Strength = 85,000 pound-force/square inch (lbf/in²)
Type 1 (1-1/8" to 1-1/2")
Proof Strength = 74,000 pound-force/square inch (lbf/in²)

Bolt Size (inch)	Threads/ Inch	Clamping Force		Standard Dry Torque	
		pound-force (lbf)	kilonewton (kN)	foot pound-force(ft lbf)	newton meter (Nm)
1/2	20	10,200	45.4	85.0	115
9/16	18	12,941	57.6	121	164
5/8	18	16,320	72.6	170	230
3/4	16	23,779	106	297	403
7/8	14	32,449	144	473	642
1	12	42,266	188	704	955
1-1/8	12	47,508	211	891	1,208
1-1/4	12	59,552	265	1,241	1,682
1-3/8	12	72,983	325	1,673	2,268
1-1/2	12	87,746	390	2,194	2,974

Grades and Types: ASTM A354 - Grade BC

Grade BC (1/4" to 1-1/2")
Proof Strength = 105,000 pound-force/square inch (lbf/in²)

Bolt Size (inch)	Threads/ Inch	Clamping Force		Standard Dry Torque	
		pound-force (lbf)	kilonewton (kN)	foot pound-force(ft lbf)	newton meter (Nm)
1/4	28	2,867	12.8	11.9	19.2
5/16	24	4,575	20.4	23.8	32.3
3/8	24	6,914	30.8	43.2	58.6
7/16	20	9,348	41.6	68.2	92.4
1/2	20	12,600	56.0	105	142
9/16	18	15,986	71.1	150	203
5/8	18	20,160	89.7	210	285
3/4	16	29,374	131	367	498
7/8	14	40,084	178	585	793
1	12	52,211	232	870	1,180
1-1/8	12	67,410	300	1,264	1,714
1-1/4	12	84,499	376	1,760	2,387

Bolt Size (inch)	Threads/Inch	pound-force (lbf)	kilonewton (kN)	foot pound-force (ft lbf)	newton meter (Nm)
1-3/8	12	103,556	461	2,373	3,218
1-1/2	12	124,504	554	3,113	4,220

Grades and Types: ASTM A354 - Grade BD

Grade BD (1/4" to 1-1/2")
Proof Strength = 120,000 pound-force/square inch (lbf/in^2)

Bolt Size (inch)	Threads/Inch	Clamping Force		Standard Dry Torque	
		pound- force (lbf)	kilonewton (kN)	foot pound-force (ft lbf)	newton meter (Nm)
1/4	28	3,276	14.6	13.7	18.5
5/16	24	5,229	23.3	27.2	36.9
3/8	24	7,902	35.1	49.4	67.0
7/16	20	10,683	47.5	77.9	106
1/2	20	14,400	64.1	120	163
9/16	18	18,270	81.3	171	232
5/8	18	23,040	102	240	325
3/4	16	33,570	149	420	569
7/8	14	45,810	204	668	906
1	12	59,670	265	995	1,348
1-1/8	12	77,040	343	1,445	1,958
1-1/4	12	96,570	430	2,012	2,728
1-3/8	12	118,350	526	2,712	3,677
1-1/2	12	142,290	633	3,557	4,823

Grades and Types: ASTM A449 - Types 1 & 2

Types 1 & 2 (1/4" to 1")
Proof Strength = 85,000 pound-force/square inch (lbf/in^2)

Type 1 (1-1/8"to 1-1/2")
Proof Strength = 74,000 pound-force/square inch (lbf/in^2)

Bolt Size (inch)	Threads/Inch	Clamping Force		Standard Dry Torque	
		pound- force (lbf)	kilonewton (kN)	foot pound-force (ft lbf)	newton meter (Nm)
1/4	28	2,321	10.3	9.67	13.1
5/16	24	3,704	16.5	19.3	26.2
3/8	24	5,597	24.9	35.0	47.4
7/16	20	7,567	33.7	55.2	74.8
1/2	20	10,200	45.4	85.0	115
9/16	18	12,941	57.6	121	164
5/8	18	16,320	72.6	170	230
3/4	16	23,779	106	297	403
7/8	14	32,449	144	473	642
1	12	42,266	188	704	955
1-1/8	12	47,508	211	891	1,208
1-1/4	12	59,552	265	1,241	1,682
1-3/8	12	72,983	325	1,673	2,268
1-1/2	12	87,746	390	2,194	2,974

Grades and Types: ASTM A490 - Types 1,2 & 3

Types 1 & 3 (1/2" to 1-1/2") & Type 2 (1/2" to 1")
Proof Strength = 120,000 pound-force/square inch (lbf/in^2)

Bolt Size (inch)	Threads/Inch	Clamping Force		Standard Dry Torque	
		pound- force (lbf)	kilonewton (kN)	foot pound-force (ft lbf)	newton meter (Nm)
1/2	20	14,400	64.1	120	163
9/16	18	18,270	81.3	170	232
5/8	18	23,040	102	240	325
3/4	16	33,570	149	420	569
7/8	14	45,810	204	668	906

1	12	59,670	265	995	1,348
1-1/8	12	77,040	343	1,445	1,958
1-1/4	12	96,570	430	2,012	2,728
1-3/8	12	118,350	526	2,712	3,677
1-1/2	12	142,290	633	3,557	4,823

Grades and Types: **ASTM A574**

(#0 to 1/2")
Proof Strength = 140,000 pound-force/square inch (lbf/in^2)

(9/16" to 1-1/2")
Proof Strength = 135,000 pound-force/square inch (lbf/in^2)

Bolt Size (# or inch)	Threads/ Inch	Clamping Force		Standard Dry Torque	
		pound-force (lbf)	kilonewton (kN)	foot pound-force(ft lbf)	newton meter (Nm)
0	80	189	0.841	0.189	0.256
1	72	292	1.30	0.355	0.482
2	64	413	1.84	0.591	0.802
3	56	549	2.44	0.906	1.23
4	48	693	3.08	1.29	1.75
5	44	873	3.88	1.82	2.46
6	40	1,065	4.74	2.45	3.32
8	36	1,547	6.88	4.23	5.73
10	32	2,100	9.34	6.65	9.02
12	28	2,709	12.1	9.75	13.2
1/4	28	3,822	17.0	15.9	21.6
5/16	24	6,101	27.1	31.8	43.1
3/8	24	9,220	41.0	57.6	78.1
7/16	20	12,460	55.4	90.9	123
1/2	20	16,800	74.7	140	190
9/16	18	20,554	91.4	193	261
5/8	18	25,920	115	270	366
3/4	16	37,766	168	472	640
7/8	14	51,536	229	752	1,019
1	12	67,129	299	1,119	1,517
1-1/8	12	86,670	386	1,625	2,203
1-1/4	12	108,641	483	2,263	3,069
1-3/8	12	133,144	592	3,051	4,137
1-1/2	12	160,076	712	4,002	5,426

Coarse METRIC-THREADED Carbon Steel Bolts

Class or Type: **ASTM F568, Class 4.6 (M5 to M100)**
ISO 898/1, Class 4.6 (M5 to M36)

Minimum Tensile Strength = 400 megapascal (MPa) = 58,000 pound-force/square inch (lbf/in²)

Bolt Size (mm)	Thread Pitch (mm)	Clamping Force		Standard Dry Torque	
		pound-force(lbf)	kilonewton (kN)	ft. pound-force(ft-lbf)	newton meter (Nm)
1.6	0.35	79.94	0.3556	0.0839	0.1138
1.8	0.35	107.1	0.4763	0.1265	0.1715
2	0.40	130.5	0.5804	0.1712	0.2322
2.2	0.45	156.2	0.6950	0.2255	0.3058
2.5	0.45	213.5	0.9495	0.3502	0.4748
3	0.50	316.8	1.409	0.6235	0.8454
3.5	0.60	426.5	1.897	0.9794	1.328
4	0.70	552.6	2.458	1.450	1.966
4.5	0.75	712.6	3.170	2.104	2.853
5	0.80	892.5	3.970	2.928	3.970
6	1.00	1,267	5.634	4.987	6.761
7	1.00	1,817	8.081	8.344	11.31
8	1.25	2,304	10.25	12.10	16.40
9	1.25	3,028	13.47	17.88	24.25
10	1.50	3,651	16.24	23.96	32.48
11	1.50	4,550	20.24	32.84	44.53
12	1.75	5,305	23.60	41.78	56.64
14	2.00	7,264	32.31	66.73	90.47
16	2.0	9,865	43.88	103.6	140.4
18	2.5	12,120	53.91	143.1	194.0
20	2.5	15,410	68.55	202.2	274.2
22	2.5	19,100	84.96	275.7	373.8
24	3.0	22,190	98.71	349.4	473.8
27	3.0	28,910	128.6	512.2	694.4
30	3.5	35,290	157.0	694.8	942.0
33	3.5	43,660	194.2	945.6	1,282
36	4.0	51,410	228.7	1,215	1,647
39	4.0	61,420	273.2	1,572	2,131
42	4.5	70,570	313.9	1,945	2,637

Class or Type: **ASTM F568, Class 4.8 (M1.6 to M16)**
ISO 898/1, Class 4.8 (M1.6 to M16)

Minimum Tensile Strength = 420 MPa = 61,000 lbf/in²

Bolt Size (mm)	Thread Pitch (mm)	Clamping Force		Standard Dry Torque	
		pound-force(lbf)	kilonewton (kN)	ft. pound-force(ft-lbf)	newton meter(Nm)
1.6	0.35	83.94	0.3734	0.0881	0.1195
1.8	0.35	112.4	0.5001	0.1328	0.1800
2	0.40	137.0	0.6095	0.1798	0.2438
2.2	0.45	164.0	0.7297	0.2368	0.3211
2.5	0.45	224.1	0.9970	0.3677	0.4985
3	0.50	332.5	1.479	0.6545	0.8874
3.5	0.60	447.8	1.992	1.028	1.394
4	0.70	580.2	2.581	1.523	2.065
4.5	0.75	748.2	3.328	2.209	2.995
5	0.80	937.2	4.169	3.075	4.169
6	1.00	1,330	5.915	5.235	7.098
7	1.00	1,908	8.485	8.762	11.88
8	1.25	2,419	10.76	12.70	17.22
9	1.25	3,181	14.15	18.79	25.47
10	1.50	3,833	17.05	25.15	34.10

Bolt Size (mm)	Thread Pitch (mm)	Clamping Force pound-force(lbf)	Kilonewton (kN)	Standard Dry Torque ft. pound-force(ft-lbf)	newton meter (Nm)
11	1.50	4,777	21.25	34.48	46.75
12	1.75	5,571	24.78	43.86	59.47
14	2.00	7,628	33.93	70.07	95.00
16	2.0	10,360	46.08	108.7	147.4
18	2.5	12,720	56.58	150.3	203.8
20	2.5	16,180	71.97	212.3	287.9
22	2.5	20,050	89.19	289.5	392.5
24	3.0	23,300	103.6	366.9	497.5
27	3.0	30,370	135.1	538.1	729.5
30	3.5	37,050	164.8	729.3	988.8
33	3.5	45,840	203.9	992.8	1,346
36	4.0	53,980	240.1	1,275	1,729
39	4.0	64,500	286.9	1,651	2,238
42	4.5	74,100	329.6	2,042	2,769

Class or Type: **ASTM F568, Class 5.8 (M5 to M24)**
ISO 898/1, Class 5.8 (M5 to M24)

Minimum Tensile Strength = 520 MPa =75,000 lbf/in²

Bolt Size (mm)	Thread Pitch (mm)	Clamping Force pound-force(lbf)	Kilonewton (kN)	Standard Dry Torque ft. pound-force(ft-lbf)	newton meter (Nm)
1.6	0.35	103.9	0.4623	0.1091	0.1479
1.8	0.35	139.2	0.6192	0.1644	0.2229
2	0.40	169.6	0.7546	0.2226	0.3018
2.2	0.45	203.1	0.9034	0.2932	0.3975
2.5	0.45	277.5	1.234	0.4552	0.6172
3	0.50	411.6	1.831	0.8103	1.099
3.5	0.60	554.4	2.466	1.273	1.726
4	0.70	718.5	3.196	1.886	2.557
4.5	0.75	926.2	4.120	2.735	3.708
5	0.80	1,160	5.162	3.807	5.162
6	1.00	1,647	7.324	6.482	8.789
7	1.00	2,362	10.50	10.85	14.71
8	1.25	2,997	13.33	15.73	21.33
9	1.25	3,939	17.52	23.26	31.54
10	1.50	4,746	21.11	31.14	42.22
11	1.50	5,915	26.31	42.69	57.88
12	1.75	6,895	30.67	54.29	73.61
14	2.00	9,444	42.01	86.76	117.6
16	2.0	12,820	57.03	134.6	182.5
18	2.5	15,750	70.06	186.1	252.3
20	2.5	20,030	89.10	262.9	356.4
22	2.5	24,830	110.4	358.4	485.9
24	3.0	28,850	128.3	454.3	615.9
27	3.0	37,590	167.2	665.9	902.9
30	3.5	45,880	204.1	903.2	1,225
33	3.5	56,740	252.5	1,230	1,667
36	4.0	66,840	297.3	1,579	2,141
39	4.0	79,850	355.2	2,044	2,771
42	4.5	91,720	408.0	2,528	3,427

Class or Type: **ISO 898/1, Class 8.8 (up to M16)**

Minimum Tensile Strength = 800 MPa = 116,000 lbf / in²

Bolt Size (mm)	Thread Pitch (mm)	Clamping Force pound-force(lbf)	Kilonewton (kN)	Standard Dry Torque ft. pound-force(ft-lbf)	newton meter (Nm)
1.6	0.35	159.9	0.7112	0.1679	0.2276
1.8	0.35	214.2	0.9526	0.2529	0.3429
2	0.40	261.0	1.161	0.3425	0.4644

2.2	0.45	312.5	1.390	0.4511	0.6116
2.5	0.45	426.9	1.899	0.7003	0.9495
3	0.50	633.3	2.817	1.247	1.690
3.5	0.60	852.9	3.794	1.959	2.656
4	0.70	1,105	4.916	2.901	3.933
4.5	0.75	1,425	6.339	4.208	5.705
5	0.80	1,785	7.941	5.857	7.941
6	1.00	2,533	11.27	9.972	13.52
7	1.00	3,633	16.16	16.69	22.63
8	1.25	4,609	20.50	24.19	32.80
9	1.25	6,059	26.95	35.78	48.51
10	1.50	7,300	32.47	47.90	64.94
11	1.50	9,098	40.47	65.67	89.03
12	1.75	10,610	47.20	83.53	113.3
14	2.00	14,530	64.63	133.5	180.9
16	2.0	19,730	87.76	207.1	280.8
18	2.5	24,230	107.8	286.2	388.1
20	2.5	30,820	137.1	404.4	548.4
22	2.5	38,200	169.9	551.4	747.6
24	3.0	44,380	197.4	698.9	947.5
27	3.0	57,840	257.3	1,025	1,389
30	3.5	70,570	313.9	1,389	1,883
33	3.5	87,320	388.4	1,890	2,563
36	4.0	102,800	457.3	2,429	3,293
39	4.0	122,800	546.2	3,143	4,262
42	4.5	141,100	627.6	3,890	5,274

Class or Type:	ASTM A325M - Types 1, 2, & 3
	ASTM F568, Class 8.8 (M16 to M36)
	ASTM F568, Class 8.8.3 (M16 to M36)
	ISO 898/1, Class 8.8 (M16 and over)

Minimum Tensile Strength = 830 MPa = 120,000 lbf / in²

Bolt Size (mm)	Thread Pitch (mm)	Clamping Force		Standard Dry Torque	
		pound-force(lbf)	Kilonewton (kN)	ft. pound-force(ft-lbf)	newton meter(Nm)
1.6	0.35	165.9	0.7379	0.1742	0.2361
1.8	0.35	222.2	0.9883	0.2624	0.3558
2	0.40	270.8	1.204	0.3553	0.4818
2.2	0.45	324.2	1.442	0.4680	0.6345
2.5	0.45	442.9	1.970	0.7266	0.9851
3	0.50	657.1	2.923	1.294	1.754
3.5	0.60	884.8	3.936	2.032	2.755
4	0.70	1,147	5.101	3.010	4.081
4.5	0.75	1,479	6.577	4.366	5.919
5	0.80	1,852	8.239	6.077	8.239
6	1.00	2,628	11.69	10.35	14.03
7	1.00	3,770	16.77	17.31	23.48
8	1.25	4,782	21.27	25.10	34.03
9	1.25	6,286	27.96	37.12	50.33
10	1.50	7,574	33.69	49.70	67.38
11	1.50	9,440	41.99	68.13	92.38
12	1.75	11,010	48.97	86.67	117.5
14	2.00	15,070	67.03	138.5	187.7
16	2.0	20,470	91.06	214.9	291.3
18	2.5	25,140	111.8	297.0	402.6
20	2.5	31,970	142.2	419.6	568.9
22	2.5	39,630	176.3	572.1	775.6
24	3.0	46,040	204.8	725.1	983.0
27	3.0	60,000	266.9	1,063	1,441
30	3.5	73,220	325.7	1,441	1,954

33	3.5	90,600	403.0	1,962	2,660
36	4.0	106,700	474.6	2,520	3,416
39	4.0	127,400	566.7	3,262	4,422
42	4.5	146,400	651.2	4,035	5,471

Class or Type: **ASTM F568, Class 9.8** (M1.6 to M16)
ISO 898/1, Class 9.8 (M1.6 to M16)

Minimum Tensile Strength = 900 MPa = 131,000 lbf/in^2

Bolt Size (mm)	Thread Pitch (mm)	Clamping Force		Standard Dry Torque	
		pound-force(lbf)	Kilonewton (kN)	ft. pound-force(ft-lbf)	newton meter(Nm)
1.6	0.35	179.9	0.8001	0.1888	0.2560
1.8	0.35	240.9	1.072	0.2845	0.3858
2	0.40	293.6	1.306	0.3853	0.5224
2.2	0.45	351.5	1.564	0.5075	0.6880
2.5	0.45	480.3	2.136	0.7878	1.068
3	0.50	712.6	3.170	1.403	1.902
3.5	0.60	959.5	4.268	2.204	2.988
4	0.70	1,243	5.531	3.264	4.425
4.5	0.75	1,603	7.132	4.734	6.419
5	0.80	2,008	8.933	6.589	8.933
6	1.00	2,850	12.68	11.22	15.211
7	1.00	4,087	18.18	18.77	25.455
8	1.25	5,184	23.06	27.21	36.896
9	1.25	6,816	30.32	40.25	54.576
10	1.50	8,212	36.53	53.89	73.060
11	1.50	10,240	45.55	73.88	100.2
12	1.75	11,940	53.11	93.98	127.4
14	2.00	16,340	72.68	150.1	203.6
16	2.0	22,190	98.71	233.0	315.9
18	2.5	27,260	121.3	322.0	436.6
20	2.5	34,670	154.2	455.0	616.9
22	2.5	42,970	191.1	620.3	841.0
24	3.0	49,930	222.1	786.2	1,066
27	3.0	65,060	289.4	1,153	1,563
30	3.5	79,400	353.2	1,563	2,119
33	3.5	98,240	437.0	2,127	2,884
36	4.0	115,700	514.7	2,732	3,704
39	4.0	138,200	614.7	3,537	4,795
42	4.5	158,800	706.4	4,375	5,932

Class or Type: **ASTM A490M - Types 1, 2, & 3**
ASTM F568, Class 10.9 (M5 to M100)
ASTM F568, Class 10.9.3 (M16 to M36)
ISO 898/1, Class 10.9 (M5 to M36)

Minimum Tensile Strength = 1,040 MPa = 151,000 lbf / in^2

Bolt Size (mm)	Thread Pitch (mm)	Clamping Force		Standard Dry Torque	
		pound-force(lbf)	Kilonewton (kN)	ft. pound-force(ft-lbf)	newton meter(Nm)
1.6	0.35	207.9	0.9246	0.2182	0.2959
1.8	0.35	278.4	1.238	0.3288	0.4458
2	0.40	339.3	1.509	0.4452	0.6036
2.2	0.45	406.2	1.807	0.5864	0.7950
2.5	0.45	555.0	2.469	0.9104	1.234
3	0.50	823.5	3.663	1.621	2.198
3.5	0.60	1,109	4.932	2.546	3.452
4	0.70	1,437	6.391	3.771	5.113
4.5	0.75	1,853	8.241	5.470	7.417
5	0.80	2,321	10.32	7.614	10.32

6	1.00	3,293	14.65	12.96	17.58
7	1.00	4,723	21.01	21.69	29.41
8	1.25	5,991	26.65	31.45	42.64
9	1.25	7,875	35.03	46.51	63.05
10	1.50	9,491	42.22	62.28	84.44
11	1.50	11,830	52.62	85.37	115.7
12	1.75	13,790	61.34	108.6	147.2
14	2.00	18,890	84.03	173.5	235.2
16	2.0	25,650	114.1	269.3	365.1
18	2.5	31,500	140.1	372.1	504.5
20	2.5	40,060	178.2	525.8	712.8
22	2.5	49,660	220.9	716.8	971.9
24	3.0	57,690	256.6	908.5	1,232
27	3.0	75,180	334.4	1,332	1,806
30	3.5	91,740	408.1	1,806	2,449
33	3.5	113,500	504.9	2,458	3,332
36	4.0	133,700	594.7	3,158	4,281
39	4.0	159,700	710.4	4,087	5,541
42	4.5	183,500	816.2	5,056	6,855

Class or Type: ASTM F568, Class 12.9 (M1.6 to M100)
ISO 898/1, Class 12.9 (M1.6 to M36)

Minimum Tensile Strength = 1,220 MPa = 177,000 lbf / in^2

Bolt Size (mm)	Thread Pitch (mm)	Clamping Force		Standard Dry Torque	
		pound-force(lbf)	Kilonewton (kN)	ft. pound-force(ft-lbf)	newton meter(Nm)
1.6	0.35	243.8	1.085	0.2560	0.3471
1.8	0.35	326.6	1.453	0.3857	0.5230
2	0.40	398.0	1.770	0.5223	0.7081
2.2	0.45	476.5	2.120	0.6879	0.9326
2.5	0.45	651.0	2.896	1.068	1.448
3	0.50	965.8	4.296	1.901	2.578
3.5	0.60	1,301	5.786	2.987	4.050
4	0.70	1,685	7.497	4.424	5.998
4.5	0.75	2,173	9.667	6.417	8.700
5	0.80	2,722	12.11	8.932	12.11
6	1.00	3,863	17.18	15.21	20.62
7	1.00	5,541	24.65	25.45	34.50
8	1.25	7,028	31.26	36.89	50.02
9	1.25	9,237	41.09	54.55	73.96
10	1.50	11,130	49.51	73.05	99.04
11	1.50	13,880	61.74	100.1	135.8
12	1.75	16,180	71.97	127.4	172.7
14	2.00	22,150	98.53	203.5	275.9
16	2.0	30,080	133.8	315.8	428.2
18	2.5	36,960	164.4	436.5	591.8
20	2.5	47,010	209.1	616.9	836.4
22	2.5	58,250	259.1	840.9	1,140
24	3.0	67,670	301.0	1,066	1,445
27	3.0	88,190	392.3	1,562	2,118
30	3.5	107,600	478.6	2,119	2,873
33	3.5	133,200	592.5	2,883	3,909
36	4.0	156,800	697.5	3,704	5,022
39	4.0	187,300	833.2	4,794	6,500
42	4.5	215,200	957.3	5,931	8,041

Effect of Anti-Seize Compounds, Lubricants, Platings, Coatings, Torque Coefficients, and Stress Levels on Torque for Carbon Steel Bolts

Anti-seize Coupmound, Lubricant, Coating, Torque Coefficient, or Stress Level	Multiply Standard Dry Torque From Tables By:
SAE J429 Grade 1 (1/4" to 1-1/2"), 70% Minimum Tensile Stress	1.70
SAE J429 Grade 2 (5/8" to 1-1/2"), 70% Minimum Tensile Stress	1.70
Zinc plating (hot-dipped galvanized)	1.60
ASTM A449 Type 1 (1-3/4" to 2"), 70% Minimum Tensile Stress	1.53
Steel (oxidized, rusted)	1.50
ASTM A325 Types 1 & 3, 70% Minimum Tensile Stress	1.32
ASTM A449 Type 1 (1/4" to 1-1/2"), 70% Minimum Tensile Stress	1.32
ASTM A449 Type 2 (1/4" to 1"), 70% Minimum Tensile Stress	1.32
SAE J429 Grade 5, 5.1 & 5.2 (all sizes), 70% Minimum Tensile Stress	1.32
SAE J429 Grade 2 (1/4" to 3/4"), 70% Minimum Tensile Stress	1.26
ASTM Type A574 (#0 to ½"), 70% Minimum Tensile Stress	1.20
ASTM Type A574 (5/8" to 2"), 70% Minimum Tensile Stress	1.18
SAE J429 Grade 7 (1/4" to 1-1/2"), 70% Minimum Tensile Stress	1.18
ASTM A354 Grade BD, 70% Minimum Tensile Stress	1.17
ASTM A490 Types 1, 2 & 3, 70% Minimum Tensile Stress	1.17
SAE J429 Grade 8 & 8.2 (all sizes), 70% Minimum Tensile Stress	1.17
ASTM A354 Grade BC, 70% Minimum Tensile Stress	1.11
80% of Proof Strength	1.07
Black oxide	1.00
Steel (clean, dry, non-plated, as-received condition)	1.00
Torque Coefficient = 0.20	1.00
75% of Proof Strength	1.00
Phosphate and oil	0.95
Torque Coefficient = 0.19	0.95
70% of Proof Strength	0.93
Dri-Lock® 204 adhesive coating	0.90
Silver grade anti-seize	0.90
Parkerized and oiled	0.90
Torque Coefficient = 0.18	0.90
65% of Proof Strength	0.87
Corro-Shield® plating (alloy of copper, zinc, and aluminum)	0.85
Grease with copper, graphite and aluminum flakes	0.85
N-1000® anti-seize	0.85

Resistoplate® TF	0.85
Torque Coefficient = 0.17	0.85
Zinc plating (electroplated)	0.85
60% of Proof Strength	0.80
C5A®, copper-graphite based anti-seize	0.80
Cadmium plating	0.80
Grease with copper and graphite flakes	0.80
Grease with graphite flakes and calcium fluoride powder	0.80
Motor oil (SAE 20W)	0.80
N-7000® anti-seize	0.80
Torque Coefficient = 0.16	0.80
WD-40®, light weight oil	0.80
Dri-Lock® 201 adhesive coating	0.75
Grease with nickel and graphite flakes	0.75
Grease with zinc dust	0.75
Motor oil (SAE 40W)	0.75
N-5000® anti-seize	0.75
Torque Coefficient = 0.15	0.75
Zinc anti-seize	0.75
55% of Proof Strength	0.73
Cadmium plating and motor oil (SAE 30W)	0.70
Graphite	0.70
Molybdenum grease	0.70
Motor oil (SAE 30W) with cadmium plating	0.70
White lead grease (lead carbonate)	0.70
50% of Proof Strength	0.67
Dri-Lock® 202 adhesive coating	0.65
Graphite-50® anti-seize	0.65
Grease with graphite flakes	0.65
Grease with graphite flakes and molybdenum disulphide powder	0.65
Moly-50® anti-seize (molybdenum disulphide)	0.65
Nickel based anti-seize	0.65
Dri-Lock® 200 adhesive coating	0.60
Molybdenum film (dry)	0.60
Oil (light weight)	0.60
Dri-Lock® 203 adhesive coating	0.55
Graphite and motor oil	0.55
Grease with molybdenum disulphide powder	0.55
Grease with molybdenum disulphide powder and graphite	0.55
M-702 MOLY® paste lubricant (molybdenum disulphide)	0.55
Moly Paste® (molybdenum disulphide)	0.55
Oil (heavy weight)	0.50
Premier ETP®	0.50
Premier Thread-Eze®	0.50
Wax (extreme pressure)	0.50
Moly-Cote® (molybdenum disulphide)	0.45
Never-sieze®	0.45
Premier® thread lubricant	0.45

Example:

You have a clean, dry, non-plated 1/2-13 coarse threaded SAE J429 Grade 8 bolt. You want the stress in the bolt to be 70% of the minimum tensile stress after you tighten the nut and you want to use WD-40® as the lubricant on the threads, nut and washer.

What is the approximate torque required to develop this stress in the bolt?

From the Clamping Force and Standard Dry Torque Table for coarse threaded bolts you read for a 1/2-13 SAE J429 Grade 8 bolt that a torque of approximately 106 foot pounds-force will develop 75% of the proof strength in this bolt.

From the Effects of Anti-seize Compounds, etc. Table you find that to develop 70% of the minimum tensile stress in an SAE J429 Grade 8 bolt you need to multiply the dry torque by 1.17 to increase the stress level in the bolt. You also find that using WD-40® as a lubricant you need to multiply the dry torque by 0.80 to reduce the torque due to lubrication.

The approximate required torque to give the desired stress level in the bolt is the product of the dry torque and the multipliers that account for different stress levels and lubricants. The approximate required torque is:

106 foot pounds-force x 1.17 x 0.80 = 99 foot pounds-force.

Trademarks:

Premier Industrial Corporation: Corro-Shield®, Resistoplate® TF, Premier ETP®, Premier Thread-Eze®, Moly-Cote® , Never-sieze®, and Premier® thread lubricant.

Locktite Corporation: C5A®, Dri-Lock®, Moly-50®, Graphite-50®, Moly Paste®, N-1000®, N-5000®, and N-7000®.

WD-40 Company: WD-40®

Clover Tool Company: M-702 MOLY®.

Standard Dry Torque for Coarse-Threaded Non-Ferrous and Stainless Steel Bolts

Nylon 6/6 (at 50% relative humidity)

Bolt Size (# or inch)	Threads/ Inch	inch pound-force (in-lbf)	foot pound-force (ft-lbf)	newton meter(Nm)
		Minimum Tensile Strength		
		Approximately 6,500 pound-force / square inch (lbf / in²)		
		Standard Dry Torque		
1	64	0.2280	0.0190	0.0258
2	56	0.3948	0.0329	0.0446
3	48	0.6324	0.0527	0.0715
4	40	0.9552	0.0796	0.1079
5	40	1.381	0.1151	0.1561
6	32	1.924	0.1603	0.2173
8	32	3.431	0.2859	0.3876
10	24	5.617	0.4681	0.6347
12	24	8.634	0.7195	0.9755
1/4	20	14.09	1.174	1.592
5/16	18	29.77	2.481	3.364
3/8	16	54.85	4.571	6.197
7/16	14	91.94	7.662	10.39
1/2	13	143.9	11.99	16.26
9/16	12	213.5	17.79	24.12
5/8	11	303.8	25.32	34.33
3/4	10	559.8	46.65	63.25

Aluminum

Bolt Size (# or inch)	Threads/ Inch	inch pound-force (in-lbf)	foot pound-force (ft-lbf)	newton meter(Nm)
		Minimum Tensile Strength		
		Approximately 55,000 pound-force / square inch (lbf / in²)		
		Standard Dry Torque		
1	64	0.9312	0.0776	0.1052
2	56	1.480	0.1233	0.1672
3	48	2.202	0.1835	0.2488
4	40	3.121	0.2601	0.3526
5	40	4.256	0.3547	0.4809
6	32	5.630	0.4692	0.6361
8	32	9.172	0.7643	1.036
10	24	13.90	1.159	1.571
12	24	19.98	1.665	2.257
1/4	20	45.06	3.755	5.091
5/16	18	83.94	6.995	9.484
3/8	16	139.5	11.63	15.76
7/16	14	214.4	17.87	24.23
1/2	13	311.1	25.93	35.15
9/16	12	432.0	36.00	48.81
5/8	11	579.5	48.29	65.48
3/4	10	963.4	80.28	108.8
7/8	9	1480	123.4	167.3
1	8	2148	179.0	242.7

Yellow Brass, (63% Cu, 37% Zn)

		Minimum Tensile Strength		
		Approximately 60,000 pound-force / square inch (lbf / in²)		
		Standard Dry Torque		
Bolt Size (# or inch)	Threads/ Inch	inch pound-force (in-lbf)	foot pound-force (ft-lbf)	newton meter(Nm)
1	64	1.315	0.1096	0.1486
2	56	2.071	0.1726	0.2340
3	48	3.059	0.2549	0.3456
4	40	4.307	0.3589	0.4866
5	40	5.839	0.4866	0.6597
6	32	7.682	0.6402	0.8679
8	32	12.40	1.033	1.401
10	24	18.64	1.553	2.106
12	24	26.60	2.217	3.005
1/4	20	61.46	5.122	6.944
5/16	18	114.3	9.525	12.91
3/8	16	189.9	15.83	21.46
7/16	14	291.6	24.30	32.95
1/2	13	422.8	35.23	47.77
9/16	12	586.7	48.89	66.29
5/8	11	786.5	65.54	88.86
3/4	10	1,249	104.1	141.1
7/8	9	1,925	160.4	217.5
1	8	2,799	233.3	316.2
1-1/8	7	3,894	324.5	440.0
1-1/4	7	5,232	436.0	591.1
1-3/8	6	6,836	569.7	772.4
1-1/2	6	8,725	727.1	985.8

Silicone Bronze - Type B (98.5% Cu, 1.5% Zn)

		Minimum Tensile Strength		
		Approximately 70,000 pound-force / square inch (lbf / in²)		
		Standard Dry Torque		
Bolt Size (# or inch)	Threads/ Inch	inch pound-force (in-lbf)	foot pound-force (ft-lbf)	newton meter(Nm)
1	64	1.445	0.1204	0.1633
2	56	2.290	0.1908	0.2587
3	48	3.402	0.2835	0.3844
4	40	4.811	0.4009	0.5436
5	40	6.550	0.5458	0.7401
6	32	8.650	0.7208	0.9773
8	32	14.05	1.171	1.587
10	24	21.24	1.770	2.400
12	24	30.46	2.538	3.442
1/4	20	68.77	5.731	7.770
5/16	18	128.6	10.72	14.53
3/8	16	214.5	17.88	24.24
7/16	14	330.5	27.54	37.34
1/2	13	480.7	40.06	54.31
9/16	12	669.0	55.75	75.59
5/8	11	899.1	74.93	101.6
3/4	10	1,416	118.0	160.0

7/8	9	2,180	181.7	246.3
1	8	3,169	264.1	358.0
1-1/8	7	4,408	367.3	498.0
1-1/4	7	5,920	493.3	668.9
1-3/8	6	7,732	644.3	873.6
1-1/2	6	9,865	822.1	1,115

18-8 Stainless Steel (Fe 68%, Cr 18%, Ni 8%)

Minimum Tensile Strength				
Approximately 75,000 pound-force / square inch (lbf / in²)				
		Standard Dry Torque		
Bolt Size (# or inch)	Threads/ Inch	inch pound-force (in-lbf)	foot pound-force (ft-lbf)	newton meter(Nm)
1	64	1.575	0.1313	0.1780
2	56	2.490	0.2075	0.2813
3	48	3.691	0.3076	0.4170
4	40	5.212	0.4343	0.5889
5	40	7.085	0.5904	0.8005
6	32	9.344	0.7787	1.056
8	32	15.14	1.262	1.711
10	24	22.85	1.904	2.582
12	24	32.70	2.725	3.695
1/4	20	75.16	6.263	8.492
5/16	18	139.9	11.66	15.81
3/8	16	232.4	19.37	26.26
7/16	14	357.0	29.75	40.34
1/2	13	517.8	43.15	58.50
9/16	12	718.8	59.90	81.21
5/8	11	963.9	80.33	108.9
3/4	10	1,530	127.5	172.9
7/8	9	2,356	196.3	266.2
1	8	3,424	285.3	386.9
1-1/8	7	4,762	396.8	538.0
1-1/4	7	6,396	533.0	722.7
1-3/8	6	8,353	696.1	943.8
1-1/2	6	10,657	888.1	1,204

316 Stainless Steel (Fe 68%, Cr 17%, Ni 12%)

Minimum Tensile Strength				
Approximately 75,000 pound-force / square inch (lbf / in²)				
		Standard Dry Torque		
Bolt Size (# or inch)	Threads/ Inch	inch pound-force (in-lbf)	foot pound-force (ft-lbf)	newton meter(Nm)
1	64	1.681	0.1401	0.1899
2	56	2.648	0.2207	0.2992
3	48	3.912	0.3260	0.4420
4	40	5.509	0.4591	0.6224
5	40	7.469	0.6224	0.8439
6	32	9.827	0.8189	1.110
8	32	15.86	1.322	1.792
10	24	23.85	1.988	2.695
12	24	34.04	2.837	3.846
1/4	20	78.75	6.563	8.898
5/16	18	146.6	12.22	16.56
3/8	16	243.6	20.30	27.52
7/16	14	374.2	31.18	42.28

1/2	13	542.8	45.23	61.33
9/16	12	753.5	62.79	85.13
5/8	11	1,010	84.17	114.1
3/4	10	1,582	131.8	178.7
7/8	9	2,443	203.6	276.0
1	8	3,560	296.7	402.2
1-1/8	7	4,961	413.4	560.5
1-1/4	7	6,677	556.4	754.4
1-3/8	6	8,734	727.8	986.8
1-1/2	6	11,162	930.2	1,261

Monel (Ni 67%, Cu 30%, Fe 1.4%)

Minimum Tensile Strength				
Approximately 82,000 pound-force / square inch (lbf / in^2)				
		Standard Dry Torque		
Bolt Size (# or inch)	Threads/ Inch	inch pound-force (in-lbf)	foot pound-force (ft-lbf)	newton meter(Nm)
1	64	1.472	0.1227	0.1663
2	56	2.406	0.2005	0.2718
3	48	3.670	0.3058	0.4147
4	40	5.313	0.4428	0.6003
5	40	7.386	0.6155	0.8345
6	32	9.937	0.8281	1.123
8	32	16.68	1.390	1.885
10	24	25.93	2.161	2.930
12	24	38.09	3.174	4.304
1/4	20	85.23	7.103	9.630
5/16	18	158.5	13.21	17.91
3/8	16	263.1	21.93	29.73
7/16	14	403.9	33.66	45.63
1/2	13	585.4	48.78	66.14
9/16	12	812.2	67.68	91.77
5/8	11	1,089	90.75	123.0
3/4	10	1,832	152.7	207.0
7/8	9	2,822	235.2	318.8
1	8	4,101	341.8	463.4
1-1/8	7	5,704	475.3	644.5
1-1/4	7	7,663	638.6	865.8
1-3/8	6	10,008	834.0	1,131
1-1/2	6	12,770	1,064	1,443

Unified Inch Screw Threads - Standard Screw Thread Series

Nominal Size	Basic Major Diameter	Threads Per Inch				
		Coarse	Fine	Extra-Fine	Miniature	Miniature Machine Screw
(# or Inch)	Inch	UNC	UNF	UNEF	UNM	NS
30	0.0118	-	-	-	318	-
35	0.0138	-	-	-	282	-
40	0.0157	-	-	-	254	-
45	0.0177	-	-	-	254	-
50	0.0197	-	-	-	203	-
0000	0.0210	-	-	-	-	160
55	0.0217	-	-	-	203	-
60	0.0236	-	-	-	169	-
70	0.0276	-	-	-	145	-
80	0.0315	-	-	-	127	-
90	0.0354	-	-	-	113	-
100	0.0394	-	-	-	102	-
110	0.0433	-	-	-	102	-
120	0.0472	-	-	-	102	-
140	0.0551	-	-	-	85	-
000	0.0340	-	-	-	-	120
00	0.0470	-	-	-	-	90 & 96
0	0.0600	-	80	-	-	-
1	0.0730	64	72	-	-	-
2	0.0860	56	64	-	-	-
3	0.0990	48	56	-	-	-
4	0.1120	40	48	-	-	-

Unified Inch Screw Threads - Standard Screw Thread Series (cont.)

Nominal Size	Basic Major Diameter	Threads Per Inch				
		Coarse	Fine	Extra-Fine	Miniature	Miniature Machine Screw
(# or Inch)	Inch	UNC	UNF	UNEF	UNM	NS
5 or 1/8	0.1250	40	44	-	-	-
6	0.1380	32	40	-	-	-
8	0.1640	32	36	-	-	-
10	0.1900	24	32	-	-	-
12	0.2160	24	28	32	-	-
1/4	0.2500	20	28	32	-	-
5/16	0.3125	18	24	32	-	-
3/8	0.3750	16	24	32	-	-
-	0.3900	-	-	-	-	-
7/16	0.4375	14	20	28	-	-
1/2	0.5000	13	20	28	-	-
9/16	0.5625	12	18	24	-	-
5/8	0.6250	11	18	24	-	-
11/16	0.6875	-	-	24	-	-
3/4	0.7500	10	16	20	-	-
13/16	0.8125	-	-	20	-	-
7/8	0.8750	9	14	20	-	-
15/16	0.9375	-	-	20	-	-
1	1.0000	8	12	20	-	-
1-1/16	1.0625	-	-	18	-	-
1-1/8	1.1250	7	12	18	-	-

Clearance Holes For Bolts and Screws - Inch Series

Bolt or Screw Size (# or inch)	Nominal Diameter (inch)	Clearance Drills					
		Close Clearance		Normal Clearance		Loose Clearance	
		Drill Size	Diameter (inch)	Drill Size	Diameter (inch)	Drill Size	Diameter (inch)
# 30	0.0118	# 83	0.0120	# 82	0.0125	#79	0.0145
# 35	0.0138	- - NA - -		#79	0.0145	# 78	0.0160
# 40	0.0157	# 78	0.0160	- - -NA- - -		# 77	0.0180
# 45	0.0177	# 77	0.0180	- - -NA- - -		# 75	0.0210
# 50	0.0197	# 76	0.0200	# 75	0.0210	# 73	0.0240
# 0000	0.0210	- NA-		# 74	0.0225	# 72	0.0250
# 55	0.0217	# 74	0.0225	# 73	0.0240	# 71	0.0260
# 60	0.0236	# 73	0.0240	# 72	0.0250	# 70	0.0280
# 70	0.0276	# 70	0.0280	# 69	0.0292	# 66	0.0330
# 80	0.0316	# 67	0.0320	# 66	0.0330	# 62	0.0380
# 000	0.0340	# 65	0.0350	# 64	0.0360	# 60	0.0400
# 90	0.0354	# 64	0.0360	# 62	0.0380	# 58	0.0420
# 100	0.0394	# 60	0.0400	# 58	0.0420	3/64	0.0469
# 110	0.0433	- - -NA- - -		# 56	0.0465	# 55	0.0520
# 00	0.0470	- - -NA- - -		- - -NA- - -		# 54	0.0550
# 120	0.0472	- - -NA- - -		- - -NA- - -		# 54	0.0550
# 140	0.0551	- - -NA- - -		# 53	0.0595	# 51	0.0670
# 0	0.0600	1/16	0.0625	# 52	0.0635	# 50	0.0700
1/16	0.0625	# 52	0.0635	# 51	0.0670	# 49	0.0730
# 1	0.0730	# 48	0.0760	5/64	0.0781	# 44	0.0860
5/64	0.0781	# 46	0.0810	# 45	0.0820	# 42	0.0935
# 2	0.0860	# 43	0.0890	# 42	0.0935	# 38	0.1015
3/32	0.0938	# 41	0.0960	# 39	0.0995	# 34	0.1110
# 3	0.0990	# 38	0.1015	# 37	0.1040	# 32	0.1160
7/64	0.1094	# 33	0.1130	# 32	0.1160	# 30	0.1285
# 4	0.1120	# 32	0.1160	# 31	0.1200	# 29	0.1360
# 5	0.1250	# 30	0.1285	# 29	0.1360	# 25	0.1490
1/8	0.1250	# 30	0.1285	# 29	0.1360	# 25	0.1490
# 6	0.1380	# 27	0.1440	# 26	0.1470	# 19	0.1660
9/64	0.1406	# 26	0.1470	# 25	0.1490	# 19	0.1660
5/32	0.1563	# 20	0.1610	# 19	0.1660	# 13	0.1850
# 8	0.1640	# 18	0.1695	# 17	0.1730	# 9	0.1960
11/64	0.1719	# 16	0.1770	# 14	0.1820	# 6	0.2040
3/16	0.1875	# 10	0.1935	# 8	0.1990	# 2	0.2210
# 10	0.1900	# 9	0.1960	# 7	0.2010	# 1	0.2280
13/64	0.2031	# 4	0.2090	# 3	0.2130	C	0.2420
# 12	0.2160	# 2	0.2210	# 1	0.2280	F	0.2570
7/32	0.2188	# 1	0.2280	A	0.2340	G	0.2610
15/64	0.2344	C	0.2420	1/4 or E	0.2500	J	0.2770
# 14	0.2420	1/4 or E	0.2500	F	0.2570	L	0.2900
1/4	0.2500	F	0.2570	17/64	0.2656	19/64	0.2969
5/16	0.3125	P	0.3230	X	0.3320	3/8	0.3750
3/8	0.3750	W	0.3860	X	0.3970	29/64	0.4531
7/16	0.4375	29/64	0.4531	15/32	0.4688	33/64	0.5156
1/2	0.5000	33/64	0.5156	17/32	0.5313	9/16	0.5938
9/16	0.5625	37/64	0.5781	19/32	0.5938	43/64	0.6719
5/8	0.6250	41/64	0.6406	21/32	0.6563	3/4	0.7500
11/16	0.6875	45/64	0.7031	47/64	0.7344	13/16	0.8125

Bolt or Screw Size (# or inch)	Nominal Diameter (inch)	Clearance Drills					
		Close Clearance		Normal Clearance		Loose Clearance	
		Drill Size	Diameter (inch)	Drill Size	Diameter (inch)	Drill Size	Diameter (inch)
3/4	0.7500	25/32	0.7813	51/64	0.7969	57/64	0.8906
13/16	0.8125	27/32	0.8438	55/64	0.8594	31/32	0.9688
7/8	0.8750	29/32	0.9063	59/64	0.9219	1-3/64	1.0469
15/16	0.9375	31/32	0.9688	1	1.0000	1-7/64	1.1094
1	1.0000	1-1/32	1.0313	1-1/16	1.0625	1-3/16	1.1875
1-1/16	1.0625	1-3/32	1.0938	1-1/8	1.1250	1-17/64	1.2656
1-1/8	1.1250	1-5/32	1.1563	1-3/16	1.1875	1-11/32	1.3438
1-3/16	1.1875	1-7/32	1.2188	1-17/64	1.2656	1-13/32	1.4063
1-1/4	1.2500	1-19/64	1.2969	1-21/64	1.3281	1-31/64	1.4844
1-5/16	1.3125	1-11/32	1.3438	1-25/64	1.3906	1-9/16	1.5625
1-3/8	1.3750	1-27/64	1.4219	1-29/64	1.4531	1-5/8	1.6250
1-7/16	1.4375	1-31/64	1.4844	1-17/32	1.5313	1-23/32	1.7188
1-1/2	1.5000	1-9/16	1.5625	1-19/32	1.5938	1-25/32	1.7813
1-9/16	1.5625	1-5/8	1.6250	1-21/32	1.6563	1-27/32	1.8438
1-5/8	1.6250	1-11/16	1.6875	1-23/32	1.7188	1-15/16	1.9375

Clearance Holes for Bolts and Screws - Metric Series

Bolt or Screw Size	Nominal Diameter millimeter	Clearance Drills					
		Close Clearance		Normal Clearance		Loose Clearance	
		Drill Size	Diameter millimeter	Drill Size	Diameter millimeter	Drill Size	Diameter millimeter
1	1.00	1.05	1.05	1.1	1.10	1.2	1.20
1.1	1.10	1.15	1.15	1.25	1.25	1.3	1.30
1.2	1.20	1.3	1.30	1.35	1.35	1.45	1.45
1.4	1.40	1.5	1.50	1.55	1.55	1.7	1.70
1.6	1.60	1.7	1.70	1.8	1.80	1.9	1.90
1.8	1.80	1.9	1.90	2	2.00	2.15	2.15
2	2.00	2.1	2.10	2.25	2.25	2.4	2.40
2.2	2.20	2.35	2.35	2.45	2.45	2.65	2.65
2.5	2.50	2.65	2.65	2.8	2.80	3	3.00
3	3.00	3.2	3.20	3.35	3.35	3.6	3.60
3.5	3.50	3.7	3.70	3.9	3.90	4.2	4.20
4	4.00	4.25	4.25	4.5	4.50	4.8	4.80
4.5	4.50	4.8	4.80	5	5.00	5.4	5.40
5	5.00	5.3	5.30	5.6	5.60	6	6.00
5.5	5.50	5.8	5.80	6.2	6.20	6.6	6.60
6	6.00	6.4	6.40	6.7	6.70	7.2	7.20
7	7.00	7.4	7.40	7.8	7.80	8.4	8.40
8	8.00	8.5	8.50	9	9.00	9.6	9.60
9	9.00	9.5	9.50	10.1	10.10	10.8	10.80
10	10.00	10.6	10.60	11.2	11.20	12	12.00
11	11.00	11.7	11.70	12.3	12.30	13.2	13.20
12	12.00	12.7	12.70	13.4	13.40	14.5	14.50
14	14.00	14.75	14.75	15.75	15.75	16.75	16.75
15	15.00	16	16.00	16.75	16.75	18	18.00
16	16.00	17	17.00	18	18.00	19	19.00
17	17.00	18	18.00	19	19.00	20	20.00
18	18.00	19	19.00	20	20.00	22	22.00

Clearance Holes for Metric Bolts and Screws (cont.)

Bolt or Screw Size	Nominal Diameter millimeter	Clearance Drills					
		Close Clearance		Normal Clearance		Loose Clearance	
		Drill Size	Diameter millimeter	Drill Size	Diameter millimeter	Drill Size	Diameter millimeter
20	20.00	21	21.00	22	22.00	24	24.00
22	22.00	23	23.00	25	25.00	26	26.00
24	24.00	25	25.00	27	27.00	29	29.00
25	25.00	26	26.00	28	28.00	30	30.00
26	26.00	28	28.00	29	29.00	31	31.00
27	27.00	29	29.00	30	30.00	32	32.00
28	28.00	30	30.00	31	31.00	34	34.00

Notes:

(1) Drill sizes in the table are based on a Clearance Ratio that is defined as: Clearance Ratio = {(Clearance Drill Diameter - Bolt/Screw Diameter)/(Bolt/Screw Diameter)} x 100.

Most drills listed under Close Clearance have Clearance Ratios between 2% and 4% for the Inch Series, and between 4% and 8% for the Metric Series.

Most drills listed under Normal Clearance have Clearance Ratios between 5% and 9% for the Inch Series, and between 10% and 14% for the Metric Series.

Most drills listed under Loose Clearance have Clearance Ratios between 17% and 20% for the Inch Series, and between 18% and 22% for the Metric Series.

(2) - NA - means Not Available. No Inch Series drills are available that provide this clearance.

(3) Similar, but less extensive, tables for the Inch Series may be found in:

IPT's Industrial Fasteners Handbook, IPT Publishing and Training, Inc., Alberta, Canada

www.evergreen.edu/user/serv_res/research/bsi/people/dawn/fabric/fraction.html

bigben.stanford.edu/docs/tapClearanceHoleInfo.html

cfa-www.harvard.edu/~masermri/screws/screw1.html

Similar, but less extensive, tables for the Metric Series may be found in:

IPT's Industrial Fasteners Handbook, IPT Publishing and Training, Inc., Alberta, Canada

Fasteners And Screw Threads, ISO Standards Handbook, ISO, Geneve, Switzerland

Graphics In Engineering Design, 3rd Edition, John Wiley & Sons, New York, NY

(4) Other drill sizes may produce acceptable results. See the Drill Number-Wire Gauge-Screw Size table in the Tools Chapter for additional drill sizes.

Head Styles

Binding
Head

Button
Head

Fillister
Head

Flange Hex
Head

Flat
Head

Flat Fillister
Head

Hex Washer
Head

Indented Hex
Head

Round
Head

Pan
Head

Truss
Head

Oval
Head

Washer
Head

Trimmed
Hex

Anchor
Head

Carpentry and Construction

Softwood Lumber Sizes 92
Softwood Lumber Grading 93
Hardwood Lumber Size and Grading 96
Wood Moisture Content...97
Plywood & Panel Grading 98
Wood Characteristics 100
Insulation Value of Materials 102
Maximum Floor Joist Spans 106
Strength of Wood Beams 126
Wood Gluing Characteristics 129
Concrete..130
Concrete and Mortar 132
Mortar 133
Rafter Length Table - Foot, Inch, 16th Inch............................135
    Notes to Rafter Length Table....................................153
Roof Pitch Table 154
    Notes to Roof Pitch Table...158
Maximum Horizontal Roof Rafter Span 159
    Notes to Maximum Horizontal Roof Rafter Span 176
Roofing materials 177
    Notes to Roofing Guide Materials.............................182
Weight of Roofing Materials 183

Softwood Lumber Sizes

Nominal Size Inches	Actual Size Dry (Inches)	(mm)	Actual Size Green (Inches)	(mm)
THICKNESS:				
1	3/4	19	25/32	20
1-1/4	1	25	1-1/32	26
1-1/2	1-1/4	32	1-9/32	33
2	1-1/2	38	1-9/16	40
2-1/2	2	51	2-1/16	52
3	2-1/2	64	2-9/16	65
3-1/2	3	76	3-1/16	78
4	3-1/2	89	3-9/16	90
4-1/2	4	102	4-1/16	103
6			5-9/16	
8	7-1/2		7-9/16	
FACE WIDTH:				
2	1-1/2	38	1-9/16	40
3	2-1/2	64	2-9/16	65
4	3-1/2	89	3-9/16	90
5	4-1/2	114	4-5/8	117
6	5-1/2	140	5-5/8	143
7	6-1/2	165	6-5/8	168
8	7-1/4	184	7-1/2	190
9	8-1/4	210	8-1/2	216
10	9-1/4	235	9-1/2	241
11	10-1/4	260	10-1/2	267
12	11-1/4	286	11-1/2	292
14	13-1/4	337	13-1/2	343
16	15-1/4	387	15-1/2	394

Dry lumber is defined as lumber with less than 19 percent moisture and unseasoned or green is greater than 19 percent. All sizes listed above, both nominal and actual, conform to standards set by the *American Softwood Lumber Standards*.

Lumber is sold by a "feet board measure" or "board foot" rating.
1 board foot =144 cubic inches (for example 12 inch x 12 inch x 1 inch or 2 inch x 6 inch x 12 inch).
Board feet = thickness (in) x face width (in) x length (in)/144
    or = thickness (in) x face width (in) x length (ft)/12

The following are quick approximations for calculating board feet:
     for a 1 x 4, divide linear length (feet) by 3
     for a 1 x 6, divide linear length (feet) by 2
     for a 1 x 8, multiply linear length (feet) by 0.66
     for a 1 x 12, linear length (feet) = board feet
     for a 2 x 4, multiply linear length (feet) by 0.66
     for a 2 x 6, linear length (feet) = board feet
     for a 2 x 8, multiply linear length (feet) by 1.33
     for a 2 x 12, multiply linear length (feet) by 2

Softwood Lumber Grading

Softwood grading is based on the appearance, strength and stiffness of lumber. Grading systems are established by a variety of associations in different parts of the country but they all must follow the US Department of Commerce American Lumber Standards. The grading system is quite long and very detailed. *If you want more detailed information on softwood grading, obtain the book "Western Lumber Grading Rules 95" by the Western Wood Products Association, 522 S.W. Fifth, Portland, Oregon, 97204, (503)224–3930. The cost is only $4.00 and it is an excellent pocket reference.*

Softwood lumber comes from "conifer" trees, which means they have needle shaped leaves that stay green all year. Hardwoods come from "deciduous" trees, which means they have broad leaves and loose their leaves in the cold months. A list of tree types and their characteristics is given later in this chapter.

The first broad softwood classification is as follows:

Rough Lumber – Sawn, trimmed, and edged, but the faces are rough and show saw marks.

Surfaced Lumber (dressed) – Rough lumber that has been smoothed by a surfacing machine. Sub-categories are based on the number of sides and edges that have been smoothed:
S1S – Surfaced 1 Side
S1E – Surfaced 1 Edge
S2S – Surfaced 2 Sides
S2E – Surfaced 2 Edges
S1S1E – Surfaced 1 Side and 1 Edge
S1S2E – Surfaced 1 Side and 2 Edges
S2S1E – Surfaced 2 Sides and 1 Edge
S4S – Surfaced 4 Sides

Worked Lumber – Surfaced lumber that has been matched, patterned, shiplapped or any combination thereof.

Another broad softwood classification (which is not a subcategory of the first classification above) is as follows:

Shop and Factory Lumber – This is millwork lumber used for applications such as molding, door jambs, and window frames.

Yard Lumber – Lumber used for house framing, concrete forms, and sheathing. It is also known as structural lumber.

Yard or structural softwood lumber is further subdivided into the following categories, based on size:

> **Boards** – Lumber must be no more than 1 inch thick and 4 to 12 inches wide.
>
> **Planks** – Lumber must be over 1 inch thick and more than 6 inches wide.
>
> **Timbers** – Lumber width and thickness must both be greater than 5 inches.

The most common softwood grading system places lumber into three main categories. Once again, bear in mind that some of these categories are very detailed and long; for example, the specific description of "#2 Common Board" is almost 2 pages long and covers details such as degree of cupping, twist, wane, knots, and raising of grain. The following descriptions cover the primary system only, see a grading manual for more detail:

1. **Select and Finish Materials** – These are "Appearance" grades and are used primarily for interior and exterior trim work, moldings, cabinets, and interior walls. Select grades are based on the best face and finish grades are based on the best face and 2 edges.

   > Select – B & BTR – 1 & 2 Clear
   > C Select
   > D Select
   > Superior Finish VG, FG or MG
   > Prime Finish VG, FG, MG
   > E Finish

2. **Boards** – Five grades referred to as "Commons" (1 Common through 5 Common) are used for general building, crafts, form lumber, flooring, sheathing, etc. "Alternate Board Grades" include the following (in order from best to worst):

   > Select Merchantable
   > Construction
   > Standard
   > Utility
   > Economy

The final category of Boards is the "Stress Related Boards". These are special use products for light trusses, rafters, and box beams for factory built and mobile homes.

3. **Dimension Lumber** – This category is limited to surfaced softwood lumber that is 2 to 4 inches thick and is to be used as framing components. Category breakdowns are as follows:

Light Framing – General framing and stud walls. Up to 4 inch wide. Grades are as follows:
Construction
Standard
Utility

Structural Light Framing – Suitable for higher stress applications such as roof trusses and concrete forms. Up to 4 inch wide. Grades are as follows:

Select Structural	No. 3
No. 1	Economy
No. 2	

Studs – Load bearing and stud walls of 2 x 4 and 2 x 6 construction. Lengths are less than 10 feet. Up to 4 inch wide; and 5 inch and over.

Structural Joists and Planks – Roof rafters, ceiling and floor joists. 5 inch and wider. Grades are as follows:

Select Structural	No. 3
No. 1	Economy
No. 2	

Timbers – Heavy beam support and floor and ceiling supports.

Select Structural	No. 2
No. 1	No. 3

If you are confused by the softwood grading scheme, don't feel bad, you're not alone! Grading is not an exact science since it deals with both visual and strength analysis. A maximum of 5% variation below grade is allowable between grades. Note that the above grading is only a small portion of the actual code; there are literally hundreds of different grades.

Hardwood Lumber Size & Grade

Hardwood comes from "deciduous" trees, which have broad leaves and lose their leaves in the cold months. Oak and walnut constitute 50% of all hardwood production. Other common hardwoods include Basswood, Beech, Birch, Butternut, Chestnut, Cherry, Elm, Gum, Hickory, Maple, Mahogany, and Yellow Poplar. See the section later in this chapter that describes wood types and their general characteristics.

Hardwood Sizes

Nominal Size (Fraction In)	Rough Size (Inches)	Surface 2 Sides Actual Size Dry (Inches)
4/4	1	13/16
5/4	1–1/4	1–1/16
6/4	1–1/2	1–5/16
7/4	1–3/4	1–1/2
8/4	2	1–3/4
10/4	2–1/2	2–1/4
12/4	3	2–3/4
14/4	3–1/2	3–1/4
16/4	4	3–3/4

Hardwood Grades

Grading is simpler than that used for Softwood and appearance is the prime consideration. Grades are based on the appearance of the poorest side, assuming that the board will be cut into pieces that are 2 to 7 feet long, each of which will have one clear face. There are numerous other requirements for grades of each of the various tree species, but the general grades of hardwood as determined by the National Hardwood Lumber Association are as follows (Listed in order from best to worst):

> **First and Second (FAS)** – The best grade. Normally required for a natural or stained finish. A FAS board must be at least 6 inches wide, 8 to 16 feet long, and 83.3% clear on the worst face.
>
> **Select – No. 1 Common** – Minimum 3 inches wide, 4 to 16 feet long, 66.66% clear wood.
>
> **Select – No. 2 Common**
>
> **Select – No. 3 Common**

For detailed information on the grading of hardwood, obtain a copy of the *Hardwood Rule Book*, National Hardwood Association, P.O. Box 34518, Memphis, Tennessee, 38184. Cost of the book is $6.00. It is an excellent source book.

Wood Moisture Content

Moisture content in wood affects both the size and strength of lumber. In general, the physical properties of wood can be improved by seasoning or drying. Although dependent on the tree species type, the strength of wood decreases as the moisture content goes up. *The following table is from Circular 108 of the U.S. Forest Service.*

MOISTURE vs. COMPRESSIVE STRENGTH		
Relative maximum crushing strength compared to wood containing 2% moisture (compression parallel to the grain)		
% Moisture	Red Spruce	Longleaf Pine	Douglas Fir
2	1.000	1.000	1.000
4	0.926	0.894	0.929
6	0.841 (c)	0.790	0.850
8	0.756	0.702	0.774
10	0.681	0.623	0.714
12	0.617	0.552	0.643
14	0.554 (b)	0.488	0.589
16	0.505	0.431	0.535
18	0.463	0.377	0.494
20	0.426	0.328(a)	0.458
22	0.394	0.278	0.428
24	0.362		0.398(a)
26	0.335		
28	0.314		
30	0.292		
32	0.271		
34	0.255		

(a) Green wood
(b) Air dried
(c) Kiln dried

The above table clearly indicates that high moisture content in wood significantly decreases the woods strength. As an example, Longleaf Pine has half the strength (0.552) with 12% moisture as it does with 2% moisture.

Additional information can be obtained from U.S. Department of Agriculture Bulletin 282 and Technical Bulletin 479.

Plywood & Panel Grading

Plywood is generally graded in terms of the quality of the veneer on both the front and back sides of the panel or by a "use type" name. Plywood is also grouped by the tree species type.

APA-- The Engineered Wood Association Veneer Grades

N .....Smooth surface "natural finish" veneer. Select, all heartwood or all sapwood. Free of open defects. Allows not more than 6 repairs, wood only, per 4 x 8 panel, made parallel to grain and well matched for grain and color. Special order.

A .....Smooth, paintable. Not more than 18 neatly made repairs, boat, sled, or router type, and parallel to grain, permitted. May be used for natural finish in less demanding applications.

B .....Solid surface. Shims, circular repair plugs and tight knots to 1 inch across grain permitted. Some minor splits permitted.

C ....Tight knots to 1–1/2 inch. Knotholes to 1 inch across grain and some to 1–1/2 inch if total width of knots and knotholes is within specified limits. Synthetic or wood repairs. Discoloration and sanding defects that do not impair strength permitted. Limited splits allowed. Stitching permitted.

C Plugged .. Improved C veneer with splits limited to 1/8-inch width and knotholes and borer holes limited to 1/4 x 1/2 inch. Admits some broken grain. Synthetic repairs permitted.

D .....Knots and knotholes to 2–1/2 inch width across grain and 1/2 inch larger within specified limits. Limited splits are permitted. Stitching permitted. Limited to Exposure 1 or Interior panels.

As an example, "C–D" grade panel would have one side conforming to the "C" grade and the other side conforming to the "D" grade. You must also specify the "Exposure Durability" (defined on the next page) to completely define the grade, e.g., EXTERIOR C–D.

NOTE: "CDX" is a very common grade of panel, but it does not have an "EXTERIOR" rating, it has an "EXPOSURE 1" rating.

A full description of the plywood and panel code can be obtained from the APA -- The Engineered Wood Association, P.O. Box 11700, Tacoma, WA 98411, (253) 565–6600.

Plywood & Panel Grading

EXPOSURE DURABILITY

EXTERIOR: Fully waterproof bond and designed for applications subject to permanent exposure to weather or moisture.

EXPOSURE 1: Fully waterproof bond but not for permanent exposure to weather or moisture.

EXPOSURE 2: Interior type with intermediate glue. Intended for protected construction applications where slight moisture exposure can be expected.

INTERIOR: Interior applications only.

GROUP CLASSIFICATION OF SPECIES

Group 1	Group 2	Group 3	Group 4	Group 5
Apitong	Cedar–Port	Alder–Red	Aspen	Basswood
Beech–Amer.	Oxford Cypress	Birch–Paper	Bigtooth	Poplar
Birch	Douglas Fir 2	Cedar-Alaska	Quaking	Balsam
Sweet	Fir	Fir-Subalpine	Cativo	
Yellow	Balsam	Hemlock- East	Cedar	
Douglas Fir 1	Calif. Red	Maple- Bigleaf	Incense	
Kapur	Grand	Pine	West Red	
Keruing	Noble	Jack	Cottonwood	
Larch–West.	Pacific-Silver	Lodgepole	Eastern	
Maple-	White	Ponderosa	Black	
Sugar	Hemlock	Spruce	West Poplar	
Pine	Lauan	Redwood	Pine	
Caribbean	Almon	Spruce	East White	
Ocote	Bagtikan	Engelmann	Sugar	
Pine South.	Mayapis	White		
Loblolly	Red			
Longleaf	Tangile			
Shortleaf	Maple–Black			
Slash	Mengkulang			
Tanoak	Meranti–Red			
	Mersawa			
	Pine			
	Pond			
	Red			
	Virginia			
	Western			
	White			
	Spruce			
	Black			
	Red			
	Sitka			
	Sweetgum			
	Tamarack			
	Yellow Poplar			

Group numbers are used to define the strength and stiffness of the panel, Group 1 being the strongest, Group 5 the weakest.

Wood Characteristics

Wood Name	1995 Cost/ Brd Ft [1]	Density Lbs per Cubic Ft	Hard	Split Resist	Grain
Alder	$3.80/5.90	25–30	Med	Good	Low
Ash	$4.25/5.60	40–45	Hard	Good	Mod open
Aspen		25	Soft	Good	Mild fine
Balsa		8	V Soft	Good	Open
Basswood	$3.60/5.90	25–28	Soft	Good	Low, fine
Beech	$5.60	45	Hard	V Good	Mod, fine
Birch	$4.35/6.15	40–45	Hard	V Good	Mod, fine
Butternut	$6.10	27	Med	Good	Mod
Cedar, East		29	M Hard	Poor	Fine, knots
Cedar, West	$3.10	25	Med	Poor	Fine
Cherry	$6.50/8.20	35	M Hard	V Good	Mod, fine
Chestnut	$26.55	30	M Hard	Good	Mod, coarse
Cottonwood	$4.10	25	Med	Good	Low, fine
Cypress		35	M Hard	Poor	Wide, fine
Ebony		50–65	V Hard	V Good	V Low, fine
Elm, American		35	M Hard	V Good	Mod, v fine
Elm, Rock		44	Hard	V Good	Mod, v fine
Fir, Douglas	$4.55	35	Med	Fair	Wide
Fir, White		25	Med	Fair	Wide
Gum, Black		36	M Hard	V Good	Mod
Gum, Blue		50	Hard	V Good	Mod, open
Gum, Red	$4.60/7.20	35	M Hard	V Good	Mod
Hackberry	$3.70	38	M Hard	Poor	Coarse
Hickory	$3.85	40–55	Hard	Good	Mod, pores
Holly		40	M Hard	V Good	None, fine
Ligum Vitae	$15/$17	80	V Hard	V Good	Mod, v fine
Madrone		45	Hard	Good	Mod, v fine
Magnolia		35	M Hard	Good	Fine
Mahogany					
African		30	M Hard	Good	Open, figure
Cuban		40	Hard	Good	Open, figure
Honduras	$6.75/9.70	35	M Hard	Good	Open, figure
Phillipine	$5.50		Not a Mahogany, see Phillipine.		
Maple (hard)	$4.45/5.90	35–44	M Hard	Good	Mod, fine
Myrtle		40	Hard	Good	Mod, fine
Oak					
Amer. Red	$4.95/6.90	45	Hard	Good	Coarse,pores
Amer. White	$4.20/6.65	47	Hard	Good	Coarse,pores
English Brown		45	Hard	Good	Coarse,pores
Pecan	$3.50	47	Hard	Good	Fine, pores
Persimmon		55	Hard	V Good	V fine
Philippine					
Red Luan	$8.05	36	M Hard	Good	Mod,coarse
Tanguile		39	M Hard	V Good	Mod,coarse

Wood Name	1995 Cost/ Brd Ft [1]	Density Lbs per Cubic Ft	Hard	Split Resist	Grain
Pine, White:					
Northern	$6.50	25	Soft	Poor	V coarse
Western	$3.10/5.15	27	Soft	Poor	Mod, fine
Poplar, Yellow	$3.25/4.25	30	M Hard	Good	Mod, v fine
Redwood	$3.10	28	Med	Poor	Fine
Rosewood:					
Bolivian	$15.70	50	Hard	Good	Swirls, pores
East Indian		55	Hard	Good	Mod
Satinwood		67	V Hard	Good	Mod, fine
Spruce		28	Med	Poor	Mod, fine
Sycamore		35	M Hard	High	Mod, fine
Teak (Burma)	$14.75/18	45	Hard	High	Mod to High
Walnut:					
Amer Black	$3.15/6.50	38	Hard	Good	Mod, fine
Claro	$18.55	30	M Hard	Good	Mod, open
European		35	M Hard	Good	Mod, open
Willow	$3.10/4.55	26	Soft	Good	Mod, fine
Zebrawood	$28.60	48	Hard	Good	High, fine

Hardness is a relative term between the different species. "V Soft" is an abbreviation for Very Soft, "V Hard" is Very Hard, and "M Hard" is moderately hard.

Split Resist refers to the susceptibility the lumber has to splitting. The scale ranges from "V Good" (Very Good) to "Good" to "Fair" to "Poor".

Grain defines the general appearance of the wood grain. "Mod" is moderate, "High" is very pronounced grain, "pores" is large open pores, "fine" is fine grained, "V fine" is very fine grained, and "coarse" is coarse grained.

(1) The cost per board foot column will sometimes contain two values instead of one. The first number represents the cost of relatively low grade lumber such as "#2 Common" and the second number represents the cost of the higher grades such as "Select 1" or "Select 2." Hardwood costs are for First & Seconds (FAS) and are surfaced 3 sides (S3S). Thicker hardwood boards are usually more expensive, e.g. 4/4 (1 inch thick) Red Oak is $4.95/board foot whereas 8/4 (2 inch thick) is $6.80/board foot. Price increases of 10% to 40% are not uncommon for double the thickness.

An excellent book on woods is "Beautiful Woods," by the Frank Paxton Lumber Co, 4837 Jackson St, Denver, CO 80216, (303)399–6810, cost $7.95 (complete with color photos!). Also, "Know Your Woods," by Albert Constantine, 1987, ISBN 0–684–14115–9.

Insulation Value of Materials

Insulation Material	Thickness (inches)	k*	C*	R Value
Air space				
non-reflective	3/4		0.99	1.01
reflective	3/4		0.29	3.48
reflective foil,				
2 reflective surfaces	1	0.72		1.39
Aluminum siding over sheathing			1.61	0.61
Architectural glass			10.00	0.10
Asbestos–cement board	4.0			0.25
	1/8		33.00	0.03
	1/4		16.50	0.06
Asphalt roll roofing	0.048		6.50	0.15
Asphalt shingle	0.048		2.27	0.44
Balsam wood	1	0.27		3.70
Brick, common	1	5.00		0.20
Brick, face	1	9.00		0.11
Built-up roofing	3/8		3.00	0.33
Carpet and fibrous pad			0.48	2.08
Carpeting with foam rubber pad			0.81	1.23
Cedar shingle			1.11	0.90
Cellose, loose fill, blown in	1	0.31		3.25
Cellular board	1	0.35		2.86
Cellular glass	1	0.38		2.63
	2		0.17	5.90
Cellulosics	1	0.29		3.50
Celotex	1	0.33		3.03
Cement fiber slab	1	0.50		2.00
Cement mortar	1	5.00		0.20
Cinder block, hollow	8		0.58	1.72
	12		0.53	1.89
Cinder block, hollow,				
with 1/2-inch of plaster	8–1/2		0.35	2.85
with 1/2-inch of plaster	12–1/2		0.33	3.03
Clay tile				
hollow, 1 cell deep	3		1.25	0.80
hollow, 1 cell deep	4		0.90	1.11
hollow, 2 cells deep	6		0.66	1.52
hollow, 2 cells deep	8		0.54	1.85
hollow, 2 cells deep	10		0.45	2.22
hollow, 3 cells deep	12		0.40	2.50
Concrete block				
hollow	8		0.90	1.11
hollow	12		0.78	1.28
hollow with:				
lightweight aggregate	8		0.50	2.00
with 1/2-inch of plaster	8–1/2		0.49	2.04
with 1/2-inch of plaster	12–1/2		0.45	2.22
Concrete, slab	4		3.13	0.32
Concrete, wall	8		1.56	0.64
Cork board	1	0.30		3.33
Cork tile	1/8		3.60	0.28
Felt, vapor-permeable			16.70	0.06

Insulation Material	Thickness (inches)	k*	C*	R Value
Fiberboard sheathing	1/2		0.76	1.32
	25/32		0.49	2.06
	1	0.42		2.36
Fiberglass batt	1	0.30		3.30
	2		0.16	6.30
	3–1/2		0.091	11.00
	6		0.053	19.00
	8		0.04	25.30
Fiberglass, loose fill	1	0.91		1.10
Floor tile, vinyl, etc			20.00	0.05
Glass fiber, organic bonded			0.25	4.00
Glass fiber board	1		0.25	4.00
Glass wool	1		0.27	3.76
Ground surface			2.00	0.50
Gypsum board	3/8		3.10	0.32
	1/2		2.22	0.45
	5/8		1.78	0.56
Gypsum plaster on gypsum lath	1/2		3.12	0.32
Hardboard	1/4		5.56	0.18
high density			0.82	1.22
high density, std tempered			1.00	1.00
medium density	1	0.73		1.37
Hardwood	1	1.10		0.91
Hardwood floor	3/4		1.47	0.68
	25/32		1.43	0.70
Linoleum or rubber tile			20.00	0.05
Mineral fiber, loose fill, blown in	1	0.31		3.25
rock or glass	1		0.38	2.60
rock or glass	3–3/4 to 5			11.00
rock or glass	6–1/2 to 8–3/4		0.05	19.00
rock or glass	10–1/4 to 13–3/4		0.03	30.00
resin binder			0.29	3.45
loosefill, blown in	7–1/2 to 10			22.0
with resin binder			0.29	3.45
Mineral fiberboard	1		0.29	3.45
(wet-felted) acoustical tile	1		0.36	2.78
(wet-felted) roof insulation	1		0.34	2.94
(wet-molded) acoustical tile	1		0.42	2.38
Mineral wool, batt	1		0.31	3.25
	1		0.24	4.16
	3 to 4		0.091	11.00
	5–1/2 to 6–1/2		0.053	19.00
	6 to 7 1/2		0.045	22.00
	9 to 10		0.033	30.00
	12 to 13		0.026	38.0
Particleboard	5/8		1.22	0.82
high density			1.18	0.85
low density			0.54	1.85
medium density	1		0.94	1.06
underlayment	5/8		1.22	0.82
Perlite, expanded	1		0.33	3.03
expanded, organic bonded			0.36	2.78
loose fill	1		0.37	2.70
Plaster	1		8.33	0.12

Insulation Material	Thickness (inches)	k*	C*	R Value
Plaster and metal lath	3/4		7.69	0.13
Plaster, cement, sand	3/8		13.3	0.08
	3/4		6.66	0.15
	1	5.00		0.20
Plaster, gypsum				
lightwt agg	1/2		3.12	0.32
lightwt agg	5/8		2.67	0.39
lightwt agg	3/4		2.13	0.47
perlite agg		1.5		0.67
sand	1/2		11.10	0.09
sand	5/8		9.10	0.11
sand	1	5.50		0.18
on metal lath	3/4		7.70	0.13
Plasterboard	3/8		3.10	0.32
	1/2		2.22	0.45
Plywood	1/4		3.20	0.31
	3/8		2.13	0.47
	1/2		1.60	0.62
	5/8		1.29	0.77
	1	0.80		1.25
Plywood (Douglas Fir)		0.80		1.25
Plywood or wood panels	3/4		1.07	0.93
Polycarbonate sheet	1/8		1.06	0.94
	3/16		1.01	0.99
	1/4		0.96	1.04
	3/8		0.88	1.14
	1/2		0.81	1.23
Polyisocyanurate, cellular	1/2		0.278	3.60
	1		0.139	7.20
	2		0.069	14.40
Polyisocyanurate, smooth skin	1	0.14		7.20
Polystyrene	1	0.28		3.57
cut cell	1	0.25		4.00
expanded, molded beads	1	0.26		3.85
foamed in place	1	0.27		3.75
smooth skin (Styrofoam)	1	0.20		5.00
Polyurethane				
expanded	1	0.14		7.00
expanded board	1	0.16		6.25
expanded, aged	1	0.16		6.30
Redwood	1	0.57		1.75
Rock cork	1	0.33		3.05
Rock wool batt	1	0.27		3.70
Roofing, 1-ply membrane	0.048		2.00	0.50
Rubber, expanded, board	1	0.22		4.55
Sawdust	1	0.41		2.44
Sawdust/shavings	1	0.45		2.20
Sheep's wool	1	0.34		2.96
Slate shingle	1/2		20.00	0.05
Softwood	1	0.80		1.25
Stone	1	12.50		0.08
Structural insulation board	1/2		0.76	1.32
Stucco	1	5.00		0.20
Terrazzo	1	12.50		0.08

Insulation Material	Thickness (inches)	k*	C*	R Value
Tile, hollow	4		1.00	1.00
Urea-formaldehyde	1	0.24		4.20
Urethane, foamed in place	1	0.16		6.30
Vapor-seal, 2-layers of mopped 15-lb felt			8.35	0.12
Vapor–seal, plastic film				Minimal
Vegetable Fiber Board				
Sheathing				
regular density	1/2		0.76	1.32
regular density	25/32		0.49	2.06
intermediate density	1/2		0.82	1.22
nail–base	1/2		0.88	1.14
Shingle backer	3/8		1.06	0.94
	5/16		1.28	0.78
sound deadening board	1/2		0.74	1.35
tile lay–in panels		0.40		2.50
	1/2		0.80	1.25
	3/4		0.53	1.89
laminated paperboard		0.50		2.00
homo. board from repulped paper		0.50		2.00
Vermiculite	1	0.47		2.13
Vermiculite, loose fill	1	0.45		2.20
Wall, vertical exterior,15 mph wind			5.88	0.17
Wall, vertical interior, still air			1.47	0.68
Wood				
bevel lap siding	1/2		1.23	0.81
bevel lap siding	3/4		0.95	1.05
drop siding	3/4		1.27	0.79
drop siding	1	1.27		0.79
fiber, soft wood	1	0.30		3.33
fiberboard	1	0.59		1.69
fiberboard, acoustical tile	1/2		0.80	1.25
fiberboard, acoustical tile	3/4		0.53	1.89
shingle			1.06	0.94
shingle siding			1.15	0.87
shingle with insulating backer board			0.71	1.40
shingle, double			0.84	1.19
subfloor	3/4		1.06	0.94
vertical tongue & groove	3/4		1.00	1.00

* "k" (in units of Btu in/ft² hr °F) is heat conductivity over a thickness of 1 inch and "C" is heat conductance (in units of Btu/ft² hr °F) over the specified thickness. "R Value" is the most common number used to compare the insulating properties of various materials and is typically marked on the wrapper or container of the insulator. The "R Value" is effectively the material's resistance to heat flow and is based on the "k" and "C" values. "R Values" are the reciprocals of "k" (which is 1/k) or "C" (which is 1/C) for a given material.

Two excellent references for information on the insulation values of various materials are as follows:
Pocket Handbook for Air Conditioning, Heating, Ventilation and Refrigeration, 1987, American Society of Heating, Refrigerating and Air-Conditioning (ASHRAE). 1791 Tullie Circle, NE, Atlanta, GA 30329

National Institute of Standards and Technology.
Quince Orchard and Clopper Roads, Gaithersburg, Maryland 20899
(301) 975-2758 Main public number
(301) 975-3058 Publications information

Maximum Floor Joist Spans

Douglas Fir - Larch: Includes Douglas fir and Western larch. See notes at end of tables.

Nominal Lumber Size (inches)	Joist Spacing Center to Center (inches)	Lumber Grade		
		Select Structural	No. 1	No. 2
		Maximum Span (feet - inches)		

Max Live load=30 lbf/ft^2; Max Dead Load=10 lbf/ft^2

Nominal Lumber Size (inches)	Joist Spacing Center to Center (inches)	Select Structural	No. 1	No. 2
2 x 6	12	12 - 06	12 - 00	11 - 10
	16	11 - 04	10 - 11	10 - 09
	24	09 - 11	09 - 07	09 - 01
2 x 8	12	16 - 06	15 - 10	15 - 07
	16	15 - 00	14 - 05	14 - 01
	24	13 - 01	12 - 04	11 - 06
2 x 10	12	21 - 00	20 - 03	19 - 10
	16	19 - 01	18 - 05	17 - 02
	24	16 - 08	15 - 00	14 - 01
2 x 12	12	25 - 07	24 - 08	23 - 00
	16	23 - 03	21 - 04	19 - 11
	24	20 - 03	17 - 05	16 - 03

Max Live load=40 lbf/ft^2; Max Dead Load=10 lbf/ft^2

Nominal Lumber Size (inches)	Joist Spacing Center to Center (inches)	Select Structural	No. 1	No. 2
2 x 6	12	11 - 04	10 - 11	10 - 09
	16	10 - 04	09 - 11	09 - 09
	24	09 - 00	08 - 08	08 - 01
2 x 8	12	15 - 00	14 - 05	14 - 02
	16	13 - 07	13 - 01	12 - 07
	24	11 - 11	11 - 00	10 - 03
2 x 10	12	19 - 01	18 - 05	17 - 09
	16	17 - 04	16 - 05	15 - 05
	24	15 - 02	13 - 05	12 - 07
2 x 12	12	23 - 03	22 - 00	20 - 07
	16	21 - 01	19 - 01	17 - 10
	24	18 - 05	15 - 07	14 - 07

Dead Load = weight of structure + fixed loads
Live Load = movable loads such as furniture, wind, snow, etc.

Maximum Floor Joist Spans (Cont.)

Douglas Fir - Larch: (cont.)

Nominal Lumber Size (inches)	Joist Spacing Center to Center (inches)	Lumber Grade		
		Select Structural	No. 1	No. 2
		Maximum Span (feet - inches)		

Max Live load=50 lbf/ft², Max Dead Load=10 lbf/ft²

Nominal Lumber Size (inches)	Joist Spacing Center to Center (inches)	Select Structural	No. 1	No. 2
2 x 8	12	13 - 11	13 - 05	13 - 01
	16	12 - 07	12 - 02	11 - 06
	24	11 - 00	10 - 00	09 - 05
2 x 10	12	17 - 09	17 - 01	16 - 03
	16	16 - 01	15 - 00	14 - 01
	24	14 - 01	12 - 03	11 - 06
2 x 12	12	21 - 07	20 - 01	18 - 10
	16	19 - 07	17 - 05	16 - 03
	24	17 - 01	14 - 03	13 - 04
2 x 14	12	25 - 05	22 - 06	21 - 00
	16	23 - 01	19 - 05	18 - 02
	24	19 - 02	15 - 11	14 - 10

Max Live load=60 lbf/ft², Max Dead Load=10 lbf/ft²

Nominal Lumber Size (inches)	Joist Spacing Center to Center (inches)	Select Structural	No. 1	No. 2
2 x 8	12	13 - 01	12 - 07	12 - 04
	16	11 - 11	11 - 05	10 - 08
	24	10 - 05	09 - 04	08 - 08
2 x 10	12	16 - 08	16 - 01	15 - 00
	16	15 - 02	13 - 11	13 - 00
	24	13 - 03	11 - 04	10 - 07
2 x 12	12	20 - 03	18 - 07	17 - 05
	16	18 - 05	16 - 01	15 - 01
	24	15 - 10	13 - 02	12 - 04
2 x 14	12	23 - 11	20 - 10	19 - 05
	16	21 - 08	18 - 00	16 - 11
	24	17 - 09	14 - 08	13 - 09

Dead Load = weight of structure + fixed loads
Live Load = movable loads such as furniture, wind, snow, etc.

Maximum Floor Joist Spans (cont.)

Douglas Fir - Larch: (cont.)

Nominal Lumber Size (inches)	Joist Spacing Center to Center (inches)	Lumber Grade		
		Select Structural	No. 1	No. 2
		Maximum Span (feet - inches)		

Max Live load=30 lbf/ft^2 , Max Dead Load=27 lbf/ft^2

Nominal Lumber Size (inches)	Joist Spacing Center to Center (inches)	Select Structural	No. 1	No. 2
2 x 6	12	12 - 06	11 - 06	10 - 09
	16	11 - 04	10 - 00	09 - 04
	24	09 - 09	08 - 02	07 - 07
2 x 8	12	16 - 06	14 - 07	13 - 07
	16	15 - 00	12 - 07	11 - 10
	24	12 - 05	10 - 04	09 - 08
2 x 10	12	21 - 00	17 - 09	16 - 08
	16	18 - 07	15 - 05	14 - 05
	24	15 - 02	12 - 07	11 - 09
2 x 12	12	24 - 10	20 - 08	19 - 04
	16	21 - 06	17 - 10	16 - 09
	24	17 - 07	14 - 07	13 - 08

Max Live load=40 lbf/ft^2 , Max Dead Load=27 lbf/ft^2

Nominal Lumber Size (inches)	Joist Spacing Center to Center (inches)	Select Structural	No. 1	No. 2
2 x 6	12	11 - 04	10 - 07	09 - 11
	16	10 - 04	09 - 02	08 - 07
	24	09 - 00	07 - 06	07 - 00
2 x 8	12	15 - 00	13 - 05	12 - 07
	16	13 - 07	11 - 08	10 - 11
	24	11 - 05	09 - 06	08 - 11
2 x 10	12	19 - 01	16 - 05	15 - 04
	16	17 - 01	14 - 03	13 - 04
	24	14 - 00	11 - 07	10 - 10
2 x 12	12	22 - 11	19 - 00	17 - 10
	16	19 - 10	16 - 06	15 - 05
	24	16 - 02	13 - 05	12 - 07

Dead Load = weight of structure + fixed loads
Live Load = movable loads such as furniture, wind, snow, etc.

Maximum Floor Joist Spans (cont.)

Douglas Fir - Larch: (cont.)

Nominal Lumber Size (inches)	Joist Spacing Center to Center (inches)	Lumber Grade		
		Select Structural	No. 1	No. 2
		Maximum Span (feet - inches)		

Max Live load=50 lbf/ft^2 , Max Dead Load=27 lbf/ft^2

2 x 8	12	13 - 11	12 - 06	11 - 09
	16	12 - 07	10 - 10	10 - 02
	24	10 - 08	08 - 10	08 - 03
2 x 10	12	17 - 09	15 - 04	14 - 04
	16	16 - 00	13 - 03	12 - 05
	24	13 - 00	10 - 10	10 - 01
2 x 12	12	21 - 04	17 - 09	16 - 07
	16	18 - 06	15 - 04	14 - 05
	24	15 - 01	12 - 07	11 - 09
2 x 14	12	23 - 11	19 - 10	18 - 07
	16	20 - 08	17 - 02	16 - 01
	24	16 - 11	14 - 00	13 - 01

Dead Load = weight of structure + fixed loads
Live Load = movable loads such as furniture, wind, snow, etc.

Notes :
1. Tabulated values developed from : Span Tables for Joists and Rafters, American Softwood Lumber Standard Sizes, 1993, American Wood Council, PO Box 5364, Madison, WI 53705-5364.
2. The tabulated values assume:
   (a) installation of at least three joists that are spaced no more than 24" on center
   (b) fully supported members, properly sheathed with adequate flooring, nailed on top edge of the joist
   (c) dry service conditions with wood moisture content not exceeding 19%
   (d) minimum bearing width of 1.5" and minimum bearing length of 1.5"
   (e) deflection is limited to span in inches divided by 360.
3. Tabulated spans apply to surfaced (S4S) lumber and are distances from face to face of supports.
4. Lumber lengths over 20' are not common.
5. Another good reference is : Western Lumber Span Tables, Western Wood Products Association, 522 SW Fifth Ave., Suite 400, Portland, OR 97204-2122.

Maximum Floor Joist Spans (con't)

Hemlock-Fir: Includes Western hemlock, California red fir, Grand fir, Noble fir, Pacific silver fir, and White fir. See notes at end of tables.

Nominal Lumber Size (inches)	Joist Spacing Center to Center (inches)	Lumber Grade		
		Select Structural	No. 1	No. 2
		Maximum Span (feet - inches)		

Max Live load=30 lbf/ft², Max Dead Load=10 lbf/ft²

Nominal Lumber Size (inches)	Joist Spacing Center to Center (inches)	Select Structural	No. 1	No. 2
2 x 6	12	11 - 10	11 - 07	11 - 00
	16	10 - 09	10 - 06	10 - 00
	24	09 - 04	09 - 02	08 - 09
2 x 8	12	15 - 07	15 - 03	14 - 06
	16	14 - 02	13 - 10	13 - 02
	24	12 - 04	12 - 00	11 - 04
2 x 10	12	19 - 10	19 - 05	18 - 06
	16	18 - 00	17 - 08	16 - 10
	24	15 - 09	14 - 08	13 - 10
2 x 12	12	24 - 02	23 - 07	22 - 06
	16	21 - 11	20 - 09	19 - 08
	24	19 - 02	17 - 00	16 - 01

Max Live load=40 lbf/ft², Max Dead Load=10 lbf/ft²

Nominal Lumber Size (inches)	Joist Spacing Center to Center (inches)	Select Structural	No. 1	No. 2
2 x 6	12	10 - 10	10 - 06	10 - 00
	16	09 - 09	09 - 06	09 - 01
	24	08 - 06	08 - 04	07 - 11
2 x 8	12	14 - 02	13 - 10	13 - 02
	16	12 - 10	12 - 07	12 - 00
	24	11 - 03	10 - 09	10 - 02
2 x 10	12	18 - 00	17 - 08	16 - 10
	16	16 - 05	16 - 00	15 - 02
	24	14 - 04	13 - 01	12 - 05
2 x 12	12	21 - 11	21 - 06	20 - 04
	16	19 - 11	18 - 07	17 - 07
	24	17 - 05	15 - 02	14 - 04

Maximum Floor Joist Spans (cont.)

Hemlock-Fir: (cont.)

Nominal Lumber Size (inches)	Joist Spacing Center to Center (inches)	Lumber Grade		
		Select Structural	No. 1	No. 2
		Maximum Span (feet - inches)		

Max Live load=50 lbf/ft², Max Dead Load=10 lbf/ft²

Nominal Lumber Size (inches)	Joist Spacing Center to Center (inches)	Select Structural	No. 1	No. 2
2 x 8	12	13 - 01	12 - 10	12 - 03
	16	11 - 11	11 - 08	11 - 01
	24	10 - 05	09 - 09	09 - 03
2 x 10	12	16 - 09	16 - 05	15 - 07
	16	15 - 02	14 - 08	13 - 10
	24	13 - 03	11 - 11	11 - 04
2 x 12	12	20 - 04	19 - 07	18 - 06
	16	18 - 06	17 - 00	16 - 01
	24	16 - 02	13 - 10	13 - 01
2 x 14	12	24 - 00	21 - 11	20 - 09
	16	21 - 09	19 - 00	17 - 11
	24	18 - 10	15 - 06	14 - 08

Max Live load=60 lbf/ft², Max Dead Load=10 lbf/ft²

Nominal Lumber Size (inches)	Joist Spacing Center to Center (inches)	Select Structural	No. 1	No. 2
2 x 8	12	12 - 04	12 - 01	11 - 06
	16	11 - 03	11 - 00	10 - 06
	24	09 - 10	09 - 01	08 - 07
2 x 10	12	15 - 09	15 - 05	14 - 08
	16	14 - 04	13 - 07	12 - 10
	24	12 - 06	11 - 01	10 - 06
2 x 12	12	19 - 02	18 - 02	17 - 02
	16	17 - 05	15 - 09	14 - 10
	24	15 - 02	12 - 10	12 - 02
2 x 14	12	22 - 07	20 - 03	19 - 02
	16	20 - 06	17 - 07	16 - 07
	24	-	14 - 04	13 - 07

Dead Load = weight of structure + fixed loads
Live Load = movable loads such as furniture, wind, snow, etc.

Maximum Floor Joist (cont.)

Hemlock-Fir: (cont.)

Nominal Lumber Size (inches)	Joist Spacing Center to Center (inches)	Lumber Grade		
		Select Structural	No. 1	No. 2
		Maximum Span (feet - inches)		

Max Live load=30 lbf/ft^2, Max Dead Load=27 lbf/ft^2

2 x 6	12	11 - 10	11 - 02	10 - 07
	16	10 - 09	09 - 08	09 - 02
	24	09 - 04	07 - 11	07 - 06
2 x 8	12	15 - 07	14 - 02	13 - 05
	16	14 - 02	12 - 04	11 - 08
	24	12 - 02	10 - 00	09 - 06
2 x 10	12	19 - 10	17 - 04	16 - 05
	16	18 - 00	15 - 00	14 - 02
	24	14 - 11	12 - 03	11 - 07
2 x 12	12	24 - 02	20 - 01	19 - 00
	16	21 - 02	17 - 05	16 - 06
	24	17 - 03	14 - 03	13 - 05

Max Live load=40 lbf/ft^2, Max Dead Load=27 lbf/ft^2

2 x 6	12	10 - 09	10 - 04	09 - 09
	16	09 - 09	08 - 11	08 - 06
	24	08 - 06	07 - 04	06 - 11
2 x 8	12	14 - 02	13 - 01	12 - 05
	16	12 - 10	11 - 04	10 - 09
	24	11 - 03	09 - 03	08 - 09
2 x 10	12	18 - 00	16 - 00	15 - 02
	16	16 - 05	13 - 10	13 - 01
	24	13 - 09	11 - 04	10 - 08
2 x 12	12	21 - 11	18 - 07	17 - 07
	16	19 - 06	16 - 01	15 - 02
	24	15 - 11	13 - 01	12 - 05

Dead Load = weight of structure + fixed loads
Live Load = movable loads such as furniture, wind, snow, etc.

Maximum Floor Joist Spans (cont.)

Hemlock-Fir: (cont.)

Nominal Lumber Size (inches)	Joist Spacing Center to Center (inches)	Lumber Grade		
		Select Structural	No. 1	No. 2
		Maximum Span (feet - inches)		

Max Live load=50 lbf/ft^2, Max Dead Load=27 lbf/ft^2

2 x 8	12	13 - 01	12 - 03	11 - 07
	16	11 - 11	10 - 07	10 - 00
	24	10 - 05	08 - 08	08 - 02
2 x 10	12	16 - 09	14 - 11	14 - 01
	16	15 - 02	12 - 11	12 - 03
	24	12 - 10	10 - 07	10 - 00
2 x 12	12	20 - 04	17 - 04	16 - 04
	16	18 - 06	15 - 00	14 - 02
	24	14 - 10	12 - 03	11 - 07
2 x 14	12	23 - 06	19 - 04	18 - 03
	16	20 - 04	16 - 09	15 - 10
	24	-	13 - 08	12 - 11

Notes :
1. Tabulated values developed from: Span Tables for Joists and Rafters, American Softwood Lumber Standard Sizes, 1993, American Wood Council, PO Box 5364, Madison, WI 53705-5364.
2. The tabulated values assume:
   (a) installation of at least three joists that are spaced no more than 24" on center
   (b) fully supported members, properly sheathed with adequate flooring, nailed on top edge of the joist
   (c) dry service conditions with wood moisture content not exceeding 19%
   (d) minimum bearing width of 1.5" and minimum bearing length of 1.5"
   (e) deflection is limited to span in inches divided by 360.
3. Tabulated spans apply to surfaced (S4S) lumber and are distances from face to face of supports
4. Lumber lengths over 20' are not common.
5. Another good reference is: Western Lumber Span Tables, Western Wood Products Association, 522 SW Fifth Ave., Suite 400, Portland, OR 97204-2122.

Maximum Floor Joist Spans (cont.)

Spruce-Pine-Fir (South): Includes Engelmann spruce, Sitka spruce, and Lodgepole pine. See notes at end of tables.

Nominal Lumber Size (inches)	Joist Spacing Center to Center (inches)	Lumber Grade		
		Select Structural	No. 1	No. 2
		Maximum Span (feet - inches)		

Max Live load=30 lbf/ft^2, Max Dead Load=10 lbf/ft^2

Nominal Lumber Size (inches)	Joist Spacing Center to Center (inches)	Select Structural	No. 1	No. 2
2 x 6	12	11 - 00	10 - 09	10 - 05
	16	10 - 00	09 - 09	09 - 06
	24	08 - 09	08 - 06	08 - 03
2 x 8	12	14 - 06	14 - 02	13 - 09
	16	13 - 02	12 - 10	12 - 06
	24	11 - 06	11 - 03	10 - 08
2 x 10	12	18 - 06	18 - 00	17 - 06
	16	16 - 10	16 - 05	15 - 11
	24	14 - 08	13 - 10	13 - 00
2 x 12	12	22 - 06	21 - 11	21 - 04
	16	20 - 06	19 - 08	18 - 06
	24	17 - 11	16 - 01	15 - 01

Max Live load=40 lbf/ft^2, Max Dead Load=10 lbf/ft^2

Nominal Lumber Size (inches)	Joist Spacing Center to Center (inches)	Select Structural	No. 1	No. 2
2 x 6	12	10 - 00	09 - 09	09 - 06
	16	09 - 01	08 - 10	08 - 07
	24	07 - 11	07 - 09	07 - 06
2 x 8	12	13 - 02	12 - 10	12 - 06
	16	12 - 00	11 - 08	11 - 04
	24	10 - 06	10 - 02	09 - 06
2 x 10	12	16 - 10	16 - 05	15 - 11
	16	15 - 03	14 - 11	14 - 03
	24	13 - 04	12 - 05	11 - 08
2 x 12	12	20 - 06	19 - 11	19 - 01
	16	18 - 07	17 - 07	16 - 06
	24	16 - 03	14 - 04	13 - 06

Maximum Floor Joist Spans (cont.)

Spruce-Pine-Fir (South): (cont.)

Nominal Lumber Size (inches)	Joist Spacing Center to Center (inches)	Lumber Grade		
		Select Structural	No. 1	No. 2
		Maximum Span (feet - inches)		

Max Live load=50 lbf/ft², Max Dead Load=10 lbf/ft²

2 x 8	12	12 - 03	11 - 11	11 - 07
	16	11 - 01	10 - 10	10 - 06
	24	09 - 09	09 - 03	08 - 08
2 x 10	12	15 - 07	15 - 02	14 - 09
	16	14 - 02	13 - 10	13 - 00
	24	12 - 05	11 - 04	10 - 07
2 x 12	12	19 - 00	18 - 06	17 - 05
	16	17 - 03	16 - 01	15 - 01
	24	15 - 01	13 - 01	12 - 04
2 x 14	12	22 - 04	20 - 09	19 - 05
	16	20 - 04	17 - 11	16 - 10
	24	-	14 - 08	13 - 09

Max Live load=60 lbf/ft², Max Dead Load=10 lbf/ft²

2 x 8	12	11 - 06	11 - 03	10 - 11
	16	10 - 06	10 - 02	09 - 10
	24	09 - 02	08 - 07	08 - 01
2 x 10	12	14 - 08	14 - 04	13 - 11
	16	13 - 04	12 - 10	12 - 00
	24	11 - 08	10 - 06	09 - 10
2 x 12	12	17 - 11	17 - 02	16 - 01
	16	16 - 03	14 - 10	14 - 00
	24	14 - 02	12 - 02	11 - 05
2 x 14	12	21 - 01	19 - 02	18 - 00
	16	19 - 02	16 - 07	15 - 07
	24	-	13 - 07	12 - 09

Dead Load = weight of structure + fixed loads
Live Load = movable loads such as furniture, wind, snow, etc.

Maximum Floor Joist Spans (cont.)

Spruce-Pine-Fir (South): (cont.)

Nominal Lumber Size (inches)	Joist Spacing Center to Center (inches)	Lumber Grade		
		Select Structural	No. 1	No. 2
		Maximum Span (feet - inches)		

Max Live load=30 lbf/ft², Max Dead Load=27 lbf/ft²

Nominal Lumber Size (inches)	Joist Spacing Center to Center (inches)	Select Structural	No. 1	No. 2
2 x 6	12	11 - 00	10 - 07	10 - 00
	16	10 - 00	09 - 02	08 - 07
	24	08 - 09	07 - 06	07 - 01
2 x 8	12	14 - 06	13 - 05	12 - 07
	16	13 - 02	11 - 08	10 - 11
	24	11 - 06	09 - 06	08 - 11
2 x 10	12	18 - 06	16 - 05	15 - 05
	16	16 - 10	14 - 02	13 - 04
	24	14 - 04	11 - 07	10 - 11
2 x 12	12	22 - 06	19 - 00	17 - 10
	16	20 - 04	16 - 06	15 - 06
	24	16 - 08	13 - 05	12 - 08

Max Live load=40 lbf/ft², Max Dead Load=27 lbf/ft²

Nominal Lumber Size (inches)	Joist Spacing Center to Center (inches)	Select Structural	No. 1	No. 2
2 x 6	12	10 - 00	09 - 09	09 - 02
	16	09 - 01	08 - 06	07 - 11
	24	07 - 11	06 - 11	06 - 06
2 x 8	12	13 - 02	12 - 05	11 - 08
	16	12 - 00	10 - 09	10 - 01
	24	10 - 06	08 - 09	08 - 03
2 x 10	12	16 - 10	15 - 02	14 - 03
	16	15 - 03	13 - 01	12 - 04
	24	13 - 03	10 - 08	10 - 01
2 x 12	12	20 - 06	17 - 07	16 - 06
	16	18 - 07	15 - 02	14 - 03
	24	-	12 - 05	11 - 08

Dead Load = weight of structure + fixed loads
Live Load = movable loads such as furniture, wind, snow, etc.

Maximum Floor Joist Spans (cont.)

Spruce-Pine-Fir (South) : (cont.)

Nominal Lumber Size (inches)	Joist Spacing Center to Center (inches)	Lumber Grade		
		Select Structural	No. 1	No. 2
		Maximum Span (feet - inches)		

Max Live load=50 lbf/ft², Max Dead Load=27 lbf/ft²

Nominal Lumber Size (inches)	Joist Spacing	Select Structural	No. 1	No. 2
2 x 8	12	12 - 03	11 - 07	10 - 10
	16	11 - 01	10 - 00	09 - 05
	24	09 - 09	08 - 02	07 - 08
2 x 10	12	15 - 07	14 - 01	13 - 03
	16	14 - 02	12 - 03	11 - 06
	24	12 - 04	10 - 00	09 - 04
2 x 12	12	19 - 00	16 - 04	15 - 04
	16	17 - 03	14 - 02	13 - 04
	24	-	11 - 07	10 - 10
2 x 14	12	22 - 04	18 - 03	17 - 02
	16	19 - 07	15 - 10	14 - 10
	24	-	12 - 11	12 - 02

Notes :
1. Tabulated values developed from Span Tables for Joists and Rafters, American Softwood Lumber Standard Sizes, 1993, American Wood Council, PO Box 5364, Madison, WI 53705-5364.
2. The tabulated values assume:
   (a) installation of at least three joists that are spaced no more than 24" on center
   (b) fully supported members, properly sheathed with adequate flooring, nailed on top edge of the joist
   (c) dry service conditions with wood moisture content not exceeding 19%
   (d) minimum bearing width of 1.5" and minimum bearing length of 1.5"
   (e) deflection is limited to span in inches divided by 360.
3. Tabulated spans apply to surfaced (S4S) lumber and are distances from face to face of supports
4. Lumber lengths over 20' are not common.
5. Another good reference is : Western Lumber Span Tables, Western Wood Products Association, 522 SW Fifth Ave., Suite 400, Portland, OR 97204-2122.

Maximum Floor Joist Spans (cont.)

Southern Pine: Includes Loblolly pine, Longleaf pine, Shortleaf pine, and Slash pine. ***Sometimes called Yellow Pine or Southern Yellow Pine.*** See notes at end of tables.

Nominal Lumber Size (inches)	Joist Spacing Center to Center (inches)	Lumber Grade		
		Select Structural	No. 1	No. 2
		Maximum Span (feet - inches)		

Max Live load=30 lbf/ft², Max Dead Load=10 lbf/ft²

Nominal Lumber Size (inches)	Joist Spacing Center to Center (inches)	Select Structural	No. 1	No. 2
2 x 6	12	12 - 03	12 - 00	11 - 10
	16	11 - 02	10 - 11	10 - 09
	24	09 - 09	09 - 07	09 - 04
2 x 8	12	16 - 02	15 - 10	15 - 07
	16	14 - 08	14 - 05	14 - 02
	24	12 - 10	12 - 07	12 - 04
2 x 10	12	20 - 08	20 - 03	19 - 10
	16	18 - 09	18 - 05	18 - 00
	24	16 - 05	16 - 01	14 - 08
2 x 12	12	25 - 01	24 - 08	24 - 02
	16	22 - 10	22 - 05	21 - 01
	24	19 - 11	19 - 06	17 - 02

Max Live load=40 lbf/ft², Max Dead Load=10 lbf/ft²

Nominal Lumber Size (inches)	Joist Spacing Center to Center (inches)	Select Structural	No. 1	No. 2
2 x 6	12	11 - 02	10 - 11	10 - 09
	16	10 - 02	09 - 11	09 - 09
	24	08 - 10	08 - 08	08 - 06
2 x 8	12	14 - 08	14 - 05	14 - 02
	16	13 - 04	13 - 01	12 - 10
	24	11 - 08	11 - 05	11 - 00
2 x 10	12	18 - 09	18 - 05	18 - 00
	16	17 - 00	16 - 09	16 - 01
	24	14 - 11	14 - 07	13 - 01
2 x 12	12	22 - 10	22 - 05	21 - 09
	16	20 - 09	20 - 04	18 - 10
	24	18 - 01	17 - 05	15 - 05

Maximum Floor Joist Spans (cont.)

Southern Pine: (cont.)

Nominal Lumber Size (inches)	Joist Spacing Center to Center (inches)	Lumber Grade		
		Select Structural	No. 1	No. 2
		Maximum Span (feet - inches)		

Max Live load=50 lbf/ft^2, Max Dead Load=10 lbf/ft^2

Nominal Lumber Size (inches)	Joist Spacing Center to Center (inches)	Select Structural	No. 1	No. 2
2 x 6	12	10 - 04	10 - 02	09 - 11
	16	09 - 05	09 - 03	09 - 01
	24	08 - 03	08 - 01	07 - 09
2 x 8	12	13 - 08	13 - 05	13 - 01
	16	12 - 05	12 - 02	11 - 11
	24	10 - 10	10 - 08	10 - 00
2 x 10	12	17 - 05	17 - 01	16 - 09
	16	15 - 10	15 - 06	14 - 08
	24	13 - 10	13 - 04	12 - 00
2 x 12	12	21 - 02	20 - 09	19 - 10
	16	19 - 03	18 - 10	17 - 02
	24	16 - 10	15 - 11	14 - 00

Max Live load=60 lbf/ft^2, Max Dead Load=10 lbf/ft^2

Nominal Lumber Size (inches)	Joist Spacing Center to Center (inches)	Select Structural	No. 1	No. 2
2 x 6	12	09 - 09	09 - 07	09 - 04
	16	08 - 10	08 - 08	08 - 06
	24	07 - 09	07 - 07	07 - 02
2 x 8	12	12 - 10	12 - 07	12 - 04
	16	11 - 08	11 - 05	11 - 03
	24	10 - 02	10 - 00	09 - 04
2 x 10	12	16 - 05	16 - 01	15 - 08
	16	14 - 11	14 - 07	13 - 07
	24	13 - 00	12 - 04	11 - 01
2 x 12	12	19 - 11	19 - 07	18 - 05
	16	18 - 01	17 - 09	15 - 11
	24	15 - 10	14 - 09	13 - 00

Dead Load = weight of structure + fixed loads
Live Load = movable loads such as furniture, wind, snow, etc.

Maximum Floor Joist Spans (cont.)

Southern Pine: (cont.)

Nominal Lumber Size (inches)	Joist Spacing Center to Center (inches)	Lumber Grade		
		Select Structural	No. 1	No. 2
		Maximum Span (feet - inches)		

Max Live load=40 lbf/ft², Max Dead Load=20 lbf/ft²

2 x 6	12	11 - 02	10 - 11	10 - 09
	16	10 - 02	09 - 11	09 - 06
	24	08 - 10	08 - 08	07 - 09
2 x 8	12	14 - 08	14 - 05	14 - 02
	16	13 - 04	13 - 01	12 - 04
	24	11 - 08	11 - 03	10 - 00
2 x 10	12	18 - 09	18 - 05	16 - 11
	16	17 - 00	16 - 04	14 - 08
	24	14 - 11	13 - 04	12 - 00
2 x 12	12	22 - 10	22 - 05	19 - 10
	16	20 - 09	19 - 06	17 - 02
	24	18 - 01	15 - 11	14 - 00

Max Live load=50 lbf/ft², Max Dead Load=20 lbf/ft²

2 x 6	12	10 - 04	10 - 02	09 - 11
	16	09 - 05	09 - 03	08 - 10
	24	08 - 03	08 - 01	07 - 02
2 x 8	12	13 - 08	13 - 05	13 - 01
	16	12 - 05	12 - 02	11 - 05
	24	10 - 10	10 - 05	09 - 04
2 x 10	12	17 - 05	17 - 01	15 - 08
	16	15 - 10	15 - 01	13 - 07
	24	13 - 10	12 - 04	11 - 01
2 x 12	12	21 - 02	20 - 09	18 - 05
	16	19 - 03	18 - 00	15 - 11
	24	16 - 10	14 - 09	13 - 00

Dead Load = weight of structure + fixed loads
Live Load = movable loads such as furniture, wind, snow, etc.

Maximum Floor Joist Spans (cont.)

Southern Pine: (cont.)

Nominal Lumber Size (inches)	Joist Spacing Center to Center (inches)	Lumber Grade		
		Select Structural	No. 1	No. 2
		Maximum Span (feet - inches)		

Max Live load=60 lbf/ft^2, Max Dead Load=20 lbf/ft^2

Nominal Lumber Size (inches)	Joist Spacing Center to Center (inches)	Select Structural	No. 1	No. 2
2 x 6	12	09 - 09	09 - 07	09 - 04
	16	08 - 10	08 - 08	08 - 03
	24	07 - 09	07 - 07	06 - 09
2 x 8	12	12 - 10	12 - 07	12 - 04
	16	11 - 08	11 - 05	10 - 08
	24	10 - 02	09 - 09	08 - 08
2 x 10	12	16 - 05	16 - 01	14 - 08
	16	14 - 11	14 - 02	12 - 08
	24	13 - 00	11 - 07	10 - 04
2 x 12	12	19 - 11	19 - 06	17 - 02
	16	18 - 01	16 - 10	14 - 11
	24	15 - 10	13 - 09	12 - 02

Notes :
1. Tabulated values developed from Span Tables for Joists and Rafters, American Softwood Lumber Standard Sizes, 1993, American Wood Council, PO Box 5364, Madison, WI 5364.
2. The tabulated values assume:
   (a) installation of at least three joists that are spaced no more than 24" on center
   (b) fully supported members, properly sheathed with adequate flooring, nailed on top edge of the joist
   (c) dry service conditions with wood moisture content not exceeding 19%
   (d) minimum bearing width of 1.5" and minimum bearing length of 1.5"
   (e) deflection is limited to span in inches divided by 360.
3. Tabulated spans apply to surfaced (S4S) lumber and are distances from face to face of supports
4. Lumber lengths over 20' are not common.
5. Another good reference is: Maximum Spans, Southern Pine Joists & Rafters, Southern Forest Products Association, PO Box 641700, Kenner, LA 70064-1700.

Maximum Floor Joist Spans (cont.)

Redwood: See notes at end of tables.

Nominal Lumber Size (inches)	Joist Spacing Center to Center (inches)	Lumber Grade		
		Select Structural	No. 1	No. 2
		Maximum Span (feet - inches)		

Max Live load=30 lbf/ft², MaDead Load=10 lbf/ft²

2 x 6	12	11 - 03	11 - 00	10 - 09
	16	10 - 03	10 - 00	09 - 09
	24	08 - 11	08 - 09	08 - 06
2 x 8	12	14 - 11	14 - 06	14 - 02
	16	13 - 06	13 - 02	12 - 10
	24	11 - 10	11 - 06	11 - 03
2 x 10	12	19 - 00	18 - 06	18 - 00
	16	17 - 03	16 - 10	16 - 05
	24	15 - 01	14 - 08	14 - 04
2 x 12	12	23 - 01	22 - 06	21 - 11
	16	21 - 00	20 - 06	19 - 11
	24	18 - 04	17 - 11	17 - 05

Max Live load=40 lbf/ft², Max Dead Load=10 lbf/ft²

2 x 6	12	10 - 03	10 - 00	09 - 09
	16	09 - 04	09 - 01	08 - 10
	24	08 - 02	07 - 11	07 - 09
2 x 8	12	13 - 06	13 - 02	12 - 10
	16	12 - 03	12 - 00	11 - 08
	24	10 - 09	10 - 06	10 - 02
2 x 10	12	17 - 03	16 - 10	16 - 05
	16	15 - 08	15 - 03	14 - 11
	24	13 - 08	13 - 04	13 - 00
2 x 12	12	21 - 00	20 - 06	19 - 11
	16	19 - 01	18 - 07	18 - 01
	24	16 - 08	16 - 03	15 - 10

Dead Load = weight of structure + fixed loads
Live Load = movable loads such as furniture, wind, snow, etc.

Maximum Floor Joist (cont.)

Redwood: (cont.)

Nominal Lumber Size (inches)	Joist Spacing Center to Center (inches)	Lumber Grade		
		Select Structural	No. 1	No. 2
		Maximum Span (feet - inches)		

Max Live load=50 lbf/ft², Max Dead Load=10 lbf/ft²

2 x 6	12	09 - 06	09 - 03	09 - 01
	16	08 - 08	08 - 05	08 - 03
	24	07 - 07	07 - 04	07 - 02
2 x 8	12	12 - 07	12 - 03	11 - 11
	16	11 - 05	11 - 01	10 - 10
	24	10 - 00	09 - 09	09 - 06
2 x 10	12	16 - 00	15 - 07	15 - 02
	16	14 - 07	14 - 02	13 - 10
	24	12 - 08	12 - 05	12 - 01
2 x 12	12	19 - 06	19 - 00	18 - 06
	16	17 - 08	17 - 03	16 - 10
	24	15 - 05	15 - 01	14 - 08

Max Live load=60 lbf/ft², Max Dead Load=10 lbf/ft²

2 x 6	12	08 - 11	08 - 09	08 - 06
	16	08 - 02	07 - 11	07 - 09
	24	07 - 01	06 - 11	06 - 09
2 x 8	12	11 - 10	11 - 06	11 - 03
	16	10 - 09	10 - 06	10 - 02
	24	09 - 04	09 - 02	08 - 11
2 x 10	12	15 - 01	14 - 08	14 - 04
	16	13 - 08	13 - 04	13 - 00
	24	11 - 11	11 - 08	11 - 04
2 x 12	12	18 - 04	17 - 11	17 - 05
	16	16 - 08	16 - 03	15 - 10
	24	14 - 07	14 - 02	13 - 10

Dead Load = weight of structure + fixed loads
Live Load = movable loads such as furniture, wind, snow, etc.

Maximum Floor Joist Spans (cont.)

Redwood: (cont.)

Nominal Lumber Size (inches)	Joist Spacing Center to Center (inches)	Lumber Grade		
		Select Structural	No. 1	No. 2
		Maximum Span (feet - inches)		

Max Live load=40 lbf/ft², Max Dead Load=20 lbf/ft²

Nominal Lumber Size (inches)	Joist Spacing Center to Center (inches)	Select Structural	No. 1	No. 2
2 x 6	12	10 - 03	10 - 00	09 - 09
	16	09 - 04	09 - 01	08 - 10
	24	08 - 02	07 - 11	07 - 09
2 x 8	12	13 - 06	13 - 02	12 - 10
	16	12 - 03	12 - 00	11 - 08
	24	10 - 09	10 - 06	10 - 02
2 x 10	12	17 - 03	16 - 10	16 - 05
	16	15 - 08	15 - 03	14 - 11
	24	13 - 08	13 - 04	13 - 00
2 x 12	12	21 - 00	20 - 09	19 - 11
	16	19 - 01	18 - 07	18 - 01
	24	16 - 08	16 - 03	15 - 10

Max Live load=50 lbf/ft², Max Dead Load=20 lbf/ft²

Nominal Lumber Size (inches)	Joist Spacing Center to Center (inches)	Select Structural	No. 1	No. 2
2 x 6	12	09 - 06	09 - 03	09 - 01
	16	08 - 08	08 - 05	08 - 03
	24	07 - 07	07 - 04	07 - 02
2 x 8	12	12 - 07	12 - 03	11 - 11
	16	11 - 05	11 - 01	10 - 10
	24	10 - 00	09 - 09	09 - 06
2 x 10	12	16 - 00	15 - 07	15 - 02
	16	14 - 07	14 - 02	13 - 10
	24	12 - 08	12 - 05	12 - 01
2 x 12	12	19 - 06	19 - 00	18 - 06
	16	17 - 08	17 - 03	16 - 10
	24	15 - 05	15 - 01	14 - 08

Dead Load = weight of structure + fixed loads
Live Load = movable loads such as furniture, wind, snow, etc.

Maximum Floor Joist Spans (cont.)

Redwood: (cont.)

Nominal Lumber Size (inches)	Joist Spacing Center to Center (inches)	Lumber Grade		
		Select Structural	No. 1	No. 2
		Maximum Span (feet - inches)		

Max Live load=60 lbf/ft^2, Max Dead Load=20 lbf/ft^2

2 x 6	12	08 - 11	08 - 09	08 - 06
	16	08 - 02	07 - 11	07 - 09
	24	07 - 01	06 - 11	06 - 09
2 x 8	12	11 - 10	11 - 06	11 - 03
	16	10 - 09	10 - 06	10 - 02
	24	09 - 04	09 - 02	08 - 11
2 x 10	12	15 - 01	14 - 08	14 - 04
	16	13 - 08	13 - 04	13 - 00
	24	11 - 11	11 - 08	11 - 04
2 x 12	12	18 - 04	17 - 11	17 - 05
	16	16 - 08	16 - 03	15 - 10
	24	14 - 07	14 - 02	13 - 10

Notes :
1. Tabulated values developed from Span Tables for Joists and Rafters, American Softwood Lumber Standard Sizes, 1993, American Wood Council, PO Box 5364, Madison, WI 53705-5364.
2. The tabulated values assume:
   (a) installation of at least three joists that are spaced no more than 24" on center
   (b) fully supported members, properly sheathed with adequate flooring, nailed on top edge of the joist
   (c) dry service conditions with wood moisture content not exceeding 19%
   (d) minimum bearing width of 1.5" and minimum bearing length of 1.5"
   (e) deflection is limited to span in inches divided by 360.
3. Tabulated spans apply to surfaced (S4S) lumber and are distances from face to face of supports
4. Span length limited to a maximum of 26' due to availability. Lumber lengths over 20' are not common.
5. Another reference is: Redwood Deck Construction, Califiornia Redwood Association, 405 Enfrente Drive, Suite 200, Novato, CA 94949.

Strength of Wood Beams

Wood Species	Stress in Pounds per Square Inch (PSI)					
	Bending		Compression			
	Horizontal Shear F_b		Perpendicular to Grain $F_{c\perp}$		Parallel to Grain F_c	
	Wet	Dry	Wet	Dry	Wet	Dry
Aspen, Big Tooth	1006	1006	177	265	725	725
Aspen, Quaking	1006	1006	177	265	725	725
Beech, American	1417	1668	477	715	960	1200
Birch, Sweet	1417	1668	477	715	960	1200
Birch, Yellow	1417	1668	477	715	960	1200
Cedar, Alaska	1150	1150	283	425	800	1000
Cedar, Incense	1150	1150	283	425	800	1000
Cedar, N. White	891	891	247	370	750	750
Cedar, Port Orford	1150	1150	283	425	800	1000
Cedar, Western Red	1150	1150	283	425	800	1000
Cottonwood	1006	1006	213	320	620	775
Fir, Alpine	1222	1438	283	425	1120	1400
Fir, Amabilis	1271	1495	247	370	1320	1650
Fir, Balsam	1222	1438	283	425	1120	1400
Fir, California Red	1369	1610	270	405	1200	1500
Fir, Douglas	1417	1668	417	625	1360	1700
Fir, Grand	1369	1610	270	405	1200	1500
Fir, Noble	1369	1610	270	405	1200	1500
Fir, Pacific Silver	1369	1610	270	405	1200	1500
Fir, White	1369	1610	270	405	1200	1500
Hemlock, Eastern	1222	1438	370	555	960	1200
Hemlock, Mountain	1006	1006	223	335	840	1050
Hemlock, Western	1271	1495	247	370	1320	1650
Hickory, Bitternut	1417	1668	477	715	960	1200
Hickory, Mockernut	1417	1668	477	715	960	1200
Hickory, Nutmeg	1417	1668	477	715	960	1200
Hickory, Pecan	1417	1668	477	715	960	1200
Hickory, Pignut	1417	1668	477	715	960	1200
Hickory, Shagbark	1417	1668	477	715	960	1200
Hickory, Shellbark	1417	1668	477	715	960	1200
Hickory, Water	1417	1668	477	715	960	1200
Larch, Western	1417	1668	417	625	1360	1700
Maple, Black	1150	1150	413	620	700	875
Maple, Red	1271	1495	410	615	880	1100
Maple, Silver	1150	1150	413	620	700	875
Maple, Sugar	978	1150	413	620	700	875

Strength of Wood Beams (cont.)

Wood Species	Stress in Pounds per Square Inch (PSI)					
	Bending		Compression			
	Horizontal Shear F_b		Perpendicular to Grain $F_{c\perp}$		Parallel to Grain F_c	
	Wet	Dry	Wet	Dry	Wet	Dry
Oak, Black	1369	1610	590	885	920	1150
Oak, Bur	1173	1380	533	800	880	1100
Oak, Cherrybark	1124	1323	547	820	800	1000
Oak, Chestnut	1173	1380	533	800	880	1100
Oak, Laurel	1124	1323	547	820	800	1000
Oak, Live	1173	1380	533	800	880	1100
Oak, Northern Red	1369	1610	590	885	920	1150
Oak, Overcup	1173	1380	533	800	880	1100
Oak, Pin	1369	1610	590	885	920	1150
Oak, Post	1173	1380	533	800	880	1100
Oak, Scarlet	1369	1610	590	885	920	1150
Oak, Southern Red	1124	1323	547	820	800	1000
Oak,Swamp Chestnut	1173	1380	533	800	880	1100
Oak, Swamp White	1173	1380	533	800	880	1100
Oak, Water	1124	1323	547	820	800	1000
Oak, White	1173	1380	533	800	880	1100
Oak, Willow	1124	1323	547	820	800	1000
Pine, Eastern White	1222	1438	223	335	960	1200
Pine, Idaho White	1006	1006	223	335	840	1050
Pine, Jack	1222	1438	283	425	1120	1400
Pine, Loblolly	1857	2185	377	565	1440	1800
Pine, Lodgeploe	1222	1438	283	425	1120	1400
Pine, Longleaf	1857	2185	377	565	1440	1800
Pine, Norway	1271	1495	223	335	960	1200
Pine, Pitch	1222	1438	223	335	960	1200
Pine, Pond	1369	1610	377	565	1240	1550
Pine, Ponderosa	1006	1006	223	335	840	1050
Pine, Red	1271	1495	223	335	960	1200
Pine, Shortleaf	1857	2185	377	565	1440	1800
Pine, Slash	1857	2185	377	565	1440	1800
Pine, Sugar	1006	1006	223	335	840	1050
Pine, Virginia	1369	1610	377	565	1240	1550
Popular, Yellow	978	1150	280	420	720	900
Redwood	1320	1553	433	650	1200	1500

Strength of Wood Beams (cont.)

Wood Species	Stress in Pounds per Square Inch (PSI)					
	Bending		Compression			
	Horizontal Shear F_b		Perpendicular to Grain $F_{c\perp}$		Parallel to Grain F_c	
	Wet	Dry	Wet	Dry	Wet	Dry
Spruce, Black	1222	1438	283	425	1120	1400
Spruce, Engelmann	1222	1438	283	425	1120	1400
Spruce, Red	1222	1438	283	425	1120	1400
Spruce, Sitka	1271	1495	223	335	960	1200
Spruce, White	1222	1438	283	425	1120	1400
Tamarack	1222	1438	370	555	960	1200

Notes:
Design conditions:
1. Visually graded dimension lumber
2. 2 to 4 inches thick
3. 12 inch nominal depth
4. Normal load duration
5. Members are used for joists, truss chords, rafters, studs, planks, or decking
6. Members in contact or spaced not more than 24 inches on centers, not less than 3 in number and joined by floor, roof or other load distributing elements to support the design load
7. Note from the above table, that all strength ratings of wood decrease dramatically when the wood is wet!

Source: Design values developed from Design Values for Wood Construction, National Design Specification, American Forest and Paper Association, Washington, D.C., 1993

Wood Gluing Characteristics

Wood gluing is a very common practice today, but there are a large number of glue types from which to choose and each of the different types of wood have different gluing properties. See the chapter on GLUE, page 282, for specific information on each of the common glue types.

The following 4 groups define the relative difficulty with which various woods can be glued:

Easy: Works with many different types of glues and under many gluing conditions.
Aspen, Western Red Cedar, Chestnut, Cottonwood, Cypress, White Fir, Larch, Redwood, Spruce, Willow, Yellow Poplar.

Moderate: More restricted gluing conditions than the Easy category. Different types of glue work fine.
Red Alder, Basswood, Butternut, Eastern Red Cedar, Douglas Fir, American and Rock Elm, Hackberry, Western Hemlock, Magnolia, Mahogany, Pine, Sweet Gum.

Difficult: Well controlled gluing conditions are required but still works with many different glue types.
White Ash, Alaskan Cedar, Cherry, Dogwood, Silver Maple (soft), Red and White Oak, Pecan, Sycamore, Black and Water Tupelo, Black Walnut.

Very Difficult: Requires special glues and very close control of gluing conditions.
American Beech, Sweet and Yellow Birch, Hickory, Sugar Maple (hard), Osage–orange, Persimmon.

"Gluing conditions" is a function of proper sanding, letting surfaces to be glued become tacky before joining, using clamps to hold glue positions, and drying in a warm, dry area. Heat lamps will sometimes aid in the drying process

In addition to the above, the following generalities are also true:
Hardwoods are more difficult to glue than softwoods.
Heartwood is more difficult to glue than sapwood.
Heavy woods are more difficult to glue than lightweight woods.

Concrete

Concrete is a mixture of aggregate (typically sand and gravel), Portland cement, and water. Characteristics of each of these components are as follows:

Aggregate: A mixture of sand and gravel ranging in size from dust to 2-1/2 inches. Rounded fragments are generally better and do not use fragments larger than 1/4 the thickness of the concrete unit you are pouring (e.g. for a 4 inch slab, don't use greater than 1 inch gravel). The larger the gravel the more cost effective the concrete and there will be less problems from shrinkage.

Portland Cement: Cement comes in 1 cubic foot bags that weigh 94 lbs. It can also be purchased in bulk trailer loads. There are 5 basic types of cement:
  Type I: The most common type sold by building suppliers.
  Type II: A "sulfate resistant" variety used in bridges & pilings.
  Type III: Quick hardening, used for rush jobs and winter use.
  Type IV: Slow hardening, low heat for large structures.
  Type V: Very high "sulfate resistance". (near water)

Water: Use clean, impurity free water, not muddy water.

Air: A fourth component of some concrete is millions of tiny air bubbles entrained in the mixture. This component helps the concrete withstand the effects of freezing and thawing and also makes the concrete lighter. Machine mixing is a must.

The strength of concrete increases when:
  1. The amount of cement in the mixture increases.
  2. The amount of water relative to cement decreases.
  3. The density of the concrete is higher.
  4. The aggregate is coarser.

The most common problems encountered in making concrete are adding too much water or sand, and poor mixing.

Other factors affecting the quality of the finished product include mixing and curing. Thorough mixing of the concrete is absolutely necessary in order to produce the strongest, most durable pour. Curing of concrete is necessary in order for the material to harden properly. The concrete must be kept moist for a period of 7 days and the temperature must not drop below 50°F. Although after 28 days, there is normally very little increase in the strength of concrete, most concrete does not completely cure for years.

Concrete (con't)
Typical Concrete Mixtures by Volume

Cement:Sand:Gravel

Ratio	Application
1:3:6	Normal static loads, no rebar; not exposed
1:2.5:5	Normal foundations & walls; exposed
1:2.5:4	Basement walls
1:2.5:3.5	Waterproof basement walls
1:2.5:3	Floors (light duty), driveways
1:2.25:3	Steps, driveways, sidewalks
1:2:4	Lintels
1:2:4	Reinforced roads, buildings, walls; exposed
1:2:3.5	Retaining walls, drive ways
1:2:3	Swimming pools, fence posts
1:1.75:4	Floors (light duty)
1:1.5:3	Watertight, reinforced tanks & columns
1:1:2	High strength columns, girders, floors
1:1:1.5	Fence posts

When mixing concrete, mix the sand and cement first until a uniform color is obtained then mix in the aggregate. Adding the correct amount of water is a difficult task. In the above table, the portion for water is about 1/2 but this will vary depending on whether the sand is dry, damp, or wet (the 1/2 ratio component is equal to about 6 gallons of water per sack of cement). Simply remember that you only want to add enough water to make the concrete mixture workable and that the less water in relation to cement, the stronger the final concrete will be.

The strength of concrete can also be increased by compacting or working the mixture into place. This is accomplished by walking in the wet mixture or tamping or vibrating. If vibrators are used be careful that you do not cause segregation of the aggregate.

Recommended Thickness of Slabs

Thickness (inches)	Application
4	Home basement floors, farm building floors
4 to 5	Home garage floors, porches
5 to 6	Sidewalks, barn and granary floors, small shed floors
6 to 8	Driveways

Concrete and Mortar

Calculating Cubic Volumes

Concrete and mortar are normally sold and used on a cubic volume basis (either cubic feet or cubic yards). Use the following to calculate the amount of concrete you need for a slab:

Cubic feet of Concrete = Slab thickness in feet x Slab width in feet x Slab length in feet

1 cubic yard = 27 cubic feet
1 cubic foot = 1,728 cubic inches

In using the above equations, note that the volume of the final concrete mixture is approximately 2/3's the volume of the original cement–aggregate mixture. This occurs because the sand and cement fill in the void spaces between the gravel fragments.

Standard Steel Reinforcing Bar (re–bar)

Bar Number	Diameter Fraction Inch	Diameter Inches	Diameter mm	Pounds per foot
2b	1/4	0.250	6.4	0.17
3	3/8	0.375	9.5	0.38
4	1/2	0.500	12.7	0.67
5	5/8	0.625	15.9	1.04
6	3/4	0.750	19.1	1.50
7	7/8	0.875	22.2	2.04
8	1	1.000	25.4	2.67
9	1–1/8	1.128	28.7	3.40
10	1–1/4	1.270	32.3	4.30
11	1–3/8	1.410	35.8	5.31
14	1–3/4	1.693	43.0	7.65
18	2–1/4	2.257	57.3	13.60

Coloring Concrete and Mortar

Color	Color material	lbs / sack Cement
Black	Black oxide or mineral Black	1 to 12
Blue	Ultramarine Blue	5 to 9
Brown–Red	Red iron oxide	5 to 9
Bright Red	Mineral Turkey Red	5 to 9
Purple–Red	Indian red	5 to 9
Brown	Metallic Brown Oxide	5 to 9
Buff to yellow	Yellow ocher or yellow oxide	2 to 9
Green	Chromium oxide or ultramarine	5 to 9

Mortar

Mortar is composed of basically the same material as concrete, except that its composition has been altered to increase the ease of workability and decrease the setting time of the mixture. As with concrete, the strength of mortar is a function of the proportions of its ingredients.

Mortar is a mixture of Portland cement, hydrated lime, sand (well graded and in a size range of 1/8 inch to 100 mesh) and water. Masonry cement, which already contains the hydrated lime, can be used instead of Portland cement.

The strength of mortar increases when:

1. The amount of cement in the mixture increases.
2. The amount of water relative to cement decreases. Unfortunately, there is no rule for the amount of water since it is a function of workability. Just use as little as possible.
3. The amount of hydrated lime decreases.
4. The amount of Portland cement relative to masonry cement increases.
5. Brick with low water absorption is used. If brick absorbs water readily, the bricks must be wetted before mortaring.
6. Clean sand is used. Organic matter and salts in the sand will drastically decrease the mortar strength. A higher percentage of coarse to fine sand increases strength.
7. Special epoxies are available that can be mixed with the mortar. These increase both the strength and bonding power of the mortar and in many cases will create mortar that is stronger than the brick. Note that this adds to the cost of the mortar.

The workability of mortar increases when:

1. The amount of hydrated lime in the mixture increases.
2. The amount of water increases.

As with concrete, thorough mixing of the mortar is imperative. A power mixer is best, but small quantities can be mixed by hand. Once the mortar has been mixed, it will begin to cure and stiffen. If the mortar begins to stiffen within 2 to 2.5 hours of mixing (above 80°F outside air temperature) you can add a small amount of water to increase workability. After the 2.5 hour time limit, the mortar should be thrown away and a new batch mixed. If the outside air temperatures are below 80°F, the 2.5 hour time limit can be increased to approximately 3.5 hours.

Mortar

Type numbers are used to define the various mortar mixes. The following are the four common types with their <u>volume</u> proportions of Portland cement (see also concrete section for different types of Portland), masonry cement (Type II unless otherwise stated), lime, and sand:

Type M: General use for foundations, walls, sidewalks and other situations in contact with the ground or below grade. 28 day compression strength 4900–5400 psi, depending on amount of water used.
Portland Mix: 1 Portland; 1/4 hydrated lime; 3 sand
Masonry Mix: 1 Portland; 1 masonry, 6 sand

Type S: General use for high resistance to sideways or lateral stress. 28 day compression strength 2100–2800 psi, depending on amount of water used.
Portland Mix: 1 Portland; 1/2 hydrated lime; 4.5 sand.
Masonry Mix: 1/2 Portland; 1 masonry; 4.5 sand

Type N: General use above grade for severe exposure walls. 28 day compression strength 800–1200 psi, depending on amount of water used.
Portland Mix: 1 Portland; 1 hydrated lime; 6 sand
Masonry Mix: 1 masonry; 3 sand

Type O: Low strength load bearing walls where excessive moisture and freezing are not present. Compression strength must be below 100 psi.
Portland Mix: 1 Portland; 2 hydrated lime; 9 sand
Masonry Mix: 1 masonry (Types I or II); 3 sand

If you need a small amount of general use mortar, the following will make about 1 cubic foot: 16 lbs Portland cement, 8.5 lbs hydrated lime, 100 lbs dry sand, and 2 to 3 gallons of water.

The amount of mortar required for a job varies tremendously, but the following average quantities may be helpful: with practice, you can lay 90–120 common bricks/hour.

Mortar required for Common Brick (8 in x 3-3/4 in x 2-1/4 in) assuming 20 bricks per cubic foot		
Joint Thickness inches	Cu ft Mortar/ 1000 brick	Cu ft Mortar/ Cu ft brick
1/4	9	0.2
3/8	14	0.3
1/2	20	0.4

Rafter Length Tables

Horizontal Span 1-5 Feet

Roof Pitch		Roof Slope degrees	Rafter Length Factor	Horizontal Span in feet															
Rise in Run Notation	Inch Rise in 12 Inch Run			1			2			3			4			5				
				Rafter Length in feet, inches, and 16th's of an inch																
				foot	inch	16th"	foot	inch	16th"	foot	inch	16th"	foot	inch	16th"	foot	inch	16th"
0 in 12		0.00	1.0000	1	0	0	2	0	0	3	0	0	4	0	0	5	0	0
1 in 12		4.76	1.0035	1	0	1	2	0	0	3	0	2	4	0	3	5	0	3
1.5 in 12		7.13	1.0078	1	0	1	2	0	3	3	0	4	4	0	6	5	0	7
2 in 12		9.46	1.0138	1	0	3	2	0	5	3	0	8	4	0	11	5	0	13
2.5 in 12		11.77	1.0215	1	0	4	2	0	8	3	0	12	4	1	0	5	1	5
3 in 12		14.04	1.0308	1	0	6	2	0	12	3	1	2	4	1	8	5	1	14
3.5 in 12		16.26	1.0417	1	0	8	2	1	0	3	1	8	4	2	0	5	2	8
4 in 12		18.43	1.0541	1	0	10	2	1	5	3	1	15	4	2	10	5	3	4
4.5 in 12		20.56	1.0680	1	0	13	2	1	10	3	2	7	4	3	4	5	4	1
5 in 12		22.62	1.0833	1	1	0	2	2	0	3	3	0	4	4	0	5	5	0
5.5 in 12		24.62	1.1000	1	1	3	2	2	6	3	3	10	4	4	13	5	6	0
6 in 12		26.57	1.1180	1	1	7	2	2	13	3	4	4	4	5	11	5	7	1
6.5 in 12		28.44	1.1373	1	1	10	2	3	5	3	5	0	4	6	9	5	8	4
7 in 12		30.26	1.1577	1	1	14	2	3	13	3	5	11	4	7	9	5	9	7
7.5 in 12		32.01	1.1792	1	2	2	2	4	5	3	6	7	4	8	10	5	10	12
8 in 12		33.69	1.2019	1	2	7	2	4	14	3	7	4	4	9	10	6	0	2
8.5 in 12		35.31	1.2255	1	2	11	2	5	7	3	8	2	4	10	13	6	1	8

RAFTER LENGTH TABLES - Horizontal Span 1-5 feet (cont.)

Roof Pitch Rise in Run Notation (Inch Rise in 12 Inch Run)	Roof Slope degrees	Rafter Length Factor	1 foot	1 inch	1 16th	2 foot	2 inch	2 16th	3 foot	3 inch	3 16th	4 foot	4 inch	4 16th	5 foot	5 inch	5 16th
9 in 12	36.87	1.2500	1	3	0	2	6	0	3	9	0	5	0	0	6	3	0
9.5 in 12	38.37	1.2754	1	3	5	2	6	10	3	9	15	5	1	4	6	4	8
10 in 12	39.81	1.3017	1	3	10	2	7	4	3	10	14	5	2	8	6	6	2
10.5 in 12	41.19	1.3288	1	3	15	2	7	14	3	11	13	5	3	12	6	7	12
11 in 12	42.51	1.3566	1	4	4	2	8	9	4	0	13	5	5	2	6	9	6
11.5 in 12	43.78	1.3851	1	4	10	2	9	4	4	1	14	5	6	8	6	11	2
12 in 12	45.00	1.4142	1	5	0	2	9	15	4	2	15	5	7	14	7	0	14
12.5 in 12	46.17	1.4440	1	5	5	2	10	10	4	4	0	5	9	5	7	2	10
13 in 12	47.29	1.4743	1	5	11	2	11	6	4	5	1	5	10	12	7	4	7
13.5 in 12	48.37	1.5052	1	6	1	3	0	2	4	6	3	6	0	4	7	6	5
14 in 12	49.40	1.5366	1	6	7	3	0	14	4	7	5	6	1	12	7	8	3
14.5 in 12	50.39	1.5685	1	6	13	3	1	10	4	8	7	6	3	5	7	10	2
15 in 12	51.34	1.6008	1	7	3	3	2	7	4	9	10	6	4	13	8	0	1
15.5 in 12	52.25	1.6335	1	7	10	3	3	3	4	10	13	6	6	7	8	2	0
16 in 12	53.13	1.6667	1	8	0	3	4	0	5	0	0	6	8	0	8	4	0
16.5 in 12	53.97	1.7002	1	8	6	3	4	13	5	1	3	6	9	10	8	6	0
17 in 12	54.78	1.7341	1	8	13	3	5	10	5	2	7	6	11	4	8	8	1
17.5 in 12	55.56	1.7683	1	9	4	3	6	7	5	3	11	7	0	14	8	10	2

RAFTER LENGTH TABLES - Horizontal Span 1-5 feet (cont.)

Rise in Run Notation — Inch Rise in 12 Inch Run	Roof Slope degrees	Rafter Length Factor	Horizontal Span in feet — Rafter Length in feet, inches, and 16th's of an inch														
			1			**2**			**3**			**4**			**5**		
			foot	inch	16th"	foot	inch	16th"	foot	inch	16th"	foot	inch	16th"	foot	inch	16th"
18 in 12	56.31	1.8028	1	9	10	3	7	4	5	4	14	7	2	4	9	0	3
18.5 in 12	57.03	1.8376	1	10	1	3	8	2	5	6	2	7	4	3	9	2	4
19 in 12	57.72	1.8727	1	10	8	3	8	15	5	7	7	7	5	14	9	4	6
19.5 in 12	58.39	1.9080	1	10	14	3	9	13	5	8	11	7	7	9	9	6	8
20 in 12	59.04	1.9437	1	11	5	3	10	10	5	10	0	7	9	5	9	8	10
20.5 in 12	59.66	1.9795	1	11	12	3	11	8	5	11	4	7	11	0	9	10	12
21 in 12	60.26	2.0156	2	0	3	4	0	6	6	0	9	8	0	12	10	0	15
21.5 in 12	60.83	2.0518	2	0	10	4	1	4	6	1	14	8	2	8	10	3	2
22 in 12	61.39	2.0883	2	1	1	4	2	2	6	3	3	8	4	4	10	5	5
22.5 in 12	61.93	2.1250	2	1	8	4	3	0	6	4	8	8	6	0	10	7	8
23 in 12	62.45	2.1619	2	1	15	4	3	14	6	5	13	8	7	12	10	9	11
23.5 in 12	62.95	2.1989	2	2	6	4	4	12	6	7	3	8	9	9	10	11	15
24 in 12	63.43	2.2361	2	2	13	4	5	11	6	8	8	8	11	5	11	2	3
24.5 in 12	63.90	2.2734	2	3	4	4	6	9	6	9	13	9	1	2	11	4	6
25 in 12	64.36	2.3109	2	3	12	4	7	7	6	11	3	9	2	15	11	6	10

RAFTER LENGTH TABLES - Horizontal Span 6-10 Feet

Rafter Length in feet, inches, and 16th's of an inch

Rise in Run Notation (Inch Rise in 12 Inch Run)	Roof Slope degrees	Rafter Length Factor	Span 6 foot	inch	16th	Span 7 foot	inch	16th	Span 8 foot	inch	16th	Span 9 foot	inch	16th	Span 10 foot	inch	16th
0 in 12	0.00	1.0000	6	0	0	7	0	0	8	0	0	9	0	0	10	0	0
1 in 12	4.76	1.0035	6	0	4	7	0	5	8	0	5	9	0	6	10	0	7
1.5 in 12	7.13	1.0078	6	0	9	7	0	10	8	0	12	9	0	13	10	0	15
2 in 12	9.46	1.0138	6	1	0	7	1	3	8	1	5	9	1	8	10	1	10
2.5 in 12	11.77	1.0215	6	1	9	7	1	13	8	2	1	9	2	5	10	2	9
3 in 12	14.04	1.0308	6	2	3	7	2	9	8	2	15	9	3	5	10	3	11
3.5 in 12	16.26	1.0417	6	3	0	7	3	0	8	4	0	9	3	4	10	5	0
4 in 12	18.43	1.0541	6	3	14	7	3	14	8	5	3	9	4	8	10	6	8
4.5 in 12	20.56	1.0680	6	4	14	7	5	11	8	6	8	9	7	6	10	8	3
5 in 12	22.62	1.0833	6	6	0	7	7	0	8	8	0	9	9	0	10	10	0
5.5 in 12	24.62	1.1000	6	7	3	7	8	6	8	9	10	9	10	13	11	0	0
6 in 12	26.57	1.1180	6	8	8	7	9	15	8	11	5	10	0	12	11	2	3
6.5 in 12	28.44	1.1373	6	9	14	7	11	9	9	1	3	10	2	13	11	4	8
7 in 12	30.26	1.1577	6	11	6	8	1	4	9	3	2	10	5	1	11	6	15
7.5 in 12	32.01	1.1792	7	0	14	8	3	1	9	5	3	10	7	6	11	9	8
8 in 12	33.69	1.2019	7	2	9	8	4	15	9	7	6	10	9	13	12	0	4
8.5 in 12	35.31	1.2255	7	4	4	8	6	15	9	9	10	11	0	6	12	3	1

RAFTER LENGTH TABLES - Horizontal Span 6-10 Feet (cont.)

Roof Pitch Rise in Run Notation — Inch Rise in 12 Inch Run	Roof Slope degrees	Rafter Length Factor	Horizontal Span in feet														
			6			7			8			9			10		
			Rafter Length in feet, inches, and 16th's of an inch														
			foot	inch	16th"	foot	inch	16th"	foot	inch	16th"	foot	inch	16th"	foot	inch	16th"
9.5 in 12	38.37	1.2754	7	7	13	8	11	2	10	2	7	11	5	12	12	9	1
10 in 12	39.81	1.3017	7	9	12	9	1	5	10	4	15	11	8	9	13	0	3
10.5 in 12	41.19	1.3288	7	11	11	9	3	10	10	7	0	11	11	8	13	3	7
11 in 12	42.51	1.3566	8	1	11	9	5	15	10	10	4	12	2	8	13	6	13
11.5 in 12	43.78	1.3851	8	3	12	9	8	6	11	0	15	12	5	9	13	10	3
12 in 12	45.00	1.4142	8	5	13	9	10	13	11	3	12	12	8	12	14	1	11
12.5 in 12	46.17	1.4440	8	7	15	10	1	5	11	6	10	12	11	15	14	5	4
13 in 12	47.29	1.4743	8	10	2	10	3	13	11	9	9	13	3	4	14	8	15
13.5 in 12	48.37	1.5052	9	0	6	10	6	7	12	0	8	13	6	9	15	0	10
14 in 12	49.40	1.5366	9	2	10	10	9	1	12	3	8	13	9	15	15	4	6
14.5 in 12	50.39	1.5685	9	4	15	10	11	12	12	6	9	14	1	6	15	8	3
15 in 12	51.34	1.6008	9	7	4	11	2	7	12	9	11	14	4	14	16	0	1
15.5 in 12	52.25	1.6335	9	9	10	11	5	3	13	0	13	14	8	7	16	4	0
16 in 12	53.13	1.6667	10	0	0	11	8	0	13	4	0	15	0	0	16	8	0
16.5 in 12	53.97	1.7002	10	2	7	11	10	13	13	7	3	15	3	10	17	0	0
17 in 12	54.78	1.7341	10	4	14	12	1	11	13	10	8	15	7	4	17	4	1
17.5 in 12	55.56	1.7683	10	7	5	12	4	9	14	1	12	15	11	0	17	8	3

RAFTER LENGTH TABLES - Horizontal Span 6-10 Feet (cont.)

Roof Pitch Rise in Run Notation Inch Rise in 12 Inch Run	Roof Slope degrees	Rafter Length Factor	Horizontal Span in feet														
			Rafter Length in feet, inches, and 16th's of an inch														
			6			7			8			9			10		
			foot	inch	16th"	foot	inch	16th"	foot	inch	16th"	foot	inch	16th"	foot	inch	16th"
18 in 12	56.31	1.8028	10	9	13	12	7	7	14	5	1	16	2	11	18	0	5
18.5 in 12	57.03	1.8376	11	0	5	12	10	6	14	8	7	16	6	7	18	4	8
19 in 12	57.72	1.8727	11	2	13	13	1	5	14	11	12	16	10	4	18	8	12
19.5 in 12	58.39	1.9080	11	5	6	13	4	4	15	3	3	17	2	1	19	0	15
20 in 12	59.04	1.9437	11	7	15	13	7	4	15	6	9	17	5	15	19	5	4
20.5 in 12	59.66	1.9795	11	10	8	13	10	4	15	10	1	17	9	13	19	9	9
21 in 12	60.26	2.0156	12	1	2	14	1	5	16	1	8	18	1	11	20	1	14
21.5 in 12	60.83	2.0518	12	3	12	14	4	6	16	5	0	18	5	10	20	6	4
22 in 12	61.39	2.0883	12	6	6	14	7	7	16	8	8	18	9	9	20	10	10
22.5 in 12	61.93	2.1250	12	9	0	14	10	8	17	0	0	19	1	8	21	3	0
23 in 12	62.45	2.1619	12	11	10	15	1	10	17	3	9	19	5	8	21	7	7
23.5 in 12	62.95	2.1989	13	2	5	15	4	11	17	7	1	19	9	8	21	11	14
24 in 12	63.43	2.2361	13	5	0	15	7	13	17	10	11	20	1	8	22	4	5
24.5 in 12	63.90	2.2734	13	7	11	15	10	15	18	2	4	20	5	8	22	8	13
25 in 12	64.36	2.3109	13	10	6	16	2	2	18	5	14	20	9	9	23	1	5

RAFTER LENGTH TABLES - Horizontal Span 11-15 Feet

Roof Pitch			Horizontal Span in feet														
Rise in Run Notation	Roof Slope	Rafter Length	11			12			13			14			15		
Inch Rise in 12 Inch Run	degrees	Factor	Rafter Length in feet, inches, and 16ths of an inch														
			foot	inch	16th"	foot	inch	16th"	foot	inch	16th"	foot	inch	16th"	foot	inch	16th"
0 in 12	0.00	1.0000	11	0	0	12	0	0	13	0	0	14	0	0	15	0	0
1 in 12	4.76	1.0035	11	0	7	12	0	8	13	0	9	14	0	9	15	0	10
1.5 in 12	7.13	1.0078	11	1	0	12	1	2	13	1	3	14	1	5	15	1	6
2 in 12	9.46	1.0138	11	1	13	12	2	0	13	2	2	14	2	5	15	2	8
2.5 in 12	11.77	1.0215	11	2	13	12	3	3	13	3	6	14	3	10	15	3	14
3 in 12	14.04	1.0308	11	4	1	12	4	7	13	4	13	14	5	3	15	5	9
3.5 in 12	16.26	1.0417	11	5	8	12	6	0	13	6	8	14	7	0	15	7	8
4 in 12	18.43	1.0541	11	7	2	12	7	13	13	8	7	14	9	1	15	9	12
4.5 in 12	20.56	1.0680	11	9	0	12	9	13	13	10	10	14	11	7	16	0	4
5 in 12	22.62	1.0833	11	11	0	13	0	0	14	1	0	15	2	1	16	3	0
5.5 in 12	24.62	1.1000	12	1	3	13	2	6	14	3	10	15	4	13	16	6	0
6 in 12	26.57	1.1180	12	3	9	13	5	0	14	6	7	15	7	13	16	9	4
6.5 in 12	28.44	1.1373	12	6	2	13	7	12	14	9	7	15	11	1	17	0	11
7 in 12	30.26	1.1577	12	8	13	13	10	11	15	0	9	16	2	8	17	4	6
7.5 in 12	32.01	1.1792	12	11	11	14	1	13	15	3	15	16	6	2	17	8	4
8 in 12	33.69	1.2019	13	2	11	14	5	1	15	7	8	16	9	15	18	0	5
8.5 in 12	35.31	1.2255	13	5	5	14	8	7	15	11	3	17	1	14	18	4	9

RAFTER LENGTH TABLES - Horizontal Span 11-15 Feet (cont.)

Roof Pitch — Rise in Run Notation (Inch Rise in 12 Inch Run)	Roof Slope degrees	Rafter Length Factor	11 foot	11 inch	11 16th"	12 foot	12 inch	12 16th"	13 foot	13 inch	13 16th"	14 foot	14 inch	14 16th"	15 foot	15 inch	15 16th"
9 in 12	36.87	1.2500	13	9	0	15	0	0	16	3	0	17	6	0	18	9	0
9.5 in 12	38.37	1.2754	14	0	6	15	3	11	16	6	15	17	10	4	19	1	9
10 in 12	39.81	1.3017	14	3	13	15	7	7	16	11	1	18	2	11	19	6	5
10.5 in 12	41.19	1.3288	14	7	6	15	11	6	17	3	5	18	7	4	19	11	3
11 in 12	42.51	1.3566	14	11	1	16	3	6	17	7	10	18	11	15	20	4	3
11.5 in 12	43.78	1.3851	15	2	13	16	7	7	18	0	1	19	4	11	20	9	5
12 in 12	45.00	1.4142	15	6	11	16	11	10	18	4	10	19	9	9	21	2	9
12.5 in 12	46.17	1.4440	15	10	10	17	3	15	18	9	4	20	2	9	21	7	15
13 in 12	47.29	1.4743	16	2	10	17	8	5	19	2	0	20	7	11	22	1	6
13.5 in 12	48.37	1.5052	16	6	11	18	0	12	19	6	13	21	0	14	22	6	15
14 in 12	49.40	1.5366	16	10	13	18	5	4	19	11	11	21	6	2	23	0	9
14.5 in 12	50.39	1.5685	17	3	1	18	9	14	20	4	11	21	11	8	23	6	5
15 in 12	51.34	1.6008	17	7	5	19	2	8	20	9	12	22	4	15	24	0	2
15.5 in 12	52.25	1.6335	17	11	10	19	7	4	21	2	13	22	10	7	24	6	0
16 in 12	53.13	1.6667	18	4	0	20	0	0	21	8	0	23	4	0	25	0	0
16.5 in 12	53.97	1.7002	18	8	7	20	4	13	22	1	4	23	9	10	25	6	1
17 in 12	54.78	1.7341	19	0	14	20	9	11	22	6	8	24	3	5	26	0	2

Horizontal Span in feet — Rafter Length in feet, inches, and 16th's of an inch

RAFTER LENGTH TABLES - Horizontal Span 11-15 Feet (cont.)

Roof Pitch — Rise in Run Notation (Inch Rise in 12 Inch Run)	Roof Slope degrees	Rafter Length Factor	Horizontal Span in feet 11			12			13			14			15		
			foot	inch	16th"	foot	inch	16th"	foot	inch	16th"	foot	inch	16th"	foot	inch	16th"
17.5 in 12	55.56	1.7683	19	5	7	21	2	10	22	11	14	24	9	1	26	6	5
18 in 12	56.31	1.8028	19	9	15	21	7	10	23	5	4	25	2	14	27	0	8
18.5 in 12	57.03	1.8376	20	2	9	22	0	10	23	10	11	25	8	11	27	6	12
19 in 12	57.72	1.8727	20	7	3	22	5	11	24	4	2	26	2	10	28	1	1
19.5 in 12	58.39	1.9080	20	11	14	22	10	12	24	9	10	26	8	9	28	7	7
20 in 12	59.04	1.9437	21	4	9	23	3	14	25	3	3	27	2	9	29	1	14
20.5 in 12	59.66	1.9795	21	9	5	23	9	1	25	8	13	27	8	9	29	8	5
21 in 12	60.26	2.0156	22	2	1	24	2	4	26	2	7	28	2	10	30	2	13
21.5 in 12	60.83	2.0518	22	6	13	24	7	7	26	8	1	28	8	11	30	9	5
22 in 12	61.39	2.0883	22	11	10	25	0	12	27	1	12	29	2	13	31	3	14
22.5 in 12	61.93	2.1250	23	4	8	25	6	0	27	7	8	29	9	0	31	10	8
23 in 12	62.45	2.1619	23	9	6	25	11	5	28	1	4	30	3	3	32	5	2
23.5 in 12	62.95	2.1989	24	2	4	26	4	10	28	7	0	30	9	7	32	11	13
24 in 12	63.43	2.2361	24	7	3	26	10	3	29	0	13	31	3	11	33	6	8
24.5 in 12	63.90	2.2734	25	0	1	27	3	6	29	6	10	31	9	15	34	1	3
25 in 12	64.36	2.3109	25	5	1	27	8	12	30	0	8	32	4	4	34	7	15

RAFTER LENGTH TABLES - Horizontal Span 16-20 Feet

Roof Pitch — Rise in Run Notation (Inch Rise in 12 Inch Run)	Roof Slope degrees	Rafter Length Factor	16 ft	16 in	16 16th"	17 ft	17 in	17 16th"	18 ft	18 in	18 16th"	19 ft	19 in	19 16th"	20 ft	20 in	20 16th"
0 in 12	0.00	1.0000	16	0	0	17	0	0	18	0	0	19	0	0	20	0	0
1 in 12	4.76	1.0035	16	0	11	17	0	11	18	0	12	19	0	13	20	0	13
1.5 in 12	7.13	1.0078	16	1	8	17	1	9	18	1	11	19	1	12	20	1	14
2 in 12	9.46	1.0138	16	2	10	17	2	13	18	3	0	19	3	2	20	3	5
2.5 in 12	11.77	1.0215	16	4	2	17	4	6	18	4	10	19	4	14	20	5	2
3 in 12	14.04	1.0308	16	5	15	17	6	4	18	6	10	19	7	0	20	7	6
3.5 in 12	16.26	1.0417	16	8	0	17	8	8	18	9	0	19	9	8	20	10	0
4 in 12	18.43	1.0541	16	10	6	17	11	1	18	11	11	20	0	5	21	1	0
4.5 in 12	20.56	1.0680	17	1	1	18	1	14	19	2	11	20	3	8	21	4	5
5 in 12	22.62	1.0833	17	4	0	18	5	0	19	6	0	20	7	0	21	8	0
5.5 in 12	24.62	1.1000	17	7	3	18	8	7	19	9	10	20	10	13	22	0	0
6 in 12	26.57	1.1180	17	10	11	19	0	1	20	1	8	21	2	15	22	4	5
6.5 in 12	28.44	1.1373	18	2	6	19	4	0	20	5	10	21	7	5	22	8	15
7 in 12	30.26	1.1577	18	6	4	19	8	3	20	10	1	21	11	15	23	1	14
7.5 in 12	32.01	1.1792	18	10	7	20	0	9	21	2	11	22	4	14	23	7	0
8 in 12	33.69	1.2019	19	2	12	20	5	3	21	7	10	22	10	0	24	0	7
8.5 in 12	35.31	1.2255	19	7	5	20	10	0	22	0	11	23	3	6	24	6	2

Rafter Length in feet, inches, and 16th's of an inch

RAFTER LENGTH TABLES - Horizontal Span 16-20 Feet (cont.)

Roof Pitch

Rise in Run Notation (Inch Rise in 12 Inch Run)	Roof Slope degrees	Rafter Length Factor	Horizontal Span in feet — Rafter Length in feet, inches, and 16th's of an inch														
			16 foot	16 inch	16 16th"	17 foot	17 inch	17 16th"	18 foot	18 inch	18 16th"	19 foot	19 inch	19 16th"	20 foot	20 inch	20 16th"
9 in 12	36.87	1.2500	20	0	0	21	3	0	22	6	0	23	9	0	25	0	0
9.5 in 12	38.37	1.2754	20	4	14	21	8	3	22	11	8	24	2	13	25	6	2
10 in 12	39.81	1.3017	20	9	15	22	1	9	23	5	3	24	8	13	26	0	7
10.5 in 12	41.19	1.3288	21	3	2	22	7	1	23	11	0	25	2	15	26	6	14
11 in 12	42.51	1.3566	21	8	8	23	0	0	24	5	5	25	9	5	27	1	9
11.5 in 12	43.78	1.3851	22	1	15	23	6	9	24	11	3	26	3	13	27	8	7
12 in 12	45.00	1.4142	22	7	8	24	0	8	25	5	8	26	10	7	28	3	7
12.5 in 12	46.17	1.4440	23	1	4	24	6	6	25	11	14	27	5	4	28	10	9
13 in 12	47.29	1.4743	23	7	1	25	0	9	26	6	7	28	0	2	29	5	13
13.5 in 12	48.37	1.5052	24	1	0	25	7	1	27	1	2	28	7	3	30	1	4
14 in 12	49.40	1.5366	24	7	7	26	1	14	27	7	14	29	1	5	30	8	13
14.5 in 12	50.39	1.5685	25	1	2	26	7	15	28	2	13	29	9	10	31	4	7
15 in 12	51.34	1.6008	25	7	6	27	2	9	28	9	12	30	5	0	32	0	3
15.5 in 12	52.25	1.6335	26	1	10	27	9	4	29	4	13	31	0	7	32	8	1
16 in 12	53.13	1.6667	26	8	0	28	4	0	30	0	0	31	8	0	33	4	0
16.5 in 12	53.97	1.7002	27	2	7	28	10	13	30	7	4	32	3	10	34	0	1
17 in 12	54.78	1.7341	27	8	15	29	5	12	31	2	9	32	11	6	34	8	3

RAFTER LENGTH TABLES - Horizontal Span 16-20 Feet (cont.)

Roof Pitch			Horizontal Span in feet												
Rise in Run Notation	Roof Slope	Rafter Length	16			17			18			19			20		
Inch Rise in 12 Inch Run	degrees	Factor	Rafter Length in feet, inches, and 16th's of an inch														
			foot	inch	16th"	foot	inch	16th"	foot	inch	16th"	foot	inch	16th"	foot	inch	16th"
17.5 in 12	55.56	1.7683	28	3	8	30	0	12	31	9	15	33	7	3	35	4	6
18 in 12	56.31	1.8028	28	10	2	30	7	12	32	5	6	34	3	1	36	0	11
18.5 in 12	57.03	1.8376	29	4	13	31	2	14	33	0	15	34	11	0	36	9	0
19 in 12	57.72	1.8727	29	11	9	31	10	0	33	8	8	35	7	0	37	5	7
19.5 in 12	58.39	1.9080	30	6	6	32	5	5	34	4	2	36	3	1	38	1	15
20 in 12	59.04	1.9437	31	1	3	33	0	8	34	11	13	36	11	2	38	10	8
20.5 in 12	59.66	1.9795	31	8	0	33	7	13	35	7	9	37	7	5	39	7	1
21 in 12	60.26	2.0156	32	3	0	34	3	3	36	3	6	38	3	9	40	3	12
21.5 in 12	60.83	2.0518	32	9	15	34	10	9	36	11	3	38	11	13	41	0	7
22 in 12	61.39	2.0883	33	4	15	35	6	8	37	7	1	39	8	2	41	9	3
22.5 in 12	61.93	2.1250	34	0	0	36	1	8	38	3	0	40	4	8	42	6	0
23 in 12	62.45	2.1619	34	7	1	36	9	9	38	10	15	41	0	14	43	2	14
23.5 in 12	62.95	2.1989	35	2	3	37	4	9	39	6	15	41	9	6	43	11	12
24 in 12	63.43	2.2361	35	9	5	38	0	0	40	3	0	42	5	13	44	8	11
24.5 in 12	63.90	2.2734	36	4	8	38	7	12	40	11	1	43	2	5	45	5	10
25 in 12	64.36	2.3109	36	11	11	39	3	7	41	7	2	43	10	14	46	2	10

RAFTER LENGTH TABLES - Horizontal Span 21-25 Feet

Roof Pitch — Rafter Length in feet, inches, and 16th's of an inch

Rise in Run Notation (Inch Rise in 12 Inch Run)	Roof Slope degrees	Rafter Length Factor	Horizontal Span 21 foot	21 inch	21 16th"	22 foot	22 inch	22 16th"	23 foot	23 inch	23 16th"	24 foot	24 inch	24 16th"	25 foot	25 inch	25 16th"
0 in 12	0.00	1.0000	21	0	0	22	0	0	23	0	0	24	0	0	25	0	0
1 in 12	4.76	1.0035	21	0	14	22	0	15	23	0	15	24	1	0	25	1	1
1.5 in 12	7.13	1.0078	21	1	15	22	2	1	23	2	2	24	2	4	25	2	5
2 in 12	9.46	1.0138	21	3	8	22	3	10	23	3	13	24	4	0	25	4	2
2.5 in 12	11.77	1.0215	21	5	7	22	5	11	23	5	15	24	6	3	25	6	7
3 in 12	14.04	1.0308	21	7	12	22	8	2	23	8	8	24	8	14	25	9	4
3.5 in 12	16.26	1.0417	21	10	8	22	11	0	23	11	8	25	0	0	26	0	8
4 in 12	18.43	1.0541	22	1	10	23	2	4	24	2	15	25	3	9	26	4	4
4.5 in 12	20.56	1.0680	22	5	2	23	5	15	24	6	12	25	7	9	26	8	6
5 in 12	22.62	1.0833	22	9	0	23	10	0	24	11	0	26	0	0	27	1	0
5.5 in 12	24.62	1.1000	23	1	3	24	2	6	25	3	10	26	4	13	27	6	0
6 in 12	26.57	1.1180	23	5	12	24	7	2	25	8	9	26	10	0	27	11	6
6.5 in 12	28.44	1.1373	23	10	10	25	0	4	26	1	14	27	3	9	28	5	3
7 in 12	30.26	1.1577	24	3	12	25	5	10	26	7	8	27	9	7	28	11	5
7.5 in 12	32.01	1.1792	24	9	3	25	11	5	27	1	7	28	3	10	29	5	12
8 in 12	33.69	1.2019	25	2	14	26	5	5	27	7	12	28	10	2	30	0	9
8.5 in 12	35.31	1.2255	25	8	13	26	11	8	28	2	4	29	4	15	30	7	10

RAFTER LENGTH TABLES - Horizontal Span 21-25 Feet (cont.)

Roof Pitch Rise in Run Notation (Inch Rise in 12 Inch Run)	Roof Slope degrees	Rafter Length Factor	21 foot	21 inch	21 16th"	22 foot	22 inch	22 16th"	23 foot	23 inch	23 16th"	24 foot	24 inch	24 16th"	25 foot	25 inch	25 16th"
9 in 12	36.87	1.2500	26	3	0	27	6	0	28	9	0	30	0	0	31	3	0
9.5 in 12	38.37	1.2754	26	9	7	28	0	11	29	4	1	30	7	5	31	10	10
10 in 12	39.81	1.3017	27	4	0	28	7	10	29	11	4	31	2	14	32	6	8
10.5 in 12	41.19	1.3288	27	10	14	29	2	13	30	6	12	31	10	11	33	2	10
11 in 12	42.51	1.3566	28	5	14	29	10	2	31	2	7	32	6	11	33	11	0
11.5 in 12	43.78	1.3851	29	1	1	30	5	11	31	10	5	33	2	14	34	7	8
12 in 12	45.00	1.4142	29	8	6	31	1	6	32	6	5	33	11	5	35	4	4
12.5 in 12	46.17	1.4440	30	3	14	31	9	3	33	2	9	34	7	14	36	1	3
13 in 12	47.29	1.4743	30	11	8	32	5	3	33	10	15	35	4	10	36	10	5
13.5 in 12	48.37	1.5052	31	7	5	33	1	6	34	7	7	36	1	8	37	7	9
14 in 12	49.40	1.5366	32	3	4	33	9	9	35	4	2	36	10	9	38	5	0
14.5 in 12	50.39	1.5685	32	11	4	34	6	1	36	0	14	37	7	11	39	2	9
15 in 12	51.34	1.6008	33	7	6	35	2	10	36	9	13	38	5	0	40	0	4
15.5 in 12	52.25	1.6335	34	3	10	35	11	4	37	6	14	39	2	7	40	10	1
16 in 12	53.13	1.6667	35	0	0	36	8	0	38	4	0	40	0	0	41	8	0
16.5 in 12	53.97	1.7002	35	8	7	37	4	14	39	1	4	40	9	10	42	6	1
17 in 12	54.78	1.7341	36	5	0	38	1	13	39	10	10	41	7	7	43	4	3

Rafter Length in feet, inches, and 16th's of an inch

RAFTER LENGTH TABLES - Horizontal Span 21-25 Feet (cont.)

Roof Pitch — Rise in Run Notation / Inch Rise in 12 Inch Run	Roof Slope degrees	Rafter Length Factor	Horizontal Span in feet 21			22			23			24			25		
			foot	inch	16th"	foot	inch	16th"	foot	inch	16th"	foot	inch	16th"	foot	inch	16th"
17.5 in 12	55.56	1.7683	37	1	10	38	10	13	40	8	1	42	5	4	44	2	8
18 in 12	56.31	1.8028	37	10	5	39	7	15	41	5	9	43	3	3	45	0	13
18.5 in 12	57.03	1.8376	38	7	1	40	5	2	42	3	10	44	1	4	45	11	4
19 in 12	57.72	1.8727	39	3	15	41	2	6	43	0	14	44	11	5	46	9	13
19.5 in 12	58.39	1.9080	40	0	13	41	11	12	43	10	10	45	9	8	47	8	7
20 in 12	59.04	1.9437	40	9	0	42	9	2	44	8	7	46	7	12	48	7	2
20.5 in 12	59.66	1.9795	41	6	13	43	6	9	45	6	5	47	6	2	49	5	14
21 in 12	60.26	2.0156	42	3	15	44	4	9	46	4	4	48	4	8	50	4	11
21.5 in 12	60.83	2.0518	43	1	1	45	1	11	47	2	5	49	2	15	51	3	9
22 in 12	61.39	2.0883	43	10	4	45	11	5	48	0	6	50	1	7	52	2	8
22.5 in 12	61.93	2.1250	44	7	8	46	9	0	48	10	8	51	0	0	53	1	8
23 in 12	62.45	2.1619	45	4	4	47	6	6	49	8	11	51	10	10	54	0	9
23.5 in 12	62.95	2.1989	46	2	2	48	4	4	50	6	14	52	9	4	54	11	11
24 in 12	63.43	2.2361	46	11	8	49	2	5	51	5	2	53	8	0	55	10	13
24.5 in 12	63.90	2.2734	47	8	14	50	0	3	52	3	7	54	6	12	56	10	0
25 in 12	64.36	2.3109	48	6	6	50	10	1	53	1	13	55	5	9	57	9	4

RAFTER LENGTH TABLES - Horizontal Span 26-30 Feet

Rafter Length in feet, inches, and 16th's of an inch

Roof Pitch — Rise in Run Notation (Inch Rise in 12 inch Run)	Roof Slope degrees	Rafter Length Factor	26 foot	26 inch	26 16th"	27 foot	27 inch	27 16th"	28 foot	28 inch	28 16th"	29 foot	29 inch	29 16th"	30 foot	30 inch	30 16th"
0 in 12	0.00	1.0000	26	0	0	27	0	0	28	0	0	29	0	0	30	0	0
1 in 12	4.76	1.0035	26	1	1	27	1	2	28	1	3	29	1	3	30	1	4
1.5 in 12	7.13	1.0078	26	2	7	27	2	8	28	2	10	29	2	11	30	2	13
2 in 12	9.46	1.0138	26	4	5	27	4	8	28	4	10	29	4	13	30	4	15
2.5 in 12	11.77	1.0215	26	6	11	27	6	15	28	7	3	29	7	8	30	7	12
3 in 12	14.04	1.0308	26	9	10	27	10	0	28	10	5	29	10	11	30	11	1
3.5 in 12	16.26	1.0417	27	1	0	28	1	8	29	2	0	30	2	8	31	3	0
4 in 12	18.43	1.0541	27	4	14	28	5	8	29	6	3	30	6	13	31	7	8
4.5 in 12	20.56	1.0680	27	9	3	28	10	1	29	10	14	30	11	11	32	0	8
5 in 12	22.62	1.0833	28	2	0	29	3	0	30	4	0	31	5	0	32	6	0
5.5 in 12	24.62	1.1000	28	7	3	29	8	7	30	9	10	31	10	13	33	0	0
6 in 12	26.57	1.1180	29	0	13	30	2	4	31	3	11	32	5	1	33	6	8
6.5 in 12	28.44	1.1373	29	6	13	30	8	8	31	10	2	32	11	12	34	1	7
7 in 12	30.26	1.1577	30	1	3	31	3	2	32	5	0	33	6	14	34	8	12
7.5 in 12	32.01	1.1792	30	7	15	31	10	1	33	0	4	34	2	6	35	4	8
8 in 12	33.69	1.2019	31	3	0	32	5	6	33	7	13	34	10	4	36	0	11
8.5 in 12	35.31	1.2255	31	10	5	33	1	1	34	3	12	35	6	7	36	9	3

RAFTER LENGTH TABLES - Horizontal Span 26-30 Feet (cont.)

Horizontal Span in feet

Rafter Length in feet, inches, and 16th's of an inch

Roof Pitch — Rise in Run Notation (Inch Rise in 12 Inch Run)	Roof Slope degrees	Rafter Length Factor	26			27			28			29			30		
			foot	inch	16th"	foot	inch	16th"	foot	inch	16th"	foot	inch	16th"	foot	inch	16th"
9 in 12	36.87	1.2500	32	6	0	33	9	0	35	0	0	36	3	0	37	6	0
9.5 in 12	38.37	1.2754	33	1	15	34	5	4	35	8	9	36	11	14	38	3	2
10 in 12	39.81	1.3017	33	10	2	35	1	12	36	5	6	37	9	0	39	0	10
10.5 in 12	41.19	1.3288	34	6	9	35	10	8	37	2	8	38	6	7	39	10	6
11 in 12	42.51	1.3566	35	3	4	36	7	8	37	11	13	39	4	1	40	8	6
11.5 in 12	43.78	1.3851	36	0	2	37	4	12	38	9	6	40	2	0	41	6	10
12 in 12	45.00	1.4142	36	9	4	38	2	3	39	7	3	41	0	2	42	5	2
12.5 in 12	46.17	1.4440	37	6	8	38	11	14	40	5	3	41	10	8	43	3	13
13 in 12	47.29	1.4743	38	4	0	39	9	11	41	3	6	42	9	1	44	2	12
13.5 in 12	48.37	1.5052	39	1	10	40	7	11	42	1	12	43	7	13	45	1	14
14 in 12	49.40	1.5366	39	11	7	41	5	14	43	0	5	44	6	12	46	1	3
14.5 in 12	50.39	1.5685	40	9	6	42	4	3	43	11	0	45	5	13	47	0	10
15 in 12	51.34	1.6008	41	7	7	43	2	10	44	9	14	46	5	1	48	0	4
15.5 in 12	52.25	1.6335	42	5	11	44	1	4	45	8	14	47	4	7	49	0	1
16 in 12	53.13	1.6667	43	4	0	45	0	0	46	8	8	48	4	0	50	0	0
16.5 in 12	53.97	1.7002	44	2	7	45	10	14	47	7	4	49	3	11	51	0	1
17 in 12	54.78	1.7341	45	1	0	46	9	13	48	6	10	50	3	7	52	0	4

RAFTER LENGTH TABLES - Horizontal Span 26-30 Feet (cont.)

Roof Pitch		Roof Slope degrees	Rafter Length Factor	Horizontal Span in feet														
Rise in Run Notation				26			27			28			29			30		
Inch Rise in 12 inch Run				Rafter Length in feet, inches, and 16th's of an inch														
				foot	inch	16th"	foot	inch	16th"	foot	inch	16th"	foot	inch	16th"	foot	inch	16th"
17.5	in 12	55.56	1.7683	45	11	11	47	8	15	49	6	2	51	3	6	53	0	9
18	in 12	56.31	1.8028	46	10	7	48	8	2	50	5	12	52	3	6	54	1	0
18.5	in 12	57.00	1.8376	47	9	5	49	7	6	51	5	7	53	3	8	55	1	9
19	in 12	57.72	1.8727	48	8	4	50	6	12	52	5	4	54	3	11	56	2	3
19.5	in 12	58.39	1.9080	49	7	5	51	6	3	53	5	2	55	4	0	57	2	14
20	in 12	59.04	1.9437	50	6	7	52	5	12	54	5	1	56	4	6	58	3	11
20.5	in 12	59.66	1.9795	51	5	10	53	5	6	55	5	2	57	4	14	59	4	10
21	in 12	60.26	2.0156	52	4	14	54	5	1	56	5	4	58	5	7	60	5	10
21.5	in 12	60.83	2.0518	53	4	3	55	4	13	57	5	7	59	6	1	61	6	11
22	in 12	61.39	2.0883	54	3	9	56	4	10	58	5	11	60	6	12	62	7	13
22.5	in 12	61.93	2.1250	55	3	0	57	4	8	59	6	0	61	7	8	63	9	0
23	in 12	62.45	2.1619	56	2	8	58	4	7	60	6	6	62	8	5	64	10	4
23.5	in 12	62.95	2.1989	57	2	2	59	4	7	61	6	13	63	9	3	65	11	10
24	in 12	63.43	2.2361	58	1	10	60	4	8	62	7	5	64	10	2	67	1	0
24.5	in 12	63.90	2.2734	59	1	5	61	4	9	63	7	14	65	11	2	68	2	7
25	in 12	64.36	2.3109	60	1	0	62	4	12	64	8	7	67	0	3	69	3	15

NOTES TO RAFTER LENGTH TABLES:

1) Rafter lengths in tables EXCLUDE any overhang length and any ridge thickness adjustments.
2) For intermediate Horizontal Span Lengths multiply the Horizontal Span Length in feet by the Rafter Length Factor to get the Rafter Length.

For example, for a horizontal span of 13 feet 7 and 3/4 inches in a roof with an 8 in 12 pitch proceed as follows. Convert the span length to decimal feet, 13 feet 7 and 3/4 inches equals 13.646 feet. Multiply by the Rafter Length Factor to get the rafter length, 13.646 times 1.2019 equals 16.401 feet. Convert decimal feet back to feet and inches, 16.401 feet equals 16 feet 4 and 13/16 inches.

SOURCES:

Rafter Length Manual, Benjamin Williams, Craftsman Books Company, Solana Beach, CA, 1979.

Timber Construction Standards, AITC 100-65, 4th Edition, American Institute Of Timber Construction, Washington, DC, 1965.

Maximum Spans, Southern Pine Joists & Rafters, Empirical Design Values, Southern Pine Council, 1995.

Construction Guide, Southern Pine Joists & Rafters, Empirical Design Values, Southern Pine Council, 1993.

The U.S. Span Book For Canadian Lumber, Canadian Wood Council, 1993.

Basic Carpentry Techniques, T. Jeff Williams, Ortho Books, San Ramon, CA, 1981.

Carpentry Framing and Finishing, 2nd Edition, Byron W. Maguire, Prentice Hall, Englewood Cliffs, NJ, 1989.

Roof Pitch
Rafter Seat Cut Graphic

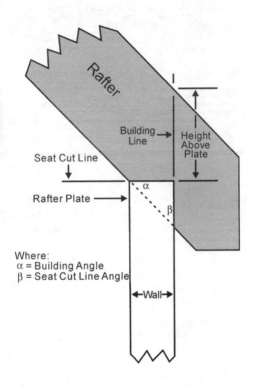

Rafter

Building Line

Height Above Plate

Seat Cut Line

Rafter Plate

α

β

Where:
α = Building Angle
β = Seat Cut Line Angle

←Wall→

Roof Pitch Table

Roof Pitch				Rafters					
Rise in Run Notation	Fraction Notation	Roof Slope	Slope Notation	Bird's Mouth Cut or Seat Cut [2] Angles		Height Above Plate or Seat Cut Height [3]		Roof Area And Gable Rafter Length Factor [4]	Regular Hip Rafter Length Factor [5]
						Rafter Size			
				Building Line	Seat Cut Line	2x4	2x6		
Inch Rise in 12 Inch Run	Rise / Span	deg. - min.		deg.	deg.	inch	inch	See Note [4]	See Note [5]
0 in 12	0/24	0 - 0	0	0.0	90.0	2-5/16	3-11/16	1.0000	1.4142
1 in 12	1/24	4 - 46	1	4.8	85.2	2-5/16	3-11/16	1.0035	1.4167
1.5 in 12	1.5/24	7 - 8	1.5	7.1	82.9	2-3/8	3-11/16	1.0078	1.4197
2 in 12	2/24 = 1/12	9 - 28	2	9.5	80.5	2-3/8	3-11/16	1.0138	1.4240
2.5 in 12	2.5/24	11 - 46	2.5	11.8	78.2	2-3/8	3-3/4	1.0215	1.4295
3 in 12	3/24 = 1/8	14 - 2	3	14.0	76.0	2-3/8	3-3/4	1.0308	1.4361
3.5 in 12	3.5/24	16 - 16	3.5	16.3	73.7	2-7/16	3-13/16	1.0417	1.4440
4 in 12	4/24 = 1/6	18 - 26	4	18.4	71.6	2-7/16	3-7/8	1.0541	1.4530
4.5 in 12	4.5/24	20 - 33	4.5	20.6	69.4	2-1/2	3-15/16	1.0680	1.4631
5 in 12	5/24	22 - 37	5	22.6	67.4	2-1/2	4	1.0833	1.4743
5.5 in 12	5.5/24	24 - 37	5.5	24.6	65.4	2-9/16	4-1/16	1.1000	1.4866
6 in 12	6/24 = 1/4	26 - 34	6	26.6	63.4	2-5/8	4-1/8	1.1180	1.5000
6.5 in 12	6.5/24	28 - 27	6.5	28.4	61.6	2-5/8	4-3/16	1.1373	1.5144
7 in 12	7/24	30 - 15	7	30.3	59.7	2-11/16	4-1/4	1.1577	1.5298
7.5 in 12	7.5/24	32 - 0	7.5	32.0	58.0	2-3/4	4-5/16	1.1792	1.5462
8 in 12	8/24 = 1/3	33 - 41	8	33.7	56.3	2-13/16	4-7/16	1.2019	1.5635

Roof Pitch Table (cont.)

Roof Pitch				Rafters				Roof Area And Gable Rafter Length Factor	Regular Hip Rafter Length Factor
Rise in Run Notation (Inch Rise in 12 Inch Run)	Fraction Notation (Rise / Span)	Roof Slope (deg. - min.)	Slope Notation	Bird's Mouth Cut or Seat Cut [2] Angles — Building Line (deg.)	Seat Cut Line (deg.)	Height Above Plate or Seat Cut Height [3] — Rafter Size 2x4 (inch)	2x6 (inch)	See Note [4]	See Note [5]
8.5 in 12	8.5/24	35 - 19	8.5	35.3	54.7	2-7/8	4-1/2	1.2255	1.5817
9 in 12	9/24 = 3/8	36 - 52	9	36.9	53.1	2-15/16	4-9/16	1.2500	1.6008
9.5 in 12	9.5/24	38 - 22	9.5	38.4	51.6	3	4-11/16	1.2754	1.6207
10 in 12	10/24 = 5/12	39 - 48	10	39.8	50.2	3-1/16	4-3/4	1.3017	1.6415
10.5 in 12	10.5/24	41 - 11	10.5	41.2	48.8	3-1/8	4-7/8	1.3288	1.6630
11 in 12	11/24	42 - 31	11	42.5	47.5	3-3/16	5	1.3566	1.6853
11.5 in 12	11.5/24	43 - 47	11.5	43.8	46.2	3-1/4	5-1/16	1.3851	1.7083
12 in 12	12/24 = 1/2	45 - 0	12	45.0	45.0	3-5/16	5-3/16	1.4142	1.7321
12.5 in 12	12.5/24	46 - 10	12.5	46.2	43.8	3-3/8	5-5/16	1.4440	1.7564
13 in 12	13/24	47 - 17	13	47.3	42.7	3-7/16	5-3/8	1.4743	1.7815
13.5 in 12	13.5/24	48 - 22	13.5	48.4	41.6	3-1/2	5-1/2	1.5052	1.8071
14 in 12	14/24 = 7/12	49 - 24	14	49.4	40.6	3-9/16	5-5/8	1.5366	1.8333
14.5 in 12	14.5/24	50 - 23	14.5	50.4	39.6	3-11/16	5-3/4	1.5685	1.8601
15 in 12	15/24	51 - 20	15	51.3	38.7	3-3/4	5-7/8	1.6008	1.8875
15.5 in 12	15.5/24	52 - 15	15.5	52.3	37.7	3-13/16	6	1.6335	1.9153
16 in 12	16/24 = 2/3	53 - 8	16	53.1	36.9	3-7/8	6-1/8	1.6667	1.9437

Roof Pitch Table (cont.)

Roof Pitch				Rafters					
Rise in Run Notation	Fraction Notation	Roof Slope	Slope Notation	Bird's Mouth Cut or Seat Cut [2] Angles		Height Above Plate or Seat Cut Height [3]		Roof Area And Gable Rafter Length Factor	Regular Hip Rafter Length Factor
						Rafter Size			
				Building Line	Seat Cut Line	2x4	2x6		
Inch Rise in 12 Inch Run	Rise / Span	deg. - min.		deg.	deg.	inch	inch	See Note [4]	See Note [5]
16.5 in 12	16.5/24	53 - 58	16.5	54.0	36.0	3-15/16	6-1/4	1.7002	1.9725
17 in 12	17/24	54 - 47	17	54.8	35.2	4-1/16	6-3/8	1.7341	2.0017
17.5 in 12	17.5/24	55 - 34	17.5	55.6	34.4	4-1/8	6-1/2	1.7683	2.0314
18 in 12	18/24 3/4	56 - 19	18	56.3	33.7	4-3/16	6-5/8	1.8028	2.0616
18.5 in 12	18.5/24	57 - 2	18.5	57.0	33.0	4-5/16	6-3/4	1.8376	2.0921
19 in 12	19/24	57 - 43	19	57.7	32.3	4-3/8	6-7/8	1.8727	2.1230
19.5 in 12	19.5/24	58 - 24	19.5	58.4	31.6	4-7/16	7	1.9080	2.1542
20 in 12	20/24 5/6	59 - 2	20	59.0	31.0	4-9/16	7-1/8	1.9437	2.1858
20.5 in 12	20.5/24	59 - 39	20.5	59.7	30.3	4-5/8	7-1/4	1.9795	2.2177
21 in 12	21/24 7/8	60 - 15	21	60.3	29.7	4-11/16	7-3/8	2.0156	2.2500
21.5 in 12	21.5/25	60 - 50	21.5	60.8	29.2	4-13/16	7-1/2	2.0518	2.2826
22 in 12	22/24 11/12	61 - 23	22	61.4	28.6	4-7/8	7-11/16	2.0883	2.3154
22.5 in 12	22.5/24	61 - 56	22.5	61.9	28.1	4-15/16	7-13/16	2.1250	2.3485
23 in 12	23/24	62 - 27	23	62.4	27.6	5	7-15/16	2.1619	2.3819
23.5 in 12	23.5/24	62 - 51	23.5	62.9	27.1	5-1/8	8-1/16	2.1989	2.4156
24 in 12	24/24 1	63 - 26	24	63.4	26.6	5-3/16	8-3/16	2.2361	2.4495
24.5 in 12	24.5/24	63 - 54	24.5	63.9	26.1	5-5/16	8-5/16	2.2734	2.4836
25 in 12	25/24	64 - 22	25	64.4	25.6	5-3/8	8-1/2	2.3109	2.5180

Notes To Roof Pitch Tables:

(1) Sources:

> *Rafter Length Manual*, Benjamin Williams, Craftsman Book Company, Solana Beach, CA, 1979.
>
> *The Roof Framer's Bible*, Barry D. Mussell, M.E.I., Stockbridge, GA, 1994.
>
> *Timber Construction Standards*, AITC 100-65, 4th Edition, American Institute Of Timber Construction, Washington, DC, 1965.
>
> *Maximum Spans*, Southern Pine Joists & Rafters, Empirical Design Values, Southern Pine Council, 1995.
>
> *Construction Guide*, Southern Pine Joists & Rafters, Empirical Design Values, Southern Pine Council, 1993.
>
> *The U.S. Span Book For Canadian Lumber*, Canadian Wood Council, 1993.
>
> *Basic Carpentry Techniques*, T. Jeff Williams, Ortho Books, San Ramon, CA, 1981.
>
> *Carpentry Framing and Finishing*, 2nd Edition, Byron C. Maguire, Prentice Hall, Englewood Cliffs, NJ, 1989.
>
> *The Contractor's Field Guide*, Paul I. Thomas, Prentice Hall, Englewood Cliffs, NJ, 1991.
>
> *Roof Framing*, Marshall Gross, 1998, Craftsman Book Company, Carlsbad, CA 92018.

(2) Confusion surrounds the spelling of "bird's mouth". Some references use two words "bird's mouth" while some use one word, "birdsmouth".

(3) Based on 2/3 the depth of the rafter above the bird's mouth cut or seat cut.

(4) To find the approximate area of the roof, multiply the area of the building at ground line in either square feet or square meters, by the Roof Area Factor shown. For example, a house measures 50 feet by 40 feet at the ground line or 2,000 square feet. The house has a gable roof with a 7 in 12 pitch. The approximate area of the roof is 2,000 times 1.1577 or 2,315 square feet. To find the approximate length of a gable rafter, multiply the horizontal span, in feet and inches or meters, by the Gable Rafter Length factor shown. For example, a house is 30 feet wide and has a gable roof with a 7 in 12 pitch. The approximate length of the rafter in the gable roof is 1/2 times 30 times 1.1577 or 17.37 feet excluding any overhang or ridge thickness adjustments.

(5) To find the approximate length of the hip rafter in a regular hip roof, multiply the horizontal span, in feet and inches or meters, by the Regular Hip Rafter Length factor shown. For example, a house is 30 feet wide and has a regular hip roof with a 7 in 12 pitch. The approximate length of the hip rafter is 1/2 times 30 times 1.5298 or 22.95 feet excluding any overhang or ridge thickness adjustments.

Maximum Horizontal Roof Rafter Span Tables

Douglas Fir - Larch:

Includes Douglas Fir and Western Larch. See Notes at end of tables

Nominal Lumber Size	Rafter Spacing, Center to Center	Lumber Grade		
		Select Structural	No.1	No. 2
		Maximum Horizontal Span		
(inches)	(inches)	(feet-inches)		
Max Live Load = 20 lbf/ft², Max Dead Load = 15 lbf/ft²				
2 x 6	12	16 - 04	15 - 09	14 - 09
	16	14 - 11	13 - 08	12 - 09
	24	13 - 00	11 - 02	10 - 05
2 x 8	12	21 - 07	19 - 11	18 - 08
	16	19 - 07	17 - 03	16 - 02
	24	17 - 00	14 - 01	13 - 02
2 x 10	12	27 - 06	24 - 04	22 - 09
	16	25 - 00	21 - 01	19 - 09
	24	20 - 09	17 - 03	16 - 01
2 x 12	12	33 - 06	28 - 03	26 - 05
	16	29 - 05	24 - 05	22 - 10
	24	24 - 00	20 - 00	18 - 08
2 x 14	12	- - -	- - -	- - -
	16	- - -	- - -	- - -
	24	- - -	- - -	- - -
Max Live Load = 30 lbf/ft², Max Dead Load = 15 lbf/ft²				
2 x 6	12	14 - 04	13 - 09	13 - 00
	16	13 - 00	12 - 00	11 - 03
	24	11 - 04	09 - 10	09 - 02
2 x 8	12	18 - 10	17 - 07	16 - 05
	16	17 - 02	15 - 03	14 - 03
	24	15 - 00	12 - 05	11 - 08
2 x 10	12	24 - 01	21 - 06	20 - 01
	16	21 - 10	18 - 07	17 - 05
	24	18 - 03	15 - 02	14 - 02
2 x 12	12	29 - 03	24 - 11	23 - 03
	16	26 - 00	21 - 07	20 - 02
	24	21 - 02	17 - 07	16 - 06
2 x 14	12	- - -	- - -	- - -
	16	- - -	- - -	- - -
	24	- - -	- - -	- - -

Maximum Horizontal Roof Rafter Span Tables (cont.)
Douglas Fir - Larch (cont.):

Nominal Lumber Size	Rafter Spacing, Center to Center	Lumber Grade		
		Select Structural	No.1	No.2
		Maximum Horizontal Span		
(inches)	(inches)	(feet -inches)		
Max Live Load = 40 lbf/ft² , Max Dead Load = 15 lbf/ft²				
2 x 6	12	13 - 00	12 - 01	11 - 09
	16	11 - 10	10 - 10	10 - 02
	24	10 - 04	08 - 11	08 - 04
2 x 8	12	17 - 00	15 - 11	14 - 10
	16	15 - 07	13 - 09	12 - 11
	24	13 - 06	11 - 03	10 - 06
2 x 10	12	21 - 10	19 - 05	18 - 02
	16	19 - 10	16 - 10	15 - 09
	24	16 - 06	13 - 09	12 - 10
2 x 12	12	26 - 07	22 - 06	21 - 01
	16	23 - 06	19 - 06	18 - 03
	24	19 - 02	15 - 11	14 - 11
2 x 14	12	- - -	- - -	- - -
	16	- - -	- - -	- - -
	24	- - -	- - -	- - -
Max Live Load = 60 lbf/ft² , Max Dead Load = 15 lbf/ft²				
2 x 6	12	- - -	- - -	- - -
	16	- - -	- - -	- - -
	24	- - -	- - -	- - -
2 x 8	12	15 - 00	13 - 07	12 - 09
	16	13 - 07	11 - 09	11 - 00
	24	11 - 07	09 - 08	09 - 00
2 x 10	12	19 - 01	16 - 08	15 - 07
	16	17 - 04	14 - 05	13 - 06
	24	14 - 02	11 - 09	11 - 00
2 x 12	12	23 - 03	19 - 03	18 - 00
	16	20 - 01	16 - 08	15 - 07
	24	16 - 05	13 - 08	12 - 09
2 x 14	12	25 - 11	21 - 07	20 - 02
	16	22 - 06	18 - 08	17 - 05
	24	18 - 04	15 - 03	14 - 03
Max Live Load = 80 lbf/ft² , Max Dead Load = 15 lbf/ft²				
2 x 6	12	- - -	- - -	- - -
	16	- - -	- - -	- - -
	24	- - -	- - -	- - -
2 x 8	12	13 - 07	12 - 01	11 - 04
	16	12 - 04	10 - 06	09 - 10
	24	10 - 04	08 - 07	08 - 00
2 x 10	12	17 - 04	14 - 09	13 - 10
	16	15 - 05	12 - 10	12 - 00
	24	12 - 07	10 - 05	09 - 09
2 x 12	12	20 - 08	17 - 02	16 - 00
	16	17 - 10	14 - 10	13 - 11
	24	14 - 07	12 - 01	11 - 04
2 x 14	12	23 - 01	19 - 02	17 - 11
	16	20 - 00	16 - 07	15 - 06
	24	16 - 04	13 - 06	12 - 08

Maximum Horizontal Roof Rafter Span Tables (cont.)
Douglas Fir - Larch (cont.):

Nominal Lumber Size (inches)	Rafter Spacing, Center to Center (inches)	Lumber Grade		
		Select Structural	No.1	No. 2
		Maximum Horizontal Span (feet -inches)		
Max Live Load = 100 lbf/ft², Max Dead Load = 15 lbf/ft²				
2 x 6	12	- - -	- - -	- - -
	16	- - -	- - -	- - -
	24	- - -	- - -	- - -
2 x 8	12	12 - 07	11 - 00	10 - 03
	16	11 - 06	09 - 06	08 - 11
	24	09 - 04	07 - 09	07 - 03
2 x 10	12	16 - 01	13 - 05	12 - 07
	16	14 - 00	11 - 08	10 - 11
	24	11 - 05	09 - 06	08 - 11
2 x 12	12	18 - 09	15 - 07	14 - 07
	16	16 - 03	13 - 06	12 - 07
	24	13 - 03	11 - 00	10 - 04
2 x 14	12	20 - 11	17 - 05	16 - 03
	16	18 - 02	15 - 01	14 - 01
	24	14 - 10	12 - 04	11 - 06
Max Live Load = 20 lbf/ft², Max Dead Load = 25 lbf/ft²				
2 x 6	12	16 - 04	13 - 11	13 - 00
	16	14 - 06	12 - 00	11 - 03
	24	11 - 10	09 - 10	09 - 02
2 x 8	12	21 - 02	17 - 07	16 - 05
	16	18 - 04	15 - 03	14 - 03
	24	15 - 00	12 - 05	11 - 08
2 x 10	12	25 - 10	21 - 06	20 - 01
	16	22 - 05	18 - 07	17 - 05
	24	18 - 03	15 - 02	14 - 02
2 x 12	12	30 - 00	24 - 11	23 - 03
	16	26 - 00	21 - 07	20 - 02
	24	21 - 02	17 - 07	16 - 06
2 x 14	12	- - -	- - -	- - -
	16	- - -	- - -	- - -
	24	- - -	- - -	- - -
Max Live Load = 30 lbf/ft², Max Dead Load = 25 lbf/ft²				
2 x 6	12	14 - 04	12 - 07	11 - 09
	16	13 - 00	10 - 10	10 - 02
	24	10 - 08	08 - 11	08 - 04
2 x 8	12	18 - 10	15 - 11	14 - 10
	16	16 - 07	13 - 09	12 - 11
	24	13 - 06	11 - 03	10 - 06
2 x 10	12	23 - 05	19 - 05	18 - 02
	16	20 - 03	16 - 10	15 - 09
	24	16 - 06	13 - 09	12 - 10
2 x 12	12	27 - 01	22 - 06	21 - 01
	16	23 - 06	19 - 06	18 - 03
	24	19 - 02	15 - 11	14 - 11
2 x 14	12	- - -	- - -	- - -
	16	- - -	- - -	- - -
	24	- - -	- - -	- - -

Maximum Horizontal Roof Rafter Span Tables (cont.)
Douglas Fir - Larch (cont.):

Nominal Lumber Size (inches)	Rafter Spacing, Center to Center (inches)	Lumber Grade		
		Select Structural	No.1	No. 2
		Maximum Horizontal Span (feet -inches)		
Max Live Load = 40 lbf/ft², Max Dead Load = 25 lbf/ft²				
2 x 6	12	13 - 00	11 - 07	10 - 10
	16	11 - 10	10 - 00	09 - 04
	24	09 - 10	08 - 02	07 - 08
2 x 8	12	17 - 02	14 - 07	13 - 08
	16	15 - 03	12 - 08	11 - 10
	24	12 - 05	10 - 04	09 - 08
2 x 10	12	21 - 06	17 - 10	16 - 09
	16	18 - 08	15 - 06	14 - 06
	24	15 - 03	12 - 08	11 - 10
2 x 12	12	24 - 11	20 - 09	19 - 05
	16	21 - 07	17 - 11	16 - 09
	24	17 - 08	14 - 08	13 - 08
2 x 14	12	- - -	- - -	- - -
	16	- - -	- - -	- - -
	24	- - -	- - -	- - -
Max Live Load = 60 lbf/ft², Max Dead Load = 25 lbf/ft²				
2 x 6	12	- - -	- - -	- - -
	16	- - -	- - -	- - -
	24	- - -	- - -	- - -
2 x 8	12	15 - 00	12 - 09	12 - 00
	16	13 - 04	11 - 01	10 - 04
	24	10 - 11	09 - 01	08 - 06
2 x 10	12	18 - 10	15 - 07	14 - 07
	16	16 - 03	13 - 06	12 - 08
	24	13 - 04	11 - 01	10 - 04
2 x 12	12	21 - 10	18 - 01	16 - 11
	16	18 - 11	15 - 08	14 - 08
	24	15 - 05	12 - 10	12 - 00
2 x 14	12	24 - 04	20 - 03	18 - 11
	16	21 - 01	17 - 06	16 - 05
	24	17 - 03	14 - 04	13 - 05
Max Live Load = 80 lbf/ft², Max Dead Load = 25 lbf/ft²				
2 x 6	12	- - -	- - -	- - -
	16	- - -	- - -	- - -
	24	- - -	- - -	- - -
2 x 8	12	13 - 07	11 - 06	10 - 09
	16	12 - 00	10 - 00	09 - 04
	24	09 - 10	08 - 02	07 - 07
2 x 10	12	16 - 11	14 - 01	13 - 02
	16	14 - 08	12 - 02	11 - 05
	24	12 - 00	09 - 11	09 - 04
2 x 12	12	19 - 08	16 - 04	15 - 03
	16	17 - 00	14 - 01	13 - 02
	24	13 - 11	11 - 06	10 - 09
2 x 14	12	21 - 11	18 - 03	17 - 00
	16	19 - 00	15 - 09	14 - 09
	24	15 - 06	12 - 11	12 - 01

Maximum Horizontal Roof Rafter Span Tables (cont.)
Douglas Fir - Larch (cont.):

Nominal Lumber Size (inches)	Rafter Spacing, Center to Center (inches)	Lumber Grade		
		Select Structural	No.1	No. 2
		Maximum Horizontal Span (feet -inches)		
Max Live Load = 100 lbf/ft², Max Dead Load = 25 lbf/ft²				
2 x 6	12	- - -	- - -	- - -
	16	- - -	- - -	- - -
	24	- - -	- - -	- - -
2 x 8	12	12 - 07	10 - 07	09 - 10
	16	11 - 00	09 - 02	08 - 07
	24	09 - 00	07 - 05	07 - 00
2 x 10	12	15 - 06	12 - 11	12 - 01
	16	13 - 05	11 - 02	10 - 05
	24	11 - 00	09 - 01	08 - 06
2 x 12	12	18 - 00	14 - 11	14 - 00
	16	15 - 07	12 - 11	12 - 01
	24	12 - 09	10 - 07	09 - 11
2 x 14	12	20 - 01	16 - 08	15 - 07
	16	17 - 05	14 - 05	13 - 06
	24	14 - 03	11 - 10	11 - 00

Maximum Horizontal Roof Rafter Span Tables (cont.)
Hemlock - Fir:
Includes Western Hemlock, California red fir, Grand fir, Noble fir, Pacific silver fir,and White fir. See Notes at end of tables.

Nominal Lumber Size (inches)	Rafter Spacing, Center to Center (inches)	Lumber Grade		
		Select Structural	No.1	No. 2
		Maximum Horizontal Span (feet -inches)		
Max Live Load = 20 lbf/ft², Max Dead Load = 15 lbf/ft²				
2 x 6	12	15 - 06	15 - 02	14 - 05
	16	14 - 01	13 - 03	12 - 07
	24	12 - 03	10 - 10	10 - 03
2 x 8	12	20 - 05	19 - 05	18 - 04
	16	18 - 06	16 - 11	15 - 11
	24	16 - 02	13 - 09	13 - 00
2 x 10	12	26 - 00	23 - 09	22 - 05
	16	23 - 08	20 - 07	19 - 05
	24	20 - 04	16 - 09	15 - 10
2 x 12	12	31 - 08	27 - 06	26 - 00
	16	28 - 09	23 - 10	22 - 06
	24	23 - 07	19 - 05	18 - 05
2 x 14	12	- - -	- - -	- - -
	16	- - -	- - -	- - -
	24	- - -	- - -	- - -

Maximum Horizontal Roof Rafter Span Tables (cont.)
Hemlock - Fir (cont.):

Nominal Lumber Size (inches)	Rafter Spacing, Center to Center (inches)	Select Structural	No.1	No. 2
		Lumber Grade		
		Maximum Horizontal Span (feet -inches)		
Max Live Load = 30 lbf/ft^2, Max Dead Load = 15 lbf/ft^2				
2 x 6	12	13 - 06	13 - 03	12 - 07
	16	12 - 03	11 - 09	11 - 01
	24	10 - 09	09 - 07	09 - 01
2 x 8	12	17 - 10	17 - 02	16 - 02
	16	16 - 02	14 - 10	14 - 00
	24	14 - 02	12 - 01	11 - 06
2 x 10	12	22 - 09	20 - 11	19 - 10
	16	20 - 08	18 - 01	17 - 02
	24	18 - 00	14 - 10	14 - 00
2 x 12	12	27 - 08	24 - 03	22 - 11
	16	25 - 01	21 - 00	19 - 11
	24	20 - 10	17 - 02	16 - 03
2 x 14	12	- - -	- - -	- - -
	16	- - -	- - -	- - -
	24	- - -	- - -	- - -
Max Live Load = 40 lbf/ft^2, Max Dead Load = 15 lbf/ft^2				
2 x 6	12	12 - 03	12 - 00	11 - 05
	16	11 - 02	10 - 07	10 - 00
	24	09 - 09	08 - 08	08 - 02
2 x 8	12	16 - 02	15 - 06	14 - 08
	16	14 - 08	13 - 05	12 - 08
	24	12 - 10	10 - 11	10 - 04
2 x 10	12	20 - 08	18 - 11	17 - 11
	16	18 - 09	16 - 05	15 - 06
	24	16 - 03	13 - 05	12 - 08
2 x 12	12	25 - 01	21 - 11	20 - 09
	16	22 - 10	19 - 00	18 - 00
	24	18 - 10	15 - 06	14 - 08
2 x 14	12	- - -	- - -	- - -
	16	- - -	- - -	- - -
	24	- - -	- - -	- - -
Max Live Load = 60 lbf/ft^2, Max Dead Load = 15 lbf/ft^2				
2 x 6	12	- - -	- - -	- - -
	16	- - -	- - -	- - -
	24	- - -	- - -	- - -
2 x 8	12	14 - 02	13 - 03	12 - 07
	16	12 - 10	11 - 06	10 - 10
	24	11 - 09	09 - 05	08 - 11
2 x 10	12	18 - 00	16 - 03	15 - 04
	16	16 - 05	14 - 00	13 - 03
	24	13 - 11	11 - 06	10 - 10
2 x 12	12	21 - 11	18 - 10	17 - 09
	16	19 - 09	16 - 03	15 - 05
	24	16 - 02	13 - 04	12 - 07
2 x 14	12	25 - 06	21 - 00	19 - 10
	16	22 - 09	18 - 02	17 - 02
	24	18 - 00 [6]	14 - 10	14 - 01

Maximum Horizontal Roof Rafter Span Tables (cont.)

Hemlock - Fir (cont.):

Nominal Lumber Size (inches)	Rafter Spacing, Center to Center (inches)	Select Structural	No.1	No. 2
		Lumber Grade		
		Maximum Horizontal Span (feet -inches)		
Max Live Load = 80 lbf/ft², Max Dead Load = 15 lbf/ft²				
2 x 6	12	- - -	- - -	- - -
	16	- - -	- - -	- - -
	24	- - -	- - -	- - -
2 x 8	12	12 - 10	11 - 09	11 - 02
	16	11 - 08	10 - 03	09 - 08
	24	10 - 01	08 - 04	07 - 11
2 x 10	12	16 - 05	14 - 05	13 - 07
	16	14 - 11	12 - 06	11 - 10
	24	12 - 04	10 - 02	09 - 08
2 x 12	12	19 - 11	16 - 08	15 - 10
	16	17 - 07	14 - 06	13 - 08
	24	14 - 04 [(6)]	11 - 10	11 - 02
2 x 14	12	22 - 08	18 - 08	17 - 08
	16	19 - 07 [(6)]	16 - 02	15 - 03
	24	16 - 00 [(6)]	13 - 02 [(6)]	12 - 06
Max Live Load = 100 lbf/ft², Max Dead Load = 15 lbf/ft²				
2 x 6	12	- - -	- - -	- - -
	16	- - -	- - -	- - -
	24	- - -	- - -	- - -
2 x 8	12	11 - 11	10 - 09	10 - 02
	16	10 - 10	09 - 03	08 - 09
	24	09 - 02	07 - 07	07 - 02
2 x 10	12	15 - 02	13 - 01	12 - 05
	16	13 - 09	11 - 04	10 - 09
	24	11 - 03 [(6)]	09 - 03	08 - 09
2 x 12	12	18 - 05	15 - 02	14 - 04
	16	16 - 00 [(6)]	13 - 02	12 - 05
	24	13 - 00 [(6)]	10 - 09 [(6)]	10 - 02
2 x 14	12	20 - 07	17 - 00	16 - 01
	16	17 - 10 [(6)]	14 - 08	13 - 11
	24	14 - 07 [(6)]	12 - 00 [(6)]	11 - 04 [(6)]
Max Live Load = 20 lbf/ft², Max Dead Load = 25 lbf/ft²				
2 x 6	12	15 - 06	13 - 06	12 - 10
	16	14 - 01	11 - 09	11 - 01
	24	11 - 07	09 - 07	09 - 01
2 x 8	12	20 - 05	17 - 02	16 - 02
	16	18 - 00	14 - 10	14 - 00
	24	14 - 08	12 - 01	11 - 06
2 x 10	12	25 - 05	20 - 11	19 - 10
	16	22 - 00	18 - 01	17 - 02
	24	18 - 00	14 - 10	14 - 00
2 x 12	12	29 - 06	24 - 03	22 - 11
	16	25 - 06	21 - 00	19 - 11
	24	20 - 10	17 - 02	16 - 03
2 x 14	12	- - -	- - -	- - -
	16	- - -	- - -	- - -
	24	- - -	- - -	- - -

Maximum Horizontal Roof Rafter Span Tables (cont.)
Hemlock - Fir (cont.):

Nominal Lumber Size (inches)	Rafter Spacing, Center to Center (inches)	Lumber Grade		
		Select Structural	No.1	No. 2
		Maximum Horizontal Span (feet -inches)		
Max Live Load = 30 lbf/ft², Max Dead Load = 25 lbf/ft²				
2 x 6	12	13 - 06	12 - 03	11 - 07
	16	12 - 03	10 - 07	10 - 00
	24	10 - 06	08 - 08	08 - 02
2 x 8	12	17 - 10	15 - 06	14 - 08
	16	16 - 02	13 - 05	12 - 08
	24	13 - 04	10 - 11	10 - 04
2 x 10	12	22 - 09	18 - 11	17 - 11
	16	19 - 11	16 - 05	15 - 06
	24	16 - 03	13 - 05	12 - 08
2 x 12	12	26 - 08	21 - 11	20 - 09
	16	23 - 01	19 - 00	18 - 00
	24	18 - 10	15 - 06	14 - 08
2 x 14	12	- - -	- - -	- - -
	16	- - -	- - -	- - -
	24	- - -	- - -	- - -
Max Live Load = 40 lbf/ft², Max Dead Load = 25 lbf/ft²				
2 x 6	12	12 - 03	11 - 03	10 - 08
	16	11 - 02	09 - 09	09 - 03
	24	09 - 08	08 - 00	07 - 06
2 x 8	12	16 - 02	14 - 03	13 - 06
	16	14 - 08	12 - 04	11 - 08
	24	12 - 03	10 - 01	09 - 06
2 x 10	12	20 - 04	17 - 05	16 - 06
	16	18 - 04	15 - 01	14 - 03
	24	14 - 11	12 - 04	11 - 08
2 x 12	12	24 - 06	20 - 02	19 - 01
	16	21 - 03	17 - 06	16 - 06
	24	17 - 04	14 - 03	13 - 06
2 x 14	12	- - -	- - -	- - -
	16	- - -	- - -	- - -
	24	- - -	- - -	- - -
Max Live Load = 60 lbf/ft², Max Dead Load = 25 lbf/ft²				
2 x 6	12	- - -	- - -	- - -
	16	- - -	- - -	- - -
	24	- - -	- - -	- - -
2 x 8	12	14 - 02	12 - 06	11 - 09
	16	12 - 10	10 - 10	10 - 03
	24	10 - 08	08 - 10	08 - 04
2 x 10	12	18 - 00	15 - 03	14 - 05
	16	16 - 00	13 - 02	12 - 06
	24	13 - 01	10 - 09	10 - 02
2 x 12	12	21 - 05	17 - 08	16 - 08
	16	18 - 07	15 - 04	14 - 06
	24	15 - 02 [6]	12 - 06	11 - 10
2 x 14	12	23 - 11	19 - 09	18 - 08
	16	20 - 09	17 - 01	16 - 02
	24	16 - 11 [6]	13 - 11	13 - 02

Maximum Horizontal Roof Rafter Span Tables (cont.)

Hemlock - Fir (cont.):

Nominal Lumber Size (inches)	Rafter Spacing, Center to Center (inches)	Select Structural	No.1	No. 2
		Lumber Grade		
		Maximum Horizontal Span (feet -inches)		
Max Live Load = 80 lbf/ft², Max Dead Load = 25 lbf/ft²				
2 x 6	12	- - -	- - -	- - -
	16	- - -	- - -	- - -
	24	- - -	- - -	- - -
2 x 8	12	12 - 10	11 - 03	10 - 07
	16	11 - 08	09 - 09	09 - 02
	24	09 - 08	07 - 11	07 - 06
2 x 10	12	16 - 05	13 - 08	13 - 00
	16	14 - 05	11 - 10	11 - 03
	24	11 - 09 (6)	09 - 08	09 - 02
2 x 12	12	19 - 03	15 - 11	15 - 00
	16	16 - 08	13 - 09	13 - 00
	24	13 - 08 (6)	11 - 03	10 - 08
2 x 14	12	21 - 07	17 - 09	16 - 09
	16	18 - 08 (6)	15 - 04	14 - 06
	24	15 - 03 (6)	12 - 07 (6)	11 - 10 (6)
Max Live Load = 100 lbf/ft², Max Dead Load = 25 lbf/ft²				
2 x 6	12	- - -	- - -	- - -
	16	- - -	- - -	- - -
	24	- - -	- - -	- - -
2 x 8	12	11 - 11	10 - 03	09 - 09
	16	10 - 10	08 - 11	08 - 05
	24	08 - 10 (6)	07 - 03	06 - 11
2 x 10	12	15 - 02	12 - 07	11 - 11
	16	13 - 02	10 - 10	10 - 03
	24	10 - 09 (6)	08 - 11	08 - 05
2 x 12	12	17 - 08	14 - 07	13 - 09
	16	15 - 04 (6)	12 - 07	11 - 11
	24	12 - 06 (6)	10 - 04 (6)	09 - 09
2 x 14	12	19 - 09 (6)	16 - 03	15 - 05
	16	17 - 01 (6)	14 - 01	13 - 04
	24	14 - 00 (6)	11 - 06 (6)	10 - 11 (6)

Maximum Horizontal Roof Rafter Span Tables (cont.)

Southern Pine:

Includes Loblolly Pine, Longleaf Pine, Shortleaf Pine, and Slash Pine. **Sometimes called Yellow Pine or Southern Yellow Pine.** See Notes at end of tables.

Nominal Lumber Size (inches)	Rafter Spacing, Center to Center (inches)	Lumber Grade		
		Select Structural	No.1	No.2
		Maximum Span (feet -inches)		
Max Live Load = 20 lbf/ft^2, Max Dead Load = 10 lbf/ft^2				
2 x 6	12	16 - 01	15 - 09	15 - 06
	16	14 - 07	14 - 04	14 - 01
	24	12 - 09	12 - 06	11 - 09
2 x 8	12	21 - 02	20 - 10	20 - 05
	16	19 - 03	18 - 11	18 - 06
	24	16 - 10	16 - 06	15 - 03
2 x 10	12	26 - 00	26 - 00	25 - 08
	16	24 - 07	24 - 01	22 - 03
	24	21 - 06	20 - 03	18 - 02
2 x 12	12	26 - 00	26 - 00	26 - 00
	16	26 - 00	26 - 00	26 - 00
	24	26 - 00	26 - 00	21 - 03
Max Live Load = 30 lbf/ft^2, Max Dead Load = 10 lbf/ft^2				
2 x 6	12	14 - 01	13 - 09	13 - 06
	16	12 - 09	12 - 06	12 - 03
	24	11 - 02	10 - 11	10 - 02
2 x 8	12	18 - 06	18 - 02	17 - 10
	16	16 - 10	16 - 06	16 - 02
	24	14 - 08	14 - 05	13 - 02
2 x 10	12	23 - 08	23 - 02	22 - 09
	16	21 - 06	21 - 01	19 - 03
	24	18 - 09	17 - 06	15 - 09
2 x 12	12	26 - 00	26 - 00	26 - 00
	16	26 - 00	25 - 07	22 - 07
	24	22 - 10	20 - 11	18 - 05
Max Live Load = 40 lbf/ft^2, Max Dead Load = 10 lbf/ft^2				
2 x 6	12	12 - 09	12 - 06	12 - 03
	16	11 - 07	11 - 05	11 - 02
	24	10 - 02	09 - 11	09 - 02
2 x 8	12	16 - 10	16 - 06	16 - 02
	16	15 - 03	15 - 00	14 - 05
	24	13 - 04	13 - 01	11 - 09
2 x 10	12	21 - 06	21 - 01	19 - 11
	16	19 - 06	19 - 02	17 - 03
	24	17 - 00	15 - 08	14 - 01
2 x 12	12	26 - 00	25 - 07	23 - 04
	16	23 - 09	22 - 10	20 - 02
	24	20 - 09	18 - 08	16 - 06

Maximum Horizontal Roof Rafter Span Tables (cont.)

Southern Pine (cont.):

Nominal Lumber Size (inches)	Rafter Spacing, Center to Center (inches)	Lumber Grade		
		Select Structural	No.1	No. 2
		Maximum Span (feet -inches)		
Max Live Load = 50 lbf/ft², Max Dead Load = 10 lbf/ft²				
2 x 6	12	11 - 10	11 - 08	11 - 05
	16	10 - 09	10 - 07	10 - 02
	24	09 - 05	09 - 03	08 - 04
2 x 8	12	15 - 07	15 - 04	15 - 00
	16	14 - 02	13 - 11	13 - 02
	24	12 - 05	12 - 00	10 - 09
2 x 10	12	19 - 11	19 - 07	18 - 02
	16	18 - 01	17 - 06	15 - 09
	24	15 - 10	14 - 04	12 - 10
2 x 12	12	24 - 03	23 - 09	21 - 03
	16	22 - 00	20 - 11	18 - 05
	24	19 - 03	17 - 01	15 - 01
Max Live Load = 20 lbf/ft², Max Dead Load = 15 lbf/ft²				
2 x 6	12	16 - 01	15 - 09	15 - 05
	16	14 - 07	14 - 04	13 - 04
	24	12 - 09	12 - 06	10 - 11
2 x 8	12	21 - 02	20 - 10	19 - 11
	16	19 - 03	18 - 11	17 - 03
	24	16 - 10	15 - 09	14 - 01
2 x 10	12	26 - 00	26 - 00	23 - 09
	16	24 - 07	22 - 11	20 - 07
	24	21 - 06	18 - 09	16 - 10
2 x 12	12	26 - 00	26 - 00	26 - 00
	16	26 - 00	26 - 00	24 - 02
	24	26 - 00	22 - 04	19 - 09
Max Live Load = 30 lbf/ft², Max Dead Load = 15 lbf/ft²				
2 x 6	12	14 - 01	13 - 09	13 - 06
	16	12 - 09	12 - 06	11 - 09
	24	11 - 02	10 - 11	09 - 07
2 x 8	12	18 - 06	18 - 02	17 - 07
	16	16 - 10	16 - 06	15 - 03
	24	14 - 08	13 - 11	12 - 05
2 x 10	12	23 - 08	23 - 02	21 - 00
	16	21 - 06	20 - 03	18 - 02
	24	18 - 09	16 - 06	14 - 10
2 x 12	12	26 - 00	26 - 00	24 - 07
	16	26 - 00	24 - 01	21 - 03
	24	22 - 10	19 - 08	17 - 05

Maximum Horizontal Roof Rafter Span Tables (cont.)
Southern Pine (cont.):

Nominal Lumber Size (inches)	Rafter Spacing, Center to Center (inches)	Lumber Grade		
		Select Structural	No.1	No. 2
		Maximum Span		
		(feet -inches)		
Max Live Load = 40 lbf/ft^2, Max Dead Load = 15 lbf/ft^2				
2 x 6	12	12 - 09	12 - 06	12 - 03
	16	11 - 07	11 - 05	10 - 08
	24	10 - 02	09 - 11	08 - 08
2 x 8	12	16 - 10	16 - 06	15 - 11
	16	15 - 03	15 - 00	13 - 09
	24	13 - 04	12 - 07	11 - 03
2 x 10	12	21 - 06	21 - 01	19 - 00
	16	19 - 06	18 - 03	16 - 05
	24	17 - 00	14 - 11	13 - 05
2 x 12	12	26 - 00	25 - 02	22 - 03
	16	23 - 09	21 - 10	19 - 03
	24	20 - 09	17 - 10	15 - 09
Max Live Load = 50 lbf/ft^2, Max Dead Load = 15 lbf/ft^2				
2 x 6	12	11 - 11	11 - 08	11 - 04
	16	10 - 09	10 - 07	09 - 10
	24	09 - 05	09 - 02	08 - 00
2 x 8	12	15 - 07	15 - 04	14 - 07
	16	14 - 02	13 - 11	12 - 08
	24	12 - 05	11 - 07	10 - 04
2 x 10	12	19 - 11	19 - 05	17 - 05
	16	18 - 01	16 - 10	15 - 01
	24	15 - 10	13 - 09	12 - 04
2 x 12	12	24 - 03	23 - 02	20 - 05
	16	22 - 00	20 - 01	17 - 09
	24	19 - 03	16 - 05	14 - 06
Max Live Load = 20 lbf/ft^2, Max Dead Load = 20 lbf/ft^2				
2 x 6	12	16 - 01	15 - 09	14 - 05
	16	14 - 07	14 - 04	12 - 06
	24	12 - 09	11 - 09	10 - 02
2 x 8	12	21 - 02	20 - 10	18 - 08
	16	19 - 03	18 - 01	16 - 02
	24	16 - 10	14 - 09	13 - 02
2 x 10	12	26 - 00	24 - 09	22 - 04
	16	24 - 07	21 - 05	19 - 03
	24	21 - 06	17 - 06	15 - 09
2 x 12	12	26 - 00	26 - 00	26 - 00
	16	26 - 00	25 - 07	22 - 07
	24	25 - 09	20 - 11	18 - 05

Maximum Horizontal Roof Rafter Span Tables (cont.)
Southern Pine (cont.):

Nominal Lumber Size (inches)	Rafter Spacing, Center to Center (inches)	Lumber Grade		
		Select Structural	No.1	No. 2
		Maximum Span (feet -inches)		
Max Live Load = 40 lbf/ft², Max Dead Load = 20 lbf/ft²				
2 x 6	12	12 - 09	12 - 06	11 - 09
	16	11 - 07	11 - 05	10 - 02
	24	10 - 02	09 - 07	08 - 04
2 x 8	12	16 - 10	16 - 06	15 - 03
	16	15 - 03	14 - 09	13 - 02
	24	13 - 04	12 - 00	10 - 09
2 x 10	12	21 - 06	20 - 03	18 - 02
	16	19 - 06	17 - 06	15 - 09
	24	17 - 00	14 - 04	12 - 10
2 x 12	12	26 - 00	24 - 01	21 - 03
	16	23 - 09	20 - 11	18 - 05
	24	20 - 09	17 - 01	15 - 01
Max Live Load = 50 lbf/ft², Max Dead Load = 20 lbf/ft²				
2 x 6	12	11 - 10	11 - 08	10 - 11
	16	10 - 09	10 - 07	09 - 05
	24	09 - 05	08 - 10	07 - 09
2 x 8	12	15 - 07	15 - 04	14 - 01
	16	14 - 02	13 - 08	12 - 02
	24	12 - 05	11 - 02	10 - 00
2 x 10	12	19 - 11	18 - 09	16 - 10
	16	18 - 01	16 - 02	14 - 07
	24	15 - 10	13 - 03	11 - 11
2 x 12	12	24 - 03	22 - 04	19 - 09
	16	22 - 00	19 - 04	17 - 01
	24	19 - 03	15 - 09	13 - 11

Maximum Horizontal Roof Rafter Span Tables (cont.)

Spruce-Pine-Fir (South):
Includes Englemann spruce, Sitka spruce, and Lodgepole pine.
See Notes at end of tables.

Nominal Lumber Size (inches)	Rafter Spacing, Center to Center (inches)	Lumber Grade		
		Select Structural	No.1	No. 2
		Maximum Horizontal Span		
		(feet-inches)		
Max Live Load = 20 lbf/ft^2, Max Dead Load = 15 lbf/ft^2				
2 x 6	12	14 - 05	14 - 01	13 - 08
	16	13 - 01	12 - 07	11 - 10
	24	11 - 05	10 - 03	09 - 08
2 x 8	12	19 - 00	18 - 04	17 - 03
	16	17 - 03	15 - 11	14 - 11
	24	15 - 01	13 - 00	12 - 02
2 x 10	12	24 - 03	22 - 05	21 - 01
	16	22 - 01	19 - 05	18 - 03
	24	19 - 03	15 - 10	14 - 11
2 x 12	12	29 - 06	26 - 00	24 - 05
	16	26 - 10	22 - 06	21 - 02
	24	22 - 09	18 - 05	17 - 03
2 x 14	12	- - -	- - -	- - -
	16	- - -	- - -	- - -
	24	- - -	- - -	- - -
Max Live Load = 30 lbf/ft^2, Max Dead Load = 15 lbf/ft^2				
2 x 6	12	12 - 07	12 - 03	11 - 11
	16	11 - 05	11 - 01	10 - 05
	24	10 - 00	09 - 07	08 - 06
2 x 8	12	16 - 07	16 - 02	15 - 03
	16	15 - 01	14 - 00	13 - 02
	24	13 - 02	11 - 06	10 - 09
2 x 10	12	21 - 02	19 - 10	18 - 07
	16	19 - 03	17 - 02	16 - 01
	24	16 - 10	14 - 00	13 - 02
2 x 12	12	25 - 09	22 - 11	21 - 07
	16	23 - 05	19 - 11	18 - 08
	24	20 - 01	16 - 03	15 - 03
2 x 14	12	- - -	- - -	- - -
	16	- - -	- - -	- - -
	24	- - -	- - -	- - -
Max Live Load = 40 lbf/ft^2, Max Dead Load = 15 lbf/ft^2				
2 x 6	12	11 - 05	11 - 02	10 - 10
	16	10 - 05	10 - 00	09 - 05
	24	09 - 01	08 - 02	07 - 08
2 x 8	12	15 - 01	14 - 08	13 - 09
	16	13 - 09	12 - 08	11 - 11
	24	12 - 00	10 - 04	09 - 09
2 x 10	12	19 - 03	17 - 11	16 - 10
	16	17 - 06	15 - 06	14 - 07
	24	15 - 03	12 - 08	11 - 11
2 x 12	12	23 - 05	20 - 09	19 - 06
	16	21 - 03	18 - 00	16 - 11
	24	18 - 02	14 - 08	13 - 09
2 x 14	12	- - -	- - -	- - -
	16	- - -	- - -	- - -
	24	- - -	- - -	- - -

Maximum Horizontal Roof Rafter Span Tables (cont.)

Spruce-Pine-Fir (South) (cont.):

Nominal Lumber Size (inches)	Rafter Spacing, Center to Center (inches)	Lumber Grade		
		Select Structural	No.1	No. 2
		Maximum Horizontal Span		
		(feet-inches)		
Max Live Load = 60 lbf/ft², Max Dead Load = 15 lbf/ft²				
2 x 6	12	- - -	- - -	- - -
	16	- - -	- - -	- - -
	24	- - -	- - -	- - -
2 x 8	12	13 - 02	12 - 07	11 - 09
	16	12 - 00	10 - 10	10 - 03
	24	10 - 06	08 - 11	08 - 04
2 x 10	12	16 - 10	15 - 04	14 - 05
	16	15 - 03	13 - 03	12 - 06
	24	13 - 04	10 - 10	10 - 02
2 x 12	12	20 - 06	17 - 09	16 - 08
	16	18 - 07	15 - 05	14 - 06
	24	15 - 07 [6]	12 - 07	11 - 10
2 x 14	12	24 - 01	19 - 10	18 - 08
	16	21 - 03 [6]	17 - 02	16 - 02
	24	17 - 04 [6]	14 - 01 [6]	13 - 02
Max Live Load = 80 lbf/ft², Max Dead Load = 15 lbf/ft²				
2 x 6	12	- - -	- - -	- - -
	16	- - -	- - -	- - -
	24	- - -	- - -	- - -
2 x 8	12	12 - 00	11 - 02	10 - 06
	16	10 - 11	09 - 08	09 - 01
	24	09 - 06	07 - 11	07 - 05
2 x 10	12	15 - 03	13 - 07	12 - 10
	16	13 - 11	11 - 10	11 - 01
	24	11 - 11 [6]	09 - 08	09 - 01
2 x 12	12	18 - 07	15 - 10	14 - 10
	16	16 - 11 [6]	13 - 08	12 - 10
	24	13 - 10 [6]	11 - 02 [6]	10 - 06
2 x 14	12	21 - 10 [6]	17 - 08	16 - 07
	16	18 - 11 [6]	15 - 03	14 - 04
	24	15 - 05 [6]	12 - 06 [6]	11 - 09 [6]
Max Live Load = 100 lbf/ft², Max Dead Load = 15 lbf/ft²				
2 x 6	12	- - -	- - -	- - -
	16	- - -	- - -	- - -
	24	- - -	- - -	- - -
2 x 8	12	11 - 01	10 - 02	09 - 06
	16	10 - 01	08 - 09	08 - 03
	24	08 - 10 [6]	07 - 02	06 - 09
2 x 10	12	14 - 02	12 - 05	11 - 08
	16	12 - 11	10 - 09	10 - 01
	24	10 - 10 [6]	08 - 09	08 - 03
2 x 12	12	17 - 03	14 - 04	13 - 06
	16	15 - 05 [6]	12 - 05	11 - 08
	24	12 - 07 [6]	10 - 02 [6]	09 - 06 [6]
2 x 14	12	19 - 10 [6]	16 - 01	15 - 01
	16	17 - 02 [6]	13 - 11 [6]	13 - 01
	24	14 - 00 [6]	11 - 04 [6]	10 - 08 [6]

Maximum Horizontal Roof Rafter Span Tables (cont.)

Spruce-Pine-Fir (South) (cont.):

Nominal Lumber Size (inches)	Rafter Spacing, Center to Center (inches)	Lumber Grade		
		Select Structural	No.1	No.2
		Maximum Horizontal Span		
		(feet-inches)		
Max Live Load = 20 lbf/ft², Max Dead Load = 25 lbf/ft²				
2 x 6	12	14 - 05	12 - 10	12 - 00
	16	13 - 01	11 - 01	10 - 05
	24	11 - 02	09 - 01	08 - 06
2 x 8	12	19 - 00	16 - 02	15 - 03
	16	17 - 03	14 - 00	13 - 02
	24	14 - 02	11 - 06	10 - 09
2 x 10	12	24 - 03	19 - 10	18 - 07
	16	21 - 02	17 - 02	16 - 01
	24	17 - 04	14 - 00	13 - 02
2 x 12	12	28 - 05	22 - 11	21 - 07
	16	24 - 07	19 - 11	18 - 08
	24	20 - 01	16 - 03	15 - 03
2 x 14	12	- - -	- - -	- - -
	16	- - -	- - -	- - -
	24	- - -	- - -	- - -
Max Live Load = 30 lbf/ft², Max Dead Load = 25 lbf/ft²				
2 x 6	12	12 - 07	11 - 07	10 - 10
	16	11 - 05	10 - 00	09 - 05
	24	10 - 00	08 - 02	07 - 08
2 x 8	12	16 - 07	14 - 08	13 - 09
	16	15 - 01	12 - 08	11 - 11
	24	12 - 10	10 - 04	09 - 09
2 x 10	12	21 - 02	17 - 11	16 - 10
	16	19 - 02	15 - 06	14 - 07
	24	15 - 08	12 - 08	11 - 11
2 x 12	12	25 - 08	20 - 09	19 - 06
	16	22 - 03	18 - 00	16 - 11
	24	18 - 02 [(6)]	14 - 08	13 - 09
2 x 14	12	- - -	- - -	- - -
	16	- - -	- - -	- - -
	24	- - -	- - -	- - -
Max Live Load = 40 lbf/ft², Max Dead Load = 25 lbf/ft²				
2 x 6	12	11 - 05	10 - 08	10 - 00
	16	10 - 05	09 - 03	08 - 08
	24	09 - 01	07 - 06	07 - 01
2 x 8	12	15 - 01	13 - 06	12 - 08
	16	13 - 09	11 - 08	11 - 00
	24	11 - 09	09 - 06	08 - 11
2 x 10	12	19 - 03	16 - 06	15 - 06
	16	17 - 06	14 - 03	13 - 05
	24	14 - 05	11 - 08	10 - 11
2 x 12	12	23 - 05	19 - 01	17 - 11
	16	20 - 05	16 - 06	15 - 06
	24	16 - 08 [(6)]	13 - 06	12 - 08
2 x 14	12	- - -	- - -	- - -
	16	- - -	- - -	- - -
	24	- - -	- - -	- - -

Maximum Horizontal Roof Rafter Span Tables (cont.)
Spruce-Pine-Fir (South) (cont.):

Nominal Lumber Size (inches)	Rafter Spacing, Center to Center (inches)	Lumber Grade		
		Select Structural	No.1	No. 2
		Maximum Horizontal Span (feet-inches)		
Max Live Load = 60 lbf/ft² , Max Dead Load = 25 lbf/ft²				
2 x 6	12	- - -	- - -	- - -
	16	- - -	- - -	- - -
	24	- - -	- - -	- - -
2 x 8	12	13 - 02	11 - 09	11 - 01
	16	12 - 00	10 - 03	09 - 07
	24	10 - 04	08 - 04	07 - 10
2 x 10	12	16 - 10	14 - 05	13 - 06
	16	15 - 03	12 - 06	11 - 09
	24	12 - 07 [6]	10 - 02	09 - 07
2 x 12	12	20 - 06	16 - 08	15 - 08
	16	17 - 11 [6]	14 - 06	13 - 07
	24	14 - 07 [6]	11 - 10	11 - 01
2 x 14	12	23 - 01	18 - 08	17 - 06
	16	20 - 00 [6]	16 - 02	15 - 02
	24	16 - 04 [6]	13 - 02 [6]	12 - 05 [6]
Max Live Load = 80 lbf/ft² , Max Dead Load = 25 lbf/ft²				
2 x 6	12	- - -	- - -	- - -
	16	- - -	- - -	- - -
	24	- - -	- - -	- - -
2 x 8	12	12 - 00	10 - 07	10 - 00
	16	10 - 11	09 - 02	08 - 08
	24	09 - 03	07 - 06	07 - 01
2 x 10	12	15 - 03	13 - 00	12 - 02
	16	13 - 11	11 - 03	10 - 07
	24	11 - 04 [6]	09 - 02	08 - 07
2 x 12	12	18 - 07	15 - 00	14 - 01
	16	16 - 01 [6]	13 - 00	12 - 03
	24	13 - 02 [6]	10 - 08 [6]	10 - 00 [6]
2 x 14	12	20 - 09 [6]	16 - 09	15 - 09
	16	18 - 00 [6]	14 - 06 [6]	13 - 08
	24	14 - 08 [6]	11 - 10 [6]	11 - 02 [6]
Max Live Load = 100 lbf/ft² , Max Dead Load = 25 lbf/ft²				
2 x 6	12	- - -	- - -	- - -
	16	- - -	- - -	- - -
	24	- - -	- - -	- - -
2 x 8	12	11 - 01	09 - 09	09 - 02
	16	10 - 01	08 - 05	07 - 11
	24	08 - 06 [6]	06 - 11	06 - 05
2 x 10	12	14 - 02 [6]	11 - 11	11 - 02
	16	12 - 09 [6]	10 - 03	09 - 08
	24	10 - 05 [6]	08 - 05 [6]	07 - 11
2 x 12	12	17 - 00 [6]	13 - 09	12 - 11
	16	14 - 09 [6]	11 - 11	11 - 02
	24	12 - 01 [6]	09 - 09 [6]	09 - 02 [6]
2 x 14	12	19 - 00 [6]	15 - 05	14 - 05
	16	16 - 06 [6]	13 - 04 [6]	12 - 06 [6]
	24	13 - 05 [6]	10 - 11 [6]	10 - 03 [6]

Notes to Maximum Horizontal Roof Rafter Span Tables:

1. Tabulated values developed from *Span Tables for Joists and Rafters*, American Softwood Lumber Standard Sizes, PS 20-70, 1993, American Wood Council, PO Box 5364, Madison, WI 53705-5364.

2. The tabulated values assume:

   (a) Maximum Horizontal Span is the horizontal projection for a sloping rafter. Use Rafter Length Tables and/or Roof Pitch Table to compute actual length of sloping rafter.

   (b) Installation of at least three rafters that are spaced no more than 24" on center.

   (c) Fully supported members, properly sheathed and nailed on top edge of the rafter.

   (d) Used in covered structures, dry service conditions with wood moisture content not exceeding 19%.

   (e) Deflections limited to span length in inches divided by 240.

   (f) Dead loads include weight of rafter, drywall ceiling, sheathing, felt, and roofing material as follows:

   - up to 10 lbf/ft^2 = light weight roofing such as asphalt shingles, wood shingles or shakes, or metal roofing;
   - over 10 lbf/ft^2 and below 15 lbf/ft^2 = medium weight roofing such as felt, tar, and gravel or slag roofing;
   - 15 lbf/ft^2 and above = heavy weight roofing such as clay tile, concrete tile, or slate roofing.

   (g) Snow loads vary greatly across North America, from no load in the Florida keys to well over 100 lbf/ft^2 in Alaska. Snow loads also increase with elevation. For example, in Mesa County, Colorado between 4,000 feet and 5,500 feet elevation the required snow load is 30 lbf/ft^2, while between 9,500 feet and 11,000 feet the required snow load is 100 lbf/ft^2. All snow loads have a load duration of 2 months. Check local building codes for required snow loading at your site.

3. Tabulated spans apply to surfaced (S4S) lumber and are distances from face to face of supports.

4. Dead load equals weight of structure plus any fixed loads.

5. Live load equals snow load plus wind load plus movable loads, such as furniture, etc.

6. Span length shown may exceed limits for deflection, horizontal shear, or compression perpendicular-to-grain. Use a shorter span, a larger member or a closer rafter spacing.

7. Southern Pine span length is limited to a maximum of 26' based on material availability. Lumber lengths over 20' are not common.

Guide To Roofing Materials

Sheathing Material	Comments
Spaced slat sheathing	1x4 or 1x6 slats of softwood lumber. Generally used for wood shingle, wood shake, concrete tile, clay tile, or metal panels. May also be used over plywood sheathing when plywood is needed for additional strength.
Plywood sheathing	Use only performance-rated panels. Minimum thickness required by code is 5/16", but 1/2" is more common. Grade of either Exterior, Exposure 1, or Exposure 2 may be used. Forms solid deck. Generally used for asphalt shingles, asphalt composite shingles, metal shingles, slate shingles, or metal shingles. Also used under spaced slat sheathing, as noted above, for additional strength. Stagger panels on 4 foot centers. Leave 1/8" gap for expansion between panels. Use panel clips on edges between panels.
OSB sheathing (Oriented Strand Board)	Same as plywood
Tongue-and-groove sheathing	2x6 tongue-and-groove roof decking is used where the sheathing is visible inside the house. A cathedral ceiling is one use for tongue-and-groove sheathing. Stagger joints and leave 1/16" for expansion. Can be used with all roofing materials.

Underlayment Material	Comments
Roofing felt	Used with asphalt shingles, asphalt composite shingles, asphalt roll roofing, wood shakes, wood shingles, concrete tile, clay tile, and slate. Sold in rolls which cover 2, 4, or 5 squares. Rolls are identified by weight. Normal weights are 15, 30, and 45 pounds per square. 30 pounds per square is common. Can be asphalt impregnated felt or asphalt impregnated felt-fiberglass composite. Two or more overlapping layers are normally required.

Guide to Roofing Materials (cont.)

Material	Durability (years)	Fire Rating (1)	Minimum Slope	Installation Labor (2)	Pros	Cons
Asphalt-fiberglass composite shingle (asphalt layers surrounding a fiberglass core)	15 to 40	A	4 in 12 or greater	1 to 1-1/2 hrs per square	Wide range of colors, weights, and textures Readily available Suitable for most residential applications Can be walked on Economical Durable Easy application Low maintenance	Apply at temperatures above 50°F Starts to deteriorate early in life-cycle Can blow off in high winds Susceptible to mildew and moss
Asphalt organic felt-base shingles (asphalt layers surrounding an organic fiber core)	12 to 20	C	4 in 12 or greater	1 to 1-1/2 hrs per square	Wide range of colors, weights, and textures Ready availability Suitable for most residential applications Can be walked on Economical Durable Easy application Low maintenance	Less durable and fire resistant than asphalt-fiberglass composite Starts to deteriorate early in life-cycle Can blow off in high winds Susceptible to mildew and moss

Guide to Roofing Materials (cont.)

Material	Durability (years)	Fire Rating (1)	Minimum Slope	Installation Labor (2)	Pros	Cons
Asphalt roll roofing	5 to 7	Varies from A to C depending on coating	1 in 12 or greater	1 to 1-1/2 hours per square	Economical	Some have poor fire rating
					Easy application	Plain appearance
Wood shingles and shakes	20 to 40	Varies from A to C depending on coatings or treatments	Shakes: 4 in 12 or greater	4 to 6 hours per square	Natural appearance	Flammable when not treated with fire-retardant
			Shingles: 3 in 12 or greater		Durable	Moderate cost
(western red cedar is most common, redwood and cypress are much less common)						May attract insects
(shakes are hand split, shingles are sawn; shakes are thicker and larger than shingles)						High maintenance Subject to mold and mildew Difficult application

Guide to Roofing Materials (cont.)

Material	Durability (years)	Fire Rating (1)	Minimum Slope	Installation Labor (2)	Pros	Cons
Concrete tile	over 50	A	3 in 12 or greater	2 to 2-1/2 hrs per square	Extremely durable Fireproof Variety of textures, shapes, and colors	High cost Can crack Can not be used in freeze/thaw areas Heavy, more framing may be needed
Clay tile	over 50	A	3 in 12 or greater	2 to 2-1/2 hrs per square	Extremely durable Fireproof Variety of textures, shapes, and colors	High cost Can crack Cannot be used in freeze/thaw areas Heavy, more framing may be needed
Concrete tile (fibrous)	30 to 50	A or B	3 in 12 or greater	2 to 2-1/2 hrs per square	Extremely durable Fireproof or fire resistant Variety of textures, shapes, and colors	Moderate cost Can not be used in freeze/thaw areas
Slate tile	over 50	A	4 in 12 or greater	2 to 2-1/2 hrs per square	Extremely durable Fireproof	Very high cost Heavy, more framing may be needed High maintenance Can not be walked on

Guide to Roofing Materials (cont.)

Material	Durability (years)	Fire Rating (1)	Minimum Slope	Installation Labor (2)	Pros	Cons
Metal shingles (aluminum)	over 50	Varies from A to C	4 in 12 or greater	4 to 6 hours per square	Lightweight Variety of colors and types Low maintenance Can be applied over existing roofing Fire resistant	Prone to scratches or dents Some systems complicated to install Can be expensive Must be insulated from non-compatible materials to stop galvanic action
Metal shingles (steel)	over 50	Varies from A to C	3 in 12 or greater	4 to 6 hours per square	Lightweight Variety of colors and types Low maintenance Can be applied over existing roofing Fire resistant	Prone to scratches or dents Some systems complicated to install Can be expensive
Metal panels (steel)	20 to 50	Varies from A to C	1 in 12 or greater		Lightweight Easy application Durable Low maintenance	Expensive application on complex roofs Some systems complicated to install

Notes To Roofing Guide Tables:

(1) Underwriter's Laboratories (UL) Fire Rating:
Class A - effective against severe fire exposure,
Class B - effective against moderate exposure,
Class C - effective against slight exposure.

(2) Approximations only; assumes experienced shinglers and installers. Roofing is sold in a unit called a "square". A "square" of roofing is enough material to cover 100 square feet.

(3) Sources:
Roofing & Siding, Sunset Books, 1994, Sunset Publishing Corp., Menlo Park, CA 94025

The Contractor's Field Guide, Paul I. Thomas, 1991, Prentice Hall, Englewood Cliffs, NJ 07632

Construction Materials, 2nd Edition, Caleb Hornbostel, John Wiley & Sons, Inc., New York, NY

www.roofingexperts.com

All About Roofs and Siding, Ortho Books, 1991, Meredith Corporation, Des Moines, IA 50309

Roofs and Siding, Time-Life Books, 1996, Time-Life Books, Inc., Alexandria, VA

Weight of Roofing Materials

Material	Average Weight (lbm/ft²)
ROOFING MATERIALS	
Light Weight Roofing	
Asphalt roll roofing	1.1
Asphalt shingle or asphalt-fiberglass composite shingle	2.7
Metal roofing; aluminum or steel; panel, sheet, or shingle	1.2
Terneplate, copper-bearing steel sheet	0.7
Wood shingle or shake	2.4
Zinc roofing	1.6
Medium Weight Roofing	
Copper-asphalt composite shingle	4.2
Felt, tar, and gravel roofing - 3-ply	4.8
Felt, tar, and gravel roofing - 4-ply	5.3
Felt, tar, and gravel roofing - 5-ply	6.1
Felt, tar, and slag roofing - 3-ply	4.5
Felt, tar, and slag roofing - 4-ply	4.8
Felt, tar, and slag roofing - 5-ply	5.3
Ceramic slate	5.8
Reconstituted slate	4.4
Heavy Weight Roofing	
Clay tile	10.8
Concrete tile	9.3
Slate, 1/4" to 3/16" thick	9.1
Slate, 3/8" thick	12.8
Slate, 1/2" thick	18.8
Slate, 3/4" thick	26.0
SHEATHING MATERIALS	
Plywood	
5/16" thick	1.0
3/8" thick	1.1
7/16" thick	1.3
15/32" thick	1.4
1/2" thick	1.5
19/32" thick	1.8
5/8" thick	1.9
23/32" thick	2.2
3/4" thick	2.3
7/8" thick	2.6
1" thick	3.0
1-1/8" thick	3.3
OSB (Oriented Strand Board) or Com-Ply	
5/16" thick	1.1
3/8" thick	1.2
7/16" thick	1.4
15/32" thick	1.5
1/2" thick	1.7
19/32" thick	2.0

Weight of Roofing Materials (cont.)	
Material	Average Weight (lbm/ft²)
OSB (Oriented Strand Board) or Com-Ply	
5/8" thick	2.1
23/32" thick	2.4
3/4" thick	2.5
7/8" thick	2.9
1" thick	3.3
1-1/8" thick	3.6
UNDERLAYMENT MATERIALS	
Asphalt impregnated felt paper	
15 pound paper	0.2
30 pound paper	0.3
45 pound paper	0.5

Sources:

ATAS International Inc., Allentown, PA 18106.

Basic Building Data, 3rd Edition, Don Graf, 1985, Van Nostrand Reinhold Company, New York, NY 10020.

CertainTeed Corporation, Valley Forge, PA 19482.

Construction Materials, 2nd Edition, Caleb Hornbostel, 1991, John Wiley & Sons, Inc., New York, NY.

Design Capacities of APA Performance Rated Structural-Use Panels, 1995, APA - The Engineered Wood Association, Tacoma, WA 98411.

Eagle Roofing Products, Rialto CA 92377

EMCO Limited, Building Products Division, London Ontario, Canada.

IKO Industries Ltd., Toronto Ontario, Canada.

Maruhachi Ceramics of America, Corona, CA 91719.

Metal Roofing of Canada, Barrie Ontario, Canada.

Roofing and Siding, 1994, Sunset Publishing Corp., Menlo Park, CA 94025.

Plywood Design Specification, 1997, APA - The Engineered Wood Association, Tacoma, WA 98411.

Roofing, Siding, and Painting Contractor's Vest Pocket Reference Book, William J. Hornung, 1984, Prentice Hall, Englewood Cliffs, NJ 07632.

Sandtoft Roof Tiles Limited, South Yorkshire, England.

Siplast Inc., Irving, TX 75039.

The Contractor's Field Guide, Paul I. Thomas, 1991, Prentice Hall, Englewood Cliffs, NJ 07632.

The Tile Man, Louisburg, NC 27549.

United States Tile Co., Corona, CA 91720.

www.roofingmall.com

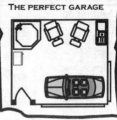

THE PERFECT GARAGE

Drafting Symbols

Electrical Symbols 186
   Lighting Outlets 186
   Panelboards, Switchboards & Related............................186
   Receptacle Outlets 187
   Remote Control Stations for Equipment...........................187
   Bus Ducts and Wireways 187
   Signaling System Outlets - Non-residential.....................188
   Signaling System Outlets - Residential 188
   Circuiting 189
   Switch Outlets 189
   Electrical Distribution, aerial..189
   Electrical Distribution, underground 189
Heating, Ventilation and Air Conditioning Symbols 190
   Heating and Ventilation Equipment...................................190
   Ductwork 191
   Heat-Power Equipment 192
   Refrigeration..192
Piping Symbols...193
   Air Conditioning...193
   Heat 193
   Plumbing 194
Household Fixtures 195

Electrical Symbols

Lighting outlets

■ Blanked Outlet	Bare Bulb fluorescent fixture	Continous Row Fluorescent Fixture
D Drop Cord	Emergency battery pack with charger and sealed beam heads (B)	(L) Outlet Controlled by low voltage switching when relay is installed in outlet box
○○○ Incandescent Track Lighting	Individual Fluorescent Fixture	⊗ Exit Light and Outlet Box
▽▽▽ Multiple floodlight assembly	(J) Junction Box	○ Individual fluorescent fixture
⊢ Outlet box and fluorescent light	○—○ Outdoor pole arm mounted fixture	(L)PS Lamp Holder with Pull switch
▬ Recessed continuous row fluorescent	Remote emergency sealed beam head	Surface mounted fluorescent
○ —○ Surface mounted light fixture		

Panels, Circuits & Related

⊠ Controller/ disconnection combination	Externally operated disconnect switch	Flush mounted panel board
TC Flush mounted terminal cabinet	(I) Instrument	Lighting Panel
⊠ Motor or other power controller	▨ Pullbox	Surface mounted panel board
TC Surface mounted terminal cabinet	▨ Switchboard power control center unit	T Transformer

Receptacle Outlets

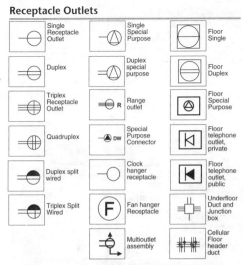

Single Receptacle Outlet	Single Special Purpose	Floor Single
Duplex	Duplex special purpose	Floor Duplex
Triplex Receptacle Outlet	Range outlet	Floor Special Purpose
Quadruplex	Special Purpose Connector DW	Floor telephone outlet, private
Duplex split wired	Clock hanger receptacle	Floor telephone outlet, public
Triplex Split Wired	Fan hanger Receptacle	Underfloor Duct and Junction box
	Multioutlet assembly	Cellular Floor header duct

Remote Control Stations for Equipment

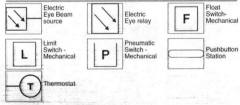

Electric Eye Beam source	Electric Eye relay	Float Switch- Mechanical
Limit Switch - Mechanical	Pneumatic Switch - Mechanical	Pushbutton Station
Thermostat		

Bus Ducts and Wireways

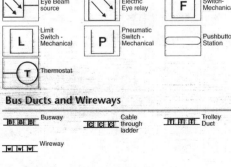

B B B	Busway	C C C	Cable through ladder	T T T	Trolley Duct
W W W	Wireway				

Signaling systems - Non-residental

Electric Clock system device	Fire Alarm system device
Nurse call device	Other signalling system devices
Paging system device	Public telephone system device
Private telephone system device	Sound System device
Staff register system device	Watchman system device

Circuiting

	Feeders
	Home Run to Panel Board
	Wiring Concealed in floor
	Wiring concealed in wall or ceiling
	Wiring, Exposed
	Wiring, turned down
	Wiring, turned up

Signaling systems - Residental

Annunciator	Bell
Bell/buzzer combination	Bell Ringing transformer (BT)
Buzzer	Chimes (CH)
Electric Door Opener (D)	Inter connection box
Inter connecting telephone	Maid's signal (M)
Outside telephone	Pushbutton
Radio Outlet (R)	TV outlet (TV)

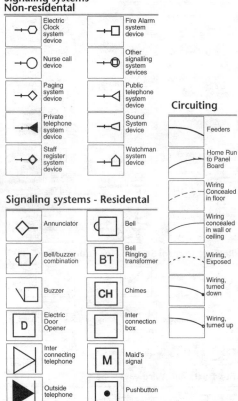

Switch Outlets

Symbol	Description	Symbol	Description	Symbol	Description
S	Single Pole	**S**F	Fused Switch	**S**RC	Remote Control
S2	Double Pole Switch	**S**D	Automatic door	⊖s	Switch and Single Receptacle
S3	Three-Way	**S**T	Time Switch	⊜s	Switch and Double receptacle
S4	Four way switch	**S**CB	Circuit Breaker	Ⓢ	Ceiling Pull Switch
SK	Key Operated switch	**S**DM	Dimmer	**S**WCB	Weatherproof Circuit Breaker
SP	Switch and Pilot Lamp	**S**LM	Master Switch for Low Voltage	**S**WF	Weatherproof Fused Switch
SL	Low Voltage Switching System	**S**MC	Momentary contact switch or pushbutton	**S**WP	Weatherproof Switch

Electrical Distribution - Aerial

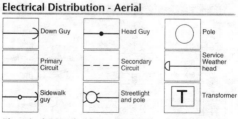

Symbol	Description	Symbol	Description	Symbol	Description
	Down Guy		Head Guy		Pole
	Primary Circuit		Secondary Circuit		Service Weather head
	Sidewalk guy		Streetlight and pole	T	Transformer

Electrical Distribution - Underground

Symbol	Description	Symbol	Description	Symbol	Description
H	Hand hole	M	Man hole		Streetlight standard fed from underground circuit
	Underground burial cable	TP	Transformer pad		
	Underground Duct Line	TM	Transformer handhole or vault		

Drafting Symbols   189

Heating, Ventilation and Air Conditioning Symbols

Heating and Ventilation Equipment

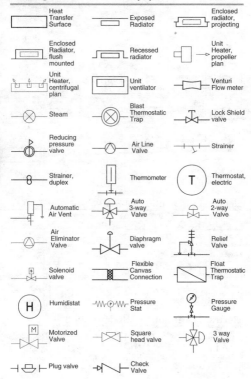

Heat Transfer Surface	Exposed Radiator	Enclosed radiator, projecting
Enclosed Radiator, flush mounted	Recessed radiator	Unit Heater, propeller plan
Unit Heater, centrifugal plan	Unit ventilator	Venturi Flow meter
Steam	Blast Thermostatic Trap	Lock Shield valve
Reducing pressure valve	Air Line Valve	Strainer
Strainer, duplex	Thermometer	Thermostat, electric
Automatic Air Vent	Auto 3-way Valve	Auto 2-way Valve
Air Eliminator Valve	Diaphragm valve	Relief Valve
Solenoid valve	Flexible Canvas Connection	Float Thermostatic Trap
Humidistat	Pressure Stat	Pressure Gauge
Motorized Valve	Square head valve	3 way Valve
Plug valve	Check Valve	

Ductwork

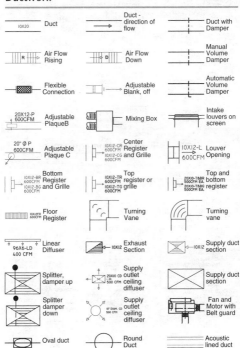

10X20 Duct	Duct - direction of flow	Duct with Damper
Air Flow Rising	Air Flow Down	Manual Volume Damper
Flexible Connection	Adjustable Blank, off	Automatic Volume Damper
20X12-P 600CFM Adjustable PlaqueB	Mixing Box	Intake louvers on screen
20" Ø P 600CFM Adjustable Plaque C	10X12-CR 600CFM 10X12-CG 600CFM Center Register and Grille	10X12-L 600CFM Louver Opening
10X12-BR 600CFM 10X12-BG 600CFM Bottom Register and Grille	10X12-TR 600CFM 10X12-TG 600CFM Top register or grille	20X10-T&BR 500CFM EA 20X10-T&BG 500CFM EA Top and bottom register
10X20FR 600CFM Floor Register	Turning Vane	Turning vane
96X6-LD 400 CFM Linear Diffuser	10X12 Exhaust Section	10X12 Supply duct section
Splitter, damper up	20X10 CD 500 CFM Supply outlet ceiling diffuser	Supply duct section
Splitter damper down	10" DIAM. CD 500 CFM Supply outlet ceiling diffuser	Fan and Motor with Belt guard
Oval duct	Round Duct	Acoustic lined duct

Heat-Power Equipment

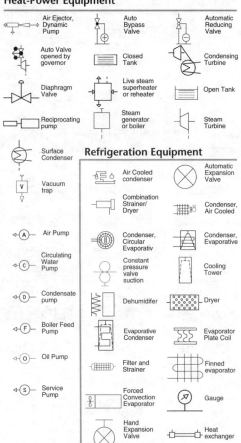

Air Ejector, Dynamic Pump	Auto Bypass Valve	Automatic Reducing Valve
Auto Valve opened by governor	Closed Tank	Condensing Turbine
Diaphragm Valve	Live steam superheater or reheater	Open Tank
Reciprocating pump	Steam generator or boiler	Steam Turbine
Surface Condenser		
Vacuum trap		

Refrigeration Equipment

Air Cooled condenser	Automatic Expansion Valve
Combination Strainer/Dryer	Condenser, Air Cooled
Condenser, Circular Evaporativ	Condenser, Evaporative
Constant pressure valve suction	Cooling Tower
Dehumidifer	Dryer
Evaporative Condenser	Evaporator Plate Coil
Filter and Strainer	Finned evaporator
Forced Convection Evaporator	Gauge
Hand Expansion Valve	Heat exchanger

Air Pump

Circulating Water Pump

Condensate pump

Boiler Feed Pump

Oil Pump

Service Pump

Refrigeration (con't)

High Side
Float Valve

Immersion
Cooling
Unit

Low Side
Float Valve

MFBT
Evaporator

MFFN
Evaporator

Scale Trap

Sight Glass

Thermal
Bulb

Thermostatic
Expansion
Valve

Water
Cooled
Condenser

Piping Symbols

Air Conditioning

Brine Return	—— BR ——
Brine Supply	—— B ——
Chilled water Return	—— CHWR ——
Chilled water supply	—— CWS ——
Condenser water return	—— CWR ——
Condenser water supply	—— CWS ——
Drain	—— D ——
Humidification Line	—— H ——
Make up Water	—— MU ——
Refrigerant Discharge	—— RD ——
Refrigerant Liquid	—— R L ——
Refrigerant Suction	—— RS ——

Heating

Air Relief Line	—— V ——
Boiler Blowoff	—— BD ——
Compressed Air	—— A ——
Condensate or Vacuum	—— VPD ——
Feedwater pump discharge	—— PPD ——
Fuel oil return	—— FOR ——
Fuel Oil Suction	—— FOS ——
Fuel Oil Vent	—— FOV ——
High pressure Return	—— HPR ——
High Pressure steam	—— HPS ——
Hot Water Heating Return	—— HWR ——
Hot Water Heating Supply	—— HW ——
Low Pressure Return	—— LPR ——
Low Pressure Steam	—— LPS ——
Make Up Water	—— MU ——
Medium Pressure Return	—— MPR ——
Medium Pressure Steam	—— MPS ——

Plumbing

Acid Vent — – AV – – —	Fire Line — F — F —	Nitrous oxide — LN —
Acid Waste — AW —	Gas, High Pressure — HG —	Oxygen — O —
Argon — AR —	Gas, Low Pressure — G — G —	Pneumatic Tube — PN —
Branch and Head Sprinkler — o — o —	Gas, Medium Pressure — MG —	Reinforced Concrete — RCP —
Cast Iron — CI —	Helium — HE —	Sanitizing Hot Water Return
Chilled Drinking Water Return — DWR —	Hot Water	Sanitizing Hot Water Supply
Chilled Drinking Water Supply — DWS —	Hot Water Return	Soft Cold Water — SW —
Clay Tile — CT —	Hydrogen — H —	Soil Waste or Leader below grade
Cold Water	Indirect Drain — IW —	Soil Waste or leader above grade
Combination Waste Vent — SV —	Industrial Cold Water — ICW —	Storm Drain — S —
Combination Standpipe — CSP —	Industrial Waste — INW —	Tempered Water Return — TWR —
Compressed Air — A —	Industrialized Hot Water Return — IHR —	Tempered Water Supply — TWS —
Culver Pipe — CP —	Industrialized Hot Water Supply — IHW —	Vacuum — V —
Drain; Tile, Open or Agricultural = = = =	Liquid Petroleum Gas — LPG —	Vacuum Cleaning — VC —
Dry Standpipe — DSP —	Liquid oxygen — LOX —	Vent
	Main Supplies Sprinkler — S —	
Ductile Iron — DI —	Nitrogen — N —	Wet Standpipe — WSP —

Household Fixtures

Elevation Views

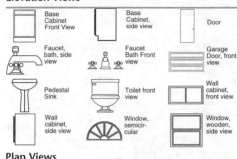

Base Cabinet Front View

Base Cabinet, side view

Door

Faucet, bath, side view

Faucet Bath Front view

Garage Door, front view

Pedestal Sink

Toilet front view

Wall cabinet, front view

Wall cabinet, side view

Window, semicircular

Window, wooden, side view

Plan Views

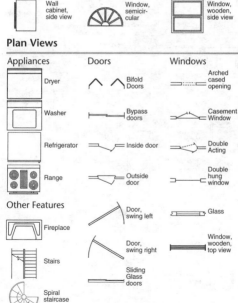

Appliances

Dryer

Washer

Refrigerator

Range

Other Features

Fireplace

Stairs

Spiral staircase

Doors

Bifold Doors

Bypass doors

Inside door

Outside door

Door, swing left

Door, swing right

Sliding Glass doors

Windows

Arched cased opening

Casement Window

Double Acting

Double hung window

Glass

Window, wooden, top view

Plumbing Fixtures

Bath tubs

Bathtub, rounded end

Bathtub, standard

Bathtub, oval

Bathtub, Whirlpool

Bidet

Sitz Bath

Grab Bars

Grab bar, corner

Grab bar, straight

Showers

Gang shower, pedestal

Shower head

Shower Stall

Sinks

Built in counter double

Built in counter triple sink

Built in counter

Commercial kitchen sink

Double kitchen sink

Corner

Floor service sink

Floor sink

Hand wash sink, half round

Pedestal

Laundry sink

Service sink

Wall hung

Wheelchair accessible

Faucets

Faucet Bath Top view

Toilets

Toilet, low profile

Toilet, tank type

Toilet, floor mounted

Detention sink and toilet

Toilet, wall mounted

Electrical

Current Carrying Capacity of Wire
    Aluminum Wire, Single...198
    Aluminum Wire, Three..199
    Copper Wire, Single...200
    Copper Wire, Three..201
Current Adjustment for More Than 3 Wires in a Cable 202
Standard Lamp and Extension Cord Current Capacities 202
Standard Wiring Color Codes...203
Wire Classes and Insulation 205
Electrical Conductors - Physical and Electrical Properties
    Solid Wires...207
    Stranded Wires 211
Voltage Drop vs Wire Size 213
Maximum Number of Conductors and Fixture Wires in Electrical
Tubing or Conduit...227
Number of Conductors in Outlet, Device, and Junction Boxes and
    Conduit Bodies..232
Electrical Connectors; NEMA Receptacle Configurations............234
Reading Electric Motor Nameplates..238
Electric Motor - Average Specs...250
Electric Motor - Three-phase Electric Motor Specs.......................252
Electric Motor - HP vs Torque vs RPM..253
Electric Motor - DC Motor Wiring Specs..256
Electric Motor - Frame Dimensions - NEMA 258
Formulas for Electricity..262

Current Carrying Capacity of Wire

ALUMINUM Wire, Single Insulated Conductor,
rated to 2,000 volts in free air @ air temperature of 86°F (30°C)

	Insulation types		
	TW, UF	RH, RHW, THHW, THW, THWN, XHHW	RHH, RHW-2, SA, SIS, TBS, THHN, THHW, THW-2, THWN-2, USE-2, XHH, XHHW, XHHW-2, ZW-2
Wire Size AWG	Conductor temperature rating		
	140°F (60°C)	167°F (75°C)	194°F (90°C)
4/0	235	280	315
3/0	200	240	275
2/0	175	210	235
1/0	150	180	205
1	130	155	175
2	110	135	150
3	95	115	130
4	80	100	110
6	60	75	80
8	45	55	60
10	35	40	40
12	25	30	35
14	-	-	-
16	-	-	-
18	-	-	-
Temperature correction factors			
Ambient Temp. (°F)	For ambient temperatures other than 86°F (30°C), multiply by the appropriate factor.		
70 to 77	1.08	1.05	1.04
78 to 86	1.00	1.00	1.00
87 to 95	0.91	0.94	0.96
96 to 104	0.82	0.88	0.91
105 to 113	0.71	0.82	0.87
114 to 122	0.58	0.75	0.82
123 to 131	0.41	0.67	0.76
132 to 140	-	0.58	0.71
141 to 158	-	0.33	0.58
159 to 176	-	-	0.41

Source: National Electrical Code, 1996, National Fire Protection Association, 1 Batterymarch Park, Quincy, MA 02269

ALUMINUM Wire, Three Insulated Conductors, rated to 2,000 volts In free air @ air temperature of 86°F (30°C)			
	Insulation types		
	TW, UF	RH, RHW, THHW, THW, THWN, XHHW, USE	RHH, RHW-2, SA, SIS, TBS, THHN, THHW, THW-2, THWN-2, USE-2, XHH, XHHW, XHHW-2, ZW-2
Wire Size AWG	Conductor temperature rating		
	140°F(60°C)	167°F (75°C)	194°F(90°C)
4/0	150	180	205
3/0	130	155	175
2/0	115	135	150
1/0	100	120	135
1	85	100	115
2	75	90	100
3	65	75	85
4	55	65	75
6	40	50	60
8	30	40	45
10	25	30	35
12	20	20	25
14	-	-	-
16	-	-	-
18	-	-	-
Temperature correction factors			
Ambient Temp. (°F)	For ambient temperatures other than 86°F (30°C), multiply by the appropriate factor.		
70 to 77	1.08	1.05	1.04
78 to 86	1.00	1.00	1.00
87 to 95	0.91	0.94	0.96
96 to 104	0.82	0.88	0.91
105 to 113	0.71	0.82	0.87
114 to 122	0.58	0.75	0.82
123 to 131	0.41	0.67	0.76
132 to 140	-	0.58	0.71
141 to 158	-	0.33	0.58
159 to 176	-		0.41

Source: National Electrical Code, 1996, National Fire Protection Association, 1 Batterymarch Park, Quincy, MA 02269

Note: The material in this table represents only a small part of the National Electrical Code. For additional information please refer directly to the Code.

COPPER Wire, Single Insulated Conductor,
rated to 2,000 volts in free air @ air temperature of 86°F (30°C)

Wire Size AWG	Insulation types		
	TW, UF	FEPW, RH, RHW, THHW, THW, THWN, XHHW, ZW	FEP, FEPB, MI RHH, RHW-2, SA THHW, THWN-2, USE-2, XHH, XHHW, XHHW-2, ZW-2
	Conductor temperature rating		
	140°F (60°C)	167°F (75°C)	194°F (90°C)
4/0	300	360	405
3/0	260	310	350
2/0	225	265	300
1/0	195	230	260
1	165	195	220
2	140	170	190
3	120	145	165
4	105	125	140
6	80	95	105
8	60	70	80
10	40	50	55
12	30	35	40
14	25	30	35
16	-	-	24
18	-	-	18

Temperature correction factors			
Ambient Temp. (°F)	For ambient temperatures other than 86°F (30°C), multiply by the appropriate factor.		
70 to 77	1.08	1.05	1.04
78 to 86	1.00	1.00	1.00
87 to 95	0.91	0.94	0.96
96 to 104	0.82	0.88	0.91
105 to 113	0.71	0.82	0.87
114 to 122	0.58	0.75	0.82
123 to 131	0.41	0.67	0.76
132 to 140	-	0.58	0.71
141 to 158	-	0.33	0.58
159 to 176	-	-	0.41

Source: National Electrical Code, 1996, National Fire Protection Association, 1 Batterymarch Park, Quincy, MA 02269

Note: The material in this table represents only a small part of the National Electrical Code. For additional information please refer directly to the Code.

COPPER Wire, Three Insulated Conductors,
rated to 2,000 volts In free air @ air temperature of 86°F (30°C)

Wire Size AWG	Insulation types		
	TW, UF	FEPW, RH, RHW, THHW, THW, THWN, USE, XHHW, ZW	FEP, FEPB, MI RHH, RHW-2, SA, SIS, TBS, THHN, THHW, THW-2, USE-2, XHH, XHHW, XHHW-2, ZW-2
	Conductor temperature rating		
	140°F (60 °C)	167°F (75°C)	194°F (90°C)
4/0	195	230	260
3/0	165	200	225
2/0	145	175	195
1/0	125	150	170
1	110	130	150
2	95	115	130
3	85	100	110
4	70	85	95
6	55	65	75
8	40	50	55
10	30	35	40
12	25	25	30
14	20	20	25
16	-	-	18
18	-	-	14

Temperature correction factors			
Ambient Temp. (°F)	For ambient temperatures other than 86°F (30°C), multiply by the appropriate factor.		
70 to 77	1.08	1.05	1.04
78 to 86	1.00	1.00	1.00
87 to 95	0.91	0.94	0.96
96 to 104	0.82	0.88	0.91
105 to 113	0.71	0.82	0.87
114 to 122	0.58	0.75	0.82
123 to 131	0.41	0.67	0.76
132 to 140	-	0.58	0.71
141 to 158	-	0.33	0.58
159 to 176	-	-	0.41

Source: National Electrical Code, 1996, National Fire Protection Association, 1 Batterymarch Park, Quincy, MA 02269

Note: The material in this table represents only a small part of the National Electrical Code. For additional information, please refer directly to the Code.

Current Adjustment for More Than Three Wires in a Cable

Number of Conductors	Percentage of amperage value listed in amperage tables on pages 198 - 201
4 to 6	80%
7 to 9	70%
10 to 20	50%
21 to 30	45%
31 to 40	40%
over 41	35%

Basically, the above table reflects the rule that the higher the temperature (more wires=higher temperature) the lower the current carrying capacity of the wire.

NOTE: In all Aluminum and Copper Clad Aluminum Wire Types listed on pages 198 through 201 (except Types TA, TBS, SA, SIS, THW-2, THWN-2, RHW-2, USE-2, XHH, XHHW-2 & ZW-2) overcurrent protection should not exceed 15 amps for 12 AWG and 25 amps for 10 AWG. This is not true if specifically permitted elsewhere in the Code.

Standard Lamp and Extension Cord Current Capacities

Wire Size AWG	Wire types SP, SPT, S, SJ, SV, ST, SJT, SVT		
	1 Conductor	2 Conductor	3 Conductor
10	30	25	20
12	25	20	16
14	18	15	12
16	13	10	8
18	10	7	6

NOTE: In all Copper Wire Types listed on page 200 (except Types MI, TA, TBS, SA, SIS, RHW-2, THW-2, THWN-2, USE-2, XHH, XHHW-2, & ZW-2) overcurrent protection should not exceed 15 amps for 14 AWG, 20 amps for 12 AWG, and 30 amps for 10 AWG. This is not true if specifically permitted elsewhere in the Code.

Standard Wiring Color Codes

Standard wire color codes are very different between electronic circuitry and household 110 Volt AC wiring.

Household Wiring (or other AC applications in the 100+ volt range) uses the following color codes:

Wire Color	Circuit type
Black	"Hot" wire. In an outlet, it is always wired to the narrow spade or brass colored terminal.
Green	"Ground" wire, always wired to the green terminal. Also called chassis ground. This wire is also sometimes green w/ yellow stripe.
Red	Second "hot" wire used in connecting 3–way switches. Connects power between the 3–way switches. Sometimes called a "traveler."
White/gray	"Neutral" wire. In an outlet, it is always wired to the wide spade or silver colored terminal.

Typically, the following color codes are used for **electronic applications** as established by the Electronic Industries Association (EIA):

Wire Color (solid)	Circuit type
Black	Chassis grounds, returns, primary leads
Blue	Plate leads, transistor collectors, FET drain
Brown	Filaments, plate start lead
Gray	AC main power leads
Green	Transistor base, finish grid, diodes, FET gate
Orange	Transistor base 2, screen grid
Red	B plus dc power supply
Violet	Power supply minus
White	B–C minus of bias supply, AVC–AGC return
Yellow	Emitters-cathode and transistor, FET source

Stereo Audio Channels are color coded as follows:

Wire Color (solid)	Circuit type
White	Left channel high side
Blue	Left channel low side
Red	Right channel high side
Green	Right channel low side

Power Transformers are color coded as follows:

Wire Color (solid)	Circuit type
Black	If a transformer does not have a tapped primary, both leads are black.
Black	If a transformer does have a tapped primary, the black is the common lead.
Black & Yellow	Tap for a tapped primary.
Black & Red	End for a tapped primary.

AF Transformers (audio) are color coded as follows:

Wire Color (solid)	Circuit type
Black	Ground line.
Blue	Plate, collector, or drain lead. End of primary winding.
Brown	Start primary loop, opposite to blue lead.
Green	High side, end secondary loop.
Red	B plus, center tap push–pull loop.
Yellow	Secondary center tap.

IF Transformers (Intermediate Frequency) are color coded as follows:

Wire Color (solid)	Circuit type
Blue	Primary high side of plate, collector, or drain lead.
Green	Secondary high side for output.
Red	Low side of primary returning B plus.
Violet	Secondary outputs.
White	Secondary low side.

Wire Classes & Insulation

Standard cable, as used in home and general construction, is classified by the wire size, number of wires, insulation type and dampness condition of the wire environment. Example: a cable with the code "12/2 with Ground – Type UF – 600V – (UL)" has the following specifications:

> Wire sizes are 14 gauge for copper, 12 gauge for aluminum (minimum size for 0 to 2000 volts), See National Electric Code.

> The " / 2 " indicates there are two wires in the cable. "Ground" indicates there is a third wire in the cable to be used as a grounding wire.

> "Type UF" indicates the insulation type and acceptable dampness rating.

> "600V" means the wire is rated at 600 volts maximum.

> "UL" indicates the wire has been certified by Under writers Laboratory to be safe.

Cables are dampness rated as follows:

> DRY: No dampness normally encountered. Indoor location above ground level.

> DAMP: Partially protected locations. Moderate amount of moisture. Indoor location below ground level.

> WET: Water saturation probable, such as underground or in concrete slabs or outside locations exposed to weather.

There are literally hundreds of different types of insulation used in wire and cable. To make things simple, the following descriptions are for wires commonly used in home wiring:

"BX"   Type "AC." Armor covered with flexible, galvanized steel. Normally used in dry locations. Not legal to use in some states, such as California.

"ROMEX" Although actually a trade name, it is used to describe a general class of plastic coated cable. Each wire is plastic wrapped except possibly the ground wire, which is sometimes bare or paper covered. Very flexible.

There are three general types:

"NM" – Dry only, 2 or 3 wire, ground wire plastic wrapped.

"NMC" – Dry, 2 or 3 wire, all wires in solid plastic.

"UF" – Wet or moist, 2 or 3 wire, all wires in solid, water resistant plastic. Use also instead of conduit. Underground feeder.

Types "NM" and "NMC" can be placed in conduit where protection from physical damage is needed.

Wire Classes & Insulation

Wire types are typically coded by the type of insulation, temperature range, dampness rating, and type and composition of the jacket. The following are some of the "Type Codes":

"T..." Very common, dry only, full current load temperature must be less than 60°C (140°F).

"F" Fixture wire. CF has cotton insulation (90°C), AF has asbestos insulation (150°C), SF has silicone insulation (200°C).

"R..." Rubber (natural, neoprene, etc) covered.

"S..." Appliance cord, stranded conductors, cotton layer between wire and insulation, jute fillers, rubber outer jacket. S is extra hard service, SJ lighter service, SV light service.

"SP..." Lamp cord, rubber insulation.

"SPT..." Lamp cord, plastic insulation.

"X..." Insulation is a cross linked synthetic polymer. Very tough and heat and moisture resistant.

"FEP..." Fluorinated ethylene propylene insulation. Rated over 90°C (194°F). Dry only.

"...B" Suffix indicating an outer braid is used, such as glass.

"...H" Suffix indicating Higher loaded current temperatures may be used, up to 75°C (167°F).

"...HH" Suffix indicating much higher loaded current temperatures may be used, up to 90°C (194°F).

"...L" Suffix indicating a seamless lead jacket.

"...N" Suffix indicating the jacket is extruded nylon or thermoplastic polyester and is very resistant to gas and oil and is very tough.

"...O" Suffix indicating neoprene jacket.

"...W" Suffix indicating WET use type.

Examples of some of the more common wire types are "T", "TW", "THWN", "THHN", "XHHW", "RHH", and "RHW".

Electrical Conductors - Physical And Electrical Properties

Solid Wires

Nominal Wire Size (AWG or kcmil)	Diameter			Cross-sectional Area			Nominal Linear Mass, Bare Wire (20°C)				Nominal Resistance, Bare Wire @ 68°F (20°C)			
							Copper (1)		Aluminum (2)		Copper (3)		Aluminum (4)	
	in.	mm	mils	sq. in.	sq. mm	cir. mils	lbs/1000 ft	kg/1000 m	lbs/1000 ft	kg/1000 m	ohms/1000 ft	ohms/1000 m	ohms/1000 ft	ohms/1000 m
500	0.7071	17.96	707.1	0.3927	253.35	500,000	1,513	2,252	460.1	684.7	0.0207	0.0680	0.0342	0.1121
400	0.6325	16.06	632.5	0.3142	202.68	400,000	1,211	1,802	368.1	547.7	0.0259	0.0851	0.0427	0.1401
350	0.5916	15.03	591.6	0.2749	177.35	350,000	1,059	1,577	322.1	479.3	0.0296	0.0972	0.0488	0.1601
300	0.5477	13.91	547.7	0.2356	152.01	300,000	908.1	1351	276.0	410.8	0.0346	0.1134	0.0569	0.1868
250	0.5000	12.70	500.0	0.1964	126.68	250,000	756.7	1126	230.0	342.3	0.0415	0.1361	0.0683	0.2241
4/0	0.4600	11.68	460.0	0.1662	107.22	211,601	640.5	953.2	194.7	289.8	0.0490	0.1608	0.0807	0.2648
3/0	0.4096	10.40	409.6	0.1318	85.011	167,773	507.8	755.8	154.4	229.7	0.0618	0.2028	0.1018	0.3340
2/0	0.3648	9.266	364.8	0.1045	67.432	133,080	402.8	599.5	122.5	182.2	0.0779	0.2557	0.1283	0.4211
1/0	0.3249	8.252	324.9	0.0829	53.488	105,560	319.5	475.5	97.13	144.5	0.0982	0.3223	0.1618	0.5308
1	0.2893	7.348	289.3	0.0657	42.409	83,695	253.3	377.0	77.01	114.6	0.1239	0.4065	0.2041	0.6695
2	0.2576	6.543	257.6	0.0521	33.624	66,358	200.9	298.9	61.06	90.87	0.1563	0.5127	0.2574	0.8445
3	0.2294	5.827	229.4	0.0413	26.665	52,625	159.3	237.1	48.42	72.06	0.1971	0.6465	0.3246	1.065
4	0.2043	5.189	204.3	0.0328	21.149	41,739	126.3	188.0	38.41	57.15	0.2485	0.8151	0.4092	1.343
5	0.1819	4.620	181.9	0.0260	16.766	33,088	100.2	149.0	30.45	45.31	0.3134	1.028	0.5162	1.694
6	0.1620	4.115	162.0	0.0206	13.298	26,244	79.44	118.2	24.15	35.94	0.3951	1.296	0.6508	2.135
7	0.1443	3.665	144.3	0.0164	10.551	20,823	63.00	93.80	19.16	28.51	0.4980	1.634	0.8203	2.691
8	0.1285	3.264	128.5	0.0130	8.3669	16,512	49.98	74.38	15.19	22.61	0.6280	2.060	1.034	3.394
9	0.1144	2.906	114.4	0.0103	6.6315	13,087	39.62	58.95	12.04	17.92	0.7924	2.600	1.305	4.282
10	0.1019	2.588	101.9	0.0082	5.2615	10,384	31.43	46.77	9.555	14.22	0.9987	3.277	1.645	5.397

Electrical Conductors - Physical And Electrical Properties

Solid Wires

Nominal Wire Size (AWG or kcmil)	Diameter			Cross-sectional Area			Nominal Linear Mass, Bare Wire (20°C)				Nominal Resistance, Bare Wire @ 68°F (20°C)			
							Copper (1)		Aluminum (2)		Copper (3)		Aluminum (4)	
	in.	mm	mils	sq. in.	sq. mm	cir. mils	lbs/1000 ft	kg/1000 m	lbs/1000 ft	kg/1000 m	ohms/1000 ft	ohms/1000 m	ohms/1000 ft	ohms/1000 m
11	0.0907	2.305	90.74	0.0065	4.1721	8,234	24.92	37.09	7.576	11.27	1.259	4.132	2.074	6.806
12	0.0808	2.053	80.81	0.0051	3.3089	6,530	19.77	29.42	6.009	8.942	1.588	5.210	2.616	8.58
13	0.0720	1.828	71.96	0.0041	2.6239	5,178	15.67	23.33	4.765	7.091	2.003	6.570	3.298	10.82
14	0.0641	1.628	64.08	0.0032	2.0807	4,106	12.43	18.50	3.778	5.623	2.525	8.285	4.160	13.65
15	0.0571	1.450	57.07	0.0026	1.6503	3,257	9.859	14.67	2.997	4.460	3.184	10.45	5.244	17.21
16	0.0508	1.291	50.82	0.0020	1.3087	2,583	7.818	11.63	2.376	3.537	4.015	13.17	6.613	21.70
17	0.0453	1.150	45.26	0.0016	1.0380	2,048	6.201	9.228	1.885	2.805	5.062	16.61	8.338	27.36
18	0.0403	1.024	40.30	0.0013	0.8229	1,624	4.916	7.316	1.494	2.224	6.385	20.95	10.52	34.50
19	0.0359	0.9116	35.89	0.0010	0.6527	1,288	3.899	5.802	1.185	1.764	8.051	26.41	13.26	43.50
20	0.0320	0.8118	31.96	0.0008	0.5176	1,021	3.092	4.601	0.9399	1.399	10.15	33.31	16.72	54.86
21	0.0285	0.7229	28.46	0.0006	0.4104	810.0	2.452	3.649	0.7453	1.109	12.80	42.00	21.09	69.18
22	0.0254	0.6439	25.35	0.0005	0.3256	642.6	1.945	2.895	0.5913	0.8800	16.14	52.94	26.58	87.2
23	0.0226	0.5733	22.57	0.0004	0.2581	509.4	1.542	2.295	0.4687	0.6976	20.36	66.79	33.53	110.0
24	0.0201	0.5105	20.10	0.0003	0.2047	404.0	1.223	1.820	0.3718	0.5532	25.67	84.21	42.28	138.7
25	0.0179	0.4547	17.90	0.0003	0.1624	320.4	0.9699	1.443	0.2948	0.4388	32.36	106.2	53.31	174.9
26	0.0159	0.4049	15.94	0.0002	0.1287	254.1	0.7691	1.145	0.2338	0.3479	40.81	133.9	67.22	220.5
27	0.0142	0.3607	14.20	0.0002	0.1022	201.6	0.6104	0.9083	0.1855	0.2761	51.43	168.7	84.71	277.9
28	0.0126	0.3211	12.64	0.0001	0.0810	159.8	0.4836	0.7197	0.1470	0.2188	64.91	212.9	106.9	350.7
29	0.0113	0.2860	11.26	0.0001	0.0642	126.8	0.3838	0.5711	0.1167	0.1736	81.79	268.3	134.7	442.0
30	0.0100	0.2548	10.03	7.901E-05	0.0510	100.6	0.3045	0.4532	0.0926	0.1378	103.1	338.2	169.8	557.0
31	0.0089	0.2268	8.928	6.260E-05	0.0404	79.71	0.2413	0.3591	0.0733	0.1092	130.1	426.8	214.3	703.0

Nominal Wire Size (AWG or kcmil)	Diameter			Cross-sectional Area			Nominal Linear Mass, Bare Wire @ 68°F (20°C)				Nominal Resistance, Bare Wire @ 68°F (20°C)			
							Copper (1)		Aluminum (2)		Copper (3)		Aluminum (4)	
	in.	mm	mils	sq. in.	sq. mm	cir. mils	lbs/1000 ft	kg/1000 m	lbs/1000 ft	kg/1000 m	ohms/1000 ft	ohms/1000 m	ohms/1000 ft	ohms/1000 m
32	0.0080	0.2019	7.950	4.964E-05	0.0320	63.20	0.1913	0.2847	0.0582	0.0865	164.1	538.3	270.2	886.6
33	0.0071	0.1798	7.080	3.937E-05	0.0254	50.13	0.1517	0.2258	0.0461	0.0686	206.9	678.7	340.7	1,118
34	0.0063	0.1601	6.305	3.122E-05	0.0201	39.75	0.1203	0.1791	0.0366	0.0544	260.9	855.8	429.7	1,410
35	0.0056	0.1426	5.615	2.476E-05	0.0160	31.53	0.0954	0.1420	0.0290	0.0432	328.9	1,079	541.7	1,777
36	0.0050	0.1270	5.000	1.963E-05	0.0127	25.00	0.0757	0.1126	0.0230	0.0342	414.8	1,361	683.2	2,241
37	0.0045	0.1131	4.453	1.557E-05	0.0101	19.83	0.0600	0.0893	0.0182	0.0272	523.0	1,716	861.4	2,826
38	0.0040	0.1007	3.965	1.235E-05	0.0080	15.72	0.0476	0.0708	0.0145	0.0215	659.6	2,164	1,086	3,564
39	0.0035	0.0897	3.531	9.792E-06	0.0063	12.47	0.0377	0.0562	0.0115	0.0171	831.7	2,729	1,370	4,494
40	0.0032	0.0799	3.145	7.768E-06	0.0050	9.891	0.0299	0.0446	0.0091	0.0135	1,048	3,440	1,727	5,665
41	0.0028	0.0711	2.800	6.158E-06	0.0040	7.840	0.0237	0.0353	0.0072	0.0107	1,323	4,340	2,179	7,148
42	0.0025	0.0635	2.500	4.909E-06	0.0032	6.250	0.0189	0.0282	0.0058	0.0086	1,659	5,444	2,733	8,970
43	0.0022	0.0559	2.200	3.801E-06	0.0025	4.840	0.0147	0.0218	0.0045	0.0066	2,143	7,029	3,529	11,580
44	0.0020	0.0508	2.000	3.142E-06	0.0020	4.000	0.0121	0.0180	0.0037	0.0055	2,592	8,510	4,270	14,010
45	0.0018	0.0447	1.760	2.433E-06	0.0016	3.098	0.0094	0.0140	0.0029	0.0042	3,348	10,980	5,514	18,090
46	0.0016	0.0399	1.570	1.936E-06	0.0013	2.465	0.0075	0.0111	0.0023	0.0034	4,207	13,800	6,929	22,730
47	0.0014	0.0356	1.400	1.539E-06	0.0010	1.960	0.0059	0.0088	0.0018	0.0027	5,291	17,360	8,714	28,590
48	0.0012	0.0315	1.240	1.208E-06	0.0008	1.538	0.0047	0.0069	0.0014	0.0021	6,744	22,130	11,108	36,440
49	0.0011	0.0282	1.110	9.677E-07	0.0006	1.232	0.0037	0.0056	0.0011	0.0017	8,416	27,610	13,862	45,480
50	0.001	0.0251	0.9801	7.698E-07	0.0005	0.9801	0.0030	0.0044	0.00090	0.0013	10,581	34,710	17,427	57,170
51	0.0009	0.0224	0.8800	6.082E-07	0.0004	0.7744	0.0023	0.0035	0.00071	0.0011	13,391	43,930	22,056	72,360
52	0.0008	0.0198	0.7800	4.778E-07	0.0003	0.6084	0.0018	0.0027	0.00056	0.0008	17,045	55,920	28,074	92,100
53	0.0007	0.0178	0.7000	3.848E-07	0.0003	0.4900	0.0015	0.0022	0.00045	0.0007	21,163	69,430	34,857	114,400

Electrical Conductors - Physical And Electrical Properties - Solid Wires (cont.)

Nominal Wire Size (AWG or kcmil)	Diameter			Cross-sectional Area			Nominal Linear Mass, Bare Wire @ 68°F (20°C)				Nominal Resistance, Bare Wire @ 68°F (20°C)			
							Copper (1)		Aluminum (2)		Copper (3)		Aluminum (4)	
	in.	mm	mils	sq. in.	sq. mm	cir. mils	lbs/1000 ft	kg/1000 m	lbs/1000 ft	kg/1000 m	ohms/1000 ft	ohms/1000 m	ohms/1000 ft	ohms/1000 m
54	0.0006	0.0157	0.6200	3.019E-07	0.00019	0.3844	0.0012	0.0017	0.00035	0.0005	26.977	88.500	44.433	145.800
55	0.0006	0.0140	0.5500	2.376E-07	0.00015	0.3025	0.0010	0.0014	0.00028	0.0004	34.281	112.500	56.463	185.200
56	0.0005	0.0124	0.4900	1.886E-07	0.00012	0.2401	0.0007	0.0011	0.00022	0.0003	43.190	141.700	71.137	233.400
57	0.0004	0.0111	0.4380	1.507E-07	0.00010	0.1918	0.0006	0.0009	0.00018	0.00026	54.054	177.300	89.030	292.100
58	0.0004	0.0099	0.3900	1.195E-07	0.00008	0.1521	0.0005	0.0007	0.00014	0.00021	68.179	223.700	112.294	368.400
59	0.0004	0.0088	0.3470	9.457E-08	0.00006	0.1204	0.0004	0.0005	0.00011	0.00016	86.123	282.600	141.849	465.400
60	0.0004	0.0078	0.3090	7.499E-08	0.00005	0.0955	0.0003	0.0004	0.00009	0.00013	108.608	356.300	178.883	586.900

NOTES:
(1) Based on specific gravity for annealed copper @ 20°C (68°F) of 8.906.
(1) Based on specific gravity for aluminum @ 20°C (68°F) of 2.707.
(3) Based on resistivity for annealed copper at 20°C (68°F) of 10.37 ohm circular mil per foot.
(4) Based on resistivity for aluminum at 20°C (68°F) of 17.08 ohm circular mil per foot.
(5) Similar tables may be found in the CRC Handbook of Chemistry and Physics, 74th Edition, 1993-1994, CRC Press, Boca Raton, FL and in the Technical Guide For Solid Bare Copper Wire, Industrial Electric Wire and Cable, Inc. at www.iewc.com.
(6) Resistance increases with increasing temperature and temperature increases with increasing amperage carried by a wire. Equation for temperature change: Resistance @ new temperature = Resistance @ 75°C [1 + a (new temperature in °C- 75°C)] where: a for copper = 0.00323 and for aluminum = 0.00330. Resistivity of copper @ 75°C is 12.60 ohm circular mil per foot. Resistivity of aluminum @ 75°C is 20.77 ohm circular mil per foot.
(7) Abbreviations: AWG = American Wire Gage, kcmil = thousand circular mil, in.=inches, mm= millimeter, m= meter, sq.= square, lbs = pounds, kg= kilograms

Electrical Conductors - Physical And Electrical Properties

Stranded Wires

Nominal Wire Size (AWG or kcmil)	Stranding Number of Strands	Strand Diameter in	Strand Diameter mm	Strand Diameter mils	Overall Wire Diameter in	Overall Wire Diameter mm	Overall Wire Diameter mils	Cross-sectional Area sq in	Cross-sectional Area sqmm	Cross-sectional Area cir mils	Nominal Direct Current Resistance 167°F (75°C) Uncoated Copper ohms/1000 ft	Uncoated Copper ohms/1000 m	Aluminum ohms/1000 ft	Aluminum ohms/1000 m
2000	127	0.126	3.20	126.0	1.632	41.45	1,632	1.5708	1,350	2,000,000	0.00643	0.02110	0.0106	0.0348
1750	127	0.117	2.97	117.0	1.526	38.76	1,526	1.3744	1,180	1,750,000	0.00735	0.02411	0.0121	0.0397
1500	91	0.128	3.25	128.0	1.412	35.86	1,412	1.1781	1,010	1,500,000	0.00858	0.02815	0.0141	0.0463
1250	91	0.117	2.97	117.0	1.289	32.74	1,289	0.9817	841.9	1,250,000	0.0103	0.0338	0.0169	0.0554
1000	61	0.128	3.25	128.0	1.152	29.26	1,152	0.7854	672.5	1,000,000	0.0129	0.0423	0.0212	0.0696
900	61	0.122	3.10	122.0	1.094	27.79	1,094	0.7069	606.4	900,000	0.0143	0.0469	0.0235	0.0771
800	61	0.114	2.90	114.0	1.030	26.16	1,030	0.6283	537.6	800,000	0.0161	0.0528	0.0265	0.0869
750	61	0.111	2.82	111.0	0.998	25.35	998.0	0.5890	504.7	750,000	0.0171	0.0561	0.0282	0.0925
700	61	0.107	2.72	107.0	0.964	24.49	964.0	0.5498	470.9	700,000	0.0184	0.0604	0.0303	0.0994
600	61	0.099	2.51	99.0	0.893	22.68	893.0	0.4712	404.1	600,000	0.0214	0.0702	0.0353	0.1158
500	37	0.116	2.95	116.0	0.813	20.65	813.0	0.3927	334.9	500,000	0.0258	0.0846	0.0424	0.1391
400	37	0.104	2.64	104.0	0.728	18.49	728.0	0.3142	268.5	400,000	0.0321	0.1053	0.0529	0.1736
350	37	0.097	2.46	97.0	0.681	17.30	681.0	0.2749	235.0	350,000	0.0367	0.1204	0.0605	0.1985
300	37	0.090	2.29	90.0	0.630	16.00	630.0	0.2356	201.1	300,000	0.0429	0.1407	0.0707	0.2320
250	37	0.082	2.08	82.0	0.575	14.61	575.0	0.1963	167.5	250,000	0.0515	0.1690	0.0847	0.2779
4/0	19	0.106	2.69	106.0	0.528	13.41	528.0	0.2190	141.3	211,600	0.0608	0.1995	0.100	0.328
3/0	19	0.094	2.39	94.0	0.470	11.94	470.0	0.1735	111.9	167,800	0.0766	0.2513	0.126	0.413
2/0	19	0.084	2.13	84.0	0.418	10.62	418.0	0.1372	88.53	133,100	0.0967	0.3173	0.159	0.522
1/0	19	0.074	1.88	74.0	0.372	9.449	372.0	0.1087	70.12	105,600	0.122	0.400	0.201	0.659

Electrical Conductors - Physical And Electrical Properties - Stranded Wires(cont.)

Nominal Wire Size (AWG or kcmil)	Stranding				Overall Wire Diameter			Cross-sectional Area			Nominal Direct Current Resistance @ 167°F (75°C)			
	Number of Strands	Strand Diameter									Uncoated Copper		Aluminum	
		in.	mm	mils	in	mm	mils	sq in	sqmm	cir mil	ohms/1000 ft	ohms/1000 m	ohms/1000 ft	ohms/1000 m
1	19	0.066	1.68	66.0	0.332	8.433	332.0	0.0866	55.85	83,690	0.154	0.505	0.253	0.830
2	7	0.097	2.46	97.0	0.292	7.417	292.0	0.0670	43.20	66,360	0.194	0.634	0.319	1.05
3	7	0.087	2.21	87.0	0.260	6.604	260.0	0.0531	34.25	52,620	0.245	0.804	0.403	1.32
4	7	0.077	1.96	77.0	0.232	5.893	232.0	0.0423	27.27	41,740	0.308	1.01	0.508	1.67
6	7	0.061	1.55	61.0	0.184	4.674	184.0	0.0266	17.16	26,240	0.491	1.61	0.808	2.65
8	7	0.049	1.24	49.0	0.146	3.708	146.0	0.0167	10.80	16,510	0.778	2.55	1.28	4.20
10	7	0.038	0.97	38.0	0.116	2.946	116.0	0.0106	6.818	10,380	1.24	4.07	2.04	6.69
12	7	0.030	0.76	30.0	0.092	2.337	92.0	0.0066	4.289	6,530	1.98	6.50	3.25	10.7
14	7	0.024	0.61	24.0	0.073	1.854	73.0	0.0042	2.700	4,110	3.14	10.3	5.17	17.0
16	7	0.019	0.48	19.0	0.058	1.473	58.0	0.0026	1.705	2,580	4.99	16.4	8.21	26.9
18	7	0.015	0.38	15.0	0.046	1.168	46.0	0.0017	1.072	1,620	7.95	26.1	13.1	43.0

NOTES:
(1) Based on resistivity for annealed copper at 75°C (167°F) of 12.87 ohm circular mil per foot.
(2) Based on resistivity for aluminum at 75°C (167°F) of 21.18 ohm circular mil per foot.
(3) A similar table may be found in the *NFPA National Electrical Code 1999*, National Fire Protection Association, Inc., Quincy, MA.
(4) Resistance increases with increasing temperature and temperature increases with increasing amperage carried by a wire.
   Equation for temperature change: Resistance @ new temperature = Resistance @ 75°C [1 + a (new temperature in °C.- 75°C))]
   where: a for copper = 0.00323 and for aluminum = 0.00330.
(5) Abbreviations: AWG = American Wire Gage, kcmil = thousand circular mil, in.=inches, mm= millimeter, m= meter, sq.= square, lbs = pounds, kg= kilograms

Voltage Drop vs. Wire Size

Voltage drop is the amount of voltage lost over the length of a circuit. Voltage drop changes as a function of the resistance of the wire and should be less than 2% if possible. If the drop is greater than 2%, efficiency of the equipment in the circuit is severely decreased and life of the equipment will be decreased. As an example, if the voltage drop on an incandescent light bulb is 10%, the light output of the bulb decreases more than 30%!

Voltage drop can be calculated using Ohm's Law, which is:

$$Voltage\ Drop = Current\ in\ amperes\ \times\ Resistance\ in\ ohms$$

For example, the voltage drop over a 200 ft. long, #14 copper, 2 wire cable supplying a 1000 watt floodlight is calculated as follows:

Current = 1000 watts / 120 volts = 8.33 amperes
Resistance of #14 solid copper wire = 2.58 ohms / 1000 feet @ 77°F
Resistance of power line = 2 x 200 feet x 0.00258 ohms/foot
       = 1.032 ohms
Voltage drop = 8.33 amperes x 1.032 ohms = 8.60 volts
Percent voltage drop = 8.60 volts / 120 volts = 7.2 %

The 7.2% drop is over the maximum 2% so either the wattage of the bulb must be decreased or the diameter of the wire must be increased (a decrease in wire gauge number). If #8 solid copper wire were used in the above example, the voltage drop would have only been 1.8%. Resistance values for various size wire are contained in the Electrical Conductors table on page 207.

A more commonly used method of calculating voltage drop is as follows:

$$Voltage\ drop = \frac{K \times P \times Wire\ length\ in\ ft. \times Current\ in\ amperes}{Wire\ area\ in\ circular\ mils}$$

K = Specific resistivity in ohm - circular mils / foot.

Wire	Temp	K	Temp	K
Solid Copper	77°-121°F	11	122°-167°F	12
Solid Aluminum	77°-121°F	18	122°-167°	20
Stranded Copper	77°-121°F	11	122°-167°F	12
Stranded Aluminum	77°-121°F	19	122°-167°F	20

P = Phase constant = 2 for single phase, 1.732 for three phase

Using values from the Ohm's Law example at the top of this page: #14 solid copper wire has an area of 4110 circular mils, then voltage drop in a single phase circuit is (11 x 2 x 200 x 8.33) / 4110 = 8.92 volts or in percent, 8.92 volts / 120 volts = 7.4%.

Wire area in circular mils is given in the Electrical Conductors table on page 207.

An interesting corollary to the above example is that if the line voltage doubles (240 volts instead of 120 volts) the voltage drop in percent decreases by a factor of 4. That means that a line can carry the same power 4 times further! Higher voltage lines are more efficient.

Wire Size vs. Voltage Drop
Copper Wire, Solid, 2-Conductor, K-11 (77°-121°F)

Amps	Volt-Amps	#14	#12	#10	#8	#6
Max Wire Feet @ 120 Volts, 1 Phase, 2% Max Voltage Drop						
1	120	450	700	1100	1800	2800
5	600	90	140	225	360	575
10	1200	45	70	115	180	285
15	1800	30	47	75	120	190
20	2400	...	36	57	90	140
25	3000	...	...	45	72	115
30	3600	...	...	38	60	95
40	4800	...	...	...	45	72
50	6000	...	...	...	...	57
Amps	Volt-Amps	#4	#2	1/0	2/0	3/0
1	120	4500	7000	...	...	...
5	600	910	1400	2250	2800	...
10	1200	455	705	1100	1400	1800
15	1800	305	485	770	965	1200
20	2400	230	365	575	725	900
25	3000	180	290	460	580	720
30	3600	150	240	385	490	600
40	4800	115	175	290	360	440
50	6000	90	145	230	290	360
60	7200	76	120	190	240	305
70	8400	65	105	165	205	260
80	9600	...	...	144	180	230

Amps	Volt-Amps	#14	#12	#10	#8	#6
Max Wire Feet @ 240 Volts, 1 Phase, 2% Max Voltage Drop						
1	240	900	1400	2200	3600	5600
5	1200	180	285	455	720	1020
10	2400	90	140	225	360	525
15	3600	60	95	150	240	350
20	4800	...	70	110	180	265
25	6000	...	...	90	144	210
30	7200	...	...	75	120	175
40	5600	...	...	...	90	130
50	12000	...	...	...	...	105
Amps	Volt-Amps	#4	#2	1/0	2/0	3/0
1	240	9000	...	...	...	...
5	1200	1750	2800	4500	5600	7000
10	2400	910	1400	2200	2800	3600
15	3600	605	965	1500	1900	2400
20	4800	455	725	1100	1400	1800
25	6000	365	580	920	1100	1440
30	7200	300	485	770	970	1200
40	5600	230	360	575	725	880
50	12000	180	290	460	580	720
60	14400	150	240	385	485	600
70	16800	130	205	330	415	520
80	19200	...	180	290	365	440
100	24000	...	...	230	280	360
150	36000	...	...	185	190	240
200	48000	...	...	...	...	180

NOTE: for K=12,(122°-167°F) multiply values in table by 0.92.

Maximum Number of Conductors and Fixture Wires
In Electrical Flexible Metal Tubing or Conduit

Insulator Type Letters	Conductor Size AWG or kcmil	Conduit Trade Sizes in inches									
		1/2	3/4	1	1-1/4	1-1/2	2	2-1/2	3	3-1/2	4
RH	14	6	10	15	24	35	62	94	135	184	240
RHH, RHW, RHW-2	12	5	8	12	19	28	50	75	108	148	193
	14	4	7	11	17	25	44	67	96	131	171
	12	3	6	9	14	21	37	55	80	109	142
	10	3	5	7	11	17	30	45	64	88	115
	8	1	2	4	6	9	15	23	34	46	60
	6	1	1	3	5	7	12	19	27	37	48
	4	1	1	2	4	5	10	14	21	29	37
	3	1	1	1	3	5	8	13	18	25	33
	2	1	1	1	3	4	7	11	16	22	28
RHH, RHW, RHW-2	1	--	1	1	1	2	5	7	10	14	19
	1/0	--	1	1	1	2	4	6	9	12	16
	2/0	--	1	1	1	1	3	5	8	11	14
	3/0	--	--	1	1	1	3	5	7	9	12
	4/0	--	--	1	1	1	2	4	6	8	10
	250	--	--	--	1	1	1	3	4	6	8
	300	--	--	--	1	1	1	2	4	5	7
	350	--	--	--	1	1	1	2	3	5	6
	400	--	--	--	1	1	1	1	3	4	6
	500	--	--	--	--	1	1	1	3	4	5

Maximum Number of Conductors and Fixture Wires (cont.)
In Electrical Flexible Metal Tubing Or Conduit

Insulator Type Letters	Conductor Size AWG or kcmil	Conduit Trade Sizes in inches									
		1/2	3/4	1	1-1/4	1-1/2	2	2-1/2	3	3-1/2	4
RH, RHH, RHW, RHW-2	600	---	---	---	---	1	1	1	2	3	4
	700	---	---	---	---	---	1	1	1	3	3
	750	---	---	---	---	---	1	1	1	2	3
	800	---	---	---	---	---	1	1	1	2	3
	900	---	---	---	---	---	1	1	1	2	3
	1000	---	---	---	---	---	1	1	1	1	3
	1250	---	---	---	---	---	---	1	1	1	1
	1500	---	---	---	---	---	---	1	1	1	1
	1750	---	---	---	---	---	---	1	1	1	1
	2000	---	---	---	---	---	---	---	1	1	1
TW	14	9	15	23	36	53	94	141	203	277	361
	12	7	11	18	28	41	72	108	156	212	277
	10	5	8	13	21	30	54	81	116	158	207
	8	3	5	7	11	17	30	45	64	88	115
RHH*, RHW*R, HW-2, THHW,T, HW, THW-2	14	6	10	15	24	35	62	94	135	184	240

In Electrical Flexible Metal Tubing Or Conduit (cont.)

Insulator Type Letters	Conductor Size AWG or kcmil	Conduit Trade Sizes in inches									
		1/2	3/4	1	1-1/4	1-1/2	2	2-1/2	3	3-1/2	4
RHH*, RHW*RHW-2*, THHW,THW	12	5	8	12	19	28	50	75	108	148	193
	10	4	6	10	15	22	39	59	85	115	151
RHH*, RHW* RHW-2* THHW,THW, THW-2	8	1	4	6	9	13	23	35	51	69	90
	6	1	3	4	7	10	18	27	39	53	69
	4	1	1	3	5	7	13	20	29	39	51
	3	1	1	3	4	6	11	17	25	34	44
	2	1	1	2	4	5	10	14	21	29	37
	1	1	1	1	2	4	7	10	15	20	26
RHH*, RHW*, RHW-2* TW, THHW, THW, THW-2	1/0	1	1	1	1	3	6	9	12	17	22
	2/0	---	1	1	1	3	5	7	10	14	19
	3/0	---	1	1	1	2	4	6	9	12	16
	4/0	---	---	1	1	1	3	5	7	10	13
	250	---	---	1	1	1	3	4	6	8	11
	300	---	---	1	1	1	2	3	5	7	9
	350	---	---	1	1	1	1	3	4	6	8
	400	---	---	---	1	1	1	3	4	6	7
	500	---	---	---	1	1	1	2	3	5	6
	600	---	---	---	---	1	1	1	3	4	5

Maximum Number of Conductors and Fixture Wires (cont.)

In Electrical Flexible Metal Tubing Or Conduit

Insulator Type Letters	Conductor Size AWG or kcmil	Conduit Trade Sizes in inches									
		1/2	3/4	1-1/4	1-1/2	2	2-1/2	3	3-1/2	4
H*, RHW*, TW, RHW-2*, THW, THHW, †THW, THW-2	700	---	---	---	---	---	1	1	2	3	4
	750	---	---	---	---	---	1	1	2	3	4
	800	---	---	---	---	---	1	1	1	3	4
	900	---	---	---	---	1	1	1	2	3	3
	1000	---	---	---	---	1	1	1	2	3	3
	1250	---	---	---	---	1	1	1	1	2	2
	1500	---	---	---	---	1	1	1	1	1	1
	1750	---	---	---	---	1	1	1	1	1	1
	2000	---	---	---	---	---	1	1	1	1	1
THHN, THWN, THWN-2	14	13	22	52	76	134	202	291	396	518
	12	9	16	38	56	98	147	212	289	378
	10	6	10	24	35	62	93	134	182	238
	8	3	6	14	20	35	53	77	105	137
	6	2	4	10	14	25	38	55	76	99
	4	1	2	6	9	16	24	34	46	61
	3	1	1	5	7	13	20	29	39	51
	2	1	1	4	6	11	17	24	33	43
	1	1	1	3	4	8	12	18	24	32
	1/0	1	1	2	4	7	10	15	20	27
	2/0	---	1	1	3	6	9	12	17	22

In Electrical Flexible Metal Tubing Or Conduit (cont.)

Insulator Type Letters	Conductor Size AWG or kcmil	Conduit Trade Sizes in inches									
		1/2	3/4	1	1-1/4	1-1/2	2	2-1/2	3	3-1/2	4
THHN, THWN, THWN-2	3/0	- - -	1	1	1	2	5	7	10	14	18
	4/0	- - -	1	1	1	1	4	6	8	12	15
	250	- - -	- - -	1	1	1	3	5	7	9	12
	300	- - -	- - -	1	1	1	3	4	6	8	11
	350	- - -	- - -	1	1	1	2	3	5	7	9
	400	- - -	- - -	1	1	1	1	3	5	6	8
	500	- - -	- - -	1	1	1	1	3	4	5	7
	600	- - -	- - -	1	1	1	1	2	3	4	5
	700	- - -	- - -	- - -	- - -	1	1	1	3	4	5
	750	- - -	- - -	- - -	- - -	1	1	1	2	3	4
	800	- - -	- - -	- - -	- - -	1	1	1	2	3	4
	900	- - -	- - -	- - -	- - -	- - -	1	1	1	3	4
	1000	- - -	- - -	- - -	- - -	- - -	1	1	1	3	3
XHH, XHHW, XHHW-2, ZW	14	9	15	23	36	53	94	141	203	277	361
	12	7	11	18	28	41	72	108	156	212	277
	10	5	8	13	21	30	54	81	116	158	207
	8	3	5	7	11	17	30	45	64	88	115
	6	1	3	5	8	12	22	33	48	65	85
	4	1	2	4	6	9	16	24	34	47	61
	3	1	1	3	5	7	13	20	29	40	52
	2	1	1	3	4	6	11	17	24	33	44

Maximum Number of Conductors and Fixture Wires (cont.)

Electrical Flexible Metal Tubing Or Conduit

Insulator Type Letters	Conductor Size AWG or kcmil	Conduit Trade Sizes in inches									
		1/2	3/4	1	1-1/4	1-1/2	2	2-1/2	3	3-1/2	4
	1	1	1	1	3	5	8	13	18	25	32
	1/0	1	1	1	2	4	7	10	15	21	27
	2/0	---	1	1	2	3	6	9	13	17	23
	3/0	---	1	1	2	3	5	7	10	14	19
	4/0	---	1	1	1	2	4	6	9	12	15
	250	---	---	1	1	1	3	5	7	10	13
	300	---	---	1	1	1	3	4	6	8	11
	350	---	---	1	1	1	2	4	5	7	9
	400	---	---	1	1	1	1	3	4	6	8
XHH, XHHW, XHHW-2	500	---	---	---	1	1	1	1	3	5	7
	600	---	---	---	1	1	1	1	3	4	5
	700	---	---	---	---	1	1	1	2	4	5
	750	---	---	---	---	---	1	1	2	3	4
	800	---	---	---	---	---	1	1	1	3	4
	900	---	---	---	---	---	1	1	1	3	4
	1000	---	---	---	---	---	1	1	1	3	3
	1250	---	---	---	---	---	1	1	1	1	3
	1500	---	---	---	---	---	1	1	1	1	3
	1750	---	---	---	---	---	---	1	1	1	2
	2000	---	---	---	---	---	---	1	1	1	1
TFN, TFFN	18	23	38	59	93	135	237	---	---	---	---
	16	17	29	45	71	103	181	---	---	---	---

Maximum Number of Conductors and Fixture Wires In Electrical Metal Tubing or Conduit

Insulator Type Letters	Conductor Size AWG or kcmil	Conduit Trade Sizes in inches										
		1/2	3/4	1	1-1/4	1-1/2	2	2-1/2	3	3-1/2	4
RH	14	6	10	16	28	39	64	112	169	221	282
	12	4	8	13	23	31	51	90	136	177	227
RHH, RHW	14	4	7	11	20	27	46	80	120	157	201
RHW-2	12	3	6	9	17	23	38	66	100	131	167
	10	2	5	8	13	18	30	53	81	105	135
	8	1	2	4	7	9	16	28	42	55	70
	6	1	1	3	5	8	13	22	34	44	56
	4	1	1	2	4	6	10	17	26	34	44
	3	1	1	1	4	5	9	15	23	30	38
	2	1	1	1	3	4	7	13	20	26	33
	1	...	1	1	1	3	5	9	13	17	22
RH, RHH, RHW, RHW-2	1/0	...	1	1	1	2	4	7	11	15	19
	2/0	...	1	1	1	2	4	6	10	13	17
	3/0	...	...	1	1	1	3	5	8	11	14
	4/0	...	...	1	1	1	3	5	7	9	12
	250	...	...	...	1	1	1	3	5	7	9
	300	...	...	...	1	1	1	3	5	6	8
	350	...	...	...	1	1	1	3	4	6	7
	400	...	...	...	1	1	1	2	4	5	7
	500	...	...	...	...	1	1	2	3	4	6

* Types RHH, RHW, and RHW-2 without outer covering.

Maximum Number of Conductors and Fixture Wires (cont.) In Electrical Metal Tubing or Conduit

Insulator Type Letters	Conductor Size AWG or kcmil	Conduit Trade Sizes in inches									
		1/2	3/4	1	1-1/4	1-1/2	2	2-1/2	3	3-1/2	4
RH, RHH, RHW, RHW-2	600	---	---	---	---	---	1	1	3	4	5
	700	---	---	---	---	---	1	1	3	3	4
	750	---	---	---	---	---	1	1	2	3	4
	800	---	---	---	---	---	1	1	2	3	4
	900	---	---	---	---	---	1	1	1	3	3
	1000	---	---	---	---	---	1	1	1	3	3
	1250	---	---	---	---	---	---	1	1	2	2
	1500	---	---	---	---	---	---	1	1	1	1
	1750	---	---	---	---	---	---	1	1	1	1
	2000	---	---	---	---	---	---	1	1	1	1
TW	14	8	15	25	43	58	96	168	254	332	424
	12	6	11	19	33	45	74	129	195	255	326
	10	5	8	14	24	33	55	96	145	190	243
	8	2	5	8	13	18	30	53	81	105	135
RHH*, RHW* RHW-2*, THHW, THW, THW-2	14	6	10	16	28	39	64	112	169	221	282
RHH*, RHW* THHW, THW-2	12	4	8	13	23	31	51	90	136	177	227
RHW-2*, THW THHW, THW	10	3	6	10	18	24	40	70	106	138	177

* Types RHH, RHW, and RHW-2 without outer covering.

In Electrical Metal Tubing or Conduit (cont.)

Insulator Type Letters	Conductor Size AWG or kcmil	Conduit Trade Sizes in inches									
		1/2	3/4	1	1-1/4	1-1/2	2	2-1/2	3	3-1/2	4
RHH*, RHW* RHW-2*, THW, THW-2	8	1	4	6	10	14	24	42	63	83	106
	6	1	3	4	8	11	18	32	48	63	81
	4	1	1	3	6	8	13	24	36	47	60
	3	1	1	3	5	7	12	20	31	40	52
	2	1	1	2	4	6	10	17	26	34	44
	1	1	1	1	3	4	7	12	18	24	31
RHH*, RHW* RHW-2* TW, THW, THW-2	1/0	- - -	1	1	2	3	6	10	16	20	26
	2/0	- - -	1	1	1	3	5	9	13	17	22
	3/0	- - -	1	1	1	2	4	7	11	15	19
	4/0	- - -	- - -	1	1	1	3	6	9	12	16
	250	- - -	- - -	1	1	1	3	5	7	10	13
	300	- - -	- - -	1	1	1	2	4	6	8	11
	350	- - -	- - -	- - -	1	1	1	4	6	7	10
	400	- - -	- - -	- - -	1	1	1	3	5	7	9
	500	- - -	- - -	- - -	1	1	1	3	4	6	7
	600	- - -	- - -	- - -	1	1	1	2	3	4	6
	700	- - -	- - -	- - -	- - -	1	1	1	3	4	5
	750	- - -	- - -	- - -	- - -	1	1	1	3	4	5
	800	- - -	- - -	- - -	- - -	1	1	1	3	3	5
	900	- - -	- - -	- - -	- - -	1	1	1	2	3	4
	1000	- - -	- - -	- - -	- - -	1	1	1	1	3	4
	1250	- - -	- - -	- - -	- - -	- - -	1	1	1	2	3
	1500	- - -	- - -	- - -	- - -	- - -	1	1	1	1	3
	1750	- - -	- - -	- - -	- - -	- - -	- - -	1	1	1	2
	2000	- - -	- - -	- - -	- - -	- - -	- - -	1	1	1	1

Maximum Number of Conductors and Fixture Wires (cont.)

In Electrical Metal Tubing or Conduit

Insulator Type Letters	Conductor Size AWG or kcmil	Conduit Trade Sizes in inches									
		1/2	3/4	1	1-1/4	1-1/2	2	2-1/2	3	3-1/2	4
THHN, THWN, THWN-2	14	12	22	35	61	84	138	241	364	476	608
	12	9	16	26	45	61	101	176	266	347	443
	10	5	10	16	28	38	63	111	167	219	279
	8	3	6	9	16	22	36	64	96	126	161
	6	2	4	7	12	16	26	46	69	91	116
	4	1	2	4	7	10	16	28	43	56	71
	3	1	1	3	6	8	13	24	36	47	60
	2	1	1	3	5	7	11	20	30	40	51
	1	1	1	1	4	5	8	15	22	29	37
	1/0	1	1	1	3	4	7	12	19	25	32
	2/0	---	1	1	2	3	6	10	16	20	26
	3/0	---	1	1	1	3	5	8	13	17	22
	4/0	---	1	1	1	2	4	7	11	14	18
	250	---	---	1	1	1	3	6	9	11	15
	300	---	---	1	1	1	3	5	7	10	13
	350	---	---	1	1	1	2	4	6	9	11
	400	---	---	1	1	1	1	4	6	8	10
	500	---	---	---	1	1	1	3	5	6	8
	600	---	---	---	1	1	1	2	4	5	7
	700	---	---	---	1	1	1	2	3	4	6

In Electrical Metal Tubing or Conduit (cont.)

Insulator Type Letters	Conductor Size AWG or kcmil	Conduit Trade Sizes in inches									
		1/2	3/4	1	1-1/4	1-1/2	2	2-1/2	3	3-1/2	4
THHN, THWN,THWN-2	750	---	---	---	---	1	1	1	3	4	5
	800	---	---	---	---	1	1	1	3	4	5
	900	---	---	---	---	1	1	1	3	3	4
	1000	---	---	---	---	1	1	1	2	3	4
	14	8	15	25	43	58	96	168	254	332	424
	12	6	11	19	33	45	74	129	195	255	326
	10	5	8	14	24	33	55	96	145	190	243
	8	2	5	8	13	18	30	53	81	105	135
XHH, XHHW XHHW-2, ZW	6	1	3	6	10	14	22	39	60	78	100
	4	1	2	4	7	10	16	28	43	56	72
	3	1	1	3	6	8	14	24	36	48	61
	2	1	1	3	5	7	11	20	31	40	51
	1	1	1	1	4	5	8	15	23	30	38

Maximum Number of Conductors and Fixture Wires (cont.)

In Electrical Metal Tubing or Conduit

Insulator Type Letters	Conductor Size AWG or kcmil	Conduit Trade Sizes in inches									
		1/2	3/4	1	1-1/4	1-1/2	2	2-1/2	3	3-1/2	4
XHH, XHHW, XHHW-2	1/0	---	1	1	3	4	7	13	19	25	32
	2/0	---	---	1	2	3	6	10	16	21	27
	3/0	---	---	1	1	3	5	9	13	17	22
	4/0	---	---	1	1	2	4	7	11	14	18
	250	---	---	1	1	1	3	6	9	12	15
	300	---	---	1	1	1	3	5	8	10	13
	350	---	---	1	1	1	2	4	7	9	11
	400	---	---	---	1	1	1	4	6	8	10
	500	---	---	---	---	1	1	3	5	6	8
	600	---	---	---	---	1	1	2	4	5	6
	700	---	---	---	---	1	1	2	3	4	6
	750	---	---	---	---	---	1	1	3	4	5
	800	---	---	---	---	---	1	1	3	3	4
	900	---	---	---	---	---	1	1	2	3	4
	1000	---	---	---	---	---	1	1	1	2	3
	1250	---	---	---	---	---	1	1	1	1	3
	1500	---	---	---	---	---	---	1	1	1	3
	1750	---	---	---	---	---	---	1	1	1	2
	2000	---	---	---	---	---	---	---	---	---	1
TFN, TFFN	18	22	38	63	108	148	244	---	---	---	---
	16	17	29	48	83	113	186	---	---	---	---

Maximum Number of Conductors and Fixture Wires In Electrical Nonmetallic Tubing or Conduit

Insulator Type Letters	Conductor Size AWG or kcmil	Conduit Trade Sizes in inches					
		1/2	3/4	1	1-1/4	1-1/2	2
RH	14	4	8	15	27	37	61
	12	3	7	12	21	29	49
RHH, RHW RHW-2	14	3	6	10	19	26	43
	12	2	5	9	16	22	36
	10	1	4	7	13	17	29
	8	1	1	3	6	9	15
	6	1	1	3	5	7	12
	4	1	1	2	4	6	9
	3	1	1	1	3	5	8
	2	---	1	1	3	4	7
RH, RHH, RHW, RHW-2	1	---	1	1	1	3	5
	1/0	---	---	1	1	2	4
	2/0	---	---	1	1	1	3
	3/0	---	---	1	1	1	3
	4/0	---	---	---	1	1	2
	250	---	---	---	1	1	1
	300	---	---	---	1	1	1
	350	---	---	---	1	1	1
	400	---	---	---	---	1	1
	500	---	---	---	---	1	1
	600	---	---	---	---	1	1
	700	---	---	---	---	---	1
	750	---	---	---	---	---	1

Maximum Number of Conductors and Fixture Wires (cont.)
In Electrical Nonmetallic Tubing or Conduit

Insulator Type Letters	Conductor Size AWG or kcmil	Conduit Trade Sizes in inches					
		1/2	3/4	1	1-1/4	1-1/2	2
RH, RHH, RHW, RHW-2	800	—	—	—	—	—	2
	900	—	—	—	—	—	1
	1000	—	—	—	—	—	1
	1250	—	—	—	—	—	—
	1500	—	—	—	—	—	—
	1750	—	—	—	—	—	—
	2000	—	—	—	—	—	—
TW	14	7	13	22	40	55	92
	12	5	10	17	31	42	71
	10	4	7	13	23	32	52
	8	2	4	7	13	17	29
RHH*, RHW*, RHW-2*, THHW, THW, THW-2	14	4	8	15	27	37	61
	12	3	7	12	21	29	49
	10	3	5	9	17	23	38
RHH*, RHW* RHW-2*, THHW, THW	8	1	3	5	10	14	23
	6	1	2	4	7	10	17
	4	1	1	3	5	8	13
	3	1	1	2	4	6	11
	2	1	1	2	4	6	9
	1	—	1	1	3	4	6
RHH*, RHW* RHW-2*, THHW, THW, THW-2	1/0	—	1	1	3	3	5
	2/0	—	—	1	2	3	5
	3/0	—	—	1	1	2	4
	4/0	—	—	1	1	1	3

In Electrical Nonmetallic Tubing or Conduit (cont.)

Insulator Type Letters	Conductor Size AWG or kcmil	Conduit Trade Sizes in inches					
		1/2	3/4	1	1-1/4	1-1/2	2
RHH*, RHW* RHW-2*, TW,THHW, THW, THW-2	250	---	---	1	1	1	2
	300	---	---	1	1	1	2
	350	---	---	1	1	1	2
	400	---	---	1	1	1	1
	500	---	---	1	1	1	1
	600	---	---	1	1	1	1
	700	---	---	---	1	1	1
	750	---	---	---	1	1	1
	800	---	---	---	---	1	1
	900	---	---	---	---	1	1
	1000	---	---	---	---	1	1
	1250	---	---	---	---	---	1
	1500	---	---	---	---	---	1
	1750	---	---	---	---	---	---
	2000	---	---	---	---	---	---
THHN, THWN, THWN-2	14	10	18	32	58	80	132
	12	7	13	23	42	58	96
	10	4	8	15	26	36	60
	8	2	5	8	15	21	35
	6	1	3	6	11	15	25
	4	1	1	4	7	9	15
	3	1	1	3	5	8	13
	2	1	1	2	5	6	11
	1	1	1	1	3	5	8

* Types RHH, RHW, and RHW-2 without outer covering.

Maximum Number of Conductors and Fixture Wires (cont.)
In Electrical Nonmetallic Tubing or Conduit (cont.)

Insulator Type Letters	Conductor Size AWG or kcmil	Conduit Trade Sizes in inches					
		1/2	3/4	1	1-1/4	1-1/2	2
THHN, THWN, THWN-2	1/0	- - -	1	1	3	4	7
	2/0	- - -	1	1	2	3	6
	3/0	- - -	1	1	1	3	5
	4/0	- - -	- - -	1	1	2	4
	250	- - -	- - -	1	1	1	4
	300	- - -	- - -	- - -	1	1	3
	350	- - -	- - -	- - -	1	1	2
	400	- - -	- - -	- - -	1	1	2
	500	- - -	- - -	- - -	1	1	1
	600	- - -	- - -	- - -	- - -	1	1
	700	- - -	- - -	- - -	- - -	1	1
	750	- - -	- - -	- - -	- - -	1	1
	800	- - -	- - -	- - -	- - -	1	1
	900	- - -	- - -	- - -	- - -	- - -	1
	1000	- - -	- - -	- - -	- - -	- - -	1
XHH, XHHW, XHHW-2, ZW	14	7	13	22	40	55	92
	12	5	10	17	31	42	71
	10	4	7	13	23	32	52
	8	1	4	7	13	17	29
	6	1	3	5	9	13	21
	4	1	1	4	7	9	15
	3	1	1	3	6	8	13
	2	1	1	2	5	6	11

In Electrical Nonmetallic Tubing or Conduit (cont.)

Insulator Type Letters	Conductor Size AWG or kcmil	Conduit Trade Sizes in inches					
		1/2	3/4	1	1-1/4	1-1/2	2
	1	- - -	1	1	3	5	8
	1/0	- - -	1	1	3	4	7
	2/0	- - -	1	1	2	3	6
	3/0	- - -	1	1	2	3	5
	4/0	- - -	- - -	1	1	2	4
	250	- - -	- - -	1	1	2	3
	300	- - -	- - -	1	1	1	3
	350	- - -	- - -	1	1	1	3
XHH, XHHW, XHHW-2	400	- - -	- - -	- - -	1	1	2
	500	- - -	- - -	- - -	1	1	1
	600	- - -	- - -	- - -	- - -	1	1
	700	- - -	- - -	- - -	- - -	1	1
	750	- - -	- - -	- - -	- - -	1	1
	800	- - -	- - -	- - -	- - -	1	1
	900	- - -	- - -	- - -	- - -	- - -	1
	1000	- - -	- - -	- - -	- - -	- - -	1
	1250	- - -	- - -	- - -	- - -	- - -	- - -
	1500	- - -	- - -	- - -	- - -	- - -	- - -
	1750	- - -	- - -	- - -	- - -	- - -	- - -
	2000	- - -	- - -	- - -	- - -	- - -	- - -

Source: National Electrical Code, 1996, National Fire Protection Association, 1 Batterymarch Park, Quincy, MA 02269

Note: The material in this table represents only a small part of the National Electrical Code. For additional information please refer directly to the Code.

Number of Conductors in Outlet, Device, and Junction Boxes and Conduit Bodies

Box Dimensions	Trade Size or Type	Min. Capacity	Maximum Number of Conductors						
			Conductor Size						
(inch)		in³	#18	#16	#14	#12	#10	#8	#6
4 x 1-1/4	round or octagonal	12.5	8	7	6	5	5	4	2
4 x 1-1/2	round or octagonal	15.5	10	8	7	6	6	5	3
4 x 2-1/8	round or octagonal	21.5	14	12	10	9	8	7	4
4 x 1-1/4	square	18.0	12	10	9	8	7	6	3
4 x 1-1/2	square	21.0	14	12	10	9	8	7	4
4 x 2-1/8	square	30.3	20	17	15	13	12	10	6
4-11/16 x 1-1/4	square	25.5	17	14	12	11	10	8	5
4-11/16 x 1-1/2	square	29.5	19	16	14	13	11	9	5
4-11/16 x 2-1/8	square	42.0	28	24	21	18	16	14	8
3 x 2 x 1-1/2	device	7.5	5	4	3	3	3	2	1
3 x 2 x 2	device	10.0	6	5	5	4	4	3	2
3 x 2 x 2-1/4	device	10.5	7	6	5	4	4	3	2
3 x 2 x 2-1/2	device	12.5	8	7	6	5	5	4	2
3 x 2 x 2-3/4	device	14.0	9	8	7	6	5	4	2
3 x 2 x 3-1/2	device	18.0	12	10	9	8	7	6	3
4 x 2-1/8 x 1-1/2	device	10.3	6	5	5	4	4	3	2
4 x 2-1/8 x 1-7/8	device	13.0	8	7	6	5	5	4	2
4 x 2-1/8 x 2-1/8	device	14.5	9	8	7	6	5	4	2
3-3/4 x 2 x 2-1/2	masonry box gang	14.0	9	8	7	6	5	4	2
3-3/4 x 2 x 3-1/2	masonry box gang	21.0	14	12	10	9	8	7	4
FS - minimum internal depth 1-3/4 inch	single cover gang	13.5	9	7	6	6	5	4	2
FD - minimum internal depth 2-3/8 inch	single cover gang	18.0	12	10	9	8	7	6	3

Number of Conductors in Outlet, Device, and Junction Boxes and Conduit Bodies (cont.)

Box Dimensions (inch)	Trade Size or Type	Min. Cap-acity in³	Maximum Number of Conductors Conductor Size						
			#18	#16	#14	#12	#10	#8	#6
FS - minimum internal depth 1-3/4 inch	multiple cover gang	18.0	12	10	9	8	7	6	3
FD - minimum internal depth 2-3/8 inch	multiple cover gang	24.0	16	13	12	10	9	8	4

Volume Required per Conductor

Size of Conductor	Free Space Within Box for Each Conductor (cubic inch)
# 18	1.50
# 16	1.75
# 14	2.00
# 12	2.25
# 10	2.50
# 8	3.00
# 6	5.00

Note: If additional devices are used in a box, each device counts as one conductor. This includes such devices as studs, clamps, or hickeys. Some devices used in a box count as two conductors. This includes such devices as straps and mounting yokes. A conductor running through a box counts as one conductor. Each conductor terminating or entering a box counts as one conductor.

Source: National Electrical Code, 1996, National Fire Protection Association, 1 Batterymarch Park, Quincy, MA 02269.

NEMA Receptacle Configurations

Straight Blade Receptacles

2 Pole, 2 Wire PLUGS-next 3 only

125V

15 Ampere (#1-15)

250 V

20 Ampere (#2-20)

30 Ampere (#2-30)

2 Pole, 3 Wire, Grounding

125V

15 Ampere (#5-15)

20 Ampere (#5-20)

30 Ampere (#5-30)

50 Ampere (#5-50)

250V

15 Ampere (#6-15)

20 Ampere (#6-20)

2 Pole, 3 Wire, Grounding (cont.)

250V (cont.)

30 Ampere (#6-30)

50 Ampere (#6-50)

277V

15 Ampere (#7-15)

20 Ampere (#7-20)

30 Ampere (#7-30)

50 Ampere (#7-50)

347 V

15 Ampere (#24-15)

20 Ampere (#24-20)

30 Ampere (#24-30)

50 Ampere (#24-50)

3 Pole, 3 Wire

125/250V

20 Ampere (#10-20)

30 Ampere (#10-30)

50 Ampere (#10-50)

3 Phase 250 V

15 Ampere (#11-15)

20 Ampere (#11-20)

30 Ampere (#11-30)

50 Ampere (#11-50)

3 Pole, 4 Wire, Grounding

125/250V

15 Ampere (#14-15)

20 Ampere (#14-20)

30 Ampere (#14-30)

Locking Receptacles

50 Ampere
(#14-50)

60 Ampere
(#14-60)

3 Phase 250V

15 Ampere
(#15-15)

20 Ampere
(#15-20)

30 Ampere
(#15-30)

50 Ampere
(#15-50)

60 Ampere
(#15-60)

4 Pole, 4 Wire
3 Phase 120/208V

15 Ampere
(#18-15)

20 Ampere
(#18-20)

30 Ampere
(#18-30)

50 Ampere
(#18-50)

60 Ampere
(#18-60)

---

2 Pole, 2 Wire
125V

15 Ampere
(#L1-15)

250 V

20 Ampere
(#L2-20)

2 Pole, 3 Wire,
Grounding
125V

15 Ampere
(#L5-15)

20 Ampere
(#L5-20)

30 Ampere
(#L5-30)

50 Ampere
(#L5-50)

60 Ampere
(#L5-60)

250V

15 Ampere
(#L6-15)

20 Ampere
(#L6-20)

30 Ampere
(#L6-30)

---

50 Ampere
(#L6-50)

60 Ampere
(#L6-60)

277 V

15 Ampere
(#L7-15)

20 Ampere
(#L7-20)

30 Ampere
(#L7-30)

50 Ampere
(#L7-50)

60 Ampere
(#L7-60)

480V

20 Ampere
(#L8-20)

30 Ampere
(#L8-30)

50 Ampere
(#L8-50)

60 Ampere
(#L8-60)

600 V

20 Ampere
(#L9-20)

600V (cont.)

30 Ampere (#L9-30)

50 Ampere (#L9-50)

60 Ampere (#L9-60)

3 Pole, 3 Wire, Grounding

125/250V

20 Ampere (#L10-20)

30 Ampere (#L10-30)

250V

15 Ampere (#L11-15)

20 Ampere (#L11-20)

30 Ampere (#L11-30)

3 Phase, 480 V

20 Ampere (#L12-20)

30 Ampere (#L12-30)

600 V 3-phase

30 Ampere (#L13-30)

3 Pole, 4 Wire, Grounding

125/250V

20 Ampere (#L14-20)

30 Ampere (#L14-30)

50 Ampere (#L14-50)

60 Ampere (#L14-60)

3 Phase, 250 V

20 Ampere (#L15-20)

30 Ampere (#L15-30)

50 Ampere (#L15-50)

60 Ampere (#L15-60)

3 Phase 480 V

20 Ampere (#L16-20)

30 Ampere (#L16-30)

50 Ampere (#L16-50)

60 Ampere (#L16-60)

3 Phase 600 V

30 Ampere (#L17-30)

50 Ampere (#L17-50)

60 Ampere (#L17-60)

4 Pole, 4 Wire

3 Phase Y, 120/208 V

20 Ampere (#L18-20)

30 Ampere (#L18-30)

3 Phase Y, 277/480V

20 Ampere (#L19-20)

30 Ampere (#L19-30)

3 Phase Y, 347/600V

20 Ampere (#L20-20)

30 Ampere (#L20-30)

4 Pole, 5 Wire, Grounding

3 Phase Y, 120/208 V

20 Ampere (#L21-20)

30 Ampere (#L21-30)

50 Ampere (#L21-50)

60 Ampere (#L21-60)

3 Phase Y, 277/480V

20 Ampere (#L22-20)

30 Ampere (#L22-30)

50 Ampere (#L22-50)

60 Ampere (#L22-60)

3 Phase Y, 347/600V

20 Ampere (#L23-20)

30 Ampere (#L23-30)

50 Ampere (#L23-50)

60 Ampere (#L23-60)

347V
20 Ampere (#L24-20)

FSL Configurations

2 Pole 3 Wire Grounding

28V DC

30 Ampere (#FSL-1)

120V/400hZ

30 Ampere (#FSL-2)

120V/400hZ, 3-Phase

30 Ampere (#FSL-3)

4 Pole 5 Wire Grounding

120/208V 3 phase Y 400 hZ

30 Ampere (#FSL-4)

Midget Locking

2 Pole 2 Wire

125 V

15 Ampere (#ML-1)

2 Pole 3 Wire Grounding

125V

15 Ampere (#ML-2)

125/250V

15 Ampere (#ML-3)

Marine Ship to Shore

2 Pole 3 Wire Grounding

125 V

50 Ampere (#SS1-50)

3 Pole, 4 Wire Grounding

125/250V

50 Ampere (#SS2-50)

Travel Trailer

2 pole, 3 Wire Grounding

120 V AC

30 Ampere (#TT)

How to Read a Motor Name Plate

This section was provided by Maintenance Troubleshooting, 273 PollyDrummond Rd, Newark, DE 19711

1. HORSEPOWER

Standard Horsepower Ratings 1 through 4000 hp			
1	30	300	1250
11/2	40	350	1500
2	50	400	1750
3	60	450	2000
5	75	500	2250
71/2	100	600	2500
10	125	700	3000
15	150	800	3500
20	200	900	4000
25	250	1000	

If the horsepower required for an application falls between two of the standard sizes given in the table, the larger size should be chosen.

This will add a safety factor and extend the life of a motor, since a reduction in the motor's operating temperature rise will result.

2. NUMBER OF PHASES

Industrial and commercial motors are usually single phase or three phase.

Because of the simplicity of the three-phase induction motor, it is the logical choice if three-phase power is available. Two-phase power may still be used in some remote locations.

3. RATED FREQUENCY

Rated frequency is the cycles per second or hertz for which the motor is designed. The abbreviation for hertz is Hz. In the United States, Canada, and foreign countries with a strong American influence, 60 hertz is used. 50 hertz is the prominent frequency in the majority of foreign countries. United States military applications often use 400 Hz motors on airplanes and ships. In addition, railroads make use of 25 Hz motors.

4. RATED VOLTAGE

Each motor is designed for optimum performance with a specific line voltage. If a motor is operated right at rated voltage it will provide the most efficient service and *longest* life.

This table lists standard voltages for polyphase induction motors:

There are special voltage requirements, such as dual voltage motors like the nameplate shown, which indicates the motor can be operated at either 230 volts or 460 volts. Also air conditioning service motors may be manufactured to operate at 208 volts.

If a motor is operated in an overvoltage condition, higher torque is developed. If shafts or couplings start to shear off, always check for overvoltage.

Within American industry it is usually less costly to choose 460 volt polyphase motors up to 200 HP, and use higher voltage motors above 200 HP. The cost savings come from not only the initial cost of the motor, but also the cost of the switchgear and wiring for the motor.

5. FULL LOAD CURRENT

As the load on a motor increases, the line current (amperage) increases. The wiring, starter, circuit breaker, and thermal overloads for a motor are all sized from nameplate amperage.

In the case of a dual voltage motor, the full load current corresponds in the same order as the voltage, i.e., this motor draws 64.0 amps at 230 volts and 32.0 amps at 460 volts.

When a motor is placed in service, the line amperage can be used to determine if the motor is *overloaded*.

Some "Rules of Thumb" for full load current are:

- At 460 volts, a 3-phase motor draws 1.25 amps/hp at rated output
- At 230 volts, a 3-phase motor draws 2.5 amps/hp at rated output
- At 230 volts, a single-phase motor draws 7 amps/hp at rated output
- At 115 volts, a single-phase motors draws 14 amps/hp at rated output

These values are only "Rules of Thumb" and should *never* be used to size switchgear, protective devices, or wire for a motor. The actual nameplate information should always be used.

6. FRAME SIZE

Motor frame dimensions have been standardized with a uniform frame size numbering system. This system was developed by NEMA and specific frame sizes have been assigned to standard motor ratings based on enclosure, horsepower and speed. See the diagram and table on page 256 for specifics.

There is one additional suffix that may be used on standard motors in the frames 284T and larger. This is an "S" inserted after the "T". This "S" stands for *short shaft*. These motors are arranged to be *directly coupled* to loads such as a centrifugal pump. They should never be used with a V-belt or chain drive.

7. ENCLOSURE TYPE

The motor nameplate enclosure is defined by the environment in which the motor operates. Different enclosures are designed to protect the windings from moisture, mechanical damage, chemical attack, or excessive heat. Explosion and ignition proof motors are designed to prevent the motor from igniting flammable gases or combustible materials.

All motor enclosures are of either Open or Totally Enclosed design.

Open Enclosure Motors (Indoor Service Only)

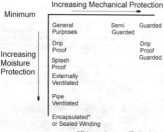

Increasing Mechanical Protection

Minimum

General Purposes	Semi Guarded	Guarded
Drip Proof		Drip Proof Guarded
Splash Proof		
Externally Ventilated		
Pipe Ventilated		
Encapsulated* or Sealed Winding		

Increasing Moisture Protection

* Not an enclosure modification, but a process of protecting random wound (encapsulated) or form wound (sealed) windings.

NEMA Electrical Enclosures

Enclosure Type	Class	Description
Type 1	general purpose	Indoor use where no oil, water or dust is present.
Type 2	Drip Tight	Indoor use where minimal dripping moisture occurs
Type 3	Rain Tight	Outdoor use for protection against snow, rain and sleet.
Type 4	Water Tight	Outdoor use for protection against massive amounts of water, such as hosing.
Type 5	Dust Tight	Protection against dust.
Type 9	Dust Tight	Protection agains dusts that are combustible.
Type 12	Industrial	Protection against oil, coolants, lints, and a variety of dusts.

Open motors

Open motors allow external air to pass directly over the windings. The windings, therefore, are exposed to ambient moisture or possible mechanical damage. The table below shows the basic types of open motors available and their relative protection from these conditions.

Open motors are best suited for clean environments and indoor service. For machinery which must be located outdoors, but will still operate in a clean environment, the motor industry has developed a "weather protected" open design. It is available in two types.

Open Enclosure Motors (Outside Service)

- **Weather Protected Type I** — Minimizes the entrance of rain, snow, or airborne particles.

- **Weather Protected Type II** — Minimizes the entrance of windborne rain, snow or particles.

Although NEMA standards define the different types of open designs, most motor manufacturers offer the open, drip proof, and guarded enclosure as standard above 200 horsepower and the Weather Protected enclosures for 200 horsepower and above. If a splash proof enclosure is required, a Totally Enclosed motor must be specified.

Totally Enclosed Motors

In totally enclosed motors, the windings and rotor are not directly exposed to external air. This design eliminates the possibility of mechanical damage to the windings. Although this enclosure is not airtight, it reduces insulation damage from ambient moisture, dirt, or chemicals.

Totally enclosed motors find applications in dirty, corrosive, or extremely wet environments. A special group of totally enclosed motors are designed to operate in atmospheres that contain flammable gases or ignitable materials.

The removal of internal heat from totally enclosed motors affects their design. The following table shows the different types of totally enclosed motors, relative to ability to operate within specific atmospheres and motor size.

Mill & Chemical Duty Motors

A mill and chemical duty motor is an especially rugged totally enclosed, fan-cooled design. Manufactured to endure the harsh environments of a smelter, mill or chemical process operation, such motors usually consist of the following:

1) Cast iron frame and end bells, with integrally cast feet. Cast iron junction box.
2) Corrosion resistant cooling fan and fan guard
3) Class F or H insulation
4) 1.15 service factor minimum
5) Sealed "lubricated-for-life" bearings
6) Automatic condensate breather at enclosure low point
7) Sealed motor leads at junction box flange
8) Epoxy paint on all exposed metal parts (except shaft)

8. TIME RATING

Most polyphase induction motors will be rated for continuous duty. Only when motors are used for some specific, well-defined applications where they will be operating for short periods of time is it possible to reduce their size, weight and cost by loading them to higher torque than would be possible if they were to operate continuously. An excellent example of a non-continuous high loading of a motor is in a residential garbage disposal. These motors usually carry a 15 minute rating.

If a motor problem develops and the nameplate on that motor indicates any *other* time rating *than continuous*, it is a good idea to time the duty cycle of the motor using a recording instrument to determine if the problem is caused by using the motor in excess of its time rating.

9. INSULATION CLASS

The four classes of insulation have an absolute temperature which cannot be exceeded without loss of insulation life. The table below defines these limits:

INSULATION CLASS	TEMPERATURE LIMIT
Class A	105° C
Class B	130° C
Class F	155° C
Class H	180° C

Class A and B insulations are hydroscopic - they absorb water. A motor with this type of insulation will rapidly degrade in outside service. In addition, when the motor is shut down, condensation can occur on the windings. Since class A and B insulations absorb moisture, the life will be shortened if condensation occurs.

Class F and H insulations are non-hydroscopic - they do not absorb moisture. If you are using a motor in an area of high ambient temperature or in an outside location, then class F and H should be used.

10. LOCKED ROTOR INDICATING LETTER

When AC motors are started with full voltage applied, they draw line currents much grater than their full load running current rating. This is commonly called the *inrush current* or *locked rotor current*. This current is a function of motor horsepower and the design characteristic of the motor.

In order to define these motor characteristics and present them in a simple fashion, a series of code letters has been established. These code letters group motors depending on the range of inrush values and express the inrush in terms of kVA (kilovolt amperes). The values for these letter code designations appear in the following table:

Code Letter	kVA/hp	Approximate Mid-Range Value
A	0.00-3.14	1.6
B	3.15-3.54	3.3
C	3.55-3.99	3.8
D	4.00-4.49	4.3
E	4.50-4.99	4.7
F	5.00-5.59	5.3
G	5.60-6.29	5.9
H	6.30-7.09	6.7
J	7.10-7.99	7.5

Code Letter	kVA/hp	Approximate Mid-Range Value
K	8.00-8.99	8.5
L	9.00-9.99	9.5
M	10.00-11.19	10.6
N	11.20-12.49	11.8
P	12.50-13.99	13.2
R	14.00-15.99	15.0

11. EFFICIENCY RATINGS

The efficiency of an electric motor is determined by how much of the electrical energy is converted into useful mechanical energy. Usually, the efficiency is expressed as a decimal on the nameplate, i.e., 87 % efficiency is expressed as .87.

In addition, NEMA has also established an index letter for efficiency rating of a motor. While some motor companies use the decimal method, others will specify an efficiency letter. The following table can be used to determine efficiency if a letter is used:

Index Letter	Nominal Efficiency	Minimum Efficiency
A	...	95.0
B	95.0	94.1
C	94.1	93.0
D	93.0	91.7
E	91.7	90.2
F	90.2	88.5
G	88.5	86.5
H	86.5	84.0
K	84.0	81.5
L	81.5	78.5
M	78.5	75.5
N	75.5	72.0
P	72.0	68.0
R	68.0	64.0
S	64.0	59.5
T	59.5	55.0
U	55.0	50.5
V	50.5	46.0
W		46.0

12. NEMA DESIGN LETTER

The NEMA Design Letter defines the *starting torque* characteristics of an induction motor. It is one of the most important pieces of information on the nameplate. Unfortunately, when a motor is being replaced the NEMA Design Letter is usually ignored.

The torque required to start the load must also be considered when selecting a new motor. Two loads with the same "load torque requirements" at operating speed can have very different "starting torque requirements." For example, fans or centrifugal pumps have starting torque requirements which increase with the square of the change in speed. In contrast, the starting torque requirements for a mixer or loaded conveyor belt with the same operating load torque requirement as the pump will change very little with speed.

NEMA Design A and B

NEMA Design A and B motors are intended for driving conventional loads such as fans, blowers and centrifugal pumps. About 80% of the induction motors used in industry today are NEMA Design B motors. They are usually an off-the-shelf item. Most loads can be accelerated by this NEMA Design due to the higher than full load locked-rotor torque and pull-up torque. However, if a motor seems to be accelerating slowly when electrical power is first applied, a motor with higher locked-rotor torque may be required.

NEMA Design C

The high locked-rotor torque and high pull-up torque of a Design C motor makes it excellently suited for "hard-to-start" applications, such as loaded conveyors or compressors. With the addition of a relatively high breakdown torque, high inertia loads such as heavy fans are also a good application for NEMA Design C motors.

NEMA Design D

With the very high locked-rotor torque, NEMA Design D motors are best used when heavy loads are suddenly applied, as with hoists, cranes, barge and rail car pullers, punch presses or machinery with flywheels. Design D motors come in different slip characteristics, grouped in *5 to 8%* slip, or *8 to 13%* slip. Actual torque characteristics may vary within these ranges. Note that the Design D motor has lower, or no, breakdown torque and full load speed will be less than an A, B or C design (slip will be higher). This loss in speed is usually not significant for the applications.

NEMA Design F

NEMA Design F motors are for "soft starts". Design F motors are most commonly used in applications requiring low starting torque to protect gears or other parts.

13. SPEED

The rated full load speed is the RPM at which the motor will run under full torque conditions when the applied voltage and frequency are held constant at the rated values.

Polyphase induction motors running unloaded operate very close to their designed synchronous speed. Under full load, squirrel cage motors operate at speeds from 1/2% to 10% below synchronous speed.

The following table lists synchronous speeds for polyphase motors at 60 hertz:

Synchronous Speed RPM at 60 Hz

*3600	720	400	277
*1800	*600	360	257
*1200	514	327	240
*900	450	300	225

Speeds marked by an asterisk(*) are common synchronous speeds for most industrial applications.

Only on rare occasions would the other speeds given in the table be found on a motor nameplate.

It is *extremely important* to recognize that the *actual speed* of a motor in operation *cannot be* determined from the nameplate RPM. If you need to know the actual speed, use of a mechanical, electrical or electronic tachometer or digital strobe tach will be required to obtain the speed within the limits of instrument accuracy.

14. SERVICE FACTOR

Motor service factor is an indication of how much overload a motor can withstand when operated under conditions of rated voltage, rated frequency and at or below maximum rated ambient temperature.

For example, if a 10 hp motor has a 1.15 service factor, then this motor is capable of operating at a 15% overload or 11.5 hp when required for a *short period of time*.

It is never a good practice to design a motor of an application which continuously loads the motor into the service factor. If the calculation of load calls for 115 hp, then a 125 hp motor should be purchased, not a 100 hp motor with a 1.15 service factor.

A service factor of 1.0 means that the motor life will be greatly shortened if overload is present.

15-16. BEARINGS

Polyphase induction motors employ either antifriction bearings or sleeve bearings. Antifriction bearings are standard in medium (integral) horsepower motor sizes up through 125 hp, 1800 RPM. Antifriction bearings are optional in 150 hp to 600 hp, 1800 RPM sizes. Sleeve bearings are standard in 500 hp, 3600 RPM and larger motors.

Antifriction Bearings

There are several ways motor bearings are identified on a motor nameplate. Before 1978, the bearing manufacturer's number was most often observed. Most bearing manufacturers use a similar method to identify basic bearing information, such as type, duty and bore. The different prefixes and suffixes used to identify bearing specifics such as seals, shields, cage design and materials, and clearances all differ between manufacturers. A bearing cross reference book is very helpful in determining the exact bearing in a motor from the manufacturer's number.

A second method of identifying bearings on a motor nameplate is becoming more common. the method employs a standard that was developed jointly by the ANSI (American National Standards Institute) and the AFBMA (Antifriction Bearing Manufacturers Association). This standard, adopted in 1978, is now used by most major motor manufacturers.

Bearing Number Nomenclature

The bearings listed on the sample nameplate are identified by their bearing number. Most bearing manufacturers still use the following nomenclature in identifying their bearings:

1. Type. The first digit (or in some instance the first two digits) identify the type of bearing. The most common antifriction bearing used in motor design is the single row, radial, deep groove, ball bearing, sometimes referred to as a *CONRAD* bearing. This bearing is primarily used to handle radial loads, but can handle moderate amounts of thrust. Standard motors up to, and including, NEMA 445U frame size can be mounted in any direction (including vertical) because of the thrust carrying capacity of this bearing. In such applications, no additional thrust can be added by the driven machinery.

Many bearing manufacturers' designation for this type of bearing is the number 6.

Since radial loads are higher at the drive end of the motor, the drive end bearing has a higher load rating. A typical nameplate might depict both bearing duties, as shown below:

Location	Bearing Number
Drive Shaft Brg.	6309 (Medium Duty)
Opp. Dr. Shaft Brg.	6207 (Light Duty)

Bearing Type - Single Row, Radial, Deep Groove, Ball Bearing

Vertical Motors with hollow shafts are usually required to carry high thrust, such as the weight of the rotating assembly in a multistage vertical pump, in addition to the weight of the motor rotor. In such motors the upper, or thrust, bearing, most often employed is a single row, angular contact ball bearing. This bearing has a high contact angle (35° or 40°). The designation for this type of bearing is the number 7.

2. Series or Duty. The next digit in the bearing number identifies the series, or duty rating, of the bearing. The common duty ratings are:

Duty Rating	Series
Extra-Light	100
Light	200
Medium	300
Heavy	400

3. Bore. The relationship between bearing number and bore can be obtained by multiplying the last two digits of the bearing number by 5. For instance, for the bearing numbers above, 6207 has a bore of 07x5 = 35 millimeters (25.4 mm equals 1 inch). The other bearing number, 6309, has a bore of 09x5=45 millimeters.

This relationship is true for bearings with a bore of 20 mm (number 05) to a bore of 480 mm (number 96).

AFBMA Designation Nomenclature

The second method used in identifying bearings on a motor nameplate employs a standard bearing designation defined by the AFBMA.

The AFBMA standard for designating bearings uses alternating sets of numbers and letters to completely identify a bearing. (See Chart on next two Pages).

17-18 MANUFACTURER'S ID NUMBERS

The manufacturer's serial number and model number can be used - often as a last resort - to identify motor characteristics. If a nameplate can no longer be read, photographic etching techniques may be used to at least determine the serial number or model number. This information can be used by the original manufacturer to supply a new nameplate for the motor.

Decoding Manufacturers ID Numbers

0000	A	A	A	00	A	AA	A	0	0

Bore

Bearing Bore in Millimeters

Type - General

B=Radial Ball
R= Cylindrical Roller
S=Self-Aligning
   (Spherical) Roller
T=Thrust, Ball or Roller

Type - Specific to "B" type

C=Single Row, Deep
   Groove (CONRAD)
L =Single Row, Filling Slot
   (Maximum Type)
N=Single Row, Angular
   Contact, Light Thrust (15°)
A=Single Row, Angular
   Contact, Medium Thrust
   (25°)
T=Single Row, Angular
   Contact, Heavy Thrust
   (35-40°)

Type - Other

Used to further define bearing types. Not normally used in motor design.

Duty Rating

02 = Light Duty
03 = Medium Duty

Decoding Manufacturers ID Numbers

<u>0000</u> <u>A</u> <u>A</u> <u>A</u> <u>00</u> <u>A</u> <u>AA</u> <u>A</u> <u>0</u> <u>0</u>

Tolerance

Defines special precision grades - not normally used in motor design

Internal Clearance

2 = Less than normal
0 = Normal
3 = Greater than normal

Special

Used to identify snap ring modifications - not normally used in motor design

Seals/Shields

E = Impervious Seal, Permanent
D = Impervious Seal, Removable
P = Shield, Permanent
A = Shield, Removable
Note: One letter used for each side, i.e.,
PP = Double Shielded Bearing

Cage Type

J = Steel, Sheet Stock, Centered by Rolling Elements
Y = nonferrous, Sheet Stock, Centered by Rolling Elements
M = Bronze or Brass Machine, Centered by Rolling Elements
T = Nonmetallic, centered by rolling elements
X = Any cage type is Acceptable

Electric Motor Specs

Note: Use the following table as a general guide only! These numbers are for normal duty applications such as fans, furnace blowers, appliances, and pumps. Exact specifications for any given motor can vary greatly from those listed below.

Specifications are for single speed, standard efficiency, 115 volt, 60 Hz, single phase, AC motors (including capacitor-start, split-phase, shaded-pole, or permanent split capacitor motors). For 230 volt motors simply divide the indicated ampreres by 2.

Motor Horsepower	RPM	Full-Load Ampere
1/20	3,000	1.5-2.9
	1,550	1.6-3.5
	1,050	2.0-3.1
1/15	5,000	1.2
	3,000	1.8-2.4
	1,550	1.3-3.2
	1,500	1.7
	1,050	1.6-4.0
	1,000	2.7
	950	3.7
1/12	1,725	2.1-2.9
	1,550	1.6
	1,450	3.1
	1,140	2.4
	1,050	1.9-3.6
	1,000	4.0
	850	3.2
1/10	10,000	1.5
	5,000	1.5
	1,550	3.1-4.6
	1,100	4.2
	1,050	3.4-4.7
	1,000	4.5
1/9	3,000	0.7
1/8	3,450	2.4
	3,000	1.8
	1,725	1.6-4.0
	1,550	4.5
	1,140	3.8
	1,075	2.3
	1,050	4.3-5.5
	850	4.6
	700	2.0
1/7	10,000	2.0
	3,450	2.0-2.4
1/6	1,725	3.0-4.2
	1,550	5.0
	1,140	3.7-4.6

Motor Horsepower	RPM	Full-Load Ampere
	1,075	2.2-2.6
1/6 (cont.)	1,050	5.6-7.1
	850	5.6-6.1
1/5	10,000	2.9-3.1
	1,050	6.0-8.0
1/4	3,450	3.5-4.1
	1,725	3.0-6.3
	1,550	7.5
	1,140	5.6-6.2
	1,075	3.3-4.0
	1,050	8.5-9.4
	850	6.9
1/3	3,450	4.9-8.6
	1,725	4.0-7.8
	1,650	5.6
	1,140	6.2-8.6
	1,075	4.2-5.1
	850	9.2
	825	4.5
1/2	10,000	6.3-7.3
	3,450	6.6-11.8
	1,725	6.3-9.6
	1,140	8.6-10.4
	1,110	8.8
	1,075	7.0
	825	6.0
3/4	3,450	9.2-14.8
	2,850	9.8
	1,725	9.8-13.3
	1,140	10.6-12.6
	1,075	9.2
1	10,000	12.1
	3,450	11.4-19.2
	1,740	13.8-14.4
	1,725	12.6-15.0
	1,140	12.6
	1,075	13.0
1-1/2	3,500	16.4
	3,450	15.4-22.0
	1,740	18.4-22.0
	1,725	14.0-20.4
2	3,500	18.8-20.8
	3,450	15.0-23.0
	1,740	19.0-25.6
	1,730	22.8
	1,725	19.0-24.6

The above general specifications are based on motor data from the 1996 Grainger Catalog, Number 387, W.W. Grainger, Inc., Chicago, IL.

Three-Phase Electric Motor Specs

HP	Full Load Amps 230V(460V)	Wire Size Minimum (AWG–Rubber) 230V(460V)	Conduit Size Inches 230V(460V)
1	3.3(1.7)	14(14)	1/2(1/2)
1.5	4.7(2.4)	14(14)	1/2(1/2)
2	6(3.0)	14(14)	1/2(1/2)
3	9(4.5)	14(14)	1/2(1/2)
5	15(7.5)	12(14)	1/2(1/2)
7.5	22(11)	8(14)	3/4(1/2)
10	27(14)	8(12)	3/4(1/2)
15	38(19)	6(10)	1-1/4(3/4)
20	52(26)	4(8)	1-1/4(3/4)
25	64(32)	3(6)	1-1/4(1-1/4)
30	77(39)	1(6)	1-1/2(1-1/4)
40	101(51)	00(4)	2(1-1/4)
50	125(63)	000(3)	2(1-1/4)
60	149(75)	200M(1)	2-1/2(1-1/2)
75	180(90)	0000(0)	2-1/2(2)
100	245(123)	500M(000)	3(2)
125	310(155)	750M(000)	3-1/2(2-1/2)
150	360(180)	1000M(300M)	4(2-1/2)
200	480(240)	NR(500M)	NR(3)
250	580(290)	NR(NR)	NR(NR)
300	696(348)	NR(NR)	NR(NR)

NR = "Not Recommended"

M = M.C.M (1000 Circular Mils).

Starting currents for the above motors can be many times the Full Load Amps, and fuses must be adjusted accordingly. If the power-line becomes too long, voltage drop will exceed safe limits and the wire size should be adjusted to the next larger (smaller AWG number) gauge wire. See the Copper Wire Specifications table (pp. 200-201) for more specific information on wire.

The above specifications are from the *National Electrical Code.*

Horsepower vs. Torque vs. RPM

	Torque in Inch Pounds-force @ Motor R.P.M.					
HP	3450	2000	1725	1550	1140	1050
1	18	32	37	41	55	60
1.5	27	47	55	61	83	90
2	37	63	73	81	111	120
3	55	95	110	122	166	180
5	91	158	183	203	276	300
7.5	137	236	274	305	415	450
10	183	315	365	407	553	600
15	274	473	548	610	829	900
20	365	630	731	813	1106	1200
25	457	788	913	1017	1382	1501
30	548	945	1096	1220	1659	1801
40	731	1261	1461	1626	2211	2401
50	913	1576	1827	2033	2764	3001
60	1096	1891	2192	2440	3317	3601
70	1279	2206	2558	2846	3870	4202
80	1461	2521	2923	3253	4423	4802
90	1644	2836	3288	3660	4976	5402
100	1827	3151	3654	4066	5529	6002
125	2284	3939	4567	5083	6911	7503
150	2740	4727	5480	6099	8293	9004
175	3197	5515	6394	7116	9675	10504
200	3654	6303	7307	8132	11057	12005
225	4110	7090	8221	9149	12439	13505
250	4567	7878	9134	10165	13821	15006
275	5024	8666	10047	11182	15203	16507
300	5480	9454	10961	12198	16586	18007
350	6394	11029	12788	14231	19350	21008
400	7307	12605	14614	16265	22114	24010
450	8221	14181	16441	18298	24878	27011
500	9134	15756	18268	20331	27643	30012
550	10047	17332	20095	22364	30407	33013
600	10961	18908	21922	24397	33171	36014

$$\text{Torque in Inch Pounds-force} = \frac{\text{Horsepower} \times 63025}{\text{Motor RPM}}$$

To convert to Foot Pounds-force, divide the torque by 12.

Horsepower vs. Torque vs. RPM   (cont.)

HP	\multicolumn{6}{c}{Torque in Inch Pounds-force @ Motor R.P.M.}
	1000	850	750	600	500	230
1	63	74	84	105	126	274
1.5	95	111	126	158	189	411
2	126	148	168	210	252	548
3	189	222	252	315	378	822
5	315	371	420	525	630	1370
7.5	473	556	630	788	945	2055
10	630	741	840	1050	1261	2740
15	945	1112	1261	1576	1891	4110
20	1261	1483	1681	2101	2521	5480
25	1576	1854	2101	2626	3151	6851
30	1891	2224	2521	3151	3782	8221
40	2521	2966	3361	4202	5042	10961
50	3151	3707	4202	5252	6303	13701
60	3782	4449	5042	6303	7563	16441
70	4412	5190	5882	7353	8824	19182
80	5042	5932	6723	8403	10084	21922
90	5672	6673	7563	9454	11345	24662
100	6303	7415	8403	10504	12605	27402
125	7878	9268	10504	13130	15756	34253
150	9454	11122	12605	15756	18908	41103
175	11029	12976	14706	18382	22059	47954
200	12605	14829	16807	21008	25210	54804
225	14181	16683	18908	23634	28361	61655
250	15756	18537	21008	26260	31513	68505
275	17332	20390	23109	28886	34664	75356
300	18908	22244	25210	31513	37815	82207
350	22059	25951	29412	36765	44118	95908
400	25210	29659	33613	42017	50420	109609
450	28361	33366	37815	47269	56723	123310
500	31513	37074	42017	52521	63025	137011
550	34664	40781	46218	57773	69328	150712
600	37815	44488	50420	63025	75630	164413

$$\text{Torque in Inch Pounds-force} = \frac{\text{Horsepower} \times 63025}{\text{Motor RPM}}$$

NOTE: Ratings below 500 RPM are for gear motors.
To convert to Foot Pounds-force, divide the torque by 12.

Horsepower vs. Torque vs. RPM (cont.)

Torque in Inch Pounds-force @ Motor R.P.M.

HP	190	155	125	100	84	68
1	332	407	504	630	750	927
1.5	498	610	756	945	1125	1390
2	663	813	1008	1261	1501	1854
3	995	1220	1513	1891	2251	2781
5	1659	2033	2521	3151	3751	4634
7.5	2488	3050	3782	4727	5627	6951
10	3317	4066	5042	6303	7503	9268
15	4976	6099	7563	9454	11254	13903
20	6634	8132	10084	12605	15006	18537
25	8293	10165	12605	15756	18757	23171
30	9951	12198	15126	18908	22509	27805
40	13268	16265	20168	25210	30012	37074
50	16586	20331	25210	31513	37515	46342
60	19903	24397	30252	37815	45018	55610
70	23220	28463	35294	44118	52521	64879
80	26537	32529	40336	50420	60024	74147
90	29854	36595	45378	56723	67527	83415
100	33171	40661	50420	63025	75030	92684
125	41464	50827	63025	78781	93787	115855
150	49757	60992	75630	94538	112545	139026
175	58049	71157	88235	110294	131302	162197
200	66342	81323	100840	126050	150060	185368
225	74635	91488	113445	141806	168817	208539
250	82928	101653	126050	157563	187574	231710
275	91220	111819	138655	173319	206332	254881
300	99513	121984	151260	189075	225089	278051
350	116099	142315	176470	220588	262604	324393
400	132684	162645	201680	252100	300119	370735
450	149270	182976	226890	283613	337634	417077
500	165855	203306	252100	315125	375149	463419
550	182441	223637	277310	346638	412664	509761
600	199026	243968	302520	378150	450179	556103

$$\text{Torque in Inch Pounds-force} = \frac{\text{Horsepower} \times 63025}{\text{Motor RPM}}$$

NOTE: Ratings below 500 RPM are for gear motors.
To convert to Foot Pounds-force, divide the torque by 12.

DC Motor Wiring Specs

HP	Full Load Amps 115V(230V)	Wire Size Minimum (AWG–Rubber) 115V(230V)	Conduit Size Inches 115V(230V)
1	8.4(4.2)	14(14)	1/2(1/2)
1.5	12.5(6.3)	12(14)	1/2(1/2)
2	16.1(8.3)	10(14)	3/4(1/2)
3	23(12.3)	8(12)	3/4(1/2)
5	40(19.8)	6(10)	1(3/4)
7.5	58(28.7)	3(6)	1-1/4(1)
10	75(38)	1(6)	1-1/2(1)
15	112(56)	00(4)	2(1-1/4)
20	140(74)	000(1)	2(1-1/2)
25	184(92)	300M(0)	2-1/2(2)
30	220(110)	400M(00)	3(2)
40	292(146)	700M(0000)	3-1/2(2-1/2)
50	360(180)	1000M(300M)	4(2-1/2)
60	NR(215)	NR(400M)	NR(3)
75	NR(268)	NR(600M)	NR(3-1/2)
100	NR(355)	NR(1000M)	NR(4)

NR = "Not Recommended"
M = M.C.M (1000 Circular Mils).

The above specifications are based on data from the *National Electrical Code.*

Electric Motor Frame Dimensions

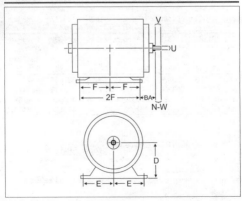

Electrical Motor Frame Dimensions (NEMA - 1984)

Frame Designation	NEMA Frame Dimensions in inches						
	D	E	2F	(BA)	(N - W)	V	U
42	2-5/8	1-3/4	11/16	2-1/16	1-1/8	- - -	3/8
42C	2-5/8	1-3/4	11/16	2-1/16	1- /8	- - -	3/8
48	3	2-1/8	2-3/4	2-1/2	1-1/2	- - -	1/2
48C	3	2-1/8	2-3/4	2-1/2	1-1/2	- - -	1/2
48H	3	2-1/8	4-3/4	2-1/2	1-1/2	- - -	1/2
56	3-1/2	2-7/16	3	2-3/4	1-7/8	- - -	5/8
56C	3-1/2	2-7/16	- - -	2-3/4	1-7/8	- - -	5/8
56H	3-1/2	2-7/16	5	2-3/4	1-7/8	- - -	5/8
56HZ	3-1/2	2-7/16	5	2-3/4	2-1/4	2	7/8
56J	3-1/2	2-7/16	- - -	2-3/4	2-7/16	- - -	5/8
66	4-1/8	2-15/16	5	3-1/8	2-1/4	- - -	3/4
140T	3-1/2	2-3/4	4	2-3/4	2-1/4	- - -	7/8
142AT	3-1/2	2-3/4	3-1/4	2-3/4	1-3/4	1-1/2	7/8
143AT	3-1/2	2-3/4	4	2-1/4	1-3/4	1-1/2	7/8
143JM	3-1/2	2-3/4	4	2-1/4	- - -	- - -	7/8
143JP	3-1/2	2-3/4	4	2-1/4	- - -	- - -	7/8
143T	3-1/2	2 - 3/4	4	2 - 1/4	2-1/4	2	7/8
143TC	3-1/2	2 - 3/4	4	2 - 3/4	2 - 1/4	- - -	7/8
143TR	3-1/2	2-3/4	4	2-1/4	2-5/8	1-3/4	7/8
144AT	3-1/2	2-3/4	4-1/2	2-3/4	1-3/4	1-1/2	7/8
145AT	3-1/2	2-3/4	5	2-3/4	1-3/4	1-1/2	7/8
145JM	3-1/2	2-3/4	5	2-1/4	- - -	- - -	7/8
145JP	3-1/2	2-3/4	5	2-1/4	- - -	- - -	7/8
145T	3-1/2	2-3/4	5	2-1/4	2-1/4	2	7/8
145TC	3-1/2	2-3/4	5	2-3/4	2-1/4	- - -	7/8
145TR	3-1/2	2-3/4	5	2-1/4	2-5/8	1-3/4	7/8
146AT	3-1/2	2-3/4	5-1/2	2-3/4	1-3/4	1-1/2	7/8
146ATC	3-1/2	2-3/4	5-1/2	2-3/4	2-1/4	- - -	7/8
147AT	3-1/2	2-3/4	6-1/4	2-3/4	1-3/4	1-1/2	7/8
148AT	3-1/2	2-3/4	7	2-3/4	1-3/4	1-1/2	7/8
149AT	3-1/2	2-3/4	8	2-3/4	1-3/4	1-1/2	7/8
1410AT	3-1/2	2-3/4	9	2-3/4	1-3/4	1-1/2	7/8
1411AT	3-1/2	2-3/4	10	2-3/4	1-3/4	1-1/2	7/8
1412AT	3-1/2	2-3/4	11	2-3/4	1-3/4	1-1/2	7/8
1412ATC	3-1/2	2-3/4	11	2-3/4	2-1/4	- - -	7/8
162AT	4	3-1/8	4	2-1/2	1-3/4	1-1/2	7/8
163AT	4	3-1/8	4-1/2	2-1/2	1-3/4	1-1/2	7/8
164AT	4	3-1/8	5	2-1/2	1-3/4	1-1/2	7/8
165AT	4	3-1/8	5-1/2	2-1/2	1-3/4	1-1/2	7/8
166AT	4	3-1/8	6-1/4	2-1/2	1-3/4	1-1/2	7/8
167AT	4	3-1/8	7	2-1/2	1-3/4	1-1/2	7/8

Electric Motor Frame Dimensions (cont.)

Frame Designation	NEMA Frame Dimensions in inches						
	D	E	2F	(BA)	(N - W)	V	U
168AT	4	3-1/8	8	2-1/2	1-3/4	1-1/2	7/8
169AT	4	3-1/8	9	2-1/2	1-3/4	1-1/2	7/8
1610AT	4	3-1/8	10	2-1/2	1-3/4	1-1/2	7/8
182	4-1/2	3-3/4	4-1/2	2-3/4	2-1/4	2	7/8
L182ACY	4-1/2	3-3/4	4-1/2	2-3/4	2-1/4	2	7/8
182AT	4-1/2	3-3/4	4-1/2	2-3/4	2-1/4	2	1-1/8
L182AT	4-1/2	3-3/4	4-1/2	2-3/4	2-1/4	2	1-1/8
182JM	4-1/2	3-3/4	4-1/2	2-3/4	- - -	- - -	7/8
182JP	4-1/2	3-3/4	4-1/2	2-3/4	- - -	- - -	7/8
182T	4-1/2	3-3/4	4-1/2	2-3/4	2-3/4	2-1/2	1-1/8
182TC	4-1/2	3-3/4	4-1/2	2-3/4	2-3/4	- - -	1-1/8
182TR	4-1/2	3-3/4	4-1/2	2-3/4	3-3/8	2-1/4	1-1/8
183AT	4-1/2	3-3/4	5	2-3/4	2-1/4	2	1-1/8
184	4-1/2	3-3/4	5-1/2	2-3/4	2-1/4	2	7/8
184AT	4-1/2	3-3/4	5-1/2	2-3/4	2-1/4	2	1-1/8
184JM	4-1/2	3-3/4	5-1/2	2-3/4	- - -	- - -	7/8
184JP	4-1/2	3-3/4	5-1/2	2-3/4	- - -	- - -	7/8
184TC	4-1/2	3-3/4	5-1/2	2-3/4	2-3/4	- - -	1-1/8
184T	4-1/2	3-3/4	5-1/2	2-3/4	2-3/4	2-1/2	1-1/8
184TR	4-1/2	3-3/4	5-1/2	2-3/4	3-3/8	2-1/4	1-1/8
185AT	4-1/2	3-3/4	6-1/4	2-3/4	2-1/4	2	1-1/8
186ACY	4-1/2	3-3/4	7	2-3/4	2-1/4	2	7/8
186AT	4-1/2	3-3/4	7	2-3/4	2-1/4	2	1-1/8
L186AT	4-1/2	3-3/4	7	2-3/4	2-1/4	2	1-1/8
186ATC	4-1/2	3-3/4	7	2-3/4	2-1/4	---	1-1/8
187AT	4-1/2	3-3/4	8	2-3/4	2-1/4	2	1-1/8
188AT	4-1/2	3-3/4	9	2-3/4	2-1/4	2	1-1/8
189AT	4-1/2	3-3/4	10	2-3/4	2-1/4	2	1-1/8
189ATC	4-1/2	3-3/4	10	2-3/4	2-1/4	---	1-1/8
1810AT	4-1/2	3-3/4	11	2-3/4	2-1/4	2	1-1/8
203	5	4	5-1/2	3-1/8	2-1/4	2	3/4
204	5	4	6-1/4	3-1/8	2-1/4	2	3/4
213	5-1/4	4-1/4	5-1/2	3-1/2	3	2-3/4	1-1/8
213AT	5-1/4	4-1/4	5-1/2	3-1/2	2-3/4	2-1/2	1-3/8
213JM	5-1/4	4-1/4	5-1/2	3-1/2	---	---	7/8
213JP	5-1/4	4-1/4	5-1/2	3-1/2	---	---	1-1/4
213T	5-1/4	4-1/4	5-1/2	3-1/2	3-3/8	3-1/8	1-3/8
213TC	5-1/4	4-1/4	5-1/2	3-1/2	3-3/8	---	1-3/8
213TR	5-1/4	4-1/4	5-1/2	3-1/2	4-1/8	2-5/8	1-3/8
214AT	5-1/4	4-1/4	6-1/4	3-1/2	2-3/4	2-1/2	1-3/8
215	5-1/4	4-1/4	7	3-1/2	3	2-3/4	1-1/8

Electric Motor Frame Dimensions (cont.)

Frame Designation	NEMA Frame Dimensions in inches						
	D	E	2F	(BA)	(N - W)	V	U
215AT	5-1/4	4-1/4	7	3-1/2	2-3/4	2-1/2	1-3/8
215JM	5-1/4	4-1/4	7	3-1/2	---	---	7/8
215JP	5-1/4	4-1/4	7	3-1/2	---	---	1-1/4
215T	5-1/4	4-1/4	7	3-1/2	3-3/8	3-1/8	1-3/8
215TC	5-1/4	4-1/4	7	3-1/2	3-3/8	---	1-3/8
215TR	5-1/4	4-1/4	7	3-1/2	4-1/8	2-5/8	1-3/8
216AT	5-1/4	4-1/4	8	3-1/2	2-3/4	2-1/2	1-3/8
217AT	5-1/4	4-1/4	9	3-1/2	2-3/4	2-1/2	1-3/8
218AT	5-1/4	4-1/4	10	3-1/2	2-3/4	2-1/2	1-3/8
219AT	5-1/4	4-1/4	11	3-1/2	2-3/4	2-1/2	1-3/8
219ATC	5-1/4	4-1/4	11	3-1/2	2-3/4	---	1-3/8
2110AT	5-1/4	4-1/4	12-1/2	3-1/2	2-3/4	2-1/2	1-3/8
2110ATC	5-1/4	4-1/4	12-1/2	3-1/2	2-3/4	---	1-3/8
224	5-1/2	4-1/2	6-3/4	3-1/2	3	2-3/4	1
225	5-1/2	4-1/2	7-1/2	3-1/2	3	2-3/4	1
253AT	6-1/4	5	7	4-1/4	3-1/4	3	1-5/8
254	6-1/4	5	8-1/4	4-1/4	3-3/8	3-1/8	1-1/8
254AT	6-1/4	5	8-1/4	4-1/4	3-1/4	3	1-5/8
254T	6-1/4	5	8-1/4	4-1/4	4	3-3/4	1-5/8
254TC	6-1/4	5	8-1/4	4-1/4	4	---	1-5/8
254TR	6-1/4	5	8-1/4	4-1/4	4-1/2	2-7/8	1-5/8
254U	6-1/4	5	8-1/4	4-1/4	3-3/4	3-1/2	1-3/8
255AT	6-1/4	5	9	4-1/4	3-1/4	3	1-5/8
256AT	6-1/4	5	10	4-1/4	3-1/4	3	1-5/8
256T	6-1/4	5	10	4-1/4	4	3-3/4	1-5/8
256TC	6-1/4	5	10	4-1/4	4	---	1-5/8
256TR	6-1/4	5	10	4-1/4	4-1/2	2-7/8	1-5/8
256U	6-1/4	5	10	4-1/4	3-3/4	3-1/2	1-3/8
257AT	6-1/4	5	11	4-1/4	3-1/4	3	1-5/8
258AT	6-1/4	5	12-1/2	4-1/4	3-1/4	3	1-5/8
259AT	6-1/4	5	14	4-1/4	3-1/4	3	1-5/8
283AT	7	5-1/2	8	4-3/4	3-3/4	3-1/2	1-7/8
284	7	5-1/2	9-1/2	4-3/4	3-3/4	3-1/2	1-1/4
284AT	7	5-1/2	9-1/2	4-3/4	3-3/4	3-1/2	1-7/8
284T	7	5-1/2	9-1/2	4-3/4	4-5/8	4-3/8	1-7/8
284TC	7	5-1/2	9-1/2	4-3/4	4-5/8	---	1-7/8
284TR	7	5-1/2	9-1/2	4-3/4	3-3/4	3-1/8	1-7/8
284TS	7	5-1/2	9-1/2	4-3/4	3-1/4	3	1-5/8
284U	7	5-1/2	9-1/2	4-3/4	4-7/8	4-5/8	1-5/8
285AT	7	5-1/2	10	4-3/4	3-3/4	3-1/2	1-7/8
286AT	7	5-1/2	11	4-3/4	3-3/4	3-1/2	1-7/8

Electric Motor Frame Dimensions (cont.)

Frame Designation	NEMA Frame Dimensions in inches						
	D	E	2F	(BA)	(N - W)	V	U
286T	7	5-1/2	11	4-3/4	4-5/8	4-3/8	1-7/8
286TC	7	5-1/2	11	4-3/4	4-5/8	---	1-7/8
286TR	7	5-1/2	11	4-3/4	4-3/4	3-1/8	1-7/8
286TS	7	5-1/2	11	4-3/4	3-1/4	3	1-5/8
286U	7	5-1/2	11	4-3/4	4-7/8	4-5/8	1-5/8
287AT	7	5-1/2	12-1/2	4-3/4	3-3/4	3-1/2	1-7/8
288AT	7	5-1/2	14	4-3/4	3-3/4	3-1/2	1-7/8
289AT	7	5-1/2	16	4-3/4	3-3/4	3-1/2	1-7/8
323AT	8	6-1/4	9	5-1/4	4-1/4	4	2-1/8
324	8	6-1/4	10-1/2	5-1/4	4-7/8	4-5/8	1-5/8
324AT	8	6-1/4	10-1/2	5-1/4	4-1/4	4	2-1/8
324TR	8	6-1/4	10-1/2	5-1/4	5-1/4	3-1/2	2-1/8
324TS	8	6-1/4	10-1/2	5-1/4	3-3/4	3-1/2	1-7/8
324U	8	6-1/4	10-1/2	5-1/4	5-5/8	5-3/8	1-7/8
325AT	8	6-1/4	11	5-1/4	4-1/4	4	2-1/8
326	8	6-1/4	12	5-1/4	4-7/8	4-5/8	1-5/8
326AT	8	6-1/4	12	5-1/4	4-1/4	4	2-1/8
326T	8	6-1/4	12	5-1/4	5-1/4	5	2-1/8
326TR	8	6-1/4	12	5-1/4	5-1/4	3-1/2	2-1/8
326TS	8	6-1/4	12	5-1/4	3-3/4	3-1/2	1-7/8
326U	8	6-1/4	12	5-1/4	5-5/8	5-3/8	1-7/8
327AT	8	6-1/4	14	5-1/4	4-1/4	4	2-1/8
328AT	8	6-1/4	16	5-1/4	4-1/4	4	2-1/8
329AT	8	6-1/4	18	5-1/4	4-1/4	4	2-1/8
363AT	9	7	10	5-7/8	4-3/4	4-1/2	2-3/8
364	9	7	11-1/4	5-7/8	5-5/8	5-3/8	1-7/8
364AT	9	7	11-1/4	5-7/8	4-3/4	4-1/2	2-3/8
364S	9	7	11-1/4	5-7/8	3-1/4	3	1-5/8
364T	9	7	11-1/4	5-7/8	5-7/8	5-7/8	2-3/8
364TR	9	7	11-1/4	5-7/8	5-3/4	3-3/4	2-3/8
364TS	9	7	11-1/4	5-7/8	3-3/4	3-1/2	1-7/8
364U	9	7	11-1/4	5-7/8	6-3/8	6-1/8	2-1/8
365	9	7	12-1/4	5-7/8	5-5/8	5-3/8	1-7/8
365AT	9	7	12-1/4	5-7/8	4-3/4	4-1/2	2-3/8
365T	9	7	12-1/4	5-7/8	5-7/8	5-7/8	2-3/8
324T	8	6-1/4	10-1/2	5-1/4	5-1/4	5	2-1/8
365TR	9	7	12-1/4	5-7/8	5-3/4	3-3/4	2-3/8
365TS	9	7	12-1/4	5-7/8	3-3/4	3-1/2	1-7/8
365U	9	7	12-1/4	5-7/8	6-3/8	6-1/8	2-1/8
366AT	9	7	14	5-7/8	4-3/4	4-1/2	2-3/8
364AT	9	7	11-1/4	5-7/8	4-3/4	4-1/2	2-3/8

Electric Motor Frame Dimensions (cont.)

Frame Designation	NEMA Frame Dimensions in inches						
	D	E	2F	(BA)	(N - W)	V	U
367AT	9	7	16	5-7/8	4-3/4	4-1/2	2-3/8
368AT	9	7	18	5-7/8	4-3/4	4-1/2	2-3/8
369AT	9	7	20	5-7/8	4-3/4	4-1/2	2-3/8
403AT	10	8	11	6-5/8	5-1/4	5	2-5/8
404AT	10	8	12-1/4	6-5/8	5-1/4	5	2-5/8
404T	10	8	12-1/4	6-5/8	7-1/4	7	2-7/8
404TR	10	8	12-1/4	6-5/8	6-5/8	4-3/8	2-7/8
404TS	10	8	12-1/4	6-5/8	4-1/4	4	2-1/8
404U	10	8	12-1/4	6-5/8	7-1/8	6-7/8	2-3/8
405AT	10	8	13-3/4	6-5/8	5-1/4	5	2-5/8
405T	10	8	13-3/4	6-5/8	7-1/4	7	2-7/8
405TR	10	8	13-3/4	6-5/8	6-5/8	4-3/8	2-7/8
405TS	10	8	13-3/4	6-5/8	4-1/4	4	2-1/8
405U	10	8	13-3/4	6-5/8	7-1/8	6-7/8	2-3/8
406AT	10	8	16	6-5/8	5-1/4	5	2-5/8
407AT	10	8	18	6-5/8	5-1/4	5	2-5/8
408AT	10	8	20	6-5/8	5-1/4	5	2-5/8
409AT	10	8	22	6-5/8	5-1/4	5	2-5/8
440	11	9	10	7-1/2	---	---	---
443AT	11	9	12-1/2	7-1/2	5-3/4	5-1/2	2-7/8
444AT	11	9	14-1/2	7-1/2	5-3/4	5-1/2	2-7/8
444T	11	9	14-1/2	7-1/2	8-1/2	8-1/4	3-3/8
444TR	11	9	14-1/2	7-1/2	7-1/2	5	3-3/8
444TS	11	9	14-1/2	7-1/2	4-3/4	4-1/2	2-3/8
444U	11	9	14-1/2	7-1/2	8-5/8	8-3/8	2-7/8
445AT	11	9	16-1/2	7-1/2	5-3/4	5-1/2	2-7/8
445T	11	9	16-1/2	7-1/2	8-1/2	8-1/4	3-3/8
445TR	11	9	16-1/2	7-1/2	7-1/2	5	3-3/8
445TS	11	9	16-1/2	7-1/2	4-3/4	4-1/2	2-3/8
445U	11	9	16-1/2	7-1/2	8-5/8	8-3/8	2-7/8
446AT	11	9	18	7-1/2	5-3/4	5-1/2	2-7/8
447AT	11	9	20	7-1/2	5-3/4	5-1/2	2-7/8
447T	11	9	20	7-1/2	8-1/2	8-1/8	3-3/8
447TS	11	9	20	7-1/2	4-3/4	4-1/2	2-3/8
448AT	11	9	22	7-1/2	5-3/4	5-1/2	2-7/8
449AT	11	9	25	7-1/2	5-3/4	5-1/2	2-7/8
449T	11	9	25	7-1/2	8-1/2	8-1/4	3-3/8
449TS	11	9	25	7-1/2	4-3/4	4-1/2	2-3/8
500	12-1/2	10	11	8-1/2	---	---	---
502AT	12-1/2	10	12-1/2	8-1/2	6-1/2	6-1/4	3-1/4
503AT	12-1/2	10	14	8-1/2	6-1/2	6-1/4	3-1/4

Electric Motor Frame Dimensions (cont.)

Frame Designation	NEMA Frame Dimensions in inches						
	D	E	2F	(BA)	(N - W)	V	U
504AT	12-1/2	10	16	8-1/2	6-1/2	6-1/4	3-1/4
505AT	12-1/2	10	18	8-1/2	6-1/2	6-1/4	3-1/4
506AT	12-1/2	10	20	8-1/2	6-1/2	6-1/4	3-1/4
507AT	12-1/2	10	22	8-1/2	6-1/2	6-1/4	3-1/4
508AT	12-1/2	10	25	8-1/2	6-1/2	6-1/4	3-1/4
509AT	12-1/2	10	28	8-1/2	6-1/2	6-1/4	3-1/4
583A	14-1/2	11-1/2	16	10	9-3/4	9-1/2	3-1/4
584A	14-1/2	11-1/2	18	10	9-3/4	9-1/2	3-1/4
585A	14-1/2	11-1/2	20	10	9-3/4	9-1/2	3-1/4
586A	14-1/2	11-1/2	22	10	9-3/4	9-1/2	3-1/4
587A	14-1/2	11-1/2	25	10	9-3/4	9-1/2	3-1/4
588A	14-1/2	11-1/2	28	10	9-3/4	9-1/2	3-1/4
683A	17	13-1/2	20	11-1/2	10-7/8	10-5/8	3-5/8
684A	17	13-1/2	22	11-1/2	10-7/8	10-5/8	3-5/8
685A	17	13-1/2	25	11-1/2	10-7/8	10-5/8	3-5/8
686A	17	13-1/2	28	11-1/2	10-7/8	10-5/8	3-5/8
687A	17	13-1/2	32	11-1/2	10-7/8	10-5/8	3-5/8
688A	17	13-1/2	36	11-1/2	10-7/8	10-5/8	3-5/8

Formulas for Electricity

(1) Ohm's Law (DC Current):

$$\text{Current in amps} = \frac{\text{Voltage in volts}}{\text{Resistance in ohms}} = \frac{\text{Power in watts}}{\text{Voltage in volts}}$$

$$\text{Current in amps} = \sqrt{\frac{\text{Power in watts}}{\text{Resistance in ohms}}}$$

Voltage in volts = Current in amps x Resistance in ohms

Voltage in volts = Power in watts / Current in amps

Voltage in volts = $\sqrt{\text{Power in watts x Resistance in ohms}}$

Power in watts = $(\text{Current in amps})^2$ x Resistance in ohms

Power in watts = Voltage in volts x Current in amps

Power in watts = $(\text{Voltage in volts})^2$ / Resistance in ohms

Resistance in ohms = Voltage in volts / Current in amps

Resistance in ohms = Power in watts / $(\text{Current in amps})^2$

(2) Resistors in Series (values in ohms):

Total Resistance = $\text{Resistance}_1 + \text{Resistance}_2 + ...\text{Resistance}_n$

Formulas for Electricity

(3) Two Resistors in Parallel (values in ohms):

$$\text{Total Resistance} = \frac{\text{Resistance}_1 \times \text{Resistance}_2}{\text{Resistance}_1 + \text{Resistance}_2}$$

(4) Multiple Resistors in Parallel (values in ohms):

$$\text{Total Resistance} = \frac{1}{1/\text{Resistance}_1 + 1/\text{Resistance}_2 + \ldots\ldots 1/\text{Resistance}_n}$$

(5) Ohm's Law (AC Current):

In the following AC Ohm's Law formulas, θ is the phase angle in degrees by which current lags voltage (in an inductive circuit) or by which current leads voltage (in a capacitive circuit). In a resonant circuit (such as normal household 120VAC) the phase angle is 0° and Impedance = Resistance.

$$\text{Current in amps} = \frac{\text{Voltage in volts}}{\text{Impedance in ohms}}$$

$$\text{Current in amps} = \sqrt{\frac{\text{Power in watts}}{\text{Impedance in ohms} \times \cos\theta}}$$

$$\text{Current in amps} = \frac{\text{Power in watts}}{\text{Voltage in volts} \times \cos\theta}$$

$$\text{Voltage in volts} = \text{Current in amps} \times \text{Impedance in ohms}$$

$$\text{Voltage in volts} = \frac{\text{Power in watts}}{\text{Current in amps} \times \cos\theta}$$

$$\text{Voltage in volts} = \sqrt{\frac{\text{Power in watts} \times \text{Impedance in ohms}}{\cos\theta}}$$

$$\text{Impedance in ohms} = \text{Voltage in volts} / \text{Current in amps}$$

$$\text{Impedance in ohms} = \text{Power in watts} / (\text{Current amps}^2 \times \cos\theta)$$

Formulas for Electricity

(5) Ohm's Law (AC Current):(cont.)

Impedance in ohms = (Voltage in volts^2 x cos θ) / Power in watts

Power in watts = Current in amps^2 x Impedance in ohms x cos θ

Power in watts = Current in amps x Voltage in volts x cos θ

Power in watts = $\dfrac{\text{(Voltage in volts)}^2 \times \cos\ \theta}{\text{impedance in ohms}}$

(6) Resonance: – f

Resonant frequency in hertz (where $X_L = X_C$) =

$$\dfrac{1}{2\pi\sqrt{\text{Inductance in henrys x Capacitance in farads}}}$$

(7) Reactance: – X

Reactance in ohms of an inductance is X_L
Reactance in ohms of a capacitance is X_C

$X_L = 2\pi(\text{frequency in hertz x Inductance in henrys})$

$X_C = 1 / (2\pi(\text{frequency in hertz x Capacitance in farads}))$

(8) Impedance: – Z

Impedance in ohms = $\sqrt{\text{Resistance in ohms}^2 + (X_L - X_C)^2}$
(series)

Impedance in ohms = $\dfrac{\text{Resistance in ohms x Reactance}}{\sqrt{\text{Resistance in ohms}^2 + \text{Reactance}^2}}$
(parallel)

(9) Susceptance: – B

Susceptance in mhos =

$$\dfrac{\text{Reactance in ohms}}{\text{Resistance in ohms}^2 + \text{Reactance in ohms}^2}$$

(10) Admittance: – Y

Admittance in mhos =

$$\dfrac{1}{\sqrt{\text{Resistance in ohms}^2 + \text{Reactance in ohms}^2}}$$

Admittance in mhos = 1 / Impedance in ohms

Formulas for Electricity

(11) Power Factor: – pf

Power Factor = cos (Phase Angle)
Power Factor = True Power / Apparent Power
Power Factor = Power in watts / (volts x current in amps)
Power Factor = Resistance in ohms / Impedance in ohms

(12) Q or Figure of Merit: – Q

Q = Inductive Reactance in ohms / Series Resistance in ohms
Q = Capacitive Reactance in ohms / Series Resistance in ohms

(13) Efficiency of any Device:

Efficiency = Output / Input

(14) Sine Wave Voltage and Current:

Effective (RMS) value = 0.707 x Peak value
Effective (RMS) value = 1.11 x Average value
Average value = 0.637 x Peak value
Average value = 0.9 x Effective (RMS) value
Peak Value = 1.414 x Effective (RMS) value
Peak Value = 1.57 x Average value

(15) Decibels: – db

db = 10 Log_{10} (Power in Watts #1 / Power in Watts #2)
db = 10 Log_{10} (Power Ratio)
db = 20 Log_{10} (Volts or Amps #1 / Volts or Amps #2)
db = 20 Log_{10} (Voltage or Current Ratio)
Power Ratio = $10^{(db/10)}$
Voltage or Current Ratio = $10^{(db/20)}$
If impedances are not equal:

$$db = 20 \text{Log}_{10} \left[(\text{Volt}_1 \sqrt{Z_2}) / (\text{Volt}_2 \sqrt{Z_1}) \right]$$

(16) Capacitors in Parallel (values in any farad):

Total Capacitance = Capacitance_1 + Capacitance_2 +
.... Capacitance_n

Formulas for Electricity

(17) Two Capacitors in Series (values in any farad):

$$\text{Total Capacitance} = \frac{\text{Capacitance}_1 \times \text{Capacitance}_2}{\text{Capacitance}_1 + \text{Capacitance}_2}$$

(18) Multiple Capacitors in Series (values in farads):

$$\text{Total Capacitance} = \frac{1}{1 / \text{Capacitance}_1 + 1 / \text{Capacitance}_2 + \ldots\ldots 1 / \text{Capacitance}_n}$$

(19) Quantity of Electricity in a Capacitor: – Q

Q in coulombs = Capacitance in farads $\times$ Volts

(20) Capacitance of a Capacitor: – C

Capacitance in picofarads =

$$0.0885 \times \frac{\text{Dielectric constant} \times \text{area in cm}^2 \times (\text{\# of plates} - 1)}{\text{thickness of dielectric in cm}}$$

(21) Self Inductance:

Use the same formulas as those for Resistance, substituting inductance for resistance. When including the effects of coupling, add 2 x mutual inductance if fields are adding and subtract 2 x mutual inductance if the fields are opposing. e.g.

Series: $L_t = L_1 + L_2 + 2M$ or $L_t = L_1 + L_2 - 2M$

Parallel: $L_t = 1 / \left[(1/L_1 + M) + (1/L_2 + M) \right]$

General Science

Elevation vs. Air and Water Properties...268
Wind Chill Factors 269
Heat - Humidity Factors..271
Firewood/Fuel Heat Comparisons..272
Sound Intensities...274
Mapping Scales and Areas 275
Temperature Conversions..277
Beaufort Wind Strength Scale..279
Richter Earthquake Scale...280

Elevation vs. Air & Water

Elevation		US Standard Atmosphere		Boiling Point H$_2$O (°F)	Speed of Sound m/sec
Meters	Feet	Temp °F	Pressure lbf/sq. in		
-1000	-3281	70.7	16.52	218.5	344.1
-500	-1640	64.9	15.59	215.2	342.2
0	0	59.0	14.70	212.0	340.3
250	820	56.1	14.26	210.4	339.3
500	1640	53.2	13.85	208.8	338.4
750	2461	50.2	13.44	207.2	337.4
1000	3281	47.3	13.03	205.7	336.4
1250	4101	44.4	12.64	204.1	335.5
1500	4921	41.5	12.26	202.6	334.5
1750	5741	38.5	11.89	201.0	333.5
2000	6562	35.6	11.53	199.5	332.5
2500	8202	29.8	10.83	196.5	330.6
3000	9843	23.9	10.17	193.5	328.6
3500	11483	18.1	9.54	190.6	326.6
4000	13123	12.2	8.94	187.7	324.6
4500	14764	6.4	8.38	184.8	322.6
5000	16404	0.5	7.84	182.0	320.5
5500	18045	-5.3	7.33	179.2	318.5
6000	19685	-11.1	6.85	176.4	316.5
6500	21325	-17.0	6.39	173.7	314.4
7000	22966	-22.8	5.96	171.0	312.3
7500	24606	-28.6	5.56	168.4	310.2
8000	26247	-34.5	5.17	165.8	308.1
8500	27887	-40.3	4.81	163.2	305.9
9000	29528	-46.2	4.47	160.7	303.8
9500	31168	-52.0	4.15	154.4	301.7
10000	32808	-57.8	3.84	151.3	299.5
11000	36089	-69.5	3.29	145.0	295.2
12000	39370	-69.5	2.81	138.9	295.1
13000	42651	-69.5	2.41	133.0	295.1
14000	45932	-69.5	2.06	127.0	295.1
15000	49213	-69.5	1.74	121.3	295.1
16000	52493	-69.5	1.50	115.7	295.1
17000	55774	-69.5	1.28	110.3	295.1
18000	59055	-69.5	1.10	104.7	295.1
19000	62336	-69.5	.94	99.7	295.1
20000	65617	-69.5	.80	94.5	295.1
25000	82021	-60.9	.37	70.5	298.4
30000	98425	-52.0	.17	49.3	301.7
32000	104987	-48.5	.13	41.5	303.0

Data in table based on ICAO Standard Atmosphere

Wind Chill Factors

To determine wind chill, find the outside air temperature on the top line, then read down the column to the measured wind speed (mph = miles per hour).

For example: When the outside air temperature is -5 degrees Fahrenheit, and the wind speed is 20 mph, equivalent wind chill temperature is -47 degrees Fahrenheit.

This wind chill temperature is in the extremely cold category where frostbite is likely.

WIND CHILL	CATEGORY	POSSIBLE EFFECTS
30 °F or greater	Chilly	Generally unpleasant
29 °F to 15 °F	Cold	Unpleasant
14 °F to 0 °F	Very cold	Very unpleasant
-1 °F to -20 °F	Bitter cold	Frostbite possible.
-21 °F to -60 °F	Extremely cold	Frostbite likely. Outdoor activity dangerous
-61°F or less	Frigidly cold	Exposed flesh will freeze within half a minute

Source: National Weather Service, www.srh.noaa.gov

To calculate wind chill factors not included on the table (next page), use the following formula:

Wind Chill Factor (°F) =

$$35.74 + 0.6216(T) - 35.75 (V^{0.16}) + 0.4275 (T) (V^{0.16})$$

Where T= air temperature in °F and V= wind speed in mph

Wind Chill Factors

Wind Speed (mph)	Outside Air Temperature (°Fahrenheit)																		
	45	40	35	30	25	20	15	10	5	0	-5	-10	-15	-20	-25	-30	-35	-40	-45
0	45	40	35	30	25	20	15	10	5	0	-5	-10	-15	-20	-25	-30	-35	-40	-45
5	42	36	31	25	19	13	7	1	-5	-11	-16	-22	-28	-34	-41	-46	-52	-57	-63
10	40	34	27	21	15	9	3	-4	-10	-16	-22	-28	-35	-41	-47	-53	-59	-66	-72
15	38	32	25	19	13	6	0	-7	-13	-19	-26	-32	-39	-45	-51	-58	-64	-71	-77
20	37	30	24	17	11	4	-2	-9	-15	-22	-29	-35	-42	-48	-55	-61	-68	-74	-81
25	36	29	23	16	9	3	-4	-11	-17	-24	-31	-37	-44	-51	-58	-64	-71	-78	-84
30	35	28	22	15	8	1	-5	-12	-19	-26	-33	-39	-46	-53	-60	-67	-73	-80	-87
35	35	28	21	14	7	0	-7	-14	-21	-27	-34	-41	-48	-55	-62	-69	-76	-82	-89
40	34	27	20	13	6	-1	-8	-15	-22	-29	-36	-43	-50	-57	-64	-71	-78	-84	-91
45	33	26	19	12	5	-2	-9	-16	-23	-30	-37	-44	-51	-58	-65	-72	-79	-86	-93
	Cold	Very Cold		Bitter Cold			Extremely Cold						Frigidly Cold						

NOTE: Wind Speeds greater than 45 mph have little additional effect on the Wind Chill Factor. At -18° and below frostbite occurs in 15 minutes or less.

Heat – Humidity Factor

In order to determine a "Heat Factor", locate the measured outside temperature row and then the humidity column and then read the corresponding apparent temperature at the intersection of the row and column. This "Heat Factor" is the combined effect of actual temperature and humidity that makes the measured outside temperature "feel" hotter. Heat exhaustion danger occurs when the "Heat Factor" is greater than 105°F.

Measured Temp °F	Percent Relative Humidity			
	0	10	20	30
70	64	65	66	67
75	69	70	72	73
80	73	75	77	78
85	78	80	82	84
90	83	85	87	90
95	87	90	93	96
100	91	95	99	104
105	95	100	105	113
110	99	105	112	123
115	103	111	120	135
120	107	116	130	148

Measured Temp °F	Percent Relative Humidity			
	40	50	60	70
70	68	69	70	70
75	74	75	76	77
80	79	81	82	85
85	86	88	90	93
90	93	96	100	106
95	101	107	114	124
100	110	120	132	144
105	123	135	149	
110	137	150		
115	151			

Measured Temp °F	Percent Relative Humidity		
	80	90	100
70	71	71	72
75	78	79	80
80	86	88	91
85	97	102	108
90	113	122	
95	136		

Firewood / Fuel Comparisons

Fuel Type	Million Btu /Unit [1]	Available Units /million Btu [2]	Comment
Coals:			.75% efficient
Anthracite	26.27/ton	0.0508	
Bituminous			
low/med volatile	28.72/ton	0.0464	
high volatile	24.74/ton	0.0539	
Subbituminous	19.19/ton	0.0695	
Lignite	13.95/ton	0.0956	
Charcoal	25.00/ton	0.0533	
Electricity: [3]	0.0034/kWh	308.5	95% efficient
Gases: [3]			
Butane	3.261/Mcf	0.3931	78% efficient
Methane	1.016/Mcf	1.230	80% efficient
Natural Gas	1.049/Mcf	1.192	80% efficient
Producer Gas	0.170/Mcf	7.347	80% efficient
Propane	2.531/Mcf	0.5065	78% efficient
Oils:			80% efficient
#1 Fuel Oil	0.1391/gallon	8.985	
#2 Fuel Oil	0.1426/gallon	8.766	
#4 Fuel Oil	0.1472/gallon	8.492	
#5 Fuel Oil	0.1508/gallon	8.289	
#6 Fuel Oil	0.1538/gallon	8.129	
Heating Oil	0.1342/gallon	9.313	
Kerosene	0.1308/gallon	9.554	
Woods:			55% efficient
Apple	28.72/cord	0.0633	L–smoke, L–spark
Ash	22.30/cord	0.0815	
Aspen	16.57/cord	0.1098	M–smoke, H–spark
Basswood	14.77/cord	0.1231	
Beech	23.33/cord	0.0779	
Birch	21.71/cord	0.0837	
Boxelder	18.10/cord	0.1005	
Buckeye	13.40/cord	0.1357	
Butternut	15.40/cord	0.1181	
Catalpa	16.40/cord	0.1109	
Cherry	21.30/cord	0.0854	
Chestnut	12.90/cord	0.1409	
Coffeetree	21.60/cord	0.0842	
Cottonwood	15.86/cord	0.1146	M–smoke, L–spark
Dogwood	27.00/cord	0.0673	
Douglas Fir	26.35/cord	0.0690	H–smoke, M–spark
Elm	19.77/cord	0.0920	M–smoke, M–spark
Hackberry	21.00/cord	0.0866	
Hemlock	16.91/cord	0.1076	
Hickory	29.21/cord	0.0622	L–smoke, L–spark
Ironwood	26.00/cord	0.0699	
Larch (Eastern)	18.65/cord	0.0975	
Locust	27.30/cord	0.0666	
Maple	21.59/cord	0.0842	L–smoke, L–spark
Mulberry	25.80/cord	0.0705	
Oak (Red & Wht)	26.39/cord	0.0689	L–smoke, L–spark

Fuel Type	Million Btu /Unit [1]	Available Units /million Btu [2]	Comment
Osage Orange	32.90/cord	0.0553	
Pine:			
Lodgepole	19.25/cord	0.0944	M–smoke, M–spark
Pinon	33.50/cord	0.0543	M–smoke, M–spark
Ponderosa	18.72/cord	0.0972	M–smoke, M–spark
Tanarack	21.15/cord	0.0860	
White	14.53/cord	0.1251	M–smoke, H–spark
Yellow	22.00/cord	0.0826	
Redcedar (East.)	19.80/cord	0.0918	
Spruce	15.98/cord	0.1138	M–smoke, H–spark
Sycamore	19.50/cord	0.0932	
Walnut (Black)	21.50/cord	0.0846	
Willow	13.15/cord	0.1383	

"L–" is Low, "M–" is Medium, and "H–" is High

To calculate the actual cost of heat for each fuel: Multiply the "Available Units/million Btu" by the current cost per unit. For example, if natural gas is currently $4.60 per Mcf, the cost of 1 million Btu is $4.60 x 1.192 = $5.48. For Pinon Pine, at $150/cord, the cost of 1 million Btu is $150 x 0.0543 = $8.15. Note that the wood efficiency can vary greatly, depending on moisture content and efficiency of the furnace, stove, or fireplace.

Notes:

(1) Million Btu/Unit defines the average amount of heat per unit that is available for that fuel, assuming 100% burning efficiency. For example, Aspen contains 16,570,000 Btu per dry cord.

(2) Available Units/million Btu defines the actual number of units required to produce 1,000,000 Btu. The efficiency of burning (shown in the Comment column) is considered, as well as the moisture content of wood (average 20% moisture for dry wood). For example, 0.1098 cords of Aspen burning at 55% efficiency will produce 1,000,000 Btu.

(3) kWh=Kilowatt Hours   Mcf=Thousand Cubic Feet

Sources:
1993 ASHRAE Handbook - Fundamentals, American Society of Heating, Refrigerating and Air-Conditioning Engineers, Inc., Atlanta, GA 30329
Blair & Ketchum's Country Journal, 1977, Country Journal Publishing Co., Brattleboro, VT 05301
Encyclopedia of Energy, 3rd Edition, 1976, McGraw-Hill, New York, NY
Energy Deskbook, Samuel Glasstone, June 1982, DOE/IR/05114-1, US Dept. of Energy, Oak Ridge, TN 37830
Energy Reference Handbook, 2nd Edition, 1977, Government Institutes, Inc., Washington, DC 20014
Firewood Fact Sheet, Colorado State Forest Service
Firewood Facts, October 1987, The Family Handyman
Fuel Oil Facts, www.fueloil.com
Heat Values of Wood, www.hearth.com
HVAC Field Manual, R.O. Parmley, 1988, McGraw-Hill, New York, NY
Mark's Standard Handbook for Mechanical Engineers, 10th Edition, 1996, McGraw-Hill, New York, NY
Mechanical Engineers' Handbook, 1986, John Wiley & Sons, New York, NY
Natural Gas Facts, www.naturalgas.com
Nebraska Fuelwood Specifications
Wood Power, Its Promises & Problems, N. Engalichev & V.K. Mathur, February 1980, University of New Hampshire, Durham, NH 03824

Sound Intensities

Degree	Decibels	Loudness or Feeling
Deafening	225	12" cannon @ 12 ft, in front & below
	194	Saturn rocket, 50# of TNT @ 10'
	140	Artillery fire, jet aircraft, ram jet
	130	Threshold of pain, >130 causes immediate ear damage. Propeller aircraft at 5 meters, Hydraulic press, pneumatic rock drill
	120	Thunder, diesel engine room, nearby riviter
	110	Close to a train, ball mill
Very Loud	100	Boiler factory, home lawn mower, car horn at 5 meters, wood saw
	90	Symphony or a band, >90 regularly can cause ear damage. Noisy factory, truck without muffler.
Loud	80	Inside a high speed auto, police whistle, electric shaver, noisy office, alarm clock
	70	Average radio, normal street noise
Moderate	60	Normal conversation, close up
	50	Normal office noise, quiet stream
	45	To awaken a sleeping person
Faint	40	Normal private office noise, residential neighborhood, no cars
	30	Quiet conversation, recording studio
Very Faint	20	Inside an empty theater, ticking of a watch, rustle of leaves, whisper
	10	Sound proof room, threshold of hearing
	0	Absolute silence

Sound intensities are typically measured in decibels (db). A decibel is defined as 10 times the logarithm of the power ratio (power ratio is the ratio of the intensity of the sound to the intensity of an arbitrary standard point.) Normally a change of 1 db is the smallest volume change detectable by the human ear.

Sound intensity is also defined in terms of energy (erg) transmitted per second over a 1 square centimeter surface. This energy is proportional to the velocity of propagation of the sound. The energy density in $erg/cm^3 = 2\pi^2$ x density in g/cm^3 x frequency^2 in Hz x amplitude^2 in cm.

Mapping Scales and Areas

Scale 1:X	Feet/ Inch	Inch/ Mile	Acres/ Sq Inch	Sq Miles/ Sq Inch
100	8.3	633.60	0.0016	0.000002
120	10.0	528.00	0.0023	0.000004
200	16.7	316.80	0.0064	0.000010
240	20.0	264.00	0.0092	0.000014
250	20.8	253.44	0.0100	0.000016
300	25.0	211.20	0.0143	0.000022
400	33.3	158.40	0.0255	0.000040
480	40.0	132.00	0.0367	0.000057
500	41.7	126.72	0.0399	0.000062
600	50.0	105.60	0.0574	0.000090
1000	83.3	63.36	0.1594	0.000249
1200	100.0	52.80	0.2296	0.000359
1500	125.0	42.24	0.3587	0.000560
2000	166.7	31.68	0.6377	0.000996
2400	200.0	26.40	0.9183	0.001435
2500	208.3	25.34	0.9964	0.001557
3000	250.0	21.12	1.4348	0.002242
3600	300.0	17.60	2.0661	0.003228
4000	333.3	15.84	2.5508	0.003986
4800	400.0	13.20	3.6731	0.005739
5000	416.7	12.67	3.9856	0.006227
6000	500.0	10.56	5.7392	0.008968
7000	583.3	9.05	7.8117	0.012206
7200	600.0	8.80	8.2645	0.012913
7920	660.0	8.00	10.0000	0.015625
8000	666.7	7.92	10.2030	0.015942
8400	700.0	7.54	11.2489	0.017576
9000	750.0	7.04	12.9132	0.020177
9600	800.0	6.60	14.6924	0.022957
10000	833.3	6.34	15.9423	0.024910
10800	900.0	5.87	18.5950	0.029055
12000	1000.0	5.28	22.9568	0.035870
13200	1100.0	4.80	27.7778	0.043403
14400	1200.0	4.40	33.0579	0.051653
15000	1250.0	4.22	35.8701	0.056047
15600	1300.0	4.06	38.7971	0.060620
15840	1320.0	4.00	40.0000	0.062500
16000	1333.3	3.96	40.8122	0.063769
16800	1400.0	3.77	44.9954	0.070305
18000	1500.0	3.52	51.6529	0.080708
19200	1600.0	3.30	58.7695	0.091827
20000	1666.7	3.17	63.7690	0.099639
20400	1700.0	3.11	66.3453	0.103664

Mapping Scales and Areas (cont.)

Scale 1:X	Feet/ Inch	Inch/ Mile	Acres/ Sq Inch	Sq Miles/ Sq Inch
21120	1760.0	3.00	71.1111	0.111111
21600	1800.0	2.93	74.3802	0.116219
22800	1900.0	2.78	82.8742	0.129491
24000	2000.0	2.64	91.8274	0.143480
25000	2083.3	2.53	99.6391	0.155686
30000	2500.0	2.11	143.4803	0.224188
31680	2640.0	2.00	160.0000	0.250000
40000	3333.3	1.58	255.0760	0.398556
45000	3750.0	1.41	322.8306	0.504423
48000	4000.0	1.32	367.3095	0.573921
50000	4166.7	1.27	398.5563	0.622744
60000	5000.0	1.06	573.9210	0.896752
62500	5208.3	1.01	622.7442	0.973038
63360	5280.0	1.00	640.0000	1.000000
80000	6666.7	0.79	1020.3041	1.594225
90000	7500.0	0.70	1291.3223	2.017691
96000	8000.0	0.66	1469.2378	2.295684
100000	8333.3	0.63	1594.2251	2.490977
125000	10416.7	0.51	2490.9767	3.892151
126720	10560.0	0.50	2560.0000	4.000000
200000	16666.7	0.32	6376.9003	9.963907
250000	20833.3	0.25	9963.9067	15.568604
253440	21120.0	0.25	10240.0000	16.000000
380160	31680.0	0.17	23040.0000	36.000000
500000	41666.7	0.13	39855.6270	62.274417
760320	63360.0	0.08	92160.0000	144.000000
1000000	83333.3	0.06	159422.5079	249.097669

Feet / Inch = Scale / 12

Meters / Inch = Scale / 39.37

Miles / Inch = Scale / 63,291.14

Chains / Inch = Scale / 792.08

Inch / Mile = 63360 / Scale

Acres / Square Inch = $Scale^2$ / 6,272,640

Square Miles / Square Inch = $Scale^2$ / 4,014,489,600

Temperature Conversions

°C	°F	°C	°F	°C	°F
10000	18032	430	806	200	392.0
9500	17132	420	788	195	383.0
9000	16232	410	770	190	374.0
8500	15332	400	752	185	365.0
8000	14432	395	743	180	356.0
7500	13532	390	734	175	347.0
7000	12632	385	725	170	338.0
6500	11732	380	716	165	329.0
6000	10832	375	707	160	320.0
5500	9932	370	698	155	311.0
5000	9032	365	689	150	302.0
4500	8132	360	680	145	293.0
4000	7232	355	671	140	284.0
3500	6332	350	662	135	275.0
3000	5432	345	653	130	266.0
2500	4532	340	644	125	257.0
2000	3632	335	635	120	248.0
1500	2732	330	626	115	239.0
1000	1832	325	617	110	230.0
950	1742	320	608	105	221.0
900	1652	315	599	100	212.0
850	1562	310	590	99	210.2
800	1472	305	581	98	208.4
750	1382	300	572	97	206.6
700	1292	295	563	96	204.8
650	1202	290	554	95	203.0
600	1112	285	545	94	201.2
590	1094	280	536	93	199.4
580	1076	275	527	92	197.6
570	1058	270	518	91	195.8
560	1040	265	509	90	194.0
550	1022	260	500	89	192.2
540	1004	255	491	88	190.4
530	986	250	482	87	188.6
520	968	245	473	86	186.8
510	950	240	464	85	185.0
500	932	235	455	84	183.2
490	914	230	446	83	181.4
480	896	225	437	82	179.6
470	878	220	428	81	177.8
460	860	215	419	80	176.0
450	842	210	410	79	174.2
440	824	205	401	78	172.4

°C = Degrees Celsius. 1 unit is 1/100 of the difference between the temperature of melting ice and boiling water at standard temperature and pressure.

°F = Degrees Fahrenheit. 1 unit is 1/180 of the difference between the temperature of melting ice and boiling water at standard temperature and pressure.

Temperature Conversions

°C	°F	°C	°F	°C	°F
77	170.6	34	93.2	−9	15.8
76	168.8	33	91.4	−10	14.0
75	167.0	32	89.6	−11	12.2
74	165.2	31	87.8	−12	10.4
73	163.4	30	86.0	−13	8.6
72	161.6	29	84.2	−14	6.8
71	159.8	28	82.4	−15	5.0
70	158.0	27	80.6	−16	3.2
69	156.2	26	78.8	−17	1.4
68	154.4	25	77.0	−18	−0.4
67	152.6	24	75.2	−19	−2.2
66	150.8	23	73.4	−20	−4.0
65	149.0	22	71.6	−21	−5.8
64	147.2	21	69.8	−22	−7.6
63	145.4	20	68.0	−23	−9.4
62	143.6	19	66.2	−24	−11.2
61	141.8	18	64.4	−25	−13.0
60	140.0	17	62.6	−26	−14.8
59	138.2	16	60.8	−27	−16.6
58	136.4	15	59.0	−28	−18.4
57	134.6	14	57.2	−29	−20.2
56	132.8	13	55.4	−30	−22.0
55	131.0	12	53.6	−31	−23.8
54	129.2	11	51.8	−32	−25.6
53	127.4	10	50.0	−33	−27.4
52	125.6	9	48.2	−34	−29.2
51	123.8	8	46.4	−35	−31.0
50	122.0	7	44.6	−36	−32.8
49	120.2	6	42.8	−37	−34.6
48	118.4	5	41.0	−38	−36.4
47	116.6	4	39.2	−39	−38.2
46	114.8	3	37.4	−40	−40.0
45	113.0	2	35.6	−50	−58.0
44	111.2	1	33.8	−60	−76.0
43	109.4	0	32.0	−70	−94.0
42	107.6	−1	30.2	−80	−112.0
41	105.8	−2	28.4	−90	−130.0
40	104.0	−3	26.6	−100	−148.0
39	102.2	−4	24.8	−125	−193.0
38	100.4	−5	23.0	−150	−238.0
37	98.6	−6	21.2	−200	−328.0
36	96.8	−7	19.4	−250	−418.0
35	95.0	−8	17.6	−273	−459.4

$$°C = 5/9 \ (°F-32) \qquad °F = 9/5 \ °C+32$$
$$\text{Absolute Zero} = 0K = −273.16°C = −459.69°F$$

K = Kelvin (Absolute temperature). This scale is based on the average kinetic energy per molecule of a perfect gas and uses the same size unit as the Celsius scale, but the degree symbol (°) is not used. Zero (0K) on the scale is the temperature at which a perfect gas has lost all of its energy.

Beaufort Wind Speed Scale

Beaufort Wind Speed Number or "Force"	Wind Speed Knots (Mile/hour) [km/hour]	Description
0	0 –1 (< 1) [< 2]	**Calm:** Still. Smoke will rise vertically. The sea is mirror smooth.
1	1–3 (1–3) [2–6]	**Light Air:** Rising smoke drifts, weather vane is inactive. Scale-like ripples on sea, no foam on wave crests.
2	4–6 (4–7) [7–11]	**Light Breeze:** Leaves rustle, can feel wind on your face, weather vane is active. Short wavelets, glassy wave crests.
3	7–10 (8–12) [12–19]	**Gentle Breeze:** Leaves and twigs move around. Light weight flags extend. Long wavelets, glassy wave crests.
4	11–16 (13–18) [20–30]	**Moderate Breeze:** Moves thin branches, raises dust and paper. Fairly frequent whitecaps occur.
5	17–21 (19–24) [31–39]	**Fresh Breeze:** Small trees sway. Moderate waves, many white foam crests.
6*	22–27 (25–31) [40–50]	**Strong Breeze:** Large tree branches move, open wires begin to "whistle", umbrellas are difficult to control. Some spray on the sea surface.
7	28–33 (32–38) [51–61]	**Moderate Gale:** Large trees begin to sway, noticeably difficult to walk. Foam from waves blown in streaks.
8	34–40 (39–46) [62–74]	**Fresh Gale:** Small branches broken from trees, walking in wind is very difficult. Long streaks of foam appear on sea.
9	41–47 (47–54) [75–87]	**Strong Gale:** Slight damage occurs to buildings, shingles are blown off roofs. High waves, crests start to roll over.
10	48–55 (55–63) [88–102]	**Whole Gale:** Large trees are uprooted, building damage is considerable. The sea takes on a white appearance.
11	56–63 (64–72) [103–117]	**Storm:** Extensive widespread damage. Exceptionally high waves, visibility affected.
12	64+ (>73) [>118]	**Hurricane:** Extreme destruction. Storm waves at sea. Air is filled with spray and foam.

* Small craft advisories are usually issued when force 6 is reached.

Earthquake Scales

Moment Magnitude	Richter Magnitude	Mercalli Intensity	Description
1.0-3.0	2	I	Usually not felt, detected by instruments.
3.0	2	II	Felt by few, especially on upper floors of buildings, detected by instruments.
3.9	3	III	Felt noticeably indoors, vibration like a passing vehicle, cars may rock.
4.0		IV	Felt indoors by many, outdoors by few, dishes & doors disturbed, like heavy truck nearby, walls–cracking sound.
4.9	4	V	Felt by most people, slight damage; some dishes & windows broken, some cracked plaster, trees disturbed.
5.0	5	VI	Felt by all, many frightened and run outdoors, damage minor to moderate.
5.9	5 to 6	VII	Everyone runs outdoors, much damage to poor design buildings, minor damage to good design buildings, some chimneys broken, noticed by people driving cars.
6.0	6	VIII	Everyone runs outdoors, damage is moderate to major. Damage minor in well designed structures, major in poor designs; chimneys, columns, & walls fall, heavy furniture turned, well water changes; sand & mud ejected.
6.9	7	IX	Major damage in all structures, ground cracked, pipes broken, shift foundation.
7.0 +	7 & 8	X	Major damage, most masonry & frame structures destroyed, ground badly cracked, landslides, water sloshed over river banks, rails bent.
	8	XI	Almost all masonry structures destroyed bridges fall, big fissures in ground, land slumps, rails bent greatly.
	8 & above	XII	Total destruction. Ground surface waves seen, objects thrown up into the air. All construction destroyed.

Richter Magnitudes (ML) are based on the movement of an instrument needle and increases logarithmically, 10 times for each number jump, so ML 8 is not twice as large as ML 4, it is 10,000 times as large! Richter Magnitude is an open-ended scale.

Moment Magnitude (MW) is the modern version of the Richter Magnitudes. Moment Magnitude is based on the energy released by an earthquake and is also logrithmic, but by a factor of 32 not 10. MW 4 releases 65,000,000 Btu while MW8 releases 69,000,000,000,000 Btu. The largest Moment Magnitude recorded to date was 9.5 and occured in Chile on 5/22/1960.

Mercalli Intensity (MM) is based on actual observations of the resulting damage, and therefore can not be measured on instruments.

Glues, Paints and Solvents

Glue Types and Applications..282
Glue Hints and General Rules..290
Paints and Finishes 291
Solvents...294

Glues & Adhesives, Types & Applications

Acrylic Resin Adhesive

onds to anything porous or nonporous, waterproof, very strong, fast setting (3 to 30 minutes), oil and gasoline resistant, good gap and hole filling. Synthetic resin based. 2 part - liquid and powder, expensive, tan. Brands: "3 Ton Adhesive" and "P.A.C. - Plastic Adhesive Cement," Tridox Labs, Philadelphia, PA and "330 Depend No-Mix Adhesive", Loctite Corporation, Rocky Hill, CT.

Acrylonitrile Adhesive

Bonds to anything porous or nonporous, not recommended for wood, flexible, waterproof, similar to rubber cement. Synthetic polymer based. 1 part liquid, flammable, brown. Brand: "Pliobond 1100-2," Ashland Chemical Company, Columbus, OH.

Albumin Glue

Used in interior-type plywood, not as strong as other animal glues, moderately resistant to water and damp atmosphere, high dry strength, applied at room temperature, cured at 250°F, not resistant to mold and fungi. Natural protein based. Made from blood and casein. Dark red to black.

Aliphatic Resin Glue (Yellow glue)

Used mainly for wood; aliphatic resin is a moisture resistant form of polyvinyl acetate glue (PVA glue); not waterproof; very strong; dries translucent; instant sticky but dries in 45 minutes to 24 hours; high resistance to solvents, heat, oil, and grease; sandable; will set at temperatures from 55°F to 110°F; dries hard; glue can be colored with water soluble dyes; not good for bonding over old glues; not good for furniture repair! Synthetic resin based. 1 part liquid, light yellow color, non-toxic, non-flammable, no stain, do not expose to lacquer thinner. Brands: "Titebond Glue," Franklin International, Columbus, OH and "DAP Weldwood Carpenter's Wood Glue," DAP Inc, Baltimore, MD (many others, very common glue).

Anaerobic Adhesive

Bonds metal. Anaerobic adhesives cure only in the absence of air and only in the presence of metal. Used for threadlocking, threadsealing, gasketing, and retaining metal parts; high resistance to chemicals and harsh environmental conditions including vibration; available in a wide range of strengths, flexibilities, viscosities, and gap filling abilities; may be used with either ferrous or non-ferrous metals. Synthetic resin based. 1 part liquid, many colors from purple to green. Brands: "103 Nutlock," Impact Adhesives, Bradford, West Yorkshire, England; "262 Threadlocker Medium to High Strength," Loctite Corporation, Rocky Hill, CT; and "Perma-Lok MM115 General Purpose Threadlocker," Permabond Engineering Adhesives, Englewood, NJ.

Bone Glue   Used mostly in making of cartons and paper boxes, there are 15 grades of bone glue based on quality of raw material, method of extraction, and material blend. Green bone glue is used for gummed paper and tapes for cartons. Bone glues are no longer made in the US. Natural protein based. Made from bones. Brand: "Bone Glue," Milligan and Higgins, Johnstown, NY.

Casein Glue   Use mainly for wood; high water resistance (not waterproof); resistant to oil, grease, and gasoline; good gap filling; sets at temperatures above 32°F; high dry strength; clamps recommended; dries in 8 hours. Very good when working with tropical hardwoods, but tough on cutting tools. Natural protein based. Made from milk curd. 1 part powder, mix with water, inexpensive, white to tan color. Brands: "No. 30 Casein Glue," National Casein Company, Chicago, IL and "Casehesive," American Casein Company, Burlington, NJ.

Cellulose Acetate Adhesive

Bonds cellulose acetate plastics, photographic film, balsa wood, porous materials including leather, paper, and fabric.

Cellulose Nitrate Adhesive

Bonds to many porous or nonporous materials, good water resistance (not waterproof), fast setting (2 hours to 24 hours), moderately high strength (up to 3500 psi), shrinks some on drying. 1 part liquid, flammable, clear to amber. Brands: "Ever Fast Liquid Cement," Ambroid Co, Taunton, MA and "Devcon Duco Cement," Chemical Development Corporation, Danvers, MA.

Ceramic Adhesive

Bonds ceramics, glass, and metal. Made with porcelain enamel grit, iron oxide, and stainless steel powder. Heat resistant to 1500°F, shear strength of 1500 psi, must be heated to 1750°F in order to cure. Common in aerospace applications.

Contact Cement (Contact adhesive)

Bonds to many porous or nonporous materials but mainly for laminates to wood, water resistant (not waterproof), requires application of a thin film to both pieces, let dry 40 minutes, then put pieces together for an instant bond, moderate to high strength. Synthetic rubber compound. 1 part liquid, flammable (solvent), adequate ventilation required. Brands: "DAP Weldwood Original Contact Cement," DAP Inc, Baltimore, MD; "Constantine's Veneer Glue," Constantine's, Bronx, NY; "3M Fastbond Contact Adhesive," Minnesota Mining and Manufacturing Company, St. Paul, MN; and "Devcon Contact Cement," Chemical Development Corporation, Danvers, MA.

Cyanoacrylate Glue (CA glue) (Super Glue)

Bonds many materials including metals, rubber, and most plastics; not a good wood glue; nonporous; oil, water, and chemical resistant; very fast setting (< 5 seconds); low viscosity formulas are not gap fillers, use high viscosity formulas for gaps; poor shock and peel resistance; no clamping needed. Chemically reacts with moisture in the material being glued, may not cure in extremely dry climates. Use extreme care when working with this glue, IT BONDS SKIN INSTANTLY! Acetone clean up. Monomer resin based. 1 part liquid, non-flammable. Brands: "Devcon Premium Super Glue II," Chemical Development Corporation, Danvers, MA; "3M Pronto Instant Adhesive CA-7," Minnesota Mining and Manufacturing Company, St. Paul, MN; "Permabond," Permabond Engineering Adhesives, Englewood, NJ; "Krazy Glue Original," Elmer's Products, Inc, Columbus, OH; "Spectrum Jet Set 41," Holdtite Adhesives Limited, Gateshead, England; and "DAP Super Glue," DAP Inc, Baltimore, MD (many others, very common glue).

Epoxy Adhesive

Bonds to many materials, porous or nonporous; waterproof; resistant to most solvents and acid; setting time ranges from very fast (5 minutes) to very long (weeks); very high dry and wet strength. Some varieties are filled with metal powder (such as steel, aluminum, brass, or titanium) to function as a metal filler. Liquid, gel, and paste formulas usually dry transparent to brown, can be thinned and cleaned with acetone, non-shrinking if no thinner is used. Putty formulas dry to a variety of colors, non-shrinking. Hardens without evaporation (result of chemical reaction and heat). Synthetic resin based. 2 part liquid, gel, paste, or putty; non-flammable; not flexible; liquid, gel, and paste are clear to tan, putty may be green, blue, gray, or black. Brands: "Scotch-Weld Epoxy Adhesive 2158," Minnesota Mining and Manufacturing Company, St. Paul, MN; "Probond Regular Epoxy" and "Elmer's Superfast Epoxy," Elmer's Products, Inc, Columbus, OH; "Fixmaster 4 Minute Epoxy," Loctite Corporation, Rocky Hill, CT; "Devcon 5-Minute Thick Gel Epoxy" and "Devcon Titanium 5 Epoxy," Chemical Development Corporation, Danvers, MA; "VR Epoxy Series," Abatron, Inc, Kenosha, WI; and "J-B Weld," "J-B Kwik," "Marineweld," "Waterweld," and "Industro Weld," J-B Weld Company, Sulphur Springs, TX. Extremely common adhesive, most major adhesive manufacturers produce epoxy adhesives.

Ethylene Vinyl Acetate Glue (EVA glue)

Bonds a variety of slick nonporous materials to porous materials, originally developed for overlays such as vinyl and metallic films. High initial tack, dries to a soft, flexible film. Synthetic resin based. 1 part liquid. Brands: "Melamine Glue," Custom-Pak Adhesives, Newark, OH; "Extreme 6001XHM," Adhesive Engineering and Supply,

Seabrooke, NH; and "0007 Waterbase Adhesive," Chembond Adhesives, Inc, Tiffin, OH.

Fish Glue   Bonds porous or nonporous materials. Used for woodworking, bellows for organs or player pianos, photographic mounting, gummed paper, household use, and in paints. Natural protein based. Made from the jelly separated from fish oil or skins. The best fish glue is made from Russian isinglass which is produced from sturgeon. High initial tack, long cure time. 1 part paste. Brands: "Fish Glue", Arndt Organ Supply, Ankeny, IA and "Cold Fish Glue", Norland Products, Inc, New Brunswick, NJ.

Furan Cement   Made with synthetic furfural alcohol resins, very strong and highly resistant to chemicals and high temperatures. Commonly used for bonding acid resistant brick and tile.

Hide Glue - Flake

Bonds wood primarily, main glue used in musical instruments and old cabinet work, known as "hot glue" because it is applied while hot, at least 15 grades of hide glue are available, non-staining, fast setting, begins to gel at about 95°F, cures by evaporation, high dry strength (2000 psi), not waterproof. Natural protein (collagen) based. Made mainly from cattle hides. Good quality hide glue has a light clean odor, the cheap stuff stinks! 1 part-dry flakes, mixed with water (about 100 grams of dry glue to 180 grams of water), non-flammable, apply hot (145°F), and be careful of "cold joints" on the work. Brands: "Constantine's Cabinet Flake (Hide) Glue", Constantine's, Bronx, NY; "Hide Glue", Milligan and Higgins, Johnstown, NY; "Hide Glue", Bjorn Industries, Inc, Charlotte, NC; and "Hide Glue", Pianotek Supply Company, Ferndale, MI.

Hide Glue - Liquid (Pearl hide glue)

Bonds wood primarily; similar to flake hide glue but requires no mixing or heating; long setting time; heat resistant; resistant to most sealers, lacquers, water, mold and varnish; high strength; not flexible but not brittle. Natural protein based. 1 part liquid, non-flammable, honey color. Brand: "Franklin Hide Glue", Franklin International, Columbus, OH.

Hot Melt Glue Formulations are available to bond most materials, porous or nonporous. Very fast setting time (< 1 minute), moderate to no flexibility, cures by cooling not evaporation, medium strength, waterproof. Sticks of hot melt glue are applied with a special electric hot melt "glue gun", thin materials with hot melt glue backings are applied with an iron. Thermoplastic resin based, a wide variety of resins are available. 1 part solid sticks, pellets, or backings; non-flammable. Brands: "3M Jet-Weld Thermoset Adhesive TE-200", Minnesota Mining and Manufacturing Company, St. Paul, MN; "Hot-Grip", Adhesive Products Corporation, Chicago, IL; "Glue Stix SS6 Slow Set - Woodworking", Arrow Fastener Company, Inc, Saddle Brooke, NJ; and "HM101 Glue Sticks", Chembond Adhesives, Inc, Tiffin, OH (many others, very common adhesive).

Latex Combo Adhesive

Sticks a variety of materials, porous or nonporous, especially good for fabric and paper, water resistant (some are waterproof), moderate to weak strength, very flexible (becomes a synthetic rubber when cured). 1 part liquid or paste, non-flammable. Brand: "Flexible Patch-Stix", Adhesive Products Corporation, Chicago, IL.

Latex Glue

Rub-off latex, used mainly in photographic mounting, does not shrink.

Latex Resin Adhesive

Bonds a wide variety of materials both porous and nonporous such as paper, wood, and metals; use at temperatures above 20°F; cures completely in 24 hours; after cure it is water and heat resistant; high strength; water clean up when wet; mineral spirits clean up when dry. Synthetic latex resin based. 1 part paste, white. Brand: "DAP Easy Bond Do-It-All Adhesive", DAP Inc, Baltimore, MD.

Neoprene Adhesive

Bonds a variety of materials, porous or nonporous, but primarily used to bond paneling to walls; water resistant; moderate to high strength; setting time is two part - apply and separate for 10 minutes to increase tack, then join parts; final set 24 hours. Synthetic rubber based. 1 part viscous liquid, flammable. Brand: "DAP Weldwood Panel Adhesive", DAP Inc, Baltimore, MD.

Polyester Resin Adhesive (Automotive body filler)
(Wood filler)

Bonds a variety of materials. Liquid is used mainly with fiberglass cloth to bond to wood or metal for boat hulls, surf boards, and car bodies; paste is mixed with a filler such as talc and used as an automotive body filler or wood filler. Waterproof, not flexible, high strength, use at temperatures from 70°F to 80°F, setting time < 30 minutes. Color of liquid is usually clear to amber but can be tinted, paste is usually gray or brown; both can be sanded and painted. Synthetic resin based. 2 part liquid or 1 part paste, flammable, amount of catalyst for 2 part liquid is critical so measure precisely. Brands: "Fiberglass Resin Jelly" and "Evercoat Rage Premium Lightweight Body Filler", Fibre Glass-Evercoat, Cincinnati, OH; "Polyester General Purpose Resin ", Fiberglass Coatings, Inc, St. Petersburg, FL; "Automotive Resin ", Kardol Quality Products, Inc, Lebanon, OH; "Bondo Body Filler", Bondo/Mar-Hyde Corporation, Cincinnati, OH; and "Minwax High Performance Wood Filler", Sherwin-Williams Company, Cleveland, OH.

Polysulfide Adhesive

Bonds to a variety of materials but is primarily for sealing seams; basically a caulking type adhesive that, when dry, is completely waterproof; setting time varies from several days to several weeks depending on humidity; medium strength; when cured it becomes a synthetic rubber; flexible. Synthetic elastomer based. 1 or 2 part. Brand: "Exide Polysulfide Caulk", Atlas Minerals and Chemicals, Mertztown, PA.

Polyurethane Glue

Bonds to virtually everything but is superior for wood bonding, pressure and moisture are necessary for optimum bonding, chemically reacts with moisture in the material being glued, expands to fill voids. Expansion can be a problem if too much glue is applied to a joint, use SPARINGLY! Use at temperatures between 40°F and 90°F. 90% cure in 1 to 4 hours, fully cured in 24 hours, clamp pieces together after 15 minutes. Waterproof when dry, accepts stains well, easy to sand, will not dull saw. Wet glue cleans up with denatured alcohol, acetone, or mineral spirits; once dry only mechanical removal (sanding) works. Eye, throat,and skin irritant; use in well ventilated area. Synthetic resin based. 1 part liquid. Amber color when wet, dries to a tan color. Brands: "Gorilla Glue", Lutz File and Tool Company, Cincinnati, OH; "Titebond Polyurethane Glue", Franklin International, Columbus, OH; "Excel One Liquid Polyurethane Adhesive", AmBel Corporation, Cottonport, LA; and "Probond Polyurethane Glue", Elmer's Products, Inc, Columbus, OH.

Polyvinyl Acetate Glue (PVA glue) (Elmer's Glue) (White glue)

Bonds wood, paper products, fabric, leather, and ceramics; not waterproof; very strong if away from moisture; setting times vary from several hours to several days; use at temperatures above 60°F; dries transparent; poor gap filling; do not use where glue must support load; corrodes metal. Does not bond well over old glues, not good for furniture repair! Synthetic resin based. 1 part liquid, non-flammable, white liquid-dries clear. Brands: "DAP Weldwood Hobby and Craft Glue", DAP Inc, Baltimore, MD and "Elmer's Glue-All", Elmer's Products, Inc, Columbus, OH (many more, very common glue).

Polyvinyl Chloride Glue (PVC glue)

Bonds glass, china, porcelain, metal, marble, hard plastics, and other materials including some porous (treat both sides for porous); not generally for wood; waterproof; resistant to gasoline, oil, and alcohol; fast setting (minutes); clean up with lacquer thinner. 1 part liquid, flammable, clear. Brand: "Sheer Magic", Miracle Adhesives Corp, Long Island, NY.

Pyroxylin Cement (Household cement)

Solution of nitrocellulose in a solvent which is sometimes mixed with resin, gum, or synthetic; poor tack but excellent adhesion to almost everything.

Rabbit-skin Glue

Bonds wood but is primarily used for gilding, artwork, and furniture repair. Natural protein based. Made from rabbit skins.

Resorcinol Resin Glue

Bonds to a variety of materials but is used mainly as a boat building glue (the main one); completely waterproof; thinning and cleanup before setting with alcohol and water; when cured it is resistant to water, salt water, gasoline, oil, acids, alkalis, and many solvents; setting time varies with temperature - 10 hours at 70°F to 3 hours at 100°F; do not use at temperatures below 70°F; very strong; cures to a very dark color; can be sanded and painted; good gap filler; do not use with copper or copper alloys. Synthetic resin based. 2 part liquid and powder, caustic powder, red. Brand: "DAP Weldwood Waterproof Resorcinol Glue", DAP Inc, Baltimore, MD.

Rice Glue   Bonds to wood, paper, fabric, leather; dry powder must be cooked with water; pre-cooked paste is available; long cure time; good initial tack; dries clear; flexible. Natural starch based. Made from rice. 1 part dry powder or paste.

Rubber Adhesive (Construction adhesive) (Elastomeric mastic)

Bonds to almost anything, porous or nonporous, will not bond two nonporous materials; water, heat, and alcohol resistant; strong bond; moderately flexible; good gap filling; setting time 24 hours; full strength is reached in 24 hours; use at temperatures above 40°F. Natural or synthetic rubber based, light gray to black color. 1 part viscous liquid, solvents, use adequate ventilation. Brands: "Black Magic Tough Glue", Miracle Adhesives Corporation, Long Island, NY; "DAP Beats The Nail All Purpose Construction Adhesive", DAP Inc, Baltimore, MD; "Devcon Rubber Adhesive", Chemical Development Corporation, Danvers, MA; and "LN-601, Liquid Nails Multi-Purpose Construction Adhesive", Macco Adhesives, Cleveland, OH.

Silicone Adhesive

Although this group is primarily a sealer or caulking compound, it does have adhesive characteristics. Bonds porous or nonporous materials, moderate to weak strength, waterproof, setting time from 2 hours to 2 days, can withstand temperatures of 400°F to 600°F, flexible, will not bond to itself, resists oil and some solvents. 1 part viscous liquid, non-flammable. Brands: "Silicone II Household Glue", General Electric Co, Waterford, NY and "Devcon Premium Silicone Adhesive", Chemical Development Corporation, Danvers, MA.

Soybean Glue   Bonds wood chip layers in interior plywood and paneling, better water resistance than most vegetable pastes and better adhesive power, moderate to low dry strength. Natural protein based. Made from soybean cake. 1 part, yellow powder mixed with water, white to tan paste.

Tapioca Glue   Also known as vegetable glue, used in cheap plywoods, postage stamps, envelopes, and labels. Quick tack and cheap, but deteriorates.

Ultraviolet Curing Adhesive

A variety of synthetic resin and polymer based adhesives that are liquid or paste on application and cure only when exposed to ultraviolet light; typically used for bonding glass to glass, metal, and plastic. Brands: "Solar 7000", Impact Adhesives, West Yorkshire, England and "352 Loctite", Loctite Corporation, Rocky Hill, CT.

Urea-Resin Glue (Plastic resin glue)

Bonds wood primarily; resistant to water, oil, gasoline, and many solvents when cured; do not use with copper or copper alloys; setting time ranges from 3 to 7 hours (less at high temperatures); very high strength (usually stronger than wood); not a gap filler; non-staining; amber or light tan to black color. Synthetic resin based. 1 part powder, mix with water to form cream or 2 part liquid resin and powder catalyst. Brand: "DAP Weldwood Plastic Resin Glue", DAP Inc, Baltimore, MD.

Vinyl Adhesive

Another caulk with adhesive properties. Bonds to a variety of construction materials including wood, concrete, tile, glass, fabric, and metal; water clean up before cure; water resistant after cure; high strength; flexible; paintable; resistant to mildew, oils, paint thinner, gasoline, asphalt, antifreeze, soap, rust, corrosion, salt water, mild acids, and mild alkalis; will bond to itself; will bond damp materials, moisture aids curing. Available in a variety of colors. Synthetic polymer based. 1 part paste, non-toxic, non-flammable. Brand: "Phenoseal Vinyl Adhesive Caulk", Gloucester Company, Franklin, MA.

Water-Phase Epoxy Adhesive

Bonds to many materials but is used primarily with fiberglass as a repair tool and as a surface coat for concrete floors, water soluble when liquid and completely waterproof when hard, medium to high strength, fast setting < 30 minutes, can be sanded and painted. 2 part liquid. Brand: "Dur-A-Poxy High Gloss Water-Based Formula", Dur-A-Flex, East Hartford, CT.

Wheat Glue

Bonds to wood, paper, fabric, and leather; mainly used in paper cartons and bottle labeling; dry powder must be cooked with water; pre-cooked paste is available; long cure time; good initial tack; dries clear; flexible. Natural starch based. Made from wheat. 1 part dry powder or paste.

NOTES:

In all of the glue descriptions, the term "wood" also refers to "wood products" such as plywood, particle board, and aspen board.

Glue Hints and General Rules

1. Apply glues and adhesives to clean, dry surfaces.

2. Drying/curing times can usually be reduced by increasing the temperature. 70°F or higher is generally preferred.

3. Be careful of the solvents and catalysts used in many adhesives, most are toxic and can also hurt your eyes, skin, and lungs. Use adequate ventilation!

4. Hardwoods require less clamping time than softwoods.

5. Domestic hardwoods are usually easier to glue than imported, tropical hardwoods.

6. The end grain of any wood is highly absorbent and will create a weak joint. To prevent this, apply a thin coat of glue to the end grain before the rest of the work and then give it a second coat when doing the normal gluing.

7. Precision alignment of parts glued with contact cement can be obtained by placing a thin sheet of paper between the work pieces after the contact cement has been applied and is no longer tacky, align the work pieces, press together, and then pull out the paper for final bonding.

8. Don't glue green wood. Damp wood may be glued with one of the adhesives that cures by reacting with water.

9. Clamp glue joints whenever possible for increased strength.

10. Don't apply too much glue, this can actually weaken a joint in some cases.

11. When all else fails READ AND FOLLOW DIRECTIONS!

RESOURCES:

Excellent books on common glues and adhesives are:

Adhesives Handbook, 3rd Edition, 1984, J. Shields, Butterworth and Co, London, England.

Home and Workshop Guide to Glues and Adhesives, 1979, George Daniels, Popular Science, Harper and Row, New York, NY.

The Glue Book, 1999, William Tandy Young, The Taunton Press, Newtown, CT.

They contain an abundance of information on glues, gluing techniques, and hints. Any of these books would be a great addition to a reference library!

On the World Wide Web see:

"The Sticky Issue of Adhesives, Glues, and Tapes" at www.naturalhandyman.com

"Adhesive Bonding of Wood Materials" by Charles B. Vick, at www.fpl.fs.fed.us/documnts/fplgtr/fplgtr113/ch09.pdf.

Paints and Finishes

House and Industrial Paints

There are basically 5 groups of house and industrial paints: oil base, alkyd, emulsion, water thinned, and catalytic. Each of these classes is subdivided into exterior and interior.

Oil Base Interior and exterior, oil vehicle, thinned by solvents such as turpentine and mineral spirits, very slow drying, strong smell. Mainly used as exterior base. Use in well ventilated area. Good adhesion to chalky surfaces.

Alkyd Synthetic oil vehicle of a resin known as alkyd. Interior and exterior enamels, easy to apply, fast drying, odorless, and produce a tough coating. Easy cleanup and thinning with mineral spirits. Excellent interior paint, not resistant to chemicals, solvents, or corrosives.

Emulsion Water based paint mixture. Latex paints fall into this category, the most common latex paints are acrylic and vinyl (PVA). Available as interior and exterior, and as flat, gloss, and semigloss enamels. Very quick drying (sometimes less than 1 hour) but do not wash for 2 to 4 weeks, paints over damp surfaces, odorless, alkali resistant, doesn't usually blister and peel. Excellent cover and blending characteristics, but poor adhesion to chalky surfaces, easy cleanup. Use special latex primers for painting bare wood. Paint at temperatures above 45°F. By far the most popular paint today.

Water-Thinned Generally a non-emulsion paint such as calcimine, casein, and white wash. These paints are used primarily on masonry surfaces. The most common water thinned paint is Portland Cement paint.

Catalytic Cures by chemical reaction, not by evaporation of a solvent or water as in the other paints. Catalytic paints are usually two-part paints: you have to mix two parts to start the curing process. Included in this class are the epoxy and polyurethane resins. Extremely tough and durable, they are highly resistant to water, wear, acids, solvents, abrasion, salt water, and chemicals. Drying times are very fast (several hours). Good ventilation is necessary when working with these paints. Catalytic paints can not be applied over other paints. Follow the manufacturer's instructions very closely, these paints are not easy to use.

House paints are further subgrouped into exterior and interior types as described below:

Exterior Paint Designed to have long life spans, good adhesion, and resistance to moisture, ultraviolet light, mildew, and sulfide and acid fumes. Also includes the varnish and stain groups described later. Never use interior paint in place of exterior paint; it will not hold up under the weather.

Interior Paint Designed to maximize the hiding ability of the paint with only 1 or 2 coats. Flat paints contain more pigment than high sheen paints but are less durable. Good interior paints can be touched up easily without major changes in the sheen or color.

Wood Finishes

Varnish

Varnish is a solution of a hard resin, a drying oil (linseed oil is most common), metallic dryers, and solvent. There are two types of resin, natural and synthetic. Natural resin varnishes are slow drying (24 to 48 hrs) and are subclassed as "long oil" (meaning high oil content; "spar" varnish is a long oil varnish) and "short oil" (meaning low oil content; "rubbing" varnish is a short oil varnish). Natural resin varnishes are tough and used mainly for exterior and marine applications. Synthetic resin varnishes contain resins such as alkyd (the most common), polyurethane, vinyl, and phenolic. They are more durable and faster drying than natural resin varnishes. Apply with natural bristle brushes; apply 3 to 4 coats total, let dry between coats, and sand with 240 grit sandpaper. Varnishes are usually transparent and are excellent sealers.

Shellac

Shellac is one of the oldest wood finishes. It is made from a mixture of the dry resinous secretions of the lac insect (*laccifer lacca*, southern Asia, mainly northern India) and alcohol. Once mixed, shellac has a very short shelf life, so store it in flake form. Keep water out of shellac! Even a few drops of water will turn shellac cloudy. Shellac is mixed in what is called a "cut." A "3 pound cut" is 3 pounds of shellac in 1 gallon of alcohol. Initial coats are typically 1 or 2 pound cuts. Shellac is applied with a brush. Better finishes use 6 to 8 coats. Each coat should be sanded with 220 to 240 grit sandpaper after it has dried (1 to 2 hours). The final coat is typically rubbed with a fine 3/0 steel wool.

Lacquer

Lacquer is a fast-drying, high gloss varnish used by most furniture manufacturers as the top-coat finish. It is very hard, dries crystal clear, and is highly resistant to alcohols, water, heat, and mild acids. Although the original lacquers came from insects and the sap of the sumac tree, almost all lacquers produced today are synthetic and are mixed with some combination of resins (better adhesion), nitrocellulose, linseed or castor oil (improves flexibility), vinyls, acrylics or synthetic polymers. The main problem with lacquer is that it dries so fast that it is sometimes difficult to get a good finish. Use a spray gun if possible; a brush does not work. Multiple coats are usually necessary. Some finishes may react with the solvents in lacquer and may need to be protected with a coat of shellac before applying lacquer.

Oil

Penetrating oils such as linseed oil, tung oil, and Danish rubbing oil make up a class of finishes that protect wood while leaving the grain and natural texture visible. Oils won't crack, chip, or scale off and provide a beautiful surface. The addition of resins such as polyurethane greatly increase the toughness of the surface and still maintain the clear finish. The oils are applied with a soft rag, left to sit for 30 minutes to allow the oil to soak in, then buffed with a soft clean rag. Buffing with fine 4/0 steel wool will improve the sheen.

Water-based Resin

Similar to synthetic resin varnish but uses water as the solvent instead of mineral spirits. Resins include acrylics and urethane. Fast drying - at 35% relative humidity and 70°F will dry to the touch in 15 to 30 minutes and can be sanded and recoated in 2 hours. Apply with natural bristle brushes, 3 to 4 coats total, let dry between coats, and sand with 240 grit sandpaper. Water-based resin finishes are usually transparent. May not be compatible with oil- or solvent-based finishes; use shellac or a clear sealer to separate the two dissimilar finishes.

Other Paints

Primers

Primers are paints intended to produce a good foundation for the overlying coats of paint. Exterior wood primers penetrate deeply into the surface, adhere tightly to the surface, and seal off the wood. Metal primers are specifically designed to adhere to the metal and stop oxidation (rusting). Automotive primers usually contain a lot of resin. Primers typically have an abundance of pigment to allow sanding if necessary.

Fire-Retardant

Paints that decompose by melting into a thick mass of cellular charred material that insulates the material it is painted on. The decomposition begins at a temperature below the combustion point of the substrate; ratings are based on the ability to suppress combustion.

Floor Paint

Specialized coatings that contain hard substances such as epoxy and phenolic modified alkyds, chlorinated rubber, and varnish. The coatings must also be water resistant.

Texture Paint

Interior house coatings for ceilings and walls that produce a matte finish. They can contain sand, styrene fragments, nut shells, perlite, volcanic ash, or any other coarse material to create a texture.

Two Part Paint

This class of paint is generally expensive and includes the epoxies, polyesters, urethanes, and styrene-solubilized polyesters. They are all thermosetting, i.e. they cure by heat once a reactant has been added. These paints are extremely tough and durable and chemically resistant.

Automotive Paints

Urethane Enamel

The best of the car finishes, lasts over 10 years, has the best look, and is the most expensive. Paint jobs can run over $1000 and paint cost alone ranges from $50 to $100 per gallon.

Polyurethane "Clear Coat"

The top coat of a two-part paint, it is applied over a base coat of acrylic enamel or acrylic lacquer producing a beautiful "wet look" finish just like a factory paint job. This type of finish is very difficult to apply and should be done by an expert. Has a life of 8 to 10 years and costs between $400 and $600.

Acrylic Lacquer Mid-range auto paint, very fast drying, much higher gloss and better durability than the alkyd enamels. Must be machine polished after drying so it is more expensive than the acrylic enamel paints. Acrylic lacquer must not be painted over acrylic enamel. Expect to pay $300 for this paint job. Life span is 5 to 7 years.

Acrylic Enamel Mid-range auto paint, very slow drying, much higher gloss and better durability than the alkyd enamels and acrylic lacquer. Acrylic enamel should not be painted over acrylic lacquer. Usually requires a heat booth to aid drying. Expect to pay $200 to $300 for a paint job.

Alkyd Enamel Cheap paint with low durability (will sometimes loose its gloss in less than 2 months). Paint life will only be 1 to 3 years. The paint job will probably only cost $100 to $200 and is commonly referred to as the "baked enamel" job since the vehicle is baked at 150°F in a heat booth to set the paint.

RESOURCES:

Excellent books and articles on paint and painting techniques include:

The Household Paint Selector, 1975, National Paint and Coatings Association, Barnes and Noble Books, New York, NY;

How To Paint Anything, 1972, Hubbard H. Cobb, Macmillan Publishing Company, Inc, New York, NY;

Paint Handbook, 1981, Guy E. Weismantel, Editor, McGraw-Hill Book Company, New York, NY;

Complete Handbook Of Home Painting, 1975, John L. Scherer, Tab Books, Blue Ridge Summit, PA;

Coloring, Finishing, and Painting Wood, Revised Edition, 1961, A. C. Newell and W. F. Holtrop, Charles A. Bennett Company, Inc, Peoria, IL;

How To Buy A New (Automotive) Paint Job, February 1987, The Family Handyman Magazine, Webb Publishing Company, St. Paul, MN;

Water-based Finishes, 1998, Andy Charron, Taunton Press, Inc, Newtown, CT.

Solvents

A solvent is a material, usually a liquid, that has the power to dissolve another material and form a homogeneous mixture known as a solution. There are literally thousands of solvents available commercially, but most are not readily available to the average consumer. The following solvents are generally available in hardware stores, paint stores, computer stores, and drug stores and provide an excellent range of capabilities. *Note that most of these are toxic, poisonous, and flammable; some are suspected carcinogens; use adequate ventilation with all solvents; exercise caution when using them; and keep out of the reach of children.*

NOTE: The solvents listed below have been arranged in approximate order of "strength", i.e., solvents at the top of the list are stronger than those at the bottom of the list.

Lacquer Thinner

An organic solvent which is a mixture of toluene, isopropanol, methyl isobutyl keytone, acetone, propylene glycol, monomethyl ether acetate, and ethyl acetate. Photochemically reactive. Used to thin lacquers and epoxies but can be used as a general cleaner and degreaser. Highly flammable; poisonous; eye and skin irritant. Dissolves or softens many plastics. **Brands:** "Klean-Strip® Lacquer Thinner," W. M. Barr and Company, Memphis, TN; "Lacquer Thinner R7K22," Sherwin-Williams Company, Cleveland, OH; and "Startex™ Lacquer Thinner," Startex Chemical, Inc, Conroe, TX.

Acetone
A volatile organic solvent for cellulose acetate and nitrocellous. Also known as dimethyl ketone, methyl ketone, dimethlyformaldehyde, ketone propane, or 2-propanone; CH_3COCH_3; soluble in water and alcohol; non-photochemically reactive; used to clean and remove polyester, epoxy resins, ink, adhesives, contact cement, and fiberglass resin. Dissolves or softens many plastics and synthetics. Irritates the eyes, nose, and throat; prolonged contact may cause skin irritation; use with adequate ventilation. **Brands:** "Klean-Strip® Acetone," W. M. Barr and Company, Memphis, TN; "Acetone R6K9," Sherwin-Williams Company, Cleveland, OH; and "Startex™ Acetone," Startex Chemical, Inc, Conroe, TX.

Finger Nail Polish Remover
An organic solvent which is a mixture of acetone, propylene carbonate, dimethyl glutarate, dimethyl succinate, and dimethyl adipate. Good for various applications, dissolves plastics. Extremely flammable; eye, nose, and throat irritant; poisonous; harmful to synthetic fabrics and wood finishes. **Brand:** "Nail Polish Remover," Topco Associates, Inc, Skokie, IL.

Adhesive Cleaners, Thinners, and Removers
Organic solvents which are mixtures of petroleum distillates (mineral spirits) and n-butyl acetate or propylene glycol monomethly ether acetate. Very powerful solvents that are typically used to clean and thin fresh adhesive, or to clean and remove dried adhesive; also removes oil, grease, and wax. These solvents will clean up brushes and tools that have dried-on adhesives if you let them soak for an hour. Dissolves or softens some plastics, rubber, paint, varnish, and asphalt. Avoid breathing fumes for long periods and use with adequate ventilation. Some are photochemically reactive. **Brands:** "DAP® Weldwood Cleaner and Thinner," DAP, Inc, Baltimore, MD and "Klean-Strip® Adhesive Remover," W. M. Barr and Company, Memphis, TN.

Contact Cement Solvent
An organic solvent which is a mixture of toluene, acetone, and hexane. A very powerful solvent that is typically used with contact cement adhesives, this solvent will clean up brushes and tools that have dried-on contact adhesives if you let them soak for an hour. Dissolves or softens some plastics. Avoid breathing fumes for long periods and use with adequate ventilation. Flammable. **Brand:** "DAP® Weldwood Standard Solvent," DAP, Inc, Baltimore, MD.

Hexane
An organic solvent from petroleum distillation. Also known as n-hexane, hexyl hydride, petroleum ether,

and petroleum naphtha; $C6H14$. Major solvent and cleaning agent; used in paint thinners, adhesives, degreasing agents, and cleaners. Highly flammable, vapor is explosive. Will soften some plastics, rubber, and synthetic coatings. Toxic; eye, nose, and throat irritant; use with adequate ventilation. **Brands:** "Aktol® Hexane," Aktol Chemicals, Cape Town, South Africa and "Exxsol® Hexane Solvent," Exxon Company USA, Houston, TX.

Toluene	An organic solvent from petroleum distillation or from the tolu tree. Also known as phenyl methane, methyl benzol, toluol, and methyl benzene; $C_6H_5CH_3$. Used as a solvent in paints, inks, adhesives, cleaning agents, and cosmetic nail products; used as a medical agent to expel or destroy roundworms and hookworms. Fast evaporation rate. Flammable; explosive; eye, nose, throat, and skin irritant; use with adequate ventilation. **Brands:** "Aktol® Toluene," Aktol Chemicals, Cape Town, South Africa; "Klean-Strip® Toluene," W. M. Barr and Company, Memphis, TN; "Toluene," Exxon Company USA, Houston, TX; "Toluol (Toluene) R2K1," Sherwin-Williams Company, Cleveland, OH; and "Startex™ Toluene," Startex Chemical, Inc, Conroe, TX.
Xylene	An organic solvent from petroleum distillation. A mixture of o-xylene, m-xylene, p-xylene, and ethylben- zene. Also known as dimethylbenzene, xylol, and mixed xylene; $C_6H_4(CH_3)_2$. Moderately soluble in water, slower evaporation rate than toluene. Flammable; eye, nose, and throat irritant; use with adequate ventilation. **Brands:** "Aktol® Xylene," Aktol Chemicals, Cape Town, South Africa; "Klean-Strip® Xylol Xylene," W. M. Barr and Company, Memphis, TN; "Xylene," Exxon Company USA, Houston, TX; "Xylol (Xylene) R2K4," Sherwin-Williams Company, Cleveland, OH; and "Startex™ Xylene," Startex Chemical, Inc, Conroe, TX.

Methyl Ethyl Keytone (MEK) (Plastic cement solvent)

An organic solvent which is also known as ethyl methyl keytone, MEK, methyl acetone, or 2-butanone; $CH_3CH_2COCH_3$. Soluble in water, alcohols, ether, acetone, and benzene; dissolves plastic and is typically used in making model airplane cement; will dissolve many plastics, resins, and rubber; used in lacquers, varnishes, polyurethanes, and enamels; used as a solvent for coatings, adhesives, magnetic tape, and printing ink. Very fast evaporation rate. Both liquid and vapor are extremely flammable; poisonous; eye, throat, and skin irritant; strong solvent smell, use with adequate ventilation. **Brands:** "Methyl Ethyl Keytone (MEK) R6K10," Sherwin-Williams Company, Cleveland, OH; "Methyl Ethyl Keytone," Wellborn Paint Manufacturing Company, Albuquerque, NM; "Methyl Ethyl Keytone," Mallinckrodt Baker, Inc, Phillipsburg, NJ; and "Startex™ M.E.K (Methyl Ethyl Ketone)," Startex Chemical, Inc, Conroe, TX.

Adhesive Remover with Methylene Chloride

An organic solvent which is a mixture of methylene chloride (also known as dichloromethane or methane dichloride; CH$_2$Cl$_2$), ethylene glycol monobutyl ether, and methanol. A strong solvent. Dissolves or softens some plastics; do not use with linoleum, rubber, asphalt tile, fiber glass or other synthetics. Use with adequate ventilation. Methylene chloride is a suspected carcinogen.

Brand: "Klean-Strip® Non-flammable Adhesive Remover with Methylene Chloride," W. M. Barr and Company, Memphis, TN.

Naphtha	Petroleum distillate also known as petroleum benzine, or coal tar. Slight odor; non-photochemically reactive; flammable; very fast evaporation rate.

Brands: "Klean-Strip® VM&P Naphtha," W. M. Barr and Company, Memphis, TN; "Naphtha With Benzine and Hexane," Exxon Company USA, Houston, TX; "VM&P Naphtha R1K3," Sherwin-Williams Company, Cleveland, OH; and "Startex™ VM&P Naphtha," Startex Chemical, Inc, Conroe, TX.

Turpentine	An organic solvent distilled from pine trees; also known as "steam distilled spirits" or "gum spirits"; used as a thinner and cleaner for oil based paint, varnish, enamel, and stain. Photochemically reactive.

Brand: "Klean-Strip® Pure Gum Spirits Turpentine," W. M. Barr and Company, Memphis, TN and "Startex™ Gum Turpentine," Startex Chemical, Inc, Conroe, TX.

D-limonene (Citrus terpene)

An organic solvent derived from the evaporation or distillation of citrus fruit oils; also called cajeputene or cinene; C$_{10}$H$_{16}$. Can also be mixed with petroleum distillates, ethers, and alcohols. Used mainly as a cleaner and degreaser; will dissolve oil, wax, grease, tar, and ink. Eye, throat, and skin irritant; flammable; use with proper ventilation.

Brands: "Citrusolv™ 40," BetCo Corporation, Toledo, OH; "Orange Solvent," CIM Supply, Inc, New Kinsington, PA; and "Orange Asphalt Remover," Orange Products Corporation, Greensboro, NC.

Paint Thinner (Mineral spirits)

An organic solvent from petroleum distillation, used as a paint thinner and cleaner, also known as Stoddard solvent, white spirits, mineral terpentine, safety solvent naphtha, and petropine. Very slow evaporation rate. Flammable; poisonous; eye and skin irritant; use with adequate ventilation.

Brands: "Klean-Strip® Odorless Mineral Spirits," "Klean-Strip® Paint Thinner," and "Gillespie® Mineral Spirits," W. M. Barr and Company, Memphis, TN; "Startex™ Paint Thinner, 100% Mineral Spirits," Startex Chemical, Inc, Conroe, TX; and "Mineral Spirits R1K4," Sherwin-Williams Company, Cleveland, OH.

Freon® TMS Cleaning Agent

NO LONGER MANUFACTURED; FREON AND OTHER CFC's MUST BE RECYCLED! Trichlortrifluoroethane, Freon® TF, non-flammable, non-conductive, low toxicity, odorless and does not attack plastic, rubber, paints or metal; low surface tension, evaporates fast. Although not commonly seen, freon is an excellent solvent and is typically used to clean electrical connectors and computer components. *Note: Depletes ozone, no longer manufactured.* **Brand:** "DuPont® Freon® TMS Cleaning Agent," DuPont Flurochemicals, Wilmington, DE.

Vetrel® Cleaning Agent

A proprietary hydrofluorocarbon fluid which can be mixed with dichloroethylene, cyclopentane, or methanol. Used mainly for vapor degreasing; can be used on most metals and plastics, and is typically used to clean electrical connectors and computer components. Nonflammable, nontoxic, mild eye and skin irritant.
Brand: "DuPont® Vertrel® Cleaning Agent," DuPont Flurochemicals, Wilmington, DE.

Methyl Alcohol (Methanol) (Solvent alcohol)

An organic solvent also called wood alcohol, CH_3OH. Non-photochemically reactive; used primarily as a thinner for shellac and shellac-based primers and in marine alcohol stoves; soluble in water and other alcohols. Can be mixed with gasoline in a tank to eliminate moisture problems (1/2 pint methanol per 15 gallons gasoline). Good cleaner for computer plastic parts. Do not use with oil or latex paints, stains, or varnishes. Poisonous, flammable ,use in well ventilated area, keep out of the reach of children.
Brands: "Methanol", Methanex Methanol Company, Dallas, TX and "Methanol R6K1," Sherwin-Williams Company, Cleveland, OH.

Denatured Alcohol (Industrial ethanol)

An organic solvent which is a mixture of ethyl alcohol (grain alcohol) and a small amount of methyl alcohol to make it unfit for drinking. Soluble in water and other alcohols; non-photochemically reactive; typically used to thin shellac, clean glass and metal, to clean ink from rubber rollers; and as a fuel in marine stoves. To clean glass, porcelain, and piano keys, mix 1:1 with water. Poisonous, flammable, use in well ventilated area, keep out of the reach of children.
Brands: "Klean-Strip® S-L-X Denatured Alcohol," W. M. Barr and Company, Memphis, TN and "Startex™ Denatured Alcohol," Startex Chemical, Inc, Conroe, TX.

Isopropyl Alcohol (Rubbing alcohol)

An organic solvent also known as 2-propanol, isopropanol, and dimethylcarbinol; $CH3CHOHCH3$. Soluble in water and other alcohols; general cleaner and disinfectant; specifically used to clean tape recorder heads and computer disk drive heads. Flammable, poisonous, use in well ventilated area, keep out of the reach of children.
Brands: "TopCare® 70% Isopropyl Alcohol," Topco Associates, Inc, Skokie, IL and "Isopropanol (Isopropyl Alcohol)," Sherwin-Williams Company, Cleveland, OH.

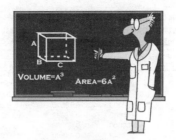

$$VOLUME = A^3 \qquad AREA = 6A^2$$

Math

Chord Length for Dividing the Circumference of a Circle
into an Equal Number of Segments 300
Circles - Diameter, Radius, Circumference, and Area 304
Convert Angles in Degrees to Degrees & Minutes,
Radians, Inches Rise in 12 Inch Run, and % Grade 307
Convert Minutes Into Decimals of a Degree.................................311
Convert Seconds into Decimals of a Degree 312
Distance Across Corners of Squares and Hexagons 313
Excess Stock and Fillet Area...316
Factors for Numbers Between 1 and 100.....................................319
Formulas and Constants for Computing Regular Polygons 320
Fractions of inches - Decimal Equivalent; Square, Cube,
Square Root, Cube Root 322
Fractions of Inches - Millimeter Equivalent; Square, Cube,
Square Root, Cube Root 324
Natural Trigonometric Functions - Angles In Degrees 327
Right Triangles 336
Oblique Triangles 337
Plane Figure Formulas 338
Solid Figure Formulas 344
Segments of Circles for Radius = 1 349
Spheres - Surface Area and Volume..354

Chord Length for Dividing the Circumference of a Circle into an Equal Number of Segments

Number of Segments, n	Center Angle, θ degrees, θ$_D$	radians, θ$_R$	Length of Chord, L
2	180.000	3.14159	1.0000000
4	90.0000	1.57080	0.7071068
6	60.0000	1.04720	0.5000000
8	45.0000	0.78540	0.3826834
10	36.0000	0.62832	0.3090170
12	30.0000	0.52360	0.2588190
14	25.7143	0.44880	0.2225209
16	22.5000	0.39270	0.1950903
18	20.0000	0.34907	0.1736482
20	18.0000	0.31416	0.1564345
22	16.3636	0.28560	0.1423148
24	15.0000	0.26180	0.1305262
26	13.8462	0.24166	0.1205367
28	12.8571	0.22440	0.1119645
30	12.0000	0.20944	0.1045285
32	11.2500	0.19635	0.0980171
34	10.5882	0.18480	0.0922684
36	10.0000	0.17453	0.0871557
38	9.4737	0.16535	0.0825793
40	9.0000	0.15708	0.0784591
42	8.5714	0.14960	0.0747301
44	8.1818	0.14280	0.0713392
46	7.8261	0.13659	0.0682424
48	7.5000	0.13090	0.0654031
50	7.2000	0.12566	0.0627905
52	6.9231	0.12083	0.0603785
54	6.6667	0.11636	0.0581448
56	6.4286	0.11220	0.0560704
57	6.3158	0.11023	0.0550878
58	6.2069	0.10833	0.0541389
59	6.1017	0.10649	0.0532222
60	6.0000	0.10472	0.0523360
61	5.9016	0.10300	0.0514788
62	5.8065	0.10134	0.0506492
63	5.7143	0.09973	0.0498459
64	5.6250	0.09817	0.0490677
66	5.4545	0.09520	0.0475819
68	5.2941	0.09240	0.0461835

Number of Segments, n	Center Angle, θ degrees, θ_D	radians, θ_R	Length of Chord, L
70	5.1429	0.08976	0.0448648
72	5.0000	0.08727	0.0436194
74	4.8649	0.08491	0.0424412
76	4.7368	0.08267	0.0413250
78	4.6154	0.08055	0.0402659
80	4.5000	0.07854	0.0392598
82	4.3902	0.07662	0.0383027
84	4.2857	0.07480	0.0373912
86	4.1860	0.07306	0.0365220
88	4.0909	0.07140	0.0356923
90	4.0000	0.06981	0.0348995
92	3.9130	0.06830	0.0341411
94	3.8298	0.06684	0.0334150
96	3.7500	0.06545	0.0327191
98	3.6735	0.06411	0.0320516
100	3.6000	0.06283	0.0314108
102	3.5294	0.06160	0.0307951
104	3.4615	0.06042	0.0302030
106	3.3962	0.05928	0.0296333
108	3.3333	0.05818	0.0290847
110	3.2727	0.05712	0.0285561
112	3.2143	0.05610	0.0280463
114	3.1579	0.05512	0.0275543
116	3.1034	0.05417	0.0270794
118	3.0508	0.05325	0.0266205
120	3.0000	0.05236	0.0261769
122	2.9508	0.05150	0.0257479
124	2.9032	0.05067	0.0253327
126	2.8571	0.04987	0.0249307
128	2.8125	0.04909	0.0245412
130	2.7692	0.04833	0.0241637
132	2.7273	0.04760	0.0237977
134	2.6866	0.04689	0.0234426
136	2.6471	0.04620	0.0230979
138	2.6087	0.04553	0.0227632
140	2.5714	0.04488	0.0224381
142	2.5352	0.04425	0.0221221
144	2.5000	0.04363	0.0218149
146	2.4658	0.04304	0.0215161
148	2.4324	0.04245	0.0212254
150	2.4000	0.04189	0.0209424
152	2.3684	0.04134	0.0206669
154	2.3377	0.04080	0.0203985

Number of Segments, n	Center Angle, θ degrees, θ_D	radians, θ_R	Length of Chord, L
156	2.3077	0.04028	0.0201371
158	2.2785	0.03977	0.0198822
160	2.2500	0.03927	0.0196337
162	2.2222	0.03879	0.0193913
164	2.1951	0.03831	0.0191549
166	2.1687	0.03785	0.0189241
168	2.1429	0.03740	0.0186989
170	2.1176	0.03696	0.0184789
172	2.0930	0.03653	0.0182641
174	2.0690	0.03611	0.0180541
176	2.0455	0.03570	0.0178490
178	2.0225	0.03530	0.0176485
180	2.0000	0.03491	0.0174524
182	1.9780	0.03452	0.0172606
184	1.9565	0.03415	0.0170730
186	1.9355	0.03378	0.0168895
188	1.9149	0.03342	0.0167098
190	1.8947	0.03307	0.0165339
192	1.8750	0.03272	0.0163617
194	1.8557	0.03239	0.0161931
196	1.8367	0.03206	0.0160278
198	1.8182	0.03173	0.0158660
200	1.8000	0.03142	0.0157073
202	1.7822	0.03110	0.0155518
204	1.7647	0.03080	0.0153994
206	1.7476	0.03050	0.0152499
208	1.7308	0.03021	0.0151032
210	1.7143	0.02992	0.0149594
212	1.6981	0.02964	0.0148183
214	1.6822	0.02936	0.0146798
216	1.6667	0.02909	0.0145439
218	1.6514	0.02882	0.0144105
220	1.6364	0.02856	0.0142795
222	1.6216	0.02830	0.0141508
224	1.6071	0.02805	0.0140245
226	1.5929	0.02780	0.0139004
228	1.5789	0.02756	0.0137785
230	1.5652	0.02732	0.0136587
232	1.5517	0.02708	0.0135409
234	1.5385	0.02685	0.0134252
236	1.5254	0.02662	0.0133114
238	1.5126	0.02640	0.0131996
240	1.5000	0.02618	0.0130896

Number of Segments, n	Center Angle, θ degrees, θ_D	radians, θ_R	Length of Chord, L
242	1.4876	0.02596	0.0129814
244	1.4754	0.02575	0.0128750
246	1.4634	0.02554	0.0127704
248	1.4516	0.02534	0.0126674
250	1.4400	0.02513	0.0125660
252	1.4286	0.02493	0.0124663
254	1.4173	0.02474	0.0123682
256	1.4063	0.02454	0.0122715
258	1.3953	0.02435	0.0121764
260	1.3846	0.02417	0.0120828
262	1.3740	0.02398	0.0119905
264	1.3636	0.02380	0.0118997
266	1.3534	0.02362	0.0118102
268	1.3433	0.02344	0.0117221
270	1.3333	0.02327	0.0116353
272	1.3235	0.02310	0.0115497
274	1.3139	0.02293	0.0114654
276	1.3043	0.02277	0.0113823
278	1.2950	0.02260	0.0113005
280	1.2857	0.02244	0.0112197
282	1.2766	0.02228	0.0111402
284	1.2676	0.02212	0.0110617
286	1.2587	0.02197	0.0109844
288	1.2500	0.02182	0.0109081
290	1.2414	0.02167	0.0108329
292	1.2329	0.02152	0.0107587
294	1.2245	0.02137	0.0106855
296	1.2162	0.02123	0.0106133
298	1.2081	0.02108	0.0105421
300	1.2000	0.02094	0.0104718
302	1.1921	0.02081	0.0104024
304	1.1842	0.02067	0.0103340
306	1.1765	0.02053	0.0102665
308	1.1688	0.02040	0.0101998
310	1.1613	0.02027	0.0101340
312	1.1538	0.02014	0.0100690
314	1.1465	0.02001	0.0100049
317	1.1356	0.01982	0.0099102
318	1.1321	0.01976	0.0098791
320	1.1250	0.01963	0.0098173
322	1.1180	0.01951	0.0097563
324	1.1111	0.01939	0.0096961
326	1.1043	0.01927	0.0096366

Number of Segments,n	Center Angle, θ degrees, θ_D	radians, θ_R	Length of Chord, L
328	1.0976	0.01916	0.0095779
330	1.0909	0.01904	0.0095198
332	1.0843	0.01893	0.0094625
334	1.0778	0.01881	0.0094058
336	1.0714	0.01870	0.0093498
338	1.0651	0.01859	0.0092945
340	1.0588	0.01848	0.0092398
342	1.0526	0.01837	0.0091858
344	1.0465	0.01827	0.0091324
346	1.0405	0.01816	0.0090796
348	1.0345	0.01806	0.0090274
350	1.0286	0.01795	0.0089759
352	1.0227	0.01785	0.0089249
354	1.0169	0.01775	0.0088744
356	1.0112	0.01765	0.0088246
358	1.0056	0.01755	0.0087753
360	1.0000	0.01745	0.0087265

Notes:

Values in the table are based on the following equations:

Diameter of Circle = 1

$\theta_D = 360°/n$

$\theta_R = 2\pi/n$

$r = D/2$

$L = 2r \times \sin(\theta_R / 2)$

Circles: Diameter, Radius, Circumference, and Area

Fraction Diameter,D inch	Decimal Diameter,D inch	Radius,r inch	Circumference,C inch	Area, A sq. inch
1/64	0.015625	0.0078125	0.0490874	0.0001917
1/32	0.031250	0.0156250	0.0981748	0.0007670
3/64	0.046875	0.0234375	0.1472622	0.0017257
1/16	0.062500	0.0312500	0.1963495	0.0030680
5/64	0.078125	0.0390625	0.2454369	0.0047937
3/32	0.093750	0.0468750	0.2945243	0.0069029
7/64	0.109375	0.0546875	0.3436117	0.0093956
1/8	0.125000	0.0625000	0.3926991	0.0122718
9/64	0.140625	0.0703125	0.4417865	0.0155316
5/32	0.156250	0.0781250	0.4908739	0.0191748
11/64	0.171875	0.0859375	0.5399612	0.0232015

Fraction Diameter, D inch	Decimal Diameter, D inch	Radius, r inch	Circumference, C inch	Area, A sq. inch
3/16	0.187500	0.0937500	0.5890486	0.0276117
13/64	0.203125	0.1015625	0.6381360	0.0324053
7/32	0.218750	0.1093750	0.6872234	0.0375825
15/64	0.234375	0.1171875	0.7363108	0.0431432
1/4	0.250000	0.1250000	0.7853982	0.0490874
17/64	0.265625	0.1328125	0.8344855	0.0554151
9/32	0.281250	0.1406250	0.8835729	0.0621262
19/64	0.296875	0.1484375	0.9326603	0.0692209
5/16	0.312500	0.1562500	0.9817477	0.0766990
21/64	0.328125	0.1640625	1.0308351	0.0845607
11/32	0.343750	0.1718750	1.0799225	0.0928058
23/64	0.359375	0.1796875	1.1290099	0.1014345
3/8	0.375000	0.1875000	1.1780972	0.1104466
25/64	0.390625	0.1953125	1.2271846	0.1198422
13/32	0.406250	0.2031250	1.2762720	0.1296214
27/64	0.421875	0.2109375	1.3253594	0.1397840
7/16	0.437500	0.2187500	1.3744468	0.1503301
29/64	0.453125	0.2265625	1.4235342	0.1612597
15/32	0.468750	0.2343750	1.4726216	0.1725728
31/64	0.484375	0.2421875	1.5217089	0.1842694
1/2	0.500000	0.2500000	1.5707963	0.1963495
33/64	0.515625	0.2578125	1.6198837	0.2088131
17/32	0.531250	0.2656250	1.6689711	0.2216602
35/64	0.546875	0.2734375	1.7180585	0.2348908
9/16	0.562500	0.2812500	1.7671459	0.2485049
37/64	0.578125	0.2890625	1.8162333	0.2625025
19/32	0.593750	0.2968750	1.8653206	0.2768835
39/64	0.609375	0.3046875	1.9144080	0.2916481
5/8	0.625000	0.3125000	1.9634954	0.3067962
41/64	0.640625	0.3203125	2.0125828	0.3223277
21/32	0.656250	0.3281250	2.0616702	0.3382428
43/64	0.671875	0.3359375	2.1107576	0.3545413
11/16	0.687500	0.3437500	2.1598449	0.3712234
45/64	0.703125	0.3515625	2.2089323	0.3882889
23/32	0.718750	0.3593750	2.2580197	0.4057379
47/64	0.734375	0.3671875	2.3071071	0.4235704
3/4	0.750000	0.3750000	2.3561945	0.4417865
49/64	0.765625	0.3828125	2.4052819	0.4603860
25/32	0.781250	0.3906250	2.4543693	0.4793690
51/64	0.796875	0.3984375	2.5034566	0.4987355
13/16	0.812500	0.4062500	2.5525440	0.5184855
53/64	0.828125	0.4140625	2.6016314	0.5386190
27/32	0.843750	0.4218750	2.6507188	0.5591360
55/64	0.859375	0.4296875	2.6998062	0.5800365
7/8	0.875000	0.4375000	2.7488936	0.6013205
57/64	0.890625	0.4453125	2.7979810	0.6229879

Fraction Diameter, D inch	Decimal Diameter, D inch	Radius, r inch	Circumference, C inch	Area, A sq. inch
29/32	0.906250	0.4531250	2.8470683	0.6450389
59/64	0.921875	0.4609375	2.8961557	0.6674734
15/16	0.937500	0.4687500	2.9452431	0.6902914
61/64	0.953125	0.4765625	2.9943305	0.7134928
31/32	0.968750	0.4843750	3.0434179	0.7370778
63/64	0.984375	0.4921875	3.0925053	0.7610462
1	1.000000	0.5000000	3.1415927	0.7853982
1-1/32	1.031250	0.5156250	3.2397674	0.8352525
1-1/16	1.062500	0.5312500	3.3379422	0.8866409
1-3/32	1.093750	0.5468750	3.4361170	0.9395632
1-1/8	1.125000	0.5625000	3.5342917	0.9940196
1-5/32	1.156250	0.5781250	3.6324665	1.0500098
1-3/16	1.187500	0.5937500	3.7306413	1.1075341
1-7/32	1.218750	0.6093750	3.8288160	1.1665924
1-1/4	1.250000	0.6250000	3.9269908	1.2271846
1-9/32	1.281250	0.6406250	4.0251656	1.2893109
1-5/16	1.312500	0.6562500	4.1233404	1.3529711
1-11/32	1.343750	0.6718750	4.2215151	1.4181652
1-3/8	1.375000	0.6875000	4.3196899	1.4848934
1/13/32	1.406250	0.7031250	4.4178647	1.5531555
1-7/16	1.437500	0.7187500	4.5160394	1.6229517
1-15/32	1.468750	0.7343750	4.6142142	1.6942818
1-1/2	1.500000	0.7500000	4.7123890	1.7671459
1-17/32	1.531250	0.7656250	4.8105638	1.8415439
1-9/16	1.562500	0.7812500	4.9087385	1.9174760
1-19/32	1.593750	0.7968750	5.0069133	1.9949420
1-5/8	1.625000	0.8125000	5.1050881	2.0739420
1-21/32	1.656250	0.8281250	5.2032628	2.1544760
1-11/16	1.687500	0.8437500	5.3014376	2.2365440
1-23/32	1.718750	0.8593750	5.3996124	2.3201459
1-3/4	1.750000	0.8750000	5.4977871	2.4052819
1-25/32	1.781250	0.8906250	5.5959619	2.4919518
1-13/16	1.812500	0.9062500	5.6941367	2.5801557
1-27/32	1.843750	0.9218750	5.7923114	2.6698936
1-7/8	1.875000	0.9375000	5.8904862	2.7611654
1-29/32	1.906250	0.9531250	5.9886610	2.8539713
1-15/16	1.937500	0.9687500	6.0868358	2.9483111
1-31/32	1.968750	0.9843750	6.1850105	3.0441849
2	2.000000	1.0000000	6.2831853	3.1415927

Notes:

Values in the table are based on the following equations:

$$r = D/2 = 0.5000\ D$$
$$C = \pi D = 2\pi r = 3.1415927\ D = 6.2831853\ r$$
$$A = \pi r^2 = \pi D^2/4 = 3.1415927\ r^2 = 0.7853982\ D^2$$

Convert Angles In Degrees to Degrees & Minutes, Radians, Inch Rise In 12 Inch Run, and Percent Grade

Angle				inch rise	
decimal degrees	degrees	minutes	radians	in run of 12 inches	percent grade
0.00	0	0	0.0000	0.0000	0.000
0.10	0	6	0.0017	0.0209	0.175
0.20	0	12	0.0035	0.0419	0.349
0.25	0	15	0.0044	0.0524	0.436
0.30	0	18	0.0052	0.0628	0.524
0.40	0	24	0.0070	0.0838	0.698
0.50	0	30	0.0087	0.1047	0.873
0.60	0	36	0.0105	0.1257	1.05
0.70	0	42	0.0122	0.1466	1.22
0.75	0	45	0.0131	0.1571	1.31
0.80	0	48	0.0140	0.1676	1.40
0.90	0	54	0.0157	0.1885	1.57
1.00	1	0	0.0175	0.2095	1.75
1.25	1	15	0.0218	0.2618	2.18
1.50	1	30	0.0262	0.3142	2.62
1.75	1	45	0.0305	0.3666	3.06
2.00	2	0	0.0349	0.4190	3.49
2.25	2	15	0.0393	0.4715	3.93
2.50	2	30	0.0436	0.5239	4.37
2.75	2	45	0.0480	0.5764	4.80
3.00	3	0	0.0524	0.6289	5.24
3.25	3	15	0.0567	0.6814	5.68
3.50	3	30	0.0611	0.7340	6.12
3.75	3	45	0.0654	0.7865	6.55
4.00	4	0	0.0698	0.8391	6.99
4.25	4	15	0.0742	0.8918	7.43
4.50	4	30	0.0785	0.9444	7.87
4.75	4	45	0.0829	0.9971	8.31
5.00	5	0	0.0873	1.050	8.75
5.25	5	15	0.0916	1.103	9.19
5.50	5	30	0.0960	1.155	9.63
5.75	5	45	0.1004	1.208	10.1
6.00	6	0	0.1047	1.261	10.5
6.25	6	15	0.1091	1.314	11.0
6.50	6	30	0.1134	1.367	11.4
6.75	6	45	0.1178	1.420	11.8
7.00	7	0	0.1222	1.473	12.3

Angle				inch rise in run of 12 inches	percent grade
decimal degrees	degrees	minutes	radians		
7.25	7	15	0.1265	1.527	12.7
7.50	7	30	0.1309	1.580	13.2
7.75	7	45	0.1353	1.633	13.6
8.00	8	0	0.1396	1.686	14.1
8.25	8	15	0.1440	1.740	14.5
8.50	8	30	0.1484	1.793	14.9
8.75	8	45	0.1527	1.847	15.4
9.00	9	0	0.1571	1.901	15.8
9.25	9	15	0.1614	1.954	16.3
9.50	9	30	0.1658	2.008	16.7
9.75	9	45	0.1702	2.062	17.2
10.00	10	0	0.1745	2.116	17.6
10.50	10	30	0.1833	2.224	18.5
11.00	11	0	0.1920	2.333	19.4
11.50	11	30	0.2007	2.441	20.3
12.00	12	0	0.2094	2.551	21.3
12.50	12	30	0.2182	2.660	22.2
13.00	13	0	0.2269	2.770	23.1
13.50	13	30	0.2356	2.881	24.0
14.00	14	0	0.2443	2.992	24.9
14.50	14	30	0.2531	3.103	25.9
15.00	15	0	0.2618	3.215	26.8
15.50	15	30	0.2705	3.328	27.7
16.00	16	0	0.2793	3.441	28.7
16.50	16	30	0.2880	3.555	29.6
17.00	17	0	0.2967	3.669	30.6
17.50	17	30	0.3054	3.784	31.5
18.00	18	0	0.3142	3.899	32.5
18.50	18	30	0.3229	4.015	33.5
19.00	19	0	0.3316	4.132	34.4
19.50	19	30	0.3403	4.249	35.4
20.00	20	0	0.3491	4.368	36.4
20.50	20	30	0.3578	4.487	37.4
21.00	21	0	0.3665	4.606	38.4
21.50	21	30	0.3752	4.727	39.4
22.00	22	0	0.3840	4.848	40.4
22.50	22	30	0.3927	4.971	41.4
23.00	23	0	0.4014	5.094	42.4
23.50	23	30	0.4102	5.218	43.5
24.00	24	0	0.4189	5.343	44.5
24.50	24	30	0.4276	5.469	45.6
25.00	25	0	0.4363	5.596	46.6

Angle				inch rise	
decimal degrees	degrees	minutes	radians	in run of 12 inches	percent grade
25.50	25	30	0.4451	5.724	47.7
26.00	26	0	0.4538	5.853	48.8
26.50	26	30	0.4625	5.983	49.9
27.00	27	0	0.4712	6.114	51.0
27.50	27	30	0.4800	6.247	52.1
28.00	28	0	0.4887	6.381	53.2
28.50	28	30	0.4974	6.515	54.3
29.00	29	0	0.5061	6.652	55.4
29.50	29	30	0.5149	6.789	56.6
30.00	30	0	0.5236	6.928	57.7
31.00	31	0	0.5411	7.210	60.1
32.00	32	0	0.5585	7.498	62.5
33.00	33	0	0.5760	7.793	64.9
34.00	34	0	0.5934	8.094	67.5
35.00	35	0	0.6109	8.402	70.0
36.00	36	0	0.6283	8.719	72.7
37.00	37	0	0.6458	9.043	75.4
38.00	38	0	0.6632	9.375	78.1
39.00	39	0	0.6807	9.717	81.0
40.00	40	0	0.6981	10.07	83.9
41.00	41	0	0.7156	10.43	86.9
42.00	42	0	0.7330	10.80	90.0
43.00	43	0	0.7505	11.19	93.3
44.00	44	0	0.7679	11.59	96.6
45.00	45	0	0.7854	12.00	100
46.00	46	0	0.8029	12.43	104
47.00	47	0	0.8203	12.87	107
48.00	48	0	0.8378	13.33	111
49.00	49	0	0.8552	13.80	115
50.00	50	0	0.8727	14.30	119
51.00	51	0	0.8901	14.82	123
52.00	52	0	0.9076	15.36	128
53.00	53	0	0.9250	15.92	133
54.00	54	0	0.9425	16.52	138
55.00	55	0	0.9599	17.14	143
56.00	56	0	0.9774	17.79	148
57.00	57	0	0.9948	18.48	154
58.00	58	0	1.0123	19.20	160
59.00	59	0	1.0297	19.97	166
60.00	60	0	1.0472	20.78	173
61.00	61	0	1.0647	21.65	180
62.00	62	0	1.0821	22.57	188

	Angle			inch rise	
decimal degrees	degrees	minutes	radians	in run of 12 inches	percent grade
63.00	63	0	1.0996	23.55	196
64.00	64	0	1.1170	24.60	205
65.00	65	0	1.1345	25.73	214
66.00	66	0	1.1519	26.95	225
67.00	67	0	1.1694	28.27	236
68.00	68	0	1.1868	29.70	248
69.00	69	0	1.2043	31.26	261
70.00	70	0	1.2217	32.97	275
71.00	71	0	1.2392	34.85	290
72.00	72	0	1.2566	36.93	308
73.00	73	0	1.2741	39.25	327
74.00	74	0	1.2915	41.85	349
75.00	75	0	1.3090	44.78	373
76.00	76	0	1.3265	48.13	401
77.00	77	0	1.3439	51.98	433
78.00	78	0	1.3614	56.46	470
79.00	79	0	1.3788	61.73	514
80.00	80	0	1.3963	68.06	567
81.00	81	0	1.4137	75.77	631
82.00	82	0	1.4312	85.38	712
83.00	83	0	1.4486	97.73	814
84.00	84	0	1.4661	114.2	951
85.00	85	0	1.4835	137.2	1,143
86.00	86	0	1.5010	171.6	1,430
87.00	87	0	1.5184	229.0	1,908
88.00	88	0	1.5359	343.6	2,864
89.00	89	0	1.5533	687.5	5,729
90.00	90	0	1.5708	infinite	infinite

Convert Minutes into Decimals of a Degree

Minute	Degree	Minute	Degree
1	0.016667	31	0.516667
2	0.033333	32	0.533333
3	0.050000	33	0.550000
4	0.066667	34	0.566667
5	0.083333	35	0.583333
6	0.100000	36	0.600000
7	0.116667	37	0.616667
8	0.133333	38	0.633333
9	0.150000	39	0.650000
10	0.166667	40	0.666667
11	0.183333	41	0.683333
12	0.200000	42	0.700000
13	0.216667	43	0.716667
14	0.233333	44	0.733333
15	0.250000	45	0.750000
16	0.266667	46	0.766667
17	0.283333	47	0.783333
18	0.300000	48	0.800000
19	0.316667	49	0.816667
20	0.333333	50	0.833333
21	0.350000	51	0.850000
22	0.366667	52	0.866667
23	0.383333	53	0.883333
24	0.400000	54	0.900000
25	0.416667	55	0.916667
26	0.433333	56	0.933333
27	0.450000	57	0.950000
28	0.466667	58	0.966667
29	0.483333	59	0.983333
30	0.500000	60	1.000000

Notes:

60 minute = 1 degree

1 minute = (1/60) degree = 0.0166667 degree

3,600 seconds = 1 degree

1 second = (1/3,600) degree = 0.0002778 degree

Convert Seconds into Decimals of a Degree

Second	Degree	Second	Degree
1	0.0002778	31	0.0086111
2	0.0005556	32	0.0088889
3	0.0008333	33	0.0091667
4	0.0011111	34	0.0094444
5	0.0013889	35	0.0097222
6	0.0016667	36	0.0100000
7	0.0019444	37	0.0102778
8	0.0022222	38	0.0105556
9	0.0025000	39	0.0108333
10	0.0027778	40	0.0111111
11	0.0030556	41	0.0113889
12	0.0033333	42	0.0116667
13	0.0036111	43	0.0119444
14	0.0038889	44	0.0122222
15	0.0041667	45	0.0125000
16	0.0044444	46	0.0127500
17	0.0047222	47	0.0130556
18	0.0050000	48	0.0133333
19	0.0052778	49	0.0136111
20	0.0055556	50	0.0138889
21	0.0058333	51	0.0141667
22	0.0061111	52	0.0144444
23	0.0063889	53	0.0147222
24	0.0066667	54	0.0150000
25	0.0069444	55	0.0152778
26	0.0072222	56	0.0155556
27	0.0075000	57	0.0158333
28	0.0077778	58	0.0161111
29	0.0080556	59	0.0163889
30	0.0083333	60	0.0166667

Notes:
60 minute = 1 degree
1 minute = (1/60) degree = 0.0166667 degree
3,600 seconds = 1 degree
1 second = (1/3,600) degree = 0.0002778 degree

Distance Across Squares and Hexagons

Values in the table are based on the following equations.
For squares: $d = a \times \sqrt{2} = 1.4142136\,a$
For hexagons: $d = a \times [\,2 / (\sqrt{3})\,] = 1.1547005\,a$
All Dimensions in Inches

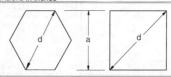

Distance Across			
Faces, *a*		Corners, *d*	
Fraction Inch	Decimal Inch	Square - Inch	Hexagon - Inch
1/16	0.0625	0.088388	0.072169
1/8	0.1250	0.176777	0.144338
3/16	0.1875	0.265165	0.216506
1/4	0.2500	0.353553	0.288675
5/16	0.3125	0.441942	0.360844
3/8	0.3750	0.530330	0.433013
7/16	0.4375	0.618718	0.505181
1/2	0.5000	0.707107	0.577350
9/16	0.5625	0.795445	0.649519
5/8	0.6250	0.883883	0.721688
11/16	0.6875	0.972272	0.793857
3/4	0.7500	1.06066	0.866025
13/16	0.8125	1.14905	0.938194
7/8	0.8750	1.23744	1.01036
15/16	0.9375	1.32583	1.08253
- - -	1.00	1.41421	1.15470
1-1/4	1.25	1.76777	1.44338
1-1/2	1.50	2.12132	1.73205
1-3/4	1.75	2.47487	2.02073
- - -	2.00	2.82843	2.30940
2-1/4	2.25	3.18198	2.59808
2-1/2	2.50	3.53553	2.88675
2-3/4	2.75	3.88909	3.17543
- - -	3.00	4.24264	3.46410
3-1/4	3.25	4.59619	3.75278
3-1/2	3.50	4.94975	4.04145
3-3/4	3.75	5.30330	4.33013
- - -	4.00	5.65685	4.61880
4-1/4	4.25	6.01041	4.90748
4-1/2	4.50	6.36396	5.19615
4-3/4	4.75	6.71751	5.48483
- - -	5.0	7.07107	5.77350
- - -	6.0	8.48528	6.92820
- - -	7.0	9.89949	8.08290

Distance Across Squares and Hexagons (cont.)

Distance Across			
Faces, *a*		Corners, *d*	
Fraction Inch	Decimal Inch	Square - Inch	Hexagon - Inch
- - -	8.0	11.3137	9.23760
- - -	9.0	12.7279	10.3923
- - -	10.0	14.1421	11.5470
- - -	11.0	15.5563	12.7017
- - -	12.0	16.9706	13.8564
- - -	13.0	18.3848	15.0111
- - -	14.0	19.7990	16.1658
- - -	15.0	21.2132	17.3205
- - -	16.0	22.6274	18.4752
- - -	17.0	24.0416	19.6299
- - -	18.0	25.4558	20.7846
- - -	19.0	26.8701	21.9393
- - -	20.0	28.2843	23.0940
- - -	21.0	29.6985	24.2487
- - -	22.0	31.1127	25.4034
- - -	23.0	32.5269	26.5581
- - -	24.0	33.9411	27.7128
- - -	25.0	35.3553	28.8675
- - -	26.0	36.7696	30.0222
- - -	27.0	38.1838	31.1769
- - -	28.0	39.5980	32.3316
- - -	29.0	41.0122	33.4863
- - -	30.0	42.4264	34.6410
- - -	31.0	43.8406	35.7957
- - -	32.0	45.2548	36.9504
- - -	33.0	46.6690	38.1051
- - -	34.0	48.0833	39.2598
- - -	35.0	49.4975	40.4145
- - -	36.0	50.9117	41.5692
- - -	37.0	52.3259	42.7239
- - -	38.0	53.7401	43.8786
- - -	39.0	55.1543	45.0333
- - -	40.0	56.5685	46.1880
- - -	41.0	57.9828	47.3427
- - -	42.0	59.3970	48.4974
- - -	43.0	60.8112	49.6521
- - -	44.0	62.2254	50.8068
- - -	45.0	63.6396	51.9615
- - -	46.0	65.0538	53.1162
- - -	47.0	66.4680	54.2709
- - -	48.0	67.8823	55.4256
- - -	49.0	69.2965	56.5803
- - -	50.0	70.7107	57.7350
- - -	51.0	72.1249	58.8897
- - -	52.0	73.5391	60.0444
- - -	53.0	74.9533	61.1991
- - -	54.0	76.3675	62.3538

Distance Across Squares and Hexagons (cont.)

Distance Across

	Faces, *a*	Corners, *d*	
Fraction Inch	Decimal Inch	Square - Inch	Hexagon - Inch
- - -	55.0	77.7817	63.5085
- - -	56.0	79.1960	64.6632
- - -	57.0	80.6102	65.8179
- - -	58.0	82.0244	66.9726
- - -	59.0	83.4386	68.1273
- - -	60.0	84.8528	69.2820
- - -	61.0	86.2670	70.4367
- - -	62.0	87.6812	71.5914
- - -	63.0	89.0955	72.7461
- - -	64.0	90.5097	73.9008
- - -	65.0	91.9239	75.0555
- - -	66.0	93.3381	76.2102
- - -	67.0	94.7523	77.3649
- - -	68.0	96.1665	78.5196
- - -	69.0	97.5807	79.6743
- - -	70.0	98.9949	80.8290
- - -	71.0	100.409	81.9837
- - -	72.0	101.823	83.1384
- - -	73.0	103.238	84.2931
- - -	74.0	104.652	85.4478
- - -	75.0	106.066	86.6025
- - -	76.0	107.480	87.7572
- - -	77.0	108.894	88.9119
- - -	78.0	110.309	90.0666
- - -	79.0	111.723	91.2213
- - -	80.0	113.137	92.3760
- - -	81.0	114.551	93.5307
- - -	82.0	115.966	94.6854
- - -	83.0	117.380	95.8401
- - -	84.0	118.794	96.9948
- - -	85.0	120.208	98.1495
- - -	86.0	121.622	99.3042
- - -	87.0	123.037	100.459
- - -	88.0	124.451	101.614
- - -	89.0	125.865	102.768
- - -	90.0	127.279	103.923
- - -	91.0	128.693	105.078
- - -	92.0	130.108	106.232
- - -	93.0	131.522	107.387
- - -	94.0	132.936	108.542
- - -	95.0	134.350	109.697
- - -	96.0	135.765	110.851
- - -	97.0	137.179	112.006
- - -	98.0	138.593	113.161
- - -	99.0	140.007	114.315
- - -	100.0	141.421	115.470
- - -	101.0	142.836	116.625

Excess Stock and Fillet Area

Based on the following equations: (radius in inches)

$$\text{Excess Stock} = r\,[(1/\sin 45°) - 1] = 0.4142136\,r$$
$$\text{Fillet Area} = r^2\,[1-(\pi/4)] = 0.2146018\,r^2$$

Radius, r		Excess Stock	Fillet Area
fractional inch	decimal inch	inch	square inch
1/64	0.01563	0.00647	0.00005
1/32	0.03125	0.01294	0.00021
3/64	0.04688	0.01942	0.00047
1/16	0.06250	0.02589	0.00084
5/64	0.07813	0.03236	0.00131
3/32	0.09375	0.03883	0.00189
7/64	0.10938	0.04530	0.00257
1/8	0.12500	0.05178	0.00335
9/64	0.14063	0.05825	0.00424
5/32	0.15625	0.06472	0.00524
11/64	0.17188	0.07119	0.00634
3/16	0.18750	0.07767	0.00754
13/64	0.20313	0.08414	0.00885
7/32	0.21875	0.09061	0.01027
15/64	0.23438	0.09708	0.01179
1/4	0.25000	0.10355	0.01341
17/64	0.26563	0.11003	0.01514
9/32	0.28125	0.11650	0.01698
19/64	0.29688	0.12297	0.01891
5/16	0.31250	0.12944	0.02096
21/64	0.32813	0.13591	0.02311
11/32	0.34375	0.14239	0.02536
23/64	0.35938	0.14886	0.02772
3/8	0.37500	0.15533	0.03018
25/64	0.39063	0.16180	0.03275
13/32	0.40625	0.16827	0.03542
27/64	0.42188	0.17475	0.03819
7/16	0.43750	0.18122	0.04108
29/64	0.45313	0.18769	0.04406
15/32	0.46875	0.19416	0.04715
31/64	0.48438	0.20063	0.05035

Excess Stock and Fillet Area (cont.)

Radius, r		Excess Stock	Fillet Area
fractional inch	decimal inch	inch	square inch
1/2	0.50000	0.20711	0.05365
33/64	0.51563	0.21358	0.05706
17/32	0.53125	0.22005	0.06057
35/64	0.54688	0.22652	0.06418
9/16	0.56250	0.23300	0.06790
37/64	0.57813	0.23947	0.07173
19/32	0.59375	0.24594	0.07566
39/64	0.60938	0.25241	0.07969
5/8	0.62500	0.25888	0.08383
41/64	0.64063	0.26536	0.08807
21/32	0.65625	0.27183	0.09242
43/64	0.67188	0.27830	0.09687
11/16	0.68750	0.28477	0.10143
45/64	0.70313	0.29124	0.10610
23/32	0.71875	0.29772	0.11086
47/64	0.73438	0.30419	0.11574
3/4	0.75000	0.31066	0.12071
49/64	0.76563	0.31713	0.12580
25/32	0.78125	0.32360	0.13098
51/64	0.79688	0.33008	0.13627
13/16	0.81250	0.33655	0.14167
53/64	0.82813	0.34302	0.14717
27/32	0.84375	0.34949	0.15278
55/64	0.85938	0.35596	0.15849
7/8	0.87500	0.36244	0.16430
57/64	0.89063	0.36891	0.17022
29/32	0.90625	0.37538	0.17625
59/64	0.92188	0.38185	0.18238
15/16	0.93750	0.38833	0.18861
61/64	0.95313	0.39480	0.19495
31/32	0.96875	0.40127	0.20140
63/64	0.98438	0.40774	0.20795
1	1.00000	0.41421	0.21460
1-1/32	1.03125	0.42716	0.22822
1-1/16	1.06250	0.44010	0.24227
1-3/32	1.09375	0.45305	0.25673
1-1/8	1.12500	0.46599	0.27161
1-5/32	1.15625	0.47893	0.28690
1-3/16	1.18750	0.49188	0.30262
1-7/32	1.21875	0.50482	0.31876
1-1/4	1.25000	0.51777	0.33532
1-9/32	1.28125	0.53071	0.35229
1-5/16	1.31250	0.54366	0.36969
1-11/32	1.34375	0.55660	0.38750
1-3/8	1.37500	0.56954	0.40573

Excess Stock and Fillet Area (cont.)

Radius, r		Excess Stock	Fillet Area
fractional inch	decimal inch	inch	square inch
1-13/32	1.40625	0.58249	0.42438
1-7/16	1.43750	0.59543	0.44345
1-15/32	1.46875	0.60838	0.46294
1-1/2	1.50000	0.62132	0.48285
1-17/32	1.53125	0.63426	0.50318
1-9/16	1.56250	0.64721	0.52393
1-19/32	1.59375	0.66015	0.54510
1-5/8	1.62500	0.67310	0.56668
1-21/32	1.65625	0.68604	0.58869
1-11/16	1.68750	0.69899	0.61111
1-23/32	1.71875	0.71193	0.63396
1-3/4	1.75000	0.72487	0.65722
1-25/32	1.78125	0.73782	0.68090
1-13/16	1.81250	0.75076	0.70500
1-27/32	1.84375	0.76371	0.72952
1-7/8	1.87500	0.77665	0.75446
1-29/32	1.90625	0.78959	0.77982
1-15/16	1.93750	0.80254	0.80560
1-31/32	1.96875	0.81548	0.83179
2	2.00000	0.82843	0.85841

Factors for Numbers from 1 to 100

Number	Factors	Number	Factors
1	P	51	17,3
2	P	52	26,13,4,2
3	P	53	P
4	2	54	27,18,9,6,3,2
5	P	55	11,5
6	3,2	56	28,14,8,7,4,2
7	P	57	19,3
8	4,2	58	29,2
9	3	59	P
10	5,2	60	30,20,15,12,10,6,5,4,3,2
11	P	61	P
12	6,4,3,2	62	31,2
13	P	63	21,9,7,3
14	7,2	64	32,16,8,4,2
15	5,3	65	13,5,
16	8,4,2	66	33,22,11,6,3,2
17	P	67	P
18	9,6,3,2	68	34,17,4,2,
19	P	69	23,3,
20	10,5,4,2	70	35,14,10,7,5,2
21	7,3	71	P
22	11,2	72	36,24,18,12,9,8,6,4,3,2
23	P	73	P
24	12,8,6,4,3,2	74	37,2,
25	5	75	25,15,5,3,
26	13,2	76	38,19,4,2,
27	9,3	77	11,7,
28	14,7,4,2	78	39,26,13,6,3,2
29	P	79	P
30	15,10,6,5,3,2	80	40,20,16,10,8,5,4,2
31	P	81	27,9,3
32	16,8,4,2	82	41,2,
33	11,3	83	P
34	17,2	84	42,28,21,14,12,7,6,4,3,2
35	7,5	85	17,5,
36	18,12,9,6,4,3,2	86	43,2,
37	P	87	29,3,
38	19,2	88	44,22,11,8,4,2
39	13,3	89	P
40	20,10,8,5,4,2	90	45,30,18,15,10,9,6,5,3,2
41	P	91	13,7,
42	21,14,7,6,3,2	92	46,23,4,2,
43	P	93	31,3,
44	22,11,4,2	94	47,2,
45	15,9,5,3	95	19,5,
46	23,2	96	48,32,24,16,12,8,6,4,3,2
47	P	97	P
48	24,16,12,8,6,4,3,2,	98	49,14,7,2,
49	7	99	33,11,9,3,
50	25,10,5,2	100	50,25,20,10,5,4,2

"P" indicates a Prime Number, that is, a number divisible only by itself and 1.

Formulas and Constants For Computing Regular Polygons

Number of Sides n	Constants						z	
	F	M	H	K	B	H	Decimal degree	degree/minute/second
3	5.196152	5.196152	0.324760	0.433013	0.384900	0.500000	120.0000	120° 00' 00"
4	4.000000	5.656854	0.500000	1.000000	0.353553	0.292893	90.0000	90° 00' 00"
5	3.632713	5.877853	0.594410	1.720477	0.340260	0.190983	72.0000	72° 00' 00"
6	3.464102	6.000000	0.649519	2.598076	0.333333	0.133975	60.0000	60° 00' 00"
7	3.371022	6.074372	0.684103	3.633912	0.329252	0.099031	51.4286	51° 25' 43"
8	3.313708	6.122935	0.707107	4.828427	0.326641	0.076120	45.0000	45° 00' 00"
9	3.275732	6.156363	0.723136	6.181824	0.324867	0.060307	40.0000	40° 00' 00"
10	3.249197	6.180340	0.734732	7.694209	0.323607	0.048943	36.0000	36° 00' 00"
11	3.229891	6.198116	0.743381	9.365640	0.322679	0.040507	32.7273	32° 43' 38"
12	3.215390	6.211657	0.750000	11.196152	0.321975	0.034074	30.0000	30° 00' 00"
13	3.204212	6.222207	0.755175	13.185768	0.321429	0.029058	27.6923	27° 41' 32"
14	3.195409	6.230586	0.759297	15.334502	0.320997	0.025072	25.7143	25° 42' 51"
15	3.188348	6.237351	0.762631	17.642363	0.320649	0.021852	24.0000	24° 00' 00"
16	3.182598	6.242890	0.765367	20.109358	0.320364	0.019215	22.5000	22° 30' 00"
17	3.177851	6.247484	0.767639	22.735492	0.320129	0.017027	21.1765	21° 10' 35"
18	3.173886	6.251334	0.769545	25.520768	0.319932	0.015192	20.0000	20° 00' 00"
19	3.170539	6.254594	0.771161	28.465189	0.319765	0.013639	18.9474	18° 56' 51"
20	3.167689	6.257379	0.772542	31.568758	0.319623	0.012312	18.0000	18° 00' 00"
21	3.165241	6.259775	0.773732	34.831474	0.319500	0.011169	17.1429	17° 08' 34"
22	3.163122	6.261853	0.774765	38.253340	0.319394	0.010179	16.3636	16° 21' 49"
23	3.161277	6.263666	0.775666	41.834357	0.319302	0.009314	15.6522	15° 39' 08"
24	3.159660	6.265257	0.776457	45.574525	0.319221	0.008555	15.0000	15° 00' 00"

Symbols:

n = Number of sides
z = Angle subtended at center by side
P = Perimeter
A = Area
C = Length of one side
D = Diameter of circumscribed circle
d = Diameter of inscribed circle

Constants:

$F = [n] \times \tan(180°/n)$
$M = [2n] \times \sin(180°/n)$
$H = [n/8] \times \sin(360°/n)$
$K = [n/4] \times \cot(180°/n)$
$B = [1/n] \times \operatorname{cosec}(180°/n)$
$H = 1 - \cos([z \times 180°]/2)$

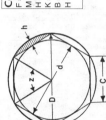

	Diameter, D	Diameter, d
	$P = (MD)/2$	$P = Fd$
	$A = HD^2$	$A = (Fd^2)/4$
	$C = (MD)/2n$	$C = (Fd)/n$
	---	$d = BFd$
	$d = (2MKD)/n^2$	---
	$h = (D/2)H$	---

Equations

You need to find:	And you know:				
	Perimeter, P	Area, A	Side, C	Diameter, D	Diameter, d
Perimeter, P	---	$P = 2\sqrt{FA}$	$P = Cn$	$P = (MD)/2$	$P = Fd$
Area, A	$A = (KP^2)/n^2$	---	$A = KC^2$	$A = HD^2$	$A = (Fd^2)/4$
Side, C	$C = P/n$	$C = [2\sqrt{FA}]/n$	---	$C = (MD)/2n$	$C = (Fd)/n$
Diameter, D	$D = BP$	$D = 2B\sqrt{FA}$	$D = nBC$	---	$D = BFd$
Diameter, d	$d = (4KP)/n^2$	$d = 4\sqrt{(AK)}/n$	$d = (4KC)/n$	$d = (2MKD)/n^2$	---
Height, h	---	---	---	$h = (D/2)H$	---

Sources: Values in the table were calculated from equations given in:
Handbook For Machine Designers, Shop Men, And Draftsmen; 2nd Edition, Frederick A. Halsey, McGraw-Hill Book Co., New York, NY, 1916
Technical Reference Handbook, E.P. Rasis, American Technical Publishers, Homewood, IL, 1984.

Fractions of Inches - Decimal Equivalents

Fraction of inch	Decimal Equivalent				
	Inch	Square	Cube	Square Root	Cube Root
1/64	0.015625	0.000244	0.000004	0.1250	0.2500
1/32	0.031250	0.000977	0.000031	0.1768	0.3150
3/64	0.046875	0.002197	0.000103	0.2165	0.3606
1/16	0.062500	0.003906	0.000244	0.2500	0.3969
5/64	0.078125	0.006104	0.000477	0.2795	0.4275
3/32	0.093750	0.008789	0.000824	0.3062	0.4543
7/64	0.109375	0.011963	0.001308	0.3307	0.4782
1/8	0.125000	0.015625	0.001953	0.3536	0.5000
9/64	0.140625	0.019775	0.002781	0.3750	0.5200
5/32	0.156250	0.024414	0.003815	0.3953	0.5386
11/64	0.171875	0.029541	0.005077	0.4146	0.5560
3/16	0.187500	0.035156	0.006592	0.4330	0.5724
13/64	0.203125	0.041260	0.008381	0.4507	0.5878
7/32	0.218750	0.047852	0.010468	0.4677	0.6025
15/64	0.234375	0.054932	0.012875	0.4841	0.6166
1/4	0.250000	0.062500	0.015625	0.5000	0.6300
17/64	0.265625	0.070557	0.018742	0.5154	0.6428
9/32	0.281250	0.079102	0.022247	0.5303	0.6552
19/64	0.296875	0.088135	0.026165	0.5449	0.6671
5/16	0.312500	0.097656	0.030518	0.5590	0.6786
21/64	0.328125	0.107666	0.035328	0.5728	0.6897
11/32	0.343750	0.118164	0.040619	0.5863	0.7005
23/64	0.359375	0.129150	0.046413	0.5995	0.7110
3/8	0.375000	0.140625	0.052734	0.6124	0.7211
25/64	0.390625	0.152588	0.059605	0.6250	0.7310
13/32	0.406250	0.165039	0.067047	0.6374	0.7406
27/64	0.421875	0.177979	0.075085	0.6495	0.7500
7/16	0.437500	0.191406	0.083740	0.6614	0.7591
29/64	0.453125	0.205322	0.093037	0.6731	0.7681
15/32	0.468750	0.219727	0.102997	0.6847	0.7768
31/64	0.484375	0.234619	0.113644	0.6960	0.7853
1/2	0.500000	0.250000	0.125000	0.7071	0.7937
33/64	0.515625	0.265869	0.137089	0.7181	0.8019
17/32	0.531250	0.282227	0.149933	0.7289	0.8099
35/64	0.546875	0.299072	0.163555	0.7395	0.8178
9/16	0.562500	0.316406	0.177979	0.7500	0.8255
37/64	0.578125	0.334229	0.193226	0.7603	0.8331
19/32	0.593750	0.352539	0.209320	0.7706	0.8405
39/64	0.609375	0.371338	0.226284	0.7806	0.8478
5/8	0.625000	0.390625	0.244141	0.7906	0.8550

Fractions of Inches - Decimal Equivalents (cont.)

Fraction of inch	Decimal Equivalent				
	Inch	Square	Cube	Square Root	Cube Root
41/64	0.640625	0.410400	0.262913	0.8004	0.8621
21/32	0.656250	0.430664	0.282623	0.8101	0.8690
43/64	0.671875	0.451416	0.303295	0.8197	0.8758
11/16	0.687500	0.472656	0.324951	0.8292	0.8826
45/64	0.703125	0.494385	0.347614	0.8385	0.8892
23/32	0.718750	0.516602	0.371307	0.8478	0.8958
47/64	0.734375	0.539307	0.396053	0.8570	0.9022
3/4	0.750000	0.562500	0.421875	0.8660	0.9086
49/64	0.765625	0.586182	0.448795	0.8750	0.9148
25/32	0.781250	0.610352	0.476837	0.8839	0.9210
51/64	0.796875	0.635010	0.506023	0.8927	0.9271
13/16	0.812500	0.660156	0.536377	0.9014	0.9331
53/64	0.828125	0.685791	0.567921	0.9100	0.9391
27/32	0.843750	0.711914	0.600677	0.9186	0.9449
55/64	0.859375	0.738525	0.634670	0.9270	0.9507
7/8	0.875000	0.765625	0.669922	0.9354	0.9565
57/64	0.890625	0.793213	0.706455	0.9437	0.9621
29/32	0.906250	0.821289	0.744293	0.9520	0.9677
59/64	0.921875	0.849854	0.783459	0.9601	0.9732
15/16	0.937500	0.878906	0.823975	0.9682	0.9787
61/64	0.953125	0.908447	0.865864	0.9763	0.9841
31/32	0.968750	0.938477	0.909149	0.9843	0.9895
63/64	0.984375	0.968994	0.953854	0.9922	0.9948
1	1.000000	1.000000	1.000000	1.0000	1.0000
1-1/32	1.031250	1.063477	1.096710	1.0155	1.0103
1-1/16	1.062500	1.128906	1.199463	1.0308	1.0204
1-3/32	1.093750	1.196289	1.308441	1.0458	1.0303
1-1/8	1.125000	1.265625	1.423828	1.0607	1.0400
1-5/32	1.156250	1.336914	1.545807	1.0753	1.0496
1-3/16	1.187500	1.410156	1.674561	1.0897	1.0590
1-7/32	1.218750	1.485352	1.810272	1.1040	1.0682
1-1/4	1.250000	1.562500	1.953125	1.1180	1.0772
1-9/32	1.281250	1.641602	2.103302	1.1319	1.0861
1-5/16	1.312500	1.722656	2.260986	1.1456	1.0949
1-11/32	1.343750	1.805664	2.426361	1.1592	1.1035
1-3/8	1.375000	1.890625	2.599609	1.1726	1.1120
1-13/32	1.406250	1.977539	2.780914	1.1859	1.1204
1-7/16	1.437500	2.066406	2.970459	1.1990	1.1286
1-15/32	1.468750	2.157227	3.168427	1.2119	1.1367
1-1/2	1.500000	2.250000	3.375000	1.2247	1.1447

Fractions of Inches - Decimal Equivalents (cont.)

Fraction of inch	Decimal Equivalent				
	Inch	Square	Cube	Square Root	Cube Root
1-17/32	1.531250	2.344727	3.590363	1.2374	1.1526
1-9/16	1.562500	2.441406	3.814697	1.2500	1.1604
1-19/32	1.593750	2.540039	4.048187	1.2624	1.1681
1-5/8	1.625000	2.640625	4.291016	1.2748	1.1757
1-21/32	1.656250	2.743164	4.543365	1.2870	1.1832
1-11/16	1.687500	2.847656	4.805420	1.2990	1.1906
1-23/32	1.718750	2.954102	5.077362	1.3110	1.1979
1-3/4	1.750000	3.062500	5.359375	1.3229	1.2051
1-25/32	1.781250	3.172852	5.651642	1.3346	1.2122
1-13/16	1.812500	3.285156	5.954346	1.3463	1.2192
1-27/32	1.843750	3.399414	6.267670	1.3578	1.2262
1-7/8	1.875000	3.515625	6.591797	1.3693	1.2331
1-29/32	1.906250	3.633789	6.926910	1.3807	1.2399
1-15/16	1.937500	3.753906	7.273193	1.3919	1.2467
1-31/32	1.968750	3.875977	7.630829	1.4031	1.2533
2	2.000000	4.000000	8.000000	1.4142	1.2599

Fractions of Inches - Millimeter Equivalents

Fraction of inch	Millimeter Equivalent				
	Millimeter	Square	Cube	Square Root	Cube Root
1/64	0.39688	0.15751	0.06251	0.62998	0.73488
1/32	0.79375	0.63004	0.50009	0.89093	0.92589
3/64	1.1906	1.4176	1.6878	1.09116	1.05988
1/16	1.5875	2.5202	4.0007	1.25996	1.16655
5/64	1.9844	3.9377	7.8140	1.40868	1.25663
3/32	2.3813	5.6704	13.503	1.54313	1.33537
7/64	2.7781	7.7180	21.442	1.66677	1.40578
1/8	3.1750	10.081	32.006	1.78185	1.46797
9/64	3.5719	12.758	45.571	1.88994	1.52862
5/32	3.9688	15.751	62.512	1.99217	1.58326
11/64	4.3656	19.059	83.203	2.08941	1.63436
3/16	4.7625	22.681	108.02	2.18232	1.68246
13/64	5.1594	26.619	137.34	2.27143	1.72795
7/32	5.5563	30.872	171.53	2.35717	1.77117
15/64	5.9531	35.440	210.98	2.43990	1.81238
1/4	6.3500	40.323	256.05	2.51992	1.85179
17/64	6.7469	45.520	307.12	2.59747	1.88959
9/32	7.1438	51.033	364.57	2.67278	1.92594
19/64	7.5406	56.861	428.77	2.74602	1.96096

Fractions of Inches - Millimeter Equivalents (cont.)

Fraction of inch	Millimeter Equivalent				
	Millimeter	Square	Cube	Square Root	Cube Root
5/16	7.9375	63.004	500.09	2.81736	1.99478
21/64	8.3344	69.462	578.92	2.88693	2.02749
11/32	8.7313	76.235	665.62	2.95487	2.05917
23/64	9.1281	83.323	760.58	3.02128	2.08991
3/8	9.5250	90.726	864.16	3.08626	2.11977
25/64	9.9219	98.444	976.75	3.14990	2.14881
13/32	10.319	106.48	1,098.7	3.21228	2.17709
27/64	10.716	114.82	1,230.4	3.27347	2.20465
7/16	11.113	123.49	1,372.3	3.33354	2.23154
29/64	11.509	132.47	1,524.6	3.39255	2.25779
15/32	11.906	141.76	1,687.8	3.45054	2.28345
31/64	12.303	151.37	1,862.3	3.50758	2.30855
1/2	12.700	161.29	2,048.4	3.56371	2.33311
33/64	13.097	171.53	2,246.5	3.61896	2.35716
17/32	13.494	182.08	2,457.0	3.67338	2.38073
35/64	13.891	192.95	2,680.2	3.72701	2.40385
9/16	14.288	204.13	2,916.5	3.77988	2.42653
37/64	14.684	215.63	3,166.4	3.83202	2.44879
19/32	15.081	227.44	3,430.1	3.88346	2.47066
39/64	15.478	239.57	3,708.1	3.93422	2.49214
5/8	15.875	252.02	4,000.7	3.98434	2.51326
41/64	16.272	264.77	4,308.4	4.03384	2.53403
21/32	16.669	277.85	4,631.4	4.08274	2.55447
43/64	17.066	291.24	4,970.1	4.13106	2.57459
11/16	17.463	304.94	5,325.0	4.17882	2.59439
45/64	17.859	318.96	5,696.4	4.22604	2.61390
23/32	18.256	333.29	6,084.6	4.27273	2.63312
47/64	18.653	347.94	6,490.2	4.31893	2.65206
3/4	19.050	362.90	6,913.3	4.36463	2.67074
49/64	19.447	378.18	7,354.4	4.40986	2.68916
25/32	19.844	393.77	7,814.0	4.45463	2.70733
51/64	20.241	409.68	8,292.2	4.49896	2.72526
13/16	20.638	425.91	8,789.6	4.54285	2.74296
53/64	21.034	442.44	9,306.6	4.58632	2.76043
27/32	21.431	459.30	9,843.3	4.62939	2.77768
55/64	21.828	476.47	10,400	4.67206	2.79472
7/8	22.225	493.95	10,978	4.71434	2.81156
57/64	22.622	511.75	11,577	4.75625	2.82820
29/32	23.019	529.86	12,197	4.79779	2.84464
59/64	23.416	548.29	12,839	4.83897	2.86089

Fractions of Inches - Millimeter Equivalents (cont.)

Fraction of inch	Millimeter Equivalent				
	Millimeter	Square	Cube	Square Root	Cube Root
15/16	23.813	567.04	13,503	4.87981	2.87697
61/64	24.209	586.09	14,189	4.92030	2.89286
31/32	24.606	605.47	14,898	4.96047	2.90859
63/64	25.003	625.16	15,631	5.00031	2.92414
1	25.400	645.16	16,387	5.03984	2.93953
1-1/32	26.194	686.11	17,972	5.11798	2.96984
1-1/16	26.988	728.33	19,656	5.19495	2.99954
1-3/32	27.781	771.80	21,442	5.27079	3.02866
1-1/8	28.575	816.53	23,332	5.34556	3.05723
1-5/32	29.369	862.52	25,331	5.41929	3.08528
1-3/16	30.163	909.78	27,441	5.49204	3.11283
1-7/32	30.956	958.29	29,665	5.56383	3.13990
1-1/4	31.750	1,008.1	32,006	5.63471	3.16651
1-9/32	32.544	1,059.1	34,467	5.70471	3.19268
1-5/16	33.338	1,111.4	37,051	5.77386	3.21843
1-11/32	34.131	1,164.9	39,761	5.84220	3.24378
1-3/8	34.925	1,219.8	42,600	5.90974	3.26873
1-13/32	35.719	1,275.8	45,571	5.97652	3.29331
1-7/16	36.513	1,333.2	48,677	6.04256	3.31752
1-15/32	37.306	1,391.8	51,921	6.10788	3.34139
1-1/2	38.100	1,451.6	55,306	6.17252	3.36492
1-17/32	38.894	1,512.7	58,836	6.23649	3.38813
1-9/16	39.688	1,575.1	62,512	6.29980	3.41102
1-19/32	40.481	1,638.7	66,338	6.36249	3.43361
1-5/8	41.275	1,703.6	70,317	6.42456	3.45591
1-21/32	42.069	1,769.8	74,452	6.48604	3.47792
1-11/16	42.863	1,837.2	78,747	6.54695	3.49966
1-23/32	43.656	1,905.9	83,203	6.60729	3.52113
1-3/4	44.450	1,975.8	87,824	6.66708	3.54234
1-25/32	45.244	2,047.0	92,614	6.72635	3.56330
1-13/16	46.038	2,119.5	97,574	6.78509	3.58402
1-27/32	46.831	2,193.2	102,709	6.84334	3.60450
1-7/8	47.625	2,268.1	108,020	6.90109	3.62475
1-29/32	48.419	2,344.4	113,512	6.95836	3.64478
1-15/16	49.213	2,421.9	119,186	7.01516	3.66459
1-31/32	50.006	2,500.6	125,047	7.07151	3.68418
2	50.800	2,580.6	131,097	7.12741	3.70358

Natural Trigonometric Functions

Angle		Sine	Cosine	Tangent	Co-tangent	Secant	Co-secant
degree	radian						
0	0.0000	0.0000	1.0000	0.0000	Infinite	1.0000	Infinite
1	0.0175	0.0175	0.9998	0.0175	57.2900	1.0002	57.2987
2	0.0349	0.0349	0.9994	0.0349	28.6363	1.0006	28.6537
3	0.0524	0.0523	0.9986	0.0524	19.0811	1.0014	19.1073
4	0.0698	0.0698	0.9976	0.0699	14.3007	1.0024	14.3356
5	0.0873	0.0872	0.9962	0.0875	11.4301	1.0038	11.4737
6	0.1047	0.1045	0.9945	0.1051	9.5144	1.0055	9.5668
7	0.1222	0.1219	0.9925	0.1228	8.1443	1.0075	8.2055
8	0.1396	0.1392	0.9903	0.1405	7.1154	1.0098	7.1853
9	0.1571	0.1564	0.9877	0.1584	6.3138	1.0125	6.3925
10	0.1745	0.1736	0.9848	0.1763	5.6713	1.0154	5.7588
11	0.1920	0.1908	0.9816	0.1944	5.1446	1.0187	5.2408
12	0.2094	0.2079	0.9781	0.2126	4.7046	1.0223	4.8097
13	0.2269	0.2250	0.9744	0.2309	4.3315	1.0263	4.4454
14	0.2443	0.2419	0.9703	0.2493	4.0108	1.0306	4.1336
15	0.2618	0.2588	0.9659	0.2679	3.7321	1.0353	3.8637
16	0.2793	0.2756	0.9613	0.2867	3.4874	1.0403	3.6280
17	0.2967	0.2924	0.9563	0.3057	3.2709	1.0457	3.4203
18	0.3142	0.3090	0.9511	0.3249	3.0777	1.0515	3.2361
19	0.3316	0.3256	0.9455	0.3443	2.9042	1.0576	3.0716
20	0.3491	0.3420	0.9397	0.3640	2.7475	1.0642	2.9238
21	0.3665	0.3584	0.9336	0.3839	2.6051	1.0711	2.7904
22	0.3840	0.3746	0.9272	0.4040	2.4751	1.0785	2.6695
23	0.4014	0.3907	0.9205	0.4245	2.3559	1.0864	2.5593
24	0.4189	0.4067	0.9135	0.4452	2.2460	1.0946	2.4586
25	0.4363	0.4226	0.9063	0.4663	2.1445	1.1034	2.3662
26	0.4538	0.4384	0.8988	0.4877	2.0503	1.1126	2.2812
27	0.4712	0.4540	0.8910	0.5095	1.9626	1.1223	2.2027
28	0.4887	0.4695	0.8829	0.5317	1.8807	1.1326	2.1301
29	0.5061	0.4848	0.8746	0.5543	1.8040	1.1434	2.0627
30	0.5236	0.5000	0.8660	0.5774	1.7321	1.1547	2.0000
31	0.5411	0.5150	0.8572	0.6009	1.6643	1.1666	1.9416
32	0.5585	0.5299	0.8480	0.6249	1.6003	1.1792	1.8871
33	0.5760	0.5446	0.8387	0.6494	1.5399	1.1924	1.8361
34	0.5934	0.5592	0.8290	0.6745	1.4826	1.2062	1.7883
35	0.6109	0.5736	0.8192	0.7002	1.4281	1.2208	1.7434
36	0.6283	0.5878	0.8090	0.7265	1.3764	1.2361	1.7013
37	0.6458	0.6018	0.7986	0.7536	1.3270	1.2521	1.6616
38	0.6632	0.6157	0.7880	0.7813	1.2799	1.2690	1.6243
39	0.6807	0.6293	0.7771	0.8098	1.2349	1.2868	1.5890

Natural Trigonometric Functions (cont.)

Angle		Sine	Cosine	Tangent	Co-tangent	Secant	Co-secant
degree	radian						
40	0.6981	0.6428	0.7660	0.8391	1.1918	1.3054	1.5557
41	0.7156	0.6561	0.7547	0.8693	1.1504	1.3250	1.5243
42	0.7330	0.6691	0.7431	0.9004	1.1106	1.3456	1.4945
43	0.7505	0.6820	0.7314	0.9325	1.0724	1.3673	1.4663
44	0.7679	0.6947	0.7193	0.9657	1.0355	1.3902	1.4396
45	0.7854	0.7071	0.7071	1.0000	1.0000	1.4142	1.4142
46	0.8029	0.7193	0.6947	1.0355	0.9657	1.4396	1.3902
47	0.8203	0.7314	0.6820	1.0724	0.9325	1.4663	1.3673
48	0.8378	0.7431	0.6691	1.1106	0.9004	1.4945	1.3456
49	0.8552	0.7547	0.6561	1.1504	0.8693	1.5243	1.3250
50	0.8727	0.7660	0.6428	1.1918	0.8391	1.5557	1.3054
51	0.8901	0.7771	0.6293	1.2349	0.8098	1.5890	1.2868
52	0.9076	0.7880	0.6157	1.2799	0.7813	1.6243	1.2690
53	0.9250	0.7986	0.6018	1.3270	0.7536	1.6616	1.2521
54	0.9425	0.8090	0.5878	1.3764	0.7265	1.7013	1.2361
55	0.9599	0.8192	0.5736	1.4281	0.7002	1.7434	1.2208
56	0.9774	0.8290	0.5592	1.4826	0.6745	1.7883	1.2062
57	0.9948	0.8387	0.5446	1.5399	0.6494	1.8361	1.1924
58	1.0123	0.8480	0.5299	1.6003	0.6249	1.8871	1.1792
59	1.0297	0.8572	0.5150	1.6643	0.6009	1.9416	1.1666
60	1.0472	0.8660	0.5000	1.7321	0.5774	2.0000	1.1547
61	1.0647	0.8746	0.4848	1.8040	0.5543	2.0627	1.1434
62	1.0821	0.8829	0.4695	1.8807	0.5317	2.1301	1.1326
63	1.0996	0.8910	0.4540	1.9626	0.5095	2.2027	1.1223
64	1.1170	0.8988	0.4384	2.0503	0.4877	2.2812	1.1126
65	1.1345	0.9063	0.4226	2.1445	0.4663	2.3662	1.1034
66	1.1519	0.9135	0.4067	2.2460	0.4452	2.4586	1.0946
67	1.1694	0.9205	0.3907	2.3559	0.4245	2.5593	1.0864
68	1.1868	0.9272	0.3746	2.4751	0.4040	2.6695	1.0785
69	1.2043	0.9336	0.3584	2.6051	0.3839	2.7904	1.0711
70	1.2217	0.9397	0.3420	2.7475	0.3640	2.9238	1.0642
71	1.2392	0.9455	0.3256	2.9042	0.3443	3.0716	1.0576
72	1.2566	0.9511	0.3090	3.0777	0.3249	3.2361	1.0515
73	1.2741	0.9563	0.2924	3.2709	0.3057	3.4203	1.0457
74	1.2915	0.9613	0.2756	3.4874	0.2867	3.6280	1.0403
75	1.3090	0.9659	0.2588	3.7321	0.2679	3.8637	1.0353
76	1.3265	0.9703	0.2419	4.0108	0.2493	4.1336	1.0306
77	1.3439	0.9744	0.2250	4.3315	0.2309	4.4454	1.0263
78	1.3614	0.9781	0.2079	4.7046	0.2126	4.8097	1.0223
79	1.3788	0.9816	0.1908	5.1446	0.1944	5.2408	1.0187
80	1.3963	0.9848	0.1736	5.6713	0.1763	5.7588	1.0154

Angle		Sine	Cosine	Tangent	Co-tangent	Secant	Co-secant
degree	radian						
81	1.4137	0.9877	0.1564	6.3138	0.1584	6.3925	1.0125
82	1.4312	0.9903	0.1392	7.1154	0.1405	7.1853	1.0098
83	1.4486	0.9925	0.1219	8.1443	0.1228	8.2055	1.0075
84	1.4661	0.9945	0.1045	9.5144	0.1051	9.5668	1.0055
85	1.4835	0.9962	0.0872	11.4301	0.0875	11.4737	1.0038
86	1.5010	0.9976	0.0698	14.3007	0.0699	14.3356	1.0024
87	1.5184	0.9986	0.0523	19.0811	0.0524	19.1073	1.0014
88	1.5359	0.9994	0.0349	28.6363	0.0349	28.6537	1.0006
89	1.5533	0.9998	0.0175	57.2900	0.0175	57.2987	1.0002
90	1.5708	1.0000	0.0000	Infinite	0.0000	Infinite	1.0000
91	1.5882	0.9998	-0.0175	-57.2900	-0.0175	-57.2987	1.0002
92	1.6057	0.9994	-0.0349	-28.6363	-0.0349	-28.6537	1.0006
93	1.6232	0.9986	-0.0523	-19.0811	-0.0524	-19.1073	1.0014
94	1.6406	0.9976	-0.0698	-14.3007	-0.0699	-14.3356	1.0024
95	1.6581	0.9962	-0.0872	-11.4301	-0.0875	-11.4737	1.0038
96	1.6755	0.9945	-0.1045	-9.5144	-0.1051	-9.5668	1.0055
97	1.6930	0.9925	-0.1219	-8.1443	-0.1228	-8.2055	1.0075
98	1.7104	0.9903	-0.1392	-7.1154	-0.1405	-7.1853	1.0098
99	1.7279	0.9877	-0.1564	-6.3138	-0.1584	-6.3925	1.0125
100	1.7453	0.9848	-0.1736	-5.6713	-0.1763	-5.7588	1.0154
101	1.7628	0.9816	-0.1908	-5.1446	-0.1944	-5.2408	1.0187
102	1.7802	0.9781	-0.2079	-4.7046	-0.2126	-4.8097	1.0223
103	1.7977	0.9744	-0.2250	-4.3315	-0.2309	-4.4454	1.0263
104	1.8151	0.9703	-0.2419	-4.0108	-0.2493	-4.1336	1.0306
105	1.8326	0.9659	-0.2588	-3.7321	-0.2679	-3.8637	1.0353
106	1.8500	0.9613	-0.2756	-3.4874	-0.2867	-3.6280	1.0403
107	1.8675	0.9563	-0.2924	-3.2709	-0.3057	-3.4203	1.0457
108	1.8850	0.9511	-0.3090	-3.0777	-0.3249	-3.2361	1.0515
109	1.9024	0.9455	-0.3256	-2.9042	-0.3443	-3.0716	1.0576
110	1.9199	0.9397	-0.3420	-2.7475	-0.3640	-2.9238	1.0642
111	1.9373	0.9336	-0.3584	-2.6051	-0.3839	-2.7904	1.0711
112	1.9548	0.9272	-0.3746	-2.4751	-0.4040	-2.6695	1.0785
113	1.9722	0.9205	-0.3907	-2.3559	-0.4245	-2.5593	1.0864
114	1.9897	0.9135	-0.4067	-2.2460	-0.4452	-2.4586	1.0946
115	2.0071	0.9063	-0.4226	-2.1445	-0.4663	-2.3662	1.1034
116	2.0246	0.8988	-0.4384	-2.0503	-0.4877	-2.2812	1.1126
117	2.0420	0.8910	-0.4540	-1.9626	-0.5095	-2.2027	1.1223
118	2.0595	0.8829	-0.4695	-1.8807	-0.5317	-2.1301	1.1326
119	2.0769	0.8746	-0.4848	-1.8040	-0.5543	-2.0627	1.1434
120	2.0944	0.8660	-0.5000	-1.7321	-0.5774	-2.0000	1.1547
121	2.1118	0.8572	-0.5150	-1.6643	-0.6009	-1.9416	1.1666
122	2.1293	0.8480	-0.5299	-1.6003	-0.6249	-1.8871	1.1792

Natural Trigonometric Functions (cont.)

Angle degree	radian	Sine	Cosine	Tangent	Co-tangent	Secant	Co-secant
123	2.1468	0.8387	-0.5446	-1.5399	-0.6494	-1.8361	1.1924
124	2.1642	0.8290	-0.5592	-1.4826	-0.6745	-1.7883	1.2062
125	2.1817	0.8192	-0.5736	-1.4281	-0.7002	-1.7434	1.2208
126	2.1991	0.8090	-0.5878	-1.3764	-0.7265	-1.7013	1.2361
127	2.2166	0.7986	-0.6018	-1.3270	-0.7536	-1.6616	1.2521
128	2.2340	0.7880	-0.6157	-1.2799	-0.7813	-1.6243	1.2690
129	2.2515	0.7771	-0.6293	-1.2349	-0.8098	-1.5890	1.2868
130	2.2689	0.7660	-0.6428	-1.1918	-0.8391	-1.5557	1.3054
131	2.2864	0.7547	-0.6561	-1.1504	-0.8693	-1.5243	1.3250
132	2.3038	0.7431	-0.6691	-1.1106	-0.9004	-1.4945	1.3456
133	2.3213	0.7314	-0.6820	-1.0724	-0.9325	-1.4663	1.3673
134	2.3387	0.7193	-0.6947	-1.0355	-0.9657	-1.4396	1.3902
135	2.3562	0.7071	-0.7071	-1.0000	-1.0000	-1.4142	1.4142
136	2.3736	0.6947	-0.7193	-0.9657	-1.0355	-1.3902	1.4396
137	2.3911	0.6820	-0.7314	-0.9325	-1.0724	-1.3673	1.4663
138	2.4086	0.6691	-0.7431	-0.9004	-1.1106	-1.3456	1.4945
139	2.4260	0.6561	-0.7547	-0.8693	-1.1504	-1.3250	1.5243
140	2.4435	0.6428	-0.7660	-0.8391	-1.1918	-1.3054	1.5557
141	2.4609	0.6293	-0.7771	-0.8098	-1.2349	-1.2868	1.5890
142	2.4784	0.6157	-0.7880	-0.7813	-1.2799	-1.2690	1.6243
143	2.4958	0.6018	-0.7986	-0.7536	-1.3270	-1.2521	1.6616
144	2.5133	0.5878	-0.8090	-0.7265	-1.3764	-1.2361	1.7013
145	2.5307	0.5736	-0.8192	-0.7002	-1.4281	-1.2208	1.7434
146	2.5482	0.5592	-0.8290	-0.6745	-1.4826	-1.2062	1.7883
147	2.5656	0.5446	-0.8387	-0.6494	-1.5399	-1.1924	1.8361
148	2.5831	0.5299	-0.8480	-0.6249	-1.6003	-1.1792	1.8871
149	2.6005	0.5150	-0.8572	-0.6009	-1.6643	-1.1666	1.9416
150	2.6180	0.5000	-0.8660	-0.5774	-1.7321	-1.1547	2.0000
151	2.6354	0.4848	-0.8746	-0.5543	-1.8040	-1.1434	2.0627
152	2.6529	0.4695	-0.8829	-0.5317	-1.8807	-1.1326	2.1301
153	2.6704	0.4540	-0.8910	-0.5095	-1.9626	-1.1223	2.2027
154	2.6878	0.4384	-0.8988	-0.4877	-2.0503	-1.1126	2.2812
155	2.7053	0.4226	-0.9063	-0.4663	-2.1445	-1.1034	2.3662
156	2.7227	0.4067	-0.9135	-0.4452	-2.2460	-1.0946	2.4586
157	2.7402	0.3907	-0.9205	-0.4245	-2.3559	-1.0864	2.5593
158	2.7576	0.3746	-0.9272	-0.4040	-2.4751	-1.0785	2.6695
159	2.7751	0.3584	-0.9336	-0.3839	-2.6051	-1.0711	2.7904
160	2.7925	0.3420	-0.9397	-0.3640	-2.7475	-1.0642	2.9238
161	2.8100	0.3256	-0.9455	-0.3443	-2.9042	-1.0576	3.0716
162	2.8274	0.3090	-0.9511	-0.3249	-3.0777	-1.0515	3.2361
163	2.8449	0.2924	-0.9563	-0.3057	-3.2709	-1.0457	3.4203

Angle		Sine	Cosine	Tangent	Co-tangent	Secant	Co-secant
degree	radian						
164	2.8623	0.2756	-0.9613	-0.2867	-3.4874	-1.0403	3.6280
165	2.8798	0.2588	-0.9659	-0.2679	-3.7321	-1.0353	3.8637
166	2.8972	0.2419	-0.9703	-0.2493	-4.0108	-1.0306	4.1336
167	2.9147	0.2250	-0.9744	-0.2309	-4.3315	-1.0263	4.4454
168	2.9322	0.2079	-0.9781	-0.2126	-4.7046	-1.0223	4.8097
169	2.9496	0.1908	-0.9816	-0.1944	-5.1446	-1.0187	5.2408
170	2.9671	0.1736	-0.9848	-0.1763	-5.6713	-1.0154	5.7588
171	2.9845	0.1564	-0.9877	-0.1584	-6.3138	-1.0125	6.3925
172	3.0020	0.1392	-0.9903	-0.1405	-7.1154	-1.0098	7.1853
173	3.0194	0.1219	-0.9925	-0.1228	-8.1443	-1.0075	8.2055
174	3.0369	0.1045	-0.9945	-0.1051	-9.5144	-1.0055	9.5668
175	3.0543	0.0872	-0.9962	-0.0875	-11.4301	-1.0038	11.4737
176	3.0718	0.0698	-0.9976	-0.0699	-14.3007	-1.0024	14.3356
177	3.0892	0.0523	-0.9986	-0.0524	-19.0811	-1.0014	19.1073
178	3.1067	0.0349	-0.9994	-0.0349	-28.6363	-1.0006	28.6537
179	3.1241	0.0175	-0.9998	-0.0175	-57.2900	-1.0002	57.2987
180	3.1416	0.0000	-1.0000	0.0000	Infinite	-1.0000	Infinite
181	3.1590	-0.0175	-0.9998	0.0175	57.2900	-1.0002	-57.2987
182	3.1765	-0.0349	-0.9994	0.0349	28.6363	-1.0006	-28.6537
183	3.1940	-0.0523	-0.9986	0.0524	19.0811	-1.0014	-19.1073
184	3.2114	-0.0698	-0.9976	0.0699	14.3007	-1.0024	-14.3356
185	3.2289	-0.0872	-0.9962	0.0875	11.4301	-1.0038	-11.4737
186	3.2463	-0.1045	-0.9945	0.1051	9.5144	-1.0055	-9.5668
187	3.2638	-0.1219	-0.9925	0.1228	8.1443	-1.0075	-8.2055
188	3.2812	-0.1392	-0.9903	0.1405	7.1154	-1.0098	-7.1853
189	3.2987	-0.1564	-0.9877	0.1584	6.3138	-1.0125	-6.3925
190	3.3161	-0.1736	-0.9848	0.1763	5.6713	-1.0154	-5.7588
191	3.3336	-0.1908	-0.9816	0.1944	5.1446	-1.0187	-5.2408
192	3.3510	-0.2079	-0.9781	0.2126	4.7046	-1.0223	-4.8097
193	3.3685	-0.2250	-0.9744	0.2309	4.3315	-1.0263	-4.4454
194	3.3859	-0.2419	-0.9703	0.2493	4.0108	-1.0306	-4.1336
195	3.4034	-0.2588	-0.9659	0.2679	3.7321	-1.0353	-3.8637
196	3.4208	-0.2756	-0.9613	0.2867	3.4874	-1.0403	-3.6280
197	3.4383	-0.2924	-0.9563	0.3057	3.2709	-1.0457	-3.4203
198	3.4558	-0.3090	-0.9511	0.3249	3.0777	-1.0515	-3.2361
199	3.4732	-0.3256	-0.9455	0.3443	2.9042	-1.0576	-3.0716
200	3.4907	-0.3420	-0.9397	0.3640	2.7475	-1.0642	-2.9238
201	3.5081	-0.3584	-0.9336	0.3839	2.6051	-1.0711	-2.7904
202	3.5256	-0.3746	-0.9272	0.4040	2.4751	-1.0785	-2.6695
203	3.5430	-0.3907	-0.9205	0.4245	2.3559	-1.0864	-2.5593
204	3.5605	-0.4067	-0.9135	0.4452	2.2460	-1.0946	-2.4586
205	3.5779	-0.4226	-0.9063	0.4663	2.1445	-1.1034	-2.3662

Natural Trigonometric Functions (cont.)

Angle		Sine	Cosine	Tangent	Co-tangent	Secant	Co-secant
degree	radian						
206	3.5954	-0.4384	-0.8988	0.4877	2.0503	-1.1126	-2.2812
207	3.6128	-0.4540	-0.8910	0.5095	1.9626	-1.1223	-2.2027
208	3.6303	-0.4695	-0.8829	0.5317	1.8807	-1.1326	-2.1301
209	3.6477	-0.4848	-0.8746	0.5543	1.8040	-1.1434	-2.0627
210	3.6652	-0.5000	-0.8660	0.5774	1.7321	-1.1547	-2.0000
211	3.6826	-0.5150	-0.8572	0.6009	1.6643	-1.1666	-1.9416
212	3.7001	-0.5299	-0.8480	0.6249	1.6003	-1.1792	-1.8871
213	3.7176	-0.5446	-0.8387	0.6494	1.5399	-1.1924	-1.8361
214	3.7350	-0.5592	-0.8290	0.6745	1.4826	-1.2062	-1.7883
215	3.7525	-0.5736	-0.8192	0.7002	1.4281	-1.2208	-1.7434
216	3.7699	-0.5878	-0.8090	0.7265	1.3764	-1.2361	-1.7013
217	3.7874	-0.6018	-0.7986	0.7536	1.3270	-1.2521	-1.6616
218	3.8048	-0.6157	-0.7880	0.7813	1.2799	-1.2690	-1.6243
219	3.8223	-0.6293	-0.7771	0.8098	1.2349	-1.2868	-1.5890
220	3.8397	-0.6428	-0.7660	0.8391	1.1918	-1.3054	-1.5557
221	3.8572	-0.6561	-0.7547	0.8693	1.1504	-1.3250	-1.5243
222	3.8746	-0.6691	-0.7431	0.9004	1.1106	-1.3456	-1.4945
223	3.8921	-0.6820	-0.7314	0.9325	1.0724	-1.3673	-1.4663
224	3.9095	-0.6947	-0.7193	0.9657	1.0355	-1.3902	-1.4396
225	3.9270	-0.7071	-0.7071	1.0000	1.0000	-1.4142	-1.4142
226	3.9444	-0.7193	-0.6947	1.0355	0.9657	-1.4396	-1.3902
227	3.9619	-0.7314	-0.6820	1.0724	0.9325	-1.4663	-1.3673
228	3.9794	-0.7431	-0.6691	1.1106	0.9004	-1.4945	-1.3456
229	3.9968	-0.7547	-0.6561	1.1504	0.8693	-1.5243	-1.3250
230	4.0143	-0.7660	-0.6428	1.1918	0.8391	-1.5557	-1.3054
231	4.0317	-0.7771	-0.6293	1.2349	0.8098	-1.5890	-1.2868
232	4.0492	-0.7880	-0.6157	1.2799	0.7813	-1.6243	-1.2690
233	4.0666	-0.7986	-0.6018	1.3270	0.7536	-1.6616	-1.2521
234	4.0841	-0.8090	-0.5878	1.3764	0.7265	-1.7013	-1.2361
235	4.1015	-0.8192	-0.5736	1.4281	0.7002	-1.7434	-1.2208
236	4.1190	-0.8290	-0.5592	1.4826	0.6745	-1.7883	-1.2062
237	4.1364	-0.8387	-0.5446	1.5399	0.6494	-1.8361	-1.1924
238	4.1539	-0.8480	-0.5299	1.6003	0.6249	-1.8871	-1.1792
239	4.1713	-0.8572	-0.5150	1.6643	0.6009	-1.9416	-1.1666
240	4.1888	-0.8660	-0.5000	1.7321	0.5774	-2.0000	-1.1547
241	4.2062	-0.8746	-0.4848	1.8040	0.5543	-2.0627	-1.1434
242	4.2237	-0.8829	-0.4695	1.8807	0.5317	-2.1301	-1.1326
243	4.2412	-0.8910	-0.4540	1.9626	0.5095	-2.2027	-1.1223
244	4.2586	-0.8988	-0.4384	2.0503	0.4877	-2.2812	-1.1126
245	4.2761	-0.9063	-0.4226	2.1445	0.4663	-2.3662	-1.1034
246	4.2935	-0.9135	-0.4067	2.2460	0.4452	-2.4586	-1.0946

Angle		Sine	Cosine	Tangent	Co-tangent	Secant	Co-secant
degree	radian						
247	4.3110	-0.9205	-0.3907	2.3559	0.4245	-2.5593	-1.0864
248	4.3284	-0.9272	-0.3746	2.4751	0.4040	-2.6695	-1.0785
249	4.3459	-0.9336	-0.3584	2.6051	0.3839	-2.7904	-1.0711
250	4.3633	-0.9397	-0.3420	2.7475	0.3640	-2.9238	-1.0642
251	4.3808	-0.9455	-0.3256	2.9042	0.3443	-3.0716	-1.0576
252	4.3982	-0.9511	-0.3090	3.0777	0.3249	-3.2361	-1.0515
253	4.4157	-0.9563	-0.2924	3.2709	0.3057	-3.4203	-1.0457
254	4.4331	-0.9613	-0.2756	3.4874	0.2867	-3.6280	-1.0403
255	4.4506	-0.9659	-0.2588	3.7321	0.2679	-3.8637	-1.0353
256	4.4680	-0.9703	-0.2419	4.0108	0.2493	-4.1336	-1.0306
257	4.4855	-0.9744	-0.2250	4.3315	0.2309	-4.4454	-1.0263
258	4.5029	-0.9781	-0.2079	4.7046	0.2126	-4.8097	-1.0223
259	4.5204	-0.9816	-0.1908	5.1446	0.1944	-5.2408	-1.0187
260	4.5379	-0.9848	-0.1736	5.6713	0.1763	-5.7588	-1.0154
261	4.5553	-0.9877	-0.1564	6.3138	0.1584	-6.3925	-1.0125
262	4.5728	-0.9903	-0.1392	7.1154	0.1405	-7.1853	-1.0098
263	4.5902	-0.9925	-0.1219	8.1443	0.1228	-8.2055	-1.0075
264	4.6077	-0.9945	-0.1045	9.5144	0.1051	-9.5668	-1.0055
265	4.6251	-0.9962	-0.0872	11.4301	0.0875	-11.4737	-1.0038
266	4.6426	-0.9976	-0.0698	14.3007	0.0699	-14.3356	-1.0024
267	4.6600	-0.9986	-0.0523	19.0811	0.0524	-19.1073	-1.0014
268	4.6775	-0.9994	-0.0349	28.6363	0.0349	-28.6537	-1.0006
269	4.6949	-0.9998	-0.0175	57.2900	0.0175	-57.2987	-1.0002
270	4.7124	-1.0000	0.0000	Infinite	0.0000	Infinite	-1.0000
271	4.7298	-0.9998	0.0175	-57.2900	-0.0175	57.2987	-1.0002
272	4.7473	-0.9994	0.0349	-28.6363	-0.0349	28.6537	-1.0006
273	4.7647	-0.9986	0.0523	-19.0811	-0.0524	19.1073	-1.0014
274	4.7822	-0.9976	0.0698	-14.3007	-0.0699	14.3356	-1.0024
275	4.7997	-0.9962	0.0872	-11.4301	-0.0875	11.4737	-1.0038
276	4.8171	-0.9945	0.1045	-9.5144	-0.1051	9.5668	-1.0055
277	4.8346	-0.9925	0.1219	-8.1443	-0.1228	8.2055	-1.0075
278	4.8520	-0.9903	0.1392	-7.1154	-0.1405	7.1853	-1.0098
279	4.8695	-0.9877	0.1564	-6.3138	-0.1584	6.3925	-1.0125
280	4.8869	-0.9848	0.1736	-5.6713	-0.1763	5.7588	-1.0154
281	4.9044	-0.9816	0.1908	-5.1446	-0.1944	5.2408	-1.0187
282	4.9218	-0.9781	0.2079	-4.7046	-0.2126	4.8097	-1.0223
283	4.9393	-0.9744	0.2250	-4.3315	-0.2309	4.4454	-1.0263
284	4.9567	-0.9703	0.2419	-4.0108	-0.2493	4.1336	-1.0306
285	4.9742	-0.9659	0.2588	-3.7321	-0.2679	3.8637	-1.0353
286	4.9916	-0.9613	0.2756	-3.4874	-0.2867	3.6280	-1.0403
287	5.0091	-0.9563	0.2924	-3.2709	-0.3057	3.4203	-1.0457
288	5.0265	-0.9511	0.3090	-3.0777	-0.3249	3.2361	-1.0515

Natural Trigonometric Functions (cont.)

Angle degree	Angle radian	Sine	Cosine	Tangent	Co-tangent	Secant	Co-secant
289	5.0440	-0.9455	0.3256	-2.9042	-0.3443	3.0716	-1.0576
290	5.0615	-0.9397	0.3420	-2.7475	-0.3640	2.9238	-1.0642
291	5.0789	-0.9336	0.3584	-2.6051	-0.3839	2.7904	-1.0711
292	5.0964	-0.9272	0.3746	-2.4751	-0.4040	2.6695	-1.0785
293	5.1138	-0.9205	0.3907	-2.3559	-0.4245	2.5593	-1.0864
294	5.1313	-0.9135	0.4067	-2.2460	-0.4452	2.4586	-1.0946
295	5.1487	-0.9063	0.4226	-2.1445	-0.4663	2.3662	-1.1034
296	5.1662	-0.8988	0.4384	-2.0503	-0.4877	2.2812	-1.1126
297	5.1836	-0.8910	0.4540	-1.9626	-0.5095	2.2027	-1.1223
298	5.2011	-0.8829	0.4695	-1.8807	-0.5317	2.1301	-1.1326
299	5.2185	-0.8746	0.4848	-1.8040	-0.5543	2.0627	-1.1434
300	5.2360	-0.8660	0.5000	-1.7321	-0.5774	2.0000	-1.1547
301	5.2534	-0.8572	0.5150	-1.6643	-0.6009	1.9416	-1.1666
302	5.2709	-0.8480	0.5299	-1.6003	-0.6249	1.8871	-1.1792
303	5.2883	-0.8387	0.5446	-1.5399	-0.6494	1.8361	-1.1924
304	5.3058	-0.8290	0.5592	-1.4826	-0.6745	1.7883	-1.2062
305	5.3233	-0.8192	0.5736	-1.4281	-0.7002	1.7434	-1.2208
306	5.3407	-0.8090	0.5878	-1.3764	-0.7265	1.7013	-1.2361
307	5.3582	-0.7986	0.6018	-1.3270	-0.7536	1.6616	-1.2521
308	5.3756	-0.7880	0.6157	-1.2799	-0.7813	1.6243	-1.2690
309	5.3931	-0.7771	0.6293	-1.2349	-0.8098	1.5890	-1.2868
310	5.4105	-0.7660	0.6428	-1.1918	-0.8391	1.5557	-1.3054
311	5.4280	-0.7547	0.6561	-1.1504	-0.8693	1.5243	-1.3250
312	5.4454	-0.7431	0.6691	-1.1106	-0.9004	1.4945	-1.3456
313	5.4629	-0.7314	0.6820	-1.0724	-0.9325	1.4663	-1.3673
314	5.4803	-0.7193	0.6947	-1.0355	-0.9657	1.4396	-1.3902
315	5.4978	-0.7071	0.7071	-1.0000	-1.0000	1.4142	-1.4142
316	5.5152	-0.6947	0.7193	-0.9657	-1.0355	1.3902	-1.4396
317	5.5327	-0.6820	0.7314	-0.9325	-1.0724	1.3673	-1.4663
318	5.5501	-0.6691	0.7431	-0.9004	-1.1106	1.3456	-1.4945
319	5.5676	-0.6561	0.7547	-0.8693	-1.1504	1.3250	-1.5243
320	5.5851	-0.6428	0.7660	-0.8391	-1.1918	1.3054	-1.5557
321	5.6025	-0.6293	0.7771	-0.8098	-1.2349	1.2868	-1.5890
322	5.6200	-0.6157	0.7880	-0.7813	-1.2799	1.2690	-1.6243
323	5.6374	-0.6018	0.7986	-0.7536	-1.3270	1.2521	-1.6616
324	5.6549	-0.5878	0.8090	-0.7265	-1.3764	1.2361	-1.7013
325	5.6723	-0.5736	0.8192	-0.7002	-1.4281	1.2208	-1.7434
326	5.6898	-0.5592	0.8290	-0.6745	-1.4826	1.2062	-1.7883
327	5.7072	-0.5446	0.8387	-0.6494	-1.5399	1.1924	-1.8361
328	5.7247	-0.5299	0.8480	-0.6249	-1.6003	1.1792	-1.8871
329	5.7421	-0.5150	0.8572	-0.6009	-1.6643	1.1666	-1.9416

Angle		Sine	Cosine	Tangent	Co-tangent	Secant	Co-secant
degree	radian						
330	5.7596	-0.5000	0.8660	-0.5774	-1.7321	1.1547	-2.0000
331	5.7770	-0.4848	0.8746	-0.5543	-1.8040	1.1434	-2.0627
332	5.7945	-0.4695	0.8829	-0.5317	-1.8807	1.1326	-2.1301
333	5.8119	-0.4540	0.8910	-0.5095	-1.9626	1.1223	-2.2027
334	5.8294	-0.4384	0.8988	-0.4877	-2.0503	1.1126	-2.2812
335	5.8469	-0.4226	0.9063	-0.4663	-2.1445	1.1034	-2.3662
336	5.8643	-0.4067	0.9135	-0.4452	-2.2460	1.0946	-2.4586
337	5.8818	-0.3907	0.9205	-0.4245	-2.3559	1.0864	-2.5593
338	5.8992	-0.3746	0.9272	-0.4040	-2.4751	1.0785	-2.6695
339	5.9167	-0.3584	0.9336	-0.3839	-2.6051	1.0711	-2.7904
340	5.9341	-0.3420	0.9397	-0.3640	-2.7475	1.0642	-2.9238
341	5.9516	-0.3256	0.9455	-0.3443	-2.9042	1.0576	-3.0716
342	5.9690	-0.3090	0.9511	-0.3249	-3.0777	1.0515	-3.2361
343	5.9865	-0.2924	0.9563	-0.3057	-3.2709	1.0457	-3.4203
344	6.0039	-0.2756	0.9613	-0.2867	-3.4874	1.0403	-3.6280
345	6.0214	-0.2588	0.9659	-0.2679	-3.7321	1.0353	-3.8637
346	6.0388	-0.2419	0.9703	-0.2493	-4.0108	1.0306	-4.1336
347	6.0563	-0.2250	0.9744	-0.2309	-4.3315	1.0263	-4.4454
348	6.0737	-0.2079	0.9781	-0.2126	-4.7046	1.0223	-4.8097
349	6.0912	-0.1908	0.9816	-0.1944	-5.1446	1.0187	-5.2408
350	6.1087	-0.1736	0.9848	-0.1763	-5.6713	1.0154	-5.7588
351	6.1261	-0.1564	0.9877	-0.1584	-6.3138	1.0125	-6.3925
352	6.1436	-0.1392	0.9903	-0.1405	-7.1154	1.0098	-7.1853
353	6.1610	-0.1219	0.9925	-0.1228	-8.1443	1.0075	-8.2055
354	6.1785	-0.1045	0.9945	-0.1051	-9.5144	1.0055	-9.5668
355	6.1959	-0.0872	0.9962	-0.0875	-11.4301	1.0038	-11.4737
356	6.2134	-0.0698	0.9976	-0.0699	-14.3007	1.0024	-14.3356
357	6.2308	-0.0523	0.9986	-0.0524	-19.0811	1.0014	-19.1073
358	6.2483	-0.0349	0.9994	-0.0349	-28.6363	1.0006	-28.6537
359	6.2657	-0.0175	0.9998	-0.0175	-57.2900	1.0002	-57.2987
360	6.2832	0.0000	1.0000	0.0000	Infinite	1.0000	Infinite

Right Triangle Trig Formulas

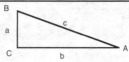

A, B, C = Angles   a, b, c = Distances

$$\sin A = \frac{a}{c} \quad , \quad \cos A = \frac{b}{c} \quad , \quad \tan A = \frac{a}{b}$$

$$\cot A = \frac{b}{a} \quad , \quad \sec A = \frac{c}{b} \quad , \quad \csc A = \frac{c}{a}$$

Area = (a b) / 2

Given a and b, Find A, B, and c

$$\tan A = \frac{a}{b} = \cot B \quad , \quad c = \sqrt{a^2 + b^2} = a\sqrt{1 + \frac{b^2}{a^2}}$$

Given a and c, Find A, B, b

$$\sin A = \frac{a}{c} = \cos B \quad , \quad b = \sqrt{(c+a)(c-a)} = c\sqrt{1 - \frac{a^2}{c^2}}$$

Given A and a, Find B, b, c

$$B = 90^\circ - A \quad , \quad b = a \cot A \quad , \quad c = \frac{a}{\sin A}$$

Given A and b, Find B, a, c

$$B = 90^\circ - A \quad , \quad a = b \tan A \quad , \quad c = \frac{b}{\cos A}$$

Given A and c, Find B, a, b

$$B = 90^\circ - A \quad , \quad a = c \sin A \quad , \quad b = c \cos A$$

Oblique Triangle Formulas

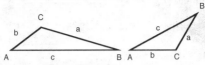

Given A, B and a, Find b, C and c

$$b = \frac{a \sin B}{\sin A} \ , \ C = 180° - (A+B) \ , \ c = \frac{a \sin C}{\sin A}$$

Given A, a and b, Find B, C and c

$$\sin B = \frac{b \sin A}{a} , C = 180° - (A+B) , c = \frac{a \sin C}{\sin A}$$

Given a, b and C, Find A, B and c

$$\tan A = \frac{a \sin C}{b - (a \cos C)} \ , \ B = 180° - (A+C)$$

$$c = \frac{a \sin C}{\sin A}$$

Given a, b and c, Find A, B and C

$$\cos A = \frac{b^2 + c^2 - a^2}{2\,bc} , \cos B = \frac{a^2 + c^2 - b^2}{2\,ac}$$

$$C = 180° - (A+B)$$

Given a, b, c, A, B and C Find Area

$$s = \frac{a+b+c}{2} \ , \ Area = \sqrt{s(s-a)(s-b)(s-c)}$$

$$Area = \frac{bc \sin A}{2} \ , \ Area = \frac{a^2 \sin B \sin C}{2 \sin A}$$

Plane Figure Formulas

Rectangle

If square, a=b

$Area = ab$

$Perimeter = 2(a+b)$, $Diagonal = \sqrt{a^2 + b^2}$

Parallelogram

All sides are
parallel
θ= degrees

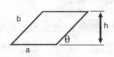

$Area = ah = ab \sin\theta$, $Perimeter = 2(a+b)$

Trapezoid

$Area = \dfrac{(a+b)}{2} h$

$Perimeter = Sum\ of\ lengths\ of\ sides$

Quadrilateral

θ = degrees

$Area = \dfrac{d_1 \times d_2 \times \sin\theta}{2}$

Trapezium

a to g = lengths

$$Perimeter = a + b + c + d$$

$$Area = \frac{(h+k)\,g + e\,h + f\,k}{2}$$

Equilateral Triangle

a = all sides equal

$$Perimeter = 3\,a \quad , \quad h = \frac{a}{2}\sqrt{3} = 0.866\,a$$

$$Area = a^2 \frac{\sqrt{3}}{4} = 0.433\,a^2$$

Annulus

$$Area = 0.7854(d^2 - f^2)$$

$$Area = \pi\,(r_1 + r_2)\,(r_2 - r_1)$$

Regular Polygons

n = *number of sides*
(all sides equal length)
θ = *degrees*

Perimeter = $n\,a$

$$Area = \frac{n\,a\,r}{2} = nr^2\,\tan\theta = \frac{nR^2}{2}\,\sin 2\theta$$

Polygon	Number of Sides	Area
Triangle, equilateral	3	0.4330 a2
Square	4	1.0000 a2
Pentagon	5	1.7205 a2
Hexagon	6	2.5981 a2
Heptagon	7	3.6339 a2
Octagon	8	4.8284 a2
Nonagon	9	6.1818 a2
Decagon	10	7.6942 a2
Undecagon	11	9.3656 a2
Dodecagon	12	11.1961 a2

Area of inscribed polygon in a circle of radius R :

$$A = \tfrac{1}{2}\,nR^2\,\sin\frac{2\pi}{n}$$

Perimeter of inscribed polygon in circle of radius R :

$$P = 2\,n\,R\,\sin\frac{\pi}{n}$$

Area of polygon circumscribing a circle of radius r :

$$A = nr^2\,\tan\frac{\pi}{n}$$

Perimeter of polygon circumscribing a circle

of radius r : P = 2\,nr\,\tan\dfrac{\pi}{n}$

Note: In all equations, π = 180°. See page 320 for more on polygons.

Circle

Z = point
X = point
θ = degrees
c,d,r,m = lengths

π = 3.14159
c = cord
r = radius

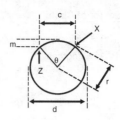

Circumference $= 2\pi r = \pi d = 3.14159\,d$

Area $= \pi r^2 = \pi\,\dfrac{d^2}{4} = 0.78539\,d^2$

Area $= \dfrac{Perimeter^2}{4\pi} = 0.07958\,Perimeter^2$

Length of arc XZ $= \theta\,\dfrac{\pi}{180}\,r = 0.017453\,\theta\,r$

$r = \dfrac{m^2 + \frac{1}{4}c^2}{2m} = \dfrac{\frac{1}{2}c}{\sin\frac{1}{2}\theta}$

$c = 2\sqrt{2mr - m^2} = 2r\,\sin\frac{1}{2}\theta$

$m = r \pm \sqrt{r^2 - \dfrac{c^2}{4}}$ (*use* + *if arc* $\geq 180°$,

$\qquad\qquad\qquad\qquad$ *use* − *if arc* < $180°$)

$m = \frac{1}{2}c\,\tan\frac{1}{4}\theta = 2r\,\sin^2\frac{1}{4}\theta$

Sector of Circle

r = radius

θ = degrees

A,B,C = points

$$Arc\ length\ AC = \frac{\pi r \theta}{180} = 0.01745\ r\ \theta$$

$$Area\ ABCA = \frac{\pi \theta r^2}{360} = 0.008727\ \theta\ r^2$$

$$Area\ ABCA = \frac{Arc\ length\ AC\ x\ r}{2}$$

Segment of Circle

r = radius

θ = degrees

A,B,C,D = points

For $\theta < 90°$

$$Area\ ACDA = \frac{r^2}{2} \left(\frac{\pi \theta}{180} - \sin \theta \right)$$

For $\theta > 90°$

$$Area\ ACDA = \frac{r^2}{2} \left(\frac{\pi \theta}{180} - \sin (180 - \theta) \right)$$

Circular Zone

Area ACDFA =
Circle Area –

Segment Area ABCA –
  Segment Area FDEF

Hollow Circle Sector

θ = degrees
A,B,C,D = points
r = radius

$$Area\ ABCDA = \frac{\pi\ \theta\ (r_1^2 - r_2^2)}{360}$$

$$Area\ ABCDA =$$
$$\frac{r_1 - r_2}{2}\ (Arc\ length\ AB + Arc\ length\ CD)$$

Fillet

r = radius
Area of fillet = 0.215 r^2

Parabola

A,B,C = points
a,b = lengths

$$Area\ ABCA = \frac{2}{3}\ a\,b$$

$$Arc\ Length\ ABC = \frac{b}{2} \sqrt{1 + \left(\frac{4\,a}{b}\right)^2}\ +$$
(approximation!)

$$\frac{b^2}{8\,a} \log_e \left[\frac{4\,a}{b} + \sqrt{1 + \left(\frac{4\,a}{b}\right)^2} \right]$$

Ellipse

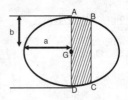

a,b = lengths
A,B,C,D,G =
  points

Area of ellipse $= \pi\, a\, b$

Perimeter of ellipse $= \pi\left[\, 1.5\,(a+b)-\sqrt{ab}\,\right]$
(approximate)

Assuming point G is the center of the ellipse, which
has (x, y) coordinates of (0, 0), and the coordinates of point B are (Bx, By) :

$$Area\ ABCDA = (B_x \times B_y) + ab\,\sin^{-1}\!\left(\frac{B_x}{a}\right)$$

Solid Figure Formulas

Parallelopiped and Cube

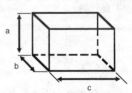

a,b,c =
  lengths

If a Cube:
  Volume $= a^3$ *Surface area* $= 6\,a^2$

If a Parallelopiped (a, b, and c can be different):
  Volume $= a\,b\,c$ *Area* $= 2\,(ab+bc+ac)$

**Prism – Right,
or oblique,
regular or
irregular**

A = area
h = length
a,b,c = length

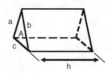

> *Volume = A h* where A is the area of the end
> plate abca. If the end plate
> has 3 or more sides, see page
> 320 for rules of calculating areas
> of polygons.

Convex Surface area = h(a + b + c +....n sides)

If end planes are parallel but not at 90° to h, the
same formulas apply but a slice at 90° through the
prism must be used to determine a, b, and c.

Right Cylinder

r = radius
h = length

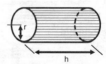

Volume $= \pi r^2 h$
Surface Area $= 2 \pi r (r + h)$
Lateral Area (shaded only) $= 2 \pi r h$

If end planes are parallel but not at 90° to h, the
same formulas apply, but a slice at 90° through the
cylinder must be used to determine r. Surface
area includes the ends; lateral area is shaded.

Frustum of a Right Cylinder

r = radius
h = height 1
k = height 2

$$Volume = \frac{\pi r^2}{2}(h+k)$$

$$Surface\ Area = \pi r\left[h+k+r+\sqrt{r^2+\left(\frac{h-k}{2}\right)^2}\right]$$

$$Lateral\ Area\,(shaded\ only) = \pi r\,(h+k)$$

Right Cone

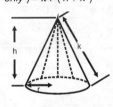

r = radius
h = height
k = side length

$$Volume = \frac{\pi r^2 h}{3}$$

$$Surface\ Area = \pi r\,(r+k) \qquad Lateral\ Area\,(shaded) = \pi r k$$

Right Pyramid

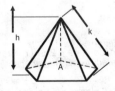

A = base plane
h = height
k = side length

$$Volume = \frac{(Area\ of\ base\ A)\,h}{3}$$

$$Surface\ Area\,(no\ base) = Perimeter\ of\ base\ A \times \frac{k}{2}$$

Use polygon areas on page 321 , if you want to include the base area

Sphere

r = radius

$Volume = \dfrac{4 \pi r^3}{3}$

$Surface\ Area = 4 \pi r^2$

Circular Ring

r = cross section radius
R = ring radius

$Volume = 2 \pi^2 R r^2$

$Surface\ Area = 4 \pi^2 R r$

Paraboloid

d = diameter
h = length

$Volume = \dfrac{\pi}{8} \times d^2 \times h$

$Surface\ Area\,(no\ base) =$

$$\dfrac{2}{3} \times \pi \times \dfrac{d}{h^2} \left[\left(\dfrac{d^2}{16} + h^2 \right)^{\frac{3}{2}} - \left(\dfrac{d}{4} \right)^3 \right]$$

Ellipsoid and Spheroid

a, b, c = axis radius

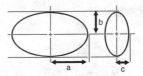

$$Volume = \frac{4}{3} \times \pi \times a \times b \times c$$

Prolate Spheroid (revolution about major axis b)

$$Volume = \frac{4}{3}(\pi \, a \, b^2)$$

Oblate Spheroid (revolution about minor axis a)

$$Volume = \frac{4}{3}(\pi \, b \, a^2)$$

Segments of Circles for Radius = 1

Values in the table are based on the following equations:

$$radius = r = 1$$
$$\theta_R = \theta_D \times \pi/180°$$
$$c = r \times \theta_R$$
$$h = r \times (1 - \cos(\theta_R/2))$$
$$l = 2r \times \sin(\theta_R/2)$$
$$A_{seg} = (r^2/2) \times (\theta_R - \sin\theta_R)$$

For other radii, multiply the values of length of arc, height above chord, and length of chord in the table by the new radius; for values of area multiply the areas in the table by the new radius squared.

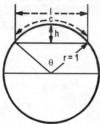

Center Angle, θ_D degrees	Center Angle, θ_R radians	Length of Arc, c	Height Above Chord, h	Length of Chord, l	Area of Segment, A_{seg}
1	0.01745	0.01745	0.0000381	0.0174531	0.0000004
2	0.03491	0.03491	0.0001523	0.0349048	0.0000035
3	0.05236	0.05236	0.0003427	0.0523539	0.0000119
4	0.06981	0.06981	0.0006092	0.0697990	0.0000283
5	0.08727	0.08727	0.0009518	0.0872388	0.0000554
6	0.10472	0.10472	0.0013705	0.1046719	0.0000956
7	0.12217	0.12217	0.0018652	0.1220971	0.0001519
8	0.13963	0.13963	0.0024359	0.1395129	0.0002266
9	0.15708	0.15708	0.0030827	0.1569182	0.0003226
10	0.17453	0.17453	0.0038053	0.1743115	0.0004424
11	0.19199	0.19199	0.0046038	0.1916915	0.0005886
12	0.20944	0.20944	0.0054781	0.2090569	0.0007639
13	0.22689	0.22689	0.0064281	0.2264064	0.0009709
14	0.24435	0.24435	0.0074538	0.2437387	0.0012121
15	0.26180	0.26180	0.0085551	0.2610524	0.0014902
16	0.27925	0.27925	0.0097319	0.2783462	0.0018077

Segments of Circles for Radius = 1 (cont.)

Center Angle, θ_D degrees	Center Angle, θ_R radians	Length of Arc, c	Height Above Chord, h	Length of Chord, l	Area of Segment, A_{seg}
17	0.29671	0.29671	0.0109841	0.2956188	0.0021671
18	0.31416	0.31416	0.0123117	0.3128689	0.0025711
19	0.33161	0.33161	0.0137144	0.3300952	0.0030222
20	0.34907	0.34907	0.0151922	0.3472964	0.0035229
21	0.36652	0.36652	0.0167451	0.3644711	0.0040756
22	0.38397	0.38397	0.0183728	0.3816180	0.0046829
23	0.40143	0.40143	0.0200753	0.3987359	0.0053473
24	0.41888	0.41888	0.0218524	0.4158234	0.0060712
25	0.43633	0.43633	0.0237040	0.4328792	0.0068570
26	0.45379	0.45379	0.0256299	0.4499021	0.0077072
27	0.47124	0.47124	0.0276301	0.4668907	0.0086242
28	0.48869	0.48869	0.0297043	0.4838438	0.0096103
29	0.50615	0.50615	0.0318524	0.5007600	0.0106679
30	0.52360	0.52360	0.0340742	0.5176381	0.0117994
31	0.54105	0.54105	0.0363695	0.5344768	0.0130070
32	0.55851	0.55851	0.0387383	0.5512747	0.0142930
33	0.57596	0.57596	0.0411803	0.5680307	0.0156598
34	0.59341	0.59341	0.0436952	0.5847434	0.0171095
35	0.61087	0.61087	0.0462830	0.6014116	0.0186444
36	0.62832	0.62832	0.0489435	0.6180340	0.0202666
37	0.64577	0.64577	0.0516763	0.6346093	0.0219784
38	0.66323	0.66323	0.0544814	0.6511363	0.0237818
39	0.68068	0.68068	0.0573585	0.6676137	0.0256790
40	0.69813	0.69813	0.0603074	0.6840403	0.0276720
41	0.71558	0.71558	0.0633278	0.7004148	0.0297630
42	0.73304	0.73304	0.0664196	0.7167359	0.0319538
43	0.75049	0.75049	0.0695824	0.7330025	0.0342466
44	0.76794	0.76794	0.0728161	0.7492132	0.0366433
45	0.78540	0.78540	0.0761205	0.7653669	0.0391457
46	0.80285	0.80285	0.0794951	0.7814623	0.0417558
47	0.82030	0.82030	0.0829399	0.7974981	0.0444755
48	0.83776	0.83776	0.0864545	0.8134733	0.0473066
49	0.85521	0.85521	0.0900387	0.8293865	0.0502509
50	0.87266	0.87266	0.0936922	0.8452365	0.0533101
51	0.89012	0.89012	0.0974147	0.8610222	0.0564860
52	0.90757	0.90757	0.1012060	0.8767423	0.0597802
53	0.92502	0.92502	0.1050656	0.8923956	0.0631945
54	0.94248	0.94248	0.1089933	0.9079810	0.0667304
55	0.95993	0.95993	0.1129892	0.9234972	0.0703895
56	0.97738	0.97738	0.1170524	0.9389431	0.0741734
57	0.99484	0.99484	0.1211829	0.9543175	0.0780836

Center Angle, θ_D degrees	Center Angle, θ_R radians	Length of Arc, c	Height Above Chord, h	Length of Chord, l	Area of Segment, A_{seg}
58	1.01229	1.01229	0.1253803	0.9696192	0.0821214
59	1.02974	1.02974	0.1296443	0.9848471	0.0862885
60	1.04720	1.04720	0.1339746	1.0000000	0.0905861
61	1.06465	1.06465	0.1383708	1.0150767	0.0950156
62	1.08210	1.08210	0.1428327	1.0300761	0.0995783
63	1.09956	1.09956	0.1473598	1.0449971	0.1042755
64	1.11701	1.11701	0.1519519	1.0598385	0.1091083
65	1.13446	1.13446	0.1566086	1.0745992	0.1140781
66	1.15192	1.15192	0.1613294	1.0892781	0.1191859
67	1.16937	1.16937	0.1661142	1.1038740	0.1244329
68	1.18682	1.18682	0.1709624	1.1183858	0.1298200
69	1.20428	1.20428	0.1758738	1.1328125	0.1353484
70	1.22173	1.22173	0.1808480	1.1471529	0.1410189
71	1.23918	1.23918	0.1858845	1.1614059	0.1468326
72	1.25664	1.25664	0.1909830	1.1755705	0.1527903
73	1.27409	1.27409	0.1961431	1.1896456	0.1588928
74	1.29154	1.29154	0.2013645	1.2036300	0.1651410
75	1.30900	1.30900	0.2066467	1.2175229	0.1715356
76	1.32645	1.32645	0.2119892	1.2313230	0.1780773
77	1.34390	1.34390	0.2173918	1.2450293	0.1847667
78	1.36136	1.36136	0.2228540	1.2586408	0.1916046
79	1.37881	1.37881	0.2283754	1.2721564	0.1985915
80	1.39626	1.39626	0.2339556	1.2855752	0.2057278
81	1.41372	1.41372	0.2395940	1.2988961	0.2130142
82	1.43117	1.43117	0.2452904	1.3121181	0.2204510
83	1.44862	1.44862	0.2510443	1.3252401	0.2280386
84	1.46608	1.46608	0.2568552	1.3382612	0.2357773
85	1.48353	1.48353	0.2627227	1.3511804	0.2436676
86	1.50098	1.50098	0.2686463	1.3639967	0.2517096
87	1.51844	1.51844	0.2746256	1.3767092	0.2599035
88	1.53589	1.53589	0.2806602	1.3893167	0.2682495
89	1.55334	1.55334	0.2867496	1.4018185	0.2767477
90	1.57080	1.57080	0.2928932	1.4142136	0.2853982
91	1.58825	1.58825	0.2990907	1.4265009	0.2942010
92	1.60570	1.60570	0.3053416	1.4386796	0.3031560
93	1.62316	1.62316	0.3116454	1.4507487	0.3122633
94	1.64061	1.64061	0.3180016	1.4627074	0.3215227
95	1.65806	1.65806	0.3244098	1.4745547	0.3309340
96	1.67552	1.67552	0.3308694	1.4862897	0.3404971
97	1.69297	1.69297	0.3373800	1.4979114	0.3502116
98	1.71042	1.71042	0.3439410	1.5094192	0.3600773
99	1.72788	1.72788	0.3505520	1.5208119	0.3700938

Segments of Circles for Radius = 1 (cont.)

Center Angle, θ_D degrees	Center Angle, θ_R radians	Length of Arc, c	Height Above Chord, h	Length of Chord, l	Area of Segment, A_{seg}
100	1.74533	1.74533	0.3572124	1.5320889	0.3802607
101	1.76278	1.76278	0.3639218	1.5432492	0.3905777
102	1.78024	1.78024	0.3706796	1.5542919	0.4010441
103	1.79769	1.79769	0.3774854	1.5652163	0.4116595
104	1.81514	1.81514	0.3843385	1.5760215	0.4224233
105	1.83260	1.83260	0.3912386	1.5867060	0.4333349
106	1.85005	1.85005	0.3981850	1.5972710	0.4443937
107	1.86750	1.86750	0.4051772	1.6077137	0.4555988
108	1.88496	1.88496	0.4122147	1.6180340	0.4669495
109	1.90241	1.90241	0.4192970	1.6282310	0.4784452
110	1.91986	1.91986	0.4264236	1.6383041	0.4900848
111	1.93732	1.93732	0.4335938	1.6482524	0.5018675
112	1.95477	1.95477	0.4408071	1.6580751	0.5137925
113	1.97222	1.97222	0.4480630	1.6677716	0.5258586
114	1.98968	1.98968	0.4553610	1.6773411	0.5380649
115	2.00713	2.00713	0.4627004	1.6867829	0.5504104
116	2.02458	2.02458	0.4700807	1.6960962	0.5628939
117	2.04204	2.04204	0.4775014	1.7052803	0.5755144
118	2.05949	2.05949	0.4849619	1.7143346	0.5882705
119	2.07694	2.07694	0.4924616	1.7232583	0.6011611
120	2.09440	2.09440	0.5000000	1.7320508	0.6141848
121	2.11185	2.11185	0.5075764	1.7407114	0.6273405
122	2.12930	2.12930	0.5151904	1.7492394	0.6406268
123	2.14675	2.14675	0.5228412	1.7576342	0.6540422
124	2.16421	2.16421	0.5305284	1.7658952	0.6675853
125	2.18166	2.18166	0.5382514	1.7740217	0.6812548
126	2.19911	2.19911	0.5460095	1.7820130	0.6950489
127	2.21657	2.21657	0.5538022	1.7898687	0.7089663
128	2.23402	2.23402	0.5616289	1.7975881	0.7230053
129	2.25147	2.25147	0.5694889	1.8051706	0.7371644
130	2.26893	2.26893	0.5773817	1.8126156	0.7514418
131	2.28638	2.28638	0.5853068	1.8199225	0.7658359
132	2.30383	2.30383	0.5932634	1.8270909	0.7803449
133	2.32129	2.32129	0.6012509	1.8341201	0.7949671
134	2.33874	2.33874	0.6092689	1.8410097	0.8097007
135	2.35619	2.35619	0.6173166	1.8477591	0.8245439
136	2.37365	2.37365	0.6253934	1.8543677	0.8394947
137	2.39110	2.39110	0.6334988	1.8608351	0.8545514
138	2.40855	2.40855	0.6416321	1.8671609	0.8697119
139	2.42601	2.42601	0.6497926	1.8733444	0.8849743
140	2.44346	2.44346	0.6579799	1.8793852	0.9003367

Center Angle, θ_D degrees	Center Angle, θ_R radians	Length of Arc, c	Height Above Chord, h	Length of Chord, l	Area of Segment, A_{seg}
141	2.46091	2.46091	0.6661931	1.8852830	0.9157969
142	2.47837	2.47837	0.6744318	1.8910372	0.9313530
143	2.49582	2.49582	0.6826953	1.8966473	0.9470029
144	2.51327	2.51327	0.6909830	1.9021130	0.9627444
145	2.53073	2.53073	0.6992942	1.9074339	0.9785755
146	2.54818	2.54818	0.7076283	1.9126095	0.9944939
147	2.56563	2.56563	0.7159847	1.9176395	1.0104975
148	2.58309	2.58309	0.7243626	1.9225234	1.0265840
149	2.60054	2.60054	0.7327616	1.9272609	1.0427513
150	2.61799	2.61799	0.7411810	1.9318517	1.0589969
151	2.63545	2.63545	0.7496200	1.9362953	1.0753188
152	2.65290	2.65290	0.7580781	1.9405915	1.0917145
153	2.67035	2.67035	0.7665546	1.9447398	1.1081816
154	2.68781	2.68781	0.7750489	1.9487401	1.1247180
155	2.70526	2.70526	0.7835604	1.9525920	1.1413210
156	2.72271	2.72271	0.7920883	1.9562952	1.1579885
157	2.74017	2.74017	0.8006321	1.9598494	1.1747179
158	2.75762	2.75762	0.8091910	1.9632544	1.1915068
159	2.77507	2.77507	0.8177645	1.9665098	1.2083528
160	2.79253	2.79253	0.8263518	1.9696155	1.2252533
161	2.80998	2.80998	0.8349524	1.9725712	1.2422060
162	2.82743	2.82743	0.8435655	1.9753767	1.2592082
163	2.84489	2.84489	0.8521906	1.9780317	1.2762575
164	2.86234	2.86234	0.8608269	1.9805361	1.2933513
165	2.87979	2.87979	0.8694738	1.9828897	1.3104871
166	2.89725	2.89725	0.8781307	1.9850923	1.3276623
167	2.91470	2.91470	0.8867968	1.9871437	1.3448744
168	2.93215	2.93215	0.8954715	1.9890438	1.3621207
169	2.94961	2.94961	0.9041542	1.9907924	1.3793987
170	2.96706	2.96706	0.9128443	1.9923894	1.3967058
171	2.98451	2.98451	0.9215409	1.9938347	1.4140393
172	3.00197	3.00197	0.9302435	1.9951281	1.4313966
173	3.01942	3.01942	0.9389515	1.9962696	1.4487751
174	3.03687	3.03687	0.9476640	1.9972591	1.4661722
175	3.05433	3.05433	0.9563806	1.9980964	1.4835852
176	3.07178	3.07178	0.9651005	1.9987817	1.5010115
177	3.08923	3.08923	0.9738231	1.9993146	1.5184484
178	3.10669	3.10669	0.9825476	1.9996954	1.5358933
179	3.12414	3.12414	0.9912735	1.9999238	1.5533435
180	3.14159	3.14159	1.0000000	2.0000000	1.5707963

Spheres - Surface Area and Volume

Fraction Diameter, D inch	Decimal Diameter, D inch	Decimal Radius, r inch	Surface Area, A square inch	Volume, V
1/64	0.015625	0.007813	0.0007670	0.0000020
1/32	0.031250	0.015625	0.0030680	0.0000160
3/64	0.046875	0.023438	0.0069029	0.0000539
1/16	0.062500	0.031250	0.0122718	0.0001278
5/64	0.078125	0.039063	0.0191748	0.0002497
3/32	0.093750	0.046875	0.0276117	0.0004314
7/64	0.109375	0.054688	0.0375825	0.0006851
1/8	0.125000	0.062500	0.0490814	0.0010227
9/64	0.140625	0.070313	0.0621262	0.0014561
5/32	0.156250	0.078125	0.0766990	0.0019974
11/64	0.171875	0.085938	0.0928058	0.0026585
3/16	0.187500	0.093750	0.1104466	0.0034515
13/64	0.203125	0.101563	0.1296214	0.0043882
7/32	0.218750	0.109375	0.1503301	0.0054808
15/64	0.234375	0.117188	0.1725728	0.0067411
1/4	0.250000	0.125000	0.1963495	0.0081812
17/64	0.265625	0.132813	0.2216602	0.0098131
9/32	0.281250	0.140625	0.2485049	0.0116487
19/64	0.296875	0.148438	0.2768835	0.0137000
5/16	0.312500	0.156250	0.3067962	0.0159790
21/64	0.328125	0.164063	0.3382428	0.0184977
11/32	0.343750	0.171875	0.3712234	0.0212680
23/64	0.359375	0.179688	0.4057379	0.0243020
3/8	0.375000	0.187500	0.4417865	0.0276117
25/64	0.390625	0.195313	0.4793690	0.0312089
13/32	0.406250	0.203125	0.5184855	0.0351058
27/64	0.421875	0.210938	0.5591360	0.0393142
7/16	0.437500	0.218750	0.6013205	0.0438463
29/64	0.453125	0.226563	0.6450389	0.0487139
15/32	0.468750	0.234375	0.6902914	0.0539290
31/64	0.484375	0.242188	0.7370778	0.0595037
1/2	0.500000	0.250000	0.7853982	0.0654498
33/64	0.515625	0.257813	0.8352525	0.0717795
17/32	0.531250	0.265625	0.8866409	0.0785047
35/64	0.546875	0.273438	0.9395632	0.0856373
9/16	0.562500	0.281250	0.9940196	0.0931893
37/64	0.578125	0.289063	1.0500098	0.1011728
19/32	0.593750	0.296875	1.1075341	0.1095997
39/64	0.609375	0.304688	1.1665924	0.1184820
5/8	0.625000	0.312500	1.2271846	0.1278317
41/64	0.640625	0.320313	1.2893109	0.1376608

Fraction Diameter, D inch	Decimal Diameter, D inch	Decimal Radius, r inch	Surface Area, A square inch	Volume, V
21/32	0.656250	0.328125	1.3529711	0.1479812
43/64	0.671875	0.335938	1.4181652	0.1588050
11/16	0.687500	0.343750	1.4848934	0.1701440
45/64	0.703125	0.351563	1.5531555	0.1820104
23/32	0.718750	0.359375	1.6229517	0.1944161
47/64	0.734375	0.367188	1.6942818	0.2073730
3/4	0.750000	0.375000	1.7671459	0.2208932
49/64	0.765625	0.382813	1.8415439	0.2349887
25/32	0.781250	0.390625	1.9174760	0.2496714
51/64	0.796875	0.398438	1.9949420	0.2649532
13/16	0.812500	0.406250	2.0739420	0.2808463
53/64	0.828125	0.414063	2.1544760	0.2973626
27/32	0.843750	0.421875	2.2365440	0.3145140
55/64	0.859375	0.429688	2.3201459	0.3323126
7/8	0.875000	0.437500	2.4052819	0.3507703
57/64	0.890625	0.445313	2.4919518	0.3698991
29/32	0.906250	0.453125	2.5801557	0.3897110
59/64	0.921875	0.460938	2.6698936	0.4102180
15/16	0.937500	0.468750	2.7611654	0.4314321
61/64	0.953125	0.476563	2.8539713	0.4533652
31/32	0.968750	0.484375	2.9483111	0.4760294
63/64	0.984375	0.492188	3.0441849	0.4994366
1	1.000000	0.500000	3.1415927	0.5235988
1-1/32	1.031250	0.515625	3.3410102	0.5742361
1-1/16	1.062500	0.531250	3.5465636	0.6280373
1-3/32	1.093750	0.546875	3.7582529	0.6850982
1-1/8	1.125000	0.562500	3.9760782	0.7455147
1-5/32	1.156250	0.578125	4.2000394	0.8093826
1-3/16	1.187500	0.593750	4.4301365	0.8767979
1-7/32	1.218750	0.609375	4.6663696	0.9478563
1-1/4	1.250000	0.625000	4.9087385	1.0226539
1-9/32	1.281250	0.640625	5.1572434	1.1012864
1-5/16	1.312500	0.656250	5.4118842	1.1838497
1-11/32	1.343750	0.671875	5.6726610	1.2704397
1-3/8	1.375000	0.687500	5.9395736	1.3611523
1-13/32	1.406250	0.703125	6.2126222	1.4560833
1-7/16	1.437500	0.718750	6.4918067	1.5553287
1-15/32	1.468750	0.734375	6.7771271	1.6589842
1-1/2	1.500000	0.750000	7.0685835	1.7671459
1-17/32	1.531250	0.765625	7.3661757	1.8799094
1-9/16	1.562500	0.781250	7.6699039	1.9973708
1-19/32	1.593750	0.796875	7.9797681	2.1196259

Spheres - Surface Area and Volume (cont.)

Fraction Diameter, D inch	Decimal Diameter, D inch	Decimal Radius, r inch	Surface Area, A square inch	Volume, V
1-5/8	1.625000	0.812500	8.2957681	2.2467705
1-21/32	1.656250	0.828125	8.6179041	2.3789006
1-11/16	1.687500	0.843750	8.9461760	2.5161120
1-23/32	1.718750	0.859375	9.2805838	2.6585006
1-3/4	1.750000	0.875000	9.6211275	2.8061622
1-25/32	1.781250	0.890625	9.9678072	2.9591928
1-13/16	1.812500	0.906250	10.3206227	3.1176881
1-27/32	1.843750	0.921875	10.6795742	3.2817442
1-7/8	1.875000	0.937500	11.0446617	3.4514568
1-29/32	1.906250	0.953125	11.4158850	3.6269218
1-15/16	1.937500	0.968750	11.7932443	3.8082351
1-31/32	1.968750	0.984375	12.1767395	3.9954926
2	2.000000	1.000000	12.5663706	4.1887902

Notes:
Values in the table are based on the following equations:

$r = D/2$

$A = \pi D^2 = 3.1415927\ D^2$

$V = (1/6)\ \pi D^3 = 0.5235988\ D^3$

Nails, Spikes & Staples

Basic Dimensions - Nails
    Box Nails 358
    Brads 359
    Casing Nails 360
    Common Nails 360
    Concrete Nails 363
    Double-Headed Nails 363
    Fine Nails 364
    Finish Nails 364
    Flooring Nails 365
    Gypsum-Wallboard Nails 365
    Joist Hanger Nails 366
    Masonry Drive Nails 367
    Masonry Nails 367
    Roofing Nails 368
    Rubber Heel Nails 371
    Shingle Nails 371
    Siding Nails 372
    Underlayment Nails 372

Basic Dimensions - Spikes
    Common Spikes 373
    Gutter Spikes 373
    Round Spikes 374

Basic Dimensions - Staples
    Cohered Flat Top Crown Staples 374
    Electrical Staples 375
    Fence Staples 376
    Flat Top Crown Staples 378
    Poultry Net Staples 382
    Preformed Hoop Staples 382
    Round or "V" Crown Staples 383
    Preformed Staples 384

Box Nails

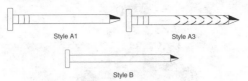

Style A1

Style A3

Style B

ASTM F 1667 Dash Number	Trade Designation pennyweight	Length inch	Body Diameter inch	Head Diameter inch	Weight number per pound
Style A					
01	2d	1	0.067	0.188	940
02	3d	1-1/4	0.076	0.219	590
03	4d	1-1/2	0.080	0.219	450
04	5d	1-3/4	0.080	0.219	390
05	6d	2	0.099	0.266	220
06	7d	2-1/4	0.099	0.266	200
07	8d	2-1/2	0.113	0.297	140
08	9d	2-3/4	0.113	0.297	120
09	10d	3	0.128	0.312	90
10	12d	3-1/4	0.128	0.312	83
11	16d	3-1/2	0.135	0.344	69
12	20d	4	0.148	0.375	50
13	30d	4-1/2	0.148	0.375	45
14	40d	5	0.162	0.406	34
Style B					
01	2d	1	0.058	0.172	1,250
02	3d	1-1/8	0.062	0.188	980
03	4d	1-3/8	0.067	0.203	680
04	5d	1-5/8	0.072	0.219	510
05	6d	1-7/8	0.086	0.250	315
06	7d	2-1/8	0.086	0.250	280
07	8d	2-3/8	0.099	0.286	190
08	9d	2-5/8	0.099	0.286	170
09	10d	2-7/8	0.113	0.297	120

Source: *American Society For Testing And Materials; Designation: F 1667-95, Standard Specification For Driven Fasteners: Nails, Spikes, and Staples*

Brads

Blunt Point   Diamond Point

ASTM F 1667 Dash Number	Length inch	Trade Designation pennyweight	Body Diameter inch	Weight number per pound
01	3/8	- - -	0.035	9,520
02	1/2	- - -	0.035	7,080
03	1/2	- - -	0.048	3,990
04	5/8	- - -	0.035	5,680
05	5/8	- - -	0.048	3,200
06	3/4	- - -	0.035	4,800
07	3/4	- - -	0.048	2,620
08	3/4	- - -	0.062	1,550
09	7/8	- - -	0.035	4,220
10	7/8	- - -	0.048	2,220
11	7/8	- - -	0.062	1,280
12	1	- - -	0.054	1,500
13	1	- - -	0.062	1,120
14	1	- - -	0.072	904
15	1-1/4	- - -	0.054	1,210
16	1-1/4	- - -	0.062	940
17	1-1/4	3d	0.080	560
18	1-1/2	- - -	0.054	1,040
19	1-1/2	- - -	0.080	470
20	1-1/2	4d	0.099	320
21	1-3/4	- - -	0.062	670
22	1-3/4	- - -	0.080	400
23	1-3/4	5d	0.099	270
24	2	- - -	0.062	580
25	2	- - -	0.080	350
26	2	6d	0.113	180
27	2-1/4	- - -	0.080	320
28	2-1/4	7d	0.113	160
29	2-1/2	- - -	0.080	290
30	2-1/2	8d	0.131	110
31	2-3/4	9d	0.131	97
32	3	10d	0.148	70
33	3-1/4	12d	0.148	65
34	3-1/2	16d	0.162	50
35	4	20d	0.192	31
36	4-1/2	30d	0.207	24
37	5	40d	0.225	18
38	5-1/2	50d	0.244	14
39	6	60d	0.262	11

Casing Nails

STM F 1667 Dash Number	Trade Designation pennyweight	Length inch	Body Diameter inch	Head Diameter inch	Weight number per pound
01	2d	1	0.067	0.099	1,090
02	3d	1-1/4	0.076	0.113	650
03	4d	1-1/2	0.080	0.120	490
04	5d	1-3/4	0.080	0.120	415
05	6d	2	0.099	0.142	245
06	7d	2-1/4	0.099	0.142	215
07	8d	2-1/2	0.113	0.155	150
08	9d	2-3/4	0.113	0.155	135
09	10d	3	0.128	0.170	95
10	12d	3-1/4	0.128	0.170	90
11	16d	3-1/2	0.135	0.177	75

Source: American Society For Testing And Materials;
Designation: F 1667-95, Standard Specification For Driven Fasteners:
Nails, Spikes, and Staples

Common Nails

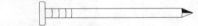

ASTM F 1667 Dash Number	Trade Designation pennyweight	Length inch	Body Diameter inch	Head Diameter inch	Weight number per pound
Aluminum					
01	4d	1-1/2	0.099	0.250	830
02	6d	2	0.120	0.266	430
03	8d	2-1/2	0.148	0.281	220
04	10d	3	0.162	0.312	170
05	16d	3-1/2	0.177	0.344	120
06	20d	4	0.199	0.406	78

Source: American Society For Testing And Materials; Designation: F 1667-95, Standard Specification For Driven Fasteners: Nails, Spikes, and Staples

ASTM F 1667 Dash Number	Trade Designation pennyweight	Length inch	Body Diameter inch	Head Diameter inch	Weight number per pound
Copper					
01	---	5/8	0.065	0.156	1,380
02	---	3/4	0.065	0.156	1,160
03	---	3/4	0.072	0.172	960
04	---	7/8	0.072	0.172	810
05	---	1	0.072	0.172	700
06	---	1-1/4	0.083	0.203	420
07	---	1-1/2	0.109	0.250	210
08	---	1-3/4	0.109	0.250	180
09	---	1-3/4	0.120	0.266	140
10	---	2	0.120	0.266	130
11	---	2	0.134	0.281	---
12	---	2-1/2	0.134	0.281	86
13	---	3	0.148	0.312	56
14	---	3-1/2	0.165	0.344	40
15	---	4	0.203	0.406	23
16	---	4-1/2	0.220	0.438	18
17	---	5	0.238	0.469	14
18	---	6	0.284	0.531	8
Steel					
01	2d	1	0.072	0.172	850
02	3d	1-1/4	0.080	0.203	540
03	4d	1-1/2	0.099	0.250	290
04	5d	1-3/4	0.099	0.250	250
05	6d	2	0.113	0.266	170
06	7d	2-1/4	0.113	0.266	150
07	8d	2-1/2	0.131	0.281	100
08	9d	2-3/4	0.131	0.281	92
09	10d	3	0.148	0.312	66
10	12d	3-1/4	0.148	0.312	61
11	16d	3-1/2	0.162	0.344	47
12	20d	4	0.192	0.406	30
13	30d	4-1/2	0.207	0.438	23
14	40d	5	0.228	0.469	17
15	50d	5-1/2	0.244	0.500	14
16	60d	6	0.262	0.531	11

ASTM F 1667 Dash Number	Trade Designation pennyweight	Length inch	Body Diameter inch	Head Diameter inch	Weight number per pound
Mechanically Driven Steel or Aluminum					
01	- - -	1-1/4	0.080	- - -	- - -
02	- - -	1-1/4	0.088	- - -	- - -
03	- - -	1-1/4	0.092	- - -	- - -
04	- - -	1-1/4	0.099	- - -	- - -
05	- - -	1-1/2	0.080	- - -	- - -
06	- - -	1-1/2	0.086	- - -	- - -
07	- - -	1-1/2	0.092	- - -	- - -
08	- - -	1-1/2	0.099	- - -	- - -
09	- - -	1-1/2	0.113	- - -	- - -
10	- - -	1-5/8	0.080	- - -	- - -
11	- - -	1-5/8	0.086	- - -	- - -
12	- - -	1-5/8	0.092	- - -	- - -
13	- - -	1-5/8	0.099	- - -	- - -
14	- - -	1-3/4	0.080	- - -	- - -
15	- - -	1-3/4	0.086	- - -	- - -
16	- - -	1-3/4	0.092	- - -	- - -
17	- - -	1-3/4	0.099	- - -	- - -
18	- - -	1-3/4	0.113	- - -	- - -
19	- - -	1-7/8	0.080	- - -	- - -
20	- - -	1-7/8	0.086	- - -	- - -
21	- - -	1-7/8	0.092	- - -	- - -
22	- - -	1-7/8	0.099	- - -	- - -
23	- - -	1-7/8	0.113	- - -	- - -
24	- - -	2	0.080	- - -	- - -
25	- - -	2	0.086	- - -	- - -
26	- - -	2	0.092	- - -	- - -
27	- - -	2	0.099	- - -	- - -
28	- - -	2	0.113	- - -	- - -
29	- - -	2	0.148	- - -	- - -
30	- - -	2-1/4	0.092	- - -	- - -
31	- - -	2-1/4	0.099	- - -	- - -
32	- - -	2-1/4	0.113	- - -	- - -
33	- - -	2-1/2	0.092	- - -	- - -
34	- - -	2-1/2	0.099	- - -	- - -
35	- - -	2-1/2	0.113	- - -	- - -
36	- - -	2-1/2	0.131	- - -	- - -
37	- - -	3-1/2	0.131	- - -	- - -

Concrete Nails

ASTM F 1667 Dash Number	Length inch	Body Diameter inch	Head Diameter inch	Weight number per pound
Smooth shank				
01	1/2	0.148	0.312	450
02	5/8	0.148	0.312	350
03	3/4	0.148	0.312	290
04	7/8	0.148	0.312	250
05	1	0.148	0.312	210
Mechanically Deformed Shank				
01	3/4	0.181	0.284	240
02	1	0.181	0.284	204
03	1-1/2	0.181	0.284	118
04	1-3/4	0.181	0.284	112
05	2	0.181	0.284	93
06	2-1/2	0.181	0.284	68
07	2-3/4	0.181	0.284	60
08	3	0.181	0.284	52

Source: American Society For Testing And Materials; Designation: F 1667-95, Standard Specification For Driven Fasteners: Nails, Spikes, and Staples

Double-Headed Nails

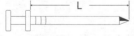

ASTM F 1667 Dash Number	Trade Designation pennyweight	Total Length inch	Body Length inch	Head Length inch	Body Diameter inch	Weight number per pound
01	6d	2	1-3/4	1/4	0.113	180
02	8d	2-1/2	2-1/4	1/4	0.131	90
03	10d	3-1/16	2-3/4	5/16	0.148	59
04	18d	3-3/8	3	3/8	0.162	45
05	20d	3-7/8	3-1/2	3/8	0.192	28
06	30d	4-7/16	4	7/16	0.207	22

Fine Nails

ASTM F 1667 Dash Number	Length inch	Trade Designation pennyweight	Body Diameter inch	Head Diameter inch	Weight number per pound
01	1-1/8	3d	0.072	0.172	760

Finish Nails

ASTM F 1667 Dash Number	Trade Designation pennyweight	Length inch	Body Diameter inch	Head Diameter inch	Weight number per pound
01	2d	1	0.058	0.086	1,470
02	3d	1-1/4	0.067	0.099	880
03	4d	1-1/2	0.072	0.106	630
04	5d	1-3/4	0.072	0.106	530
05	6d	2	0.092	0.135	290
06	7d	2-1/4	0.092	0.135	250
07	8d	2-1/2	0.099	0.142	190
08	9d	2-3/4	0.099	0.142	180
09	10d	3	0.113	0.155	120
10	12d	3-1/4	0.113	0.155	110
11	18d	3-1/2	0.120	0.162	93
12	20d	4	0.135	0.177	85

Source: American Society For Testing And Materials; Designation: F 1667-95, Standard Specification For Driven Fasteners: Nails, Spikes, and Staples

Flooring Nails

ASTM F 1667 Dash Number	Trade Designation pennyweight	Length inch	Body Diameter inch	Head Diameter inch	Weight number per pound
Smooth and Deformed					
01	2d	1	0.072	0.141	840
02	3d	1-1/4	0.072	0.141	700
03	4d	1-1/2	0.080	0.156	430
04	4d	1-1/2	0.092	0.156	370
05	5d	1-3/4	0.092	0.156	310
06	6d	2	0.113	0.203	180
07	7d	2-1/4	0.113	0.203	150
08	8d	2-1/2	0.135	0.177	100
09	8d	2-1/2	0.113	0.203	110
10	10d	3	0.135	0.250	82
11	12d	3-1/4	0.135	0.250	75
12	16d	3-1/2	0.148	0.281	58

Gypsum Wallboard Nails

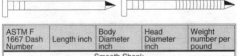

ASTM F 1667 Dash Number	Length inch	Body Diameter inch	Head Diameter inch	Weight number per pound
Smooth Shank				
01	1-1/8	0.092	0.297	470
02	1-1/8	0.092	0.375	450
03	1-1/4	0.092	0.297	420
04	1-1/4	0.108	0.375	310
05	1-3/4	0.092	0.375	290
Mechanically Deformed Shank				
01	1-1/8	0.099	0.250	380
02	1-1/4	0.099	0.250	340
03	1-3/8	0.099	0.250	320
04	1-1/2	0.099	0.250	290
05	1-5/8	0.099	0.250	270

Joist Hanger Nails

ASTM F 1667 Dash Number	Trade Designation pennyweight	Length inch	Body Diameter inch	Steel Type	Maker*	Weight number per pound
Smooth Shank						
- - -	8d	1-1/4	- - -	B	SMP	230
- - -	8d	1-1/2	0.131	G	USP	175
- - -	8d	1-1/2	0.131	G	SSTC	152
- - -	8d	1-1/2	0.131	S	SSTC	152
- - -	8d	1-1/2	0.131	S	USP	143
- - -	8d	2-1/2	0.131	S	SSTC	94
- - -	10d	1-1/2	0.148	G	USP	128
- - -	10d	1-1/2	- - -	B	SMP	128
- - -	10d	1-1/2	0.148	G	SSTC	119
- - -	10d	1-1/2	0.148	S	SSTC	122
- - -	10d	1-1/2	0.148	S	USP	112
- - -	10d	3	0.148	S	SSTC	67
- - -	16d	2-1/2	0.162	G	USP	66
- - -	16d	2-1/2	- - -	B	SMP	65
- - -	16d	2-1/2	0.162	S	SSTC	44
- - -	16d	2-1/2	0.162	S	SSTC	63
Mechanically Deformed Shank						
- - -	10d	3	0.132	B	SSTC	- - -
- - -	20d	1-3/4	0.192	G	USP	65
- - -	20d	1-3/4	0.192	B	SSTC	63
- - -	20d	1-3/4	- - -	B	SMP	63
- - -	20d	2-1/8	- - -	B	SMP	50
- - -	20d	2-1/2	0.192	G	USP	46
- - -	- - -	2-1/2	0.250	B	SMP	27
- - -	- - -	3	0.250	B	SSTC	27
- - -	- - -	3	0.250	B	USP	22

Steel Type: B= Bright, G=Galvanized, S= Stainless

* Makers:

SMP   Silver Metal Products, Inc.
         2150 Kitty Hawk Road, Livermore, CA 94550

SSTC   Simpson Strong-Tie Company, Inc.
         4637 Chabot Dr., Suite 200, Pleasanton, CA 94588

USP   United Steel Products Company, Inc.
         703 Rogers Drive, PO Box 80, Montgomery, MN 56069

Masonry Drive Nails

ASTM F 1667 Dash Number	Length (inch)	Head Length (inch)	Thread Diameter (inch)
01	3/4	3/32	0.125
02	3/4	1/8	0.156
03	1	5/32	0.188
04	1-1/4	3/16	0.215
05	1-1/2	1/4	0.258
06	2	5/16	0.330

Masonry Nails

ASTM F 1667 Dash Number	Length (inch)	Body Diameter (inch)	Head Diameter (inch)	Weight number per pound
		Standard		
01	1/2	0.148	0.312	340
02	3/4	0.148	0.312	280
03	1	0.148	0.312	170
04	1-1/4	0.148	0.312	140
05	1-1/2	0.148	0.312	130
06	1-3/4	0.148	0.312	110
07	2	0.148	0.312	98
08	2-1/4	0.148	0.312	84
09	2-1/2	0.148	0.312	78
10	2-3/4	0.148	0.312	70
11	3	0.148	0.312	67
12	3-1/4	0.148	0.312	60
13	3-1/2	0.162	0.344	48
14	3-3/4	0.162	0.344	45
15	4	0.177	0.375	35
		Heavy		
01	1	0.250	0.582	53
02	1-1/4	0.250	0.582	47
03	1-1/2	0.250	0.582	43
04	1-3/4	0.250	0.582	39
05	2	0.250	0.582	34
06	2-1/2	0.250	0.582	27
07	3-1/2	0.250	0.582	19
08	3	0.250	0.582	24

Source: *American Society For Testing And Materials; Designation: F 1667-95, Standard Specification For Driven Fasteners: Nails, Spikes, and Staples*

Roofing Nails

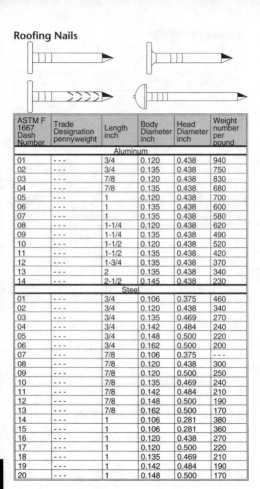

ASTM F 1667 Dash Number	Trade Designation pennyweight	Length inch	Body Diameter inch	Head Diameter inch	Weight number per pound
Aluminum					
01	- - -	3/4	0.120	0.438	940
02	- - -	3/4	0.135	0.438	750
03	- - -	7/8	0.120	0.438	830
04	- - -	7/8	0.135	0.438	680
05	- - -	1	0.120	0.438	700
06	- - -	1	0.135	0.438	600
07	- - -	1	0.135	0.438	580
08	- - -	1-1/4	0.120	0.438	620
09	- - -	1-1/4	0.135	0.438	490
10	- - -	1-1/2	0.120	0.438	520
11	- - -	1-1/2	0.135	0.438	420
12	- - -	1-3/4	0.135	0.438	370
13	- - -	2	0.135	0.438	340
14	- - -	2-1/2	0.145	0.438	230
Steel					
01	- - -	3/4	0.106	0.375	460
02	- - -	3/4	0.120	0.438	340
03	- - -	3/4	0.135	0.469	270
04	- - -	3/4	0.142	0.484	240
05	- - -	3/4	0.148	0.500	220
06	- - -	3/4	0.162	0.500	200
07	- - -	7/8	0.106	0.375	- - -
08	- - -	7/8	0.120	0.438	300
09	- - -	7/8	0.120	0.500	250
10	- - -	7/8	0.135	0.469	240
11	- - -	7/8	0.142	0.484	210
12	- - -	7/8	0.148	0.500	190
13	- - -	7/8	0.162	0.500	170
14	- - -	1	0.106	0.281	380
15	- - -	1	0.106	0.281	360
16	- - -	1	0.120	0.438	270
17	- - -	1	0.120	0.500	220
18	- - -	1	0.135	0.469	210
19	- - -	1	0.142	0.484	190
20	- - -	1	0.148	0.500	170

ASTM F 1667 Dash Number	Trade Designation pennyweight	Length inch	Body Diameter inch	Head Diameter inch	Weight number per pound
		Steel (cont.)			
21	- - -	1	0.162	0.500	150
22	- - -	1-1/8	0.106	0.375	320
23	- - -	1-1/8	0.120	0.438	240
24	- - -	1-1/8	0.135	0.469	190
25	- - -	1-1/8	0.142	0.484	170
26	- - -	1-1/8	0.148	0.500	160
27	- - -	1-1/8	0.162	0.500	140
28	- - -	1-1/4	0.106	0.375	300
29	- - -	1-1/4	0.120	0.312	240
30	- - -	1-1/4	0.120	0.438	220
31	- - -	1-1/4	0.120	0.500	- - -
32	- - -	1-1/4	0.135	0.469	180
33	- - -	1-1/4	0.142	0.484	160
34	- - -	1-1/4	0.148	0.500	140
35	- - -	1-1/4	0.162	0.500	120
36	- - -	1-1/2	0.106	0.375	- - -
37	- - -	1-1/2	0.120	0.438	180
38	- - -	1-1/2	0.120	0.500	160
39	- - -	1-1/2	0.135	0.489	150
40	- - -	1-1/2	0.142	0.484	130
41	- - -	1-1/2	0.148	0.500	120
42	- - -	1-1/2	0.162	0.500	110
43	- - -	1-3/4	0.106	0.375	220
44	- - -	1-3/4	0.120	0.438	160
45	- - -	1-3/4	0.120	0.500	140
46	- - -	1-3/4	0.135	0.469	130
47	- - -	1-3/4	0.142	0.484	120
48	- - -	1-3/4	0.148	0.500	110
49	- - -	1-3/4	0.162	0.500	92
		Steel, Copper-clad			
01	2d	1	0.120	0.375	280
02	3d	1-1/4	0.120	0.375	220
03	4d	1-1/2	0.120	0.375	190
04	5d	1-3/4	0.120	0.375	160
05	6d	2	0.120	0.375	140
06	7d	2-1/4	0.120	0.375	130
		Steel, Leak-resistant, Convex Head			
01	- - -	1-3/4	0.135	0.500	110
02	- - -	2	0.135	0.500	98
		Steel, Reinforced Head			
01	- - -	3/4	0.106	0.625	190
02	- - -	3/4	0.120	0.625	170
03	- - -	7/8	0.106	0.625	180
04	- - -	7/8	0.120	0.625	160

ASTM F 1667 Dash Number	Trade Designation pennyweight	Length inch	Body Diameter inch	Head Diameter inch	Weight number per pound
Steel, Reinforced Head (cont.)					
05	- - -	1	0.106	0.625	170
06	- - -	1	0.120	0.625	150
07	- - -	1-1/8	0.106	0.625	170
08	- - -	1-1/8	0.120	0.625	140
09	- - -	1-1/4	0.106	0.625	160
10	- - -	1-1/4	0.106	0.625	140
Steel, Mechanically Deformed Shank					
01	- - -	1/2	0.106	- - -	130
02	- - -	5/8	0.106	- - -	120
03	- - -	3/4	0.106	- - -	115
04	- - -	7/8	0.106	- - -	110
05	- - -	1	0.106	- - -	110
06	- - -	1-1/8	0.106	- - -	110
07	- - -	1-1/4	0.106	- - -	100
08	- - -	1-1/2	0.106 - 0.120	- - -	96 - 84
09	- - -	1-3/4	0.106 - 0.120	- - -	94 - 85
10	- - -	2	0.106 - 0.120	- - -	90 - 74
11	- - -	2-1/2	0.106 - 0.120	- - -	80 - 61
12	- - -	3	0.106	- - -	70
Steel, Cast Lead Head, Smooth Shank					
01	- - -	1-1/2	0.148	- - -	98
02	- - -	1-3/4	0.148	- - -	87
03	- - -	2	0.148	- - -	79
Steel, Cast Lead Head, Barbed Shank					
01	- - -	1-1/2	0.135	- - -	110
02	- - -	1-3/4	0.135	- - -	110
03	- - -	2	0.135	- - -	93
Aluminum, Neoprene Washer, Smooth Shank					
01	- - -	1-3/4	0.135	0.438	320
02	- - -	2	0.135	0.438	280
03	- - -	2-1/4	0.135	0.438	240
04	- - -	2-1/2	0.135	0.438	210
Aluminum, Neoprene Washer, Deformed Shank					
01	- - -	1-3/4	0.145	0.438	290
02	- - -	2	0.145	0.438	280
03	- - -	2-1/4	0.145	0.438	230
04	- - -	2-1/2	0.145	0.438	210

Source: American Society For Testing And Materials; Designation: F 1667-95, Standard Specification For Driven Fasteners: Nails, Spikes, and Staples

Rubber Heel Nails

ASTM F 1667 Dash Number	Length (inch)	Body Diameter (inch)	Head Diameter (inch)	Weight number per pound
01	5/8	0.080	0.154	- - -
02	3/4	0.080	0.154	- - -
03	7/8	0.080	0.154	- - -
04	1	0.080	0.154	- - -
05	1-1/8	0.080	0.154	- - -
06	1-1/4	0.080	0.154	- - -

Shingle Nails

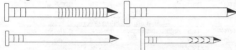

ASTM F 1667 Dash Number	Trade Designation pennyweight	Length inch	Body Diameter inch	Head Diameter inch	Weight number per pound
Aluminum, Deformed Shank					
01	- - -	1-1/4	0.101	0.191	1,060
02	- - -	1-1/2	0.101	0.191	860
03	- - -	1-3/4	0.105	0.191	720
04	- - -	2	0.105	0.191	610
05	- - -	2-1/4	0.113	0.200	180
06	- - -	2-1/2	0.113	0.200	130
Aluminum, Smooth Shank					
01	- - -	7/8	0.099	0.281	1,310
02	- - -	1-1/4	0.080	0.219	1,460
03	- - -	1-1/4	0.099	0.281	1,010
04	- - -	1-1/4	0.113	0.312	780
05	- - -	1-1/2	0.113	0.312	660
06	- - -	1-3/4	0.113	0.312	610
Steel, Smooth Shank					
01	3d	1-1/4	0.092	0.250	410
02	3.5d	1-3/8	0.099	0.281	310
03	4d	1-1/2	0.108	0.281	260
Steel, Barbed Shank					
01	- - -	1-1/4	0.113	0.406	250
02	- - -	1-1/2	0.113	0.406	210
03	- - -	1-3/4	0.113	0.406	180
04	- - -	2	0.113	0.406	162

Siding Nails

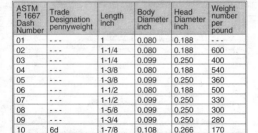

ASTM F 1667 Dash Number	Trade Designation pennyweight	Length inch	Body Diameter inch	Head Diameter inch	Weight number per pound
Aluminum, Flat Head					
01	- - -	1-1/2	0.113	0.219	700
02	- - -	1-1/2	0.113	0.312	680
03	- - -	2	0.113	0.219	490
04	- - -	2-1/2	0.135	0.219	290
Aluminum, Casing Head					
01	6d	1-7/8	0.106	0.141	600
02	7d	2-1/8	0.113	0.141	470
03	8d	2-3/8	0.128	0.158	320
04	9d	2-5/8	0.148	0.189	200
Aluminum, Countersunk Head					
01	6d	1-7/8	0.106	0.266	600
02	7d	2-1/8	0.113	0.286	470
03	8d	2-3/8	0.128	0.297	320
04	9d	2-5/8	0.148	0.312	200

Underlayment Nails

ASTM F 1667 Dash Number	Trade Designation pennyweight	Length inch	Body Diameter inch	Head Diameter inch	Weight number per pound
01	- - -	1	0.080	0.188	- - -
02	- - -	1-1/4	0.080	0.188	600
03	- - -	1-1/4	0.099	0.250	400
04	- - -	1-3/8	0.080	0.188	540
05	- - -	1-3/8	0.099	0.250	360
06	- - -	1-1/2	0.080	0.188	500
07	- - -	1-1/2	0.099	0.250	330
08	- - -	1-5/8	0.099	0.250	300
09	- - -	1-3/4	0.099	0.250	280
10	6d	1-7/8	0.108	0.266	170
11	7d	2-1/8	0.108	0.266	170
12	8d	2-3/8	0.113	0.297	140

Source: American Society For Testing And Materials; Designation: F 1667-95, Standard Specification For Driven Fasteners: Nails, Spikes, and Staples

Basic Dimensions - Spikes

Common Spikes

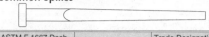

ASTM F 1667 Dash Number	Length inch	Trade Designation pennyweight
01	4	20d
02	4-1/2	30d
03	5	40d
04	5-1/2	50d
05	6	60d
06	7	80d
07	8	100d

Gutter Spikes

ASTM F 1667 Dash Number	Length	Body Diameter inch	Head Diameter
Flat Head			
01	6-1/2	0.250	0.562
02	7	0.250	0.562
03	8	0.250	0.562
04	8-1/2	0.250	0.562
05	9	0.250	0.562
06	10	0.250	0.562
07	10-1/2	0.250	0.562
Oval Head			
01	6-1/2	0.250	0.531
02	7	0.250	0.531
03	8	0.250	0.531
04	8-1/2	0.250	0.531
05	9	0.250	0.531
06	10	0.250	0.531
07	10-1/2	0.250	0.531

Source: American Society For Testing And Materials; Designation: F 1667-95, Standard Specification For Driven Fasteners: Nails, Spikes, and Staples

Round Spikes

ASTM F 1667Dash Number	Length (inch)	Trade Designation pennyweight	Body Diameter (inch)	Head Diameter (inch)
Flat Head				
01	8	- - -	0.312	0.625
02	8	- - -	0.312	0.750
03	9	- - -	0.312	0.750
04	10	- - -	0.312	0.750
Oval Head				
01	5	40d	0.2625	0.531
02	5-1/2	50d	0.283	0.562
03	6	60d	0.283	0.562
04	7	- - -	0.312	0.625

Basic Dimensions - Staples

Cohered Flat Top Crown Staples

ASTM F 1667 Dash Number	Leg Length	Crown Width	Wire Dimensions Thickness	Width
(inch)				
01	3/16	0.500	0.020	0.030
02	1/4	0.500	0.020	0.030
03	5/16	0.500	0.020	0.030
04	1/4	0.500	0.020	0.050
05	5/16	0.500	0.020	0.050
06	3/8	0.500	0.020	0.050
07	1/2	0.500	0.020	0.050
08	3/8	0.437	0.020	0.050
09	1/2	0.437	0.020	0.050
10	9/16	0.437	0.020	0.050
11	3/8	0.164	0.030	0.050
12	1/2	0.164	0.030	0.050
13	5/8	0.164	0.030	0.050
14	3/4	0.164	0.030	0.050
15	7/8	0.164	0.030	0.050
16	1	0.164	0.030	0.050
17	1-1/8	0.164	0.030	0.050
18	1-1/4	0.164	0.030	0.050

Source: American Society For Testing And Materials; Designation: F 1667-95, Standard Specification For Driven Fasteners: Nails, Spikes, and Staples

Electrical Staples

ASTM F 1667 Dash Number	Leg Length	Crown Width	Body Dimensions		Point Length	Point Angle	Weight number per pound
			Diameter	Flatten			
			(inch)			degree	
01	3/8	5/32	0.067	0.048	1/4	12	1,440
02	1/2	3/16	0.072	0.057	1/4	12	990
03	5/8	1/4	0.072	0.057	5/16	12	740
04	3/4	3/16	0.083	0.060	11/32	12	480
05	3/4	1/4	0.083	0.060	11/32	12	450
06	7/8	1/4	0.083	0.060	11/32	12	400
07	7/8	7/16	0.083	0.060	11/32	12	370
08	1	1/2	0.120	.050 X .215	3/8	18	- - -
09	1-1/4	5/8	0.120	.050 X .215	3/8	18	- - -

Source: American Society For Testing And Materials; Designation: F 1667-95, Standard Specification For Driven Fasteners: Nails, Spikes, and Staples

Fence Staples

ASTM F 1667 Dash Number	Leg Length (inch)	Body Diameter (inch)	Weight number per pound
01	7/8	0.1483	120
02	1	0.1483	110
03	1-1/8	0.1483	97
04	1-1/4	0.1483	87
05	1-1/2	0.1483	72
06	1-3/4	0.1483	61

Source: American Society For Testing And Materials; Designation: F 1667-95, Standard Specification For DrivenFasteners: Nails, Spikes, and Staples

Flat Top Crown Staples

ASTM F 1667 Dash Number	Leg Length (inch)	Crown Width (inch)	Wire Gage
01	3/8	3/16	18
02	1/2	3/16	18
03	5/8	3/16	18
04	3/4	3/16	18
05	7/8	3/16	18
06	1	3/16	18
07	1-1/8	3/16	18
08	1-1/4	3/16	18
09	3/8	3/8	14
10	1/2	3/8	14
11	5/8	3/8	14
12	3/4	3/8	14
13	7/8	3/8	14
14	1-1/8	3/8	14
15	1-1/4	3/8	14
16	1-3/8	3/8	14
17	1-1/2	3/8	14
18	1-5/8	3/8	14
19	1-3/4	3/8	14
20	1-7/8	3/8	16
21	1/2	3/8	16
22	5/8	3/8	16

ASTM F 1667 Dash Number	Leg Length	Crown Width	Wire Gage
	(inch)		
23	3/4	3/8	16
24	7/8	3/8	16
25	1-1/8	3/8	16
26	1-1/4	3/8	16
27	1-3/8	3/8	16
28	1-1/2	3/8	16
29	1-5/8	3/8	16
30	1-3/4	3/8	16
31	3/8	3/8	18
32	1/2	3/8	18
33	5/8	3/8	18
34	3/4	3/8	18
35	7/8	3/8	18
36	1	3/8	18
37	1-1/8	3/8	18
38	1-1/4	3/8	18
39	1-1/2	3/8	18
40	1-5/8	3/8	18
41	1-3/4	3/8	18
42	3/8	7/16	14
43	1/2	7/16	14
44	5/8	7/16	14
45	3/4	7/16	14
46	7/8	7/16	14
47	1	7/16	14
48	1-1/8	7/16	14
49	1-1/4	7/16	14
50	1-3/8	7/16	14
51	1-1/2	7/16	14
52	1-5/8	7/16	14
53	1-3/4	7/16	14
54	1-7/8	7/16	14
55	2	7/16	14
56	2-1/4	7/16	14
57	2-1/2	7/16	14
58	3/8	7/16	15
59	1/2	7/16	15
60	5/8	7/16	15
61	3/4	7/16	15
62	7/8	7/16	15
63	1	7/16	15
64	1-1/8	7/16	15
65	1-1/4	7/16	15

Flat-top Crown Staples (cont.)

ASTM F 1667 Dash Number	Leg Length	Crown Width	Wire Gage
	(inch)		
66	1-3/8	7/16	15
67	1-1/2	7/16	15
68	1-5/8	7/16	15
69	1-3/4	7/16	15
70	1-7/8	7/16	15
71	2	7/16	15
72	2-1/4	7/16	15
73	2-1/2	7/16	15
74	3/8	7/16	16
75	1/2	7/16	16
76	5/8	7/16	16
77	3/4	7/16	16
78	7/8	7/16	16
79	1	7/16	16
80	1-1/8	7/16	16
81	1-1/4	7/16	16
82	1-3/8	7/16	16
83	1-1/2	7/16	16
84	1-5/8	7/16	16
85	1-3/4	7/16	16
86	1-7/8	7/16	16
87	2	7/16	16
88	2-1/4	7/16	16
89	2-1/2	7/16	16
90	1/2	1/2	14
91	5/8	1/2	14
92	3/4	1/2	14
93	7/8	1/2	14
94	1	1/2	14
95	1-1/8	1/2	14
96	1-1/4	1/2	14
97	1-3/8	1/2	14
98	1-1/2	1/2	14
99	1-5/8	1/2	14
100	1-3/4	1/2	14
101	1-7/8	1/2	14
102	2	1/2	14
103	2-1/4	1/2	14
104	2-1/2	1/2	14
105	1/2	1/2	15
106	5/8	1/2	15

ASTM F 1667 Dash Number	Leg Length	Crown Width	Wire Gage
	(inch)		
107	3/4	1/2	15
108	7/8	1/2	15
109	1	1/2	15
110	1-1/8	1/2	15
111	1-1/4	1/2	15
112	1-3/8	1/2	15
113	1-1/2	1/2	15
114	1-5/8	1/2	15
115	1-3/4	1/2	15
116	1-7/8	1/2	15
117	2	1/2	15
118	2-1/4	1/2	15
119	2-1/2	1/2	15
120	1/2	1/2	16
121	5/8	1/2	16
122	3/4	1/2	16
123	7/8	1/2	16
124	1	1/2	16
125	1-1/8	1/2	16
126	1-1/4	1/2	16
127	1-3/8	1/2	16
128	1-1/2	1/2	16
129	1-5/8	1/2	16
130	1-3/4	1/2	16
131	1-7/8	1/2	16
132	2	1/2	16
133	2-1/4	1/2	16
134	2-1/2	1/2	16
135	1/2	3/4	14
136	5/8	3/4	14
137	3/4	3/4	14
138	7/8	3/4	14
139	1	3/4	14
140	1-1/8	3/4	14
141	1-1/4	3/4	14
142	1-3/8	3/4	14
143	1-1/2	3/4	14
144	1-5/8	3/4	14
145	1-3/4	3/4	14
146	1-7/8	3/4	14
147	2	3/4	14
148	1/2	3/4	16
149	5/8	3/4	16

Flat-top Crown Staples (cont.)

ASTM F 1667 Dash Number	Leg Length	Crown Width	Wire Gage
	(inch)		
150	3/4	3/4	16
151	7/8	3/4	16
152	1	3/4	16
153	1-1/8	3/4	16
154	1-1/4	3/4	16
155	1-3/8	3/4	16
156	1-1/2	3/4	16
157	1-5/8	3/4	16
158	1-3/4	3/4	16
159	1-7/8	3/4	16
160	2	3/4	16
161	1/2	7/8	14
162	5/8	7/8	14
163	3/4	7/8	14
164	7/8	7/8	14
165	1	7/8	14
166	1-1/8	7/8	14
167	1-1/4	7/8	14
168	1-3/8	7/8	14
169	1-1/2	7/8	14
170	1-5/8	7/8	14
171	1-3/4	7/8	14
172	1-7/8	7/8	14
173	2	7/8	14
174	1/2	7/8	16
175	5/8	7/8	16
176	3/4	7/8	16
177	7/8	7/8	16
178	1	7/8	16
179	1-1/8	7/8	16
180	1-1/4	7/8	16
181	1-3/8	7/8	16
182	1-1/2	7/8	16
183	1-5/8	7/8	16
184	1-3/4	7/8	16
185	1-7/8	7/8	16
186	2	7/8	16
187	1/2	15/16	14
188	5/8	15/16	14
189	3/4	15/16	14
190	7/8	15/16	14

ASTM F 1667 Dash Number	Leg Length	Crown Width	Wire Gage
	(inch)		
191	1	15/16	14
192	1-1/8	15/16	14
193	1-1/4	15/16	14
194	1-3/8	15/16	14
195	1-1/2	15/16	14
196	1/2	15/16	16
197	5/8	15/16	16
198	3/4	15/16	16
199	7/8	15/16	16
200	1	15/16	16
201	1-1/8	15/16	16
202	1-1/4	15/16	16
203	1-3/8	15/16	16
204	1-1/2	15/16	16
205	1/2	1	14
206	5/8	1	14
207	3/4	1	14
208	7/8	1	14
209	1	1	14
210	1-1/8	1	14
211	1-1/4	1	14
212	1-3/8	1	14
213	1-1/2	1	14
214	1/2	1	16
215	5/8	1	16
216	3/4	1	16
217	7/8	1	16
218	1	1	16
219	1-1/8	1	16
220	1-1/4	1	16
221	1-3/8	1	16
222	1-1/2	1	16
223	3/4	1-3/8	12
224	3/4	1-3/8	12
225	1	2-1/8	10

Source: American Society For Testing And Materials; Designation: F 1667-95, Standard Specification For Driven Fasteners: Nails, Spikes, and Staples

Poultry Net Staples

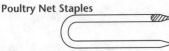

ASTM F 1667 Dash Number	Leg Length	Body Diameter	Weight number per pound
	(inch)		
01	3/4	0.080	500

Preformed Hoop Staples

ASTM F 1667 Dash Number	Leg Length	Crown Width	Body Dimensions Diameter	Flatten	Weight number per pound
			(inch)		
01	1/2	1/2	0.072	0.057	720
02	1/2	1/2	0.083	0.060	470
03	5/8	1/2	0.072	0.057	580
04	5/8	1/2	0.083	0.060	430
05	3/4	1/2	0.072	0.057	490
06	3/4	1/2	0.083	0.060	370
07	1/2	5/8	0.072	0.057	670
08	1/2	5/8	0.083	0.060	470
09	5/8	5/8	0.072	0.057	530
10	5/8	5/8	0.083	0.060	400
11	3/4	5/8	0.072	0.057	460
12	3/4	5/8	0.083	0.060	340
13	1/2	3/4	0.072	0.057	580
14	1/2	3/4	0.083	0.060	430
15	1/2	3/4	0.109	0.083	260
16	5/8	3/4	0.072	0.057	490
17	5/8	3/4	0.083	0.060	370
18	5/8	3/4	0.109	0.083	220
19	3/4	3/4	0.072	0.057	430
20	3/4	3/4	0.083	0.060	320
21	3/4	3/4	0.109	0.083	190
22	1	3/4	0.072	0.057	350
23	1	3/4	0.083	0.060	260
24	1	3/4	0.109	0.083	150
25	1/2	7/8	0.072	0.057	530
26	1/2	7/8	0.083	0.060	400
27	5/8	7/8	0.072	0.057	460
28	5/8	7/8	0.083	0.060	340

ASTM F 1667 Dash Number	Leg Length	Crown Width	Body Dimensions		Weight number per pound
			Diameter	Flatten	
		(inch)			
29	3/4	7/8	0.072	0.057	410
30	3/4	7/8	0.083	0.060	300
31	7/8	7/8	0.072	0.057	360
32	7/8	7/8	0.083	0.060	270
33	5/8	1	0.083	0.060	320
34	5/8	1	0.109	0.083	200
35	3/4	1	0.083	0.060	290
36	3/4	1	0.109	0.083	180
37	7/8	1	0.083	0.060	260
38	7/8	1	0.109	0.083	160
39	1	1	0.083	0.060	240
40	1	1	0.109	0.083	140
41	3/4	1-1/4	0.083	0.060	220
42	3/4	1-1/4	0.109	0.083	130
43	- - -	1-1/4	0.083	0.060	180
44	1	1-1/4	0.109	0.083	140

Source: American Society For Testing And Materials; Designation: F 1667-95, Standard Specification For Driven Fasteners: Nails, Spikes, and Staples

Round or "V" Crown Staples

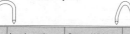

ASTM F 1667 Dash Number	Leg Length (inch)	Crown Width (inch)	Wire Gage
01	1/2	0.346	16
02	9/16	0.346	16
03	5/8	0.346	16
04	3/4	0.346	16
05	7/8	0.346	16
06	1	0.346	16
07	1/2	0.435	16
08	9/16	0.435	16
09	5/8	0.435	16
10	3/4	0.435	16
11	7/8	0.435	16
12	1	0.435	16

Source: American Society For Testing And Materials; Designation: F 1667-95, Standard Specification For Driven Fasteners: Nails, Spikes, and Staples

Preformed Staples

ASTM F 1667 Dash Number	Leg Length	Crown Width	Body Dimensions		Point Length	Point Angle degree	Weight number per pound
			Diam.	Flatten			
			inch				
01	3/8	7/32	0.054	0.040	3/16	13	1,920
02	13/32	3/16	0.067	0.048	3/16	12	1,380
03	7/16	7/32	0.067	0.048	1/4	12	1,250
04	1/2	1/4	0.072	0.057	1/4	12	860
05	9/16	9/32	0.072	0.057	5/16	12	800
06	5/8	5/16	0.072	0.057	5/16	12	670
07	11/16	3/4	0.083	0.060	11/32	12	540
08	3/4	3/4	0.083	0.060	11/32	12	410

Source: American Society For Testing And Materials;
Designation: F 1667-95, Standard Specification For Driven
Fasteners: Nails, Spikes, and Staples

Pipes and Fittings

Introduction to Pipe Tables...386

Tables - Properties and Friction Loss in Pipes and Fittings
  Acrylonitrile-Butadiene-Styrene (ABS) Pipe 392
  Aluminum Pipe and Tube...397
  Brass Pipe and Tube..412
  Chlorinated Poly(vinyl Chloride)(CPVC) Pipe 428
  Copper Pipe and Tube..433
  PolyVinyl Chloride (PVC) Pipe..443
  Polybutylene (PB) Pipe, controlled on Inside Diameter 451
  Polybutylene (PB) Pipe, controlled on Outside Diameter.........453
  Polyethylene (PE) Pipe, controlled on Inside Diameter 456
  Polyethylene (PE Pipe, controlled on Outside Diameter.........460
  Steel Pipe..468

Friction Loss in Pipe Fittings
  Plastic Pipe 508
  Steel Pipe..510

Pipe Tables

The **Pipe and Tube Tables** have been compiled after an exhaustive search of industry literature, consensus standards, and manufactures catalogs. See **References** for a complete list. The editors at Sequoia Publishing have made every attempt to provide accurate data in these tables, however, due to the amount of data; the values given can not be guaranteed and should be used only as a guide. Pipe and tube sizes listed are as complete as possible but may not contain all available sizes. A listing in the tables does not guarantee availability. Some pipe and tubing listed in the table is intended for use as structural elements and are not intended be used in fluid handling applications. For dimensional and weight data, size and availability, and appropriate uses for a specific product check with the manufacturer.

Pipes and tubes are manufactured using either the inside or outside diameter as the controlling dimension. Steel pipe, for instance, is manufactured only with a controlled outside diameter while vitrified clay pipe is manufactured only with a controlled inside diameter. For pipe or tube controlled on the outside diameter, the actual outside diameter is usually not equal to the nominal or standard pipe size. For example, steel pipe in nominal sizes smaller than 14 inches have actual outside diameters that are larger than the nominal size. The same is true for cast iron and ductile iron pipe of all sizes. Some plastic pipe, such as polyethylene pipe (PE pipe), can be manufactured using either diameter as the controlling dimension. Be sure to select the proper table for your type of pipe or tube.

The **Pipe Tables** are arranged in columns:

- The first column is always the nominal or standard pipe size, this is the dimension used by industry to identify and specify pipe or tube size.

- The second column is always the actual controlled diameter, either inside or outside.

- The columns to the right of the controlled diameter; one, two, or three columns depending on the type of pipe or tube; contain additional identifying information. This information can include pipe use, wall type, wall strength, designation, pressure class, thickness class, dimension ratio, schedule number, pipe series, or weight class for the pipe or tube.

- The next column is the nominal wall thickness.

- The column to the right of the wall thickness is the uncontrolled diameter, either inside or outside. These values are calculated using the controlled diameter and the nominal wall thickness.

- The column to the right of the uncontrolled diameter is the approximate weight per foot of pipe, not including joints, fittings, collars, or other devices.

- The last six columns on the right-hand side of each table contain flow data. This part of the table can be used to estimate flow rate in a given size pipe or tube while limiting the head loss due to friction to a specified value. The flow data were computed using the Hazen-Williams equation for flow of water in pipes. The Hazen-Williams equation is based on the inside diameter, the energy loss due to friction in the pipe, and a friction loss coefficient that varies with the material in the pipe wall. The friction loss coefficients used in the tables are 100 for concrete and steel; 110 for vitrified clay; 130 for aluminum, brass, copper, and plastic; and 140 for cast and ductile iron. The Hazen-Williams equation assumes that the pipe is flowing full, that the pipe carries clear water at approximately 60°F (15.6°C), and that the water flows at velocities generally less than 10 feet per second. The Hazen-Williams equation works well for moderately smooth pipes, but it is not as accurate for rough pipes, small pipes, or laminar flow. These tables should be used only for estimating friction head loss in a pipe or tube. Final pipe design should be done using more accurate methods such as the Darcy-Weisbach formula or Manning equation.

Pipe Sizing Example Using The Pipe Tables

Let's size a pipe and find out how to use of the **Pipe and Tube Tables**.

Size a steel pipe to carry approximately 300 gallons (US liquid) per minute through a 10,000-foot long pipeline and limit the total head loss to 1 foot. One foot of head loss in 1,000 feet of pipe is equivalent to 0.1 feet of head loss in 100 feet of pipe (see calculations below). In the steel pipe table, scan down the head loss column labeled "0.1 (feet)". Find that the 10-inch nominal, schedule 30, steel pipe will deliver 299 gallons (US liquid) per minute at a head loss of 0.1 feet in 100 feet of pipe, close enough to the required 300.

Now check the flow velocity. Flow velocity is equal to the flow rate divided by the flow area. In the steel pipe table, again find the 10-inch nominal, schedule 30, pipe and in the seventh column find that the inside diameter is 10.136 inches. Calculate the cross-sectional area of the pipe using the equation on page 533 and find that the cross-sectional area is 80.691 square inches (see calculations below). A flow rate of 299 gallons (US liquid) per minute is equal to 1,151 cubic inches/second (see calculations below). A flow rate of 1,151 cubic inches/second in an area of 80.69 square inches yields an average velocity of 14.3 inches per second or 1.2 feet per second (see calculations below). This is well within the assumption of 10 feet per second or less made in the Hazen-Williams equation. A 10-inch nominal, schedule 30, steel pipe is a good first estimate of the required pipe.

Calculations used in the example:

Equivalent Head Loss: $\left(\dfrac{1ft}{1,000ft}\right) * (100ft) = 0.1ft$

Cross-sectional Area: $\pi * \left(\dfrac{ID^2}{4}\right) = \pi * \dfrac{(10.136\ in)^2}{4} = 80.69\ in^2$

Convert Flow Rate: $\dfrac{299 gallon}{1\ min} * \dfrac{231 in^3}{1 gallon} * \dfrac{1\ min}{60\ sec} = 1,151 in^3\ /\ sec$

Compute and Convert Velocity: $\left(\dfrac{1,151 \frac{in^3}{sec}}{80.69 in^2}\right) = 14.3\ \dfrac{in}{sec} * \dfrac{1ft}{12 in} = 1.2\ \dfrac{ft}{sec}$

NOTE: Be very careful when scanning across the Theoretical Flow Rate portion of the Pipe Table. The values of Head Loss, at the tope of each column, increase by factors of 2 or 5 as you move from one column to the next. Be sure to account for environmental and design conditions that the pipe may encounter; such as corrosion, temperature, pressure, low vacuum, pH, liquids other than water, etc. Adjust the type and size of pipe accordingly. Also account for minor head loss caused by valves, elbows or other fittings in the pipeline and contractions or expansions of the pipe diameter.

Typical Uses For Various Types of Pipe

Aluminum Pipe

water (ASTM B 210 and B 241)

Brass Pipe

plumbing and boiler feed lines (ASTM B 43)

Chlorinated Poly (Vinyl Chloride) (CPVC) Pipe

water (ASTM F 441 and F 442)

Clay Pipe (Vitrified)

sewage, industrial wastes, storm water, underdrainage, filter fields, and leaching fields (ASTM C 700 and C 1208)

Concrete Pipe

sewage, industrial wastes, and storm water (ASTM C 14 and C 76)

irrigation water at pressures of 30 feet of water head (ASTM C 118)

irrigation water at pressures less than 30 feet of water head (ASTM C 505)

drainage (ASTM C 118)

water at pressures not exceeding 125 feet of water head (ASTM C 361)

water (AWWA C 300)

Copper Pipe

plumbing and boiler feed lines (ASTM B 42)

general plumbing (ASTM B 88)

air conditioning and refrigeration (ASTM B 280)

drainage tubing (ASTM B 306)

natural and LP gas (ASTM B 837)

Iron Pipe (Cast and Ductile)

water (AWWA C 115 and C 151)

gravity sewer line (ASTM A 746)

gravity soil pipe – drain, waste, vent, storm drain (ASTM A 74)

water, gas, and other liquids under pressure (ASTM A 377)

raw and potable water, sewage, slurries, and process chemicals (Ductile Iron Pipe Research Association)

Polybutylene (PB) Pipe

water (AWWA C 902; ASTM D 3000 and D 2662)

water, municipal sewage, industrial process liquids, effluents, and slurries in pressure and nonpressure systems (ASTM F 809)

Polyethylene (PE) Pipe

water (AWWA C 901 and C 906; ASTM D 2447, D 2104, and D 2239)

water, industrial process liquids, effluents, slurries, and municipal sewage (ASTM D 3035 and F 714)

irrigation water (ASTM F 771)

Poly(Vinyl Chloride) (PVC) Pipe

subsurface drainage (ASTM F 758)

water (AWWA C 900 and C 905; ASTM D 1785 and D 2241)

water, sewage, and drainage (ASTM F 891)

Steel Pipe

Black and Hot-Dipped Galvanized Steel:

fluids under pressure including steam, vapor, water, gas, and air (ASTM A 53, A 795, and A 135)

high-temperature service (ASTM A 106)

water-wells (ASTM A 589)

atmospheric pressure and low-temperature (ASTM A 524)

high-pressure pipe-type electrical cable conduit (ASTM A 523)

Stainless Steel:

high-temperature and corrosive services (ASTM A 814, A 954, A 813, A 943, A 949, A 790, A 409, and A 312)

Low-carbon Steel:

chemical services (ASTM A 587)

References

Standards:

American Society for Testing and Materials:
ASTM Designations:
A 53 - 96, *Pipe, Steel, Black and Hot-Dipped, Zinc-Coated, Welded and Seamless*
A 74 - 98, *Cast Iron Soil Pipe and Fittings*
A 106 - 95, *Seamless Carbon Steel Pipe for High-Temperature Service*
A 135 - 95, *Electric-Resistance-Welded Steel Pipe*
A 312/A 312M - 95a, *Seamless and Welded Austenitic Stainless Steel Pipes*
A 377 - 95, *Ductile-Iron Pressure Pipe*
A 409/A 409M - 95a, *Welded Large Diameter Austenitic Steel Pipe for Corrosive or High-Temperature Service*
A 523 - 93, *Plain End Seamless and Electric-Resistance-Welded Steel Pipe for High-Pressure Pipe-Type Cable Circuits*
A 524 - 93, *Seamless Carbon Steel Pipe for Atmospheric and Low Temperatures*
A 587 - 93, *Electric-Resistance-Welded Low-Carbon Steel Pipe for the Chemical Industry*
A 589 - 95a, *Seamless and Welded Carbon Steel Water-Well Pipe*
A 746 - 93, *Ductile Iron Gravity Sewer Pipe*
A 790/A 790M - 95, *Seamless and Welded Ferritic/Austenitic Stainless Steel Pipe*
A 795 - 96, *Black and Hot-Dipped Zinc-Coated (Galvanized) Welded and Seamless Steel Pipe for Fire Protection Use*
A 813/A 813M - 95, *Single- or Double-Welded Austenitic Stainless Steel Pipe*
A 814/A 814M - 96, *Cold-Worked Welded Austenitic Stainless Steel Pipe*
A 943/A 943M - 95, *Spray-Formed Seamless Austenitic Stainless Steel Pipes*
A 949/A 949M - 95, *Spray-Formed Seamless Ferritic/Austenitic Stainless Steel Pipe*
A 954 - 96, *Austenitic Chromium-Nickel-Silicon Alloy Steel Seamless and Welded Pipe*
B 42 - 96, *Seamless Copper Pipe, Standard Sizes*
B 43 - 98, *Seamless Red Brass Pipe, Standard Sizes*
B 88 - 96, *Seamless Copper Water Tube*
B 161 - 93, *Nickel Seamless Pipe and Tube*
B 165 - 93, *Nickel-Copper Alloy (UNS N04400) Seamless Pipe and Tube*
B 210 - 95, *Aluminum and Aluminum-Alloy Drawn Seamless Tubes*
B 210M - 95, *Aluminum and Aluminum-Alloy Drawn Seamless Tubes [Metric]*

B 221 - 96, Aluminum and Aluminum-Alloy Extruded Bars, Rods, Wire, Profiles, and Tubes

B 221M - 96, Aluminum and Aluminum-Alloy Extruded Bars, Rods, Wire, Profiles, and Tubes [Metric]

B 280 - 97, Seamless Copper Tube for Air Conditioning and Refrigeration Field Service

B 302 - 97, Threadless Copper Pipe

B 306 - 96, Copper Drainage Tube (DWV)

B 429 - 95, Aluminum and Aluminum-Alloy Extruded Structural Pipe and Tube

B 587 - 97, Welded Brass Pipe

B 837 - 95, Seamless Copper Tube for Natural Gas and Liquified Petroleum (LP) Gas Fuel Distribution Systems

C 14 - 95, Concrete Sewer, Storm Drain, and Culvert Pipe

C 76 - 95a, Reinforced Concrete Culvert, Storm Drain, and Sewer Pipe

C 118 - 95, Concrete Pipe for Irrigation or Drainage

C 361 - 96, Reinforced Concrete Low-Head Pressure Pipe

C 505 - 95, Nonreinforced Concrete Irrigation Pipe With Rubber Gasket Joints

C 700 - 96, Vitrified Clay Pipe, Extra Strength, Standard Strength, and Perforated

C 1208 - 95, Vitrified Clay Pipe and Joints for Use in Jacking, Sliplining, and Tunnels

D 1785 - 96a, Poly(Vinyl Chloride) (PVC) Plastic Pipe, Schedules 40, 80, and 120

D 1527 - 96a, Acrylonitrile-Butadiene-Styrene (ABS) Plastic Pipe, Schedules 40 and 80

D 2104 - 95, Polyethylene (PE) Plastic Pipe, Schedule 40

D 2239 - 96a, Polyethylene (PE) Plastic Pipe (SIDR-PR) Based on Controlled Inside Diameter

D 2241 - 96a, Poly(Vinyl Chloride) (PVC) Pressure-Rated Pipe (SDR Series)

D 2282 - 96a, Acrylonitrile-Butadiene-Styrene (ABS) Plastic Pipe, (SDR-PR)

D 2447 - 95, Polyethylene (PE) Plastic Pipe, Schedules 40 and 80, Based on Outside Diameter

D 2662 - 96a, Polybutylene (PB) Plastic Pipe (SIDR-PR) Based on Controlled Inside Diameter

D 3000 - 95a, Polybutylene (PB) Plastic Pipe (SDR-PR) Based on Outside Diameter

D 3035 - 95, Polyethylene (PE) Plastic Pipe, (DR-PR) Based on Controlled Outside Diameter

F 441/F 441M - 96b, Chlorinated Poly(Vinyl Chloride) (CPVC) Plastic Pipe, Schedules 40 and 80

F 442/F 442M - 96b, Chlorinated Poly(Vinyl Chloride) (CPVC) Plastic Pipe (SDR-PR)

F 714 - 95, Polyethylene (PE) Plastic Pipe, (SDR-PR) Based on Outside Diameter

F 758 - 95, Smooth-wall Poly(Vinyl Chloride) (PVC) Plastic Underdrain Systems for Highway, Airport, and Similar Drainage

F 771 - 95, Polyethylene (PE) Thermoplastic High-Pressure Irrigation Pipeline Systems

F 809/F 809M - 95, Large Diameter Polybutylene Plastic Pipe

F 891 - 96, Coextruded Poly(Vinyl Chloride) (PVC) Plastic Pipe With a Cellular Core

American National Standards Institute/American Water Works Association:

ANSI/AWWA Standards:

C115/A21.15 - 94, Flanged Ductile-Iron Pipe With Ductile-Iron or Gray-Iron Threaded Flanges

C151/A21.51 - 96, Ductile-Iron Pipe, Centrifugally Cast, For Water

C300 - 97, Reinforced Concrete Pressure Pipe, Steel-Cylinder Type

C900 - 89, Polyvinyl Chloride (PVC) Pressure Pipe, 4 Inch Through 12 Inch, For Water Distribution

C901 - 96, Polyethylene (PE) Pressure Pipe and Tubing, 1/2 Inch (13 mm) Through 3 Inch (76 mm) For Water Service

C902 - 88, Polybutylene (PB) Pressure Pipe and Tubing, 1/2 Inch Through 3 Inch, For Water

C905 - 88, Polyvinyl Chloride (PVC) Water Transmission Pipe, Nominal Diameters 14 Inch Through 36 Inch.

C906 - 90, Polyethylene (PE) Pressure Pipe and Fittings, 4 Inch Through 63 Inch., For Water Distribution

Handbooks:

Clay Pipe Engineering Manual, Clay Sewer Pipe Association, Inc., 1960

Handbook of Ductile Iron Pipe, Sixth Edition, Ductile Iron Pipe Research Association, 1984

Handbook of Cast Iron Pipe, Third Edition, Cast Iron Research Association, 1967

Mark's Standard Handbook for Mechanical Engineers, Ninth Edition, McGraw-Hill Book Company, 1986

Concrete Pipe Design Manual, American Concrete Pipe Association, 1980

Aluminum Data Book, Reynolds Metals Company, 1965

ASM Metals Reference Book, ASM International, 1997

Copper Tube Handbook, Copper Development Association, 1999

Pipe And Tube Bending Handbook, Copper and Brass Research Association, 1943.

Catalogs:

Central Steel and Wire Company, Chicago, IL, 1997.

Alaskan Copper and Brass Company, Seattle, WA, 1999.

Acrylonitrile-Butadiene-Styrene (ABS) Pipe

Controlled On Outside Diameter - Properties and Friction Loss

Nom. Pipe Size	Outside Diameter	Dimension Ratio - (DR) or Schedule Number*	Minimum Wall Thickness	Inside Diameter	Theoretical Weight Per Foot**	Theoretical Flow Rate (Gallons per Minute) Which Will Cause A Head Loss (H_L) In 100 Feet of Pipe						
						H_L						
						0.1	0.5	1.0	5.0	10.0	50.0	
(inch)	(inch)		(inch)	(inch)	(pound)	(feet)	(feet)	(feet)	(feet)	(feet)	(feet)	
1/8	0.405	Schedule 80	0.095	0.215	0.04	0.015	0.037	0.053	0.127	0.185	0.442	
		Schedule 40	0.068	0.269	0.03	0.028	0.066	0.096	0.230	0.334	0.796	
		DR 13.5	0.060	0.285	0.03	0.032	0.077	0.112	0.267	0.389	0.927	
1/4	0.540	Schedule 80	0.119	0.302	0.07	0.038	0.090	0.131	0.311	0.453	1.08	
		Schedule 40	0.088	0.364	0.06	0.062	0.147	0.213	0.509	0.740	1.76	
		DR 13.5	0.060	0.420	0.04	0.090	0.214	0.311	0.741	1.08	2.57	
3/8	0.675	Schedule 80	0.126	0.423	0.10	0.091	0.218	0.317	0.755	1.10	2.62	
		Schedule 40	0.091	0.493	0.08	0.137	0.326	0.474	1.13	1.64	3.92	
		DR 13.5	0.060	0.555	0.05	0.187	0.445	0.647	1.54	2.24	5.35	
1/2	0.840	Schedule 80	0.147	0.546	0.14	0.179	0.426	0.620	1.48	2.15	5.13	
		Schedule 40	0.109	0.622	0.11	0.252	0.601	0.873	2.08	3.03	7.22	
		DR 13.5	0.062	0.716	0.07	0.364	0.868	1.26	3.01	4.38	10.4	
		DR 17	0.060	0.720	0.07	0.370	0.883	1.28	3.06	4.45	10.6	
3/4	1.050	Schedule 80	0.154	0.742	0.20	0.401	0.955	1.39	3.31	4.82	11.5	
		Schedule 40	0.113	0.824	0.15	0.528	1.26	1.83	4.36	6.34	15.1	
		DR 13.5	0.078	0.894	0.11	0.655	1.56	2.27	5.41	7.87	18.8	
		DR 17	0.062	0.926	0.09	0.718	1.71	2.49	5.94	8.63	20.6	
		DR 21	0.060	0.930	0.08	0.725	1.73	2.52	6.00	8.72	20.8	

Nom. Pipe Size	Outside Diameter	Dimension Ratio - (DR) or Schedule Number *	Minimum Wall Thickness	Inside Diameter	Theoretical Weight Per Foot **	Theoretical Flow Rate (Gallons per Minute) Which Will Cause A Head Loss (Hₗ) In 100 Feet of Pipe					
						H_L					
						0.1	0.5	1.0	5.0	10.0	50.0
(inch)	(inch)		(inch)	(inch)	(pound)	(feet)	(feet)	(feet)	(feet)	(feet)	(feet)
1	1.315	Schedule 80	0.179	0.957	0.29	0.782	1.87	2.71	6.47	9.40	22.4
		Schedule 40	0.133	1.049	0.22	1.00	2.37	3.45	8.23	12.0	28.5
		DR 13.5	0.097	1.120	0.17	1.18	2.82	4.10	9.79	14.2	33.9
		DR 17	0.077	1.160	0.14	1.30	3.10	4.50	10.7	15.6	37.2
		DR 21	0.063	1.190	0.11	1.39	3.31	4.81	11.5	16.7	39.8
		DR 26	0.060	1.195	0.11	1.40	3.35	4.86	11.6	16.9	40.2
1-1/4	1.660	Schedule 80	0.191	1.278	0.40	1.67	3.99	5.80	13.8	20.1	48.0
		Schedule 40	0.140	1.380	0.30	2.05	4.88	7.10	16.9	24.6	58.7
		DR 13.5	0.123	1.414	0.27	2.18	5.21	7.57	18.1	26.3	62.6
		DR 17	0.098	1.465	0.22	2.40	5.71	8.31	19.8	28.8	68.7
		DR 21	0.079	1.502	0.18	2.56	6.10	8.87	21.2	30.8	73.4
		DR 26	0.064	1.532	0.15	2.70	6.43	9.35	22.3	32.4	77.3
1-1/2	1.900	Schedule 80	0.200	1.500	0.48	2.55	6.08	8.84	21.1	30.7	73.1
		Schedule 40	0.145	1.610	0.36	3.07	7.33	10.7	25.4	36.9	88.1
		DR 13.5	0.141	1.619	0.35	3.12	7.43	10.8	25.8	37.5	89.3
		DR 17	0.112	1.676	0.28	3.42	8.15	11.8	28.3	41.1	98.0
		DR 21	0.090	1.719	0.23	3.65	8.70	12.7	30.2	43.9	105
		DR 26	0.073	1.754	0.19	3.85	9.18	13.3	31.8	46.3	110
2	2.375	Schedule 80	0.218	1.939	0.67	5.01	11.9	17.4	41.4	60.2	144
		DR 13.5	0.176	2.023	0.55	5.60	13.4	19.4	46.3	67.4	161
		Schedule 40	0.154	2.067	0.49	5.93	14.1	20.6	49.0	71.3	170

Acrylonitrile-Butadiene-Styrene (ABS) Pipe
Controlled On Outside Diameter - Properties And Friction Loss (cont.)

Nom. Pipe Size	Outside Diameter	Dimension Ratio - (DR) or Schedule Number	Minimum Wall Thickness	Inside Diameter	Theoretical Weight Per Foot**	Theoretical Flow Rate (Gallons per Minute) Which Will Cause A Head Loss (HL) In 100 Feet of Pipe					
						H_L					
						0.1	0.5	1.0	5.0	10.0	50.0
(inch)	(inch)		(inch)	(inch)	(pound)	(feet)	(feet)	(feet)	(feet)	(feet)	(feet)
2	2.375	DR 17	0.140	2.096	0.44	6.15	14.7	21.3	50.8	73.9	176
		DR 21	0.113	2.149	0.36	6.56	15.7	22.8	54.3	78.9	188
		DR 26	0.091	2.192	0.30	6.92	16.5	24.0	57.2	83.2	198
2-1/2	2.875	Schedule 80	0.276	2.323	1.0	8.06	19.2	27.9	66.6	96.9	231
		DR 13.5	0.213	2.449	0.81	9.26	22.1	32.1	76.6	111	265
		Schedule 40	0.203	2.469	0.77	9.46	22.6	32.8	78.2	114	271
		DR 17	0.169	2.537	0.65	10.2	24.2	35.2	84.0	122	291
		DR 21	0.137	2.601	0.53	10.8	25.9	37.6	89.7	130	311
		DR 26	0.111	2.654	0.44	11.4	27.3	39.7	94.6	137	328
3	3.500	Schedule 80	0.300	2.900	1.4	14.4	34.4	50.1	119	174	414
		DR 13.5	0.259	2.981	1.2	15.5	37.0	53.9	128	187	445
		Schedule 40	0.216	3.068	1.0	16.7	39.9	58.1	138	201	480
		DR 17	0.206	3.088	0.97	17.0	40.6	59.1	141	205	489
		DR 21	0.167	3.167	0.79	18.2	43.4	63.1	150	219	522
		DR 26	0.135	3.231	0.64	19.2	45.8	66.5	159	231	550
3-1/2	4.000	Schedule 80	0.318	3.364	1.7	21.3	50.9	74.0	176	257	612
		DR 13.5	0.296	3.407	1.6	22.1	52.6	76.5	182	265	633
		DR 17	0.235	3.529	1.3	24.2	57.7	83.9	200	291	694
		Schedule 40	0.226	3.548	1.2	24.5	58.5	85.1	203	295	704

Nom. Pipe Size	Outside Diameter	Dimension Ratio - (DR) or Schedule Number*	Minimum Wall Thickness	Inside Diameter	Theoretical Weight Per Foot**	Theoretical Flow Rate (Gallons per Minute) Which Will Cause A Head Loss (H$_f$) In 100 Feet of Pipe					
						H$_f$					
						0.1	0.5	1.0	5.0	10.0	50.0
(inch)	(inch)		(inch)	(inch)	(pound)	(feet)	(feet)	(feet)	(feet)	(feet)	(feet)
3-1/2	4.000	DR 21	0.190	3.619	1.0	25.9	61.7	89.7	214	311	741
		DR 26	0.154	3.692	0.84	27.3	65.0	94.5	225	328	781
4	4.500	Schedule 80	0.337	3.826	2.0	29.9	71.4	104	247	360	858
		DR 13.5	0.333	3.833	2.0	30.1	71.7	104	249	362	862
		DR 17	0.265	3.971	1.6	33.0	78.7	114	273	397	946
		Schedule 40	0.237	4.026	1.4	34.2	81.6	119	283	411	981
		DR 21	0.214	4.071	1.3	35.2	84.1	122	291	424	1,010
		DR 26	0.173	4.154	1.1	37.2	88.6	129	307	447	1,070
5	5.563	DR 13.5	0.412	4.739	3.0	52.5	125	182	434	632	1,510
		Schedule 80	0.375	4.813	2.8	54.7	131	190	453	658	1,570
		DR 17	0.327	4.909	2.4	57.6	137	200	477	693	1,650
		DR 21	0.265	5.033	2.0	61.6	147	213	509	740	1,770
		Schedule 40	0.258	5.047	1.9	62.0	148	215	513	746	1,780
		DR 26	0.214	5.135	1.6	64.9	155	225	537	780	1,860
6	6.625	DR 13.5	0.491	5.644	4.3	83.2	198	288	688	1,000	2,390
		Schedule 80	0.432	5.761	3.8	87.8	209	305	726	1,060	2,520
		DR 17	0.390	5.846	3.5	91.3	218	316	755	1,100	2,620
		DR 21	0.315	5.994	2.8	97.5	232	338	806	1,170	2,790
		Schedule 40	0.280	6.065	2.5	101	240	349	831	1,210	2,880
		DR 26	0.255	6.115	2.3	103	245	356	850	1,240	2,950

Acrylonitrile-Butadiene-Styrene (ABS) Pipe Controlled On Outside Diameter - Properties And Friction Loss (cont.)

Nom. Pipe Size	Outside Diameter	Dimension Ratio - (DR) or Schedule Number*	Minimum Wall Thickness	Inside Diameter	Theoretical Weight Per Foot**	Theoretical Flow Rate (Gallons per Minute) Which Will Cause A Head Loss (H_t) In 100 Feet of Pipe					
						0.1	0.5	1.0	5.0	10.0	50.0
(inch)	(inch)		(inch)	(inch)	(pound)	(feet)	(feet)	(feet)	(feet)	(feet)	(feet)
8	8.625	Schedule 80	0.500	7.625	5.8	184	438	636	1,520	2,210	5,260
		DR 21	0.411	7.804	4.8	195	465	676	1,610	2,350	5,590
		DR 26	0.332	7.962	3.9	206	490	713	1,700	2,470	5,900
		Schedule 40	0.322	7.981	3.8	207	494	718	1,710	2,490	5,930
10	10.750	Schedule 80	0.593	9.564	8.6	333	794	1,150	2,750	4,000	9,550
		DR 21	0.512	9.726	7.5	348	830	1,210	2,880	4,190	9,980
		DR 26	0.413	9.923	6.1	367	875	1,270	3,030	4,410	10,500
		Schedule 40	0.365	10.020	5.4	377	898	1,310	3,110	4,530	10,800
12	12.750	Schedule 80	0.687	11.376	12	526	1,250	1,820	4,350	6,320	15,100
		DR 21	0.607	11.536	10	545	1,300	1,890	4,510	6,560	15,600
		DR 26	0.490	11.769	8.6	575	1,370	1,990	4,750	6,910	16,500
		Schedule 40	0.406	11.938	7.1	597	1,420	2,070	4,930	7,170	17,100

Notes:

1 * Dimension Ratio = Outside Diameter / Wall Thickness / Wall Thickness = Outside Diameter / Dimension Ratio

2 ** Based on an average density of 65.2 pounds per cubic foot for acrylonitrile-butadiene-styrene. Actual weight may vary by ± 3%.

3 Diameter and wall thickness data from : ASTM Designations D 1527 - 96a, D 2282 - 96a

Aluminum Pipe and Tube - Properties and Friction Loss

Nominal or Standard Pipe Size	Outside Diameter	Pipe Schedule Number or Weight Class *		Minimum Wall Thickness	Inside Diameter	Theoretical Weight Per Foot**	Theoretical Flow Rate (Gallons per Minute) Which Will Cause A Head Loss (H_h) In 100 Feet of Pipe H_h					
		a	b				0.1	0.5	1.0	5.0	10.0	50.0
(inch)	(inch)			(inch)	(inch)	(pound)	(feet)	(feet)	(feet)	(feet)	(feet)	(feet)
1/8	0.405	80	XS	0.095	0.215	0.109	0.015	0.037	0.053	0.127	0.185	0.442
		40	S	0.068	0.269	0.085	0.028	0.066	0.096	0.230	0.334	0.796
3/16	0.1875	Seamless tube		0.049	0.0895	0.025	0.002	0.004	0.005	0.013	0.018	0.044
				0.035	0.1175	0.020	0.003	0.008	0.011	0.026	0.038	0.090
1/4	0.250	Seamless tube		0.058	0.134	0.041	0.004	0.011	0.015	0.037	0.053	0.127
				0.049	0.152	0.036	0.006	0.015	0.021	0.051	0.074	0.177
				0.035	0.180	0.028	0.010	0.023	0.033	0.080	0.116	0.277
	0.540	80	XS	0.119	0.302	0.185	0.038	0.090	0.131	0.311	0.453	1.08
		40	S	0.088	0.364	0.147	0.062	0.147	0.213	0.509	0.740	1.76
5/16	0.3125	Seamless tube		0.091	0.1305	0.074	0.004	0.010	0.014	0.034	0.050	0.119
				0.058	0.1965	0.055	0.012	0.029	0.042	0.101	0.146	0.349
				0.049	0.2145	0.048	0.015	0.037	0.053	0.127	0.184	0.439
				0.035	0.2425	0.036	0.021	0.050	0.073	0.175	0.254	0.606
3/8	0.375	Seamless tube		0.065	0.245	0.074	0.022	0.052	0.075	0.180	0.261	0.623
				0.058	0.259	0.068	0.025	0.060	0.087	0.208	0.302	0.721
				0.049	0.277	0.059	0.030	0.072	0.104	0.248	0.361	0.860
				0.035	0.305	0.044	0.039	0.092	0.134	0.320	0.465	1.11
				0.028	0.319	0.036	0.043	0.104	0.151	0.360	0.523	1.25

Aluminum Pipe and Tube - Properties and Friction Loss (cont.)

Nominal or Standard Pipe Size	Outside Diameter	Pipe Schedule Number or Weight Class *		Minimum Wall Thickness	Inside Diameter	Theoretical Weight Per Foot**	Theoretical Flow Rate (Gallons per Minute) Which Will Cause A Head Loss (H_L) In 100 Feet of Pipe					
							H_L					
		a	b				0.1	0.5	1.0	5.0	10.0	50.0
(inch)	(inch)			(inch)	(inch)	(pound)	(feet)	(feet)	(feet)	(feet)	(feet)	(feet)
3/8	0.675	80	XS	0.126	0.423	0.256	0.091	0.218	0.317	0.755	1.10	2.62
		40	S	0.091	0.493	0.196	0.137	0.326	0.474	1.13	1.64	3.92
7/16	0.4375	Seamless tube		0.065	0.3075	0.089	0.039	0.094	0.137	0.327	0.475	1.13
				0.049	0.3395	0.070	0.051	0.122	0.178	0.424	0.616	1.47
				0.035	0.3675	0.052	0.063	0.151	0.219	0.522	0.759	1.81
	0.500	Seamless tube		0.120	0.260	0.168	0.025	0.061	0.088	0.210	0.305	0.73
				0.065	0.370	0.104	0.064	0.153	0.223	0.531	0.772	1.84
				0.058	0.384	0.095	0.071	0.169	0.246	0.586	0.852	2.03
				0.049	0.402	0.082	0.080	0.191	0.277	0.661	0.961	2.29
				0.035	0.430	0.060	0.095	0.227	0.331	0.789	1.15	2.73
				0.028	0.444	0.049	0.104	0.247	0.360	0.858	1.25	2.98
1/2	0.840	160	--	0.187	0.466	0.451	0.118	0.281	0.409	0.975	1.42	3.38
		80	XS	0.147	0.546	0.376	0.179	0.426	0.620	1.48	2.15	5.13
		40	S	0.109	0.622	0.294	0.252	0.601	0.873	2.08	3.03	7.22
		10	--	0.083	0.674	0.232	0.311	0.742	1.08	2.57	3.74	8.92
		5	--	0.065	0.710	0.186	0.357	0.851	1.24	2.95	4.29	10.2
5/8	0.625			0.065	0.495	0.134	0.138	0.329	0.479	1.14	1.66	3.96
				0.058	0.509	0.121	0.149	0.354	0.515	1.23	1.79	4.26

Nominal or Standard Pipe Size	Outside Diameter	Pipe Schedule Number or Weight Class *		Minimum Wall Thickness	Inside Diameter	Theoretical Weight Per Foot**	Theoretical Flow Rate (Gallons per Minute) Which Will Cause A Head Loss (H_L) In 100 Feet of Pipe					
		a	b				H_L					
							0.1	0.5	1.0	5.0	10.0	50.0
(inch)	(inch)			(inch)	(inch)	(pound)	(feet)	(feet)	(feet)	(feet)	(feet)	(feet)
5/8	0.625	Seamless tube		0.049	0.527	0.104	0.163	0.388	0.565	1.35	1.96	4.67
				0.035	0.555	0.076	0.187	0.445	0.647	1.54	2.24	5.35
				0.028	0.569	0.062	0.199	0.475	0.691	1.65	2.40	5.71
3/4	0.750	Seamless tube		0.083	0.584	0.205	0.213	0.509	0.740	1.76	2.57	6.12
				0.065	0.620	0.164	0.250	0.596	0.866	2.07	3.00	7.16
				0.058	0.634	0.148	0.265	0.632	0.918	2.19	3.18	7.59
				0.049	0.652	0.127	0.285	0.680	0.988	2.36	3.43	8.17
				0.035	0.680	0.092	0.318	0.759	1.10	2.63	3.83	9.13
3/4	1.050	160	---	0.218	0.614	0.670	0.243	0.581	0.844	2.01	2.93	6.98
		80	XS	0.154	0.742	0.510	0.401	0.955	1.39	3.31	4.82	11.5
		40	S	0.113	0.824	0.391	0.528	1.26	1.83	4.36	6.34	15.1
		10	---	0.083	0.884	0.297	0.635	1.51	2.20	5.25	7.63	18.2
		5	---	0.065	0.920	0.237	0.705	1.68	2.44	5.83	8.48	20.2
---	0.860	---	---	0.062	0.736	0.183	0.392	0.935	1.36	3.24	4.71	11.2
7/8	0.875	Seamless tube		0.156	0.563	0.414	0.194	0.462	0.672	1.60	2.33	5.56
				0.065	0.745	0.195	0.405	0.965	1.40	3.35	4.87	11.6
				0.062	0.751	0.186	0.413	0.986	1.43	3.42	4.97	11.9
				0.058	0.759	0.175	0.425	1.01	1.47	3.52	5.11	12.2
				0.049	0.777	0.150	0.452	1.08	1.57	3.74	5.44	13.0
				0.035	0.805	0.109	0.496	1.18	1.72	4.10	5.97	14.2

Aluminum Pipe and Tube - Properties and Friction Loss

Nominal or Standard Pipe Size	Outside Diameter	Pipe Schedule Number or Weight Class * (a)	(b)	Minimum Wall Thickness	Inside Diameter	Theoretical Weight Per Foot**	Theoretical Flow Rate (Gallons per Minute) Which Will Cause A Head Loss (H_h, in 100 Feet of Pipe) H_f					
							0.1	0.5	1.0	5.0	10.0	50.0
(inch)	(inch)			(inch)	(inch)	(pound)	(feet)	(feet)	(feet)	(feet)	(feet)	(feet)
1	1.000	Extruded tube		0.250	0.500	0.693	0.142	0.338	0.492	1.17	1.71	4.07
				0.220	0.560	0.634	0.191	0.456	0.663	1.58	2.30	5.48
				0.125	0.750	0.404	0.412	0.983	1.43	3.41	4.95	11.8
	1.000	Seamless tube		0.083	0.834	0.281	0.545	1.30	1.89	4.50	6.55	15.6
				0.080	0.840	0.272	0.555	1.32	1.92	4.59	6.67	15.9
				0.065	0.870	0.225	0.609	1.45	2.11	5.03	7.32	17.5
				0.058	0.884	0.202	0.635	1.51	2.20	5.25	7.63	18.2
				0.049	0.902	0.172	0.669	1.60	2.32	5.54	8.05	19.2
				0.035	0.930	0.125	0.725	1.73	2.52	6.00	8.72	20.8
	1.315	160	---	0.250	0.815	0.984	0.513	1.22	1.78	4.24	6.16	14.7
		80	XS	0.179	0.957	0.751	0.782	1.87	2.71	6.47	9.40	22.4
		40	S	0.133	1.049	0.581	1.00	2.37	3.45	8.23	12.0	28.5
		10	---	0.109	1.097	0.486	1.12	2.67	3.88	9.26	13.5	32.1
		5	---	0.065	1.185	0.300	1.37	3.27	4.76	11.3	16.5	39.3
1-1/8	1.125	Seamless tube		0.090	0.945	0.344	0.757	1.80	2.62	6.26	9.10	21.7
				0.065	0.995	0.255	0.866	2.07	3.00	7.16	10.4	24.8
				0.058	1.009	0.229	0.899	2.14	3.12	7.43	10.8	25.8
				0.035	1.055	0.141	1.011	2.41	3.50	8.36	12.2	29.0

Nominal or Standard Pipe Size	Outside Diameter	Pipe Schedule Number or Weight Class *		Minimum Wall Thickness	Inside Diameter	Theoretical Weight Per Foot**	Theoretical Flow Rate (Gallons per Minute) Which Will Cause A Head Loss (H_h, In 100 Feet of Pipe)					
							H_h					
		a	b				0.1	0.5	1.0	5.0	10.0	50.0
(inch)	(inch)			(inch)	(inch)	(pound)	(feet)	(feet)	(feet)	(feet)	(feet)	(feet)
1-1/4	1.250	Extruded tube		0.250	0.750	0.924	0.412	0.983	1.43	3.41	4.95	11.8
				0.175	0.900	0.695	0.665	1.59	2.31	5.50	8.00	19.1
				0.125	1.000	0.520	0.878	2.09	3.04	7.26	10.6	25.2
				0.120	1.010	0.501	0.901	2.15	3.13	7.45	10.8	25.8
		Seamless tube		0.090	1.070	0.386	1.05	2.50	3.64	8.67	12.6	30.1
				0.083	1.084	0.358	1.09	2.59	3.76	8.98	13.1	31.1
				0.075	1.100	0.326	1.13	2.69	3.91	9.33	13.6	32.3
				0.070	1.110	0.305	1.16	2.76	4.01	9.55	13.9	33.1
				0.065	1.120	0.285	1.18	2.82	4.10	9.78	14.2	33.9
				0.058	1.134	0.255	1.22	2.91	4.24	10.1	14.7	35.0
				0.049	1.152	0.217	1.27	3.04	4.42	10.5	15.3	36.5
				0.042	1.166	0.187	1.31	3.14	4.56	10.9	15.8	37.7
				0.035	1.180	0.157	1.36	3.24	4.70	11.2	16.3	38.9
	1.660	80	XS	0.191	1.278	1.037	1.67	3.99	5.80	13.8	20.1	48.0
		40	S	0.140	1.380	0.786	2.05	4.88	7.10	16.9	24.6	58.7
		10	---	0.109	1.442	0.625	2.30	5.48	7.97	19.0	27.6	65.9
		5	---	0.065	1.530	0.383	2.69	6.41	9.32	22.2	32.3	77.0
1-3/8	1.375	Extruded tube		0.125	1.125	0.577	1.20	2.85	4.15	9.90	14.4	34.3
		Seamless tube		0.095	1.185	0.449	1.37	3.27	4.76	11.3	16.5	39.3

Aluminum Pipe and Tube - Properties and Friction Loss (cont.)

Nominal or Standard Pipe Size	Outside Diameter	Pipe Schedule Number or Weight Class * (a)	(b)	Minimum Wall Thickness	Inside Diameter	Theoretical Weight Per Foot **	Theoretical Flow Rate (Gallons per Minute) Which Will Cause A Head Loss (H_n In 100 Feet of Pipe) — H_f — 0.1	0.5	1.0	5.0	10.0	50.0
(inch)	(inch)			(inch)	(inch)	(pound)	(feet)	(feet)	(feet)	(feet)	(feet)	(feet)
1-3/8	1.375	Seamless tube		0.080	1.215	0.383	1.47	3.49	5.08	12.1	17.6	42.0
				0.058	1.259	0.282	1.61	3.84	5.58	13.3	19.3	46.1
				0.049	1.277	0.240	1.67	3.98	5.79	13.8	20.1	47.9
				0.035	1.305	0.173	1.77	4.22	6.13	14.6	21.3	50.7
	1.500	Extruded tube		0.406	0.688	1.641	0.328	0.783	1.14	2.72	3.95	9.41
				0.250	1.000	1.155	0.878	2.09	3.04	7.26	10.6	25.2
				0.125	1.250	0.635	1.58	3.77	5.47	13.1	19.0	45.3
		Seamless tube		0.095	1.310	0.493	1.79	4.26	6.19	14.8	21.5	51.2
				0.083	1.334	0.435	1.87	4.47	6.50	15.5	22.5	53.7
				0.065	1.370	0.345	2.01	4.79	6.97	16.6	24.2	57.6
				0.058	1.384	0.309	2.06	4.92	7.16	17.1	24.8	59.2
				0.049	1.402	0.263	2.14	5.09	7.40	17.7	25.7	61.2
				0.042	1.416	0.226	2.19	5.23	7.60	18.1	26.4	62.8
				0.035	1.430	0.189	2.25	5.36	7.80	18.6	27.0	64.5
1-1/2	1.900	160	---	0.281	1.338	1.681	1.89	4.50	6.55	15.6	22.7	54.1
		80	XS	0.200	1.500	1.256	2.55	6.08	8.84	21.1	30.7	73.1
		40	S	0.145	1.610	0.940	3.07	7.33	10.7	25.4	36.9	88.1
		10	---	0.109	1.682	0.721	3.45	8.22	12.0	28.5	41.4	98.8

Nominal or Standard Pipe Size	Outside Diameter	Pipe Schedule Number or Weight Class *		Minimum Wall Thickness	Inside Diameter	Theoretical Weight Per Foot**	Theoretical Flow Rate (Gallons per Minute) Which Will Cause A Head Loss (H_n In 100 Feet of Pipe) H_f					
		a	b				0.1	0.5	1.0	5.0	10.0	50.0
(inch)	(inch)			(inch)	(inch)	(pound)	(feet)	(feet)	(feet)	(feet)	(feet)	(feet)
1-1/2	1.900	---	---	0.105	1.690	0.696	3.49	8.32	12.1	28.9	42.0	100
			5	0.065	1.770	0.441	3.94	9.40	13.7	32.6	47.4	113
1-5/8	1.625	Seamless tube		0.312	1.001	1.513	0.880	2.10	3.05	7.28	10.6	25.2
				0.250	1.125	1.270	1.20	2.85	4.15	9.90	14.4	34.3
				0.175	1.275	0.937	1.66	3.97	5.77	13.8	20.0	47.7
				0.125	1.375	0.693	2.03	4.84	7.03	16.8	24.4	58.2
				0.095	1.435	0.537	2.27	5.41	7.87	18.8	27.3	65.1
				0.058	1.509	0.336	2.59	6.18	8.98	21.4	31.1	74.3
				0.035	1.555	0.206	2.80	6.69	9.72	23.2	33.7	80.4
1-3/4	1.750	Extruded tube		0.469	0.812	2.220	0.508	1.21	1.76	4.20	6.10	14.6
				0.281	1.188	1.525	1.38	3.29	4.79	11.4	16.6	39.6
				0.250	1.250	1.385	1.58	3.77	5.47	13.1	19.0	45.3
				0.125	1.500	0.750	2.55	6.08	8.84	21.1	30.7	73.1
	1.750	Seamless tube		0.090	1.570	0.552	2.88	6.86	9.97	23.8	34.6	82.4
				0.083	1.584	0.511	2.94	7.02	10.2	24.3	35.4	84.4
				0.065	1.620	0.405	3.12	7.45	10.8	25.8	37.5	89.5
				0.058	1.634	0.363	3.19	7.62	11.1	26.4	38.4	91.6
				0.035	1.680	0.222	3.44	8.19	11.9	28.4	41.3	98.5
---	1.765	---	---	0.070	1.625	0.438	3.15	7.51	10.9	26.0	37.8	90.3
---	1.840	---	---	0.110	1.620	0.703	3.12	7.45	10.8	25.8	37.5	89.5

Aluminum Pipe and Tube - Properties and Friction Loss (cont.)

Nominal or Standard Pipe Size	Outside Diameter	Pipe Schedule Number or Weight Class *		Minimum Wall Thickness	Inside Diameter	Theoretical Weight Per Foot **	Theoretical Flow Rate (Gallons per Minute) Which Will Cause A Head Loss (H_f in 100 Feet of Pipe)					
		a	b				H_f					
							0.1	0.5	1.0	5.0	10.0	50.0
(inch)	(inch)			(inch)	(inch)	(pound)	(feet)	(feet)	(feet)	(feet)	(feet)	(feet)
1-7/8	1.875	Seamless tube		0.273	1.329	1.616	1.86	4.42	6.43	15.3	22.3	53.2
---	1.988	---	---	0.058	1.759	0.389	3.88	9.25	13.4	32.1	46.6	111
				0.105	1.778	0.730	3.99	9.51	13.8	33.0	48.0	114
---	2.000	Extruded tube		0.531	0.938	2.882	0.742	1.77	2.57	6.14	8.92	21.3
				0.250	1.500	1.616	2.55	6.08	8.84	21.1	30.7	73.1
				0.188	1.624	1.259	3.14	7.50	10.9	26.0	37.8	90.1
				0.125	1.750	0.866	3.83	9.12	13.3	31.6	46.0	110
		Seamless tube		0.083	1.834	0.588	4.33	10.3	15.0	35.8	52.0	124
				0.065	1.870	0.465	4.55	10.9	15.8	37.7	54.8	131
				0.058	1.884	0.416	4.64	11.1	16.1	38.4	55.8	133
				0.050	1.900	0.360	4.75	11.3	16.5	39.3	57.1	136
				0.049	1.902	0.353	4.76	11.4	16.5	39.4	57.3	137
				0.035	1.930	0.254	4.95	11.8	17.2	40.9	59.5	142
2	2.375	160	---	0.343	1.689	2.575	3.48	8.31	12.1	28.8	41.9	99.9
		80	XS	0.218	1.939	1.737	5.01	11.9	17.4	41.4	60.2	144
		40	S	0.154	2.067	1.264	5.93	14.1	20.6	49.0	71.3	170
		10	---	0.109	2.157	0.913	6.63	15.8	23.0	54.8	79.7	190
		5	---	0.065	2.245	0.555	7.37	17.6	25.5	60.9	88.5	211

Nominal or Standard Pipe Size	Outside Diameter	Pipe Schedule Number or Weight Class *		Minimum Wall Thickness	Inside Diameter	Theoretical Weight Per Foot**	Theoretical Flow Rate (Gallons per Minute) Which Will Cause A Head Loss H_h In 100 Feet of Pipe					
		a	b				0.1	0.5	1.0	5.0	10.0	50.0
(inch)	(inch)			(inch)	(inch)	(pound)	(feet)	(feet)	(feet)	(feet)	(feet)	(feet)
2-1/8	2.125	---	---	0.250	1.625	1.732	3.15	7.51	10.9	26.0	37.8	90.3
2-1/4	2.250	Seamless tube		0.250	1.750	1.847	3.83	9.12	13.3	31.6	46.0	110
	2.250	Seamless tube		0.083	2.084	0.664	6.06	14.4	21.0	50.1	72.8	174
				0.065	2.120	0.525	6.34	15.1	22.0	52.4	76.2	182
				0.049	2.152	0.398	6.59	15.7	22.8	54.5	79.2	189
---	2.300	---	---	0.188	1.924	1.467	4.91	11.7	17.0	40.6	59.0	141
---	2.310	---	---	0.500	1.310	3.344	1.79	4.26	6.19	14.8	21.5	51.2
---	2.500	Extruded tube		0.500	1.500	3.695	2.55	6.08	8.84	21.1	30.7	73.1
				0.250	2.000	2.078	5.43	13.0	18.8	44.9	65.3	156
				0.125	2.250	1.097	7.41	17.7	25.7	61.3	89.1	212
2-1/2	2.500	Seamless tube		0.083	2.334	0.741	8.16	19.5	28.3	67.5	98.1	234
				0.065	2.370	0.585	8.49	20.3	29.4	70.2	102	244
				0.049	2.402	0.444	8.80	21.0	30.5	72.8	106	252
	2.875	160	---	0.375	2.125	3.464	6.37	15.2	22.1	52.7	76.6	183
		80	XS	0.276	2.323	2.650	8.06	19.2	27.9	66.6	96.9	231
		40	S	0.203	2.469	2.004	9.46	22.6	32.8	78.2	114	271
		10	---	0.120	2.635	1.221	11.2	26.8	38.9	92.8	135	322
		5	---	0.083	2.709	0.856	12.1	28.8	41.9	99.8	145	346
---	2.655	---	---	0.430	1.795	3.535	4.09	9.75	14.2	33.8	49.2	117
---	2.688	---	---	0.125	2.438	1.184	9.15	21.8	31.7	75.7	110	262

Aluminum Pipe and Tube - Properties and Friction Loss (cont.)

Nominal or Standard Pipe Size	Outside Diameter	Pipe Schedule Number or Weight Class * (a)	Pipe Schedule Number or Weight Class * (b)	Minimum Wall Thickness	Inside Diameter	Theoretical Weight** Per Foot	Theoretical Flow Rate (Gallons per Minute) Which Will Cause A Head Loss (Hh, In 100 Feet of Pipe) — Hf, 0.1	0.5	1.0	5.0	10.0	50.0
(inch)	(inch)			(inch)	(inch)	(pound)	(feet)	(feet)	(feet)	(feet)	(feet)	(feet)
---	2.700	---	---	0.518	1.664	4.176	3.35	7.99	11.6	27.7	40.3	96.1
2-3/4	2.750	Extruded tube		0.625	1.500	4.907	2.55	6.08	8.84	21.1	30.7	73.1
		Extruded tube		0.500	1.750	4.156	3.83	9.12	13.3	31.6	46.0	110
	3.000	Extruded tube		0.750	1.500	6.234	2.55	6.08	8.84	21.1	30.7	73.1
		Extruded tube		0.500	2.000	4.618	5.43	13.0	18.8	44.9	65.3	156
		Extruded tube		0.375	2.250	3.637	7.41	17.7	25.7	61.3	89.1	212
		Extruded tube		0.313	2.374	3.107	8.53	20.3	29.6	70.5	103	245
		Extruded tube		0.250	2.500	2.540	9.77	23.3	33.9	80.8	118	280
		Extruded tube		0.125	2.750	1.328	12.6	29.9	43.5	104	151	360
		Seamless tube		0.083	2.834	0.894	13.6	32.4	47.1	112	163	390
		Seamless tube		0.065	2.870	0.705	14.1	33.5	48.7	116	169	403
3	3.500	---	---	0.750	2.000	7.620	5.43	13.0	18.8	44.9	65.3	156
		---	---	0.500	2.500	5.542	9.77	23.3	33.9	80.8	118	280
		160		0.437	2.626	4.945	11.1	26.5	38.6	92.0	134	319
		80	XS	0.300	2.900	3.547	14.4	34.4	50.1	119	174	414
		40	S	0.216	3.068	2.621	16.7	39.9	58.1	138	201	480
		---	---	0.188	3.124	2.300	17.6	41.9	60.9	145	211	504
		---	---	0.156	3.188	1.927	18.5	44.2	64.2	153	223	531

Nominal or Standard Pipe Size	Outside Diameter	Pipe Schedule Number or Weight Class *		Minimum Wall Thickness	Inside Diameter	Theoretical Weight Per Foot**	Theoretical Flow Rate (Gallons per Minute) Which Will Cause A Head Loss (H_L, in 100 Feet of Pipe)					
		a	b				H_L					
							0.1	0.5	1.0	5.0	10.0	50.0
(inch)	(inch)			(inch)	(inch)	(pound)	(feet)	(feet)	(feet)	(feet)	(feet)	(feet)
3	3.500	10	- - -	0.120	3.260	1.498	19.6	46.8	68.1	162	236	563
		- - -	- - -	0.093	3.314	1.171	20.5	48.9	71.1	170	247	588
		5	- - -	0.083	3.334	1.048	20.8	49.7	72.3	172	251	597
3-1/4	3.250	Extruded tube		0.500	2.250	5.080	7.41	17.7	25.7	61.3	89.1	212
				0.375	2.500	3.983	9.77	23.3	33.9	80.8	118	280
- - -	3.490			0.120	3.250	1.494	19.5	46.5	67.6	161	234	559
	3.500	Extruded tube		0.750	2.000	7.620	5.43	13.0	18.8	44.9	65.3	156
				0.500	2.500	5.542	9.77	23.3	33.9	80.8	118	280
	4.000	- - -	- - -	0.750	2.500	9.005	9.77	23.3	33.9	80.8	118	280
		- - -	- - -	0.500	3.000	6.465	15.8	37.6	54.7	131	190	453
		80	XS	0.318	3.364	4.326	21.3	50.9	74.0	176	257	612
3-1/2		40	S	0.250	3.500	3.464	23.7	56.5	82.1	196	285	679
		- - -	- - -	0.226	3.548	3.151	24.5	58.5	85.1	203	295	704
		- - -	- - -	0.125	3.750	1.790	28.4	67.7	98.4	235	341	814
		10	- - -	0.120	3.760	1.720	28.6	68.2	99.1	236	344	820
		5	- - -	0.083	3.834	1.201	30.1	71.8	104	249	362	863
		- - -	- - -	0.072	3.856	1.045	30.6	72.9	106	253	367	876
		- - -	- - -	0.050	3.900	0.730	31.5	75.1	109	260	378	902
- - -	3.540	- - -	- - -	0.295	2.950	3.537	15.1	36.0	52.4	125	182	433
- - -	3.565	- - -	- - -	0.250	3.065	3.062	16.7	39.8	57.9	138	201	479

Aluminum Pipe and Tube - Properties and Friction Loss (cont.)

Nominal or Standard Pipe Size	Outside Diameter	Pipe Schedule Number or Weight Class * (a)	(b)	Minimum Wall Thickness	Inside Diameter	Theoretical Weight Per Foot**	Theoretical Flow Rate (Gallons per Minute) Which Will Cause A Head Loss (H_h) In 100 Feet of Pipe — H_f = 0.1	0.5	1.0	5.0	10.0	50.0
(inch)	(inch)	(inch)		(inch)	(inch)	(pound)	(feet)	(feet)	(feet)	(feet)	(feet)	(feet)
3-3/4	3.750	Extruded tube	---	0.500	2.750	6.004	12.6	29.9	43.5	104	151	360
---	3.953	---	---	0.101	3.751	1.437	28.4	67.8	98.5	235	342	815
---	4.438	---	---	0.375	3.688	5.629	27.2	64.8	94.2	225	327	779
	4.000	Extruded tube		0.750	2.500	9.005	9.77	23.3	33.9	80.8	118	280
				0.500	3.000	6.465	15.8	37.6	54.7	131	190	453
				0.250	3.500	3.464	23.7	56.5	82.1	196	285	679
				0.125	3.750	1.790	28.4	67.7	98.4	235	341	814
	4.000	Seamless tube		0.065	3.870	0.945	30.8	73.6	107	255	371	884
	4.500	---	---	0.750	3.000	10.39	15.8	37.6	54.7	131	190	453
		160		0.531	3.438	7.786	22.6	53.9	78.3	187	272	648
		---	---	0.500	3.500	7.389	23.7	56.5	82.1	196	285	679
		120		0.437	3.626	6.560	26.0	62.0	90.1	215	312	745
		80	XS	0.337	3.826	5.183	29.9	71.4	104	247	360	858
		---	---	0.312	3.876	4.827	31.0	73.9	107	256	372	888
4		40	S	0.237	4.026	3.733	34.2	81.6	119	283	411	981
		---	---	0.188	4.124	2.995	36.5	86.9	126	301	438	1,050
		---	---	0.125	4.250	2.020	39.5	94.1	137	326	474	1,130
		10		0.120	4.260	1.942	39.7	94.7	138	328	477	1,140
		5		0.083	4.334	1.354	41.5	99.1	144	344	499	1,190

Nominal or Standard Pipe Size (inch)	Outside Diameter (inch)	Pipe Schedule Number or Weight Class *		Minimum Wall Thickness (inch)	Inside Diameter (inch)	Theoretical Weight Per Foot ** (pound)	Theoretical Flow Rate (Gallons per Minute) Which Will Cause A Head Loss (H_L) In 100 Feet of Pipe					
		a	b				0.1 (feet)	0.5 (feet)	1.0 (feet)	5.0 (feet)	10.0 (feet)	50.0 (feet)
4-1/2	4.500	Extruded tube		0.750	3.000	10.391	15.8	37.6	54.7	131	190	453
				0.500	3.500	7.389	23.7	56.5	82.1	196	285	679
---	4.938	---	---	0.250	4.438	4.330	44.2	105	153	366	532	1,270
5	5.000	Ext ruded tube		1.000	3.000	14.778	15.8	37.6	54.7	131	190	453
				0.750	3.500	11.776	23.7	56.5	82.1	196	285	679
				0.500	4.000	8.313	33.6	80.2	117	278	404	965
				0.250	4.500	4.387	47.5	109	159	379	551	1,310
	5.000	Seamless tube		0.219	4.562	3.868	47.5	113	165	393	572	1,360
				0.105	4.790	1.899	54.0	129	187	447	650	1,550
				0.078	4.844	1.418	55.7	133	193	460	669	1,600
				0.051	4.898	0.932	57.3	137	199	474	689	1,640
	5.563	160		0.625	4.313	11.40	41.0	97.8	142	339	493	1,180
		120		0.500	4.563	9.353	47.6	113	165	393	572	1,360
		80	XS	0.375	4.813	7.188	54.7	131	190	453	658	1,570
		40	S	0.258	5.047	5.057	62.0	148	215	513	746	1,780
		10	---	0.134	5.295	2.688	70.3	168	244	582	846	2,020
		5	---	0.109	5.345	2.196	72.1	172	250	596	867	2,070
5-3/8	5.375	---	---	0.188	4.999	3.603	60.5	144	210	500	727	1,730
5-1/2	5.500	Extruded tube		1.000	3.500	16.63	23.7	56.5	82.1	196	285	679
				0.750	4.000	13.16	33.6	80.2	117	278	404	965
				0.500	4.500	9.24	45.9	109	159	379	551	1,310
				0.250	5.000	4.85	60.5	144	210	500	727	1,730

Aluminum Pipe and Tube - Properties and Friction Loss (cont.)

Nominal or Standard Pipe Size	Outside Diameter	Pipe Schedule Number or Weight Class a	b	Minimum Wall Thickness	Inside Diameter	Theoretical Weight Per Foot**	Theoretical Flow Rate (Gallons per Minute) Which Will Cause A Head Loss (Hn In 100 Feet of Pipe)					
							0.1	0.5	1.0	5.0	10.0	50.0
(inch)	(inch)			(inch)	(inch)	(pound)	(feet)	(feet)	(feet)	(feet)	(feet)	(feet)
6	6.000	Extruded tube		1.000	4.000	18.47	33.6	80.2	117	278	404	965
		Extruded tube		0.750	4.500	14.55	45.9	109	159	379	551	1,310
		Extruded tube		0.500	5.000	10.16	60.5	144	210	500	727	1,730
		Extruded tube		0.250	5.500	5.311	77.7	185	270	643	935	2,230
	6.000	Seamless tube		0.083	5.834	1.814	90.8	216	315	751	1,090	2,600
		Seamless tube		0.058	5.884	1.273	92.8	221	322	768	1,120	2,660
		Seamless tube		0.051	5.898	1.121	93.4	223	324	772	1,120	2,680
	6.625	160		0.718	5.189	15.67	66.7	159	231	552	802	1,910
		120		0.562	5.501	12.59	77.8	185	270	643	935	2,230
		80	XS	0.432	5.761	9.884	87.8	209	305	726	1,060	2,520
		40	S	0.280	6.065	6.564	101	240	349	831	1,210	2,880
		10		0.134	6.357	3.213	114	271	394	941	1,370	3,260
		5		0.109	6.407	2.624	116	277	403	960	1,400	3,330
6-1/2	6.500	Extruded tube		1.000	4.500	20.32	45.9	109	159	379	551	1,310
7	7.000	Extruded tube		1.000	5.000	22.17	60.5	144	210	500	727	1,730
		Extruded tube		0.750	5.500	17.32	77.7	185	270	643	935	2,230
		Extruded tube		0.500	6.000	12.01	97.7	233	339	808	1,170	2,800
8	8.000	Extruded tube		1.000	6.000	25.86	97.7	233	339	808	1,170	2,800
		Extruded tube		0.750	6.500	20.09	121	288	418	997	1,450	3,460
		Extruded tube		0.500	7.000	13.85	147	350	508	1,210	1,760	4,200
		Extruded tube		0.250	7.500	7.158	176	419	609	1,450	2,110	5,040

Nominal or Standard Pipe Size	Outside Diameter	Pipe Schedule Number or Weight Class *		Minimum Wall Thickness *	Inside Diameter	Theoretical Weight Per Foot **	Theoretical Flow Rate (Gallons per Minute) Which Will Cause A Head Loss (Hf) In 100 Feet of Pipe					
		a	b				Hf					
							0.1	0.5	1.0	5.0	10.0	50.0
(inch)	(inch)			(inch)	(inch)	(pound)	(feet)	(feet)	(feet)	(feet)	(feet)	(feet)
8	8.000	Seamless tube		0.094	7.812	2.746	196	467	678	1,620	2,350	5,610
		Seamless tube		0.083	7.834	2.428	197	470	683	1,630	2,370	5,650
		Seamless tube		0.064	7.872	1.876	200	476	692	1,650	2,400	5,720
		Seamless tube		0.051	7.898	1.498	201	480	698	1,660	2,420	5,770
	8.625	160		0.906	6.813	25.84	137	326	473	1,130	1,640	3,910
		140		0.812	7.001	23.44	147	350	508	1,210	1,760	4,200
		120		0.718	7.189	20.97	157	375	545	1,300	1,890	4,510
		100		0.593	7.439	17.60	172	410	596	1,420	2,070	4,930
		80	XS	0.500	7.625	15.01	184	438	636	1,520	2,210	5,260
		60		0.406	7.813	12.33	196	467	679	1,620	2,350	5,610
		40	S	0.322	7.981	9.878	207	494	718	1,710	2,490	5,930
		30		0.277	8.071	8.543	213	508	739	1,760	2,560	6,110
		20		0.250	8.125	7.735	217	517	752	1,790	2,610	6,220
		10		0.148	8.329	4.635	232	552	803	1,910	2,780	6,640
		5		0.109	8.407	3.429	237	566	823	1,960	2,850	6,800

Notes:

(1) * Schedule Numbers and Weight Classes:
column a = Schedule numbers from ANSI Standard B36.10 for Steel Pipe. Schedule numbers can be 10, 20, 30, 40, 60, 80, 100, 120, 140, or 160.
column b = Weight classes from ANSI Standard B36.10 for Steel Pipe Wall Thickness. Weight classes are Standard Wall (S) or Extra-Strong Wall (XS).
Extra-Heavy-Wall is sometimes known as Extra-Heavy-Wall.

(2) ** Based on a density of 169.344 pounds per cubic foot for 6061, 6062, and 6063 aluminum.

(3) Diameter and wall thickness data from: ASTM Designation B 429 - 95; ASM Metals Reference Book, Third Edition, ASM International, 1997; Aluminum Data Book, Reynolds Metals Company, 1965; Alaskan Copper and Brass Company, Seattle, WA Central Steel and Wire Company, Chicago, IL

Brass Pipe and Tube - Properties and Friction Loss

Nominal or Standard Pipe Size	Outside Diameter	Pipe or Tube Designation	Wall Thickness	Inside Diameter	Theoretical Weight Per Foot	Theoretical Flow Rate (Gallons per Minute) Which Will Cause A Head Loss (H_f) In 100 Feet of Pipe					
						H_f					
						0.1	0.5	1.0	5.0	10.0	50.0
(inch)	(inch)		(inch)	(inch)	(pound)	(feet)	(feet)	(feet)	(feet)	(feet)	(feet)
1/8	0.125	Seamless tube	0.016	0.093	0.0202	0.002	0.004	0.006	0.014	0.020	0.049
			0.020	0.085	0.0243	0.001	0.003	0.005	0.011	0.016	0.038
			0.025	0.075	0.0289	0.001	0.002	0.003	0.008	0.012	0.028
			0.030	0.065	0.0330	0.001	0.002	0.002	0.005	0.008	0.019
			0.032	0.061	0.0344	0.001	0.001	0.002	0.005	0.007	0.016
	0.405	Regular Pipe	0.062	0.281	0.2533	0.031	0.074	0.108	0.258	0.375	0.893
		Ex. Hvy/Ex. Strong	0.100	0.205	0.3633	0.014	0.032	0.047	0.112	0.163	0.390
5/32	0.15625	Seamless tube	0.016	0.12425	0.0260	0.004	0.009	0.013	0.030	0.044	0.104
			0.020	0.11625	0.0315	0.003	0.007	0.011	0.025	0.037	0.088
			0.025	0.10625	0.0380	0.002	0.006	0.008	0.020	0.029	0.069
			0.030	0.09625	0.0438	0.002	0.004	0.006	0.015	0.022	0.053
			0.032	0.09225	0.0460	0.002	0.004	0.006	0.014	0.020	0.048
			0.040	0.07625	0.0538	0.001	0.002	0.003	0.008	0.012	0.029
3/16	0.1875	Seamless tube	0.016	0.1555	0.0318	0.007	0.016	0.023	0.054	0.079	0.188
			0.020	0.1475	0.0388	0.006	0.014	0.020	0.047	0.069	0.164
			0.025	0.1375	0.0470	0.005	0.011	0.016	0.039	0.057	0.136
			0.030	0.1275	0.0547	0.004	0.009	0.014	0.032	0.047	0.112
			0.032	0.1235	0.0576	0.004	0.009	0.012	0.030	0.043	0.103
			0.040	0.1075	0.0683	0.002	0.006	0.009	0.021	0.030	0.071
			0.050	0.0875	0.0796	0.001	0.003	0.005	0.012	0.017	0.042

Nominal or Standard Pipe Size (inch)	Outside Diameter (inch)	Pipe or Tube Designation	Wall Thickness (inch)	Inside Diameter (inch)	Theoretical Weight Per Foot (pound)	Theoretical Flow Rate (Gallons per Minute) Which Will Cause A Head Loss (H_f) In 100 Feet of Pipe					
						H_f					
						0.1 (feet)	0.5 (feet)	1.0 (feet)	5.0 (feet)	10.0 (feet)	50.0 (feet)
7/32	0.21875	Seamless tube	0.020	0.17875	0.0460	0.009	0.023	0.033	0.078	0.114	0.272
			0.025	0.16875	0.0561	0.008	0.019	0.028	0.067	0.098	0.234
			0.032	0.15875	0.0655	0.007	0.017	0.024	0.057	0.083	0.199
			0.032	0.15475	0.0692	0.006	0.015	0.023	0.054	0.078	0.186
			0.040	0.13875	0.0828	0.005	0.012	0.017	0.040	0.059	0.140
			0.050	0.11875	0.0977	0.003	0.008	0.011	0.027	0.039	0.093
1/4	0.250	Seamless tube	0.020	0.210	0.0532	0.014	0.035	0.050	0.120	0.174	0.415
			0.025	0.200	0.0651	0.013	0.030	0.044	0.105	0.153	0.365
			0.028	0.194	0.0719	0.012	0.028	0.041	0.097	0.141	0.337
			0.030	0.190	0.0764	0.011	0.027	0.039	0.092	0.134	0.319
			0.032	0.186	0.0807	0.011	0.025	0.037	0.087	0.127	0.302
			0.040	0.170	0.0972	0.008	0.020	0.029	0.069	0.100	0.238
			0.051	0.148	0.1175	0.006	0.014	0.020	0.048	0.069	0.165
			0.060	0.130	0.1320	0.004	0.010	0.014	0.034	0.049	0.118
			0.065	0.120	0.1392	0.003	0.008	0.012	0.027	0.040	0.095
	0.540	Regular Pipe	0.082	0.376	0.4474	0.067	0.160	0.232	0.554	0.806	1.92
		Ex. Hvy/Ex. Strong	0.123	0.294	0.6110	0.035	0.084	0.122	0.290	0.422	1.01
5/16	0.3125	Seamless Tube	0.020	0.2725	0.0677	0.035	0.069	0.100	0.238	0.346	0.824
			0.025	0.2625	0.0832	0.026	0.062	0.090	0.215	0.313	0.747
			0.030	0.2525	0.0981	0.024	0.056	0.082	0.194	0.283	0.674
			0.032	0.2485	0.1039	0.023	0.054	0.078	0.186	0.271	0.647
			0.040	0.2325	0.1262	0.019	0.045	0.066	0.157	0.228	0.543

Brass Pipe and Tube - Properties and Friction Loss (cont.)

Nominal or Standard Pipe Size	Outside Diameter	Pipe or Tube Designation	Wall Thickness	Inside Diameter	Theoretical Weight Per Foot	Theoretical Flow Rate (Gallons per Minute) Which Will Cause A Head Loss (H_f) In 100 Feet of Pipe					
						H_f					
						0.1	0.5	1.0	5.0	10.0	50.0
(inch)	(inch)		(inch)	(inch)	(pound)	(feet)	(feet)	(feet)	(feet)	(feet)	(feet)
5/16	0.3125	Seamless tube	0.051	0.2105	0.1544	0.015	0.035	0.051	0.121	0.175	0.418
			0.058	0.1965	0.1710	0.012	0.029	0.042	0.101	0.146	0.349
			0.065	0.1825	0.1862	0.010	0.024	0.035	0.083	0.120	0.287
			0.070	0.1725	0.1960	0.009	0.021	0.030	0.071	0.104	0.248
			0.078	0.1563	0.2120	0.007	0.016	0.023	0.055	0.080	0.191
			0.080	0.1525	0.2150	0.006	0.015	0.022	0.052	0.075	0.179
			0.091	0.1305	0.2333	0.004	0.010	0.014	0.034	0.050	0.119
			0.020	0.335	0.0822	0.049	0.118	0.172	0.409	0.595	1.42
			0.025	0.325	0.1013	0.046	0.109	0.158	0.378	0.549	1.31
			0.030	0.315	0.1200	0.042	0.100	0.146	0.348	0.506	1.21
			0.032	0.311	0.1270	0.041	0.097	0.141	0.336	0.489	1.17
			0.035	0.305	0.1377	0.039	0.092	0.134	0.320	0.465	1.11
			0.040	0.295	0.1551	0.035	0.084	0.123	0.293	0.426	1.02
3/8	0.375	Seamless tube	0.045	0.285	0.1720	0.032	0.077	0.112	0.267	0.389	0.927
			0.051	0.273	0.1912	0.029	0.069	0.100	0.239	0.347	0.828
			0.058	0.259	0.2128	0.025	0.060	0.087	0.208	0.302	0.721
			0.065	0.245	0.2332	0.022	0.052	0.075	0.180	0.261	0.623
			0.072	0.231	0.2525	0.019	0.044	0.065	0.154	0.224	0.534
			0.078	0.219	0.2680	0.016	0.038	0.056	0.133	0.194	0.462
			0.081	0.213	0.2756	0.015	0.036	0.052	0.124	0.181	0.431
			0.091	0.193	0.2991	0.012	0.028	0.040	0.096	0.139	0.333

Nominal or Standard Pipe Size (inch)	Outside Diameter (inch)	Pipe or Tube Designation	Wall Thickness (inch)	Inside Diameter (inch)	Theoretical Weight Per Foot (pound)	Theoretical Flow Rate (Gallons per Minute) Which Will Cause A Head Loss (H_f) In 100 Feet of Pipe					
						H_f					
						0.1 (feet)	0.5 (feet)	1.0 (feet)	5.0 (feet)	10.0 (feet)	50.0 (feet)
3/8	0.675	Regular Pipe	0.090	0.495	0.6272	0.138	0.329	0.479	1.14	1.66	3.96
		Ex. Heavy/Ex. Strong Pipe	0.127	0.421	0.8291	0.090	0.215	0.313	0.746	1.08	2.59
7/16	0.4375	Seamless tube	0.020	0.3975	0.0966	0.078	0.185	0.269	0.641	0.933	2.22
			0.025	0.3875	0.1194	0.073	0.173	0.252	0.600	0.872	2.08
			0.030	0.3775	0.1410	0.068	0.162	0.235	0.560	0.814	1.94
			0.032	0.3735	0.1502	0.066	0.157	0.228	0.545	0.792	1.89
			0.040	0.3575	0.1840	0.059	0.140	0.204	0.485	0.706	1.68
			0.045	0.3475	0.2040	0.054	0.130	0.189	0.450	0.655	1.56
			0.051	0.3355	0.2281	0.050	0.118	0.172	0.411	0.597	1.42
			0.060	0.3175	0.2620	0.043	0.102	0.149	0.355	0.517	1.23
			0.065	0.3075	0.2802	0.039	0.094	0.137	0.327	0.475	1.13
			0.070	0.2975	0.2980	0.036	0.086	0.126	0.299	0.435	1.04
			0.081	0.2755	0.3342	0.030	0.071	0.103	0.245	0.356	0.848
1/2	0.500	Seamless tube	0.020	0.460	0.1111	0.114	0.272	0.395	0.942	1.37	3.27
			0.025	0.450	0.1374	0.108	0.256	0.373	0.889	1.29	3.08
			0.030	0.440	0.1630	0.101	0.242	0.351	0.838	1.22	2.91
			0.032	0.436	0.1733	0.099	0.236	0.343	0.818	1.19	2.84
			0.035	0.430	0.1884	0.095	0.227	0.331	0.789	1.15	2.73
			0.040	0.420	0.2130	0.090	0.214	0.311	0.741	1.08	2.57
			0.045	0.410	0.2370	0.084	0.201	0.292	0.696	1.01	2.41
			0.051	0.398	0.2650	0.078	0.186	0.270	0.644	0.936	2.23
			0.060	0.380	0.3060	0.069	0.164	0.239	0.570	0.829	1.98

Brass Pipe and Tube - Properties and Friction Loss (cont.)

Nominal or Standard Pipe Size (inch)	Outside Diameter (inch)	Pipe or Tube Designation	Wall Thickness (inch)	Inside Diameter (inch)	Theoretical Weight Per Foot (pound)	Theoretical Flow Rate (Gallons per Minute) Which Will Cause A Head Loss (H_f) In 100 Feet of Pipe					
						H_f					
						0.1 (feet)	0.5 (feet)	1.0 (feet)	5.0 (feet)	10.0 (feet)	50.0 (feet)
1/2	0.500	Seamless tube	0.065	0.370	0.3272	0.064	0.153	0.223	0.531	0.772	1.84
			0.070	0.360	0.3480	0.060	0.143	0.207	0.494	0.719	1.71
			0.081	0.338	0.3928	0.051	0.121	0.176	0.419	0.609	1.45
			0.091	0.318	0.4308	0.043	0.103	0.150	0.357	0.519	1.24
			0.100	0.300	0.4630	0.037	0.088	0.128	0.306	0.445	1.06
			0.120	0.260	0.5280	0.025	0.061	0.088	0.210	0.305	0.728
			0.128	0.244	0.5511	0.021	0.051	0.075	0.178	0.258	0.616
	0.840	Regular Pipe	0.107	0.626	0.9343	0.256	0.611	0.888	2.12	3.08	7.34
		Ex. Heavy/Ex. Strong Pipe	0.149	0.542	1.227	0.175	0.418	0.608	1.45	2.11	5.03
		Double Extra Heavy	0.294	0.252	1.910	0.023	0.056	0.081	0.193	0.281	0.671
9/16	0.5625	Seamless tube	0.025	0.5125	0.1555	0.151	0.361	0.525	1.25	1.82	4.34
			0.032	0.4985	0.1965	0.141	0.336	0.488	1.16	1.69	4.03
			0.040	0.4825	0.2420	0.129	0.308	0.448	1.07	1.55	3.70
			0.051	0.4605	0.3019	0.114	0.272	0.396	0.945	1.37	3.28
			0.065	0.4325	0.3743	0.097	0.231	0.336	0.801	1.16	2.78
			0.080	0.4025	0.4470	0.080	0.191	0.278	0.663	0.964	2.30
			0.090	0.3825	0.4920	0.070	0.167	0.243	0.580	0.843	2.01
			0.100	0.3625	0.5350	0.061	0.145	0.211	0.503	0.732	1.75
			0.120	0.3225	0.6150	0.045	0.107	0.155	0.370	0.538	1.28
			0.128	0.3065	0.6437	0.039	0.093	0.136	0.324	0.471	1.12

Handyman In~Your~Pocket

Nominal or Standard Pipe Size	Outside Diameter	Pipe or Tube Designation	Wall Thickness	Inside Diameter	Theoretical Weight Per Foot	Theoretical Flow Rate (Gallons per Minute) Which Will Cause A Head Loss (H_f) In 100 Feet of Pipe					
						H_f					
						0.1	0.5	1.0	5.0	10.0	50.0
(inch)	(inch)		(inch)	(inch)	(pound)	(feet)	(feet)	(feet)	(feet)	(feet)	(feet)
5/8	0.625	Seamless tube	0.020	0.585	0.1400	0.214	0.511	0.743	1.77	2.58	6.15
			0.025	0.575	0.1736	0.205	0.488	0.710	1.69	2.46	5.87
			0.028	0.569	0.1935	0.199	0.475	0.691	1.65	2.40	5.71
			0.030	0.565	0.2070	0.196	0.466	0.678	1.62	2.35	5.61
			0.032	0.561	0.2196	0.192	0.458	0.666	1.59	2.31	5.50
			0.035	0.555	0.2390	0.187	0.445	0.647	1.54	2.24	5.35
			0.040	0.545	0.2708	0.178	0.424	0.617	1.47	2.14	5.10
			0.045	0.535	0.3020	0.169	0.404	0.588	1.40	2.04	4.86
			0.051	0.523	0.3388	0.160	0.381	0.554	1.32	1.92	4.58
			0.058	0.509	0.3806	0.149	0.354	0.515	1.23	1.79	4.26
			0.060	0.505	0.3920	0.146	0.347	0.505	1.20	1.75	4.17
			0.065	0.495	0.4213	0.138	0.329	0.479	1.14	1.66	3.96
			0.078	0.469	0.4940	0.120	0.285	0.415	0.990	1.44	3.43
			0.081	0.463	0.5100	0.116	0.276	0.402	0.958	1.39	3.32
			0.091	0.443	0.5624	0.103	0.246	0.358	0.853	1.24	2.96
			0.100	0.425	0.6080	0.093	0.221	0.321	0.765	1.11	2.65
			0.120	0.385	0.7010	0.071	0.170	0.247	0.590	0.858	2.05
			0.128	0.369	0.7363	0.064	0.152	0.221	0.527	0.767	1.83
11/16	0.6875	Seamless Tube	0.020	0.6475	0.1545	0.280	0.668	0.971	2.31	3.37	8.03
			0.025	0.6375	0.1917	0.269	0.641	0.932	2.22	3.23	7.70
			0.028	0.6315	0.2140	0.262	0.625	0.909	2.17	3.15	7.51
			0.032	0.6235	0.2428	0.253	0.604	0.879	2.10	3.05	7.27

Brass Pipe and Tube - Properties and Friction Loss (cont.)

Nominal or Standard Pipe Size	Outside Diameter	Pipe or Tube Designation	Wall Thickness	Inside Diameter	Theoretical Weight Per Foot	Theoretical Flow Rate (Gallons per Minute) Which Will Cause A Head Loss (H_f) In 100 Feet of Pipe					
						H_f					
						0.1	0.5	1.0	5.0	10.0	50.0
(inch)	(inch)		(inch)	(inch)	(pound)	(feet)	(feet)	(feet)	(feet)	(feet)	(feet)
11/16	0.6875	Seamless tube	0.040	0.6075	0.2998	0.237	0.564	0.821	1.96	2.85	6.79
			0.050	0.5875	0.3690	0.217	0.517	0.752	1.79	2.61	6.21
			0.060	0.5675	0.4360	0.198	0.472	0.686	1.64	2.38	5.67
			0.065	0.5575	0.4683	0.189	0.450	0.655	1.56	2.27	5.41
			0.080	0.5275	0.5620	0.163	0.389	0.566	1.35	1.96	4.68
			0.090	0.5075	0.6220	0.147	0.352	0.511	1.22	1.77	4.23
			0.100	0.4875	0.6800	0.133	0.316	0.460	1.10	1.60	3.80
			0.120	0.4475	0.7880	0.106	0.253	0.367	0.876	1.27	3.04
			0.128	0.4315	0.8289	0.096	0.230	0.334	0.796	1.16	2.76
3/4	0.750	Seamless tube	0.025	0.700	0.2098	0.344	0.819	1.19	2.84	4.13	9.85
			0.028	0.694	0.2340	0.336	0.801	1.16	2.78	4.04	9.63
			0.030	0.690	0.2500	0.331	0.789	1.15	2.74	3.98	9.49
			0.032	0.686	0.2659	0.326	0.777	1.13	2.69	3.92	9.34
			0.040	0.670	0.3287	0.306	0.730	1.06	2.53	3.68	8.78
			0.047	0.656	0.3820	0.290	0.692	1.01	2.40	3.49	8.31
			0.051	0.648	0.4126	0.280	0.669	0.973	2.32	3.37	8.04
			0.060	0.630	0.4790	0.260	0.621	0.903	2.15	3.13	7.47
			0.065	0.620	0.5153	0.250	0.596	0.866	2.07	3.00	7.16
			0.070	0.610	0.5510	0.239	0.571	0.830	1.98	2.88	6.86
			0.081	0.588	0.6272	0.217	0.518	0.753	1.80	2.61	6.23
			0.091	0.568	0.6941	0.198	0.473	0.688	1.64	2.38	5.69

Nominal or Standard Pipe Size	Outside Diameter	Pipe or Tube Designation	Wall Thickness	Inside Diameter	Theoretical Weight Per Foot	Theoretical Flow Rate (Gallons per Minute) Which Will Cause A Head Loss (H_f) In 100 Feet of Pipe					
						H_f					
						50.0	10.0	5.0	1.0	0.5	0.1
(inch)	(inch)		(inch)	(inch)	(pound)	(feet)	(feet)	(feet)	(feet)	(feet)	(feet)
3/4	0.750	Seamless tube	0.100	0.550	0.7520	5.22	2.19	1.51	0.632	0.435	0.182
			0.120	0.510	0.8750	4.28	1.80	1.24	0.518	0.356	0.149
			0.128	0.494	0.9215	3.94	1.65	1.14	0.476	0.328	0.137
	1.050	Regular Pipe	0.114	0.822	1.271	15.0	6.30	4.34	1.82	1.25	0.524
		Ex. Heavy/Ex. Strong Pipe	0.157	0.736	1.670	11.2	4.71	3.24	1.36	0.935	0.392
		Double Extra Heavy	0.308	0.434	2.720	2.80	1.18	0.808	0.339	0.233	0.098
13/16	0.8125	Seamless tube	0.025	0.7625	0.2279	12.3	5.17	3.56	1.49	1.03	0.430
			0.028	0.7565	0.2540	12.1	5.07	3.48	1.46	1.01	0.421
			0.032	0.7485	0.2891	11.8	4.93	3.39	1.42	0.977	0.410
			0.035	0.7425	0.3150	11.5	4.82	3.32	1.39	0.957	0.401
			0.040	0.7325	0.3580	11.1	4.66	3.20	1.34	0.923	0.387
			0.045	0.7225	0.4000	10.7	4.49	3.09	1.29	0.891	0.373
			0.050	0.7125	0.4410	10.3	4.33	2.98	1.25	0.859	0.360
			0.060	0.6925	0.5230	9.58	4.02	2.76	1.16	0.797	0.334
			0.065	0.6825	0.5623	9.22	3.87	2.66	1.11	0.767	0.321
7/8	0.875	Seamless tube	0.020	0.835	0.1979	15.7	6.57	4.52	1.89	1.30	0.546
			0.025	0.825	0.2459	15.2	6.36	4.38	1.84	1.26	0.529
			0.032	0.811	0.3122	14.5	6.08	4.18	1.75	1.21	0.506
			0.040	0.795	0.3866	13.8	5.77	3.97	1.67	1.15	0.480
			0.050	0.775	0.4770	13.9	5.40	3.71	1.56	1.07	0.449
			0.065	0.745	0.6094	11.6	4.87	3.35	1.40	0.965	0.405

Brass Pipe and Tube - Properties and Friction Loss (cont.)

Nominal or Standard Pipe Size	Outside Diameter	Pipe or Tube Designation	Wall Thickness	Inside Diameter	Theoretical Weight Per Foot	Theoretical Flow Rate (Gallons per Minute) Which Will Cause A Head Loss (Hf) In 100 Feet of Pipe					
									Hf		
(inch)	(inch)		(inch)	(inch)	(pound)	0.1 (feet)	0.5 (feet)	1.0 (feet)	5.0 (feet)	10.0 (feet)	50.0 (feet)
7/8	0.875	Seamless Tube	0.080	0.715	0.7360	0.363	0.866	1.26	3.00	4.37	10.4
			0.091	0.693	0.8257	0.335	0.798	1.16	2.77	4.02	9.60
			0.100	0.675	0.8970	0.312	0.745	1.08	2.58	3.75	8.95
			0.120	0.635	1.050	0.266	0.634	0.922	2.20	3.20	7.62
			0.128	0.619	1.107	0.249	0.593	0.862	2.06	2.99	7.13
15/16	0.9375	Seamless tube	0.032	0.8735	0.3354	0.615	1.47	2.13	5.09	7.40	17.6
			0.040	0.8575	0.4150	0.586	1.40	2.03	4.85	7.05	16.8
			0.050	0.8375	0.5140	0.551	1.31	1.91	4.55	6.62	15.8
			0.060	0.8175	0.6090	0.517	1.23	1.79	4.27	6.21	14.8
			0.065	0.8075	0.6564	0.500	1.19	1.73	4.14	6.02	14.3
			0.070	0.7975	0.7030	0.484	1.15	1.68	4.00	5.82	13.9
			0.080	0.7775	0.7940	0.453	1.08	1.57	3.75	5.45	13.0
			0.090	0.7575	0.8830	0.423	1.01	1.47	3.50	5.08	12.1
			0.100	0.7375	0.9690	0.394	0.940	1.37	3.26	4.74	11.3
			0.120	0.6975	1.140	0.340	0.812	1.18	2.81	4.09	9.76
			0.128	0.6815	1.199	0.320	0.764	1.11	2.65	3.85	9.18
1	1.000	Seamless Tube	0.020	0.960	0.2268	0.789	1.88	2.73	6.52	9.48	22.6
			0.025	0.950	0.2821	0.767	1.83	2.66	6.34	9.22	22.0
			0.032	0.936	0.3585	0.738	1.76	2.56	6.10	8.87	21.2
			0.040	0.920	0.4444	0.705	1.68	2.44	5.83	8.48	20.2
			0.045	0.910	0.4970	0.685	1.63	2.38	5.67	8.24	19.6

Nominal or Standard Pipe Size	Outside Diameter	Pipe or Tube Designation	Wall Thickness	Inside Diameter	Theoretical Weight Per Foot	Theoretical Flow Rate (Gallons per Minute) Which Will Cause A Head Loss (H_f) In 100 Feet					
						0.1	0.5	1.0	5.0	10.0	50.0
(inch)	(inch)		(inch)	(inch)	(pound)	(feet)	(feet)	(feet)	(feet)	(feet)	(feet)
1	1.000	Seamless tube	0.051	0.898	0.5602	0.662	1.58	2.29	5.47	7.95	19.0
			0.060	0.880	0.6530	0.627	1.50	2.18	5.19	7.54	18.0
			0.065	0.870	0.7034	0.609	1.45	2.11	5.03	7.32	17.5
			0.070	0.860	0.7530	0.590	1.41	2.05	4.88	7.10	16.9
			0.080	0.840	0.8520	0.555	1.32	1.92	4.59	6.67	15.9
			0.091	0.818	0.9574	0.518	1.23	1.79	4.28	6.22	14.8
			0.100	0.800	1.040	0.488	1.16	1.69	4.04	5.87	14.0
			0.120	0.760	1.220	0.427	1.02	1.48	3.53	5.13	12.2
			0.128	0.744	1.292	0.403	0.962	1.40	3.34	4.85	11.6
	1.315	Regular Pipe	0.126	1.063	1.785	1.03	2.46	3.57	8.53	12.4	29.6
		Ex. Heavy/Ex. Strong Pipe	0.182	0.951	2.457	0.769	1.83	2.67	6.36	9.25	22.1
		Double Extra Hvy	0.358	0.599	4.080	0.228	0.544	0.791	1.89	2.74	6.54
1-1/16	1.0625	Seamless tube	0.025	1.0125	0.3002	0.907	2.16	3.15	7.50	10.9	26.0
			0.032	0.9985	0.3817	0.875	2.09	3.03	7.23	10.5	25.1
			0.040	0.9825	0.4730	0.838	2.00	2.91	6.93	10.1	24.0
			0.050	0.9625	0.5860	0.794	1.89	2.75	6.57	9.55	22.8
			0.065	0.9325	0.7504	0.731	1.74	2.53	6.04	8.78	20.9
			0.080	0.9025	0.9100	0.670	1.60	2.32	5.54	8.06	19.2
			0.090	0.8825	1.010	0.632	1.51	2.19	5.23	7.60	18.1
			0.100	0.8625	1.110	0.595	1.42	2.06	4.92	7.15	17.1
			0.120	0.8225	1.310	0.525	1.25	1.82	4.34	6.31	15.1
			0.128	0.8065	1.384	0.499	1.19	1.73	4.12	6.00	14.3

Brass Pipe and Tube - Properties and Friction Loss (cont.)

Nominal or Standard Pipe Size	Outside Diameter	Pipe or Tube Designation	Wall Thickness	Inside Diameter	Theoretical Weight Per Foot	Theoretical Flow Rate (Gallons per Minute) Which Will Cause A Head Loss (H_f) In 100 Feet of Pipe					
						\(H_f\)					
						0.1	0.5	1.0	5.0	10.0	50.0
(inch)	(inch)		(inch)	(inch)	(pound)	(feet)	(feet)	(feet)	(feet)	(feet)	(feet)
1-1/8	1.125	Seamless tube	0.032	1.061	0.4048	1.03	2.45	3.56	8.48	12.3	29.4
			0.040	1.045	0.5023	0.986	2.35	3.42	8.15	11.9	28.3
			0.050	1.025	0.6220	0.937	2.23	3.25	7.75	11.3	26.9
			0.065	0.995	0.7974	0.866	2.07	3.00	7.16	10.4	24.8
			0.080	0.965	0.9680	0.799	1.91	2.77	6.61	9.61	22.9
			0.090	0.945	1.080	0.757	1.80	2.62	6.26	9.10	21.7
			0.100	0.925	1.190	0.715	1.71	2.48	5.91	8.60	20.5
			0.120	0.885	1.400	0.637	1.52	2.21	5.26	7.66	18.3
			0.128	0.869	1.477	0.607	1.45	2.10	5.02	7.30	17.4
1-3/16	1.1875	Seamless tube	0.032	1.1235	0.4279	1.19	2.84	4.14	9.86	14.3	34.2
			0.040	1.1075	0.5310	1.15	2.74	3.98	9.50	13.8	32.9
			0.050	1.0875	0.6580	1.09	2.61	3.80	9.05	13.2	31.4
			0.065	1.0575	0.8444	1.02	2.43	3.53	8.41	12.2	29.2
			0.080	1.0275	1.030	0.943	2.25	3.27	7.80	11.3	27.0
			0.090	1.0075	1.140	0.895	2.14	3.10	7.40	10.8	25.7
			0.100	0.9875	1.260	0.849	2.03	2.95	7.02	10.2	24.4
			0.120	0.9475	1.480	0.762	1.82	2.64	6.30	9.16	21.8
			0.128	0.9315	1.570	0.729	1.74	2.53	6.02	8.76	20.9
1/1/4	1.250	Seamless tube	0.025	1.200	0.3544	1.42	3.38	4.92	11.7	17.1	40.7
			0.032	1.186	0.4511	1.38	3.28	4.77	11.4	16.5	39.4
			0.045	1.160	0.6280	1.30	3.09	4.50	10.7	15.6	37.2

Nominal or Standard Pipe Size	Outside Diameter	Pipe or Tube Designation	Wall Thickness	Inside Diameter	Theoretical Weight Per Foot	Theoretical Flow Rate (Gallons per Minute) Which Will Cause A Head Loss (H_f) in 100 Feet of Pipe					
						H_f					
						0.1	0.5	1.0	5.0	10.0	50.0
(inch)	(inch)		(inch)	(inch)	(pound)	(feet)	(feet)	(feet)	(feet)	(feet)	(feet)
1-1/4	1.250	Seamless tube	0.051	1.148	0.7077	1.26	3.01	4.38	10.4	15.2	36.2
			0.065	1.120	0.8915	1.18	2.82	4.10	9.78	14.2	33.9
			0.080	1.090	1.080	1.10	2.63	3.82	9.11	13.2	31.6
			0.100	1.050	1.330	1.00	2.38	3.46	8.25	12.0	28.6
			0.120	1.010	1.570	0.901	2.15	3.13	7.45	10.8	25.8
			0.128	0.994	1.662	0.864	2.06	3.00	7.15	10.4	24.8
	1.660	Regular Pipe	0.146	1.368	2.633	2.00	4.77	6.94	16.6	24.1	57.4
		Ex. Heavy/Ex. Strong Pipe	0.194	1.272	3.388	1.65	3.94	5.73	13.7	19.9	47.4
		Double Extra Hvy	0.382	0.896	5.820	0.658	1.57	2.28	5.44	7.91	18.9
1-5/16	1.3125	Seamless tube	0.032	1.249	0.4742	1.57	3.75	5.46	13.0	18.9	45.1
			0.040	1.233	0.5890	1.52	3.63	5.28	12.6	18.3	43.6
			0.050	1.213	0.7310	1.46	3.48	5.05	12.1	17.5	41.8
1-3/8	1.375	Seamless tube	0.032	1.311	0.4974	1.79	4.27	6.21	14.8	21.5	51.3
			0.045	1.285	0.6930	1.70	4.05	5.89	14.0	20.4	48.7
			0.051	1.273	0.7815	1.66	3.95	5.74	13.7	19.9	47.5
			0.065	1.245	0.9855	1.56	3.73	5.42	12.9	18.8	44.8
			0.080	1.215	1.200	1.47	3.49	5.08	12.1	17.6	42.0
			0.100	1.175	1.480	1.34	3.20	4.65	11.1	16.1	38.5
			0.120	1.135	1.740	1.22	2.92	4.25	10.1	14.7	35.1
			0.128	1.119	1.847	1.18	2.81	4.09	9.76	14.2	33.8
1-1/2	1.50	Seamless Tube	0.025	1.450	0.4268	2.33	5.56	8.09	19.3	28.0	66.9
			0.032	1.436	0.5437	2.27	5.42	7.89	18.8	27.3	65.2

Brass Pipe and Tube - Properties and Friction Loss (cont.)

Nominal or Standard Pipe Size	Outside Diameter	Pipe or Tube Designation	Wall Thickness	Inside Diameter	Theoretical Weight Per Foot	Theoretical Flow Rate (Gallons per Minute) Which Will Cause A Head Loss (H_f) In 100 Feet of Pipe					
						0.1	0.5	1.0 H_f	5.0	10.0	50.0
(inch)	(inch)		(inch)	(inch)	(pound)	(feet)	(feet)	(feet)	(feet)	(feet)	(feet)
1-1/2	1.500	Seamless tube	0.035	1.430	0.5934	2.25	5.36	7.80	18.6	27.0	64.5
			0.040	1.420	0.6759	2.21	5.27	7.66	18.3	26.5	63.3
			0.051	1.398	0.8553	2.12	5.05	7.35	17.5	25.5	60.8
			0.065	1.370	1.080	2.01	4.79	6.97	16.6	24.2	57.6
			0.080	1.340	1.310	1.90	4.52	6.57	15.7	22.8	54.4
			0.091	1.318	1.484	1.81	4.33	6.29	15.0	21.8	52.0
			0.100	1.300	1.620	1.75	4.17	6.07	14.5	21.0	50.2
			0.120	1.260	1.920	1.61	3.85	5.59	13.3	19.4	46.2
			0.128	1.244	2.033	1.56	3.72	5.41	12.9	18.7	44.7
	1.900	Regular Pipe	0.150	1.600	3.127	3.02	7.21	10.5	25.0	36.3	86.6
		Ex. Heavy/Ex. Strong Pipe	0.203	1.494	4.104	2.52	6.02	8.75	20.9	30.3	72.4
		Double Extra Heavy	0.400	1.100	7.150	1.13	2.69	3.91	9.33	13.6	32.3
1-5/8	1.625	Seamless tube	0.040	1.545	0.7338	2.76	6.57	9.56	22.8	33.1	79.0
			0.050	1.525	0.9110	2.66	6.35	9.24	22.0	32.0	76.4
			0.065	1.495	1.174	2.53	6.03	8.77	20.9	30.4	72.5
			0.080	1.465	1.430	2.40	5.72	8.31	19.8	28.8	68.7
			0.095	1.435	1.680	2.27	5.41	7.87	18.8	27.3	65.1
			0.120	1.385	2.090	2.07	4.93	7.17	17.1	24.9	59.3
			0.128	1.369	2.218	2.01	4.78	6.95	16.6	24.1	57.5

Nominal or Standard Pipe Size	Outside Diameter	Pipe or Tube Designation	Wall Thickness	Inside Diameter	Theoretical Weight Per Foot	Theoretical Flow Rate (Gallons per Minute) Which Will Cause A Head Loss (H_f) In 100 Feet of Pipe					
						H_f					
						0.1	0.5	1.0	5.0	10.0	50.0
(inch)	(inch)		(inch)	(inch)	(pound)	(feet)	(feet)	(feet)	(feet)	(feet)	(feet)
1-3/4	1.750	Seamless tube	0.032	1.686	0.6363	3.47	8.27	12.0	28.7	41.7	99.4
			0.040	1.670	0.7916	3.38	8.07	11.7	28.0	40.7	97.0
			0.051	1.648	1.003	3.27	7.79	11.3	27.0	39.3	93.7
			0.065	1.620	1.268	3.12	7.45	10.8	25.8	37.5	89.5
			0.090	1.570	1.730	2.88	6.86	10.0	23.8	34.6	82.4
			0.100	1.550	1.910	2.78	6.63	9.64	23.0	33.4	79.7
			0.120	1.510	2.260	2.60	6.19	9.00	21.5	31.2	74.4
			0.128	1.494	2.403	2.52	6.02	8.75	20.9	30.3	72.4
1-7/8	1.875	Seamless tube	0.032	1.811	0.6826	4.19	9.98	14.5	34.6	50.3	120
			0.045	1.785	0.9530	4.03	9.61	14.0	33.3	48.5	116
			0.065	1.745	1.362	3.80	9.05	13.2	31.4	45.6	109
			0.090	1.695	1.860	3.52	8.39	12.2	29.1	42.3	101
			0.100	1.675	2.050	3.41	8.13	11.8	28.2	41.0	97.7
			0.128	1.619	2.588	3.12	7.43	10.8	25.8	37.5	89.4
			0.140	1.595	2.810	3.00	7.15	10.4	24.8	36.0	85.9
			0.160	1.555	3.180	2.80	6.69	9.72	23.2	33.7	80.4
			0.187	1.501	3.662	2.55	6.09	8.86	21.1	30.7	73.3
2	2.000	Seamless tube	0.032	1.936	0.7289	4.99	11.9	17.3	41.3	60.0	143
			0.040	1.920	0.9070	4.88	11.6	16.9	40.4	58.7	140
			0.051	1.898	1.150	4.74	11.3	16.4	39.2	56.9	136
			0.065	1.870	1.456	4.55	10.9	15.8	37.7	54.8	131
			0.080	1.840	1.780	4.36	10.4	15.1	36.1	52.5	125

Brass Pipe and Tube - Properties and Friction Loss (cont.)

Nominal or Standard Pipe Size	Outside Diameter	Pipe or Tube Designation	Wall Thickness	Inside Diameter	Theoretical Weight Per Foot	Theoretical Flow Rate (Gallons per Minute) Which Will Cause A Head Loss (H_f) In 100 Feet of Pipe					
						0.1	0.5	1.0	5.0	10.0	50.0
(inch)	(inch)		(inch)	(inch)	(pound)	(feet)	(feet)	(feet)	(feet)	(feet)	(feet)
2	2.000	Seamless tube	0.100	1.800	2.200	4.12	9.82	14.3	34.1	49.5	118
			0.120	1.760	2.610	3.88	9.26	13.5	32.1	46.7	111
			0.128	1.744	2.773	3.79	9.04	13.1	31.3	45.6	109
	2.375	Regular Pipe	0.156	2.063	4.124	5.90	14.1	20.4	48.8	70.9	169
		Ex. Heavy/Ex. Strong Pipe	0.221	1.933	5.671	4.97	11.9	17.2	41.1	59.7	142
		Double Extra Hvy	0.436	1.503	10.07	2.56	6.11	8.89	21.2	30.8	73.5
2-1/8	2.125	Seamless tube	0.051	2.023	1.224	5.60	13.4	19.4	46.3	67.3	161
			0.065	1.995	1.550	5.40	12.9	18.7	44.6	64.9	155
			0.080	1.965	1.890	5.19	12.4	18.0	42.9	62.4	149
			0.100	1.925	2.340	4.92	11.7	17.0	40.6	59.1	141
			0.120	1.885	2.780	4.65	11.1	16.1	38.5	55.9	133
			0.128	1.869	2.958	4.55	10.8	15.8	37.6	54.7	130
			0.160	1.805	3.640	4.15	9.90	14.4	34.3	49.9	119
			0.187	1.751	4.205	3.83	9.14	13.3	31.7	46.1	110
2-1/4	2.250	Seamless tube	0.051	2.148	1.298	6.56	15.6	22.7	54.2	78.8	188
			0.065	2.120	1.644	6.34	15.1	22.0	52.4	76.2	182
			0.080	2.090	2.010	6.10	14.6	21.2	50.5	73.4	175
			0.100	2.050	2.490	5.80	13.8	20.1	48.0	69.7	166
			0.120	2.010	2.960	5.51	13.1	19.1	45.5	66.2	158
			0.128	1.994	3.144	5.39	12.9	18.7	44.6	64.8	155

Nominal or Standard Pipe Size	Outside Diameter	Pipe or Tube Designation	Wall Thickness	Inside Diameter	Theoretical Weight Per Foot	Theoretical Flow Rate (Gallons per Minute) Which Will Cause A Head Loss (H_f) In 100 Feet of Pipe					
						H_f					
						0.1	0.5	1.0	5.0	10.0	50.0
(inch)	(inch)		(inch)	(inch)	(pound)	(feet)	(feet)	(feet)	(feet)	(feet)	(feet)
2-3/8	2.375	Seamless tube	0.050	2.275	1.350	7.63	18.2	26.4	63.1	91.7	219
			0.065	2.245	1.738	7.37	17.6	25.5	60.9	88.5	211
			0.080	2.215	2.120	7.11	17.0	24.7	58.8	85.5	204
2-1/2	2.500	Seamless tube	0.065	2.370	1.832	8.49	20.3	29.4	70.2	102	244
			0.080	2.340	2.240	8.21	19.6	28.5	67.9	98.7	235
			0.100	2.300	2.780	7.85	18.7	27.2	64.9	94.4	225
			0.120	2.260	3.310	7.50	17.9	26.0	62.0	90.1	215
			0.128	2.244	3.514	7.36	17.5	25.5	60.8	88.4	211
			0.160	2.180	4.330	6.82	16.3	23.6	56.4	82.0	195
			0.180	2.140	4.830	6.49	15.5	22.5	53.7	78.1	186
			0.200	2.100	5.320	6.18	14.7	21.4	51.1	74.3	177
	2.875	Regular Pipe	0.187	2.501	5.988	9.78	23.3	33.9	80.9	118	281
		Ex. Heavy/Ex. Strong Pipe	0.280	2.315	8.656	7.98	19.0	27.7	66.0	96.0	229
		Double Extra Hvy	0.552	1.771	15.27	3.95	9.41	13.7	32.6	47.5	113

(1) Diameter, wall thickness, and weight data from:
ASTM Designations B 43 - 98 and B 587 - 97
Alaskan Copper and Brass Company, Seattle, WA.
Central Steel and Wire Company, Chicago, IL.
Pipe And Tube Bending Handbook, Copper & Brass Research Association, New York, NY.
(2) The abbreviation "Ex." means "Extra.""Hvy" means "Heavy."

Chlorinated Poly (Vinyl Chloride) (CPVC) Pipe -
Controlled On Outside Diameter - Properties And Friction Loss

Nominal Pipe Size	Outside Diameter	Dimension Ratio - (DR) or Schedule Number*	Minimum Wall Thickness	Inside Diameter	Theoretical Weight Per Foot*	Theoretical Flow Rate (Gallons per Minute) Which Will Cause A Head Loss (H_f) In 100 Feet of Pipe						
						0.1	0.5	1.0	5.0	10.0	50.0	
(inch)	(inch)		(inch)	(inch)	(pound)	(feet)	(feet)	(feet)	(feet)	(feet)	(feet)	
1/4	0.540	Schedule 80	0.119	0.302	0.10	0.038	0.090	0.131	0.311	0.453	1.08	
		Schedule 40	0.088	0.364	0.08	0.062	0.147	0.213	0.509	0.740	1.76	
		DR 11	0.060	0.420	0.06	0.090	0.214	0.311	0.741	1.08	2.57	
		DR 13.5	0.060	0.420	0.06	0.090	0.214	0.311	0.741	1.08	2.57	
3/8	0.675	Schedule 80	0.126	0.423	0.14	0.091	0.218	0.317	0.755	1.10	2.62	
		Schedule 40	0.091	0.493	0.11	0.137	0.326	0.474	1.13	1.64	3.92	
		DR 11	0.061	0.552	0.08	0.184	0.439	0.639	1.52	2.21	5.28	
		DR 13.5	0.060	0.555	0.08	0.187	0.445	0.647	1.54	2.24	5.35	
1/2	0.840	Schedule 80	0.147	0.546	0.21	0.179	0.426	0.620	1.48	2.15	5.13	
		Schedule 40	0.109	0.622	0.17	0.252	0.601	0.873	2.08	3.03	7.22	
		DR 11	0.076	0.687	0.12	0.327	0.781	1.14	2.71	3.94	9.39	
		DR 13.5	0.062	0.716	0.10	0.364	0.868	1.26	3.01	4.38	10.4	
3/4	1.050	Schedule 80	0.154	0.742	0.29	0.401	0.955	1.39	3.31	4.82	11.5	
		Schedule 40	0.113	0.824	0.22	0.528	1.26	1.83	4.36	6.34	15.1	
		DR 11	0.095	0.859	0.19	0.589	1.40	2.04	4.87	7.08	16.9	
		DR 13.5	0.078	0.894	0.16	0.655	1.56	2.27	5.41	7.87	18.8	
		DR 17	0.062	0.926	0.13	0.718	1.71	2.49	5.94	8.63	20.6	
		DR 21	0.060	0.930	0.12	0.725	1.73	2.52	6.00	8.72	20.8	

Nominal Pipe Size	Outside Diameter	Dimension Ratio - (DR) or Schedule Number*	Minimum Wall Thickness	Inside Diameter	Theoretical Weight** Per Foot*	Theoretical Flow Rate (Gallons per Minute) Which Will Cause A Head Loss (H_f) Per 100 Feet of Pipe					
						H_f					
(inch)	(inch)		(inch)	(inch)	(pound)	0.1 (feet)	0.5 (feet)	1.0 (feet)	5.0 (feet)	10.0 (feet)	50.0 (feet)
1	1.315	Schedule 80	0.179	0.957	0.43	0.782	1.87	2.71	6.47	9.40	22.4
		Schedule 40	0.133	1.049	0.33	1.00	2.37	3.45	8.23	12.0	28.5
		DR 11	0.120	1.076	0.30	1.06	2.54	3.69	8.80	12.8	30.5
		DR 13.5	0.097	1.120	0.25	1.18	2.82	4.10	9.79	14.2	33.9
		DR 17	0.077	1.160	0.20	1.30	3.10	4.50	10.7	15.6	37.2
		DR 21	0.063	1.190	0.16	1.39	3.31	4.81	11.5	16.7	39.8
		DR 26	0.060	1.195	0.16	1.40	3.35	4.86	11.6	16.9	40.2
1-1/4	1.660	Schedule 80	0.191	1.278	0.59	1.67	3.99	5.80	13.8	20.1	48.0
		DR 11	0.151	1.358	0.48	1.96	4.68	6.81	16.2	23.6	56.3
		Schedule 40	0.140	1.380	0.44	2.05	4.88	7.10	16.9	24.6	58.7
		DR 13.5	0.123	1.414	0.40	2.18	5.21	7.57	18.1	26.3	62.6
		DR 17	0.098	1.465	0.32	2.40	5.71	8.31	19.8	28.8	68.7
		DR 21	0.079	1.502	0.26	2.56	6.10	8.87	21.2	30.8	73.4
		DR 26	0.064	1.532	0.21	2.70	6.43	9.35	22.3	32.4	77.3
1-1/2	1.900	Schedule 80	0.200	1.500	0.71	2.55	6.08	8.84	21.1	30.7	73.1
		DR 11	0.173	1.555	0.62	2.80	6.68	9.71	23.2	33.7	80.3
		Schedule 40	0.145	1.610	0.53	3.07	7.33	10.7	25.4	36.9	88.0
		DR 13.5	0.141	1.619	0.52	3.12	7.43	10.8	25.8	37.5	89.3
		DR 17	0.112	1.676	0.42	3.42	8.15	11.8	28.3	41.1	98.0
		DR 21	0.090	1.719	0.34	3.65	8.70	12.7	30.2	43.9	105
		DR 26	0.073	1.754	0.28	3.85	9.18	13.3	31.8	46.3	110

Nominal Pipe Size (inch)	Outside Diameter (inch)	Dimension Ratio - (DR) or Schedule Number*	Minimum Wall Thickness (inch)	Inside Diameter (inch)	Theoretical Weight Per Foot* (pound)	Theoretical Flow Rate (Gallons per Minute) Which Will Cause A Head Loss (Ht) In 100 Feet of Pipe					
						0.1 (feet)	0.5 (feet)	1.0 (feet)	5.0 (feet)	10.0 (feet)	50.0 (feet)
2	2.375	Schedule 80	0.218	1.943	0.98	5.01	11.9	17.4	41.4	60.2	144
		DR 11	0.216	1.943	0.97	5.04	12.0	17.5	41.7	60.6	144
		DR 13.5	0.176	2.023	0.81	5.60	13.4	19.4	46.3	67.4	161
		Schedule 40	0.154	2.067	0.72	5.93	14.1	20.6	49.0	71.3	170
		DR 17	0.140	2.096	0.65	6.15	14.7	21.3	50.8	73.9	176
		DR 21	0.113	2.149	0.53	6.56	15.7	22.8	54.3	78.9	188
		DR 26	0.091	2.192	0.44	6.92	16.5	24.0	57.2	83.2	198
2-1/2	2.875	Schedule 80	0.276	2.323	1.5	8.06	19.2	27.9	66.6	96.9	231
		DR 11	0.261	2.352	1.4	8.33	19.9	28.9	68.9	100	239
		DR 13.5	0.213	2.449	1.2	9.26	22.1	32.1	76.6	111	265
		Schedule 40	0.203	2.469	1.1	9.46	22.6	32.8	78.2	114	271
		DR 17	0.169	2.537	1.0	10.2	24.2	35.2	84.0	122	291
		DR 21	0.137	2.601	0.78	10.8	25.9	37.6	89.7	130	311
		DR 26	0.111	2.654	0.64	11.4	27.3	39.7	94.6	137	328
3	3.500	DR 11	0.318	2.864	2.1	14.4	33.3	48.4	116	168	401
		Schedule 80	0.300	2.900	2.0	14.4	34.4	50.1	119	174	414
		DR 13.5	0.259	2.981	1.8	15.5	37.0	53.9	128	187	445
		Schedule 40	0.216	3.068	1.5	16.7	39.9	58.1	138	201	480
		DR 17	0.206	3.088	1.4	17.0	40.6	59.1	141	205	489
		DR 21	0.167	3.167	1.2	18.2	43.4	63.1	150	219	522
		DR 26	0.135	3.231	0.95	19.2	45.8	66.5	159	231	550
		DR 32.5	0.108	3.285	0.76	20.0	47.8	69.5	166	241	574

Chlorinated Poly (Vinyl Chloride) (CPVC) Pipe - Controlled On Outside Diameter (cont.)

Nominal Pipe Size	Outside Diameter	Dimension Ratio - (DR) or Schedule Number*	Minimum Wall Thickness	Inside Diameter	Theoretical Weight Per Foot**	Theoretical Flow Rate (Gallons per Minute) Which Will Cause A Head Loss (H$_f$) In 100 Feet of Pipe					
						H$_f$					
(inch)	(inch)		(inch)	(inch)	(pound)	0.1 (feet)	0.5 (feet)	1.0 (feet)	5.0 (feet)	10.0 (feet)	50.0 (feet)
3-1/2	4.000	DR 11	0.364	3.273	2.8	19.8	47.3	68.8	164	239	569
		Schedule 80	0.318	3.364	2.4	21.3	50.9	74.0	176	257	612
		DR 13.5	0.296	3.407	2.3	22.1	52.6	76.5	182	265	633
		DR 17	0.235	3.529	1.9	24.1	57.7	83.9	200	291	694
		Schedule 40	0.226	3.548	1.8	24.5	58.5	85.1	203	295	704
		DR 21	0.190	3.619	1.5	25.9	61.7	89.7	214	311	741
		DR 26	0.154	3.692	1.2	27.3	65.0	94.5	225	328	781
		DR 32.5	0.123	3.754	1.0	28.5	67.9	98.7	235	342	816
4	4.500	DR 11	0.409	3.682	3.5	27.1	64.5	93.8	224	325	776
		Schedule 80	0.337	3.826	2.9	29.9	71.4	104	247	360	858
		DR 13.5	0.333	3.833	2.9	30.1	71.7	104	249	362	862
		DR 17	0.265	3.971	2.3	33.0	78.7	114	273	397	946
		Schedule 40	0.237	4.026	2.1	34.2	81.6	119	283	411	981
		DR 21	0.214	4.071	1.9	35.2	84.1	122	291	424	1,010
		DR 26	0.173	4.154	1.6	37.2	88.6	129	307	447	1,070
		DR 32.5	0.138	4.223	1.3	38.8	92.5	135	321	467	1,110
5	5.000	DR 11	0.506	4.552	5.3	47.3	113	164	391	568	1,350
		DR 13.5	0.412	4.739	4.4	52.5	125	182	434	632	1,510
		Schedule 80	0.375	4.813	4.1	54.7	131	190	453	658	1,570
6	5.563	DR 17	0.327	4.909	3.6	57.6	137	200	477	693	1,650
		DR 21	0.265	5.033	2.9	61.6	147	213	509	740	1,770
		Schedule 40	0.258	5.047	2.9	62.0	148	215	513	746	1,780
		DR 26	0.214	5.135	2.4	64.9	155	225	537	780	1,860
		DR 32.5	0.171	5.221	1.9	67.8	162	235	560	815	1,940

Nominal Pipe Size	Outside Diameter	Dimension Ratio -(DR) or Schedule Number*	Minimum Wall Thickness	Inside Diameter	Theoretical Weight Per Foot **	Theoretical Flow Rate (Gallons per Minute) Which Will Cause A Head Loss (H$_f$) In 100 Feet of Pipe					
						H$_f$					
						0.1	0.5	1.0	5.0	10.0	50.0
(inch)	(inch)		(inch)	(inch)	(pound)	(feet)	(feet)	(feet)	(feet)	(feet)	(feet)
6	6.625	DR 11	0.602	5.420	7.6	74.8	178	259	619	900	2,150
		DR 13.5	0.491	5.644	6.3	83.2	198	288	688	1,000	2,390
		Schedule 80	0.432	5.761	5.6	87.8	209	305	726	1,060	2,520
		DR 17	0.390	5.846	5.1	91.3	218	316	755	1,100	2,620
		DR 21	0.315	5.994	4.2	97.5	232	338	806	1,170	2,790
		Schedule 40	0.280	6.065	3.7	101	240	349	831	1,210	2,880
		DR 26	0.255	6.115	3.4	103	245	356	850	1,240	2,950
		DR 32.5	0.204	6.217	2.7	107	256	372	887	1,290	3,080
8	8.625	DR 11	0.784	7.057	13	150	357	519	1,240	1,800	4,290
		DR 13.5	0.639	7.347	11	166	397	577	1,380	2,000	4,770
		DR 17	0.507	7.610	8.6	183	436	633	1,510	2,200	5,240
		Schedule 80	0.500	7.625	8.5	184	438	636	1,520	2,210	5,260
		DR 21	0.411	7.804	7.1	195	465	676	1,610	2,350	5,590
		DR 26	0.332	7.962	5.8	206	490	713	1,700	2,470	5,900
		Schedule 40	0.322	7.981	5.6	207	494	718	1,710	2,490	5,930
		DR 32.5	0.265	8.094	4.6	215	512	745	1,780	2,580	6,160

Notes:
(1) * Dimension Ratio = Outside Diameter / Wall Thickness or Wall Thickness = Outside Diameter / Dimension Ratio
(2) ** Based on an average density of 75.3 pounds per cubic foot for chlorinated poly(vinyl chloride). Actual weight may vary by ± 3%.
(3) Diameter and wall thickness data from :.
ASTM Designations F 441/F 441M - 96b, F 442/F 442M - 96b

Copper Pipe and Tube - Properties and Friction Loss

Nominal or Standard Pipe Size	Outside Diameter	Pipe or Tube Designation	Wall Thickness	Inside Diameter	Theoretical Weight Per Foot	Theoretical Flow Rate (Gallons per Minute) Which Will Cause A Head Loss (H_f) In 100 Feet of Pipe					
						H_f					
(inch)	(inch)		(inch)	(inch)	(pound)	0.1 (feet)	0.5 (feet)	1.0 (feet)	5.0 (feet)	10.0 (feet)	50.0 (feet)
1/8	0.125	Seamless tube	0.025	0.075	0.030	0.001	0.001	0.002	0.008	0.012	0.028
		ACR Tube - Type A	0.030	0.065	0.035	0.001	0.002	0.002	0.005	0.008	0.019
		Seamless tube	0.032	0.061	0.036	0.001	0.001	0.002	0.005	0.007	0.016
		Seamless tube	0.040	0.045	0.041	0.000	0.001	0.001	0.002	0.003	0.007
	0.405	Regular Pipe	0.062	0.281	0.259	0.031	0.074	0.108	0.258	0.375	0.893
		Ex. Hvy/Ex. Strong	0.100	0.205	0.371	0.014	0.032	0.047	0.112	0.163	0.390
3/16	0.1875	Seamless tube	0.025	0.1375	0.050	0.005	0.011	0.016	0.039	0.057	0.136
		ACR Tube - Type A	0.030	0.1275	0.058	0.004	0.009	0.014	0.032	0.047	0.112
		Seamless tube	0.032	0.1235	0.061	0.004	0.008	0.012	0.030	0.043	0.103
		Seamless tube	0.035	0.1175	0.065	0.003	0.008	0.011	0.026	0.038	0.090
		Seamless tube	0.040	0.1075	0.072	0.002	0.006	0.009	0.021	0.030	0.071
1/4	0.250	Seamless tube	0.020	0.210	0.056	0.014	0.035	0.050	0.120	0.174	0.415
		Seamless tube	0.025	0.200	0.069	0.013	0.030	0.044	0.105	0.153	0.365
		ACR Tube - Type A	0.030	0.190	0.080	0.011	0.027	0.039	0.092	0.134	0.319
		Seamless tube	0.032	0.186	0.085	0.011	0.023	0.037	0.087	0.127	0.302
		Seamless tube	0.035	0.180	0.092	0.010	0.023	0.033	0.080	0.12	0.277
		Seamless tube	0.049	0.152	0.120	0.006	0.015	0.021	0.051	0.074	0.177
		Seamless tube	0.065	0.120	0.146	0.003	0.008	0.012	0.027	0.040	0.095

Copper Pipe and Tube - Properties and Friction Loss (cont.)

Nominal or Standard Pipe Size	Outside Diameter	Pipe or Tube Designation	Wall Thickness	Inside Diameter	Theoretical Weight Per Foot	Theoretical Flow Rate (Gallons per Minute) Which Will Cause A Head Loss (H_f) In 100 Feet of Pipe					
						H_f					
						0.1	0.5	1.0	5.0	10.0	50.0
(inch)	(inch)		(inch)	(inch)	(pound)	(feet)	(feet)	(feet)	(feet)	(feet)	(feet)
1/4	0.375	Type L Tube	0.030	0.315	0.126	0.042	0.100	0.146	0.348	0.506	1.21
		Type K Tube	0.035	0.305	0.145	0.039	0.092	0.134	0.320	0.465	1.11
	0.540	Threadless Pipe (TP)	0.065	0.410	0.376	0.084	0.201	0.292	0.696	1.01	2.41
		Regular Pipe	0.082	0.376	0.457	0.067	0.160	0.232	0.554	0.806	1.92
		Ex. Hvy/Ex. Strong	0.123	0.294	0.625	0.035	0.084	0.122	0.290	0.422	1.01
5/16	0.3125	Seamless tube	0.025	0.2625	0.088	0.026	0.062	0.090	0.215	0.313	0.747
		ACR Tube - Type A	0.032	0.2485	0.109	0.023	0.054	0.078	0.186	0.271	0.647
		Seamless tube	0.049	0.2145	0.157	0.015	0.037	0.053	0.127	0.184	0.439
		Seamless tube	0.060	0.1925	0.184	0.012	0.027	0.040	0.095	0.139	0.330
3/8	0.375	Seamless tube	0.025	0.325	0.107	0.046	0.109	0.158	0.378	0.549	1.31
		Type G Tube	0.030	0.315	0.126	0.042	0.100	0.146	0.348	0.506	1.21
		ACR Tube - Type D	0.030	0.315	0.126	0.042	0.100	0.146	0.348	0.506	1.21
		ACR Tube - Type A	0.032	0.311	0.134	0.041	0.097	0.141	0.338	0.489	1.17
		Seamless tube	0.049	0.277	0.195	0.030	0.072	0.104	0.248	0.361	0.860
		Seamless tube	0.058	0.259	0.224	0.025	0.060	0.087	0.208	0.302	0.721
		Seamless tube	0.065	0.245	0.245	0.022	0.052	0.075	0.180	0.261	0.623
		Seamless tube	0.072	0.231	0.266	0.019	0.044	0.065	0.154	0.224	0.534
		Seamless tube	0.080	0.215	0.287	0.015	0.037	0.053	0.127	0.185	0.442

Nominal or Standard Pipe Size	Outside Diameter	Pipe or Tube Designation	Wall Thickness	Inside Diameter	Theoretical Weight Per Foot	Theoretical Flow Rate (Gallons per Minute) Which Will Cause A Head Loss (H_f) in 100 Feet of Pipe					
						H_f					
						0.1	0.5	1.0	5.0	10.0	50.0
(inch)	(inch)		(inch)	(inch)	(pound)	(feet)	(feet)	(feet)	(feet)	(feet)	(feet)
3/8	0.500	Type M Tube	0.025	0.450	0.145	0.108	0.256	0.373	0.889	1.29	3.08
		Type L Tube	0.035	0.430	0.198	0.095	0.227	0.331	0.789	1.15	2.73
		Type K Tube	0.049	0.402	0.269	0.080	0.191	0.277	0.661	0.961	2.29
	0.675	Threadless Pipe (TP) Regular Pipe	0.065	0.545	0.483	0.178	0.424	0.617	1.47	2.14	5.10
		Ex. Hvy/Ex. Strong	0.090	0.495	0.641	0.138	0.329	0.479	1.14	1.66	3.96
			0.127	0.421	0.848	0.090	0.215	0.313	0.746	1.08	2.59
7/16	0.4375	Seamless tube	0.025	0.3875	0.126	0.073	0.173	0.252	0.600	0.872	2.08
		Seamless tube	0.032	0.3735	0.158	0.066	0.157	0.228	0.545	0.792	1.89
		Seamless tube	0.045	0.3475	0.215	0.054	0.130	0.189	0.450	0.655	1.56
1/2	0.500	Seamless tube	0.028	0.444	0.161	0.104	0.247	0.360	0.858	1.25	2.98
		ACR Tube - Type A	0.032	0.436	0.182	0.099	0.236	0.343	0.818	1.19	2.84
		Type G Tube	0.035	0.430	0.198	0.095	0.227	0.331	0.789	1.15	2.73
		ACR Tube - Type D	0.035	0.430	0.198	0.095	0.227	0.331	0.789	1.15	2.73
		Seamless tube	0.049	0.402	0.269	0.080	0.191	0.277	0.661	0.961	2.29
		Seamless tube	0.058	0.384	0.312	0.071	0.169	0.246	0.586	0.852	2.03
		Seamless tube	0.065	0.370	0.344	0.064	0.153	0.223	0.531	0.772	1.84
		Seamless tube	0.072	0.356	0.375	0.058	0.138	0.201	0.480	0.698	1.66
	0.625	Type M Tube	0.028	0.569	0.204	0.199	0.475	0.691	1.65	2.40	5.71
		Type L Tube	0.040	0.545	0.285	0.178	0.424	0.617	1.47	2.14	5.10
		Type K Tube	0.049	0.527	0.344	0.163	0.388	0.565	1.35	1.96	4.67

Copper Pipe and Tube - Properties and Friction Loss (cont.)

Nominal or Standard Pipe Size	Outside Diameter	Pipe or Tube Designation	Wall Thickness	Inside Diameter	Theoretical Weight Per Foot	Theoretical Flow Rate (Gallons per Minute) Which Will Cause A Head Loss (Hf) In 100 Feet of Pipe					
						Hf					
(inch)	(inch)		(inch)	(inch)	(pound)	0.1 (feet)	0.5 (feet)	1.0 (feet)	5.0 (feet)	10.0 (feet)	50.0 (feet)
1/2	0.840	Threadless Pipe (TP)	0.065	0.710	0.613	0.357	0.851	1.24	2.95	4.29	10.2
		Regular Pipe	0.107	0.626	0.955	0.256	0.611	0.888	2.12	3.08	7.34
		Ex. Heavy/Ex. Strong	0.149	0.542	1.25	0.175	0.418	0.608	1.45	2.11	5.03
		Double Extra Hvy.	0.294	0.252	1.95	0.023	0.056	0.081	0.193	0.281	0.671
5/8	0.625	Seamless tube	0.032	0.561	0.231	0.192	0.458	0.666	1.59	2.31	5.50
		ACR Tube - Type A	0.035	0.555	0.251	0.187	0.445	0.647	1.54	2.24	5.35
		Type G Tube	0.040	0.545	0.285	0.178	0.424	0.617	1.47	2.14	5.10
		ACR Tube - Type D	0.040	0.545	0.285	0.178	0.424	0.617	1.47	2.14	5.10
		Seamless tube	0.049	0.527	0.344	0.163	0.388	0.565	1.35	1.96	4.67
		Seamless tube	0.065	0.495	0.443	0.138	0.329	0.479	1.14	1.66	3.96
	0.750	Type L Tube	0.042	0.666	0.362	0.301	0.719	1.05	2.49	3.62	8.64
		Type K Tube	0.049	0.652	0.418	0.285	0.680	0.988	2.36	3.43	8.17
3/4	0.750	Seamless tube	0.032	0.686	0.280	0.326	0.777	1.13	2.69	3.92	9.34
		ACR Tube - Type A	0.035	0.680	0.305	0.318	0.759	1.10	2.63	3.83	9.13
		Type G Tube	0.042	0.666	0.362	0.301	0.719	1.05	2.49	3.62	8.64
		ACR Tube - Type A	0.042	0.666	0.362	0.301	0.719	1.05	2.49	3.62	8.64
		ACR Tube - Type D	0.042	0.666	0.362	0.301	0.719	1.05	2.49	3.62	8.64
		Seamless tube	0.049	0.652	0.418	0.285	0.680	0.988	2.36	3.43	8.17
		Seamless tube	0.065	0.620	0.542	0.250	0.596	0.866	2.07	3.00	7.16
		Seamless tube	0.128	0.494	0.970	0.137	0.328	0.476	1.14	1.65	3.94

Nominal or Standard Pipe Size (inch)	Outside Diameter (inch)	Pipe or Tube Designation	Wall Thickness (inch)	Inside Diameter (inch)	Theoretical Weight Per Foot (pound)	Theoretical Flow Rate (Gallons per Minute) Which Will Cause A Head Loss (H_f) In 100 Feet of Pipe					
						H_f					
						0.1 (feet)	0.5 (feet)	1.0 (feet)	5.0 (feet)	10.0 (feet)	50.0 (feet)
3/4	0.875	Type M Tube	0.032	0.811	0.328	0.506	1.21	1.75	4.18	6.08	14.5
		Type L Tube	0.045	0.785	0.455	0.465	1.11	1.61	3.84	5.58	13.3
		Type K Tube	0.065	0.745	0.641	0.405	0.965	1.40	3.35	4.87	11.6
	1.050	Threadless Pipe (TP)	0.065	0.920	0.780	0.705	1.68	2.44	5.83	8.48	20.2
		Regular Pipe	0.114	0.822	1.30	0.524	1.25	1.82	4.34	6.30	15.0
		Ex. Heavy/Ex. Strong	0.157	0.736	1.71	0.392	0.935	1.36	3.24	4.71	11.2
		Double Extra Heavy	0.308	0.434	2.78	0.098	0.233	0.339	0.808	1.18	2.80
7/8	0.875	Seamless tube	0.028	0.819	0.289	0.519	1.21	1.80	4.29	6.24	14.9
		Seamless tube	0.032	0.811	0.329	0.506	1.21	1.75	4.18	6.08	14.5
		Type G Tube	0.045	0.785	0.455	0.465	1.11	1.61	3.84	5.58	13.3
		ACR Tube - Type A	0.045	0.785	0.455	0.465	1.11	1.61	3.84	5.58	13.3
		ACR Tube - Type D	0.045	0.785	0.455	0.465	1.11	1.61	3.84	5.58	13.3
		Seamless tube	0.065	0.745	0.641	0.405	0.965	1.40	3.35	4.87	11.6
		Seamless tube	0.072	0.731	0.704	0.385	0.918	1.34	3.18	4.63	11.0
1	1.000	Seamless tube	0.028	0.944	0.331	0.755	1.80	2.62	6.24	9.07	21.6
		Seamless tube	0.032	0.936	0.377	0.738	1.76	2.56	6.10	8.87	21.2
		Seamless tube	0.065	0.870	0.740	0.609	1.45	2.11	5.03	7.32	17.5
		Seamless tube	0.090	0.820	0.997	0.521	1.24	1.81	4.31	6.26	14.9
		Seamless tube	0.128	0.744	1.36	0.403	0.962	1.40	3.34	4.85	11.6

Copper Pipe and Tube - Properties and Friction Loss (cont.)

Nominal or Standard Pipe Size	Outside Diameter	Pipe or Tube Designation	Wall Thickness	Inside Diameter	Theoretical Weight Per Foot	Theoretical Flow Rate (Gallons per Minute) Which Will Cause A Head Loss (Hf) In 100 Feet of Pipe					
						Hf					
						0.1	0.5	1.0	5.0	10.0	50.0
(inch)	(inch)		(inch)	(inch)	(pound)	(feet)	(feet)	(feet)	(feet)	(feet)	(feet)
1	1.125	Type M Tube	0.035	1.055	0.465	1.01	2.41	3.50	8.4	12.2	29.0
		Type L Tube	0.050	1.025	0.655	0.94	2.23	3.25	7.7	11.3	26.9
		Type K Tube	0.065	0.995	0.839	0.87	2.07	3.00	7.2	10.4	24.8
	1.315	Threadless Pipe (TP)	0.065	1.185	0.989	1.37	2.46	4.76	11.3	16.5	39.3
		Regular Pipe	0.126	1.063	1.82	1.03	2.23	3.57	8.53	12.4	29.6
		Ex. Heavy/Ex. Strong	0.182	0.951	2.51	0.769	1.83	2.67	6.36	9.25	22.1
		Double Extra Heavy	0.358	0.599	4.17	0.228	0.544	0.791	1.89	2.74	6.54
1-1/8	1.125	Seamless tube	0.028	1.069	0.374	1.05	2.50	3.63	8.65	12.6	30.0
		Seamless tube	0.032	1.061	0.426	1.03	2.45	3.56	8.48	12.3	29.4
		Type G Tube	0.050	1.025	0.655	0.937	2.23	3.25	7.75	11.3	26.9
		ACR Tube - Type A	0.050	1.025	0.655	0.937	2.23	3.25	7.75	11.3	26.9
		ACR Tube - Type D	0.065	0.995	0.839	0.866	2.07	3.00	7.16	10.4	24.8
		Seamless tube	0.080	0.965	1.02	0.799	1.91	2.77	6.61	9.61	22.9
1-1/4	1.250	Seamless tube	0.028	1.194	0.417	1.40	3.34	4.85	11.6	16.8	40.1
		Seamless tube	0.032	1.186	0.475	1.38	3.28	4.77	11.4	16.5	39.4
		Seamless tube	0.065	1.120	0.938	1.18	2.82	4.10	9.78	14.2	33.9
		Seamless tube	0.083	1.084	1.18	1.09	2.59	3.76	8.98	13.1	31.1
		Seamless tube	0.095	1.060	1.34	1.02	2.44	3.55	8.46	12.3	29.3
		Seamless tube	0.128	0.994	1.75	0.864	2.06	3.00	7.15	10.4	24.8

Nominal or Standard Pipe Size	Outside Diameter	Pipe or Tube Designation	Wall Thickness	Inside Diameter	Theoretical Weight Per Foot	Theoretical Flow Rate (Gallons per Minute) Which Will Cause A Head Loss (H_f) In 100 Feet of Pipe					
						H_f					
						0.1	0.5	1.0	5.0	10.0	50.0
(inch)	(inch)		(inch)	(inch)	(pound)	(feet)	(feet)	(feet)	(feet)	(feet)	(feet)
1-1/4	1.375	Type DWV	0.040	1.295	0.650	1.73	4.13	6.01	14.3	20.8	49.7
		Type M Tube	0.042	1.291	0.682	1.72	4.10	5.96	14.2	20.7	49.3
		Type L Tube	0.055	1.265	0.884	1.63	3.89	5.65	13.5	19.6	46.7
		Type K Tube	0.065	1.245	1.04	1.56	3.73	5.42	12.9	18.8	44.8
	1.660	Threadless Pipe (TP)	0.065	1.530	1.26	2.69	6.41	9.32	22.2	32.3	77.0
		Regular Pipe	0.146	1.368	2.69	2.00	4.77	6.94	16.6	24.1	57.4
		Ex. Heavy/Ex. Strong	0.194	1.272	3.46	1.65	3.94	5.73	13.7	19.9	47.4
		Double Extra Heavy	0.382	0.896	5.95	0.658	1.57	2.28	5.44	7.91	18.9
1-3/8	1.375	Seamless tube	0.028	1.319	0.459	1.82	4.34	6.31	15.0	21.9	52.1
		ACR Tube - Type A	0.055	1.265	0.884	1.63	3.89	5.65	13.5	19.6	46.7
		ACR Tube - Type D	0.055	1.265	0.884	1.63	3.89	5.65	13.5	19.6	46.7
		Seamless tube	0.070	1.235	1.11	1.53	3.65	5.30	12.6	18.4	43.9
1-1/2	1.500	Seamless tube	0.065	1.370	1.14	2.01	4.79	6.97	16.6	24.2	57.6
		Seamless tube	0.080	1.340	1.38	1.90	4.52	6.57	15.7	22.8	54.4
		Seamless tube	0.095	1.310	1.63	1.79	4.26	6.19	14.8	21.5	51.2
		Seamless tube	0.120	1.260	2.02	1.61	3.85	5.59	13.3	19.4	46.2
		Seamless tube	0.128	1.244	2.14	1.56	3.72	5.41	12.9	18.7	44.7
	1.625	Type DWV	0.042	1.541	0.809	2.74	6.53	9.49	22.6	32.9	78.5
		Type M Tube	0.049	1.527	0.940	2.67	6.37	9.27	22.1	32.1	76.6
		Type L Tube	0.060	1.505	1.14	2.57	6.14	8.92	21.3	30.9	73.8
		Type K Tube	0.072	1.481	1.36	2.47	5.88	8.55	20.4	29.7	70.7

Copper Pipe and Tube - Properties and Friction Loss (cont.)

Nominal or Standard Pipe Size	Outside Diameter	Pipe or Tube Designation	Wall Thickness	Inside Diameter	Theoretical Weight Per Foot	Theoretical Flow Rate (Gallons per Minute) Which Will Cause A Head Loss (H_f) In 100 Feet of Pipe					
						H_f					
(inch)	(inch)		(inch)	(inch)	(pound)	0.1 (feet)	0.5 (feet)	1.0 (feet)	5.0 (feet)	10.0 (feet)	50.0 (feet)
1-1/2	1.900	Threadless Pipe (TP)	0.065	1.770	1.45	3.94	9.40	13.7	32.6	47.4	113
		Regular Pipe	0.150	1.600	3.20	3.02	7.21	10.5	25.0	36.3	86.6
		Ex. Heavy/Ex. Strong	0.203	1.494	4.20	2.52	6.02	8.75	20.9	30.3	72.4
		Double Extra Heavy	0.400	1.100	7.30	1.13	2.69	3.91	9.33	13.6	32.3
1-5/8	1.625	Seamless tube	0.030	1.565	0.583	2.85	6.80	9.89	23.6	34.3	81.8
		ACR Tube - Type A	0.060	1.505	1.14	2.57	6.14	8.92	21.3	30.9	73.8
		ACR Tube - Type D	0.060	1.505	1.14	2.57	6.14	8.92	21.3	30.9	73.8
		Seamless tube	0.070	1.485	1.33	2.48	5.92	8.61	20.5	29.9	71.2
		Seamless tube	0.100	1.425	1.86	2.23	5.31	7.73	18.4	26.8	63.9
1-3/4	1.750	Seamless tube	0.050	1.650	1.04	3.28	7.81	11.4	27.1	39.4	94.0
		Seamless tube	0.065	1.620	1.33	3.12	7.45	10.8	25.8	37.5	89.5
		Seamless tube	0.090	1.570	1.82	2.88	6.86	10.0	23.8	34.6	82.4
	2.000	Seamless tube	0.050	1.900	1.19	4.75	11.3	16.5	39.3	57.1	136
		Seamless tube	0.065	1.870	1.53	4.55	10.9	15.8	37.7	54.8	131
		Seamless tube	0.090	1.820	2.09	4.24	10.1	14.7	35.1	51.0	122
2	2.125	Type DWV	0.042	2.041	1.07	5.73	13.7	19.9	47.4	68.9	164
		Type M Tube	0.058	2.009	1.46	5.50	13.1	19.1	45.5	66.1	158
		Type L Tube	0.070	1.985	1.75	5.33	12.7	18.5	44.1	64.1	153
		Type K Tube	0.083	1.959	2.06	5.15	12.3	17.8	42.6	61.9	148

Nominal or Standard Pipe Size (inch)	Outside Diameter (inch)	Pipe or Tube Designation	Wall Thickness (inch)	Inside Diameter (inch)	Theoretical Weight Per Foot (pound)	Theoretical Flow Rate (Gallons per Minute) Which Will Cause A Head Loss (H_f) in 100 Feet of Pipe					
						H_f					
						0.1 (feet)	0.5 (feet)	1.0 (feet)	5.0 (feet)	10.0 (feet)	50.0 (feet)
2	2.375	Threadless Pipe (TP)	0.065	2.245	1.83	7.37	17.6	25.5	60.9	88.5	211
		Regular Pipe	0.156	2.063	4.22	5.90	14.1	20.4	48.8	70.9	169
		Ex. Heavy/Ex. Strong	0.221	1.933	5.80	4.97	11.9	17.2	41.1	59.7	142
		Double Extra Heavy	0.436	1.503	10.3	2.56	6.11	8.89	21.2	30.8	73.5
2-1/8	2.125	Seamless tube	0.050	2.025	1.26	5.62	13.4	19.5	46.4	67.5	161
		ACR Tube - Type D	0.070	1.985	1.75	5.33	12.7	18.5	44.1	64.1	153
		Seamless tube	0.090	1.945	2.23	5.05	12.0	17.5	41.8	60.7	145
	2.500	Seamless tube	0.050	2.400	1.49	8.78	20.9	30.4	72.6	106	252
		Type M Tube	0.065	2.370	1.93	8.49	20.3	29.4	70.2	102	244
		Seamless tube	0.090	2.320	2.64	8.03	19.1	27.8	66.4	96.5	230
2-1/2	2.625	Type M Tube	0.065	2.495	2.03	9.72	23.2	33.7	80.4	117	279
		Type L Tube	0.080	2.465	2.48	9.42	22.5	32.7	77.9	113	270
		Type K Tube	0.095	2.435	2.93	9.12	21.7	31.6	75.4	110	261
	2.875	Threadless Pipe (TP)	0.065	2.745	2.22	12.5	29.8	43.3	103	150	358
		Regular Pipe	0.187	2.501	6.12	9.78	23.3	33.9	80.9	118	281
		Ex. Heavy/Ex. Strong	0.280	2.315	8.85	7.98	19.0	27.7	66.0	96.0	229
		Double Extra Heavy	0.552	1.771	15.6	3.95	9.41	13.7	32.6	47.5	113
2-5/8	2.625	Seamless tube	0.050	2.525	1.57	10.0	23.9	34.8	83.0	121	288
		ACR Tube - Type D	0.080	2.465	2.48	9.42	22.5	32.7	77.9	113	270
		Seamless tube	0.100	2.425	3.07	9.02	21.5	31.3	74.6	108	259

Copper Pipe and Tube - Properties and Friction Loss (cont.)

Nominal or Standard Pipe Size	Outside Diameter	Pipe or Tube Designation	Wall Thickness	Inside Diameter	Theoretical Weight Per Foot	Theoretical Flow Rate (Gallons per Minute) Which Will Cause A Head Loss (H_f) In 100 Feet of Pipe					
						H_f					
						0.1	0.5	1.0	5.0	10.0	50.0
(inch)	(inch)		(inch)	(inch)	(pound)	(feet)	(feet)	(feet)	(feet)	(feet)	(feet)
	3.000	Seamless tube	0.050	2.900	1.80	14.4	34.4	50.1	119	174	414
		Seamless tube	0.065	2.870	2.32	14.1	33.5	48.7	116	169	403
		Seamless tube	0.090	2.820	3.19	13.4	32.0	46.5	111	161	385
	3.125	Type DWV	0.045	3.035	1.69	16.3	38.8	56.4	135	196	467
		Type M Tube	0.072	2.981	2.68	15.5	37.0	53.8	128	187	445
		Type L Tube	0.090	2.945	3.33	15.0	35.9	52.1	124	181	431
3		Type K Tube	0.109	2.907	4.00	14.5	34.7	50.4	120	175	417
	3.500	Threadless Pipe (TP)	0.083	3.334	3.45	20.8	49.7	72.3	172	251	597
		Regular Pipe	0.219	3.062	8.76	16.7	39.7	57.8	138	200	478
		Ex. Heavy/Ex. Strong	0.304	2.892	11.8	14.3	34.2	49.7	119	172	411
		Double Extra Heavy	0.600	2.300	21.2	7.85	18.7	27.2	64.9	94.4	225

Notes:
(1). Abbreviations used: ACR - air conditioning and refrigeration. DWV - drain, waste, and vent. Ex. - extra Hvy - Heavy
(2). Diameter, wall thickness, and weight data from: ASTM Designations B 42 - 96; B 88 - 96; B 280 - 97; B 302 - 97; B 306 - 96; and B 837 - 95.
Fluid Power Data Book, Ninth Edition, Womack Educational Publications, Dallas, TX, 1995
Copper Tube Handbook, Copper Development Association, Inc., New York, NY (see www.tubebook.copper.org)
Alaskan Copper and Brass Company, Seattle, WA
Central Steel and Wire Company, Chicago, IL

Poly(Vinyl Chloride) (PVC) Pipe
Controlled On Outside Diameter - Properties And Friction Loss

Nominal Pipe Size	Outside Diameter	Dimension Ratio (DR) or Schedule Number (PS) or Pipe Series or Sewer & Drain Pipe Series (SDPS)	Minimum Wall Thickness	Inside Diameter	Theoretical Weight Per Foot**	Theoretical Flow Rate (Gallons per Minute) Which Will Cause A Head Loss (Hf) In 100 Feet of Pipe					
						Hf					
						0.1	0.5	1.0	5.0	10.0	50.0
(inch)	(inch)		(inch)	(inch)	(pound)	(feet)	(feet)	(feet)	(feet)	(feet)	(feet)
1/8	0.405	Schedule 80	0.095	0.215	0.058	0.015	0.037	0.053	0.127	0.185	0.442
		Schedule 40	0.068	0.269	0.045	0.028	0.066	0.096	0.230	0.334	0.796
		DR 13.5	0.060	0.285	0.041	0.032	0.077	0.112	0.267	0.389	0.927
1/4	0.540	Schedule 80	0.119	0.302	0.098	0.038	0.090	0.131	0.311	0.453	1.08
		Schedule 40	0.088	0.364	0.078	0.062	0.147	0.213	0.509	0.740	1.76
		DR 13.5	0.060	0.420	0.056	0.090	0.214	0.311	0.741	1.08	2.57
3/8	0.675	Schedule 80	0.126	0.423	0.136	0.091	0.218	0.317	0.755	1.10	2.62
		Schedule 40	0.091	0.493	0.104	0.137	0.326	0.474	1.13	1.64	3.92
		DR 13.5	0.060	0.555	0.072	0.187	0.445	0.647	1.54	2.24	5.35
1/2	0.840	Schedule 120	0.170	0.500	0.223	0.142	0.338	0.492	1.17	1.71	4.07
		Schedule 80	0.147	0.546	0.200	0.179	0.426	0.620	1.48	2.15	5.13
		Schedule 40	0.109	0.622	0.156	0.252	0.601	0.873	2.08	3.03	7.22
		DR 13.5	0.062	0.716	0.095	0.365	0.870	1.26	3.02	4.38	10.5
3/4	1.050	Schedule 120	0.170	0.710	0.293	0.357	0.851	1.24	2.95	4.29	10.2
		Schedule 80	0.154	0.742	0.271	0.401	0.955	1.39	3.31	4.82	11.5
		Schedule 40	0.113	0.824	0.208	0.528	1.26	1.83	4.36	6.34	15.1
		DR 13.5	0.078	0.894	0.149	0.654	1.56	2.27	5.41	7.86	18.7
		DR 17	0.062	0.926	0.120	0.717	1.71	2.49	5.93	8.62	20.6
		DR 21	0.060	0.930	0.116	0.725	1.73	2.52	6.00	8.72	20.8

Poly(Vinyl Chloride) (PVC) Pipe Controlled On Outside Diameter (cont.)

Nominal Pipe Size (inch)	Outside Diameter (inch)	Dimension Ratio (DR) or Schedule Number or Pipe Series (PS) Sewer & Drain Pipe Series (SDPS)	Minimum Wall Thickness (inch)	Theoretical Weight Per Foot** (pound)	Inside Diameter (inch)	Theoretical Flow Rate (Gallons per Minute) Which Will Cause A Head Loss (Hf) In 100 Feet of Pipe					
						0.1 (feet)	0.5 (feet)	1.0 (feet)	5.0 (feet)	10.0 (feet)	50.0 (feet)
1	1.315	Schedule 120	0.200	0.437	0.915	0.695	1.66	2.41	5.75	8.36	19.9
		Schedule 80	0.179	0.399	0.957	0.782	1.87	2.71	6.47	9.40	22.4
		Schedule 40	0.133	0.308	1.049	0.996	2.37	3.45	8.23	12.0	28.5
		DR 13.5	0.097	0.232	1.121	1.19	2.83	4.11	9.80	14.3	34.0
		DR 17	0.077	0.187	1.161	1.30	3.10	4.51	10.8	15.6	37.3
		DR 21	0.063	0.155	1.189	1.38	3.30	4.80	11.4	16.6	39.7
		DR 26	0.060	0.148	1.195	1.40	3.35	4.86	11.6	16.9	40.2
1-1/4	1.660	Schedule 120	0.215	0.609	1.230	1.51	3.61	5.25	12.5	18.2	43.4
		Schedule 80	0.191	0.550	1.278	1.67	3.99	5.80	13.8	20.1	48.0
		Schedule 40	0.140	0.417	1.380	2.05	4.88	7.10	16.9	24.6	58.7
		DR 13.5	0.123	0.371	1.414	2.18	5.21	7.57	18.1	26.3	62.6
		DR 17	0.098	0.300	1.464	2.39	5.71	8.30	19.8	28.8	68.6
		DR 21	0.079	0.245	1.502	2.56	6.10	8.87	21.2	30.8	73.4
		DR 26	0.064	0.200	1.532	2.70	6.43	9.35	22.3	32.4	77.3
		DR 32.5	0.060	0.188	1.540	2.73	6.52	9.48	22.6	32.9	78.4
1-1/2	1.900	Schedule 120	0.225	0.739	1.450	2.33	5.56	8.09	19.3	28.0	66.9
		Schedule 80	0.200	0.667	1.500	2.55	6.08	8.84	21.1	30.7	73.1
		Schedule 40	0.145	0.499	1.610	3.07	7.33	10.7	25.4	36.9	88.1
		DR 13.5	0.141	0.486	1.618	3.11	7.42	10.8	25.7	37.4	89.2
		DR 17	0.112	0.393	1.676	3.41	8.14	11.8	28.2	41.1	97.9
		DR 21	0.090	0.319	1.720	3.66	8.72	12.7	30.2	43.9	105

Nominal Pipe Size	Outside Diameter	Dimension Ratio (DR)* or Schedule Number or Pipe Series (PS) or Sewer & Drain Pipe Series (SDPS)	Minimum Wall Thickness	Inside Diameter	Theoretical Weight Per Foot**	Theoretical Flow Rate (Gallons per Minute) Which Will Cause A Head Loss (Hf) in 100 Feet of Pipe					
						H_f					
						0.1	0.5	1.0	5.0	10.0	50.0
(inch)	(inch)		(inch)	(inch)	(pound)	(feet)	(feet)	(feet)	(feet)	(feet)	(feet)
1-1/2	1.90	DR 26	0.073	1.754	0.262	3.85	9.18	13.3	31.8	46.3	110
		DR 32.5	0.060	1.780	0.217	4.00	9.54	13.5	33.1	48.1	115
		Schedule 120	0.250	1.875	1.04	4.59	10.9	15.9	37.9	55.1	131
		Schedule 80	0.218	1.939	0.922	5.01	11.9	16.7	41.4	60.2	144
		DR 13.5	0.176	2.023	0.759	5.60	13.4	19.4	46.3	67.3	161
2	2.375	Schedule 40	0.154	2.067	0.671	5.93	14.1	20.6	49.0	71.3	170
		DR 17	0.140	2.095	0.614	6.14	14.6	21.3	50.8	73.8	176
		DR 21	0.113	2.149	0.501	6.57	15.7	22.8	54.3	78.9	188
		PS 100	0.100	2.175	0.446	6.78	16.2	23.5	56.0	81.5	194
		DR 26	0.091	2.193	0.408	6.92	16.5	24.0	57.3	83.3	199
		DR 32.5	0.073	2.229	0.330	7.23	17.2	25.1	59.8	86.9	207
		Schedule 120	0.300	2.275	1.52	7.63	18.2	26.4	63.1	91.7	219
		Schedule 80	0.276	2.323	1.41	8.06	19.2	27.9	66.6	96.9	231
		DR 13.5	0.213	2.449	1.11	9.26	22.1	32.1	76.6	111	265
2-1/2	2.875	Schedule 40	0.203	2.469	1.06	9.46	22.6	32.8	78.2	114	271
		DR 17	0.169	2.537	0.897	10.2	24.2	35.2	84.0	122	291
		DR 21	0.137	2.601	0.736	10.8	25.9	37.6	89.7	130	311
		DR 26	0.110	2.655	0.597	11.4	27.3	39.7	94.7	138	328
		DR 32.5	0.088	2.699	0.481	12.0	28.5	41.5	98.9	144	343
3	3.250	SDPS 100	0.120	3.010	0.737	15.9	38.0	55.2	132	191	457
		SDPS 50	0.100	3.050	0.618	16.5	39.3	57.2	136	198	473
		Schedule 120	0.350	2.800	2.16	13.2	31.4	45.7	109	158	378
		Schedule 80	0.300	2.900	1.88	14.4	34.4	50.1	119	174	414

Poly(Vinyl Chloride) (PVC) Pipe Controlled On Outside Diameter (cont.)

Nominal Pipe Size (inch)	Outside Diameter (inch)	Dimension Ratio (DR) or Schedule Number or Pipe Series (PS) or Cast Iron & Drain Pipe Series (SDPS)	Minimum Wall Thickness (inch)	Inside Diameter (inch)	Theoretical Weight Per Foot** (pound)	Theoretical Flow Rate (Gallons per Minute) Which Will Cause A Head Loss (H_L) In 100 Feet of Pipe					
						0.1 (feet)	0.5 (feet)	1.0 (feet)	5.0 (feet)	10.0 (feet)	50.0 (feet)
3	3.500	DR 13.5	0.259	2.982	1.65	15.5	37.1	53.9	128	187	446
		Schedule 40	0.216	3.068	1.39	16.7	39.9	58.1	138	201	480
		DR 17	0.206	3.088	1.33	17.0	40.6	59.1	141	205	488
		DR 21	0.167	3.166	1.09	18.2	43.4	63.1	150	219	522
		DR 26	0.135	3.230	0.891	19.2	45.7	66.5	159	231	550
		PS 100	0.130	3.240	0.859	19.3	46.1	67.0	160	232	554
		DR 32.5	0.108	3.284	0.718	20.0	47.8	69.4	166	241	574
		PS 50	0.103	3.294	0.686	20.2	48.1	70.0	167	243	579
		DR 41	0.085	3.330	0.569	20.8	49.5	72.0	172	250	596
3-1/2	4.000	Schedule 120	0.350	3.300	2.51	20.3	48.4	70.3	168	244	582
		Schedule 80	0.318	3.364	2.30	21.3	50.9	74.0	176	257	612
		DR 13.5	0.298	3.404	2.16	22.0	52.5	76.3	182	265	631
		DR 17	0.235	3.530	1.74	24.2	57.8	84.0	200	291	694
		Schedule 40	0.226	3.548	1.67	24.5	58.5	85.1	203	295	704
		DR 21	0.190	3.620	1.42	25.9	61.7	89.7	214	311	742
		DR 26	0.154	3.692	1.16	27.5	65.0	94.5	225	328	781
		PS 100	0.148	3.704	1.12	27.5	65.5	95.3	227	330	788
		DR 32.5	0.123	3.754	0.935	28.5	67.9	98.7	235	342	816
		PS 50	0.118	3.764	0.898	28.7	68.4	99.4	237	345	822
		PS 25	0.100	3.800	0.765	29.4	70.1	102	243	353	843
		DR 41	0.098	3.804	0.750	29.5	70.3	102	244	354	845

Nominal Pipe Size	Outside Diameter	Dimension Ratio (DR)* or Schedule Number or Pipe Series (PS) or Sewer & Drain Pipe Series (SDPS)	Minimum Wall Thickness	Inside Diameter	Theoretical Weight Per Foot**	Theoretical Flow Rate (Gallons per Minute) Which Will Cause A Head Loss (H_f) In 100 Feet of Pipe				
						0.1	0.5	5.0	10.0	50.0
(inch)	(inch)		(inch)	(inch)	(pound)	(feet)	(feet)	(feet)	(feet)	(feet)
4	4.215	SDPS 100	0.156	3.903	1.24	31.5	75.2	261	379	900
		SDPS 50	0.124	3.967	0.995	32.9	78.5	272	396	940
		PS 46	0.120	3.975	0.964	33.1	78.9	274	398	950
		PS 28	0.103	4.009	0.831	33.8	80.7	280	407	970
		SDPS 25	0.100	4.015	0.807	34.0	81.0	281	408	970
	4.500	Schedule 120	0.437	3.626	3.48	26.0	62.0	215	312	745
		Schedule 80	0.337	3.826	2.75	29.9	71.4	247	360	858
		DR 13.5	0.333	3.834	2.72	30.1	71.8	249	362	863
		DR 17	0.265	3.970	2.20	33.0	78.7	273	397	946
		Schedule 40	0.237	4.026	1.98	34.2	81.6	283	411	981
		DR 21	0.214	4.072	1.80	35.3	84.1	292	424	1,010
		DR 26	0.173	4.154	1.47	37.2	88.6	307	447	1,070
		PS 100	0.167	4.166	1.42	37.4	89.3	310	450	1,070
		DR 32.5	0.138	4.224	1.18	38.8	92.6	321	467	1,110
		PS 50	0.133	4.234	1.14	39.1	93.2	323	470	1,120
		DR 41	0.110	4.280	0.947	40.2	95.9	332	483	1,150
		PS 25	0.106	4.288	0.913	40.4	96.3	334	486	1,160
		DR 64	0.070	4.360	0.608	42.2	101	349	507	1,210
	4.800	DR 14	0.343	4.114	3.00	36.2	86.4	300	436	1,040
		DR 18	0.267	4.266	2.37	39.9	95.0	330	479	1,140
		DR 25	0.192	4.416	1.74	43.6	104	361	525	1,250

Poly(Vinyl Chloride) (PVC) Pipe Controlled On Outside Diameter - Properties And Friction Loss

Nominal Pipe Size	Outside Diameter	Dimension Ratio (DR)* or Schedule Number (PS) or Pipe Series (PS) or Sewer & Drain Pipe Series (SDPS)	Minimum Wall Thickness	Inside Diameter	Theoretical Weight Per Foot**	Theoretical Flow Rate (Gallons per Minute) Which Will Cause A Head Loss (H_L) In 100 Feet of Pipe					
						H_L					
						0.1	0.5	1.0	5.0	10.0	50.0
(inch)	(inch)		(inch)	(inch)	(pound)	(feet)	(feet)	(feet)	(feet)	(feet)	(feet)
5	5.563	Schedule 120	0.500	4.563	4.96	47.6	113	165	393	572	1,360
		DR 13.5	0.412	4.739	4.16	52.5	125	182	434	632	1,510
		Schedule 80	0.375	4.813	3.82	54.7	131	190	453	658	1,570
		DR 17	0.327	4.909	3.36	57.7	137	200	477	693	1,650
		DR 21	0.265	5.033	2.75	61.6	147	213	509	740	1,760
		Schedule 40	0.258	5.047	2.68	62.0	148	215	513	746	1,780
		DR 26	0.214	5.135	2.25	64.9	155	225	537	780	1,860
		PS 100	0.206	5.151	2.16	65.4	156	227	541	787	1,880
		DR 32.5	0.171	5.221	1.81	67.8	162	235	561	815	1,940
		PS 50	0.164	5.235	1.74	68.3	163	237	565	821	1,960
		DR 41	0.136	5.291	1.45	70.2	167	243	581	844	2,010
		PS 25	0.131	5.301	1.40	70.6	168	245	583	848	2,020
		DR 64	0.087	5.389	0.934	73.7	176	255	609	886	2,110
6	6.275	SDPS 100	0.232	5.811	2.93	90	214	312	743	1,080	2,580
		SDPS 50	0.185	5.905	2.36	94	223	325	775	1,130	2,690
		PS 46	0.180	5.915	2.29	94	224	326	778	1,130	2,700
		PS 28	0.153	5.969	1.96	96	230	334	797	1,160	2,760
		SDPS 25	0.148	5.979	1.90	97	231	336	801	1,160	2,780
		SDPS 12.5	0.118	6.039	1.52	99	237	345	822	1,200	2,850
	6.625	Schedule 120	0.562	5.501	7.12	77.8	185	270	643	935	2,230
		DR 13.5	0.491	5.643	6.30	83.2	198	288	688	1,000	2,380

Nominal Pipe Size (inch)	Outside Diameter (inch)	Dimension Ratio (DR) or Schedule Number or Pipe Series (PS) or Sewer & Drain Pipe Series (SDPS)	Minimum Wall Thickness (inch)	Inside Diameter (inch)	Theoretical Weight Per Foot** (pound)	Theoretical Flow Rate (Gallons per Minute) Which Will Cause A Head Loss (H_L) In 100 Feet of Pipe					
						H_L					
						0.1 (feet)	0.5 (feet)	1.0 (feet)	5.0 (feet)	10.0 (feet)	50.0 (feet)
6	6.625	Schedule 80	0.432	5.761	5.59	87.8	209	305	726	1,060	2,520
		DR 17	0.390	5.845	5.08	91.2	218	316	754	1,100	2,620
		DR 21	0.316	5.993	4.17	97.4	232	338	806	1,170	2,790
		Schedule 40	0.280	6.065	3.71	101	240	349	831	1,210	2,880
		DR 26	0.255	6.115	3.40	103	245	356	849	1,240	2,950
		PS 100	0.245	6.135	3.27	104	247	359	857	1,250	2,970
		DR 32.5	0.204	6.217	2.74	107	256	372	887	1,290	3,080
		PS 50	0.195	6.235	2.62	108	258	375	894	1,300	3,100
		DR 41	0.162	6.301	2.19	111	265	385	919	1,340	3,190
		PS 25	0.156	6.313	2.11	112	266	387	924	1,340	3,200
		DR 64	0.104	6.417	1.42	117	278	404	964	1,400	3,340
	6.900	DR 14	0.493	5.914	6.60	94.1	224	326	778	1,130	2,700
		DR 18	0.383	6.134	5.22	104	247	359	856	1,250	2,970
		DR 25	0.276	6.348	3.82	113	270	393	937	1,360	3,250
8	8.400	SDPS 100	0.310	7.780	5.24	194	462	671	1,600	2,330	5,550
		SDPS 50	0.248	7.904	4.23	202	481	700	1,670	2,430	5,780
		PS 46	0.240	7.920	4.09	203	484	703	1,680	2,440	5,820
		PS 28	0.205	7.990	3.51	208	495	720	1,720	2,500	5,950
		SDPS 25	0.198	8.004	3.40	209	497	723	1,720	2,510	5,980
	8.625	Schedule 120	0.718	7.189	11.9	157	375	545	1,300	1,890	4,510
		DR 17	0.508	7.609	8.62	183	435	633	1,510	2,190	5,230
		Schedule 80	0.500	7.625	8.49	184	438	636	1,520	2,210	5,260
		DR 21	0.410	7.805	7.04	195	465	677	1,610	2,350	5,600

Nominal Pipe Size	Outside Diameter	Dimension Ratio (DR)* or Schedule Number or Pipe Series (PS) or Sewer & Drain Pipe Series (SDPS)	Minimum Wall Thickness	Inside Diameter	Theoretical Weight Per Foot**	Theoretical Flow Rate (Gallons per Minute) Which Will Cause A Head Loss (H_f) In 100 Feet of Pipe					
						H_f					
						0.1	0.5	1.0	5.0	10.0	50.0
(inch)	(inch)		(inch)	(inch)	(pound)	(feet)	(feet)	(feet)	(feet)	(feet)	(feet)
8	8.625	DR 26	0.332	7.961	5.76	206	490	713	1,700	2,470	5,890
		Schedule 40	0.322	7.981	5.59	207	494	718	1,710	2,490	5,930
		DR 32.5	0.265	8.095	4.63	215	512	745	1,780	2,580	6,160
		DR 41	0.210	8.205	3.69	223	531	772	1,840	2,680	6,380
		DR 64	0.135	8.355	2.40	233	557	809	1,930	2,810	6,690
	9.050	DR 14	0.646	7.758	11.3	192	458	666	1,590	2,310	5,510
		DR 18	0.503	8.044	8.99	211	504	733	1,750	2,540	6,060
		DR 25	0.362	8.326	6.58	231	552	802	1,910	2,780	6,630

Notes:
(1) * Dimension Ratio = Outside Diameter / Wall Thickness or Wall Thickness = Outside Diameter / Dimension Ratio
(2) ** Based on an average density of 89.9 pounds per cubic foot for poly(vinyl chloride). Actual weight may vary by ± 3%.
(3) Diameter and wall thickness data from :
ANSI / AWWA Standards C900-89, C905-88
ASTM Designations D 1785 - 96a, D 2241 - 96a, F 758 - 95, F 891 - 96

Polybutylene (PB) Pipe - Controlled on Inside Diameter - Properties and Friction Loss

Nominal Pipe Size	Inside Diameter	Dimension Ratio (DR)*	Minimum Wall Thickness	Outside Diameter	Theoretical Weight Per Foot**	Theoretical Flow Rate (Gallons per Minute) Which Will Cause A Head Loss (H_L) in 100 Feet of Pipe					
						H_L					
						0.1	0.5	1.0	5.0	10.0	50.0
(inch)	(inch)		(inch)	(inch)	(pound)	(feet)	(feet)	(feet)	(feet)	(feet)	(feet)
1/2	0.622	DR 7	0.089	0.800	0.079	0.252	0.601	0.873	2.08	3.03	7.22
		DR 9	0.069	0.760	0.060						
		DR 11.5	0.062	0.746	0.053						
		DR 15	0.062	0.746	0.053						
3/4	0.824	DR 7	0.118	1.059	0.139	0.528	1.26	1.83	4.36	6.34	15.1
		DR 9	0.092	1.007	0.105						
		DR 11.5	0.072	0.967	0.080						
		DR 15	0.062	0.948	0.069						
1	1.049	DR 7	0.150	1.349	0.225	0.996	2.37	3.45	8.23	12.0	28.5
		DR 9	0.117	1.282	0.170						
		DR 11.5	0.091	1.231	0.130						
		DR 15	0.070	1.189	0.098						
1-1/4	1.380	DR 7	0.197	1.774	0.389	2.05	4.88	7.10	16.9	24.6	58.7
		DR 9	0.153	1.687	0.294						
		DR 11.5	0.120	1.620	0.225						
		DR 15	0.092	1.564	0.169						
1-1/2	1.610	DR 7	0.230	2.070	0.529	3.07	7.33	10.7	25.4	36.9	88.1
		DR 9	0.179	1.968	0.400						
		DR 11.5	0.140	1.890	0.306						
		DR 15	0.107	1.825	0.230						

Polybutylene (PB) Pipe - Controlled On Inside Diameter - Properties And Friction Loss (cont.)

Nominal Pipe Size	Inside Diameter	Dimension Ratio - (DR)*	Minimum Wall Thickness	Outside Diameter	Theoretical Weight Per Foot**	Theoretical Flow Rate (Gallons per Minute) Which Will Cause A Head Loss (H_f) In 100 Feet Of Pipe					
						H_f 0.1	0.5	1.0	5.0	10.0	50.0
(inch)	(inch)		(inch)	(inch)	(pound)	(feet)	(feet)	(feet)	(feet)	(feet)	(feet)
2	2.067	DR 7	0.295	2.658	0.872	5.93	14.1	20.6	49.0	71.3	170
		DR 9	0.230	2.526	0.659						
		DR 11.5	0.180	2.426	0.505						
		DR 15	0.138	2.343	0.380						
2-1/2	2.469	DR 7	0.353	3.174	1.24	9.46	22.6	32.8	78.2	114	271
		DR 9	0.274	3.018	0.940						
		DR 11.5	0.215	2.898	0.720						
		DR 15	0.165	2.798	0.542						
3	3.068	DR 7	0.438	3.945	1.92	16.7	39.9	58.1	138	201	480
		DR 9	0.341	3.750	1.45						
		DR 11.5	0.267	3.602	1.11						
		DR 15	0.205	3.477	0.836						
4	4.026	DR 11.5	0.350	4.726	1.91	34.2	81.6	119	283	411	981
		DR 15	0.268	4.563	1.44						
6	6.065	DR 11.5	0.527	7.120	4.34	101	240	349	831	1,210	2,880
		DR 15	0.404	6.874	3.27						

Notes:
1 * Dimension Ratio = Inside Diameter / Wall Thickness = Inside Diameter / Dimension Ratio
2 ** Based on an average density of 57.3 pounds per cubic foot for polybutylene. Actual weight may vary by ± 3%.
3 Diameter and wall thickness data from: ANSI / AWWA Standard C902-88 and ASTM Designation D 2662 - 96a

Polybutylene (PB) Pipe - Controlled on Outside Diameter - Properties and Friction Loss

Nominal Pipe Size	Outside Diameter	Dimension Ratio-(DR)*	Minimum Wall Thickness	Inside Diameter	Theoretical Weight Per Foot**	Theoretical Flow Rate (Gallons per Minute) Which Will Cause A Head Loss (Hf) In 100 Feet of Pipe					
						Hf					
						0.1	0.5	1.0	5.0	10.0	50.0
(inch)	(inch)		(inch)	(inch)	(pound)	(feet)	(feet)	(feet)	(feet)	(feet)	(feet)
1/2	0.840	DR 9	0.093	0.653	0.089	0.287	0.683	0.994	2.37	3.45	8.22
		DR 11	0.076	0.687	0.074	0.327	0.781	1.14	2.71	3.94	9.39
		DR 13.5	0.062	0.716	0.062	0.364	0.868	1.26	3.01	4.38	10.4
		DR 17	0.062	0.716	0.062	0.365	0.870	1.26	3.02	4.38	10.5
3/4	1.050	DR 9	0.117	0.817	0.136	0.515	1.23	1.79	4.26	6.20	14.8
		DR 11	0.095	0.859	0.114	0.589	1.40	2.04	4.87	7.08	16.9
		DR 13.5	0.078	0.894	0.094	0.655	1.56	2.27	5.41	7.87	18.8
		DR 17	0.062	0.926	0.076	0.718	1.71	2.49	5.94	8.63	20.6
1	1.315	DR 9	0.146	1.023	0.213	0.932	2.22	3.23	7.70	11.2	26.7
		DR 11	0.120	1.076	0.179	1.06	2.54	3.69	8.80	12.8	30.5
		DR 13.5	0.097	1.120	0.148	1.18	2.82	4.10	9.79	14.2	33.9
		DR 17	0.077	1.160	0.120	1.30	3.10	4.50	10.7	15.6	37.2
1-1/4	1.660	DR 9	0.184	1.291	0.340	1.72	4.10	5.96	14.2	20.7	49.3
		DR 11	0.151	1.358	0.285	1.96	4.68	6.81	16.2	23.6	56.3
		DR 13.5	0.123	1.414	0.236	2.18	5.21	7.57	18.1	26.3	62.6
		DR 17	0.098	1.465	0.191	2.40	5.71	8.31	19.8	28.8	68.7
1-1/2	1.900	DR 9	0.211	1.478	0.446	2.45	5.85	8.50	20.3	29.5	70.3
		DR 11	0.173	1.555	0.373	2.80	6.68	9.71	23.2	33.7	80.3
		DR 13.5	0.141	1.619	0.309	3.12	7.43	10.8	25.8	37.5	89.3

Polybutylene (PB) Pipe - Controlled On Outside Diameter - Properties And Friction Loss (cont.)

Nominal Pipe Size	Outside Diameter	Dimension Ratio-(DR)*	Minimum Wall Thickness	Inside Diameter	Theoretical Weight Per Foot**	Theoretical Flow Rate (Gallons per Minute) Which Will Cause A Head Loss (Hf) In 100 Feet of Pipe					
						Hf					
						0.1	0.5	1.0	5.0	10.0	50.0
(inch)	(inch)		(inch)	(inch)	(pound)	(feet)	(feet)	(feet)	(feet)	(feet)	(feet)
2	2.375	DR 9	0.264	1.847	0.696	4.41	10.5	15.3	36.5	53.0	126
		DR 11	0.216	1.943	0.583	5.04	12.0	17.5	41.7	60.6	144
		DR 13.5	0.176	2.023	0.483	5.60	13.4	19.4	46.3	67.4	161
		DR 17	0.140	2.096	0.390	6.15	14.7	21.3	50.8	73.9	176
2-1/2	2.875	DR 9	0.319	2.236	1.02	7.29	17.4	25.3	60.3	87.6	209
		DR 11	0.261	2.352	0.854	8.33	19.9	28.9	68.4	100	239
		DR 13.5	0.213	2.449	0.708	9.26	22.1	32.1	76.6	111	265
		DR 17	0.169	2.537	0.572	10.2	24.2	35.2	84.0	122	291
3	3.500	DR 9	0.389	2.722	1.51	12.2	29.2	42.4	101	147	351
		DR 11	0.318	2.864	1.27	14.0	33.3	48.4	116	168	401
		DR 13.5	0.259	2.981	1.05	15.5	37.0	53.9	128	187	445
		DR 17	0.206	3.088	0.847	17.0	40.6	59.1	141	205	489
		DR 21	0.167	3.167	0.694	18.2	43.4	63.1	150	219	522
		DR 26	0.135	3.231	0.566	19.2	45.8	66.5	159	231	550
4	4.500	DR 9	0.500	3.500	2.50	23.7	56.5	82.1	196	285	679
		DR 11	0.409	3.682	2.09	27.1	64.5	93.8	224	325	776
		DR 13.5	0.333	3.833	1.74	30.1	71.7	104	249	362	862
		DR 17	0.265	3.971	1.40	33.0	78.7	114	273	397	946
		DR 21	0.214	4.071	1.15	35.2	84.1	122	291	424	1,010
		DR 26	0.173	4.154	0.936	37.2	88.6	129	307	447	1,070
		DR 32.5	0.138	4.223	0.755	38.8	92.5	135	321	467	1,110

Nominal Pipe Size	Outside Diameter	Dimension Ratio-(DR)*	Minimum Wall Thickness	Inside Diameter	Theoretical Weight Per Foot**	Theoretical Flow Rate (Gallons per Minute) Which Will Cause A Head Loss (Hf) In 100 Feet of Pipe					
						Hf					
(inch)	(inch)		(inch)	(inch)	(pound)	0.1 (feet)	0.5 (feet)	1.0 (feet)	5.0 (feet)	10.0 (feet)	50.0 (feet)
5	5.563	DR 11	0.506	4.552	3.20	47.3	113	164	391	568	1,350
		DR 13.5	0.412	4.739	2.65	52.5	125	182	434	632	1,510
		DR 17	0.327	4.909	2.14	57.6	137	200	477	693	1,650
		DR 21	0.265	5.033	1.75	61.6	147	213	509	740	1,770
		DR 26	0.214	5.135	1.43	64.9	155	225	537	780	1,860
		DR 32.5	0.171	5.221	1.15	67.8	162	235	560	815	1,940
6	6.625	DR 9	0.736	5.153	5.42	65.5	156	227	542	787	1,880
		DR 11	0.602	5.420	4.53	74.8	178	259	619	900	2,150
		DR 13.5	0.491	5.644	3.76	83.2	198	288	688	1,000	2,390
		DR 17	0.390	5.846	3.04	91.3	218	316	755	1,100	2,620
		DR 21	0.315	5.994	2.49	97.5	232	338	806	1,170	2,790
		DR 26	0.255	6.115	2.03	103	245	356	850	1,240	2,950
		DR 32.5	0.204	6.217	1.64	107	256	372	887	1,290	3,080
8	8.625	DR 11	0.784	7.057	7.68	150	357	519	1,240	1,800	4,290
		DR 13.5	0.639	7.347	6.38	166	397	577	1,380	2,000	4,770
		DR 17	0.507	7.610	5.15	183	436	633	1,510	2,200	5,240
		DR 21	0.411	7.804	4.22	195	465	676	1,610	2,350	5,590
		DR 26	0.332	7.962	3.44	206	490	713	1,700	2,470	5,900
		DR 32.5	0.265	8.094	2.77	215	512	745	1,780	2,580	6,160

Notes:
1 * Dimension Ratio = Outside Diameter / Wall Thickness or Wall Thickness = Outside Diameter / Dimension Ratio
2 ** Based on an average density of 57.3 pounds per cubic foot for polybutylene. Actual weight may vary by ± 3%.
3 Diameter and wall thickness data from: ANSI / AWWA Standard C902-88 and ASTM Designations D 3000 - 95a, F 809/F 809M - 95

Polyethylene (PE) Pipe - Controlled on Inside Diameter - Properties and Friction Loss

Nominal Pipe Size	Inside Diameter	Dimension Ratio - (DR) or Schedule Number*	Minimum Wall Thickness	Outside Diameter	Theoretical Weight Per Foot**	Theoretical Flow Rate (Gallons per Minute) Which Will Cause A Head Loss (H_f) In 100 Feet of Pipe H_f					
						0.1	0.5	1.0	5.0	10.0	50.0
(inch)	(inch)		(inch)	(inch)	(pound)	(feet)	(feet)	(feet)	(feet)	(feet)	(feet)
1/2	0.622	DR 5.3	0.117	0.857	0.111	0.252	0.601	0.873	2.08	3.03	7.22
		Schedule 40	0.109	0.840	0.102						
		DR 7	0.089	0.800	0.081						
		DR 9	0.069	0.760	0.061						
		DR 11.5	0.060	0.742	0.052						
		DR 15	0.060	0.742	0.052						
		DR 19	0.060	0.742	0.052						
3/4	0.824	DR 5.3	0.155	1.135	0.194	0.528	1.258	1.83	4.36	6.34	15.1
		DR 7	0.118	1.059	0.142						
		Schedule 40	0.113	1.050	0.135						
		DR 9	0.092	1.007	0.107						
		DR 11.5	0.072	0.967	0.082						
		DR 15	0.060	0.944	0.068						
		DR 19	0.060	0.944	0.068						
1	1.049	DR 5.3	0.198	1.445	0.315	0.996	2.37	3.45	8.23	12.0	28.5
		DR 7	0.150	1.349	0.229						
		Schedule 40	0.133	1.315	0.201						
		DR 9	0.117	1.282	0.173						
		DR 11.5	0.091	1.231	0.133						
		DR 15	0.070	1.189	0.100						
		DR 19	0.060	1.169	0.085						

Nominal Pipe Size (inch)	Inside Diameter (inch)	Dimension Ratio - (DR) or Schedule Number*	Minimum Wall Thickness (inch)	Outside Diameter (inch)	Theoretical Weight Per Foot** (pound)	Theoretical Flow Rate (Gallons per Minute) Which Will Cause A Head Loss (H$_f$) In 100 Feet of Pipe					
						H$_f$					
						0.1 (feet)	0.5 (feet)	1.0 (feet)	5.0 (feet)	10.0 (feet)	50.0 (feet)
1-1/4	1.380	DR 5.3	0.260	1.901	0.545	2.05	4.88	7.10	16.9	24.6	58.7
		DR 7	0.197	1.774	0.397						
		DR 9	0.153	1.687	0.300						
		Schedule 40	0.140	1.660	0.272						
		DR 11.5	0.120	1.620	0.230						
		DR 15	0.092	1.564	0.173						
		DR 19	0.073	1.525	0.135						
1-1/2	1.610	DR 5.3	0.304	2.218	0.742	3.07	7.33	10.7	25.4	36.9	88.1
		DR 7	0.230	2.070	0.540						
		DR 9	0.179	1.968	0.409						
		Schedule 40	0.145	1.900	0.325						
		DR 11.5	0.140	1.890	0.313						
		DR 15	0.107	1.825	0.235						
		DR 19	0.085	1.779	0.183						
2	2.067	DR 5.3	0.390	2.847	1.22	5.93	14.1	20.6	49.0	71.3	170
		DR 7	0.295	2.658	0.891						
		DR 9	0.230	2.526	0.673						
		DR 11.5	0.180	2.426	0.516						
		Schedule 40	0.154	2.375	0.437						
		DR 15	0.138	2.343	0.388						
		DR 19	0.109	2.285	0.302						

Polyethylene (PE) Pipe - Controlled On Inside Diameter - Properties And Friction Loss (cont.)

Nominal Pipe Size (inch)	Inside Diameter (inch)	Dimension Ratio - (DR) or Schedule Number*	Minimum Wall Thickness (inch)	Outside Diameter (inch)	Theoretical Weight Per Foot** (pound)	Theoretical Flow Rate (Gallons per Minute) Which Will Cause A Head Loss (H_f) In 100 Feet of Pipe — H_f					
						0.1 (feet)	0.5 (feet)	1.0 (feet)	5.0 (feet)	10.0 (feet)	50.0 (feet)
2-1/2	2.469	DR 5.3	0.466	3.401	1.75	9.46	22.6	32.8	78.2	114	271
		DR 7	0.353	3.175	1.27						
		DR 9	0.272	3.013	0.952						
		DR 11.5	0.215	2.898	0.736						
		Schedule 40	0.203	2.875	0.693						
		DR 15	0.165	2.798	0.554						
		DR 19	0.130	2.729	0.431						
3	3.068	DR 5.3	0.579	4.226	2.70	16.7	39.9	58.1	138	201	480
		DR 7	0.438	3.944	1.96						
		DR 9	0.341	3.750	1.48						
		DR 11.5	0.267	3.602	1.14						
		Schedule 40	0.216	3.500	0.906						
		DR 15	0.205	3.477	0.855						
		DR 19	0.161	3.391	0.666						
4	4.026	DR 11.5	0.350	4.726	1.96	34.2	81.6	119	283	411	981
		DR 15	0.268	4.563	1.47						
		Schedule 40	0.237	4.500	1.29						
		DR 19	0.212	4.450	1.15						

Nominal Pipe Size	Inside Diameter	Dimension Ratio - (DR) or Schedule Number*	Minimum Wall Thickness	Outside Diameter	Theoretical Weight Per Foot**	Theoretical Flow Rate (Gallons per Minute) Which Will Cause A Head Loss (H_f) in 100 Feet of Pipe					
						H_f					
						0.1	0.5	1.0	5.0	10.0	50.0
(inch)	(inch)		(inch)	(inch)	(pound)	(feet)	(feet)	(feet)	(feet)	(feet)	(feet)
6	6.065	DR 11.5	0.527	7.120	4.44	101	240	349	831	1,210	2,880
		DR 15	0.404	6.874	3.34						
		DR 19	0.319	6.703	2.60						
		Schedule 40	0.280	6.625	2.27						

Notes:

1* Dimension Ratio = Inside Diameter/Wall Thickness or Wall Thickness = Inside Diameter/Dimension Ratio

2** Based on an average density of 58.5 pounds per cubic foot for polyethylene. Actual weight may vary by ± 3%.

3 Diameter and wall thickness data from: ANSI/ AWWA Standard C901-96; ASTM Designations D 2104 - 95, D 2239 - 96a, F 771 - 95

Polyethylene (PE) Pipe - Controlled On Outside Diameter - Properties And Friction Loss

Nominal Pipe Size	Outside Diameter	Dimension Ratio - (DR) or Schedule Number*	Minimum Wall Thickness	Inside Diameter	Theoretical Weight Per Foot**	Theoretical Flow Rate (Gallons per Minute) Which Will Cause A Head Loss (H_f) In 100 Feet of Pipe H_f					
						0.1	0.5	1.0	5.0	10.0	50.0
(inch)	(inch)		(inch)	(inch)	(pound)	(feet)	(feet)	(feet)	(feet)	(feet)	(feet)
1/2	0.840	Schedule 80	0.147	0.546	0.130	0.179	0.426	0.620	1.48	2.15	5.13
		DR 7	0.120	0.600	0.110	0.229	0.546	0.794	1.89	2.75	6.57
		Schedule 40	0.109	0.622	0.102	0.252	0.601	0.873	2.08	3.03	7.22
		DR 9	0.093	0.653	0.089	0.287	0.683	0.994	2.37	3.45	8.22
		DR 9.3	0.090	0.659	0.086	0.294	0.700	1.02	2.43	3.53	8.42
		DR 11	0.076	0.687	0.074	0.327	0.781	1.14	2.71	3.94	9.39
		DR 13.5	0.062	0.716	0.062	0.364	0.868	1.26	3.01	4.38	10.4
		DR 15.5	0.062	0.716	0.062	0.365	0.870	1.26	3.02	4.38	10.5
		DR 17	0.062	0.716	0.062	0.365	0.870	1.26	3.02	4.38	10.5
		DR 21	0.062	0.716	0.062	0.365	0.870	1.26	3.02	4.38	10.5
		DR 26	0.062	0.716	0.062	0.365	0.870	1.26	3.02	4.38	10.5
		DR 32.5	0.062	0.716	0.062	0.365	0.870	1.26	3.02	4.38	10.5
3/4	1.050	Schedule 80	0.154	0.742	0.176	0.401	0.955	1.39	3.31	4.82	11.5
		DR 7	0.150	0.750	0.172	0.412	0.983	1.43	3.41	4.95	11.8
		DR 9	0.117	0.817	0.139	0.515	1.23	1.79	4.26	6.20	14.8
		DR 9.3	0.113	0.824	0.135	0.528	1.26	1.83	4.37	6.35	15.1
		Schedule 40	0.113	0.824	0.135	0.528	1.26	1.83	4.36	6.34	15.1
		DR 11	0.095	0.859	0.116	0.589	1.40	2.04	4.87	7.08	16.9
		DR 13.5	0.078	0.894	0.097	0.655	1.56	2.27	5.41	7.87	18.8
		DR 15.5	0.068	0.915	0.085	0.694	1.66	2.41	5.74	8.34	19.9

Nominal Pipe Size	Outside Diameter	Dimension Ratio - (DR) or Schedule Number*	Minimum Wall Thickness	Inside Diameter	Theoretical Weight Per Foot**	Theoretical Flow Rate (Gallons per Minute) Which Will Cause A Head Loss (Hf) In 100 Feet of Pipe					
						Hf					
						0.1	0.5	1.0	5.0	10.0	50.0
(inch)	(inch)		(inch)	(inch)	(pound)	(feet)	(feet)	(feet)	(feet)	(feet)	(feet)
3/4	1.050	DR 17	0.062	0.926	0.078	0.718	1.71	2.49	5.94	8.63	20.6
		DR 21	0.062	0.926	0.078	0.717	1.71	2.49	5.93	8.62	20.6
		DR 26	0.062	0.926	0.078	0.717	1.71	2.49	5.93	8.62	20.6
		DR 32.5	0.062	0.926	0.078	0.717	1.71	2.49	5.93	8.62	20.6
1	1.315	DR 7	0.188	0.939	0.270	0.745	1.78	2.58	6.16	8.95	21.3
		Schedule 80	0.179	0.957	0.260	0.782	1.87	2.71	6.47	9.40	22.4
		DR 9	0.146	1.023	0.218	0.932	2.22	3.23	7.70	11.2	26.7
		DR 9.3	0.141	1.032	0.212	0.954	2.28	3.31	7.89	11.5	27.4
		Schedule 40	0.133	1.049	0.201	1.00	2.37	3.45	8.23	12.0	28.5
		DR 11	0.120	1.076	0.182	1.06	2.54	3.69	8.80	12.8	30.5
		DR 13.5	0.097	1.120	0.151	1.18	2.82	4.10	9.79	14.2	33.9
		DR 15.5	0.085	1.145	0.133	1.25	2.99	4.35	10.4	15.1	36.0
		DR 17	0.077	1.160	0.122	1.30	3.10	4.50	10.7	15.6	37.2
		DR 21	0.063	1.190	0.100	1.39	3.31	4.81	11.5	16.7	39.8
		DR 26	0.062	1.191	0.099	1.39	3.32	4.82	11.5	16.7	39.9
		DR 32.5	0.062	1.191	0.099	1.39	3.32	4.82	11.5	16.7	39.9
1-1/4	1.660	DR 7	0.237	1.186	0.431	1.37	3.28	4.76	11.4	16.5	39.4
		Schedule 80	0.191	1.278	0.358	1.67	3.99	5.80	13.8	20.1	48.0
		DR 9	0.184	1.291	0.348	1.72	4.10	5.96	14.2	20.7	49.3
		DR 9.3	0.178	1.303	0.338	1.76	4.20	6.11	14.6	21.2	50.5
		DR 11	0.151	1.358	0.291	1.96	4.68	6.81	16.2	23.6	56.3
		Schedule 40	0.140	1.380	0.272	2.05	4.88	7.10	16.9	24.6	58.7
		DR 13.5	0.123	1.414	0.241	2.18	5.21	7.57	18.1	26.3	62.6

Polyethylene (PE) Pipe - Controlled On Outside Diameter - Properties and Friction Loss (cont.)

Nominal Pipe Size	Outside Diameter	Dimension Ratio - (DR) or Schedule Number*	Minimum Wall Thickness	Inside Diameter	Theoretical Weight Per Foot**	Theoretical Flow Rate (Gallons per Minute) Which Will Cause A Head Loss (H$_f$) In 100 Feet of Pipe					
						H$_f$					
(inch)	(inch)		(inch)		(pound)	0.1 (feet)	0.5 (feet)	1.0 (feet)	5.0 (feet)	10.0 (feet)	50.0 (feet)
1-1/4	1.660	DR 15.5	0.107	1.446	0.212	2.32	5.52	8.03	19.1	27.8	66.4
		DR 17	0.098	1.465	0.195	2.40	5.71	8.31	19.8	28.8	68.7
		DR 21	0.079	1.502	0.160	2.56	6.10	8.87	21.2	30.8	73.4
		DR 26	0.064	1.532	0.130	2.70	6.43	9.35	22.3	32.4	77.3
		DR 32.5	0.062	1.536	0.127	2.71	6.47	9.41	22.4	32.6	77.8
1-1/2	1.900	DR 7	0.271	1.357	0.564	1.96	4.67	6.80	16.2	23.6	56.2
		DR 9	0.211	1.478	0.455	2.45	5.85	8.50	20.3	29.5	70.3
		DR 9.3	0.204	1.491	0.442	2.51	5.99	8.71	20.8	30.2	72.0
		Schedule 80	0.200	1.500	0.434	2.55	6.08	8.84	21.1	30.7	73.1
		DR 11	0.173	1.555	0.381	2.80	6.68	9.71	23.2	33.7	80.3
		Schedule 40	0.145	1.610	0.325	3.07	7.33	10.7	25.4	36.9	88.1
		DR 13.5	0.141	1.619	0.316	3.12	7.43	10.8	25.8	37.5	89.3
		DR 15.5	0.123	1.655	0.278	3.30	7.88	11.5	27.3	39.7	94.7
		DR 17	0.112	1.676	0.255	3.42	8.15	11.8	28.3	41.1	98.0
		DR 21	0.090	1.719	0.209	3.65	8.70	12.7	30.2	43.9	105
		DR 26	0.073	1.754	0.170	3.85	9.18	13.3	31.8	46.3	110
		DR 32.5	0.062	1.776	0.146	3.98	9.48	13.8	32.9	47.8	114
2	2.375	DR 7	0.339	1.696	0.882	3.53	8.41	12.2	29.1	42.4	101
		DR 9	0.264	1.847	0.711	4.41	10.5	15.3	36.5	53.0	126
		DR 9.3	0.255	1.864	0.691	4.52	10.8	15.7	37.4	54.3	130
		Schedule 80	0.218	1.939	0.600	5.01	11.9	17.4	41.4	60.2	144
		DR 11	0.216	1.943	0.595	5.04	12.0	17.5	41.7	60.6	144

Nominal Pipe Size (inch)	Outside Diameter (inch)	Dimension Ratio - (DR) or Schedule Number*	Minimum Wall Thickness (inch)	Inside Diameter (inch)	Theoretical Weight Per Foot** (pound)	Theoretical Flow Rate (Gallons per Minute) Which Will Cause A Head Loss (H_f) In 100 Feet of Pipe					
						H_f					
						0.1 (feet)	0.5 (feet)	1.0 (feet)	5.0 (feet)	10.0 (feet)	50.0 (feet)
2	2.375	DR 13.5	0.176	2.023	0.494	5.60	13.4	19.4	46.3	67.4	161
		Schedule 40	0.154	2.067	0.437	5.93	14.1	20.6	49.0	71.3	170
		DR 15.5	0.153	2.069	0.435	5.94	14.2	20.6	49.1	71.4	170
		DR 17	0.140	2.096	0.399	6.15	14.7	21.3	50.8	73.9	176
		DR 21	0.113	2.149	0.327	6.56	15.7	22.8	54.3	78.9	188
		DR 26	0.091	2.192	0.266	6.92	16.5	24.0	57.2	83.2	198
		DR 32.5	0.073	2.229	0.215	7.23	17.2	25.1	59.8	86.9	207
2-1/2	2.875	Schedule 80	0.276	2.323	0.916	8.06	19.2	27.9	66.6	96.9	231
		Schedule 40	0.203	1.969	1.40	5.22	12.4	18.1	43.1	62.7	150
3	3.500	DR 7	0.500	2.500	1.92	9.77	23.3	33.9	80.8	118	280
		DR 7.3	0.479	2.541	1.85	10.2	24.3	35.4	84.4	123	293
		DR 8.3	0.422	2.657	1.66	11.5	27.3	39.8	94.8	138	329
		DR 9	0.389	2.722	1.54	12.2	29.2	42.4	101	147	351
		DR 9.3	0.376	2.747	1.50	12.5	29.9	43.4	104	151	359
		DR 11	0.318	2.864	1.29	14.0	33.3	48.4	116	168	401
		Schedule 80	0.300	2.900	1.23	14.4	34.4	50.1	119	174	414
		DR 13.5	0.259	2.981	1.07	15.5	37.0	53.9	128	187	445
		DR 15.5	0.226	3.048	0.944	16.5	39.3	57.1	136	198	472
		Schedule 40	0.216	3.068	0.906	16.7	39.9	58.1	138	201	480
		DR 17	0.206	3.088	0.866	17.0	40.6	59.1	141	205	489
		DR 21	0.167	3.167	0.709	18.2	43.4	63.2	150	219	522
		DR 26	0.135	3.231	0.578	19.2	45.8	66.5	159	231	550
		DR 32.5	0.108	3.285	0.466	20.0	47.8	69.5	166	241	574

Polyethylene (PE) Pipe - Controlled On Outside Diameter - Properties and Friction Loss (cont.)

Nominal Pipe Size	Outside Diameter	Dimension Ratio - (DR) or Schedule Number*	Minimum Wall Thickness	Inside Diameter	Theoretical Weight Per Foot**	Theoretical Flow Rate (Gallons per Minute) Which Will Cause A Head Loss (H_f) In 100 Feet of Pipe					
						H_f					
(inch)	(inch)		(inch)	(inch)	(pound)	0.1	0.5	1.0	5.0	10.0	50.0
						(feet)	(feet)	(feet)	(feet)	(feet)	(feet)
3-1/2	4.000	Schedule 80	0.318	3.364	1.50	21.3	50.9	74.0	176	257	612
		Schedule 40	0.226	3.548	1.09	24.5	58.5	85.1	203	295	704
4	4.500	DR 7	0.643	3.214	3.17	18.9	45.1	65.6	157	228	543
		DR 7.3	0.616	3.267	3.06	19.8	47.1	68.5	163	238	566
		DR 8.3	0.542	3.416	2.74	22.2	53.0	77.0	184	267	637
		DR 9	0.500	3.500	2.55	23.7	56.5	82.1	196	285	679
		DR 9.3	0.484	3.532	2.48	24.3	57.9	84.1	201	292	696
		DR 11	0.409	3.682	2.14	27.1	64.5	93.8	224	325	776
		Schedule 80	0.337	3.826	1.79	29.9	71.4	104	247	360	858
		DR 13.5	0.333	3.833	1.77	30.1	71.7	104	249	362	862
		DR 15.5	0.290	3.919	1.56	30.7	76.0	111	264	383	914
		DR 17	0.265	3.971	1.43	33.0	78.7	114	273	397	946
		Schedule 40	0.237	4.026	1.29	34.2	81.6	119	283	411	981
		DR 21	0.214	4.071	1.17	35.2	84.1	122	291	424	1,010
		DR 26	0.173	4.154	0.956	37.2	88.6	129	307	447	1,070
		DR 32.5	0.138	4.223	0.771	38.8	92.5	135	321	467	1,110
5	5.375	DR 7.3	0.736	3.902	4.36	31.5	75.2	109	261	379	904
		DR 8.3	0.648	4.080	3.91	35.4	84.5	123	293	426	1,020
		DR 9	0.597	4.181	3.64	37.8	90.1	131	312	454	1,080
		DR 9.3	0.578	4.219	3.54	38.7	92.3	134	320	465	1,110
		DR 11	0.489	4.398	3.05	43.2	103	150	357	519	1,240

Nominal Pipe Size	Outside Diameter	Dimension Ratio - (DR) or Schedule Number*	Minimum Wall Thickness	Inside Diameter	Theoretical Weight Per Foot**	Theoretical Flow Rate (Gallons per Minute) Which Will Cause A Head Loss (H_f) In 100 Feet of Pipe					
						0.1	0.5	1.0	5.0	10.0	50.0
(inch)	(inch)		(inch)		(pound)	(feet)	(feet)	(feet)	(feet)	(feet)	(feet)
5	5.375	DR 13.5	0.398	4.579	2.53	48.0	114	166	397	577	1,380
		DR 15.5	0.347	4.681	2.23	50.9	121	176	421	612	1,460
		DR 17	0.316	4.743	2.04	52.7	126	183	435	633	1,510
		DR 21	0.256	4.863	1.67	56.2	134	195	465	676	1,610
		DR 26	0.207	4.962	1.36	59.3	141	206	490	713	1,700
		DR 32.5	0.165	5.044	1.10	61.9	148	215	512	744	1,780
	5.563	DR 7	0.795	3.974	4.84	33.1	78.8	115	273	397	948
		DR 7.3	0.762	4.039	4.67	34.5	82.3	120	285	415	989
		DR 8.3	0.670	4.223	4.19	38.8	92.5	135	321	466	1,110
		DR 9	0.618	4.327	3.90	41.4	98.6	143	342	497	1,190
		DR 9.3	0.598	4.367	3.79	42.4	101	147	350	509	1,210
		DR 11	0.506	4.552	3.27	47.3	113	164	391	568	1,350
		DR 13.5	0.412	4.739	2.71	52.5	125	182	434	632	1,510
		Schedule 80	0.375	4.813	2.48	54.7	131	190	453	658	1,570
		DR 15.5	0.359	4.845	2.38	55.7	133	193	461	670	1,600
		DR 17	0.327	4.909	2.19	57.6	137	200	477	693	1,650
		DR 21	0.265	5.033	1.79	61.6	147	213	509	740	1,770
	5.563	Schedule 40	0.258	5.047	1.75	62.0	148	215	513	746	1,780
		DR 26	0.214	5.135	1.46	64.9	155	225	537	780	1,860
		DR 32.5	0.171	5.221	1.18	67.8	162	235	560	815	1,940
6	6.625	DR 7	0.946	4.732	6.86	52.3	125	182	433	629	1,500
		DR 7.3	0.908	4.810	6.63	54.6	130	189	452	657	1,570

Polyethylene (PE) Pipe - Controlled On Outside Diameter - Properties and Friction Loss (cont.)

Nominal Pipe Size	Outside Diameter	Dimension Ratio - (DR) or Schedule Number*	Minimum Wall Thickness	Inside Diameter	Theoretical Weight Per Foot**	Theoretical Flow Rate (Gallons per Minute) Which Will Cause A Head Loss (Hf) In 100 Feet of Pipe					
						Hf					
						0.1	0.5	1.0	5.0	10.0	50.0
(inch)	(inch)		(inch)	(inch)	(pound)	(feet)	(feet)	(feet)	(feet)	(feet)	(feet)
6	6.625	DR 8.3	0.798	5.029	5.94	61.4	146	213	508	738	1,760
		DR 9	0.736	5.153	5.53	65.5	156	227	542	787	1,880
		DR 9.3	0.712	5.200	5.38	67.1	160	233	555	807	1,920
		DR 11	0.602	5.420	4.63	74.8	178	259	619	900	2,150
		DR 13.5	0.491	5.644	3.84	83.2	198	288	688	1,000	2,390
		Schedule 80	0.432	5.761	3.42	87.8	209	305	726	1,060	2,520
		DR 15.5	0.427	5.770	3.38	88.2	210	306	729	1,060	2,530
		DR 17	0.390	5.846	3.10	91.3	218	316	755	1,100	2,620
		DR 21	0.315	5.994	2.54	97.5	232	338	806	1,170	2,790
		Schedule 40	0.280	6.065	2.27	101	240	349	831	1,210	2,880
		DR 26	0.255	6.115	2.07	103	245	356	850	1,240	2,950
		DR 32.5	0.204	6.217	1.67	107	256	372	887	1,290	3,080
7	7.125	DR 7.3	0.976	5.173	7.66	66.2	158	229	547	795	1,900
		DR 8.3	0.858	5.408	6.87	74.4	177	258	615	894	2,130
		DR 9	0.792	5.542	6.40	79.3	189	275	656	953	2,270
		DR 9.3	0.766	5.593	6.22	81.2	194	282	672	977	2,330
		DR 11	0.648	5.830	5.36	90.6	216	314	749	1,090	2,600
		DR 13.5	0.528	6.069	4.45	101	240	349	833	1,210	2,890
		DR 15.5	0.460	6.206	3.91	107	255	370	883	1,280	3,060
		DR 17	0.419	6.287	3.59	110	264	383	914	1,330	3,170
		DR 21	0.339	6.446	2.94	118	281	409	976	1,420	3,380

Nominal Pipe Size	Outside Diameter	Dimension Ratio - (DR) or Schedule Number*	Minimum Wall Thickness	Inside Diameter	Theoretical Weight Per Foot **	Theoretical Flow Rate (Gallons per Minute) Which Will Cause A Head Loss (Hf) In 100 Feet of Pipe					
						H_f					
						0.1	0.5	1.0	5.0	10.0	50.0
(inch)	(inch)		(inch)	(inch)	(pound)	(feet)	(feet)	(feet)	(feet)	(feet)	(feet)
7	7.125	DR 26	0.274	6.577	2.40	124	297	431	1,030	1,500	3,570
		DR 32.5	0.219	6.687	1.93	130	310	451	1,070	1,560	3,730
8	8.625	DR 7	1.232	6.161	11.6	105	250	363	866	1,260	3,000
		DR 7.3	1.182	6.262	11.2	109	261	379	904	1,310	3,140
		DR 8.3	1.039	6.547	10.1	123	293	426	1,020	1,480	3,520
		DR 9	0.958	6.708	9.38	131	313	454	1,080	1,580	3,760
		DR 9.3	0.927	6.770	9.12	134	320	466	1,110	1,610	3,850
		DR 11	0.784	7.057	7.85	150	357	519	1,240	1,800	4,290
		DR 13.5	0.639	7.347	6.51	166	397	577	1,380	2,000	4,770
		DR 15.5	0.556	7.512	5.73	176	421	612	1,460	2,120	5,060
		DR 17	0.507	7.610	5.26	183	436	633	1,510	2,200	5,240
		DR 21	0.411	7.804	4.31	195	465	676	1,610	2,350	5,590
		DR 26	0.332	7.962	3.51	206	490	713	1,700	2,470	5,900
		Schedule 40	0.322	7.981	3.41	207	494	718	1,710	2,490	5,930
		DR 32.5	0.265	8.094	2.83	215	512	745	1,780	2,580	6,160

(1) * Dimension Ratio = Outside Diameter / Wall Thickness or Wall Thickness = Outside Diameter / Dimension Ratio

(2) ** Based on an average density of 58.5 pounds per cubic foot for polyethylene. Actual weight may vary by ± 3%.

(3) Diameter and wall thickness data from : ANSI / AWWA Standards C901-96, C906-90 and ASTM Designations D 2447 - 95, D 3035 - 95, F 714 - 95, F 771 - 95

Steel Pipe and Tube - Properties and Friction Loss

Nominal or Standard Pipe Size (inch)	Outside Diameter (inch)	Pipe Schedule Number or Weight Class* a	b	c	Wall Thickness (inch)	Inside Diameter (inch)	Weight Per Foot ** (pound)	Theoretical Flow Rate (Gallons per Minute) Which Will Cause A Head Loss (H_L) In 100 Feet of Pipe H_L 0.1 (feet)	0.5 (feet)	1.0 (feet)	5.0 (feet)	10.0 (feet)	50.0 (feet)
1/8	0.125		Tube		0.022	0.081	0.024	0.0009	0.002	0.003	0.008	0.011	0.026
					0.028	0.069	0.029	0.0006	0.001	0.002	0.005	0.007	0.017
					0.032	0.061	0.032	0.0003	0.001	0.001	0.004	0.005	0.012
					0.035	0.055	0.034	0.0003	0.0008	0.001	0.003	0.004	0.009
					0.049	0.027	0.040	0.0001	0.0001	0.0002	0.0004	0.0006	0.001
	0.405	10	---	10S	0.049	0.307	0.186	0.030	0.072	0.105	0.250	0.364	0.867
		40	S	40S	0.068	0.269	0.245	0.021	0.051	0.074	0.177	0.257	0.613
		80	XS	80S	0.095	0.215	0.315	0.012	0.028	0.041	0.098	0.143	0.340
1/4	0.250		Tube		0.022	0.206	0.054	0.011	0.025	0.037	0.088	0.127	0.304
					0.025	0.200	0.060	0.010	0.023	0.034	0.081	0.118	0.281
					0.028	0.194	0.066	0.009	0.022	0.031	0.075	0.109	0.259
					0.032	0.186	0.075	0.008	0.019	0.028	0.067	0.097	0.232
					0.035	0.180	0.080	0.007	0.018	0.026	0.061	0.089	0.213
					0.042	0.166	0.093	0.006	0.014	0.021	0.050	0.072	0.172
					0.049	0.152	0.105	0.005	0.011	0.017	0.039	0.057	0.137
					0.058	0.134	0.119	0.003	0.008	0.012	0.028	0.041	0.098
					0.065	0.120	0.128	0.003	0.006	0.009	0.021	0.031	0.073
					0.083	0.084	0.148	0.001	0.002	0.003	0.008	0.012	0.029
					0.095	0.060	0.157	0.0004	0.001	0.001	0.003	0.005	0.012
	0.540	10	---	10S	0.065	0.410	0.330	0.065	0.154	0.224	0.535	0.778	1.86
		40	S	40S	0.088	0.364	0.425	0.047	0.113	0.164	0.391	0.569	1.36
		80	XS	80S	0.119	0.302	0.535	0.029	0.069	0.100	0.240	0.348	0.831

Nominal or Standard Pipe Size	Outside Diameter	Pipe Schedule Number or Weight Class			Wall Thickness	Inside Diameter	Weight Per Foot	Theoretical Flow Rate (Gallons per Minute) Which Will Cause A Head Loss (Hf) In 100 Feet of Pipe					
		a	b	c				Hf					
(inch)	(inch)				(inch)	(inch)	(pound)	0.1 (feet)	0.5 (feet)	1.0 (feet)	5.0 (feet)	10.0 (feet)	50.0 (feet)
3/8	0.375		Tube		0.022	0.331	0.083	0.037	0.088	0.128	0.305	0.443	1.06
					0.028	0.319	0.104	0.033	0.080	0.116	0.277	0.402	0.959
					0.032	0.311	0.117	0.031	0.075	0.109	0.259	0.376	0.897
					0.035	0.305	0.127	0.030	0.071	0.103	0.246	0.357	0.853
					0.042	0.291	0.149	0.026	0.063	0.091	0.217	0.316	0.753
					0.049	0.277	0.171	0.023	0.055	0.080	0.191	0.278	0.662
					0.058	0.259	0.196	0.019	0.046	0.067	0.160	0.233	0.555
					0.065	0.245	0.215	0.017	0.040	0.058	0.138	0.201	0.479
					0.072	0.231	0.233	0.014	0.034	0.050	0.118	0.172	0.410
					0.083	0.209	0.259	0.011	0.026	0.038	0.091	0.132	0.315
					0.095	0.185	0.284	0.008	0.019	0.028	0.066	0.096	0.229
					0.109	0.157	0.310	0.005	0.012	0.018	0.043	0.062	0.149
					0.125	0.125	0.334	0.003	0.007	0.010	0.024	0.034	0.082
					0.134	0.107	0.345	0.002	0.005	0.007	0.016	0.023	0.054
	0.675	10	---	10S	0.065	0.545	0.423	0.137	0.326	0.475	1.13	1.65	3.92
		40	S	40S	0.091	0.493	0.568	0.105	0.251	0.365	0.869	1.26	3.01
		80	XS	80S	0.126	0.423	0.739	0.070	0.168	0.244	0.581	0.845	2.01
1/2	0.500		Tube		0.022	0.456	0.112	0.086	0.204	0.297	0.708	1.029	2.46
					0.028	0.444	0.141	0.080	0.190	0.277	0.660	0.960	2.29
					0.032	0.436	0.160	0.076	0.181	0.264	0.629	0.915	2.18
					0.035	0.430	0.174	0.073	0.175	0.254	0.607	0.882	2.10
					0.049	0.402	0.236	0.061	0.147	0.213	0.508	0.739	1.76
					0.058	0.384	0.274	0.054	0.130	0.189	0.451	0.655	1.56

Steel Pipe and Tube - Properties and Friction Loss (cont.)

Nominal or Standard Pipe Size	Outside Diameter	Pipe Schedule Number or Weight Class a	b	c	Wall Thickness	Inside Diameter	Weight Per Foot	Theoretical Flow Rate (Gallons per Minute) Which Will Cause A Head Loss (Hf) In 100 Feet of Pipe Hf 0.1	0.5	1.0	5.0	10.0	50.0
(inch)	(inch)				(inch)	(inch)	(pound)	(feet)	(feet)	(feet)	(feet)	(feet)	(feet)
1/2	0.500		Tube		0.065	0.370	0.302	0.049	0.118	0.171	0.409	0.594	1.42
					0.072	0.356	0.329	0.045	0.106	0.155	0.369	0.537	1.28
					0.083	0.334	0.370	0.038	0.090	0.131	0.312	0.454	1.08
					0.095	0.310	0.411	0.031	0.074	0.108	0.257	0.373	0.89
					0.109	0.282	0.455	0.024	0.058	0.084	0.200	0.291	0.69
					0.120	0.260	0.487	0.020	0.047	0.068	0.162	0.235	0.56
					0.125	0.250	0.501	0.018	0.042	0.061	0.146	0.212	0.51
					0.134	0.232	0.524	0.014	0.035	0.050	0.120	0.174	0.42
					0.156	0.188	0.573	0.008	0.020	0.029	0.069	0.100	0.24
					0.188	0.124	0.626	0.003	0.007	0.010	0.023	0.034	0.08
	0.840	5		5S	0.065	0.710	0.538	0.274	0.654	0.951	2.27	3.30	7.87
		10		10S	0.083	0.674	0.671	0.239	0.571	0.830	1.98	2.88	6.86
				40S	0.103	0.634	0.811	0.204	0.486	0.706	1.68	2.45	5.84
		40	S		0.109	0.622	0.851	0.194	0.462	0.672	1.60	2.33	5.55
					0.140	0.560	1.05	0.147	0.351	0.510	1.22	1.77	4.21
		80	XS	80S	0.147	0.546	1.09	0.138	0.328	0.477	1.14	1.65	3.94
		160			0.188	0.464	1.31	0.090	0.214	0.311	0.741	1.08	2.57
				XXS	0.294	0.252	1.71	0.018	0.043	0.062	0.149	0.216	0.516
5/8	0.625		Tube		0.022	0.581	0.142	0.162	0.386	0.561	1.34	1.95	4.64
					0.028	0.569	0.179	0.153	0.366	0.531	1.27	1.84	4.39
					0.032	0.561	0.203	0.148	0.352	0.512	1.22	1.78	4.23
					0.035	0.555	0.221	0.144	0.342	0.498	1.19	1.73	4.12

Nominal or Standard Pipe Size	Outside Diameter	Pipe Schedule Number or Weight Class*			Wall Thickness	Inside Diameter	Weight Per Foot **	Theoretical Flow Rate (Gallons per Minute) Which Will Cause A Head Loss (Hf) In 100 Feet of Pipe					
		a	b	c				Hf					
								0.1	0.5	1.0	5.0	10.0	50.0
(inch)	(inch)				(inch)	(inch)	(pound)	(feet)	(feet)	(feet)	(feet)	(feet)	(feet)
5/8	0.625	Tube			0.042	0.541	0.262	0.134	0.320	0.465	1.11	1.61	3.85
					0.049	0.527	0.301	0.125	0.299	0.434	1.04	1.51	3.59
					0.058	0.509	0.351	0.114	0.273	0.396	0.945	1.37	3.28
					0.065	0.495	0.389	0.106	0.253	0.368	0.879	1.28	3.05
					0.072	0.481	0.425	0.099	0.235	0.342	0.815	1.18	2.83
					0.083	0.459	0.480	0.087	0.208	0.302	0.720	1.05	2.50
					0.095	0.435	0.538	0.076	0.180	0.262	0.625	0.909	2.17
					0.109	0.407	0.601	0.064	0.151	0.220	0.525	0.763	1.82
					0.120	0.385	0.647	0.055	0.131	0.190	0.454	0.660	1.57
					0.125	0.375	0.668	0.051	0.122	0.178	0.423	0.616	1.47
					0.134	0.357	0.703	0.045	0.107	0.156	0.372	0.541	1.29
					0.156	0.313	0.781	0.032	0.076	0.110	0.263	0.383	0.913
					0.188	0.249	0.877	0.017	0.042	0.060	0.144	0.210	0.500
					0.219	0.187	0.950	0.008	0.020	0.028	0.068	0.099	0.235
3/4	0.750	Tube			0.022	0.706	0.171	0.270	0.645	0.937	2.24	3.25	7.75
					0.028	0.694	0.216	0.258	0.616	0.896	2.14	3.11	7.41
					0.035	0.680	0.267	0.245	0.584	0.849	2.03	2.94	7.02
					0.049	0.652	0.367	0.219	0.523	0.760	1.81	2.64	6.29
					0.058	0.634	0.429	0.204	0.486	0.706	1.68	2.45	5.84
					0.065	0.620	0.476	0.192	0.458	0.666	1.59	2.31	5.51
					0.072	0.606	0.521	0.181	0.431	0.627	1.50	2.17	5.19
					0.083	0.584	0.591	0.164	0.391	0.569	1.36	1.97	4.71
					0.095	0.560	0.665	0.147	0.351	0.510	1.22	1.77	4.21

Steel Pipe and Tube - Properties and Friction Loss (cont.)

Nominal or Standard Pipe Size	Outside Diameter	Pipe Schedule Number or Weight Class*			Wall Thickness	Inside Diameter	Weight Per Foot **	Theoretical Flow Rate (Gallons per Minute) Which Will Cause A Head Loss (Hf) In 100 Feet of Pipe					
								0.1	0.5	1.0	5.0	10.0	50.0
(inch)	(inch)	a	b	c	(inch)	(inch)	(pound)	(feet)	(feet)	(feet)	(feet)	(feet)	(feet)
3/4	0.750		Tube		0.109	0.532	0.746	0.128	0.306	0.445	1.06	1.54	3.68
					0.120	0.510	0.807	0.115	0.274	0.399	0.950	1.38	3.30
					0.125	0.500	0.834	0.109	0.260	0.378	0.902	1.31	3.13
					0.134	0.482	0.882	0.099	0.236	0.344	0.819	1.19	2.84
					0.156	0.438	0.990	0.077	0.184	0.267	0.637	0.926	2.21
					0.172	0.406	1.062	0.063	0.150	0.219	0.522	0.759	1.81
					0.188	0.374	1.128	0.051	0.121	0.176	0.420	0.611	1.46
					0.219	0.312	1.242	0.032	0.075	0.109	0.261	0.379	0.905
					0.250	0.250	1.335	0.018	0.042	0.061	0.146	0.212	0.505
	1.050	5	---	5S	0.065	0.920	0.684	0.542	1.29	1.88	4.48	6.52	15.6
		10	---	10S	0.083	0.884	0.857	0.488	1.16	1.69	4.04	5.87	14.0
		---	---	40S	0.108	0.834	1.09	0.419	1.00	1.45	3.46	5.04	12.0
		40	S	---	0.113	0.824	1.13	0.406	0.968	1.41	3.36	4.88	11.6
		---	---	80S	0.147	0.756	1.42	0.324	0.772	1.12	2.68	3.89	9.28
		80	XS	---	0.154	0.742	1.47	0.308	0.735	1.07	2.55	3.70	8.83
		160	---	---	0.219	0.612	1.94	0.186	0.443	0.644	1.54	2.23	5.32
		---	XXS	---	0.308	0.434	2.44	0.075	0.179	0.261	0.622	0.904	2.16
7/8	0.875		Tube		0.028	0.819	0.253	0.399	0.953	1.39	3.30	4.80	11.5
					0.032	0.811	0.288	0.389	0.928	1.35	3.22	4.68	11.2
					0.035	0.805	0.314	0.382	0.910	1.32	3.16	4.59	10.9
					0.049	0.777	0.432	0.348	0.829	1.21	2.88	4.18	9.97

Nominal or Standard Pipe Size (inch)	Outside Diameter (inch)	Pipe Schedule Number or Weight Class ** a	b	c	Wall Thickness (inch)	Inside Diameter (inch)	Weight Per Foot ** (pound)	Theoretical Flow Rate (Gallons per Minute) Which Will Cause A Head Loss (H_L) In 100 Feet of Pipe — H_L 0.1 (feet)	0.5 (feet)	1.0 (feet)	5.0 (feet)	10.0 (feet)	50.0 (feet)
7/8	0.875		Tube		0.058	0.759	0.506	0.327	0.780	1.13	2.70	3.93	9.38
					0.065	0.745	0.562	0.311	0.743	1.08	2.57	3.74	8.93
					0.072	0.731	0.617	0.296	0.706	1.03	2.45	3.56	8.49
					0.083	0.709	0.702	0.273	0.652	0.948	2.26	3.29	7.84
					0.095	0.685	0.791	0.250	0.595	0.866	2.06	3.00	7.16
					0.109	0.657	0.892	0.224	0.534	0.776	1.85	2.69	6.41
					0.120	0.635	0.968	0.205	0.488	0.709	1.69	2.46	5.87
					0.125	0.625	1.00	0.196	0.468	0.680	1.62	2.36	5.63
					0.134	0.607	1.06	0.182	0.433	0.630	1.50	2.18	5.21
					0.156	0.563	1.20	0.149	0.355	0.517	1.23	1.79	4.27
					0.188	0.499	1.38	0.109	0.259	0.376	0.897	1.30	3.11
					0.219	0.437	1.53	0.077	0.183	0.265	0.633	0.920	2.20
					0.250	0.375	1.67	0.051	0.122	0.178	0.423	0.616	1.47
					0.281	0.313	1.78	0.032	0.076	0.110	0.263	0.383	0.913
					0.313	0.249	1.88	0.017	0.042	0.060	0.144	0.210	0.500
1	1.000		Tube		0.028	0.944	0.291	0.580	1.38	2.01	4.80	6.98	16.6
					0.032	0.936	0.331	0.568	1.35	1.97	4.69	6.82	16.3
					0.035	0.930	0.361	0.558	1.33	1.93	4.61	6.71	16.0
					0.049	0.902	0.498	0.515	1.23	1.79	4.26	6.19	14.8
					0.058	0.884	0.584	0.488	1.16	1.69	4.04	5.87	14.0
					0.065	0.870	0.649	0.468	1.12	1.62	3.87	5.63	13.4
					0.072	0.856	0.714	0.449	1.07	1.56	3.71	5.39	12.9
					0.083	0.834	0.813	0.419	1.00	1.45	3.46	5.04	12.0
					0.095	0.810	0.918	0.388	0.925	1.35	3.21	4.67	11.1

Steel Pipe and Tube - Properties and Friction Loss (cont.)

Nominal or Standard Pipe Size	Outside Diameter	Pipe Schedule Number or Weight Class*			Wall Thickness	Inside Diameter	Weight Per Foot **	Theoretical Flow Rate (Gallons per Minute) Which Will Cause A Head Loss (H_f) In 100 Feet of Pipe					
		a	b	c				0.1	0.5	1.0	5.0	10.0	50.0
(inch)	(inch)				(inch)	(inch)	(pound)	(feet)	(feet)	(feet)	(feet)	(feet)	(feet)
	1.000		Tube		0.109	0.782	1.04	0.354	0.844	1.23	2.92	4.25	10.1
					0.120	0.760	1.13	0.328	0.783	1.14	2.71	3.95	9.41
					0.125	0.750	1.17	0.317	0.756	1.10	2.62	3.81	9.09
					0.134	0.732	1.24	0.297	0.709	1.03	2.46	3.57	8.52
					0.156	0.688	1.41	0.253	0.602	0.876	2.09	3.04	7.24
					0.172	0.656	1.52	0.223	0.531	0.773	1.84	2.68	6.39
					0.180	0.640	1.58	0.209	0.498	0.724	1.73	2.51	5.99
					0.188	0.624	1.63	0.195	0.466	0.677	1.62	2.35	5.60
					0.219	0.562	1.83	0.148	0.354	0.514	1.23	1.78	4.25
					0.250	0.500	2.00	0.109	0.260	0.378	0.902	1.31	3.13
					0.281	0.438	2.16	0.077	0.184	0.267	0.637	0.926	2.21
					0.313	0.374	2.30	0.051	0.121	0.176	0.420	0.611	1.46
					0.344	0.312	2.41	0.032	0.075	0.109	0.261	0.379	0.905
					0.375	0.250	2.50	0.018	0.042	0.061	0.146	0.212	0.505
	1.315	5	---	5S	0.065	1.185	0.868	1.06	2.52	3.66	8.73	12.7	30.3
		10	---	10S	0.109	1.097	1.40	0.862	2.05	2.99	7.12	10.4	24.7
		---	---	---	0.126	1.063	1.60	0.793	1.89	2.75	6.56	9.54	22.7
		40	S	40S	0.133	1.049	1.68	0.766	1.83	2.66	6.33	9.21	22.0
		---	---	---	0.171	0.973	2.09	0.628	1.50	2.18	5.20	7.56	18.0
		80	XS	80S	0.179	0.957	2.17	0.602	1.43	2.09	4.97	7.23	17.3
		160	---	---	0.250	0.815	2.84	0.394	0.940	1.37	3.26	4.74	11.3
		---	XXS	---	0.358	0.599	3.66	0.175	0.418	0.608	1.45	2.11	5.03

Nominal or Standard Pipe Size	Outside Diameter	Pipe Schedule Number or Weight Class*			Wall Thickness	Inside Diameter	Weight Per Foot **	Theoretical Flow Rate (Gallons per Minute) Which Will Cause A Head Loss (H$_L$) In 100 Feet of Pipe					
		a	b	c				H$_L$					
								0.1	0.5	1.0	5.0	10.0	50.0
(inch)	(inch)				(inch)	(inch)	(pound)	(feet)	(feet)	(feet)	(feet)	(feet)	(feet)
1-1/8	1.125	Tube			0.022	1.081	0.259	0.829	1.98	2.87	6.85	9.97	23.8
					0.028	1.069	0.328	0.805	1.92	2.79	6.66	9.68	23.1
					0.035	1.055	0.407	0.778	1.85	2.70	6.43	9.35	22.3
					0.049	1.027	0.563	0.724	1.73	2.51	5.99	8.71	20.8
					0.058	1.009	0.661	0.691	1.65	2.40	5.72	8.31	19.8
					0.065	0.995	0.736	0.667	1.59	2.31	5.51	8.01	19.1
					0.083	0.959	0.924	0.605	1.44	2.10	5.00	7.27	17.3
					0.095	0.935	1.05	0.566	1.35	1.96	4.68	6.80	16.2
					0.109	0.907	1.18	0.522	1.25	1.81	4.32	6.28	15.0
					0.120	0.885	1.29	0.490	1.17	1.70	4.05	5.89	14.0
					0.125	0.875	1.34	0.475	1.13	1.65	3.93	5.72	13.6
					0.134	0.857	1.42	0.450	1.07	1.56	3.72	5.41	12.9
					0.156	0.813	1.61	0.392	0.934	1.36	3.24	4.71	11.2
					0.172	0.781	1.75	0.353	0.841	1.22	2.92	4.24	10.1
					0.188	0.749	1.88	0.316	0.753	1.10	2.61	3.80	9.05
					0.219	0.687	2.12	0.252	0.600	0.872	2.08	3.03	7.21
					0.250	0.625	2.34	0.196	0.468	0.680	1.62	2.36	5.63
					0.281	0.563	2.53	0.149	0.355	0.517	1.23	1.79	4.27
					0.313	0.499	2.71	0.109	0.259	0.376	0.897	1.30	3.11
					0.375	0.375	3.00	0.051	0.122	0.178	0.423	0.616	1.47
1-1/4	1.250	Tube			0.028	1.194	0.365	1.077	2.57	3.73	8.90	12.9	30.9
					0.035	1.180	0.454	1.044	2.49	3.62	8.63	12.5	29.9
					0.049	1.152	0.629	0.980	2.34	3.40	8.10	11.8	28.1

Steel Pipe and Tube - Properties and Friction Loss (cont.)

Nominal or Standard Pipe Size	Outside Diameter	Pipe Schedule Number or Weight Class*			Wall Thickness	Inside Diameter	Weight Per Foot **	Theoretical Flow Rate (Gallons per Minute) Which Will Cause A Head Loss (Hf) In 100 Feet of Pipe					
								Hf					
		a	b	c				0.1	0.5	1.0	5.0	10.0	50.0
(inch)	(inch)				(inch)	(inch)	(pound)	(feet)	(feet)	(feet)	(feet)	(feet)	(feet)
	1.250		Tube		0.058	1.134	0.738	0.940	2.24	3.26	7.77	11.3	27.0
					0.065	1.120	0.823	0.910	2.17	3.15	7.52	10.9	26.1
					0.072	1.106	0.906	0.880	2.10	3.05	7.28	10.6	25.2
					0.083	1.084	1.03	0.835	1.99	2.90	6.90	10.0	23.9
					0.095	1.060	1.17	0.787	1.88	2.73	6.51	9.46	22.6
					0.109	1.032	1.33	0.734	1.75	2.54	6.07	8.82	21.0
					0.120	1.010	1.45	0.693	1.65	2.40	5.73	8.34	19.9
					0.125	1.000	1.50	0.675	1.61	2.34	5.58	8.12	19.4
					0.134	0.982	1.60	0.644	1.54	2.23	5.32	7.74	18.5
					0.156	0.938	1.82	0.571	1.36	1.98	4.72	6.86	16.4
					0.188	0.874	2.13	0.474	1.13	1.64	3.92	5.70	13.6
					0.219	0.812	2.41	0.391	0.931	1.35	3.23	4.70	11.2
					0.250	0.750	2.67	0.317	0.756	1.10	2.62	3.81	9.09
					0.281	0.688	2.91	0.253	0.602	0.876	2.09	3.04	7.24
					0.313	0.624	3.13	0.195	0.466	0.677	1.62	2.35	5.60
					0.344	0.562	3.33	0.148	0.354	0.514	1.23	1.78	4.25
					0.375	0.500	3.50	0.109	0.260	0.378	0.902	1.31	3.13
					0.438	0.374	3.80	0.051	0.121	0.176	0.420	0.611	1.46
1-1/4	1.660	5	---	5S	0.065	1.530	1.11	2.07	4.93	7.17	17.1	24.8	59.3
		10	---	10S	0.109	1.442	1.81	1.77	4.22	6.13	14.6	21.3	50.7
		---	S	---	0.132	1.396	2.15	1.62	3.87	5.63	13.4	19.5	46.6
		40	S	40S	0.140	1.380	2.27	1.58	3.76	5.46	13.0	18.9	45.2

Nominal or Standard Pipe Size	Outside Diameter	Pipe Schedule Number or Weight Class			Wall Thickness	Inside Diameter	Weight Per Foot **	Theoretical Flow Rate (Gallons per Minute) Which Will Cause A Head Loss (H$_L$) In 100 Feet of Pipe — H$_L$					
		a	b	c				0.1	0.5	1.0	5.0	10.0	50.0
(inch)	(inch)				(inch)	(inch)	(pound)	(feet)	(feet)	(feet)	(feet)	(feet)	(feet)
1-1/4	1.660	--	--	--	0.182	1.296	2.87	1.34	3.19	4.63	11.0	16.1	38.3
		80	XS	80S	0.191	1.278	3.00	1.29	3.07	4.46	10.6	15.5	36.9
		160	--	--	0.250	1.160	3.76	1.00	2.38	3.46	8.25	12.0	28.6
		--	XXS	--	0.382	0.896	5.21	0.506	1.21	1.75	4.18	6.08	14.5
1-1/2	1.500	Tube			0.028	1.444	0.440	1.78	4.23	6.15	14.7	21.3	50.9
					0.035	1.430	0.548	1.73	4.13	6.00	14.3	20.8	49.6
					0.049	1.402	0.759	1.64	3.92	5.70	13.6	19.7	47.1
					0.058	1.384	0.893	1.59	3.79	5.50	13.1	19.1	45.5
					0.065	1.370	0.996	1.55	3.69	5.36	12.8	18.6	44.3
					0.072	1.356	1.10	1.50	3.59	5.22	12.4	18.1	43.1
					0.083	1.334	1.26	1.44	3.44	5.00	11.9	17.3	41.3
					0.095	1.310	1.43	1.37	3.28	4.76	11.4	16.5	39.4
					0.109	1.282	1.62	1.30	3.10	4.50	10.7	15.6	37.2
					0.120	1.260	1.77	1.24	2.96	4.30	10.3	14.9	35.6
					0.125	1.250	1.84	1.21	2.90	4.21	10.0	14.6	34.8
					0.134	1.232	1.95	1.17	2.79	4.05	9.67	14.1	33.5
					0.156	1.188	2.24	1.06	2.53	3.68	8.79	12.8	30.5
					0.188	1.124	2.63	0.918	2.19	3.18	7.59	11.0	26.3
					0.219	1.062	3.00	0.791	1.89	2.74	6.54	9.51	22.7
					0.250	1.000	3.34	0.675	1.61	2.34	5.58	8.12	19.4
					0.281	0.938	3.66	0.571	1.36	1.98	4.72	6.86	16.4
					0.313	0.874	3.97	0.474	1.13	1.64	3.92	5.70	13.6
					0.344	0.812	4.25	0.391	0.931	1.35	3.23	4.70	11.2
					0.375	0.750	4.51	0.317	0.756	1.10	2.62	3.81	9.09

Steel Pipe and Tube - Properties and Friction Loss (cont.)

Nominal or Standard Pipe Size	Outside Diameter	Pipe Schedule Number or Weight Class*			Wall Thickness	Inside Diameter	Weight Per Foot **	Theoretical Flow Rate (Gallons per Minute) Which Will Cause A Head Loss (H$_f$) In 100 Feet of Pipe					
		a	b	c				50.0	10.0	5.0	1.0	0.5	0.1
(inch)	(inch)				(inch)	(inch)	(pound)	(feet)	(feet)	(feet)	(feet)	(feet)	(feet)
1-1/2	1.500	Tube			0.438	0.624	4.97	5.60	2.35	1.62	0.677	0.466	0.195
	1.500	Tube			0.500	0.500	5.34	3.13	1.31	0.902	0.378	0.260	0.109
	1.900	5	--	5S	0.065	1.770	1.27	86.9	36.5	25.1	10.5	7.23	3.03
	1.900	10	--	10S	0.109	1.682	2.08	76.0	31.9	21.9	9.19	6.32	2.65
	1.900	40	S	40S	0.145	1.610	2.72	67.8	28.4	19.5	8.19	5.64	2.36
	1.900				0.158	1.584	2.94	64.9	27.2	18.7	7.85	5.40	2.26
	1.900				0.190	1.520	3.47	58.2	24.4	16.8	7.04	4.84	2.03
	1.900	80	XS	80S	0.200	1.500	3.63	56.2	23.6	16.2	6.80	4.68	1.96
	1.900				0.281	1.338	4.86	41.6	17.5	12.0	5.04	3.46	1.45
	1.900	160	--	--	0.400	1.100	6.41	24.9	10.4	7.18	3.01	2.07	0.868
	1.900	--	XXS	--	0.525	0.850	7.71	12.6	5.30	3.64	1.53	1.05	0.440
	1.900				0.650	0.600	8.68	5.05	2.12	1.46	0.611	0.420	0.176
1-5/8	1.625	Tube			0.035	1.555	0.594	61.8	25.9	17.8	7.48	5.14	2.16
	1.625	Tube			0.049	1.527	0.825	59.0	24.7	17.0	7.13	4.90	2.06
	1.625	Tube			0.058	1.509	0.971	57.1	24.0	16.5	6.91	4.75	1.99
	1.625	Tube			0.065	1.495	1.08	55.8	23.4	16.1	6.74	4.64	1.94
	1.625	Tube			0.083	1.459	1.37	52.3	21.9	15.1	6.32	4.35	1.82
	1.625	Tube			0.095	1.435	1.55	50.1	21.0	14.4	6.05	4.16	1.75
	1.625	Tube			0.109	1.407	1.76	47.5	19.9	13.7	5.75	3.95	1.66
	1.625	Tube			0.120	1.385	1.93	45.6	19.1	13.2	5.52	3.79	1.59
	1.625	Tube			0.125	1.375	2.00	44.7	18.8	12.9	5.41	3.72	1.56
	1.625	Tube			0.134	1.357	2.13	43.2	18.1	12.5	5.23	3.59	1.51

Nominal or Standard Pipe Size	Outside Diameter	Pipe Schedule Number or Weight Class*			Wall Thickness	Inside Diameter	Weight Per Foot **	Theoretical Flow Rate (Gallons per Minute) Which Will Cause A Head Loss (H_f) In 100 Feet of Pipe					
		a	b	c				0.1	0.5	1.0	5.0	10.0	50.0
(inch)	(inch)				(inch)	(inch)	(pound)	(feet)	(feet)	(feet)	(feet)	(feet)	(feet)
1-5/8	1.625	Tube			0.156	1.313	2.45	1.38	3.30	4.79	11.4	16.6	39.6
					0.172	1.281	2.67	1.30	3.09	4.49	10.7	15.6	37.1
					0.188	1.249	2.89	1.21	2.89	4.20	10.0	14.6	34.7
					0.219	1.187	3.29	1.06	2.53	3.68	8.77	12.7	30.4
					0.250	1.125	3.67	0.921	2.20	3.19	7.61	11.1	26.4
					0.281	1.063	4.03	0.793	1.89	2.75	6.56	9.54	22.7
					0.313	0.999	4.39	0.674	1.61	2.34	5.57	8.10	19.3
					0.375	0.875	5.01	0.475	1.13	1.65	3.93	5.72	13.6
					0.438	0.749	5.55	0.316	0.753	1.10	2.61	3.80	9.05
					0.500	0.625	6.01	0.196	0.468	0.680	1.62	2.36	5.63
1-3/4	1.750	Tube			0.035	1.680	0.641	2.64	6.30	9.16	21.9	31.8	75.8
					0.049	1.652	0.890	2.53	6.03	8.77	20.9	30.4	72.5
					0.065	1.620	1.17	2.40	5.73	8.33	19.9	28.9	68.9
					0.083	1.584	1.48	2.26	5.40	7.85	18.7	27.2	64.9
					0.095	1.560	1.68	2.18	5.19	7.54	18.0	26.1	62.4
					0.109	1.532	1.91	2.07	4.95	7.19	17.1	24.9	59.5
					0.120	1.510	2.09	2.00	4.76	6.92	16.5	24.0	57.2
					0.125	1.500	2.17	1.96	4.68	6.80	16.2	23.6	56.2
					0.134	1.482	2.31	1.90	4.53	6.59	15.7	22.8	54.5
					0.156	1.438	2.66	1.76	4.19	6.09	14.5	21.1	50.3
					0.188	1.374	3.14	1.56	3.71	5.40	12.9	18.7	44.7
					0.219	1.312	3.58	1.38	3.29	4.78	11.4	16.6	39.6
					0.250	1.250	4.01	1.21	2.90	4.21	10.0	14.6	34.8

Steel Pipe and Tube - Properties and Friction Loss (cont.)

Nominal or Standard Pipe Size	Outside Diameter	Pipe Schedule Number or Weight Class*			Wall Thickness	Inside Diameter	Weight Per Foot **	Theoretical Flow Rate (Gallons per Minute) Which Will Cause A Head Loss (H_L) In 100 Feet of Pipe					
		a	b	c				H_L					
(inch)	(inch)				(inch)	(inch)	(pound)	0.1 (feet)	0.5 (feet)	1.0 (feet)	5.0 (feet)	10.0 (feet)	50.0 (feet)
1-3/4	1.750	Tube			0.281	1.188	4.41	1.06	2.53	3.68	8.79	12.8	30.5
					0.313	1.124	4.80	0.918	2.19	3.18	7.59	11.0	26.3
					0.375	1.000	5.51	0.675	1.61	2.34	5.58	8.12	19.4
					0.438	0.874	6.14	0.474	1.13	1.64	3.92	5.70	13.6
					0.500	0.750	6.68	0.317	0.756	1.10	2.62	3.81	9.09
					0.563	0.624	7.14	0.195	0.466	0.677	1.62	2.35	5.60
					0.625	0.500	7.51	0.109	0.260	0.378	0.902	1.31	3.13
1-7/8	1.875	Tube			0.049	1.777	0.956	3.06	7.31	10.6	25.3	36.8	87.8
					0.065	1.745	1.26	2.92	6.96	10.1	24.1	35.1	83.7
					0.083	1.709	1.59	2.76	6.59	9.59	22.9	33.2	79.3
					0.095	1.685	1.81	2.66	6.35	9.24	22.0	32.0	76.4
					0.109	1.657	2.06	2.55	6.08	8.84	21.1	30.6	73.1
					0.120	1.635	2.25	2.46	5.87	8.53	20.3	29.6	70.6
					0.125	1.625	2.34	2.42	5.77	8.40	20.0	29.1	69.4
					0.134	1.607	2.49	2.35	5.61	8.15	19.4	28.3	67.4
					0.138	1.599	2.56	2.32	5.53	8.05	19.2	27.9	66.5
					0.156	1.563	2.86	2.19	5.21	7.58	18.1	26.3	62.7
					0.188	1.499	3.39	1.96	4.67	6.79	16.2	23.5	56.1
					0.190	1.495	3.42	1.94	4.64	6.74	16.1	23.4	55.8
					0.219	1.437	3.87	1.75	4.18	6.08	14.5	21.1	50.2
					0.250	1.375	4.34	1.56	3.72	5.41	12.9	18.8	44.7
					0.281	1.313	4.78	1.38	3.30	4.79	11.4	16.6	39.6

Nominal or Standard Pipe Size	Outside Diameter	Pipe Schedule Number or Weight Class*			Wall Thickness	Inside Diameter	Weight Per Foot **	Theoretical Flow Rate (Gallons per Minute) Which Will Cause A Head Loss (Ht) In 100 Feet of Pipe					
		a	b	c				Ht					
								0.1	0.5	1.0	5.0	10.0	50.0
(inch)	(inch)				(inch)	(inch)	(pound)	(feet)	(feet)	(feet)	(feet)	(feet)	(feet)
1-7/8	1.875		Tube		0.313	1.249	5.22	1.21	2.89	4.20	10.0	14.6	34.7
					0.375	1.125	6.01	0.921	2.20	3.19	7.61	11.1	26.4
					0.438	0.999	6.72	0.674	1.61	2.34	5.57	8.10	19.3
					0.500	0.875	7.34	0.475	1.13	1.65	3.93	5.72	13.6
					0.563	0.749	7.89	0.316	0.753	1.10	2.61	3.80	9.05
2	2.000		Tube		0.035	1.930	0.735	3.81	9.08	13.2	31.5	45.8	109
					0.049	1.902	1.02	3.66	8.74	12.7	30.3	44.0	105
					0.065	1.870	1.34	3.50	8.35	12.1	29.0	42.1	100
					0.083	1.834	1.70	3.33	7.94	11.5	27.5	40.0	95.4
					0.095	1.810	1.93	3.22	7.67	11.1	26.6	38.7	92.2
					0.109	1.782	2.20	3.09	7.36	10.7	25.5	37.1	88.5
					0.120	1.760	2.41	2.99	7.12	10.4	24.7	35.9	85.6
					0.125	1.750	2.50	2.94	7.02	10.2	24.3	35.4	84.4
					0.134	1.732	2.67	2.86	6.83	9.93	23.7	34.4	82.1
					0.156	1.688	3.07	2.68	6.38	9.28	22.1	32.2	76.7
					0.180	1.640	3.50	2.48	5.92	8.60	20.5	29.8	71.1
					0.188	1.624	3.64	2.42	5.77	8.38	20.0	29.1	69.3
					0.219	1.562	4.17	2.18	5.20	7.57	18.0	26.2	62.6
					0.250	1.500	4.67	1.96	4.68	6.80	16.2	23.6	56.2
					0.281	1.438	5.16	1.76	4.19	6.09	14.5	21.1	50.3
					0.313	1.374	5.64	1.56	3.71	5.40	12.9	18.7	44.7
					0.344	1.312	6.08	1.38	3.29	4.78	11.4	16.6	39.6
					0.375	1.250	6.51	1.21	2.90	4.21	10.0	14.6	34.8

Steel Pipe and Tube - Properties and Friction Loss (cont.)

Nominal or Standard Pipe Size	Outside Diameter	Pipe Schedule Number or Weight Class*			Wall Thickness	Inside Diameter	Weight Per Foot **	Theoretical Flow Rate (Gallons per Minute) Which Will Cause A Head Loss (H$_L$) In 100 Feet of Pipe					
		a	b	c				|← H$_L$ →|					
(inch)	(inch)				(inch)	(inch)	(pound)	0.1 (feet)	0.5 (feet)	1.0 (feet)	5.0 (feet)	10.0 (feet)	50.0 (feet)
2	2.000		Tube		0.438	1.124	7.31	0.918	2.19	3.18	7.59	11.0	26.3
					0.500	1.000	8.01	0.675	1.61	2.34	5.58	8.12	19.4
					0.563	0.874	8.64	0.474	1.13	1.64	3.92	5.70	13.6
					0.625	0.750	9.18	0.317	0.756	1.10	2.62	3.81	9.09
					0.750	0.500	10.0	0.109	0.260	0.38	0.90	1.31	3.13
	2.375	5		5S	0.065	2.245	1.60	5.67	13.5	19.6	46.8	68.1	162
		10		10S	0.083	2.209	2.03	5.43	12.9	18.8	44.9	65.3	156
					0.109	2.157	2.64	5.10	12.2	17.7	42.2	61.3	146
					0.125	2.125	3.00	4.90	11.7	17.0	40.5	59.0	141
					0.141	2.093	3.36	4.71	11.2	16.3	39.0	56.6	135
					0.147	2.081	3.50	4.64	11.1	16.1	38.4	55.8	133
		40	S	40S	0.154	2.067	3.65	4.56	10.9	15.8	37.7	54.8	131
					0.167	2.041	3.94	4.41	10.5	15.3	36.5	53.0	126
					0.172	2.031	4.05	4.35	10.4	15.1	36.0	52.3	125
					0.188	1.999	4.39	4.18	10.0	14.5	34.5	50.2	120
					0.208	1.959	4.81	3.96	9.44	13.7	32.7	47.6	114
					0.218	1.939	5.02	3.85	9.19	13.4	31.9	46.3	110
		80	XS	80S	0.250	1.875	5.67	3.53	8.41	12.2	29.2	42.4	101
					0.281	1.813	6.28	3.23	7.70	11.2	26.7	38.8	92.6
		160			0.344	1.687	7.46	2.67	6.37	9.27	22.1	32.1	76.6
			XXS		0.436	1.503	9.03	1.97	4.70	6.84	16.3	23.7	56.5
					0.562	1.251	10.9	1.22	2.90	4.22	10.1	14.6	34.9
					0.687	1.001	12.4	0.677	1.61	2.35	5.60	8.14	19.4

Nominal or Standard Pipe Size	Outside Diameter	Pipe Schedule Number or Weight Class*			Wall Thickness	Inside Diameter	Weight Per Foot**	Theoretical Flow Rate (Gallons per Minute) Which Will Cause A Head Loss (Ht) In 100 Feet of Pipe.					
		a	b	c				Ht					
								0.1	0.5	1.0	5.0	10.0	50.0
(inch)	(inch)				(inch)	(inch)	(pound)	(feet)	(feet)	(feet)	(feet)	(feet)	(feet)
2-1/4	2.250	Tube			0.035	2.180	0.828	5.24	12.5	18.2	43.4	63.1	150
					0.049	2.152	1.15	5.07	12.1	17.6	41.9	60.9	145
					0.065	2.120	1.52	4.87	11.6	16.9	40.3	58.6	140
					0.083	2.084	1.92	4.66	11.1	16.2	38.5	56.0	134
					0.095	2.060	2.19	4.52	10.8	15.7	37.4	54.3	130
					0.109	2.032	2.49	4.36	10.4	15.1	36.0	52.4	125
					0.120	2.010	2.73	4.24	10.1	14.7	35.0	50.9	121
					0.125	2.000	2.84	4.18	9.97	14.5	34.6	50.3	120
					0.134	1.982	3.03	4.08	9.74	14.2	33.8	49.1	117
					0.156	1.938	3.49	3.85	9.18	13.3	31.8	46.3	110
					0.188	1.874	4.14	3.52	8.40	12.2	29.1	42.4	101
					0.219	1.812	4.75	3.22	7.69	11.2	26.7	38.8	92.5
					0.250	1.750	5.34	2.94	7.02	10.2	24.3	35.4	84.4
					0.281	1.688	5.91	2.68	6.38	9.28	22.1	32.2	76.7
					0.313	1.624	6.48	2.42	5.77	8.38	20.0	29.1	69.3
					0.344	1.562	7.00	2.18	5.20	7.57	18.0	26.2	62.6
					0.375	1.500	7.51	1.96	4.68	6.80	16.2	23.6	56.2
					0.406	1.438	8.00	1.76	4.19	6.09	14.5	21.1	50.3
					0.438	1.374	8.48	1.56	3.71	5.40	12.9	18.7	44.7
					0.500	1.250	9.35	1.21	2.90	4.21	10.0	14.6	34.8
					0.563	1.124	10.1	0.918	2.19	3.18	7.59	11.0	26.3
					0.625	1.000	10.8	0.675	1.61	2.34	5.58	8.12	19.4
					0.750	0.750	12.0	0.317	0.756	1.10	2.62	3.81	9.09

Steel Pipe and Tube - Properties and Friction Loss (cont.)

Nominal or Standard Pipe Size	Outside Diameter	Pipe Schedule Number or Weight Class*			Wall Thickness	Inside Diameter	Weight Per Foot **	Theoretical Flow Rate (Gallons per Minute) Which Will Cause A Head Loss (Hf) In 100 Feet of Pipe					
		a	b	c				H_f					
								0.1	0.5	1.0	5.0	10.0	50.0
(inch)	(inch)				(inch)	(inch)	(pound)	(feet)	(feet)	(feet)	(feet)	(feet)	(feet)
2-1/2	2.500	Tube			0.049	2.402	1.28	6.77	16.1	23.5	56.0	81.4	194
					0.065	2.370	1.69	6.53	15.6	22.7	54.0	78.5	187
					0.083	2.334	2.14	6.28	15.0	21.8	51.9	75.4	180
					0.095	2.310	2.44	6.11	14.6	21.2	50.5	73.4	175
					0.109	2.282	2.78	5.91	14.1	20.5	48.9	71.1	170
					0.120	2.260	3.05	5.77	13.7	20.0	47.7	69.3	165
					0.125	2.250	3.17	5.70	13.6	19.8	47.1	68.5	163
					0.134	2.232	3.39	5.58	13.3	19.3	46.1	67.1	160
					0.156	2.188	3.91	5.30	12.6	18.4	43.8	63.7	152
					0.180	2.140	4.46	5.00	11.9	17.3	41.3	60.1	143
					0.188	2.124	4.64	4.90	11.7	17.0	40.5	58.9	140
					0.219	2.062	5.34	4.53	10.8	15.7	37.5	54.5	130
					0.250	2.000	6.01	4.18	10.0	14.5	34.6	50.3	120
					0.281	1.938	6.66	3.85	9.18	13.3	31.8	46.3	110
					0.313	1.874	7.31	3.52	8.40	12.2	29.1	42.4	101
					0.344	1.812	7.92	3.22	7.69	11.2	26.7	38.8	92.5
					0.375	1.750	8.51	2.94	7.02	10.2	24.3	35.4	84.4
					0.438	1.624	9.65	2.42	5.77	8.38	20.0	29.1	69.3
					0.500	1.500	10.7	1.96	4.68	6.80	16.2	23.6	56.2
					0.563	1.374	11.6	1.56	3.71	5.40	12.9	18.7	44.7
					0.625	1.250	12.5	1.21	2.90	4.21	10.0	14.6	34.8
					0.750	1.000	14.0	0.675	1.61	2.34	5.58	8.12	19.4

Nominal or Standard Pipe Size (inch)	Outside Diameter (inch)	Pipe Schedule Number or Weight Class* a	b	c	Wall Thickness (inch)	Inside Diameter (inch)	Weight Per Foot ** (pound)	Theoretical Flow Rate (Gallons per Minute) Which Will Cause A Head Loss (H_L) In 100 Feet of Pipe — H_L 0.1 (feet)	0.5 (feet)	1.0 (feet)	5.0 (feet)	10.0 (feet)	50.0 (feet)
2-1/2	2.875	5		5S	0.083	2.709	2.47	9.29	21.0	30.2	76.8	112	266
		10		10S	0.109	2.657	3.22	8.82	21.0	30.6	73.0	106	253
					0.120	2.635	3.53	8.63	20.6	29.9	71.4	104	248
					0.125	2.625	3.67	8.55	20.4	29.6	70.7	103	245
					0.141	2.593	4.12	8.28	19.7	28.7	68.4	100	237
		40	S	40S	0.156	2.563	4.53	8.03	19.1	27.8	66.4	96.5	230
					0.172	2.531	4.97	7.77	18.5	26.9	64.2	93.4	223
					0.188	2.499	5.40	7.51	17.9	26.0	62.1	90.3	215
		80	XS	80S	0.203	2.469	5.79	7.28	17.4	25.2	60.2	87.5	209
					0.216	2.443	6.13	7.08	16.9	24.5	58.5	85.1	203
		160			0.250	2.375	7.01	6.57	15.7	22.8	54.3	79.0	188
			XXS		0.276	2.323	7.66	6.20	14.8	21.5	51.3	74.5	178
					0.375	2.125	10.0	4.90	11.7	17.0	40.5	59.0	141
					0.552	1.771	13.7	3.04	7.24	10.5	25.1	36.5	87.1
					0.675	1.525	15.9	2.05	4.89	7.10	16.9	24.6	58.7
					0.800	1.275	17.7	1.28	3.05	4.44	10.6	15.4	36.7
2-3/4	2.750		Tube		0.049	2.652	1.41	8.78	20.9	30.4	72.6	106	252
					0.065	2.620	1.86	8.51	20.3	29.5	70.3	102	244
					0.083	2.584	2.36	8.20	19.6	28.4	67.8	98.6	235
					0.095	2.560	2.69	8.00	19.1	27.7	66.2	96.2	229
					0.120	2.510	3.37	7.60	18.1	26.3	62.8	91.3	218
					0.125	2.500	3.50	7.52	17.9	26.1	62.2	90.4	216
					0.134	2.482	3.74	7.38	17.6	25.6	61.0	88.7	212

Steel Pipe and Tube - Properties and Friction Loss (cont.)

Nominal or Standard Pipe Size	Outside Diameter	Pipe Schedule Number or Weight Class			Wall Thickness	Inside Diameter	Weight Per Foot	Theoretical Flow Rate (Gallons per Minute) Which Will Cause A Head Loss (Hf) In 100 Feet of Pipe					
		a	b	c				Hf					
								0.1	0.5	1.0	5.0	10.0	50.0
(inch)	(inch)				(inch)	(inch)	(pound)	(feet)	(feet)	(feet)	(feet)	(feet)	(feet)
2-3/4	2.750		Tube		0.156	2.438	4.32	7.04	16.8	24.4	58.2	84.6	202
					0.188	2.374	5.14	6.56	15.6	22.8	54.3	78.9	188
					0.219	2.312	5.92	6.12	14.6	21.2	50.6	73.6	176
					0.250	2.250	6.68	5.70	13.6	19.8	47.1	68.5	163
					0.281	2.188	7.41	5.30	12.6	18.4	43.8	63.7	152
					0.313	2.124	8.15	4.90	11.7	17.0	40.5	58.9	140
					0.344	2.062	8.84	4.53	10.8	15.7	37.5	54.5	130
					0.375	2.000	9.51	4.18	10.0	14.5	34.6	50.3	120
					0.438	1.874	10.8	3.52	8.40	12.2	29.1	42.4	101
					0.500	1.750	12.0	2.94	7.02	10.2	24.3	35.4	84.4
					0.563	1.624	13.2	2.42	5.77	8.38	20.0	29.1	69.3
					0.625	1.500	14.2	1.96	4.68	6.80	16.2	23.6	56.2
					0.688	1.374	15.2	1.56	3.71	5.40	12.9	18.7	44.7
					0.750	1.250	16.0	1.21	2.90	4.21	10.0	14.6	34.8
					0.875	1.000	17.5	0.675	1.61	2.34	5.58	8.12	19.4
3	3.000		Tube		0.049	2.902	1.54	11.1	26.5	38.6	92.0	134	319
					0.065	2.870	2.04	10.8	25.8	37.5	89.4	130	310
					0.083	2.834	2.59	10.5	24.9	36.3	86.5	126	300
					0.095	2.810	2.95	10.2	24.4	35.5	84.5	123	293
					0.109	2.782	3.37	9.96	23.7	34.5	82.0	120	286
					0.120	2.760	3.69	9.75	23.3	33.8	80.6	117	280
					0.125	2.750	3.84	9.66	23.0	33.5	79.9	116	277

Nominal or Standard Pipe Size (inch)	Outside Diameter (inch)	Pipe Schedule Number or Weight Class* a	b	c	Wall Thickness (inch)	Inside Diameter (inch)	Weight Per Foot ** (pound)	Theoretical Flow Rate (Gallons per Minute) Which Will Cause A Head Loss (H_f) In 100 Feet of Pipe 0.1 (feet)	0.5 (feet)	1.0 (feet)	5.0 (feet)	10.0 (feet)	50.0 (feet)
3	3.000		Tube		0.134	2.732	4.10	9.49	22.6	32.9	78.5	114	272
					0.156	2.688	4.74	9.10	21.7	31.5	75.2	109	261
					0.180	2.640	5.42	8.68	20.7	30.1	71.7	104	249
					0.188	2.624	5.65	8.54	20.4	29.6	70.6	103	245
					0.219	2.562	6.50	8.02	19.1	27.8	66.3	96.4	230
					0.250	2.500	7.34	7.52	17.9	26.1	62.2	90.4	216
					0.281	2.438	8.16	7.04	16.8	24.4	58.2	84.6	202
					0.313	2.374	8.98	6.56	15.6	22.8	54.3	78.9	188
					0.344	2.312	9.76	6.12	14.6	21.2	50.6	73.6	176
					0.375	2.250	10.5	5.70	13.6	19.8	47.1	68.5	163
					0.438	2.124	12.0	4.90	11.7	17.0	40.5	58.9	140
					0.500	2.000	13.4	4.18	10.0	14.5	34.6	50.3	120
					0.563	1.874	14.7	3.52	8.40	12.2	29.1	42.4	101
					0.625	1.750	15.9	2.94	7.02	10.2	24.3	35.4	84.4
					0.688	1.624	17.0	2.42	5.77	8.38	20.0	29.1	69.3
					0.750	1.500	18.0	1.96	4.68	6.80	16.2	23.6	56.2
					0.875	1.250	19.9	1.21	2.90	4.21	10.0	14.6	34.8
					1.000	1.000	21.4	0.675	1.61	2.34	5.58	8.12	19.4
	3.500	5	---	5S	0.083	3.334	3.03	16.0	38.2	55.6	133	193	460
		---	---	---	0.109	3.282	3.95	15.4	36.7	53.3	127	185	441
		10	---	10S	0.120	3.260	4.33	15.1	36.0	52.4	125	182	433
		---	---	---	0.125	3.250	4.51	15.0	35.7	52.0	124	180	430

Steel Pipe and Tube - Properties and Friction Loss (cont.)

Nominal or Standard Pipe Size	Outside Diameter	Pipe Schedule Number or Weight Class*			Wall Thickness	Inside Diameter	Weight Per Foot **	Theoretical Flow Rate (Gallons per Minute) Which Will Cause A Head Loss (Hf) In 100 Feet of Pipe					
		a	b	c				Hf					
(inch)	(inch)				(inch)	(inch)	(pound)	0.1 (feet)	0.5 (feet)	1.0 (feet)	5.0 (feet)	10.0 (feet)	50.0 (feet)
3	3.500	--	--	--	0.141	3.218	5.06	14.6	34.8	50.6	121	176	419
		--	--	--	0.156	3.188	5.57	14.2	34.0	49.4	118	171	409
		--	--	--	0.172	3.156	6.11	13.9	33.1	48.1	115	167	398
		40	S	40S	0.188	3.124	6.65	13.5	32.2	46.8	112	162	387
		--	--	--	0.206	3.088	7.25	13.1	31.2	45.4	108	158	376
		--	--	--	0.216	3.068	7.58	12.9	30.7	44.7	107	155	369
		--	--	--	0.250	3.000	8.68	12.1	29.0	42.1	100	146	348
		80	XS	80S	0.281	2.938	9.66	11.5	27.4	39.9	95.1	138	330
		--	--	--	0.286	2.928	9.82	11.4	27.2	39.5	94.2	137	327
		--	--	--	0.300	2.900	10.3	11.1	26.5	38.5	91.9	134	318
		160			0.438	2.624	14.3	8.54	20.4	29.6	70.6	103	245
		--	--	--	0.600	2.300	18.6	6.04	14.4	20.9	49.9	72.6	173
			XXS		0.725	2.050	21.5	4.46	10.6	15.5	36.9	53.6	128
		--	--	--	0.850	1.800	24.1	3.17	7.56	11.0	26.2	38.1	90.9
3-1/4	3.250		Tube		0.065	3.120	2.21	13.5	32.1	46.7	111	162	386
					0.095	3.060	3.20	12.8	30.5	44.4	106	154	367
					0.120	3.010	4.01	12.3	29.2	42.5	101	147	351
					0.125	3.000	4.17	12.1	29.0	42.1	100	146	348
					0.156	2.938	5.15	11.5	27.4	39.9	95.1	138	330
					0.188	2.874	6.15	10.8	25.9	37.6	89.7	130	311
					0.219	2.812	7.09	10.2	24.4	35.5	84.7	123	294
					0.250	2.750	8.01	9.66	23.0	33.5	79.9	116	277

Nominal or Standard Pipe Size	Outside Diameter	Pipe Schedule Number or Weight Class*			Wall Thickness	Inside Diameter	Weight Per Foot **	Theoretical Flow Rate (Gallons per Minute) Which Will Cause A Head Loss (H$_L$) In 100 Feet of Pipe					
		a	b	c				H$_L$					
								0.1	0.5	1.0	5.0	10.0	50.0
(inch)	(inch)				(inch)	(inch)	(pound)	(feet)	(feet)	(feet)	(feet)	(feet)	(feet)
3-1/4	3.250		Tube		0.281	2.688	8.91	9.10	21.7	31.5	75.2	109	261
					0.313	2.624	9.82	8.54	20.4	29.6	70.6	103	245
					0.344	2.562	10.7	8.02	19.1	27.8	66.3	96.4	230
					0.375	2.500	11.5	7.52	17.9	26.1	62.2	90.4	216
					0.438	2.374	13.2	6.56	15.6	22.8	54.3	78.9	188
					0.500	2.250	14.7	5.70	13.6	19.8	47.1	68.5	163
					0.563	2.124	16.2	4.90	11.7	17.0	40.5	58.9	140
					0.625	2.000	17.5	4.18	10.0	14.5	34.6	50.3	120
					0.750	1.750	20.0	2.94	7.02	10.2	24.3	35.4	84.4
					0.875	1.500	22.2	1.96	4.68	6.80	16.2	23.6	56.2
					1.000	1.250	24.0	1.21	2.90	4.21	10.0	14.6	34.8
3-1/2	3.500		Tube		0.049	3.402	1.81	16.9	40.3	58.6	140	203	485
					0.065	3.370	2.38	16.5	39.3	57.2	136	198	473
					0.083	3.334	3.03	16.0	38.2	55.6	133	193	460
					0.095	3.310	3.45	15.7	37.5	54.5	130	189	451
					0.120	3.260	4.33	15.1	36.0	52.4	125	182	433
					0.125	3.250	4.51	15.0	35.7	52.0	124	180	430
					0.134	3.232	4.82	14.8	35.2	51.2	122	178	424
					0.156	3.188	5.57	14.2	34.0	49.4	118	171	409
					0.180	3.140	6.38	13.7	32.7	47.5	113	165	393
					0.188	3.124	6.65	13.5	32.2	46.8	112	162	387
					0.219	3.062	7.67	12.8	30.6	44.4	106	154	367
					0.250	3.000	8.68	12.1	29.0	42.1	100	146	348

Steel Pipe and Tube - Properties and Friction Loss (cont.)

Nominal or Standard Pipe Size	Outside Diameter	Pipe Schedule Number or Weight Class*			Wall Thickness	Inside Diameter	Weight Per Foot **	Theoretical Flow Rate (Gallons per Minute) Which Will Cause A Head Loss (Hf) In 100 Feet of Pipe					
		a	b	c				H_f					
(inch)	(inch)				(inch)	(inch)	(pound)	50.0 (feet)	10.0 (feet)	5.0 (feet)	1.0 (feet)	0.5 (feet)	0.1 (feet)
3-1/2	3.500		Tube		0.281	2.938	9.66	330	138	95.1	39.9	27.4	11.5
					0.313	2.874	10.7	311	130	89.7	37.6	25.9	10.8
					0.344	2.812	11.6	294	123	84.7	35.5	24.4	10.2
					0.375	2.750	12.5	277	116	79.9	33.5	23.0	9.66
					0.438	2.624	14.3	245	103	70.6	29.6	20.4	8.54
					0.500	2.500	16.0	216	90.4	62.2	26.1	17.9	7.52
					0.563	2.374	17.7	188	78.9	54.3	22.8	15.6	6.56
					0.625	2.250	19.2	163	68.5	47.1	19.8	13.6	5.70
					0.750	2.000	22.0	120	50.3	34.6	14.5	10.0	4.18
					0.875	1.750	24.5	84.4	35.4	24.3	10.2	7.02	2.94
					1.000	1.500	26.7	56.2	23.6	16.2	6.80	4.68	1.96
4	4.000	5	---	5S	0.083	3.834	3.47	664	278	191	80.3	55.2	23.2
			---		0.109	3.782	4.53	640	269	185	77.4	53.2	22.3
		10	---	10S	0.120	3.760	4.97	631	264	182	76.3	52.4	22.0
			---		0.125	3.750	5.17	626	263	181	75.7	52.1	21.8
			---		0.134	3.732	5.53	618	259	178	74.8	51.4	21.6
			---		0.141	3.718	5.81	612	257	177	74.0	50.9	21.4
			---		0.156	3.688	6.40	599	251	173	72.5	49.8	20.9
			---		0.172	3.656	7.03	586	246	169	70.8	48.7	20.4
			---		0.188	3.624	7.65	572	240	165	69.2	47.6	20.0
		40	S	40S	0.226	3.548	9.11	541	227	156	65.5	45.0	18.9
			---		0.250	3.500	10.0	522	219	151	63.2	43.4	18.2

Nominal or Standard Pipe Size	Outside Diameter	Pipe Schedule Number or Weight Class			Wall Thickness	Inside Diameter	Weight Per Foot **	Theoretical Flow Rate (Gallons per Minute) Which Will Cause A Head Loss (H$_f$) In 100 Feet of Pipe					
		a	b	c				0.1	0.5	1.0	5.0	10.0	50.0
(inch)	(inch)				(inch)	(inch)	(pound)	(feet)	(feet)	(feet)	(feet)	(feet)	(feet)
3-1/2	4.000	---	---	---	0.281	3.438	11.2	17.4	41.4	60.3	144	209	498
		80	XS	80S	0.318	3.364	12.5	16.4	39.1	56.9	136	197	471
		---	XXS	---	0.636	2.728	22.9	9.46	22.6	32.8	78.2	114	271
3-3/4	3.750		Tube		0.065	3.620	2.56	19.9	47.5	69.0	165	239	571
					0.095	3.560	3.71	19.0	45.4	66.0	158	229	546
					0.120	3.510	4.65	18.4	43.8	63.6	152	221	526
					0.125	3.500	4.84	18.2	43.4	63.2	151	219	522
					0.134	3.482	5.18	18.0	42.9	62.3	149	216	515
					0.188	3.374	7.15	16.5	39.4	57.4	137	199	474
					0.219	3.312	8.26	15.8	37.6	54.6	130	189	452
					0.250	3.250	9.35	15.0	35.7	52.0	124	180	430
					0.313	3.124	11.5	13.5	32.2	46.8	112	162	387
					0.344	3.062	12.5	13.0	30.6	44.4	106	154	367
					0.375	3.000	13.5	12.1	29.0	42.1	100	146	348
					0.438	2.874	15.5	10.8	25.9	37.6	89.7	130	311
					0.500	2.750	17.4	9.66	23.0	33.5	79.9	116	277
					0.563	2.624	19.2	8.54	20.4	29.6	70.6	103	245
					0.625	2.500	20.9	7.52	17.9	26.1	62.2	90.4	216
					0.688	2.374	22.5	6.56	15.6	22.8	54.3	78.9	188
					0.750	2.250	24.0	5.70	13.6	19.8	47.1	68.5	163
					0.875	2.000	26.9	4.18	10.0	14.5	34.6	50.3	120
					1.000	1.750	29.4	2.94	7.02	10.2	24.3	35.4	84.4

Steel Pipe and Tube - Properties and Friction Loss (cont.)

Nominal or Standard Pipe Size	Outside Diameter	Pipe Schedule Number or Weight Class			Wall Thickness	Inside Diameter	Weight Per Foot **	Theoretical Flow Rate (Gallons per Minute) Which Will Cause A Head Loss (HL) In 100 Feet of Pipe					
		a	b	c				H_L					
								0.1	0.5	1.0	5.0	10.0	50.0
(inch)	(inch)				(inch)	(inch)	(pound)	(feet)	(feet)	(feet)	(feet)	(feet)	(feet)
4	4.000		Tube		0.065	3.870	2.73	23.7	56.6	82.3	196	285	680
					0.083	3.834	3.47	23.2	55.2	80.3	191	278	664
					0.095	3.810	3.96	22.8	54.3	79.0	188	274	653
					0.109	3.782	4.53	22.3	53.3	77.4	185	269	640
					0.125	3.760	4.97	22.0	52.4	76.3	182	264	631
					0.120	3.750	5.17	21.8	52.1	75.7	181	263	626
					0.134	3.732	5.53	21.6	51.4	74.8	178	259	618
					0.156	3.688	6.40	20.9	49.8	72.5	173	251	599
					0.180	3.640	7.34	20.2	48.2	70.0	167	243	579
					0.188	3.624	7.65	20.0	47.6	69.2	165	240	572
					0.219	3.562	8.84	19.1	45.5	66.1	158	229	547
					0.250	3.500	10.0	18.2	43.4	63.2	151	219	522
					0.281	3.438	11.2	17.4	41.4	60.3	144	209	498
					0.313	3.374	12.3	16.5	39.4	57.4	137	199	474
					0.375	3.250	14.5	15.0	35.7	52.0	124	180	430
					0.438	3.124	16.7	13.5	32.2	46.8	112	162	387
					0.500	3.000	18.7	12.1	29.0	42.1	100	146	348
					0.563	2.874	20.7	10.8	25.9	37.6	89.7	130	311
					0.625	2.750	22.5	9.66	23.0	33.5	79.9	116	277
					0.688	2.624	24.3	8.54	20.4	29.6	70.6	103	245
					0.750	2.500	26.0	7.52	17.9	26.1	62.2	90.4	216
					0.875	2.250	29.2	5.70	13.6	19.8	47.1	68.5	163

Nominal or Standard Pipe Size (inch)	Outside Diameter (inch)	Pipe Schedule Number or Weight Class*			Wall Thickness (inch)	Inside Diameter (inch)	Weight Per Foot (pound)	Theoretical Flow Rate (Gallons per Minute) Which Will Cause A Head Loss (HL) In 100 Feet of Pipe HL					
		a	b	c				0.1 (feet)	0.5 (feet)	1.0 (feet)	5.0 (feet)	10.0 (feet)	50.0 (feet)
	4.000		Tube		1.000	2.000	32.0	4.18	10.0	14.5	34.6	50.3	120
					1.125	1.750	34.5	2.94	7.02	10.2	24.3	35.4	84.4
					1.250	1.500	36.7	1.96	4.68	6.80	16.2	23.6	56.2
	4.500	5	---	5S	0.083	4.334	3.92	32.0	76.2	111	264	384	916
		---	---	---	0.109	4.282	5.11	31.0	73.8	107	256	372	888
		10	---	10S	0.120	4.260	5.61	30.5	72.8	106	253	367	876
		---	---	---	0.125	4.250	5.84	30.4	72.4	105	251	365	870
		---	---	---	0.141	4.218	6.56	29.8	71.0	103	246	358	853
		---	---	---	0.142	4.216	6.61	29.7	70.9	103	246	357	852
		---	---	---	0.156	4.188	7.24	29.2	69.6	101	241	351	837
		---	---	---	0.172	4.156	7.95	28.6	68.3	99.2	237	344	821
		---	---	---	0.188	4.124	8.66	28.0	66.9	97.2	232	337	804
		40	S	40S	0.203	4.094	9.32	27.5	65.6	95.4	227	331	789
		---	---	---	0.219	4.062	10.0	26.9	64.3	93.4	223	324	773
		---	---	---	0.226	4.048	10.3	26.7	63.7	92.6	221	321	766
		---	---	---	0.237	4.026	10.8	26.3	62.8	91.3	218	316	755
		---	---	---	0.250	4.000	11.3	25.9	61.7	89.7	214	311	742
		---	---	---	0.281	3.938	12.7	24.8	59.2	86.1	205	299	712
		---	---	---	0.312	3.876	14.0	23.8	56.8	82.6	197	286	683
		80	XS	80S	0.322	3.856	14.4	23.5	56.0	81.5	194	283	674
4		---	---	---	0.337	3.826	15.0	23.0	54.9	79.8	190	277	660
		120	---	---	0.438	3.624	19.0	20.0	47.6	69.2	165	240	572
		---	---	---	0.500	3.500	21.4	18.2	43.4	63.2	151	219	522

Steel Pipe and Tube - Properties and Friction Loss (cont.)

Nominal or Standard Pipe Size	Outside Diameter	Pipe Schedule Number or Weight Class[a]			Wall Thickness	Inside Diameter	Weight Per Foot [b]	Theoretical Flow Rate (Gallons per Minute) Which Will Cause A Head Loss (HL) In 100 Feet of Pipe					
		a	b	c				0.1	0.5	1.0	5.0	10.0	50.0
(inch)	(inch)				(inch)	(inch)	(pound)	(feet)	(feet)	(feet)	(feet)	(feet)	(feet)
4	4.500	160	---	---	0.531	3.438	22.5	17.4	41.4	60.3	144	209	498
		---	XXS	---	0.674	3.152	27.5	13.8	33.0	48.0	114	166	397
		---	---	---	0.800	2.900	31.6	11.1	26.5	38.5	91.9	134	318
		---	---	---	0.925	2.650	35.3	8.76	20.9	30.4	72.5	105	251
4-1/4	4.250	Tube			0.065	4.120	2.91	28.0	66.7	97.0	231	336	802
					0.095	4.060	4.22	26.9	64.2	93.3	223	324	772
					0.120	4.010	5.29	26.1	62.1	90.3	215	313	747
					0.125	4.000	5.51	25.9	61.7	89.7	214	311	742
					0.156	3.938	6.82	24.8	59.2	86.1	205	299	712
					0.180	3.890	7.82	24.0	57.4	83.4	199	289	690
					0.188	3.874	8.16	23.8	56.7	82.4	197	286	682
					0.250	3.750	10.7	21.8	52.1	75.7	181	263	626
					0.313	3.624	13.2	20.0	47.6	69.2	165	240	572
					0.344	3.562	14.4	19.1	45.5	66.1	158	229	547
					0.375	3.500	15.5	18.2	43.4	63.2	151	219	522
					0.438	3.374	17.8	16.5	39.4	57.4	137	199	474
					0.500	3.250	20.0	15.0	35.7	52.0	124	180	430
					0.625	3.000	24.2	12.1	28.9	42.1	100	146	348
					0.688	2.874	26.2	10.8	25.9	37.6	89.7	130	311
					0.750	2.750	28.0	9.66	23.0	33.5	79.9	116	277
					0.875	2.500	31.5	7.52	17.9	26.1	62.2	90.4	216
					1.000	2.250	34.7	5.70	13.6	19.8	47.1	68.5	163
					1.125	2.000	37.5	4.18	10.0	14.5	34.6	50.3	120
					1.250	1.750	40.1	2.94	7.02	10.2	24.3	35.4	84.4

Nominal or Standard Pipe Size	Outside Diameter	Pipe Schedule Number or Weight Class*			Wall Thickness	Inside Diameter	Weight Per Foot **	Theoretical Flow Rate (Gallons per Minute) Which Will Cause A Head Loss (HL) in 100 Feet of Pipe					
		a	b	c				HL					
(inch)	(inch)				(inch)	(inch)	(pound)	0.1 (feet)	0.5 (feet)	1.0 (feet)	5.0 (feet)	10.0 (feet)	50.0 (feet)
4-1/2	4.500		Tube		0.065	4.370	3.08	32.7	77.9	113	270	393	936
					0.083	4.334	3.92	32.0	76.2	111	264	384	916
					0.095	4.310	4.47	31.5	75.1	109	260	379	903
					0.120	4.260	5.61	30.5	72.8	106	253	367	876
					0.125	4.250	5.84	30.4	72.4	105	251	365	870
					0.134	4.232	6.25	30.0	71.6	104	248	361	861
					0.156	4.188	7.24	29.2	69.6	101	241	351	837
					0.180	4.140	8.30	28.3	67.6	98.2	234	341	812
					0.188	4.124	8.66	28.0	67.0	97.2	232	337	804
					0.219	4.062	10.0	26.9	64.3	93.4	223	324	773
					0.250	4.000	11.3	25.9	61.7	89.7	214	311	742
					0.313	3.874	14.0	23.8	56.7	82.5	197	286	682
					0.375	3.750	16.5	21.8	52.1	75.7	181	263	626
					0.438	3.624	19.0	20.0	47.6	69.2	165	240	572
					0.500	3.500	21.4	18.2	43.4	63.2	151	219	522
					0.563	3.374	23.7	16.5	39.4	57.4	137	199	474
					0.625	3.250	25.9	15.0	35.7	52.0	124	180	430
					0.688	3.124	28.0	13.5	32.2	46.8	112	162	387
					0.750	3.000	30.0	12.1	29.0	42.1	100	146	348
					0.875	2.750	33.9	9.66	23.0	33.5	79.9	116	277
					1.000	2.500	37.4	7.52	17.9	26.1	62.2	90.4	216
					1.125	2.250	40.6	5.70	13.6	19.8	47.1	68.5	163
					1.250	2.000	43.4	4.18	10.0	14.5	34.6	50.3	120
					1.500	1.500	48.1	1.96	4.68	6.80	16.2	23.6	56.2

Steel Pipe and Tube - Properties and Friction Loss (cont.)

Nominal or Standard Pipe Size	Outside Diameter	Pipe Schedule Number or Weight Class			Wall Thickness	Inside Diameter	Weight Per Foot **	Theoretical Flow Rate (Gallons per Minute) Which Will Cause A Head Loss (Hf) In 100 Feet of Pipe					
		a	b	c				H_f					
(inch)	(inch)				(inch)	(inch)	(pound)	0.1 (feet)	0.5 (feet)	1.0 (feet)	5.0 (feet)	10.0 (feet)	50.0 (feet)
4-3/4	4.750		Tube		0.120	4.510	5.93	35.5	84.6	123	293	427	1,020
					0.125	4.500	6.17	35.3	84.1	122	292	424	1,010
					0.188	4.374	9.16	32.7	78.1	114	271	394	939
					0.250	4.250	12.0	30.4	72.4	105	251	365	870
					0.313	4.124	14.8	28.0	66.9	97.2	232	337	804
					0.375	4.000	17.5	25.9	61.7	89.7	214	311	742
					0.438	3.874	20.2	23.8	56.7	82.5	197	286	682
					0.500	3.750	22.7	21.8	52.1	75.7	181	263	626
					0.563	3.624	25.2	20.0	47.6	69.2	165	240	572
					0.625	3.500	27.5	18.2	43.4	63.2	151	219	522
					0.750	3.250	32.0	15.0	35.7	52.0	124	180	430
					0.875	3.000	36.2	12.1	29.0	42.1	100	146	348
					1.000	2.750	40.1	9.66	23.0	33.5	79.9	116	277
					1.250	2.250	46.7	5.70	13.6	19.8	47.1	68.5	163
5	5.000		Tube		0.065	4.870	3.43	43.4	104	151	359	522	1,250
					0.083	4.834	4.36	42.6	102	148	352	512	1,220
					0.120	4.760	6.25	40.9	97.5	142	338	492	1,170
					0.125	4.750	6.51	40.7	97.0	141	336	489	1,170
					0.180	4.640	9.27	38.2	91.2	133	316	460	1,100
					0.188	4.624	9.66	37.9	90.4	131	313	456	1,090
					0.250	4.500	12.7	35.3	84.1	122	292	424	1,010
					0.313	4.374	15.7	32.7	78.1	114	271	394	939

Nominal or Standard Pipe Size (inch)	Outside Diameter (inch)	Pipe Schedule Number or Weight Class*			Wall Thickness (inch)	Inside Diameter (inch)	Weight Per Foot ** (pound)	Theoretical Flow Rate (Gallons per Minute) Which Will Cause A Head Loss (Hf) In 100 Feet of Pipe					
		a	b	c				Hf					
								0.1 (feet)	0.5 (feet)	1.0 (feet)	5.0 (feet)	10.0 (feet)	50.0 (feet)
5	5.000	Tube			0.375	4.250	18.5	30.4	72.4	105	251	365	870
					0.438	4.124	21.3	28.0	66.9	97.2	232	337	804
					0.500	4.000	24.0	25.9	61.7	89.7	214	311	742
					0.563	3.874	26.7	23.8	56.7	82.5	197	286	682
					0.625	3.750	29.2	21.8	52.1	75.7	181	263	626
					0.750	3.500	34.0	18.2	43.4	63.2	151	219	522
					0.875	3.250	38.5	15.0	35.7	52.0	124	180	430
					1.000	3.000	42.7	12.1	29.0	42.1	100	146	348
					1.125	2.750	46.6	9.66	23.0	33.5	79.9	116	277
					1.250	2.500	50.1	7.52	17.9	26.1	62.2	90.4	216
					1.500	2.000	56.1	4.18	10.0	14.5	34.6	50.3	120
	5.563				0.083	5.397	4.86	56.9	136	197	470	684	1,630
		5		5S	0.109	5.345	6.35	55.5	132	192	459	667	1,590
					0.125	5.313	7.26	54.6	130	189	451	656	1,570
		10		10S	0.134	5.295	7.77	54.1	129	188	447	651	1,550
					0.156	5.251	9.01	52.9	126	184	438	636	1,520
					0.188	5.187	10.8	51.3	122	178	424	616	1,470
					0.219	5.125	12.5	49.7	118	172	411	597	1,420
		40	S	40S	0.258	5.047	14.6	47.7	114	165	394	573	1,370
					0.281	5.001	15.9	46.6	111	161	385	560	1,340
					0.312	4.939	17.5	45.1	107	156	373	542	1,290
					0.344	4.875	19.2	43.5	104	151	360	524	1,290
		80	XS	80S	0.375	4.813	20.8	42.1	100	146	348	506	1,210

Steel Pipe and Tube - Properties and Friction Loss (cont.)

Nominal or Standard Pipe Size	Outside Diameter	Pipe Schedule Number or Weight Class*			Wall Thickness	Inside Diameter	Weight Per Foot **	Theoretical Flow Rate (Gallons per Minute) Which Will Cause A Head Loss (H_L) In 100 Feet of Pipe					
											H_L		
		a	b	c				0.1	0.5	1.0	5.0	10.0	50.0
(inch)	(inch)				(inch)	(inch)	(pound)	(feet)	(feet)	(feet)	(feet)	(feet)	(feet)
5	5.563	120	---	---	0.500	4.563	27.0	36.6	87.3	127	303	440	1,050
		160	---	---	0.625	4.313	33.0	31.6	75.2	109	261	379	905
		---	XXS	---	0.750	4.063	38.6	27.0	64.3	93.5	223	324	773
		---	---	---	0.875	3.813	43.8	22.8	54.4	79.1	189	274	654
		---	---	---	1.000	3.563	48.7	19.1	45.5	66.2	158	230	547
		Tube			0.065	5.370	3.77	56.2	134	195	464	675	1,610
					0.120	5.260	6.90	53.2	127	184	440	639	1,520
					0.125	5.250	7.18	52.9	126	183	438	636	1,520
					0.154	5.192	8.79	51.4	123	178	425	618	1,470
					0.188	5.124	10.7	49.6	118	172	410	597	1,420
					0.250	5.000	14.0	46.5	111	161	385	560	1,330
					0.313	4.874	17.3	43.5	104	151	360	523	1,250
	5.500				0.375	4.750	20.5	40.7	97.0	141	336	489	1,170
					0.438	4.624	23.7	37.9	90.4	131	313	456	1,090
					0.500	4.500	26.7	35.3	84.1	122	292	424	1,010
					0.625	4.250	32.5	30.4	72.4	105	251	365	870
					0.750	4.000	38.0	25.9	61.7	89.7	214	311	742
					0.875	3.750	43.2	21.8	52.1	75.7	181	263	626
					1.000	3.500	48.1	18.2	43.4	63.2	151	219	522
5-1/2					1.250	3.000	56.7	12.1	29.0	42.1	100	146	348
					1.500	2.500	64.1	7.52	17.9	26.1	62.2	90.4	216

Nominal or Standard Pipe Size	Outside Diameter	Pipe Schedule Number or Weight Class*			Wall Thickness	Inside Diameter	Weight Per Foot **	Theoretical Flow Rate (Gallons per Minute) Which Will Cause A Head Loss (Hf) In 100 Feet of Pipe					
		a	b	c				Hf					
(inch)	(inch)				(inch)	(inch)	(pound)	0.1 (feet)	0.5 (feet)	1.0 (feet)	5.0 (feet)	10.0 (feet)	50.0 (feet)
6	6.000		Tube		0.065	5.870	4.12	71.0	169	246	577	853	2,030
					0.083	5.834	5.25	69.8	167	242	567	840	2,000
					0.120	5.760	7.54	67.5	161	234	558	812	1,940
					0.125	5.750	7.84	67.2	160	233	556	808	1,930
					0.134	5.732	8.40	66.7	159	231	551	801	1,910
					0.164	5.672	10.2	64.8	155	225	536	780	1,860
					0.180	5.640	11.2	63.9	152	222	528	768	1,830
					0.188	5.624	11.7	63.4	151	220	524	762	1,820
					0.250	5.500	15.4	59.8	143	207	494	719	1,710
					0.313	5.374	19.0	56.3	134	195	465	676	1,610
					0.375	5.250	22.5	52.9	126	183	438	636	1,520
					0.500	5.000	29.4	46.5	111	161	385	560	1,330
					0.563	4.874	32.7	43.5	104	151	360	523	1,250
					0.625	4.750	35.9	40.7	97.0	141	336	489	1,170
					0.750	4.500	42.1	35.3	84.1	122	292	424	1,010
					0.875	4.250	47.9	30.4	72.4	105	251	365	870
					1.000	4.000	53.4	25.9	61.7	89.7	214	311	742
					1.250	3.500	63.4	18.2	43.4	63.2	151	219	522
					1.500	3.000	72.1	12.1	29.0	42.1	100	146	348
6	6.625	--	--	5S	0.083	6.459	5.80	91.3	218	316	755	1,100	2,620
		5	--	--	0.109	6.407	7.59	89.3	213	310	739	1,070	2,560
		--	--	10S	0.125	6.375	8.68	88.2	210	306	729	1,060	2,530
		10	--	--	0.134	6.357	9.29	87.5	209	303	724	1,050	2,510
		--	--	--	0.141	6.343	9.76	87.0	208	302	719	1,050	2,490

Steel Pipe and Tube - Properties and Friction Loss (cont.)

Nominal or Standard Pipe Size	Outside Diameter	Pipe Schedule Number or Weight Class			Wall Thickness	Inside Diameter	Weight Per Foot **	Theoretical Flow Rate (Gallons per Minute) Which Will Cause A Head Loss (H_L) In 100 Feet of Pipe					
								H_L					
		a	b	c				0.1	0.5	1.0	5.0	10.0	50.0
(inch)	(inch)				(inch)	(inch)	(pound)	(feet)	(feet)	(feet)	(feet)	(feet)	(feet)
6	6.625	--	--	--	0.156	6.313	10.8	85.9	205	298	711	1,030	2,460
		--	--	--	0.172	6.281	11.9	84.8	202	294	701	1,020	2,430
		--	--	--	0.185	6.255	12.7	83.9	200	291	694	1,010	2,400
		--	--	--	0.188	6.249	12.9	83.7	200	290	692	1,010	2,400
		--	--	--	0.203	6.219	13.9	82.6	197	286	683	990	2,370
		--	--	--	0.219	6.187	15.0	81.5	194	283	674	980	2,340
		--	--	--	0.250	6.125	17.0	79.4	189	275	656	954	2,280
		--	--	--	0.267	6.091	18.1	78.2	187	271	647	940	2,240
		40	S	40S	0.280	6.065	19.0	77.3	184	268	639	930	2,220
		--	--	--	0.312	6.001	21.0	75.2	179	261	622	904	2,160
		--	--	--	0.344	5.937	23.1	73.1	174	254	605	879	2,100
		--	--	--	0.375	5.875	25.0	71.1	170	247	588	855	2,040
		--	--	--	0.412	5.801	27.3	68.8	164	239	569	827	1,970
		80	XS	80S	0.432	5.761	28.6	67.6	161	234	559	812	1,940
		--	--	--	0.500	5.625	32.7	63.4	151	220	525	763	1,820
		120	--	--	0.562	5.501	36.4	59.8	143	207	495	719	1,720
		--	--	--	0.625	5.375	40.1	56.3	134	195	465	677	1,610
		160	--	--	0.719	5.187	45.4	51.3	122	178	424	616	1,470
		--	XXS	--	0.864	4.897	53.2	44.1	105	153	364	530	1,260
		--	--	--	1.000	4.625	60.1	37.9	90.4	131	313	456	1,090
		--	--	--	1.125	4.375	66.1	32.8	78.1	114	271	394	939

Nominal or Standard Pipe Size	Outside Diameter	Pipe Schedule Number or Weight Class*			Wall Thickness	Inside Diameter	Weight Per Foot **	Theoretical Flow Rate (Gallons per Minute) Which Will Cause A Head Loss (H$_L$) In 100 Feet of Pipe					
		a	b	c							H$_L$		
								0.1	0.5	1.0	5.0	10.0	50.0
(inch)	(inch)				(inch)	(inch)	(pound)	(feet)	(feet)	(feet)	(feet)	(feet)	(feet)
6-1/2	6.500	Tube			0.134	6.232	9.11	83.1	198	288	687	999	2,380
					0.188	6.124	12.7	79.3	189	275	656	954	2,270
					0.250	6.000	16.7	75.2	179	261	622	904	2,160
					0.375	5.750	24.5	67.2	160	233	556	808	1,930
					0.500	5.500	32.0	59.8	143	207	494	719	1,710
					0.625	5.250	39.2	52.9	126	183	438	636	1,520
					0.750	5.000	46.1	46.5	111	161	385	560	1,330
					0.875	4.750	52.6	40.7	97.0	141	336	489	1,170
					1.000	4.500	58.7	35.3	84.1	122	292	424	1,010
					1.250	4.000	70.1	25.9	61.7	89.7	214	311	740
					1.500	3.500	80.1	18.2	43.4	63.2	151	219	520
7	7.000	Tube			0.058	6.884	4.30	108	257	374	892	1,300	3,090
					0.072	6.856	5.33	107	255	370	883	1,280	3,060
					0.125	6.750	9.18	102	244	355	847	1,230	2,940
					0.188	6.624	13.7	97.5	233	338	806	1,170	2,800
					0.250	6.500	18.0	92.8	221	322	767	1,120	2,660
					0.375	6.250	26.5	83.7	200	290	692	1,010	2,400
					0.500	6.000	34.7	75.2	179	261	622	900	2,160
					0.625	5.750	42.6	67.2	160	233	556	810	1,930
					0.750	5.500	50.1	59.8	143	207	494	720	1,710
					1.000	5.000	64.1	46.5	111	161	385	560	1,330
					1.250	4.500	76.8	35.3	84.1	122	292	420	1,010
					1.500	4.000	88.1	25.9	61.7	89.7	214	310	740
					1.875	3.250	103	15.0	35.7	52.0	124	180	430
					2.000	3.000	107	12.1	29.0	42.1	100	150	350

Nominal or Standard Pipe Size	Outside Diameter	Pipe Schedule Number or Weight Class*			Wall Thickness	Inside Diameter	Weight Per Foot **	Theoretical Flow Rate (Gallons per Minute) Which Will Cause A Head Loss (H₁) In 100 Feet of Pipe H_1					
		a	b	c				0.1	0.5	1.0	5.0	10.0	50.0
(inch)	(inch)				(inch)	(inch)	(pound)	(feet)	(feet)	(feet)	(feet)	(feet)	(feet)
7-1/2	7.500		Tube		0.250	7.000	19.4	113	269	391	932	1,360	3,230
					0.375	6.750	28.5	102	244	355	847	1,230	2,940
					0.500	6.500	37.4	92.8	221	322	767	1,120	2,660
					0.625	6.250	45.9	83.7	200	290	692	1,010	2,400
					0.750	6.000	54.1	75.2	179	261	622	900	2,160
					1.000	5.500	69.4	59.8	143	207	494	720	1,710
					1.250	5.000	83.4	46.5	111	161	385	560	1,330
					1.500	4.500	96.1	35.3	84.1	122	292	420	1,010
8	8.000		Tube		0.058	7.884	4.92	154	368	535	1,270	1,850	4,420
					0.072	7.856	6.10	153	364	530	1,260	1,840	4,380
					0.109	7.782	9.19	149	355	517	1,230	1,790	4,270
					0.125	7.750	10.5	147	351	511	1,220	1,770	4,230
					0.134	7.732	11.3	146	349	508	1,210	1,760	4,200
					0.188	7.624	15.7	141	337	489	1,170	1,700	4,050
					0.250	7.500	20.7	135	322	469	1,120	1,630	3,880
					0.375	7.250	30.5	124	295	429	1,020	1,490	3,550
					0.500	7.000	40.1	113	269	391	930	1,360	3,230
					0.625	6.750	49.2	102	244	355	850	1,230	2,940
					0.750	6.500	58.1	92.8	221	322	770	1,120	2,660
					1.000	6.000	74.8	75.2	179	261	620	900	2,160
					1.125	5.750	82.6	67.2	160	233	560	810	1,930
					1.250	5.500	90.1	59.8	143	207	490	720	1,710

Nominal or Standard Pipe Size (inch)	Outside Diameter (inch)	Pipe Schedule Number or Weight Class* a	b	c	Wall Thickness (inch)	Inside Diameter (inch)	Weight Per Foot (pound)	Theoretical Flow Rate (Gallons per Minute) Which Will Cause A Head Loss (H_L) In 100 Feet of Pipe — H_L = 0.1 (feet)	0.5 (feet)	1.0 (feet)	5.0 (feet)	10.0 (feet)	50.0 (feet)
8	8.000		Tube		1.500	5.000	104	46.5	111	161	380	560	1,330
					2.000	4.000	128	25.9	61.7	89.7	210	310	740
	8.625			5S	0.109	8.407	9.91	183	435	633	1,510	2,190	5,230
					0.125	8.375	11.3	181	431	627	1,490	2,170	5,180
		10		10S	0.148	8.329	13.4	178	425	618	1,470	2,140	5,110
					0.156	8.313	14.1	177	423	614	1,470	2,130	5,080
					0.188	8.249	16.9	174	414	602	1,440	2,090	4,980
					0.203	8.219	18.3	172	410	596	1,420	2,070	4,930
					0.219	8.187	19.7	170	406	590	1,410	2,050	4,880
		20			0.250	8.125	22.4	167	398	579	1,380	2,010	4,780
		30			0.277	8.071	24.7	164	391	569	1,360	1,970	4,700
					0.308	8.009	27.4	161	383	557	1,330	1,930	4,610
					0.312	8.001	27.7	160	382	556	1,330	1,930	4,590
		40	S	40S	0.322	7.981	28.6	159	380	552	1,320	1,910	4,560
					0.344	7.937	30.4	157	374	544	1,300	1,890	4,500
					0.354	7.917	31.3	156	372	540	1,290	1,870	4,470
					0.375	7.875	33.0	154	367	533	1,270	1,850	4,410
		60			0.406	7.813	35.6	151	359	522	1,240	1,810	4,320
					0.438	7.749	38.3	147	351	511	1,220	1,770	4,220
					0.478	7.669	41.6	143	342	497	1,190	1,720	4,110
		80	XS	80S	0.500	7.625	43.4	141	337	490	1,170	1,700	4,050
					0.562	7.501	48.4	135	323	469	1,120	1,630	3,880
					0.594	7.437	50.9	132	315	458	1,090	1,590	3,790
		100			0.625	7.375	53.4	129	308	448	1,070	1,560	3,710

Steel Pipe and Tube - Properties and Friction Loss (cont.)

Nominal or Standard Pipe Size	Outside Diameter	Pipe Schedule Number or Weight Class*			Wall Thickness	Inside Diameter	Weight Per Foot*	Theoretical Flow Rate (Gallons per Minute) Which Will Cause A Head Loss (HL) In 100 Feet of Pipe					
		a	b	c				H_L					
(inch)	(inch)				(inch)	(inch)	(pound)	0.1 (feet)	0.5 (feet)	1.0 (feet)	5.0 (feet)	10.0 (feet)	50.0 (feet)
8	8.625	120	--	--	0.719	7.187	60.7	121	288	419	1,000	1,450	3,470
		140	--	--	0.812	7.001	67.8	113	269	391	933	1,360	3,230
		--	XXS	--	0.875	6.875	72.4	108	256	373	889	1,290	3,080
		160	--	--	0.906	6.813	74.7	105	250	364	868	1,260	3,010
		--	--	--	1.000	6.625	81.4	97.6	233	338	807	1,170	2,800
		--	--	--	1.125	6.375	90.1	88.2	210	306	729	1,060	2,530
8-1/2	8.500	Tube			0.250	8.000	22.0	160	382	555	1,320	1,930	4,590
					0.375	7.750	32.5	147	351	511	1,220	1,770	4,230
					0.500	7.500	42.7	135	322	469	1,120	1,630	3,880
					0.625	7.250	52.6	124	295	429	1,020	1,490	3,550
					0.750	7.000	62.1	113	269	391	930	1,360	3,230
					1.000	6.500	80.1	92.8	221	322	770	1,120	2,660
					1.250	6.000	96.8	75.2	179	261	620	900	2,160
					1.500	5.500	112	59.8	143	207	490	720	1,710
					2.000	4.500	139	35.3	84.1	122	290	420	1,010
9	9.000	Tube			0.250	8.500	23.4	188	448	652	1,550	2,260	5,390
					0.500	8.000	45.4	160	382	555	1,320	1,930	4,590
					0.750	7.500	66.1	135	322	469	1,120	1,630	3,880
					1.000	7.000	85.4	113	269	391	930	1,360	3,230
					1.250	6.500	103	92.8	221	322	770	1,120	2,660
					1.500	6.000	120	75.2	179	261	620	900	2,160
					2.000	5.000	150	46.5	111	161	380	560	1,330

Nominal or Standard Pipe Size	Outside Diameter	Pipe Schedule Number or Weight Class*			Wall Thickness	Inside Diameter	Weight Per Foot **	Theoretical Flow Rate (Gallons per Minute) Which Will Cause A Head Loss (H_f) In 100 Feet of Pipe					
		a	b	c				H_f					
								0.1	0.5	1.0	5.0	10.0	50.0
(inch)	(inch)				(inch)	(inch)	(pound)	(feet)	(feet)	(feet)	(feet)	(feet)	(feet)
9-1/2	9.500	Tube			0.250	9.000	24.7	218	521	757	1,810	2,630	6,260
					0.375	8.750	36.5	203	484	703	1,680	2,440	5,810
					0.500	8.500	48.1	188	448	652	1,550	2,260	5,390
					0.625	8.250	59.2	174	414	602	1,440	2,090	4,980
					0.750	8.000	70.1	160	382	555	1,320	1,930	4,590
					1.000	7.500	90.8	135	322	469	1,120	1,630	3,880
					1.125	7.250	101	124	295	429	1,020	1,490	3,550
					1.500	6.500	128	92.8	221	322	770	1,120	2,660
					2.000	5.500	160	59.8	143	207	490	720	1,710
10	10.000	Tube			0.072	9.856	7.63	277	661	962	2,290	3,330	7,950
					0.109	9.782	11.5	272	648	943	2,250	3,270	7,790
					0.134	9.732	14.1	268	640	930	2,220	3,220	7,690
					0.188	9.624	19.7	260	621	903	2,150	3,130	7,470
					0.250	9.500	26.0	252	600	873	2,080	3,030	7,220
					0.375	9.250	38.5	235	560	814	1,940	2,820	6,730
					0.500	9.000	50.7	218	521	757	1,810	2,630	6,260
					0.750	8.500	74.1	188	448	652	1,550	2,260	5,390
					1.000	8.000	96.1	160	382	555	1,320	1,930	4,590
					1.125	7.750	107	147	351	511	1,220	1,770	4,230
					1.250	7.500	117	135	322	469	1,120	1,630	3,880
					1.500	7.000	136	113	269	391	930	1,360	3,230
					2.000	6.000	171	75.2	179	261	620	900	2,160

Nominal or Standard Pipe Size	Outside Diameter	Pipe Schedule Number or Weight Class			Wall Thickness	Inside Diameter	Weight Per Foot**	Theoretical Flow Rate (Gallons per Minute) Which Will Cause A Head Loss (H_f) In 100 Feet of Pipe					
								H_f					
		a	b	c				0.1	0.5	1.0	5.0	10.0	50.0
(inch)	(inch)				(inch)	(inch)	(pound)	(feet)	(feet)	(feet)	(feet)	(feet)	(feet)
10	10.750	--	--	5S	0.134	10.482	15.2	326	778	1,130	2,700	3,920	9,350
		--	--	--	0.156	10.438	17.7	322	769	1,120	2,670	3,880	9,250
		--	--	10S	0.165	10.420	18.7	321	766	1,110	2,650	3,860	9,200
		--	--	--	0.188	10.374	21.2	317	757	1,100	2,620	3,810	9,100
		10	--	--	0.203	10.344	22.9	315	751	1,090	2,600	3,790	9,030
		--	--	--	0.219	10.312	24.6	312	745	1,080	2,580	3,760	8,960
		20	--	--	0.250	10.250	28.0	307	733	1,070	2,540	3,700	8,810
		--	--	--	0.279	10.192	31.2	303	722	1,050	2,500	3,640	8,680
		30	--	--	0.307	10.136	34.2	299	712	1,040	2,470	3,590	8,560
		--	--	--	0.344	10.062	38.2	293	698	1,020	2,420	3,520	8,400
		--	--	--	0.348	10.054	38.7	292	697	1,010	2,420	3,510	8,380
		40	S	40S	0.365	10.020	40.5	290	691	1,000	2,390	3,480	8,300
		--	--	--	0.438	9.874	48.2	279	665	966	2,300	3,350	7,990
		60	XS	80S	0.500	9.750	54.7	270	643	935	2,230	3,240	7,730
		--	--	--	0.562	9.626	61.2	261	622	904	2,160	3,130	7,470
		--	--	--	0.567	9.616	61.7	260	620	901	2,150	3,120	7,450
		80	--	--	0.594	9.562	64.4	256	611	888	2,120	3,080	7,340
		--	--	--	0.625	9.500	67.6	252	600	873	2,080	3,030	7,220
		--	--	--	0.719	9.312	77.0	239	570	828	1,980	2,870	6,850
		100	--	--	0.812	9.126	86.2	227	540	785	1,870	2,720	6,490

Nominal or Standard Pipe Size	Outside Diameter	Pipe Schedule Number or Weight Class			Wall Thickness	Inside Diameter	Weight Per Foot **	Theoretical Flow Rate (Gallons per Minute) Which Will Cause A Head Loss (H_t) In 100 Feet of Pipe					
		a	b	c				0.1	0.5	1.0	5.0	10.0	50.0
(inch)	(inch)				(inch)	(inch)	(pound)	(feet)	(feet)	(feet)	(feet)	(feet)	(feet)
10	10.750	120	---	---	0.844	9.062	89.3	222	530	771	1,840	2,670	6,380
		---	XXS	---	0.875	9.000	92.3	218	521	757	1,810	2,630	6,260
		140	---	---	1.000	8.750	104	203	484	703	1,680	2,440	5,810
		---	---	---	1.125	8.500	116	188	448	652	1,550	2,260	5,390
		160	---	---	1.250	8.250	127	174	414	602	1,440	2,090	4,980
		---	---	---	1.500	7.750	148	147	351	511	1,220	1,770	4,230

Notes:
* Schedule Numbers and Weight Classes:
Column a = Schedule numbers from ANSI Standard B36.10 for Steel Pipe. Schedule numbers can be 10, 20, 30, 40, 60, 80, 100, 120, 140, or 160.
Column b = Weight classes from ANSI Standard B36.10 for Steel Pipe Wall Thickness. Weight classes are Standard Wall (S), Extra-Strong Wall (XS), or Double-Extra-Strong-Wall is sometimes known as Extra-Heavy-Wall; Double-Extra-Strong-Wall (XXS). Extra-Strong-Wall is sometimes known as Double-Extra-Strong-Wall.
Column c = Schedule numbers from ANSI Standard B36.19 for Stainless Steel Pipe. Schedule numbers can be 5S, 10S, 40S, or 80S. The "S" designates "Stainless Steel".

** Weight per foot based on a density of 489.54 pounds per cubic foot (0.2833 pounds per cubic inch).

3 Diameter and wall thickness data from: ANSI Standards B 36.10, B 36.19
ASTM Designations A 53 - 96, A 106 - 95, A 135 - 96, A 312/A 312M - 95a, A 409/A 409M - 95a, A 523 - 93, A 524 - 93, A 587 - 93, A 589 - 95a, A 790/A 790M - 95, A 795 - 96, A 813/A 813M - 95, A 814/A 814M - 95, A 943/A 943M - 95, A 949/A 949M - 95, A 954 - 96, B 161 - 93, B 165 - 93
Standard Handbook for Mechanical Engineers, Ninth Edition, McGraw-Hill Book Company, 1978
ASM Metals Reference Book, Third Edition, ASM International, 1997
Fluid Power Data Book, Ninth Edition, Womack Educational Publications, Dallas, TX, 1995
Alaskan Copper and Brass Company, Seattle, WA
Central Steel and Wire Company, Chicago, IL.

Friction Loss In Pipe Fittings - Plastic Pipe, Schedule 80

Friction Loss for Water in Terms of Equivalent Length of Straight Pipe - feet

Fitting	Condition	Nominal Pipe Size, inch											
		1/8	1/4	3/8	1/2	3/4	1	1-1/4	1-1/2	2	2-1/2	3	3-1/2
	Actual Inside Pipe Diameter, inch	0.215	0.302	0.423	0.546	0.742	0.957	1.278	1.500	1.939	2.323	2.900	3.364
90° Standard Elbow	- - -	0.64	0.90	1.25	1.60	2.10	2.60	3.50	4.00	5.50	6.20	7.70	8.91
90° Long Radius Elbow	- - -	0.43	0.60	0.81	1.00	1.70	2.10	2.30	2.70	4.30	5.10	6.30	7.30
90° Street Elbow	- - -	1.07	1.50	2.06	2.60	3.40	4.40	5.80	6.70	8.60	10.3	12.8	14.8
90° Square Corner Elbow	- - -	1.21	1.70	2.35	3.00	3.90	5.00	6.50	7.60	9.80	11.7	14.6	16.9
45° Standard Elbow	- - -	0.36	0.50	0.66	0.80	1.10	1.40	1.80	2.10	2.80	3.30	4.10	4.75
45° Street Elbow	- - -	0.57	0.80	1.06	1.30	1.80	2.30	3.00	3.50	4.50	5.40	6.60	7.65
Standard Tee	Thru Flow	0.43	0.60	0.81	1.00	1.40	1.70	2.30	2.70	4.30	5.10	6.30	7.30
	Branch Flow	1.28	1.80	2.81	4.00	5.10	6.00	8.10	9.60	12.0	14.3	16.3	19.2
Angle Valve	Full Open - No Obstruction	3.13	4.40	5.99	7.50	10.0	12.7	16.7	19.5	25.0	29.8	37.1	42.9
	Full Open - Disc	4.34	6.10	8.30	10.4	13.7	17.5	23.0	26.8	34.5	41.2	51.1	59.1
Gate Valve	Full Open	0.28	0.40	0.55	0.70	0.90	1.10	1.50	1.70	2.20	2.70	3.30	3.85
	3/4 Open	0.78	1.10	1.47	1.80	2.40	3.10	4.00	4.70	6.00	7.20	8.90	10.3
	1/2 Open	3.49	4.90	6.65	8.30	11.0	14.0	18.4	21.5	27.6	32.9	40.9	47.3
	1/4 Open	19.4	27.3	36.8	45.7	61.8	78.7	104	121	155	185	230	266
Globe Valve, Full Open	Conventional - No obstruction	7.33	10.3	14.0	17.6	23.3	29.7	39.1	45.6	58.6	70.0	86.9	101
	Conventional w/ disc	9.75	13.7	18.6	23.3	30.9	39.3	51.8	60.4	77.5	92.6	115	133
	Y-pattern, stem at 60°	3.77	5.30	7.24	9.10	12.0	15.3	20.1	23.5	30.1	36.0	44.7	51.7
	Y-pattern, stem at 45°	3.13	4.40	5.99	7.50	10.0	12.7	16.7	19.5	25.0	29.8	37.1	42.9

Friction Loss In Pipe Fittings - Plastic Pipe, Schedule 80

Friction Loss for Water in Terms of Equivalent Length of Straight Pipe - feet

Fitting	Condition	Nominal Pipe Size, inch										
		4	5	6	8	10	12	14	16	18	20	24
		Actual Inside Pipe Diameter, inch										
		3.826	4.813	5.761	7.625	9.564	11.376	12.500	14.314	16.126	17.938	21.564
90° Standard Elbow	- - -	10.1	12.7	15.2	20.0	25.1	29.8	32.8	37.5	42.3	47.0	56.5
90° Long Radius Elbow	- - -	8.3	10.4	12.5	16.5	20.7	24.7	27.1	31.0	35.0	38.9	46.7
90° Street Elbow	- - -	16.8	21.1	25.3	33.3	41.8	49.7	54.6	62.5	70.5	78.4	94.2
90° Square Corner Elbow	- - -	19.1	24.0	28.8	37.9	47.6	56.7	62.3	71.3	80.3	89.3	107
45° Standard Elbow	- - -	5.4	6.8	8.1	10.6	13.4	15.9	17.5	20.0	22.6	25.1	30.2
45° Street Elbow	- - -	8.7	10.9	13.1	17.3	21.7	25.9	28.4	32.5	36.7	40.8	49.0
Standard Tee	Thru Flow	8.3	10.4	12.5	16.5	20.7	24.7	27.1	31.0	35.0	38.9	46.7
	Branch Flow	22.1	27.4	32.2	39.9	50.1	59.7	65.5	75.1	84.6	94.1	113
Angle Valve	Full Open	48.6	61.2	73.3	96.4	121	144	158	181	204	227	273
	Full Open - Disc	67.1	84.4	101	133	167	199	218	250	282	314	377
Gate Valve	3/4 Open	4.4	5.5	6.6	8.6	10.9	12.9	14.2	16.3	18.3	20.4	24.5
	1/2 Open	11.7	14.8	17.7	23.3	29.2	34.8	38.2	43.7	49.3	54.8	65.9
	1/4 Open	53.7	67.6	80.9	106	134	159	175	200	225	251	302
Globe Valve, Full Open	Straight - No obstruction	114	144	172	226	284	338	371	425	479	533	641
	Straight w/ disc	302	380	455	599	752	895	983	1,130	1,270	1,410	1,700
	Y-pattern, Stem at 60°	151	190	227	299	376	448	492	563	634	705	848
	Y-pattern, Stem at 45°	58.7	73.8	88.4	116	146	174	191	219	247	274	330

This table was originally developed from tests on PVC [poly(vinyl chloride)] pipe, but the values apply to all thermoplastic piping materials with equally smooth interior surfaces.

Friction Loss in Pipe Fittings - Steel Pipe, Schedule 40

Friction Loss for Water in Terms of Equivalent Length of Straight Pipe - feet

Fitting	Condition	L_E/d	Nominal Pipe Size, inch												
			1/4	3/8	1/2	3/4	1	1-1/4	1-1/2	2	2-1/2	3	3-1/2	4	5
			Actual Inside Pipe Diameter, inch												
			0.364	0.493	0.622	0.824	1.049	1.380	1.610	2.067	2.469	3.068	3.548	4.026	5.047
90° Standard Elbow	- - -	30	0.91	1.23	1.56	2.06	2.62	3.45	4.03	5.17	6.17	7.67	8.87	10.1	12.6
90° Long Radius Elbow	- - -	18	0.55	0.74	0.93	1.24	1.57	2.07	2.42	3.10	3.70	4.60	5.32	6.04	7.57
90° Sharp Elbow	- - -	60	1.82	2.47	3.11	4.12	5.25	6.90	8.05	10.3	12.3	15.3	17.7	20.1	25.2
90° Street Elbow	- - -	50	1.52	2.05	2.59	3.43	4.37	5.75	6.71	8.61	10.3	12.8	14.8	16.8	21.0
90° Sharp Corner Street Elbow	- - -	57	1.73	2.34	2.95	3.91	4.98	6.56	7.65	9.82	11.7	14.6	16.9	19.1	24.0
45° Standard Elbow	- - -	15	0.46	0.62	0.78	1.03	1.31	1.73	2.01	2.58	3.09	3.84	4.44	5.03	6.31
45° Street Elbow	- - -	26	0.79	1.07	1.35	1.79	2.27	2.99	3.49	4.48	5.35	6.65	7.69	8.72	10.9
90° Bends, Pipe Bends, Flanged Elbows, Butt-welded Elbows	r/d = 1	18	0.55	0.74	0.93	1.24	1.57	2.07	2.42	3.10	3.70	4.60	5.32	6.04	7.57
	r/d = 1-1/2	12	0.36	0.49	0.62	0.82	1.05	1.38	1.61	2.07	2.47	3.07	3.55	4.03	5.05
	r/d = 2	10	0.30	0.41	0.52	0.69	0.87	1.15	1.34	1.72	2.06	2.56	2.96	3.36	4.21
	r/d = 3	11	0.33	0.45	0.57	0.76	0.96	1.27	1.48	1.89	2.26	2.81	3.25	3.69	4.63
	r/d = 4	11	0.33	0.45	0.57	0.76	0.96	1.27	1.48	1.89	2.26	2.81	3.25	3.69	4.63
	r/d = 6	13	0.39	0.53	0.67	0.89	1.14	1.50	1.74	2.24	2.67	3.32	3.84	4.36	5.47
	r/d = 8	16	0.49	0.66	0.83	1.10	1.40	1.84	2.15	2.76	3.29	4.09	4.73	5.37	6.7
	r/d = 10	30	0.91	1.23	1.56	2.06	2.62	3.45	4.03	5.17	6.17	7.67	8.87	10.1	12.6
	r/d = 12	34	1.03	1.40	1.76	2.33	2.97	3.91	4.56	5.86	7.00	8.69	10.1	11.4	14.3
	r/d = 14	38	1.15	1.56	1.97	2.61	3.32	4.37	5.10	6.55	7.82	9.72	11.2	12.7	16.0

r/d = bend radius/ pipe diameter

Friction Loss for Water in Terms of Equivalent Length of Straight Pipe - feet

Fitting	Condition	L_E/d	Nominal Pipe Size, inch												
			1/4	3/8	1/2	3/4	1	1-1/4	1-1/2	2	2-1/2	3	3-1/2	4	5
			Actual Inside Pipe Diameter, inch												
			0.364	0.493	0.622	0.824	1.049	1.380		2.067	2.469	3.068	3.548	4.026	5.047
90° Bends, Pipe Bends, Flanged Elbows, Butt-welded Elbows	r/d = 16	42	1.27	1.73	2.18	2.88	3.67	4.83	5.64	7.23	8.64	10.7	12.4	14.1	17.7
	r/d = 18	45	1.37	1.85	2.33	3.09	3.93	5.18	6.04	7.75	9.26	11.5	13.3	15.1	18.9
	r/d = 20	50	1.52	2.05	2.59	3.43	4.37	5.75	6.71	8.61	10.3	12.8	14.8	16.8	21.0
Mitre Bends	a = 0°	2	0.06	0.08	0.10	0.14	0.17	0.23	0.27	0.34	0.41	0.51	0.59	0.67	0.84
	a = 15°	4	0.12	0.16	0.21	0.27	0.35	0.46	0.54	0.69	0.82	1.02	1.18	1.34	1.68
	a = 30°	8	0.24	0.33	0.41	0.55	0.70	0.92	1.07	1.38	1.65	2.05	2.37	2.68	3.36
	a = 45°	15	0.46	0.62	0.78	1.03	1.31	1.73	2.01	2.58	3.09	3.84	4.44	5.03	6.31
	a = 60°	27	0.82	1.11	1.40	1.85	2.36	3.11	3.62	4.65	5.56	6.90	7.98	9.06	11.4
	a = 75°	40	1.21	1.64	2.07	2.75	3.50	4.60	5.37	6.89	8.23	10.2	11.8	13.4	16.8
	a = 90°	60	1.82	2.47	3.11	4.12	5.25	6.90	8.05	10.34	12.3	15.3	17.7	20.1	25.2
	2-90°	20	0.61	0.82	1.04	1.37	1.75	2.30	2.68	3.45	4.12	5.11	5.91	6.71	8.41
	3-90°	15	0.46	0.62	0.78	1.03	1.31	1.73	2.01	2.58	3.09	3.84	4.44	5.03	6.31
180° Bend (Close Return Bend)	Small Radius	75	2.28	3.08	3.89	5.15	6.56	8.63	10.1	12.9	15.4	19.2	22.2	25.2	31.5
	Large Radius	50	1.52	2.05	2.59	3.43	4.37	5.75	6.71	8.61	10.3	12.8	14.8	16.8	21.0
Standard Tee	Thru Flow	20	0.61	0.82	1.04	1.37	1.75	2.30	2.68	3.45	4.12	5.11	5.91	6.71	8.41
	Branch Flow	60	1.82	2.47	3.11	4.12	5.25	6.90	8.05	10.3	12.3	15.3	17.7	20.1	25.2
Welding Tee	Forged	45	1.37	1.85	2.33	3.09	3.93	5.18	6.04	7.75	9.26	11.5	13.3	15.1	18.9
	Mitre	60	1.82	2.47	3.11	4.12	5.25	6.90	8.05	10.3	12.3	15.3	17.7	20.1	25.2
Angle Valve	Full Open	158	4.79	6.49	8.19	10.8	13.8	18.2	21.2	27.2	32.5	40.4	46.7	53.0	66.5
	Full Open - Disc	200	6.07	8.22	10.4	13.7	17.5	23.0	26.8	34.5	41.2	51.1	59.1	67.1	84.1

Friction Loss in Pipe Fittings - Steel Pipe, Schedule 40

Friction Loss for Water in Terms of Equivalent Length of Straight Pipe - feet

Fitting	Condition	L_E/d	1/4	3/8	1/2	3/4	1	1-1/4	1-1/2	2	2-1/2	3	3-1/2	4	5
			Nominal Pipe Size, inch												
			0.364	0.493	0.622	0.824	1.049	1.380	1.610	2.067	2.469	3.068	3.548	4.026	5.047
			Actual Inside Pipe Diameter, inch												
Ball Valve	Full Open	3	0.09	0.12	0.16	0.21	0.26	0.35	0.40	0.52	0.62	0.77	0.89	1.01	1.26
Butterfly Valve	Full Open, α=0°	40	1.21	1.64	2.07	2.75	3.50	4.60	5.37	6.89	8.23	10.2	11.8	13.4	16.8
	α=5°	3	0.09	0.12	0.16	0.21	0.26	0.35	0.40	0.52	0.62	0.77	0.89	1.01	1.26
	α=10°	16	0.49	0.66	0.83	1.10	1.40	1.84	2.15	2.76	3.29	4.09	4.73	5.37	6.73
	α=20°	85	2.58	3.49	4.41	5.84	7.43	9.78	11.4	14.6	17.5	21.7	25.1	28.5	35.7
	α=40°	950	28.8	39.0	49.2	65.2	83.0	109	127	164	195	243	281	319	400
Check Valve, Full Open	Ball	150	4.55	6.16	7.78	10.3	13.1	17.3	20.1	25.8	30.9	38.4	44.0	50.0	60.0
	Clearway	50	1.52	2.05	2.59	3.43	4.37	5.75	6.71	8.61	10.3	12.8	14.8	16.8	20.0
	Conventional	133	4.03	5.46	6.89	9.13	11.6	15.3	17.8	22.9	27.4	34.0	40.0	40.0	60.0
	Disk	500	15.2	20.5	25.9	34.3	43.7	57.5	67.1	86.1	103	128	148	168	210
	Hinged	110	3.34	4.52	5.70	7.55	9.62	12.7	14.8	18.9	22.6	28.1	32.5	36.9	46.3
	Swing	92	2.79	3.78	4.77	6.32	8.04	10.6	12.3	15.8	18.9	23.5	27.2	30.9	38.7
Cock Valve	Full Open, Thru Flow	18	0.55	0.74	0.93	1.24	1.57	2.07	2.42	3.10	3.70	4.60	5.32	6.04	7.57
	Three-way, Straight Thru	44	1.33	1.81	2.28	3.02	3.85	5.06	5.90	7.58	9.05	11.2	13.0	14.8	18.5
	Three-way, Branch	140	4.25	5.75	7.26	9.61	12.2	16.1	18.8	24.1	28.8	35.8	41.4	47.0	58.9
Diaphragm Valve	Full Open	125	3.79	5.14	6.48	8.58	10.9	14.4	16.8	21.5	25.7	32.0	37.0	41.9	52.6
	3/4 Open	140	4.25	5.75	7.26	9.61	12.2	16.1	18.8	24.1	28.8	35.8	41.4	47.0	58.9
	1/2 Open	235	7.13	9.65	12.2	16.1	20.5	27.0	31.5	40.5	48.4	60.1	69.5	78.8	98.8

Friction Loss for Water in Terms of Equivalent Length of Straight Pipe - feet

Fitting	Condition	L_E/d	Nominal Pipe Size, inch												
			1/4	3/8	1/2	3/4	1	1-1/4	1-1/2	2	2-1/2	3	3-1/2	4	5
			Actual Inside Pipe Diameter, inch												
			0.364	0.493	0.622	0.824	1.049	1.380	1.610	2.067	2.469	3.068	3.548	4.026	5.047
Foot Valve w/ Strainer	With poppet lift-type disc	420	12.7	17.3	21.8	28.8	36.7	48.3	56.4	72.3	86.4	107	124	141	177
	With hinged disc	75	2.28	3.08	3.89	5.15	6.56	8.63	10.1	12.9	15.4	19.2	22.2	25.2	31.5
Gate Valve	Full Open	10	0.30	0.41	0.52	0.69	0.87	1.15	1.34	1.72	2.06	2.56	2.96	3.36	4.21
	3/4 Open	35	1.06	1.44	1.81	2.40	3.06	4.03	4.70	6.03	7.20	8.95	10.3	11.7	14.7
	1/2 Open	160	4.85	6.57	8.29	11.0	14.0	18.4	21.5	27.6	32.9	40.9	47.3	53.7	67.3
	1/4 Open	900	27.3	37.0	46.7	61.8	78.7	104	121	155	185	230	266	302	379
Globe Valve, Full Open	Straight	340	10.3	14.0	17.6	23.3	29.7	39.1	45.6	58.6	70.0	86.9	100.5	114	143
	Straight - 1/2 Open	470	14.3	19.3	24.4	32.3	41.1	54.1	63.1	81.0	96.7	120	139	158	198
	Wing or Pin Guided Disc	450	13.7	18.5	23.3	30.9	39.3	51.8	60.4	77.5	92.6	115	133	151	189
	Y-pattern, Stem at 60°	175	5.31	7.19	9.07	12.0	15.3	20.1	23.5	30.1	36.0	44.7	51.7	58.7	73.6
	Y-pattern, Stem at 45°	145	4.40	5.96	7.52	10.0	12.7	16.7	19.5	25.0	29.8	37.1	42.9	48.6	61.0
Plug Valve	90° Branch	170	5.16	6.98	8.80	11.7	14.9	19.6	22.8	29.3	35.0	43.5	50.3	57.0	71.5
	Branch	90	2.73	3.70	4.67	6.18	7.87	10.4	12.1	15.5	18.5	23.0	26.6	30.2	37.9
	Straight Thru	18	0.55	0.74	0.93	1.24	1.57	2.07	2.42	3.10	3.70	4.60	5.32	6.04	7.57
	3-way Thru Flow	30	0.91	1.23	1.56	2.06	2.62	3.45	4.03	5.17	6.17	7.67	8.87	10.1	12.6
Water Meters	Wheel	300	9.10	12.3	15.6	20.6	26.2	34.5	40.3	51.7	61.7	76.7	88.7	101	126
	Disk	400	12.1	16.4	20.7	27.5	35.0	46.0	53.7	68.9	82.3	102	118	134	168
	Piston	600	18.2	24.7	31.1	41.2	52.5	69.0	80.5	103	123	153	177	201	252

Friction Loss in Pipe Fittings - Steel Pipe, Schedule 40

Friction Loss for Water in Terms of Equivalent Length of Straight Pipe - feet

Fitting	Condition	L_E/d	Nominal Pipe Size, inch												
			6	8	10	12	14	16	18	20	24	30	32	34	36
			Actual Inside Pipe Diameter, inch												
			6.065	7.981	10.02	11.94	13.12	15.00	16.88	18.81	22.62	28.50	30.62	32.62	34.50
90° Standard Elbow	- - -	30	15.2	20.0	25.1	29.8	32.8	37.5	42.2	47.0	56.6	71.3	76.6	81.6	86.3
90° Long Radius Elbow	- - -	18	9.10	12.0	15.0	17.9	19.7	22.5	25.3	28.2	33.9	42.8	45.9	48.9	51.8
90° Sharp Elbow	- - -	60	30.3	39.9	50.1	59.7	65.6	75.0	84.4	94.1	113	143	153	163	173
90° Street Elbow	- - -	50	25.3	33.8	41.8	49.7	54.7	62.5	70.3	78.4	94.3	119	128	136	144
90° Sharp Corner Street Elbow	- - -	57	28.8	37.9	47.6	56.7	62.3	71.3	80.2	89.4	107	135	145	155	164
45° Standard Elbow	- - -	15	7.58	9.98	12.5	14.9	16.4	18.8	21.1	23.5	28.3	35.6	38.3	40.8	43.1
45° Street Elbow	- - -	26	13.1	17.3	21.7	25.9	28.4	32.5	36.6	40.8	49.0	61.8	66.4	70.7	74.8
90° Bends, Pipe Bends, Flanged Elbows, Butt-welded Elbows	r/d = 1	18	9.10	12.0	15.0	17.9	19.7	22.5	25.3	28.2	33.9	42.8	45.9	48.9	51.8
	r/d = 1-1/2	12	6.07	7.98	10.0	11.9	13.1	15.0	16.9	18.8	22.6	28.5	30.6	32.6	34.5
	r/d = 2	10	5.05	6.65	8.35	9.95	10.9	12.5	14.1	15.7	18.9	23.8	25.5	27.2	28.8
	r/d = 3	11	5.56	7.32	9.19	10.9	12.0	13.8	15.5	17.2	20.7	26.1	28.1	29.9	31.6
	r/d = 4	11	5.56	7.32	9.19	10.9	12.0	13.8	15.5	17.2	20.7	26.1	28.1	29.9	31.6
	r/d = 6	13	6.57	8.65	10.9	12.9	14.2	16.3	18.3	20.4	24.5	30.9	33.2	35.3	37.4
	r/d = 8	16	8.09	10.6	13.4	15.9	17.5	20.0	22.5	25.1	30.2	38.0	40.8	43.5	46.0
r/d = bend radius/ pipe diameter	r/d = 10	30	15.2	20.0	25.1	29.8	32.8	37.5	42.2	47.0	56.6	71.3	76.6	81.6	86.3
	r/d = 12	34	17.2	22.6	28.4	33.8	37.2	42.5	47.8	53.3	64.1	80.8	86.8	92.4	97.8
	r/d = 14	38	19.2	25.3	31.7	37.8	41.6	47.5	53.4	59.6	71.6	90.3	97.0	103	109

Fitting	Condition	L_E/d	6	8	10	12	14	16	18	20	24	30	32	34	36
			6.065	7.981	10.02	11.94	13.12	15.00	16.88	18.81	22.62	28.50	30.62	32.62	34.50
90° Bends, Pipe Bends, Flanged Elbows, Butt-welded Elbows	r/d = 16	42	21.2	27.9	35.1	41.8	45.9	52.5	59.1	65.8	79.2	99.8	107	114	121
	r/d = 18	45	22.7	29.9	37.6	44.8	49.2	56.3	63.3	70.5	84.8	107	115	122	129
	r/d = 20	50	25.3	33.3	41.8	49.7	54.7	62.5	70.3	78.4	94.3	119	128	136	144
Mitre Bends	a = 0°	2	1.01	1.33	1.67	1.99	2.19	2.50	2.81	3.14	3.77	4.75	5.10	5.44	5.75
	a = 15°	4	2.02	2.66	3.34	3.98	4.37	5.00	5.63	6.27	7.54	9.50	10.2	10.9	11.5
	a = 30°	8	4.04	5.32	6.68	7.96	8.75	10.0	11.3	12.5	15.1	19.0	20.4	21.7	23.0
	a = 45°	15	7.58	10.0	12.5	14.9	16.4	18.8	21.1	23.5	28.3	35.6	38.3	40.8	43.1
	a = 60°	27	13.6	18.0	22.5	26.9	29.5	33.8	38.0	42.3	50.9	64.1	68.9	73.4	77.6
	a = 75°	40	20.2	26.6	33.4	39.8	43.7	50.0	56.3	62.7	75.4	95.0	102	109	115
	a = 90°	60	30.3	39.9	50.1	59.7	65.6	75.0	84.4	94.1	113	143	153	163	173
	2-90°	20	10.1	13.3	16.7	19.9	21.9	25.0	28.1	31.4	37.7	47.5	51.0	54.4	57.5
	3-90°	15	7.6	10.0	12.5	14.9	16.4	18.8	21.1	23.5	28.3	35.6	38.3	40.8	43.1
180° Bend (Close Return Bend)	Small Radius	75	37.9	49.9	62.6	74.6	82.0	93.8	105	118	141	178	191	204	216
	Large Radius	50	25.3	33.3	41.8	49.7	54.7	62.5	70.3	78.4	94.3	119	128	136	144
Standard Tee	Thru Flow	20	10.1	13.3	16.7	19.9	21.9	25.0	28.1	31.4	37.7	47.5	51.0	54.4	57.5
	Branch Flow	60	30.3	39.9	50.1	59.7	65.6	75.0	84.4	94.1	113	143	153	163	173
Welding Tee	Forged	45	22.7	29.9	37.6	44.8	49.2	56.3	63.3	70.5	84.8	107	115	122	129
	Mitre	60	30.3	39.9	50.1	59.7	65.6	75.0	84.4	94.1	113	143	153	163	173
Angle Valve	Full Open	158	79.9	105	132	157	173	198	222	248	298	375	403	430	454
	Full Open - Disc	200	101	133	167	199	219	250	280	310	380	480	510	540	580

Friction Loss for Water in Terms of Equivalent Length of Straight Pipe - feet

Nominal Pipe Size, inch

Actual Inside Pipe Diameter, inch

Friction Loss in Pipe Fittings - Steel Pipe. Schedule 40

Friction Loss for Water in Terms of Equivalent Length of Straight Pipe - feet

Fitting	Condition	L_E/d	6	8	10	12	14	16	18	20	24	30	32	34	36
			Nominal Pipe Size, inch												
			6.065	7.981	10.02	11.94	13.12	15.00	16.88	18.81	22.62	28.50	30.62	32.62	34.50
Ball Valve	Full Open	3	1.52	2.00	2.51	2.98	3.28	3.75	4.22	4.70	5.66	7.13	7.66	8.16	8.63
Butterfly Valve	Full Open, α=0°	40	20.2	26.6	33.4	39.8	43.7	50.0	56.3	62.7	75.4	100	100	110	120
	α=5°	3	1.52	2.00	2.51	2.98	3.28	3.75	4.22	4.70	5.66	7.13	7.66	8.16	8.63
	α=10°	16	8.09	10.6	13.4	15.9	17.5	20.0	22.5	25.1	30.2	38.0	40.8	43.5	46.0
	α=20°	85	43.0	56.5	71.0	84.6	93.0	106	120	133	160	202	217	231	244
	α=40°	950	480	632	793	945	1,040	1,190	1,340	1,490	1,790	2,260	2,420	2,580	2,730
Check Valve, Full Open	Ball	150	75.8	99.8	125	149	164	188	211	235	283	356	383	408	431
	Clearway	50	25.3	33.3	41.8	49.7	54.7	62.5	70.3	78.4	94.3	119	128	136	144
	Conventional	133	67.2	88.5	111	132	145	166	187	208	251	316	339	362	382
	Disk	500	253	333	418	497	547	625	703	784	943	1,190	1,280	1,360	1,400
	Hinged	110	55.6	73.2	91.9	109	120	138	155	172	207	261	281	299	316
	Swing	92	46.5	61.2	76.8	91.5	101	115	129	144	173	219	235	250	265
Cock Valve	Full Open, Thru Flow	18	9.10	12.0	15.0	17.9	19.7	22.5	25.3	28.2	33.9	42.8	45.9	48.9	51.8
	Three-way, Straight Thru	44	22.2	29.3	36.7	43.8	48.1	55.0	61.9	69.0	83.0	105	112	120	127
	Three-way, Branch	140	70.8	93.1	117	139	153	175	197	219	264	333	357	381	403
Diaphragm Valve	Full Open	125	63.2	83.1	104	124	137	156	176	196	236	297	319	340	359
	3/4 Open	140	70.8	93.1	117	139	153	175	197	219	264	333	357	381	403
	1/2 Open	235	119	156	196	234	257	294	330	368	443	558	600	639	676

Friction Loss for Water in Terms of Equivalent Length of Straight Pipe - feet

Fitting	Condition	L_E/d	Nominal Pipe Size, inch												
			6	8	10	12	14	16	18	20	24	30	32	34	36
			Actual Inside Pipe Diameter, inch												
			6.065	7.981	10.02	11.94	13.12	15.00	16.88	18.81	22.62	28.50	30.62	32.62	34.50
Foot Valve w/ Strainer	With poppet lift-type disc	420	212	279	351	418	459	525	591	658	792	1,000	1,070	1,140	1,210
	With hinged disc	75	37.9	49.9	62.6	74.6	82.0	93.8	105	118	141	178	191	204	216
Gate Valve	Full Open	10	5.05	6.65	8.35	9.95	10.9	12.5	14.1	15.7	18.9	23.8	25.5	27.2	28.8
	3/4 Open	35	17.7	23.3	29.2	34.8	38.3	43.8	49.2	54.9	66.0	83.1	89.3	95.2	101
	1/2 Open	160	80.9	106	134	159	175	200	225	251	302	380	408	435	460
	1/4 Open	900	455	599	752	895	984	1,130	1,270	1,410	1,700	2,140	2,300	2,450	2,590
Globe Valve, Full Open	Straight	340	172	226	284	338	372	425	478	533	641	808	868	924	978
	Straight - 1/2 Open	470	238	313	392	468	514	588	661	737	886	1,120	1,200	1,280	1,350
	Wing or Pin Guided Disc	450	227	299	376	448	492	563	633	705	848	1,070	1,150	1,220	1,290
	Y-pattern, Stem at 60°	175	88.4	116	146	174	191	219	246	274	330	416	447	476	503
	Y-pattern, Stem at 45°	145	73.3	96.4	121	144	159	181	204	227	273	344	370	394	417
Plug Valve	90° Branch	170	85.9	113	142	169	186	213	239	267	321	404	434	462	489
	Straight Thru Branch	90	45.5	59.9	75.2	89.5	98.4	113	127	141	170	214	230	245	259
	3-way Straight Thru Flow	18	9.10	12.0	15.0	17.9	19.7	22.5	25.3	28.2	33.9	42.8	45.9	48.9	51.8
		30	15.2	20.0	25.1	29.8	32.8	37.5	42.2	47.0	56.6	71.3	76.6	81.6	86.3
Water Meters	Wheel	300	152	200	251	298	328	375	422	470	566	713	766	816	863
	Disk	400	202	266	334	398	437	500	563	627	754	950	1,020	1,090	1,150
	Piston	600	303	399	501	597	656	750	844	941	1,130	1,430	1,530	1,630	1,730

Notes for Friction Loss in Pipe Fittings:

Values in **Friction Loss in Pipe Fittings, Plastic Pipe, Schedule 80** were compiled, adapted, and extrapolated from:

Industrial Thermoplastic and Thermoset Piping Systems: A Manual For Consulting Engineers, Plant Engineers, Process Engineers, Pollution Control Engineers, Piping Estimators, 1980, PPS, Inc., 225 Old Brunswick Road, Piscataway, NJ 08854

Values in **Friction Loss in Pipe Fittings, Steel Pipe, Schedule 40**, are based on the equation: $L_E = (L_E/d)*(d/12)$; where L_E is the Equivalent Length in feet and d is the actual Inside Diameter in inches.

L_E/d was compiled from several sources including:

Flow of Fluids Through Valves, Fittings, and Pipe, Technical Paper No. 410, Crane Company, Chicago, IL, 1969.

Analysis of Water Distribution Systems, Thomas M. Walski, Van Nostrand Reinhold Company, 1984.

Lyon's Encyclopedia of Valves, Jerry L. Lyons and Carl Askland, Van Nostrand Reinhold Company, 1975.

PUMP.NET

Piping Handbook, Sabin Crocker, McGraw-Hill Book Company, 1945.

SST.TEES.AC.UK

Pumps & Tanks

Commonly Available Pumps and Their Characteristics
    Centrifugal...520
    Rotary..521
    Reciprocating...522
    Special Purpose...522

Practical Lift for Centrifugal Pumps 523

Practical Lift for Reciprocating Pumps 525

Pump Relationships: Impeller Velocity, Specific Gravity,
Head, and Pressure

Affinity Laws and Formulas for Centrifugal Pumps 529

Relationship Between Absolute Pressure and Gauge
Pressure..530

Equivalents and Equations For Pipe Flow and Pumps 531

How to Size a Centrifugal Pump 535

Horsepower Needed to Elevate Water to Various Heights 542

Horizontal Cylinder Fillage 544

Capacities of Tanks and Cylinders...............................545

Commonly Available Pumps

| Pump Configuration | Range of Maximum Flow | Range of Maximum Total Dynamic Head (TDH) | Range of Maximum Pressure Rating (Working) | Temperature Range | | Capacity | Vacuum In Hg |
| | | | | Minimum | Maximum | | |
	gpm (US)	ft	psig	°F	°F	ft^3 / min	(absolute)
Centrifugal Pumps							
Horizontal, Overhung Impeller, Close Coupled, Single & Double Stage	30 to 15,000	11 to 5,500	20 to 5,000	-180	1,200	- - -	- - -
Horizontal, Overhung Impeller, Separately Coupled, Single & Double Stage	30 to 120,000	35 to 5,500	19 to 5,000	-400	1,500	- - -	- - -
Horizontal, Impeller Between Bearings, Single & Double Stage	5 to 180,000	23 to 2,600	75 to 3,000	-350	850	- - -	- - -
Horizontal, Impeller Between Bearings, Multi-Stage	18 to 140,000	260 to 15,000	145 to 7,000	-400	850	- - -	- - -
Vertical In-Line, Overhung Impeller	20 to 140,000	15 to 6,900	100 to 5,000	-350	842	- - -	- - -
Vertical In-Line, Impeller Between Bearings	40 to 120,000	48 to 1,500	250 to 653	-65	350	- - -	- - -

Commonly Available Pumps (cont.)

Pump Configuration	Range of Maximum Flow gpm (US)	Range of Maximum Total Dynamic Head (TDH) ft	Range of Maximum Pressure Rating (Working) psig	Temperature Range		Capacity ft³/min	Vacuum In Hg (absolute)
				Minimum °F	Maximum °F		
Centrifugal Pumps (cont.)							
Vertically Suspended, Single Stage, Separate Discharge	8 to 60,000	10 to 1,000	- - -	-150	1,200	- - -	- - -
Vertically Suspended, Multi-Stage, Discharge Through Column	500 to 600,000	50 to 7,200	- - -	-350	1,000	- - -	- - -
Vertically Suspended, Axial Flow	10,000 to 1,000,000	10 to 3,500	- - -	-50	1,000	- - -	- - -
Submersible, Single Stage	20 to 100,000	14 to 1,300	- - -	-100	2,000	- - -	- - -
Submersible, Multi-Single Stage Turbine	1,100 to 220,000	100 to 4,000	- - -	-50	700	- - -	- - -
Rotary Pumps							
Vane, Flexible and Sliding	11 to 1,000	- - -	20 to 350	-100	600	- - -	- - -
Gear, External and Internal	1 to 120,000	- - -	90 to 10,000	-100	950	- - -	- - -
Piston	680 to 1,800	- - -	300 to 20,000	-150	800	- - -	- - -
Lobe	40 to 3,000	- - -	100 to 450	-40	500	- - -	- - -
Progressing Cavity	2 to 4,000	- - -	125 to 2,100	-20	1,300	- - -	- - -

Pump Configuration	Range of Maximum Flow gpm (US)	Range of Maximum Total Dynamic Head (TDH) ft	Range of Maximum Pressure Rating (Working) psig	Temperature Range Minimum °F	Temperature Range Maximum °F	Capacity ft³/min	Vacuum In Hg (absolute)
Rotary Pumps (cont.)							
Peristaltic	1 to 412	- - -	20 to 690	-60	300	- - -	- - -
Screw, Two and Three	35 to 15,000	- - -	580 to 6,900	-40	800	- - -	- - -
Reciprocating Pumps							
Power, Plunger/Piston	1 to 5,000	- - -	22 to 100,000	-300	700	- - -	- - -
Power, Diaphragm	1 to 3,000	25 to 7,623	11 to 17,200	-300	850	- - -	- - -
Special Purpose Pumps							
Metering Reciprocating, Controlled Volume	1 to 18,240	- - -	7 to 60,000	- - -	- - -	- - -	- - -
Vacuum	2 to 2,000	- - -	4 to 14,000	-70	1,450	1 to 14,000	up to 29
Non-Electric, Gas or Vapor Driven	4 to 5,000	20 to 23,000	15 to 10,000	-40	650	- - -	- - -
Cryogenic	1 to 21,400	25 to 2,500	600 to 17,000	-413	892	- - -	- - -
Hydrostatic Test	3 to 300	- - -	1,200 to 100,000	-40	600	- - -	- - -
Drum/Carboy	1 to 220	15 to 289	- - -	-50	325	- - -	- - -

Practical Lift For Centrifugal Pumps

Pumping Water at Various Altitudes and Temperatures

Altitude Feet Above Sea Level	Practical Pump Lift in feet															
	Temperature of Water in °F															
	60	65	70	75	80	85	90	95	100	105	110	115	120	125	130	135
0	-15.0	-14.0	-13.0	-11.5	-10.0	-9.0	-8.0	-7.0	-6.0	-5.0	-4.0	-2.5	-1.0	0.0	1.0	2.0
500	-14.3	-13.3	-12.3	-10.9	-9.5	-8.5	-7.5	-6.5	-5.5	-4.4	-3.3	-1.9	-0.5	0.5	1.5	2.5
1,000	-13.5	-12.5	-11.5	-10.3	-9.0	-8.0	-7.0	-6.0	-5.0	-3.8	-2.5	-1.3	0.0	1.0	2.0	3.0
1,500	-12.8	-11.8	-10.8	-9.6	-8.5	-7.5	-6.5	-5.5	-4.5	-3.1	-1.8	-0.6	0.5	1.5	2.5	3.5
2,000	-12.0	-11.0	-10.0	-9.0	-8.0	-7.0	-6.0	-5.0	-4.0	-2.5	-1.0	0.0	1.0	2.0	3.0	4.0
2,500	-11.5	-10.5	-9.5	-8.5	-7.5	-6.4	-5.3	-4.3	-3.3	-1.9	-0.5	0.5	1.5	2.6	3.8	4.8
3,000	-11.0	-10.0	-9.0	-8.0	-7.0	-5.8	-4.5	-3.5	-2.5	-1.3	0.0	1.0	2.0	3.3	4.5	5.5
3,500	-10.5	-9.5	-8.5	-7.5	-6.5	-5.1	-3.8	-2.8	-1.8	-0.6	0.5	1.5	2.5	3.9	5.3	6.3
4,000	-10.0	-9.0	-8.0	-7.0	-6.0	-4.5	-3.0	-2.0	-1.0	0.0	1.0	2.0	3.0	4.5	6.0	7.0
4,500	-9.5	-8.5	-7.5	-6.5	-5.5	-4.0	-2.5	-1.5	-0.5	0.5	1.5	2.5	3.5	5.0	6.5	7.5
5,000	-9.0	-8.0	-7.0	-6.0	-5.0	-3.5	-2.0	-1.0	0.0	1.0	2.0	3.0	4.0	5.5	7.0	8.0
5,500	-8.5	-7.5	-6.5	-5.5	-4.5	-3.0	-1.5	0.0	0.5	1.5	2.5	3.5	4.5	6.0	7.5	8.5
6,000	-8.0	-7.0	-6.0	-5.0	-4.0	-2.5	-1.0	0.0	1.0	2.0	3.0	4.0	5.0	6.5	8.0	9.0
6,500	-7.5	-6.5	-5.5	-4.5	-3.5	-2.0	-0.5	0.5	1.5	2.5	3.5	4.5	5.5	7.0	8.5	9.5
7,000	-7.0	-6.0	-5.0	-4.0	-3.0	-1.5	0.0	1.0	2.0	3.0	4.0	5.0	6.0	7.5	9.0	10.0
7,500	-6.5	-5.5	-4.5	-3.5	-2.5	-1.0	0.5	1.5	2.5	3.5	4.5	5.5	6.5	8.0	9.5	10.5
8,000	-6.0	-5.0	-4.0	-3.0	-2.0	-0.5	1.0	2.0	3.0	4.0	5.0	6.0	7.0	8.5	10.0	11.0
8,500	-5.5	-4.5	-3.5	-2.5	-1.5	0.0	1.5	2.5	3.5	4.5	5.5	6.5	7.5	8.9	10.3	11.4
9,000	-5.0	-4.0	-3.0	-2.0	-1.0	0.5	2.0	3.0	4.0	5.0	6.0	7.0	8.0	9.3	10.5	11.8
9,500	-4.5	-3.5	-2.5	-1.5	-0.5	1.0	2.5	3.5	4.5	5.5	6.5	7.5	8.5	9.6	10.8	12.1
10,000	-4.0	-3.0	-2.0	-1.0	0.0	1.5	3.0	4.0	5.0	6.0	7.0	8.0	9.0	10.0	11.0	12.5

Practical Pump Lift in feet

Altitude Feet Above Sea Level	Temperature of Water in °F													
	140	145	150	155	160	165	170	175	180	185	190	195	200	205
0	3.0	4.0	5.0	6.0	7.0	8.5	10.0	11.0	12.0	13.0	14.0	15.5	17.0	18.0
500	3.5	4.6	5.8	6.8	7.8	9.3	10.8	11.6	12.5	13.6	14.8	16.1	17.5	--
1,000	4.0	5.3	6.5	7.5	8.5	10.0	11.5	12.3	13.0	14.3	15.5	16.8	18.0	--
1,500	4.5	5.9	7.3	8.3	9.3	10.8	12.3	12.9	13.5	14.9	16.3	17.4	--	--
2,000	5.0	6.5	8.0	9.0	10.0	11.5	12.9	13.6	14.0	15.5	17.0	18.0	--	--
2,500	5.8	7.1	8.5	9.5	10.5	12.3	13.6	14.3	14.8	16.1	17.5	--	--	--
3,000	6.5	7.8	9.0	10.0	11.0	12.9	14.3	14.9	15.5	16.8	18.0	--	--	--
3,500	7.3	8.4	9.5	10.5	11.5	13.6	14.9	15.5	16.3	17.4	--	--	--	--
4,000	8.0	9.0	10.0	11.0	12.0	14.3	15.5	16.1	17.0	18.0	--	--	--	--
4,500	8.5	9.5	10.5	11.5	12.5	14.9	16.1	16.8	17.5	--	--	--	--	--
5,000	9.0	10.0	11.0	12.0	13.0	15.5	16.8	17.4	18.0	--	--	--	--	--
5,500	9.5	10.5	11.5	12.5	13.5	16.1	17.4	18.0	--	--	--	--	--	--
6,000	10.0	11.0	12.0	13.0	14.0	16.8	18.0	--	--	--	--	--	--	--
6,500	10.5	11.5	12.5	13.5	14.5	17.4	--	--	--	--	--	--	--	--
7,000	11.0	12.0	13.0	14.0	15.0	18.0	--	--	--	--	--	--	--	--
7,500	11.5	12.5	13.5	14.5	15.5	--	--	--	--	--	--	--	--	--
8,000	12.0	13.0	14.0	15.0	16.0	--	--	--	--	--	--	--	--	--
8,500	12.5	13.5	14.5	15.5	16.5	--	--	--	--	--	--	--	--	--
9,000	13.0	14.0	15.0	16.0	17.0	--	--	--	--	--	--	--	--	--
9,500	13.5	14.5	15.5	16.5	17.5	--	--	--	--	--	--	--	--	--
10,000	14.0	15.0	16.0	17.0	18.0	--	--	--	--	--	--	--	--	--

Negative numbers are lift, positive numbers are head.

Adapted and expanded from tables in Pumps, 5th Edition, Harry L. Stewart, Macmillan Publishing Company, 1991and Water Well Handbook, 4th Edition, 6th Printing, Keith E. Anderson, Missouri Water Well & Pump Contractors Assn., Inc., Belle, MO, 1971.

Practical Lift For Reciprocating Pumps

Pumping Water At Various Altitudes And Temperatures

Practical Pump Lift in feet

Temperature of Water in °F

Altitude Feet Above Sea Level	60	65	70	75	80	85	90	95	100	105	110	115	120	125	130	135
0	-22.0	-21.0	-20.0	-18.5	-17.0	-16.0	-15.0	-14.0	-13.0	-12.0	-11.0	-9.5	-8.0	-7.0	-6.0	-5.0
500	-21.3	-20.3	-19.3	-17.9	-16.5	-15.5	-14.5	-13.5	-12.5	-11.4	-10.3	-8.9	-7.5	-6.5	-5.5	-4.5
1,000	-20.5	-19.5	-18.5	-17.3	-16.0	-15.0	-14.0	-13.0	-12.0	-10.8	-9.5	-8.3	-7.0	-6.0	-5.0	-4.0
1,500	-19.8	-18.8	-17.8	-16.6	-15.5	-14.5	-13.5	-12.5	-11.5	-10.1	-8.8	-7.6	-6.5	-5.5	-4.5	-3.5
2,000	-19.0	-18.0	-17.0	-16.0	-15.0	-14.0	-13.0	-12.0	-11.0	-9.5	-8.0	-7.0	-6.0	-5.0	-4.0	-3.0
2,500	-18.5	-17.5	-16.5	-15.5	-14.5	-13.4	-12.3	-11.3	-10.3	-8.9	-7.5	-6.5	-5.5	-4.4	-3.3	-2.3
3,000	-18.0	-17.0	-16.0	-15.0	-14.0	-12.8	-11.5	-10.5	-9.5	-8.3	-7.0	-6.0	-5.0	-3.8	-2.5	-1.5
3,500	-17.5	-16.5	-15.5	-14.5	-13.5	-12.1	-10.5	-9.8	-8.8	-7.6	-6.5	-5.5	-4.5	-3.1	-1.8	-0.8
4,000	-17.0	-16.0	-15.0	-14.0	-13.0	-11.5	-10.0	-9.0	-8.0	-7.0	-6.0	-5.0	-4.0	-2.5	-1.0	0.0
4,500	-16.5	-15.5	-14.5	-13.5	-12.5	-11.0	-9.5	-8.5	-7.5	-6.5	-5.5	-4.5	-3.5	-2.0	-0.5	0.5
5,000	-16.0	-15.0	-14.0	-13.0	-12.0	-10.5	-9.0	-8.0	-7.0	-6.0	-5.0	-4.0	-3.0	-1.5	0.0	1.0
5,500	-15.5	-14.5	-13.5	-12.5	-11.5	-10.0	-8.5	-7.5	-6.5	-5.5	-4.5	-3.5	-2.5	-1.0	0.5	1.5
6,000	-15.0	-14.0	-13.0	-12.0	-11.0	-9.5	-8.0	-7.0	-6.0	-5.0	-4.0	-3.0	-2.0	-0.5	1.0	2.0
6,500	-14.5	-13.5	-12.5	-11.5	-10.5	-9.0	-7.5	-6.5	-5.5	-4.5	-3.5	-2.5	-1.5	0.0	1.5	2.5
7,000	-14.0	-13.0	-12.0	-11.0	-10.0	-8.5	-7.0	-6.0	-5.0	-4.0	-3.0	-2.0	-1.0	0.5	2.0	3.0
7,500	-13.5	-12.5	-11.5	-10.5	-9.5	-8.0	-6.5	-5.5	-4.5	-3.5	-2.5	-1.5	-0.5	1.0	2.5	3.5
8,000	-13.0	-12.0	-11.0	-10.0	-9.0	-7.5	-6.0	-5.0	-4.0	-3.0	-2.0	-1.0	0.0	1.5	3.0	4.0
8,500	-12.5	-11.5	-10.5	-9.5	-8.5	-7.0	-5.5	-4.5	-3.5	-2.5	-1.5	-0.5	0.5	1.9	3.3	4.4
9,000	-12.0	-11.0	-10.0	-9.0	-8.0	-6.5	-5.0	-4.0	-3.0	-2.0	-1.0	0.0	1.0	2.3	3.5	4.8
9,500	-11.5	-10.5	-9.5	-8.5	-7.5	-6.0	-4.5	-3.5	-2.5	-1.5	-0.5	0.5	1.5	2.6	3.8	5.1
10,000	-11.0	-10.0	-9.0	-8.0	-7.0	-5.5	-4.0	-3.0	-2.0	-1.0	0.0	1.0	2.0	3.0	4.0	5.5

Altitude Feet Above Sea Level	Practical Pump Lift in feet — Temperature of Water in °F															
	140	145	150	155	160	165	170	175	180	185	190	195	200	205	210	- - -
0	-4.0	-3.0	-2.0	-1.0	0.0	1.5	3.0	4.0	5.0	6.0	7.0	8.5	10.0	11.0	12.0	- - -
500	-3.5	-2.4	-1.3	-0.3	1.0	2.3	3.8	4.6	5.5	6.0	7.8	9.1	10.5	11.6	12.8	- - -
1,000	-3.0	-1.8	-0.5	0.5	1.5	3.0	4.5	5.3	6.0	7.3	8.5	9.8	11.0	12.3	13.5	- - -
1,500	-2.5	-1.1	0.3	1.3	2.3	3.8	5.3	5.9	6.5	7.9	9.3	10.4	11.5	12.9	14.3	- - -
2,000	-2.0	-0.5	1.0	2.0	3.0	4.0	5.0	6.0	7.0	8.5	10.0	11.0	12.0	13.5	15.0	- - -
2,500	-1.3	0.1	1.5	2.5	3.5	4.5	5.5	6.6	7.8	9.1	10.5	11.5	12.5	- - -	- - -	- - -
3,000	-0.5	0.8	2.0	3.0	4.0	5.0	6.0	7.3	8.5	9.8	11.0	12.0	13.0	- - -	- - -	- - -
3,500	0.3	1.4	2.5	3.5	4.5	5.5	6.5	7.9	9.3	10.4	11.5	12.5	13.5	- - -	- - -	- - -
4,000	1.0	2.0	3.0	4.0	5.0	6.0	7.0	8.5	10.0	11.0	12.0	13.0	14.0	- - -	- - -	- - -
4,500	1.5	2.5	3.5	4.5	5.5	6.6	7.8	9.1	10.5	11.5	12.5	13.5	14.5	- - -	- - -	- - -
5,000	2.0	3.0	4.0	5.0	6.0	7.3	8.5	9.8	11.0	12.0	13.0	14.0	15.0	- - -	- - -	- - -
5,500	2.5	3.5	4.5	5.5	6.5	7.9	9.3	10.4	11.5	12.5	13.5	14.5	15.5	- - -	- - -	- - -
6,000	3.0	4.0	5.0	6.0	7.0	8.5	10.0	11.0	12.0	13.0	14.0	15.0	16.0	- - -	- - -	- - -
6,500	3.5	4.5	5.5	6.5	7.5	9.0	10.5	11.5	12.5	13.5	14.5	- - -	- - -	- - -	- - -	- - -
7,000	4.0	5.0	6.0	7.0	8.0	9.5	11.0	12.0	13.0	14.0	15.0	- - -	- - -	- - -	- - -	- - -
7,500	4.5	5.5	6.5	7.5	8.5	10.0	11.5	12.5	13.5	14.5	15.5	- - -	- - -	- - -	- - -	- - -
8,000	5.0	6.0	7.0	8.0	9.0	10.5	12.0	13.0	14.0	15.0	16.0	- - -	- - -	- - -	- - -	- - -
8,500	5.5	6.5	7.5	8.5	9.5	11.0	12.5	13.5	14.5	15.5	16.5	- - -	- - -	- - -	- - -	- - -
9,000	6.0	7.0	8.0	9.0	10.0	11.5	13.0	14.0	15.0	16.0	17.0	- - -	- - -	- - -	- - -	- - -
9,500	6.5	7.5	8.5	9.5	10.5	12.0	13.5	14.5	15.5	16.5	17.5	- - -	- - -	- - -	- - -	- - -
10,000	7.0	8.0	9.0	10.0	11.0	12.5	14.0	15.0	16.0	17.0	18.0	- - -	- - -	- - -	- - -	- - -

Pump Relationships:
Impeller Velocity, Specific Gravity, Head, and Pressure

The total head developed by a centrifugal pump depends only on the velocity of the periphery of the impeller as shown in the following equation: $H = \dfrac{v^2}{2g}$

where:
  H is the total head, at zero flow rate, developed by the pump in feet of liquid;

  v is the velocity of the periphery of the impeller in feet per second;

  g is the acceleration of free fall, 32.1740486 feet per second squared.

Note that the total head does <u>not</u> depend on the density or specific gravity of the liquid pumped.

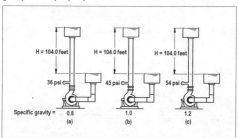

Figure 1 - Press/head relationships of identical pumps handling liquids of differing specific gravities.

Figure 1 shows three identical pumps, each designed to develop 104.0 feet of head based on water. The head is the same for each pump regardless of whether the liquid being pumped is

  (a) JP1 jet fuel with a specific gravity of 0.8 at 68°F,

  (b) water with a specific gravity of 1.0 at 39°F,

  (c) corn starch solution (24 baumé) with a specific gravity of 1.2 at 60°F, or

  (d) or a liquid with some other specific gravity.

While the total head in feet is the same for each pump, the pressure head in psi is different for each liquid. The pressure head measured by a gauge placed as shown in Figure 1 will be different for each liquid, although the pump's impeller velocity and diameter are unchanged for each fluid.

The pressure head in each example can be found using the following equation: $P = \dfrac{H \bullet SpG}{2.3108}$

This equation can be rearranged to determine the total head developed by the pump in feet of liquid as follows: $H = \dfrac{2.3108 \cdot P}{SpG}$

Where, in either equation:

P is the pressure head in psi;

H is the total head developed by the pump in feet of liquid;

SpG is the specific gravity of the liquid being pumped;

2.3108 is a constant to handle unit conversions.

These relationships can also be stated as follows:

(1) pressure head (in psi) is proportional to both total head (in feet of liquid) and density or specific gravity of the liquid, and

(2) total head (in feet of liquid) is proportional to pressure head (in psi) and inversely proportional to the density or specific gravity of the liquid.

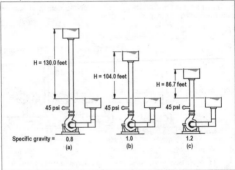

Figure 2 - Pressure head relationships for pumps delivering the same pressure head, and handling liquids of different specific gravity.

In Figure 2, all three pumps are conveying liquids at a pressure of 45 psi. Since the density or specific gravity of each liquid is different, each pump develops a different total head in feet. Therefore, if the impeller velocity for all three pumps is the same, the impeller diameters must be different. The pump in figure 2(a) must have the largest diameter impeller and the pump in figure 2(c) must have the smallest.

In both figures, losses to friction, etc., have been ignored.

SOURCES:

Pump Users Handbook, 4th Edition, R. Rayner, Elsevier Science Publishers, Ltd., 1995.

Hydraulic Handbook, 6th Edition, Colt Industries, Pump Division, Kansas City, KS, 1971.

Cameron Hydraulic Data, Ingersoll-Rand Co., Phillipsburg, NJ, 1979.

Affinity Laws and Formulas For Centrifugal Pumps

Vendor supplied pump performance curves give the relationship between flow rate or pump capacity and total dynamic head. The curves are usually developed for different impeller diameters at a constant impeller speed. At times it may be necessary to estimate pump performance at an impeller diameter or speed not shown on the original performance curves. The Affinity Laws can be used to make these estimates.

The Affinity Laws relate the flow rate or pump capacity, total dynamic head, and brake horsepower to impeller diameter, impeller speed, or to both diameter and speed as follows:

Change In Diameter Only	Change In Speed Only	Change In Both Diameter and Speed
$Q_m = Q_o \left(\dfrac{D_m}{D_o} \right)$	$Q_m = Q_o \left(\dfrac{N_m}{N_o} \right)$	$Q_m = Q_o \left(\dfrac{N_m \, x D_m}{N_o \, x D_o} \right)$
$H_m = H_o \left(\dfrac{Dm}{D_o} \right)^2$	$H_m = H_o \left(\dfrac{N_m}{N_o} \right)^2$	$H_m = H_o \left(\dfrac{N_m \, x D_m}{N_o \, x D_o} \right)$
$bhp_m = bhp_o \left(\dfrac{D_m}{D_o} \right)^3$	$bhp_m = bhp_o \left(\dfrac{N_m}{N_o} \right)^3$	$bhp_m = bhp_o \left(\dfrac{N_m x D_m}{N_o \, x D_o} \right)^3$

Where:

bhp	= Brake horsepower in horsepower or kilowatts
D	= impeller diameter in inches or millimeters
H	= total dynamic head in feet or meters
N	= impeller speed in revolutions per minute or revolutions per second
Q	= flow rate or pump capacity in gallons per minute or liters per second
o	indicates original condition
m	indicates the modified condition

Relationship Between Absolute Pressure and Gauge Pressure

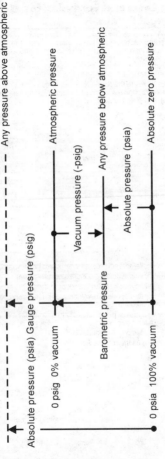

Any pressure above atmospheric

Atmospheric pressure

Vacuum pressure (-psig)

Any pressure below atmospheric

Absolute pressure (psia)

Absolute zero pressure

Absolute pressure (psia) Gauge pressure (psig)

0 psig   0% vacuum

Barometric pressure

0 psia   100% vacuum

Absolute pressure (psia) = Barometric pressure ± Gauge pressure (psig)

Equivalents and Equations for Pipe Flow and Pumps

Abbreviations and symbols:

A	= Inside area of pipe in ft^2.
a	= Inside area of pipe in in^2.
atm	= Atmospheric pressure in psi.
BHP	= Brake horsepower.
BPH	= Flow rate in barrels (petroleum) per hr.
Btu	= British thermal unit.
C	= Specific heat of liquid; 1.0 for water, 0.5 for hydrocarbons
CMPS	= Flow rate in m^3 per sec.
°C	= Degree Celsius.
eff	= Efficiency.
°F	= Degree Fahrenheit.
ft	= Foot.
ft^2	= Square foot.
ft^3	= Cubic foot.
g	= Acceleration due to gravity at sea level, 9.80665 m per sec^2 = 32.1740486 ft per sec^2.
GPM	= Flow rate in gallons (US, liquid) per min.
h	= Head in ft.
HP	= Horsepower.
hr	= Hour.
h_v	= Velocity head in ft.
ID	= Inside diameter of pipe.
IDf	= Inside diameter of pipe in ft.
IDi	= Inside diameter of pipe in in.
IDM	= Inside diameter of pipe in mm.
IDm	= Inside diameter of pipe in mm.
IMD	= Pump impeller diameter in in.
in	= Inch.
in^2	= Square inch.
in^3	= Cubic inch.
kg	= Kilogram.
LPM	= Flow rate in liters per min.
m	= Meter.
m^2	= Square meter.
m^3	= Cubic meter.
min	= Minute.
mm	= Millimeter.
N_s	= Specific speed at the best efficiency point.
P	= Pressure in psi.
Pa	= Pascal.

pcf	= Pound per ft^3.
PPH	= Pound per hr.
psi	= Pound-force per in^2.
psia	= Absolute pressure in psi.
psig	= Gauge pressure in psi.
Q	= Flow rate in ft^3 per sec.
RPM	= Speed of pump in revolutions per minute.
sec	= Second.
SpG	= Specific gravity.
TH	= Total head in ft.
T_r	= Temperature rise in °F.
V	= Average velocity in ft per sec.
w	= Specific weight of liquid in pounds per ft^3.
π	= Constant, approximately 3.141592654.
•	= Multiply.

Equivalents:

Density of water at 4°C (39.2°F) = 62.42640 pcf = 999.9750 kg/m^3

Density of water at 68°F (20.0°C) = 62.31598 pcf = 998.2063 kg/m^3

Atmospheric pressure (standard) = 1.01325 bars = 14.695949 psi = 101,325 Pa

1 bar = 0.9869233 atmospheres (standard) = 14.503774 psi = 100,000 Pa

1 ft of water at 68°F = 2,983.7054 Pa = 0.432749888 psi

1 psi = 2.3066587 ft of water at 4°C (39.2°F) = 2.3108036 ft of water at 68°F (20.0°C)

1 psi = 6,894.7573 pascal = 0.068046 atmospheres (standard) = 0.0689476 bars

1 pascal = .00014503774 psi = 0.00001 bars = 9.8692327E-06 atmospheres (standard)

1 barrel (petroleum) = 42 gallons (US, liquid)

1 gallon (US, liquid) = 0.1336806 ft^3 = 231 in^3 = 0.0037854 m^3

1 ft^3 = 1,728 in^3 = 0.0283168 m^3

1 m^3 = 1,000 liters = 6.2898108 barrel (petroleum) = 35.314667 ft^3 = 264.17205 gallon (US, liquid)

1 ft^2 = 144 in^2 = 0.092903 m^2

1 ft = 12 in = 0.3048 m

1 meter = 1,000 millimeters = 3.2808399 ft

1 hr = 60 min

1 min = 60 sec

1 HP = 550 foot pound-force per sec = 33,000 foot pound-force per min

1 HP = 745.69987 watts = 745.69987 joules per sec = 2,545 Btu per hr at 15°C

Equations for Area of Pipes or Circles:
(Note: the • symbol below indicates multiplication)

$$A = \frac{\pi \cdot ID^2}{4} = 0.785398 \cdot V \cdot IDf^2 = 0.005454 \cdot V \cdot IDi^2$$

Equations for Flow Rate in Pipes:

$$Q = V \cdot A = 0.785398 \cdot V \cdot IDf^2 = 0.005454 \cdot V \cdot IDi^2$$

$$GPM = \frac{PPH}{500 \cdot SpG} \quad \text{(at 60 to 65°F)}$$

Equations for Head:

$$h = \frac{2.3018 \cdot P}{SpG} = \frac{P \cdot 143.913}{w} \quad \text{(at 68°F)}$$

Equations for Pressure:

$$P = \frac{h \cdot SpG}{2.3108} = \frac{h \cdot w}{143.913} \quad \text{(at 68°F)}$$

Equations for Pumps:

$$BHP = \frac{GPM \cdot (0.1337 ft^3 / gallon) \cdot (62.33 pounds / ft^3) \cdot SpG \cdot h}{33,000 \cdot eff}$$

$$BHP = \frac{GPM \cdot h \cdot SpG}{3,960 \cdot eff} = \frac{GPM \cdot P}{1,714 \cdot eff} = \frac{PPH \cdot P}{857,000 \cdot eff} \cdot \frac{1}{SpG}$$

$$\frac{Btu}{hr} = \frac{P \cdot GPM}{1.5}$$

$$eff = \frac{HP}{BHP} \cdot 100$$

$$HP = \frac{Torque \cdot RPM}{5,252} = \frac{GPM \cdot P}{1,714} = \frac{GPM \cdot TH}{3,960} = \frac{GPM \cdot h \cdot SpG}{3,960}$$

$$= \frac{w \cdot Q \cdot TH}{550} = \frac{PPH \cdot h}{33,000}$$

(Note: the • symbol below indicates multiplication)

$$IMD = \frac{1,840 \cdot h^{0.5}}{RPM}$$

$$N_s = \frac{RPM \cdot GPM^{0.5}}{h^{0.75}}$$

$$Torque = \frac{5,252 \cdot HP}{RPM}$$

$$T_r = \frac{TH}{778 \cdot C} \cdot \left(\frac{1}{eff} - 1 \right) = \frac{TH \cdot (1 - eff)}{778 \cdot C \cdot eff} = \frac{2,545 \cdot (BHP - HP)}{PPH \cdot C}$$

Equations for Velocity in Pipes:

$$V = \frac{Q}{A} = \frac{4 \cdot Q}{\pi \cdot ID^2} = 1.273240 \cdot \frac{Q}{IDf^2} = 183.346 \cdot \frac{Q}{IDi^2}$$

$$V = 0.285948 \cdot \frac{BPH}{IDi^2} = 4.177295 \cdot \frac{CMPS}{IDM^2} = 0.3208333 \cdot \frac{GPM}{a}$$

$$V = 0.0028368 \cdot \frac{GPM}{IDf^2} = 0.408497 \cdot \frac{GPM}{IDi^2}$$

$$V = 69.63798 \cdot \frac{LPM}{IDm^2} = 0.0019858 \cdot \frac{BPH}{IDf^2}$$

Equations for Velocity Head:

$$h_v = \frac{V^2}{2 \cdot g} = 0.0155405 \cdot V^2 = 0.0012707 \cdot \frac{BPH^2}{IDi^4}$$

$$h_v = 0.2711785 \cdot \frac{CMPS^2}{IDM^2} = 0.0025932 \cdot \frac{GPM^2}{IDi^4}$$

Sources and References:

Cameron Hydraulic Data, 16th Edition, Ingersoll-Rand Company, 1979.

Centrifugal Pump Clinic, Igor J. Karassik, Marcel Dekker, Inc., New York, 1981.

Centrifugal Pumps, Selection, Operation, and Maintenance, Igor J. Karassik and Roy Carter, F.W. Dodge Corporation, New York, 1960.

Flow of Fluids Through Valves, Fittings, and Pipe, Technical Paper No. 410, 13th Printing, Crane Company, New York, 1973.

Fluid Power Data Book, 9th Edition, 10th Printing, Womack Educational Publications, Dallas, Texas, 1995.

Fundamentals and Application of Centrifugal Pumps For The Practicing Engineer, Alfred Benaroya, Petroleum Publishing Company, Tulsa, Oklahoma, 1978.

HVAC Pump Handbook, James B. Rishel, McGraw-Hill, New York, 1996.

Hydraulic Field Manual, Robert O. Parmley, McGraw-Hill, Inc., New York, 1992.

Hydraulic Handbook, 6th Edition, Colt Industries Pump Division, Kansas City, Kansas, 1971.

Hydraulic Institute Standards For Centrifugal, Rotary, and Reciprocating Pumps, 14th edition, Hydraulic Institute, Cleveland, Ohio, 1983.

Practical Introduction to Pumping Technology, Uno Wahren, Gulf Publishing Company, Houston Texas, 1997.

www.pumpline.com/operatio.htm, 1999.

How To Size A Centrifugal Pump

Centrifugal pumps are the most common pumps used today. Here are 11 steps to follow when sizing a centrifugal pump and the piping and fittings needed to convey a liquid.

Step 1. Draw a sketch of the pump, piping, and fittings.

The sketch should include the location and elevation of the source of the liquid being pumped; the location and elevation of the destination for the liquid being pumped; the location and elevation of the pump; the total length of pipe including the suction pipe and discharge pipe; and the number and location of all valves, bends, and other fittings.

Step 2. Determine the liquid that will be pumped and the type of pump.

The viscosity and density of a liquid effect the type and size of pump.

The viscosity has an effect on selecting the type of pump. Reciprocating pumps can handle liquids with viscosities up to 3,000 SSU (Saybolt Seconds Universal) or 600 cSt (centistokes); centrifugal pumps can handle viscosities up to 4,550 SSU (1,000 cSt); and rotary pumps can handle viscosities up to 6,800,000 SSU (1,500,000 cSt).

The specific gravity or density of the liquid determines the Total Dynamic Head (TDH) the pump will produce.

Step 3. Determine the amount of liquid to be pumped.

The amount of liquid is referred to as "capacity" or "flow rate". Generally, the greater the required flow rate, the larger the size of the pump. Pumps are available with flow rates ranging from less than 1 gallon (US) per minute to 1,000,000 gallons (US) per minute. See Commonly Available Pumps on page 520 for more information.

Step 4. Determine the Static Discharge Head (SDH) that the pump must overcome.

Static Discharge Head (SDH) is the height, in feet, from the centerline of the pump to the surface of the liquid in the container into which the pump will discharge.

Step 5. Determine the Static Suction Lift (SSL) that the pump will be required to produce.

Static Suction Lift (SSL) is the height in feet from the centerline of the pump to the surface of the liquid in the container from which the pump is drawing liquid. Static Suction Lift (SSL) is produced by atmospheric pressure. A centrifugal pump creates an area of low pressure (vacuum or suction) in the volute. Liquid is then pushed toward the area of low pressure by the higher atmospheric pressure. At 60°F, suction lift for water is limited to about fifteen feet at sea level for a well sealed centrifugal pump. For a reciprocating pump, the suction lift is limited to about 22 feet for water at 60°F at sea level. These values decrease with increasing temperature and increasing elevation (see *Practical Lift For Centrifugal Pumps* on page 523 and *Practical Lift For Reciprocating Pumps* on page). If the source of liquid is above the centerline of the pump, SSL is negative because it reduces the Total Dynamic Head (TDH). If the source of liquid is below the centerline of the pump, SSL is positive because it increases the Total Dynamic Head (TDH).

Step 6. Determine the total length of pipe.

Water flowing through pipe and fittings causes an energy or head loss due to friction. Friction head loss is proportional to the length and diameter of pipe. The energy required to overcome friction must be accounted for in the Total Dynamic Head (TDH) produced by the pump.

Step 7. Determine the type and size of pipe and fittings.

Using the *Pipe - Properties and Friction Loss* tables starting on page 392 you can estimate the type and size of pipe. The size of the fittings are then matched to the size of the pipe.

Step 8. Determine the Friction Head Loss (Hf) for the pipe and fittings.

Using the *Pipe - Properties and Friction Loss* tables starting on page 392 and the *Friction Loss in Pipe Fittings* tables starting on page 508, you can estimate the friction head loss (Hf) for all components.

Step 9. Determine the Velocity Head Loss (Hv) for the liquid.

In addition to friction head loss, liquid in motion loses energy or head as it works against gravity. This head loss is related to the velocity of the liquid. Velocity head loss is calculated as $Hv = V^2 / 2g$, where Hv is the velocity head loss in feet, V is the velocity in feet per second, and g is the acceleration of gravity equal to 32.174 feet per second squared at sea level.

Step 10. Determine the Total Dynamic Head (TDH) the pump needs to produce.

Total Dynamic Head (TDH) is the sum of the Static Discharge Head (SDH), the Static Suction Lift (SSL), the Friction Head Loss (Hf), and the Velocity Head Loss (Hv).

Step 11. Determine size of the pump.

The size of the pump can be determined from the required flow rate and the Total Dynamic Head (TDH). Pump manufacturers publish pump rating or pump performance curves for each pump they manufacture. Performance curves show a plot of capacity or flow rate versus Total Dynamic Head (TDH).

Example

In this example, all elevations are in feet above mean sea level.

Step 1: Draw a sketch of the pump, piping, and fittings.

We want to pump water from a small stream to an elevated holding tank. The elevation of the surface of the water in the stream is 55 feet and the elevation of the surface of the water in the holding tank is 120 feet. We have determined that the centerline of the pump will be set at an elevation of 60 feet. We will use a suction or intake pipe which is 7 feet long, an offset intake pipe which is 5 feet long from the 90° elbow to the pump, a discharge pipeline which is 5 feet long from the gate valve to the 45° standard elbow, and 82 feet long to the second 45° standard elbow, and a discharge pipe which is 7 feet long. We will use a foot valve with a strainer at the intake, a gate valve on the discharge side of the pump, one 90° standard elbow, and two 45° standard elbows. The foot valve will be set 2 feet below the water level in the stream and the discharge pipe will be 2 feet below the water level in the holding tank. See the sketch.

Step 2: Determine the liquid that will be pumped and the type of pump.

We will pump clean, sediment-free, water at a temperature between 60° and 70°F. Water has a specific gravity of 1.0 in this temperature range, a density of 62.4 pounds per cubic foot at 60°F, and a viscosity of 32 SSU (1 cSt) at 70°F. For water in this temperature range, the most commonly selected pump is a centrifugal pump.

Step 3: Determine the amount of liquid to be pumped.

We want to pump 200 gallons (US) per minute.

Step 4: Determine the Static Discharge Head (SDH) that the pump must overcome.

The Static Discharge Head (SDH) is equal to 120 feet minus 60 feet, or 60 feet.

Step 5: Determine the Static Suction Lift (SSL) that the pump will be required to produce.

The SSL is equal to 60 feet minus 55 feet, or 5 feet.

Step 6: Determine the total length of pipe.

We will use the following pipe sections:

- Intake side of pump: intake pipe = 7 feet,
  intake offset pipe = 5 feet.

- Discharge side of pump: discharge pipeline = 87 feet,
  discharge pipe = 7 feet.

- Total length of pipe = 106 feet.

Step 7: Determine the type and size of pipe and fittings.

We will use schedule 40 steel pipe because it is durable and available in a wide range of sizes. There are three factors to consider when selecting the type and size of pipe:

- flow rate
- velocity, and
- Availability

Pump Selection Example - All schedule 40 steel pipe

Pump Selection - Flow Rate Table

Nominal ID inch	Actual ID inch	Flow Rate (gallons (US) per minute)					
		Friction Head Loss (feet/100 feet)					
		0.1	0.5	1	5	10	50
2-1/2	2.469	7	17	25	60	88	209
3	3.068	13	31	45	107	155	369
3-1/2	3.548	19	45	66	156	227	541
4	4.026	26	63	91	218	316	755
5	5.047	48	114	165	394	573	1370

Pump Selection - Velocity Table

Nominal ID inch	Actual ID inch	Velocity (feet per second)					
		Friction Head Loss (feet/100 feet)					
		0.1	0.5	1	5	10	50
2-1/2	2.469	0.5	1.2	1.7	4.0	5.9	14.0
3	3.068	0.6	1.3	1.9	4.6	6.7	16.0
3-1/2	3.548	0.6	1.5	2.1	5.1	7.4	17.6
4	4.026	0.7	1.6	2.3	5.5	8.0	19.0
5	5.047	0.8	1.8	2.6	6.3	9.2	22.0

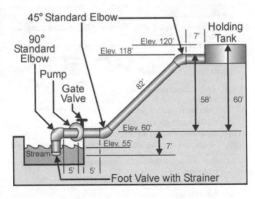

The first factor to consider in selecting the correct pipe size is the **flow rate**. In the *Steel Pipe - Properties and Friction Loss* table starting on page 468, scan down the Theoretical Flow Rate columns until flow rates around 200 gallons (US) per minute are located. The first entry we come to is 209 gallons (US) per minute at 50 feet of head loss per 100 feet of pipe. Reading across to the left we find a 2-1/2 inch nominal diameter pipe will produce this flow rate. Further down in the table we find that a 3 inch nominal diameter pipe will produce 155 gallons (US) per minute at 10 feet of head loss per 100 feet of pipe and 369 gallons (US) per minute at 50 feet of head loss per 100 feet of pipe. Still further in the table we find a 4 inch nominal diameter pipe will produce 218 gallons (US) per minute at 5 feet of head loss per 100 feet of pipe and 316 gallons (US) per minute at 10 feet of head loss per 100 feet of pipe. How do we decide which size is best? We use the second factor, velocity.

It is generally accepted that the velocity in the discharge pipe should be between 4 feet per second and 8 feet per second. The velocity can be determined from the flow rate and the inside diameter of the pipe. Go to the section on Equivalents and Equations For Pipe Flow and Pumps starting on page 531. Find the section titled Equations for Velocity in Pipes. The eigth relationship in this section reads: $V = 0.408497 \cdot GPM/IDi^2$, where V is the average velocity in feet per second, GPM is the flow rate in gallons (US) per minute, and IDi is the inside diameter of the pipe in inches. We will use this relationship to calculate velocity.

We construct a table of flow rates and velocities (see attached table). In the first part of the table we have gathered the flow rate/friction head loss data from the Steel Pipe - Properties and Friction Loss table for schedule 40 steel pipe ranging from 2-1/2 inch nominal diameter to 5 inch nominal diameter. In the second part of the table we have calculated the velocity for each of the flow rates. We find that only two columns, the 5 feet per 100 feet column and the 10 feet per 100 feet column, meet the velocity criteria. It can also be seen that the 2-1/2 inch nominal and 3 inch nominal pipe sizes can be eliminated because the flow rates at these velocities are below the required flow rate of 200 gallons (US) per minute. We now consider the third factor, availability.

Four inch nominal steel pipe is much more common than either the 3-1/2 inch nominal or the 5 inch nominal diameters. So we choose to use 4-inch nominal diameter pipe (inside diameter is 4.026 inches) with 4-inch nominal fittings on the discharge side of the pump.

Most large centrifugal pumps have an intake port which is larger than the discharge port. Commonly intake ports are from 1.2 to 2.0 times larger than the discharge port. With this in mind, we will use a factor of 1.5 (or 1.5 times 4.026 equals 6.0), and on the intake side of the pump we will use 6-inch nominal schedule 40 steel pipe (inside diameter is 6.065 inches) and 6-inch nominal fittings.

Step 8: Determine the Friction Head Loss (Hf) for the pipe and fittings.

We have 94 feet of 4-inch nominal schedule 40 steel pipe on the discharge side of the pump. In the *Steel Pipe - Properties and Friction Loss* table, scan down the Nominal Pipe Size column to find 4-inch diameter pipe. Under the Schedule Number Column, locate schedule 40 and read across to the right to find 218 gallons (US) per minute as the Theoretical Flow Rate that will cause 5 feet of head loss per 100 feet of pipe. This is the reverse of what we did in Step 7. The flow rate of 218 gallons (US) per minute is close enough to our required flow rate of 200 gallons (US) per minute that we will use 5 feet of head loss per 100 feet of pipe. The friction loss in the pipe on the discharge side can be calculated as 94 feet divided by 100 feet of pipe, times 5 feet of head loss or 4.70 feet of head loss.

We also have 12 feet of 6-inch nominal schedule 40 steel pipe on the intake side of the pump. In the *Steel Pipe - Properties and Friction Loss* table, scan down the Nominal Pipe Size column to find 6-inch diameter pipe. Under the Schedule Number Column, locate schedule 40 and read across to the right to find 184 gallons (US) per minute as the Theoretical Flow Rate that will cause 0.5 feet of head loss per 100 feet of pipe. A flow rate of 184 gallons (US) per minute is close enough to our required flow rate of 200 gallons (US) per minute that we will use 0.5 feet of head loss per 100 feet of pipe. The friction loss in the pipe on the intake side can be calculated as 12 feet of pipe divided by 100 feet of pipe, times 0.5 feet of head loss, or 0.06 feet of head loss.

We also have several pipe fittings: 2 fittings in the 6-inch intake pipe and 3 fittings in the 4-inch discharge pipe. In the *Friction Loss in Pipe Fittings* table for steel pipe, in the column for 4-inch nominal pipe, we find a 45° standard elbow is equivalent to 5.03 feet of pipe and a fully opened gate valve is equivalent to 3.36 feet of pipe. In the column for 6-inch nominal pipe, we find a 90° standard elbow is equivalent to 15.2 feet of pipe and a foot valve with strainer and hinged disc is equivalen to 37.9 feet of pipe.

The friction head loss for the fittings is calculated as the equivalent pipe length times the friction loss per 100 feet of pipe. The equivalent pipe length for the 4-inch fittings is 5.03 feet of pipe plus 5.03 feet of pipe, plus 3.36 feet of pipe equals 13.42 feet of pipe. 13.42 feet of pipe divided by 100 feet of pipe, times 5 feet of head loss equals 0.67 feet of head loss in the 4-inch fittings. For the 6-inch fittings, the friction head loss is 15.2 feet of pipe plus 37.9 feet of pipe which equals 53.1 feet of pipe divided by 100 feet of pipe times 0.5 feet of head loss equals 0.27 feet of head loss in the 6-inch fittings. The total head loss in all the fittings is 0.67 feet plus 0.27 feets, equals 0.94 feet of head loss in the fittings.

The total friction head loss (Hf) for the system is the sum of the head losses for the pipe and fittings. The total is calculated as 4.70 feet for the discharge pipe, plus 0.06 for the intake pipe, plus 0.94 feet for the fittings, for a total of 5.7 feet of friction head loss (Hf).

Step 9: Determine the Velocity Head Loss (Hv) for the liquid.

The velocity can be determined using the velocity equation shown in Step 7.

On the discharge side of the pump, we calculate the average velocity in 4-inch nominal pipe as 0.408497 times 200, divided by 4.026 squared, or 5.04 feet per second. We then calculate the velocity head loss (Hv) as 5.04 squared divided by 2 times 32.174 or 0.39 feet.

On the intake side of the pump, we calculate that the average velocity in 6 inch nominal pipe as 0.408497 times 200 divided by 6.065 squared, or 2.22 feet per second. We then calculate the velocity head loss (Hv) as 2.22 squared divided by 2 times 32.174 or 0.08 feet.

The total velocity head loss (Hv) is 0.39 feet plus 0.08 feet, or 0.47 feet.

Step 10: Determine the Total Dynamic Head (TDH) the pump needs to produce.

The Total Dynamic Head (TDH) equals SDH of 60.0 feet, plus SSL of 5.0 feet, plus Hf of 5.7 feet, and Hv of 0.47 feet for a TDH of 71.17 feet which can be rounded down to 71 feet.

Step 11: Determine size of the pump.

Pump size is commonly designated by a series of numbers indicating the discharge port diameter (DPD), intake port diameter (IPD), and impeller diameter (IMD). The designation looks like DPD x IPD - IMD. For most pumps sold in the US, these dimensions will be in inches. So we will look in our pump catalogs for a 4 x 6 pump that produces 200 gallons (US) per minute at 71 feet of Total Dynamic Head (TDH).

Pump Performance Curve

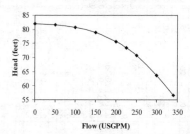

After looking through many pump catalogs and performance curves we finally find a 4 x 6 - 8 (4 inch discharge, 6 inch intake, 8 inch impeller) centrifugal pump that produces about 225 gallons (US) per minute at a Total Dynamic Head (TDH) of 73 feet.

This pump produces about 13% more flow and 3% more head than we need but the extra capacity and head provide for minor entrance and exit losses which were not taken into account and for minor losses which will occur as the pump, pipe, and fittings age.

Horsepower Needed To Raise Water To Various Heights

Flow Gals. Per Minute	Height of Water in Feet										
	5	10	15	20	25	30	35	40	45	50	60
1	0.001	0.003	0.004	0.005	0.006	0.008	0.009	0.010	0.011	0.013	0.015
2	0.003	0.005	0.008	0.010	0.013	0.015	0.018	0.020	0.023	0.025	0.030
4	0.005	0.010	0.015	0.020	0.025	0.030	0.035	0.040	0.045	0.050	0.060
5	0.006	0.013	0.019	0.025	0.031	0.038	0.044	0.050	0.057	0.063	0.076
10	0.013	0.025	0.038	0.050	0.063	0.076	0.088	0.101	0.113	0.126	0.151
15	0.019	0.038	0.057	0.076	0.094	0.113	0.132	0.151	0.170	0.189	0.227
20	0.025	0.050	0.076	0.101	0.126	0.151	0.176	0.202	0.227	0.252	0.302
25	0.031	0.063	0.094	0.126	0.157	0.189	0.220	0.252	0.283	0.315	0.378
30	0.038	0.076	0.113	0.151	0.189	0.227	0.265	0.302	0.340	0.378	0.454
35	0.044	0.088	0.132	0.176	0.220	0.265	0.309	0.353	0.397	0.441	0.529
40	0.050	0.101	0.151	0.202	0.252	0.302	0.353	0.403	0.454	0.504	0.605
45	0.057	0.113	0.170	0.227	0.283	0.340	0.397	0.454	0.510	0.567	0.680
50	0.063	0.126	0.189	0.252	0.315	0.378	0.441	0.504	0.567	0.630	0.756
60	0.076	0.151	0.227	0.302	0.378	0.454	0.529	0.605	0.680	0.756	0.907
75	0.094	0.189	0.283	0.378	0.472	0.567	0.661	0.756	0.850	0.945	1.13
100	0.126	0.252	0.378	0.504	0.630	0.756	0.882	1.01	1.13	1.26	1.51
125	0.157	0.315	0.472	0.630	0.787	0.945	1.10	1.26	1.42	1.57	1.89
150	0.189	0.378	0.567	0.756	0.945	1.13	1.32	1.51	1.70	1.89	2.27
175	0.220	0.441	0.661	0.882	1.10	1.32	1.54	1.76	1.98	2.20	2.65
200	0.252	0.504	0.756	1.01	1.26	1.51	1.76	2.02	2.27	2.52	3.02
250	0.315	0.630	0.945	1.26	1.57	1.89	2.20	2.52	2.83	3.15	3.78
300	0.378	0.756	1.13	1.51	1.89	2.27	2.65	3.02	3.40	3.78	4.54
350	0.441	0.882	1.32	1.76	2.20	2.65	3.09	3.53	3.97	4.41	5.29
400	0.504	1.01	1.51	2.02	2.52	3.02	3.53	4.03	4.54	5.04	6.05
500	0.630	1.26	1.89	2.52	3.15	3.78	4.41	5.04	5.67	6.30	7.56

Handyman In~Your~Pocket

Horsepower Needed To Raise Water To Various Heights

Flow Gals. Per Minute	Height of Water in feet												
	75	100	125	150	175	200	250	300	350	400	500
1	0.019	0.025	0.031	0.038	0.044	0.050	0.063	0.076	0.088	0.101	0.126
2	0.038	0.050	0.063	0.076	0.088	0.101	0.126	0.151	0.176	0.202	0.252
4	0.076	0.101	0.126	0.151	0.176	0.202	0.252	0.302	0.353	0.403	0.504
5	0.094	0.126	0.157	0.189	0.220	0.252	0.315	0.378	0.441	0.504	0.630
10	0.189	0.252	0.315	0.378	0.441	0.504	0.630	0.756	0.882	1.01	1.26
15	0.283	0.378	0.472	0.567	0.661	0.756	0.945	1.13	1.32	1.51	1.89
20	0.378	0.504	0.630	0.756	0.882	1.01	1.26	1.51	1.76	2.02	2.52
25	0.472	0.630	0.787	0.945	1.10	1.26	1.57	1.89	2.20	2.52	3.15
30	0.567	0.756	0.945	1.13	1.32	1.51	1.89	2.27	2.65	3.02	3.78
35	0.661	0.882	1.10	1.32	1.54	1.76	2.20	2.65	3.09	3.53	4.41
40	0.756	1.01	1.26	1.51	1.76	2.02	2.52	3.02	3.53	4.03	5.04
45	0.850	1.13	1.42	1.70	1.98	2.27	2.83	3.40	3.97	4.54	5.67
50	0.945	1.26	1.57	1.89	2.20	2.52	3.15	3.78	4.41	5.04	6.30
60	1.13	1.51	1.89	2.27	2.65	3.02	3.78	4.54	5.29	6.05	7.56
75	1.42	1.89	2.36	2.83	3.31	3.78	4.72	5.67	6.61	7.56	9.45
100	1.89	2.52	3.15	3.78	4.41	5.04	6.30	7.56	8.82	10.1	12.6
125	2.36	3.15	3.94	4.72	5.51	6.30	7.87	9.45	11.0	12.6	15.7
150	2.83	3.78	4.72	5.67	6.61	7.56	9.45	11.3	13.2	15.1	18.9
175	3.31	4.41	5.51	6.61	7.72	8.82	11.0	13.2	15.4	17.6	22.0
200	3.78	5.04	6.30	7.56	8.82	10.1	12.6	15.1	17.6	20.2	25.2
250	4.72	6.30	7.87	9.45	11.0	12.6	15.7	18.9	22.0	25.2	31.5
300	5.67	7.56	9.45	11.3	13.2	15.1	18.9	22.7	26.5	30.2	37.8
350	6.61	8.82	11.0	13.2	15.4	17.6	22.0	26.5	30.9	35.3	44.1
400	7.56	10.1	12.6	15.1	17.6	20.2	25.2	30.2	35.3	40.3	50.4
500	9.45	12.6	15.7	18.9	22.0	25.2	31.5	37.8	44.1	50.4	63.0

Notes: Values in the table were calculated using the following equation:

thp = (head x capacity x weight x SpG) / 33,000

Where: thp is theoretical horsepower; head is head of water in feet; capacity is pump capacity in gallons per minute; weight is the weight in pounds of one gallon of the liquid being pumped; SpG is the specific gravity of the liquid being pumped; and 33,000 is the constant to convert foot pound-force per minute to horsepower.

Values in the table are theoretical horsepower (also called water horsepower, liquid horsepower, or hydraulic horsepower).

Values in the table are for water at 68°F (20°C), at which 1 gallon of water weighs 8.3304 pounds and has a specific gravity of 0.9982.

To determine actual required horsepower (also called brake horsepower) divide the values in the table by the pump's efficiency expressed as a decimal.

Horizontal Cylinder Fillage

The following equation can be used to calculate the number of gallons remaining in a horizontal tank if the height of the liquid remaining in the tank and the diameter of the tank are known.

Gallons Remaining = Depth Factor $\times$ *Total Tank Gallons*

Use the formula $Ratio = \dfrac{H}{D}$ and then the following table in order to calculate the Depth Factor.

Ratio	Depth Factor	Ratio	Depth Factor
0.02	0.0047728	0.52	0.5254580
0.04	0.0134171	0.54	0.5508752
0.06	0.0244963	0.56	0.5762106
0.08	0.0374780	0.58	0.6014229
0.10	0.0520440	0.60	0.6264700
0.12	0.0679724	0.62	0.6513090
0.14	0.0850946	0.64	0.6758962
0.16	0.1032755	0.66	0.7001861
0.18	0.1224023	0.68	0.7241318
0.20	0.1423785	0.70	0.7476842
0.22	0.1631194	0.72	0.7707919
0.24	0.1845494	0.74	0.7934001
0.26	0.2065999	0.76	0.8154506
0.28	0.2292081	0.78	0.8368806
0.30	0.2523158	0.80	0.8576215
0.32	0.2758682	0.82	0.8775977
0.34	0.2998139	0.84	0.8967245
0.36	0.3241038	0.86	0.9149054
0.38	0.3486910	0.88	0.9320276
0.40	0.3735300	0.90	0.9479560
0.42	0.3985771	0.92	0.9625220
0.44	0.4237894	0.94	0.9755037
0.46	0.4491248	0.96	0.9865829
0.48	0.4745420	0.98	0.9952272
0.50	0.5000000	1.00	1.0000000

Capacities of Tanks and Cylinders

Diameter of Tank or Cylinder (inch)	Length of Tank or Cylinder — Capacity in US gallons											
	inch									feet		
	1	2	3	4	5	6	8	10	12	1	2	3
1	0.003	0.007	0.010	0.014	0.017	0.020	0.027	0.034	0.041	0.041	0.082	0.122
2	0.014	0.027	0.041	0.054	0.068	0.082	0.109	0.136	0.163	0.163	0.326	0.490
3	0.031	0.061	0.092	0.122	0.153	0.184	0.245	0.306	0.367	0.367	0.734	1.10
4	0.054	0.109	0.163	0.218	0.272	0.326	0.435	0.544	0.653	0.653	1.31	1.96
5	0.085	0.170	0.255	0.340	0.425	0.510	0.680	0.850	1.02	1.02	2.04	3.06
6	0.122	0.245	0.367	0.490	0.612	0.734	0.979	1.22	1.47	1.47	2.94	4.41
7	0.167	0.333	0.500	0.666	0.833	1.00	1.33	1.67	2.00	2.00	4.00	6.00
8	0.218	0.435	0.653	0.870	1.09	1.31	1.74	2.18	2.61	2.61	5.22	7.83
9	0.275	0.551	0.826	1.10	1.38	1.65	2.20	2.75	3.30	3.30	6.61	9.91
10	0.340	0.680	1.02	1.36	1.70	2.04	2.72	3.40	4.08	4.08	8.16	12.2
11	0.411	0.823	1.23	1.65	2.06	2.47	3.29	4.11	4.94	4.94	9.87	14.8
12	0.490	0.979	1.47	1.96	2.45	2.94	3.92	4.90	5.88	5.88	11.8	17.6
13	0.575	1.15	1.72	2.30	2.87	3.45	4.60	5.75	6.90	6.90	13.8	20.7
14	0.666	1.33	2.00	2.67	3.33	4.00	5.33	6.66	8.00	8.00	16.0	24.0
15	0.765	1.53	2.29	3.06	3.82	4.59	6.12	7.65	9.18	9.18	18.4	27.5
16	0.870	1.74	2.61	3.48	4.35	5.22	6.96	8.70	10.4	10.4	20.9	31.3
17	0.983	1.97	2.95	3.93	4.91	5.90	7.86	9.83	11.8	11.8	23.6	35.4
18	1.10	2.20	3.30	4.41	5.51	6.61	8.81	11.0	13.2	13.2	26.4	39.7
19	1.23	2.45	3.68	4.91	6.14	7.36	9.82	12.3	14.7	14.7	29.5	44.2

Capacities of Tanks and Cylinders (cont.)

| Diameter of Tank or Cylinder | Capacity in US gallons — Length of Tank or Cylinder | | | | | | | | | | | |
| | inch | | | | | | | | | feet | | |
inch	1	2	3	4	5	6	8	10	12	1	2	3
20	1.36	2.72	4.08	5.44	6.80	8.16	10.9	13.6	16.3	16.3	32.6	49.0
21	1.50	3.00	4.50	6.00	7.50	9.00	12.0	15.0	18.0	18.0	36.0	54.0
22	1.65	3.29	4.94	6.58	8.23	9.87	13.2	16.5	19.7	19.7	39.5	59.2
23	1.80	3.60	5.40	7.19	8.99	10.8	14.4	18.0	21.6	21.6	43.2	64.7
24	1.96	3.92	5.88	7.83	9.79	11.8	15.7	19.6	23.5	23.5	47.0	70.5
25	2.12	4.25	6.37	8.50	10.6	12.7	17.0	21.2	25.5	25.5	51.0	76.5
26	2.30	4.60	6.90	9.19	11.5	13.8	18.4	23.0	27.6	27.6	55.2	82.7
27	2.48	4.96	7.44	9.91	12.4	14.9	19.8	24.8	29.7	29.7	59.5	89.2
28	2.67	5.33	8.00	10.7	13.3	16.0	21.3	26.7	32.0	32.0	64.0	96.0
29	2.86	5.72	8.58	11.4	14.3	17.2	22.9	28.6	34.3	34.3	68.6	103
30	3.06	6.12	9.18	12.2	15.3	18.4	24.5	30.6	36.7	36.7	73.4	110
32	3.48	6.96	10.4	13.9	17.4	20.9	27.9	34.8	41.8	41.8	83.6	125
34	3.93	7.86	11.8	15.7	19.7	23.6	31.4	39.3	47.2	47.2	94.3	141
36	4.41	8.81	13.2	17.6	22.0	26.4	35.3	44.1	52.9	52.9	106	159
38	4.91	9.82	14.7	19.6	24.5	29.5	39.3	49.1	58.9	58.9	118	177
40	5.44	10.9	16.3	21.8	27.2	32.6	43.5	54.4	65.3	65.3	131	196
42	6.00	12.0	18.0	24.0	30.0	36.0	48.0	60.0	72.0	72.0	144	216
44	6.58	13.2	19.7	26.3	32.9	39.5	52.7	65.8	79.0	79.0	158	237
46	7.19	14.4	21.6	28.8	36.0	43.2	57.6	71.9	86.3	86.3	173	259

Diameter of Tank or Cylinder	Capacity in US gallons											
	Length of Tank or Cylinder											
inch	inch									feet		
	1	2	3	4	5	6	8	10	12	1	2	3
48	7.83	15.7	23.5	31.3	39.2	47.0	62.7	78.3	94.0	94.0	188	282
50	8.50	17.0	25.5	34.0	42.5	51.0	68.0	85.0	102	102	204	306
52	9.19	18.4	27.6	36.8	46.0	55.2	73.5	91.9	110	110	221	331
54	9.91	19.8	29.7	39.7	49.6	59.5	79.3	99.1	119	119	238	357
56	10.7	21.3	32.0	42.6	53.3	64.0	85.3	107	128	128	256	384
58	11.4	22.9	34.3	45.8	57.2	68.6	91.5	114	137	137	275	412
60	12.2	24.5	36.7	49.0	61.2	73.4	97.9	122	147	147	294	441
62	13.1	26.1	39.2	52.3	65.3	78.4	105	131	157	157	314	471
64	13.9	27.9	41.8	55.7	69.6	83.6	111	139	167	167	334	501
66	14.8	29.6	44.4	59.2	74.1	88.9	118	148	178	178	355	533
68	15.7	31.4	47.2	62.9	78.6	94.3	126	157	189	189	377	566
70	16.7	33.3	50.0	66.6	83.3	100	133	167	200	200	400	600
72	17.6	35.3	52.9	70.5	88.1	106	141	176	212	212	423	635

Capacities of Tanks and Cylinders (cont.)

| Diameter of Tank or Cylinder | Capacity in US gallons — Length of Tank or Cylinder | | | | | | | | | | | |
| | 4 | 5 | 6 | 8 | 10 | 12 | 14 | 16 | 18 | 20 | 22 | 24 |
inch	feet											
1	0.163	0.204	0.245	0.326	0.408	0.490	0.571	0.653	0.734	0.816	0.898	0.979
2	0.653	0.816	0.979	1.31	1.63	1.96	2.28	2.61	2.94	3.26	3.59	3.92
3	1.47	1.84	2.20	2.94	3.67	4.41	5.14	5.88	6.61	7.34	8.08	8.81
4	2.61	3.26	3.92	5.22	6.53	7.83	9.14	10.4	11.8	13.1	14.4	15.7
5	4.08	5.10	6.12	8.16	10.2	12.2	14.3	16.3	18.4	20.4	22.4	24.5
6	5.88	7.34	8.81	11.75	14.7	17.6	20.6	23.5	26.4	29.4	32.3	35.3
7	8.00	10.0	12.0	15.99	20.0	24.0	28.0	32.0	36.0	40.0	44.0	48.0
8	10.4	13.1	15.7	20.9	26.1	31.3	36.6	41.8	47.0	52.2	57.4	62.7
9	13.2	16.5	19.8	26.4	33.0	39.7	46.3	52.9	59.5	66.1	72.7	79.3
10	16.3	20.4	24.5	32.6	40.8	49.0	57.1	65.3	73.4	81.6	89.8	97.9
11	19.7	24.7	29.6	39.5	49.4	59.2	69.1	79.0	88.9	98.7	109	118
12	23.5	29.4	35.3	47.0	58.8	70.5	82.3	94.0	106	118	129	141
13	27.6	34.5	41.4	55.2	69.0	82.7	96.5	110	124	138	152	165
14	32.0	40.0	48.0	64.0	80.0	96.0	112	128	144	160	176	192
15	36.7	45.9	55.1	73.4	91.8	110	129	147	165	184	202	220
16	41.8	52.2	62.7	83.6	104	125	146	167	188	209	230	251
17	47.2	59.0	70.7	94.3	118	141	165	189	212	236	259	283
18	52.9	66.1	79.3	106	132	159	185	212	238	264	291	317
19	58.9	73.6	88.4	118	147	177	206	236	265	295	324	353

| Diameter of Tank or Cylinder | Capacity in US gallons — Length of Tank or Cylinder | | | | | | | | | | | |
inch	4	5	6	8	10	12 feet	14	16	18	20	22	24
20	65.3	81.6	97.9	131	163	196	228	261	294	326	359	392
21	72.0	90.0	108	144	180	216	252	288	324	360	396	432
22	79.0	98.7	118	158	197	237	276	316	355	395	434	474
23	86.3	108	129	173	216	259	302	345	388	432	475	518
24	94.0	118	141	188	235	282	329	376	423	470	517	564
25	102	127	153	204	255	306	357	408	459	510	561	612
26	110	138	165	221	276	331	386	441	496	552	607	662
27	119	149	178	238	297	357	416	476	535	595	654	714
28	128	160	192	256	320	384	448	512	576	640	704	768
29	137	172	206	275	343	412	480	549	618	686	755	824
30	147	184	220	294	367	441	514	588	661	734	808	881
32	167	209	251	334	418	501	585	668	752	836	919	1,003
34	189	236	283	377	472	566	660	755	849	943	1,038	1,132
36	212	264	317	423	529	635	740	846	952	1,058	1,163	1,269
38	236	295	353	471	589	707	825	943	1,060	1,178	1,296	1,414
40	261	326	392	522	653	783	914	1,044	1,175	1,306	1,436	1,567
42	288	360	432	576	720	864	1,008	1,152	1,295	1,439	1,583	1,727
44	316	395	474	632	790	948	1,106	1,264	1,422	1,580	1,738	1,896
46	345	432	518	691	863	1,036	1,209	1,381	1,554	1,727	1,899	2,072
48	376	470	564	752	940	1,128	1,316	1,504	1,692	1,880	2,068	2,256

Capacities of Tanks and Cylinders (cont.)

Diameter of Tank or Cylinder	Capacity in US gallons											
	Length of Tank or Cylinder											
inch	4	5	6	8	10	12	14	16	18	20	22	24
							feet					
50	408	510	612	816	1,020	1,224	1,428	1,632	1,836	2,040	2,244	2,448
52	441	552	662	883	1,103	1,324	1,545	1,765	1,986	2,206	2,427	2,648
54	476	595	714	952	1,190	1,428	1,666	1,904	2,142	2,379	2,617	2,855
56	512	640	768	1,024	1,279	1,535	1,791	2,047	2,303	2,559	2,815	3,071
58	549	686	824	1,098	1,373	1,647	1,922	2,196	2,471	2,745	3,020	3,294
60	588	734	881	1,175	1,469	1,763	2,056	2,350	2,644	2,938	3,231	3,525
62	627	784	941	1,255	1,568	1,882	2,196	2,509	2,823	3,137	3,450	3,764
64	668	836	1,003	1,337	1,671	2,005	2,340	2,674	3,008	3,342	3,677	4,011
66	711	889	1,066	1,422	1,777	2,133	2,488	2,844	3,199	3,554	3,910	4,265
68	755	943	1,132	1,509	1,887	2,264	2,641	3,019	3,396	3,773	4,150	4,528
70	800	1,000	1,200	1,599	1,999	2,399	2,799	3,199	3,599	3,998	4,398	4,798
72	846	1,058	1,269	1,692	2,115	2,538	2,961	3,384	3,807	4,230	4,653	5,076

Notes: Values in the table were calculated using the equation: Capacity = [(π/4) x D^2 x L] / 231.

Where: Capacity is in US gallons, D is the tank or cylinder diameter in inches,
L is the tank or cylinder length in inches, and 231 converts cubic inches to US gallons.

To convert values in the table to cubic inches, multiply by 231.
To convert values in the table to cubic feet, multiply by 0.13368056.
To convert values in the table to liters, multiply by 3.7854118.
To convert values in the table to cubic meters, multiply by 0.003785418.

Rope, Chain and Cable

Cable Clips For Wire Rope..552
   U-Bolt Clips...552
   Twin-base Clips...553

Chain, Strength and Weight...554

Feet of Wire Rope on a Drum or Reel...........................558

Load Capacity Loss due to Line Angle..........................559

Rope, Strength and Weight
   Natural and Synthetic Fiber..............................560
   Manila Rope, 3 strand.......................................560
   Nylon Rope, 3 strand and 8 strand 560
   Polyester Rope, 3 strand and 8 strand.............561
   Polyester/Polyolefin Dual Fiber Rope, 3 strand ...562
   Polypropylene Fiber Rope, 3 strand and 8 strand....563
   Sisal Rope, 3 strand..564

Wire Rope, Strength and Weight
   6 Strand x 19 Wire 566
   6 Strand x 37 Wire 570

Cable Clips for Wire Rope

U-Bolt Clips

Wire Rope & Clip Size	U-Bolt Diam.	Number of Clips	Clip Spacing	Rope Turn Back	Bolt Torque	Approx. Weight
inch	inch		inch	inch	ft-lbf	lbm
1/8	7/32	2	1-5/8	3-1/4	4.5	0.05
3/16	1/4	2	2	3-3/4	7.5	0.08
1/4	5/16	2	2-3/8	4-3/4	15	0.17
5/16	3/8	2	2-5/8	5-1/4	30	0.30
3/8	7/16	2	3-1/4	6-1/2	45	0.41
7/16	1/2	2	3-1/2	7	65	0.65
1/2	1/2	3	3-3/4	11-1/2	65	0.75
9/16	9/16	3	4	12	95	1.00
5/8	9/16	3	4	12	95	1.00
3/4	5/8	4	4-1/2	18	130	1.40
7/8	3/4	4	5-1/4	19	225	2.40
1	3/4	5	6	26	225	2.50
1-1/8	3/4	6	6-3/4	34	225	3.00
1-1/4	7/8	7	7-1/2	44	360	4.50
1-3/8	7/8	7	8-1/4	44	360	5.20
1-1/2	7/8	8	9	54	360	5.90
1-5/8	1	8	9-3/4	58	43s0	7.30
1-3/4	1-1/8	8	10-1/2	61	590	9.80
2	1-1/4	8	12	71	750	13.40
2-1/4	1-1/4	8	13-1/2	73	750	15.70
2-1/2	1-1/4	9	15	84	750	17.90
2-3/4	1-1/4	10	19	100	750	23.00
3	1-1/2	10	21	106	1,200	31.00
3-1/2	1-1/2	12	35	149	1,200	40.00

Notes:

(1) Wire rope clips are about 80% efficient.

(2) The correct usage of wire rope clips is illustrated on the next page.

(3) References: Similar tables can be found in the following sources:
General Purpose Catalog, Bethlehem Wire Rope, Williamsport Wirerope Works, Inc, Williamsport, PA, 2000
(see www.wwwrope.com)
Wire Rope Users Manual, Third Edition, Wire Rope Technical Board, 1993.
Crosby Clips, The Crosby Group, Inc, Tulsa, OK (see www.thecrosbygroup.com)
Materials Handling Handbook, Second Edition, John Wiley & Sons, 1985.
CooperTools Materials Handling Products Catalog, CooperTools, Apex, NC, 1995.

Twin-base Clips (Double-saddle, Chair, or Fist Grip Clips)

Wire Rope & Clip Size	Nut Size or Stud Diam.	Number of Clips	Clip Spacing	Rope Turn Back	Bolt Torque	Approx. Weight
inch	inch		inch	inch	ft-lbf	lbm
3/16	3/8	2	1-7/8	4	30	0.23
1/4	3/8	2	1-7/8	4	30	0.23
5/16	3/8	2	2-1/8	5	30	0.28
3/8	7/16	2	2-1/4	5-1/4	45	0.40
7/16	1/2	2	2-5/8	6-1/2	65	0.62
1/2	1/2	2	3	11	65	0.62
9/16	5/8	3	3-3/8	12-3/4	130	1.03
5/8	5/8	3	3-3/4	13-1/2	130	1.03
3/4	3/4	3	4-1/2	16	225	1.75
7/8	3/4	4	5-1/4	26	225	2.25
1	3/4	5	6	37	225	3.00
1-1/8	7/8	5	6-3/4	41	360	4.00
1-1/4	7/8	6	7-1/2	55	360	4.00
1-3/8	1	6	8-1/4	62	500	7.00
1-1/2	1	7	9	78	500	7.00

When placing cable clamps on the wire, the U-bolt side of the clip MUST be placed on the short, turn-back side while the saddle goes on the long side (the "live" end). Torque the nuts down to the specified torque for the particular U-bolt diameter, place a load on the wire, and then re-torque the clamps.

U-bolt Clip

Correct Attachment

Incorrect Attachment

Incorrect Attachment

Twin-base Clip

Chain - Strength and Weight

Chain Size or Trade Size		Material Diameter		Strength Working Load		Weight	
Fractional inch	mm	inch	mm	lbf	kN	lbm/ft	kg/m
Grade 100 Steel Chain (Alloy Steel Heat Treated)							
7/32	5.5	0.217	5.5	2,700	12.0	0.32	0.47
9/32	7	0.276	7	4,300	19.1	0.74	1.10
5/16	8.0	0.315	8.0	5,700	25.4	0.89	1.33
3/8	10	0.394	10	8,800	39.1	1.48	2.20
1/2	13	0.512	13	15,000	66.7	2.50	3.72
5/8	16	0.630	16	22,600	101	3.79	5.64
3/4	20	0.787	20	35,300	157	5.98	8.90
7/8	22	0.866	22	42,700	190	7.05	10.49
Grade 80 Steel Chain (Alloy Steel Heated Treated)							
7/32	5.5	0.217	5.5	2,100	9.34	0.43	0.64
9/32	7	0.276	7	3,500	15.6	0.70	1.04
5/16	8.0	0.315	8.0	5,100	22.7	0.92	1.37
3/8	10	0.394	10	7,100	31.6	1.42	2.11
1/2	13	0.512	13	12,000	53.4	2.44	3.63
5/8	16	0.630	16	18,100	80.5	3.56	5.30
3/4	20	0.787	20	28,300	126	5.62	8.36
7/8	22	0.866	22	34,200	152	7.50	11.16
1	26	1.024	26	47,700	212	9.65	14.36
1-1/4	32	1.260	32	72,300	322	15.25	22.69
1-1/2	38	1.500	38	80,000	356	21.40	31.85
Grade 70 Steel Chain (Transport Chain) (Carbon Steel Heat Treated)							
1/4	7	0.31	7	3,150	14.0	0.94	1.40
5/16	8	0.34	9	4,700	20.9	1.11	1.65
3/8	10	0.39	10	6,600	29.4	1.42	2.11
7/16	12	0.47	12	8,750	38.9	2.12	3.15
1/2	13	0.51	13	11,300	50.3	2.38	3.54
Grades 40 & 43 Steel Chain (High Test Chain) (Carbon Steel)							
1/4	7	0.28	7	2,600	11.6	1.06	1.58
5/16	9	0.34	9	3,900	17.3	1.06	1.58
3/8	10	0.39	10	5,400	24.0	1.53	2.27
7/16	12	0.47	12	7,200	32.0	2.11	3.14
1/2	13	0.51	13	9,200	40.9	2.47	3.68
5/8	17	0.66	17	11,500	51.2	3.69	5.49
3/4	20	0.78	20	16,200	72.1	5.67	8.43
Grade 30 Steel Chain (Proof Coil Chain) (Low Carbon Steel)							
1/8	4	0.16	4	375	1.67	0.21	0.31
3/16	6	0.22	6	800	3.56	0.38	0.57
1/4	7	0.28	7	1,300	5.78	0.64	0.95
5/16	8	0.32	8	1,900	8.45	0.91	1.35
7/16	12	0.47	12	3,500	15.6	2.10	3.13
1/2	13	0.51	13	4,500	20.0	2.51	3.74
3/8	10	0.39	10	2,650	11.8	1.37	2.03

Chain Size or Trade Size		Material Diameter		Strength		Weight	
fractional inch	mm	inch	mm	Working Load			
				lbf	kN	lbm/ft	kg/m
Grade 30 Steel Chain (Proof Coil Chain) (Low Carbon Steel)							
5/8	17	0.66	17	6,900	30.7	3.86	5.74
3/4	20	0.78	20	10,600	47.2	5.44	8.10
7/8	23	0.91	23	12,800	56.9	7.48	11.12
1	26	1.02	26	17,900	79.6	10.25	15.25
Stainless Steel Chain							
1/8	4	0.16	4	410	1.82	0.21	0.31
7/32	5	0.22	5	1,200	5.34	0.41	0.61
9/32	7	0.28	7	2,000	8.90	0.75	1.12
5/16	8	0.31	8	2,400	10.7	0.95	1.41
3/8	10	0.38	10	3,550	15.8	1.38	2.05
1/2	13	0.50	13	6,500	28.9	2.45	3.65
Aluminum Chain							
17/64	7	0.26	7	550	2.45	0.19	0.28
5/16	9	0.34	9	850	3.78	0.36	0.54
3/8	10	0.41	10	1,200	5.34	0.54	0.80
Straight Link Machine Chain (Low Carbon Steel)							
4	3	0.12	3	215	0.96	0.11	0.16
3	3	0.14	3	270	1.20	0.15	0.22
2	4	0.15	4	325	1.45	0.19	0.28
1	4	0.16	4	390	1.73	0.23	0.34
1/0	4	0.18	4	465	2.07	0.27	0.40
2/0	5	0.19	5	545	2.42	0.33	0.49
3/0	5	0.21	5	635	2.82	0.37	0.55
4/0	6	0.23	6	700	3.11	0.44	0.65
5/0	6	0.25	6	925	4.11	0.53	0.79
Twisted Link Machine Chain (Low Carbon Steel)							
4	3	0.12	3	205	0.91	0.13	0.19
3	3	0.14	3	255	1.13	0.16	0.24
2	4	0.15	4	310	1.38	0.20	0.30
1	4	0.16	4	370	1.65	0.25	0.37
1/0	4	0.18	4	440	1.96	0.29	0.43
2/0	5	0.19	5	520	2.31	0.34	0.51
3/0	5	0.21	5	605	2.69	0.36	0.54
4/0	6	0.23	6	670	2.98	0.45	0.67
5/0	6	0.25	6	880	3.91	0.56	0.83
Straight Link Coil Chain (Low Carbon Steel)							
4	3	0.12	3	205	0.91	0.10	0.15
3	3	0.14	3	255	1.13	0.13	0.19
2	4	0.15	4	310	1.38	0.15	0.22
1	4	0.16	4	370	1.65	0.19	0.28
1/0	4	0.18	4	440	1.96	0.22	0.33
2/0	5	0.19	5	520	2.31	0.27	0.40

Chain Size or Trade Size		Material Diameter		Strength		Weight	
fractional inch	mm	inch	mm	Working Load			
				lbf	kN	lbm/ft	kg/m
Straight Link Coil Chain (Low Carbon Steel) (cont.)							
3/0	5	0.21	5	605	2.69	0.31	0.46
4/0	6	0.23	6	670	2.98	0.35	0.52
5/0	6	0.25	6	880	3.91	0.46	0.68
Twisted Link Coil Chain (Low Carbon Steel)							
4	3	0.12	3	195	0.87	0.10	0.15
3	3	0.14	3	240	1.07	0.13	0.19
2	4	0.15	4	295	1.31	0.16	0.24
1	4	0.16	4	350	1.56	0.20	0.30
1/0	4	0.18	4	415	1.85	0.23	0.34
2/0	5	0.19	5	495	2.20	0.28	0.42
3/0	5	0.21	5	575	2.56	0.33	0.49
4/0	6	0.23	6	635	2.82	0.37	0.55
5/0	6	0.25	6	835	3.71	0.49	0.73
Passing Link Chain (Low Carbon Steel)							
2/0	5	0.19	5	450	2.00	0.32	0.48
4/0	6	0.22	6	600	2.67	0.43	0.64
End Welded Sash Chain (Low Carbon Steel)							
14	2	0.08	2	75	0.33	0.04	0.07
Handy Link Utility Chain (Low Carbon Steel)							
135	3	0.14	3	255	1.13	0.10	0.15
Lock Link, Single Loop Chain (Low Carbon Steel)							
2	2	0.09	2	155	0.69	0.09	0.13
1/0	3	0.12	3	265	1.18	0.16	0.24
2/0	3	0.14	3	340	1.51	0.23	0.39
3/0	4	0.15	4	405	1.80	0.26	0.39
4/0	4	0.16	4	485	2.16	0.29	0.43
5/0	4	0.18	4	580	2.58	0.34	0.51
Double Loop Chain (Inco or Tenso Chain) (Low Carbon Steel)							
5	2	0.06	2	55	0.24	0.04	0.06
4	2	0.07	2	70	0.31	0.05	0.07
3	2	0.08	2	90	0.40	0.06	0.09
2	2	0.09	2	115	0.51	0.08	0.12
1	3	0.11	3	155	0.69	0.10	0.15
1/0	3	0.12	3	200	0.89	0.13	0.19
2/0	3	0.14	3	255	1.13	0.16	0.24
3/0	4	0.15	4	305	1.36	0.20	0.30
4/0	4	0.16	4	365	1.62	0.25	0.37
8/0	6	0.23	6	705	3.14	0.51	0.76
Single Jack Chain (Low Carbon Steel or Brass)							
20	1	0.03	1	3	0.013	0.01	0.01
18	1	0.05	1	5	0.022	0.02	0.03
16	2	0.06	2	10	0.044	0.03	0.04
14	2	0.08	2	16	0.071	0.04	0.06

Chain Size or Trade Size		Material Diameter		Strength		Weight	
				Working Load			
fractional inch	mm	inch	mm	lbf	kN	lbm/ft	kg/m
Single Jack Chain (Low Carbon Steel or Brass) (cont.)							
12	3	0.11	3	29	0.13	0.09	0.13
10	3	0.14	3	43	0.19	0.14	0.21
8	4	0.16	4	60	0.27	0.21	0.31
6	5	0.19	5	80	0.36	0.30	0.45
Double Jack Chain (Low Carbon Steel or Brass)							
16	2	0.06	2	11	0.049	0.04	0.06
Sash Chain (Low Carbon Steel or Stainless Steel)							
8	1	0.04	1	75	0.334	0.04	0.06
25	1	0.04	1	94	0.418	0.05	0.07
30	1	0.03	1	81	0.360	0.05	0.07
35	1	0.04	1	106	0.472	0.06	0.09
40	1	0.04	1	131	0.58	0.07	0.10
45	1	0.05	1	175	0.78	0.09	0.13
50	2	0.06	2	225	1.00	0.11	0.16
Sash Chain (Bronze)							
8	1	0.04	1	68	0.302	0.04	0.06
25	1	0.04	1	80	0.356	0.05	0.07
30	1	0.03	1	75	0.334	0.05	0.07
35	1	0.04	1	100	0.445	0.06	0.09
40	1	0.04	1	125	0.56	0.07	0.10
45	1	0.05	1	163	0.73	0.09	0.13
50	2	0.06	2	210	0.93	0.11	0.16
Safety Chain (Plumber's Chain) (Brass)							
2/0	1	0.02	1	23	0.102	0.02	0.02
1/0	1	0.02	1	35	0.156	0.02	0.03
1	1	0.03	1	45	0.200	0.04	0.05
2	1	0.03	1	50	0.222	0.04	0.05

Notes:

(1) Abbreviations used: lbf = pound-force, lbm/ft = pound-mass/foot, kg/m = kilogram/meter, kN = kilonewton, mm = millimeter

(2) Conversions: 2,000 pounds-force = 1 short ton-force and 1 short ton-force = 0.90718474 metric ton-force.

(3) Only Grade 100 and Grade 80 Alloy Steel Chain should be used for overhead lifting.

(4) References: Similar tables may be found in:

ASTM A 391/A 391M - 98, Grade 80 Alloy Steel Chain, American Society For Testing And Materials, West Conshohocken, PA, 1998.
ASTM A 973/A 973M - 00, Grade 100 Alloy Steel Chain, American Society For Testing And Materials, West Conshohocken, PA, 2000.
Materials Handling Products Catalog, CooperTools, Apex, NC, 1995.
Acco Chain And Accessories, Acco Chain & Lifting Products Division, York, PA, 1996.

Feet of Wire Rope on a Drum or Reel

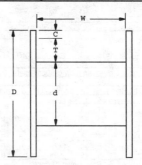

Values in the table can be used in the equation:
L = (T + d) x T x W x K
Where:
L = length of wire rope (feet)
T = thickness of wire rope on drum or reel (inches), T = ½(D - d) - C
W = width of drum or reel (inches)
d = diameter of drum or reel barrel (inches)
K = constant = 0.2618/wire rope diameter squared
D = diameter of drum or reel flange (inches)
C = clearance (inches)

Wire Rope Diameter		Value of K For wire rope Manufactured		Wire Rope Diameter		Value of K For wire rope Manufactured	
Fractional inch	inch	After 1993	Before 1993	Fractional inch	inch	After 1993	before 1993
1/16	0.0625	57.5	29.8	13/16	0.8125	0.360	0.354
3/32	0.0938	25.5	16.8	7/8	0.8750	0.310	0.308
1/8	0.1250	14.4	10.7	1	1.0000	0.237	0.239
5/32	0.1563	9.37	7.45	1-1/8	1.1250	0.188	0.191
3/16	0.1875	6.50	5.47	1-1/4	1.2500	0.152	0.152
7/32	0.2188	4.87	4.19	1-3/8	1.3750	0.126	0.127
1/4	0.2500	3.73	3.31	1-1/2	1.5000	0.106	0.107
5/16	0.3125	2.39	2.22	1-5/8	1.6250	0.0899	0.0886
3/8	0.3750	1.69	1.59	1-3/4	1.7500	0.0775	0.0770
7/16	0.4375	1.24	1.19	1-7/8	1.8750	0.0675	0.0675
1/2	0.5000	0.950	0.928	2	2.0000	0.0594	0.0597
9/16	0.5625	0.750	0.743	2-1/8	2.1250	0.0526	0.0532
5/8	0.6250	0.608	0.608	2-1/4	2.2500	0.0469	0.0477
11/16	0.6875	0.502	0.507	2-3/8	2.3750	0.0421	0.0419
3/4	0.7500	0.422	0.429	2-1/2	2.5000	0.0380	0.0380

NOTES:

(1) Values of K are based on the maximum allowable oversize for wire rope. Prior to 1993 oversize was specified as a fixed fraction of an inch, such as +1/32" for wire rope smaller than 3/4" diameter. In 1993 the oversize specifications were changed to percentages of the wire rope diameter, such as +8% for wire rope 1/8" and smaller.

(2) Clearance should be about 2 inches unless wire rope end fittings require more space.

(3) Equation is based on uniform wire rope winding on the drum or reel. It will not give correct lengths if the winding is non-uniform.

(4) Values calculated using the above method are approximate.

(5) References: Similar tables can be found in:
Wire Rope Users Manual, Third Edition, Wire Rope Technical Board, 1993.
Riggers Bible, R.P. Leach, Moore Printing, 1976.

Southwest Wire Rope, Houston, TX, (see www.southwestwirerope.com)

Load Capacity Loss due to Line Angle

Line angle with load degrees		Load Loss Factor
α	β	K
0	90	1.0000
5	85	0.9962
10	80	0.9848
15	75	0.9659
20	70	0.9397
25	65	0.9063
30	60	0.8660
35	55	0.8192
40	50	0.7660
45	45	0.7071
50	40	0.6428
55	35	0.5736
60	30	0.5000
65	25	0.4226
70	20	0.3420
75	15	0.2588
80	10	0.1736
85	5	0.0872

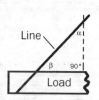

Notes:

(1). Load carrying capacity of a line (cable, rope, sling, or wire rope) decreases by the Load Factor, K, as the Line Angle, α, increases.

(2). Based on the equation $K = \cos \alpha$.

Synthetic and Natural Fiber Rope

Manila Rope, 3-Strand

| Rope Diameter | | | Strength | | | | Weight | |
| | | | Minimum Breaking Strength | | Safe Load FS = 12 | | | |
inch		mm	lbf	kN	lbf	kN	lbm/ft	kg/m
3/16	0.188	5	405	1.80	33.8	0.150	0.014	0.020
1/4	0.250	6	540	2.40	45.0	0.200	0.018	0.027
5/16	0.313	8	900	4.00	75.0	0.334	0.026	0.039
3/8	0.375	10	1,215	5.40	101	0.450	0.038	0.056
7/16	0.438	11	1,575	7.01	131	0.584	0.049	0.072
1/2	0.500	12	2,385	10.6	199	0.884	0.070	0.104
9/16	0.563	14	3,105	13.8	259	1.15	0.096	0.143
5/8	0.625	16	3,960	17.6	330	1.47	0.127	0.189
3/4	0.750	18	4,860	21.6	405	1.80	0.159	0.237
13/16	0.813	20	5,850	26.0	488	2.17	0.186	0.277
7/8	0.875	22	6,930	30.8	578	2.57	0.214	0.318
1	1.000	24	8,100	36.0	675	3.00	0.257	0.382
1-1/16	1.063	26	9,450	42.0	788	3.50	0.298	0.443
1-1/8	1.125	28	10,800	48.0	900	4.00	0.343	0.510
1-1/4	1.250	30	12,150	54.0	1,010	4.49	0.397	0.591
1-3/8	1.375	32	13,500	60.1	1,130	5.03	0.456	0.679
1-1/2	1.500	36	16,650	74.1	1,390	6.18	0.570	0.848
1-5/8	1.625	40	20,250	90.1	1,690	7.52	0.711	1.06
1-3/4	1.750	44	23,850	110	1,990	8.85	0.850	1.26
2	2.000	48	27,900	120	2,330	10.4	1.02	1.52
2-1/8	2.125	52	32,400	140	2,700	12.0	1.20	1.79
2-1/4	2.250	56	36,900	160	3,080	13.7	1.39	2.07
2-1/2	2.500	60	42,300	190	3,530	15.7	1.64	2.44
2-5/8	2.625	64	46,800	210	3,900	17.3	1.82	2.71
2-7/8	2.875	68	54,900	240	4,580	20.4	2.15	3.20
3	3.000	72	57,500	260	4,790	21.3	2.30	3.42
3-5/16	3.313	80	69,500	310	5,790	25.8	2.84	4.23
3-5/8	3.625	88	81,900	360	6,830	30.4	3.49	5.19
4	4.000	96	94,500	420	7,880	35.1	4.14	6.16

Nylon Rope, 3-Strand and 8-Strand

| Rope Diameter | | | Strength | | | | Weight | |
| | | | Minimum Breaking Strength | | Safe Load FS = 12 | | | |
inch		mm	lbf	kN	lbf	kN	lbm/ft	kg/m
3/16	0.19	5	880	3.91	73.3	0.326	0.009	0.013
1/4	0.25	6	1,486	6.61	124	0.551	0.016	0.023
5/16	0.31	8	2,295	10.2	191	0.851	0.025	0.036
3/8	0.38	10	3,240	14.4	270	1.20	0.036	0.053

Nylon Rope, 3-Strand and 8-Strand (cont.)

Rope Diameter			Minimum Breaking Strength		Safe Load FS = 12		Weight	
inch		mm	lbf	kN	lbf	kN	lbm/ft	kg/m
7/16	0.44	11	4,320	19.2	360	1.60	0.048	0.071
1/2	0.50	12	5,670	25.2	473	2.10	0.063	0.094
9/16	0.56	14	7,200	32.0	600	2.67	0.080	0.119
5/8	0.63	16	8,910	39.6	743	3.30	0.099	0.147
3/4	0.75	18	12,780	56.8	1,070	4.76	0.143	0.213
7/8	0.88	22	17,280	76.9	1,440	6.41	0.195	0.290
1	1.00	24	22,230	98.9	1,850	8.23	0.253	0.377
1-1/16	1.06	26	25,200	112	2,100	9.34	0.287	0.427
1-1/8	1.13	28	28,260	126	2,360	10.5	0.322	0.479
1-1/4	1.25	30	34,830	155	2,900	12.9	0.397	0.591
1-5/16	1.31	32	38,250	170	3,190	14.2	0.437	0.650
1-1/2	1.50	36	48,600	216	4,050	18.0	0.570	0.848
1-5/8	1.63	40	57,375	255	4,780	21.3	0.673	1.00
1-3/4	1.75	44	66,150	294	5,510	24.5	0.780	1.16
2	2.00	48	84,600	376	7,050	31.4	1.00	1.49
2-1/8	2.13	52	95,400	424	7,950	35.4	1.13	1.68
2-1/4	2.25	56	107,100	476	8,930	39.7	1.27	1.89
2-1/2	2.50	60	131,400	584	11,000	48.9	1.57	2.34
2-5/8	2.63	64	144,000	641	12,000	53.4	1.73	2.57
2-3/4	2.75	68	171,000	761	14,300	63.6	2.08	3.10
3	3.00	72	185,400	825	15,500	68.9	2.26	3.36
3-1/4	3.25	80	224,100	1,000	18,700	83.2	2.75	4.09
3-1/2	3.50	88	267,300	1,190	22,300	99.2	3.29	4.90
4	4.00	96	324,000	1,440	27,000	120	4.00	5.95
4-1/4	4.25	104	369,000	1,640	30,800	137	4.60	6.85
4-1/2	4.50	112	418,500	1,860	34,900	155	5.25	7.81
5	5.00	120	480,600	2,140	40,100	178	6.10	9.08
5-5/16	5.31	128	532,800	2,370	44,400	198	6.85	10.2
5-5/8	5.63	136	589,500	2,620	49,100	218	7.67	11.4
6	6.00	144	660,600	2,940	55,100	245	8.70	12.9

Polyester Rope, 3-Strand and 8-Strand

Rope Diameter			Minimum Breaking Strength		Safe Load FS = 12		Weight	
inch		mm	lbf	kN	lbf	kN	lbm/ft	kg/m
3/16	0.19	5	765	3.40	63.8	0.284	0.011	0.016
1/4	0.25	6	1,315	5.85	110	0.487	0.020	0.029
5/16	0.31	8	2,050	9.1	171	0.760	0.031	0.045
3/8	0.38	10	2,900	12.9	242	1.07	0.044	0.065
7/16	0.44	11	3,915	17.4	326	1.45	0.059	0.088

Polyester Rope, 3-Strand and 8-Strand (cont.)

Rope Diameter			Strength Minimum Breaking Strength		Safe Load FS = 12		Weight	
inch		mm	lbf	kN	lbf	kN	lbm/ft	kg/m
1/2	0.50	12	5,085	22.6	424	1.88	0.077	0.115
9/16	0.56	14	6,435	28.6	536	2.39	0.098	0.146
5/8	0.63	16	7,825	34.8	652	2.90	0.120	0.179
3/4	0.75	18	11,200	49.8	933	4.15	0.172	0.256
7/8	0.88	22	15,225	67.7	1,270	5.65	0.234	0.348
1	1.00	24	19,775	88.0	1,650	7.34	0.304	0.452
1-1/16	1.06	26	22,225	99	1,850	8.23	0.342	0.509
1-1/8	1.13	28	24,800	110	2,070	9.21	0.385	0.573
1-1/4	1.25	30	29,800	133	2,480	11.0	0.465	0.692
1-5/16	1.31	32	32,500	145	2,710	12.1	0.51	0.759
1-1/2	1.50	36	42,200	188	3,520	15.7	0.67	0.997
1-5/8	1.63	40	49,250	219	4,100	18.2	0.78	1.16
1-3/4	1.75	44	57,000	254	4,750	21.1	0.91	1.35
2	2.00	48	72,000	320	6,000	26.7	1.17	1.74
2-1/8	2.13	52	81,000	360	6,750	30.0	1.33	1.98
2-1/4	2.25	56	90,500	403	7,540	33.5	1.49	2.22
2-1/2	2.50	60	110,000	489	9,170	40.8	1.84	2.74
2-5/8	2.63	64	121,000	538	10,100	44.9	2.03	3.02
2-3/4	2.75	68	144,000	641	12,000	53.4	2.43	3.62
3	3.00	72	156,000	694	13,000	57.8	2.64	3.93
3-1/4	3.25	80	188,500	838	15,700	69.8	3.23	4.81
3-1/2	3.50	88	225,000	1,000	18,800	83.6	3.87	5.76
4	4.00	96	270,000	1,200	22,500	100	4.70	6.99
4-1/4	4.25	104	310,000	1,380	25,800	115	5.47	8.14
4-1/2	4.50	112	355,000	1,580	29,600	132	6.30	9.38
5	5.00	120	410,000	1,820	34,200	152	7.32	10.9
5-5/16	5.31	128	459,000	2,040	38,300	170	8.25	12.3
5-5/8	5.63	136	508,500	2,260	42,400	189	9.25	13.8
6	6.00	144	567,000	2,520	47,300	210	10.5	15.6

Polyester/Polyolefin Dual Fiber Rope, 3-Strand

Rope Diameter			Strength Minimum Breaking Strength		Safe Load FS = 12		Weight	
inch		mm	lbf	kN	lbf	kN	lbm/ft	kg/m
1/4	0.25	6	1,200	5.34	100	0.445	0.016	0.024
5/16	0.31	8	1,870	8.3	156	0.693	0.025	0.037
3/8	0.38	10	2,700	12.0	225	1.00	0.036	0.054
7/16	0.44	11	3,500	15.6	292	1.30	0.048	0.071
1/2	0.50	12	4,400	19.6	367	1.63	0.062	0.092

Polyester/Polyolefin Dual Fiber Rope, 3-Strand(cont.)

Rope Diameter			Strength Minimum Breaking Strength		Safe Load FS = 12		Weight	
inch		mm	lbf	kN	lbf	kN	lbm/ft	kg/m
9/16	0.56	14	5,200	23.1	433	1.93	0.079	0.118
5/8	0.63	16	6,100	27.1	508	2.26	0.095	0.141
3/4	0.75	18	8,400	37.4	700	3.11	0.135	0.201
7/8	0.88	22	11,125	49.5	927	4.12	0.180	0.268
1	1.00	24	13,175	58.6	1,100	4.89	0.218	0.324
1-1/16	1.06	26	14,775	66	1,230	5.47	0.245	0.365
1-1/8	1.13	28	16,325	73	1,360	6.05	0.271	0.403
1-1/4	1.25	30	19,900	89	1,660	7.38	0.334	0.497
1-5/16	1.31	32	21,950	98	1,830	8.14	0.365	0.543
1-1/2	1.50	36	28,250	126	2,350	10.5	0.470	0.699
1-5/8	1.63	40	32,950	147	2,750	12.2	0.550	0.818
1-3/4	1.75	44	36,850	164	3,070	13.7	0.620	0.923
2	2.00	48	48,050	214	4,000	17.8	0.810	1.21
2-1/8	2.13	52	53,950	240	4,500	20.0	0.910	1.35
2-1/4	2.25	56	59,950	267	5,000	22.2	1.01	1.50
2-1/2	2.50	60	73,550	327	6,130	27.3	1.24	1.85
2-5/8	2.63	64	80,650	359	6,720	29.9	1.36	2.02
2-3/4	2.75	68	95,400	424	7,950	35.4	1.61	2.40
3	3.00	72	102,900	458	8,580	38.2	1.74	2.59
3-1/4	3.25	80	122,800	546	10,200	45.4	2.12	3.15
3-1/2	3.50	88	144,800	644	12,100	53.8	2.50	3.72
4	4.00	96	171,000	761	14,300	63.6	3.00	4.46
4-1/4	4.25	104	195,800	871	16,300	72.5	3.45	5.13
4-1/2	4.50	112	224,800	1,000	18,700	83.2	3.95	5.88
5	5.00	120	254,700	1,130	21,200	94.3	4.55	6.77
5-5/16	5.31	128	282,600	1,260	23,600	105	5.06	7.53
5-5/8	5.63	136	312,300	1,390	26,000	116	5.62	8.36
6	6.00	144	351,000	1,560	29,300	130	6.35	9.45

Polypropylene Fiber Rope, 3-Strand and 8-Strand

Rope Diameter			Strength Minimum Breaking Strength		Safe Load FS = 12		Weight	
inch		mm	lbf	kN	lbf	kN	lbm/ft	kg/m
3/16	0.19	5	650	2.89	54.2	0.241	0.01	0.01
1/4	0.25	6	1,125	5.00	93.8	0.417	0.01	0.02
5/16	0.31	8	1,710	7.61	143	0.634	0.02	0.03
3/8	0.38	10	2,430	10.8	203	0.90	0.03	0.04
7/16	0.44	11	3,150	14.0	263	1.17	0.04	0.05
1/2	0.50	12	3,780	16.8	315	1.40	0.05	0.07

Polypropylene Fiber Rope, 3-Strand and 8-Strand (cont.)

Rope Diameter			Strength				Weight	
			Minimum Breaking Strength		Safe Load FS = 12			
inch		mm	lbf	kN	lbf	kN	lbm/ft	kg/m
9/16	0.56	14	4,590	20.4	383	1.70	0.06	0.09
5/8	0.63	16	5,580	24.8	465	2.07	0.07	0.11
3/4	0.75	18	7,650	34.0	638	2.84	0.10	0.15
7/8	0.88	22	10,350	46.0	863	3.84	0.14	0.21
1	1.00	24	12,825	57.0	1,070	4.76	0.18	0.27
1-1/16	1.06	26	14,400	64.1	1,200	5.34	0.20	0.30
1-1/8	1.13	28	16,000	71.2	1,330	5.92	0.23	0.34
1-1/4	1.25	30	19,350	86.1	1,610	7.16	0.28	0.41
1-5/16	1.31	32	21,150	94.1	1,760	7.83	0.30	0.45
1-1/2	1.50	36	27,350	122	2,280	10.1	0.39	0.59
1-5/8	1.63	40	31,950	142	2,660	11.8	0.46	0.68
1-3/4	1.75	44	36,900	164	3,080	13.7	0.53	0.79
2	2.00	48	46,800	208	3,900	17.3	0.69	1.03
2-1/8	2.13	52	52,650	234	4,390	19.5	0.78	1.16
2-1/4	2.25	56	59,400	264	4,950	22.0	0.88	1.31
2-1/2	2.50	64	72,000	320	6,000	26.7	1.07	1.59
2-5/8	2.63	64	80,500	358	6,710	29.8	1.20	1.79
2-3/4	2.75	68	94,500	420	7,880	35.1	1.41	2.10
3	3.00	72	102,600	456	8,550	38.0	1.53	2.28
3-1/4	3.25	80	121,500	540	10,100	44.9	1.86	2.77
3-1/2	3.50	88	144,000	641	12,000	53.4	2.23	3.32
4	4.00	96	171,900	765	14,300	63.6	2.72	4.05
4-1/4	4.25	104	198,000	881	16,500	73.4	3.15	4.69
4-1/2	4.50	112	223,200	993	18,600	82.7	3.60	5.36
5	5.00	120	256,500	1,140	21,400	95.2	4.20	6.25
5-5/16	5.31	128	287,100	1,280	23,900	106	4.74	7.05
5-5/8	5.63	136	319,500	1,420	26,600	118	5.31	7.90
6	6.00	144	358,200	1,590	29,900	133	6.03	8.97

Sisal Rope, 3-Strand

Nominal Rope Diameter			Strength				Weight	
			Minimum Breaking Strength		Safe Load FS = 12			
inch		mm	lbf	kN	lbf	kN	lbm/ft	kg/m
3/16	0.19	5	290	1.29	24.2	0.11	0.01	0.02
1/4	0.25	6	385	1.71	32.1	0.14	0.02	0.03
5/16	0.31	8	640	2.85	53.3	0.24	0.03	0.04
3/8	0.38	10	865	3.85	72.1	0.32	0.04	0.06
7/16	0.44	11	1,120	4.98	93.3	0.42	0.05	0.07
1/2	0.50	12	1,700	7.56	142	0.63	0.07	0.10
9/16	0.56	14	2,210	9.83	184	0.82	0.10	0.14

Sisal Rope, 3-Strand(cont.)

Nominal Rope Diameter			Strength					Weight	
			Minimum Breaking Strength		Safe Load FS = 12				
inch		mm	lbf	kN	lbf	kN		lbm/ft	kg/m
5/8	0.63	16	2,815	12.5	235	1.04		0.13	0.19
3/4	0.75	18	3,455	15.4	288	1.28		0.16	0.24
7/8	0.88	22	4,930	21.9	411	1.83		0.21	0.32
1	1.00	24	5,760	25.6	480	2.14		0.27	0.40
1-1/16	1.06	26	6,720	29.9	560	2.49		0.30	0.44
1-1/8	1.13	28	7,680	34.2	640	2.85		0.34	0.51
1-1/4	1.25	30	8,640	38.4	720	3.20		0.40	0.59
1-5/16	1.31	32	9,600	42.7	800	3.56		0.46	0.68
1-1/2	1.50	36	11,840	52.7	987	4.39		0.57	0.85
1-5/8	1.63	40	14,440	64.2	1,200	5.34		0.71	1.06
1-3/4	1.75	44	16,960	75.4	1,410	6.27		0.85	1.26
2	2.00	48	19,840	88.3	1,650	7.34		1.02	1.52
2-1/4	2.25	56	26,240	117	2,190	9.74		1.39	2.07
2-5/8	2.63	64	33,280	148	2,770	12.3		1.82	2.71
3	3.00	72	40,960	182	3,410	15.2		2.30	3.42

Notes:
(1) Abbreviations used:
  lbf = pound-force, lbm/ft = pound-mass/foot, kg/m = kilogram/meter,
  kN = kilonewton, mm = millimeter, FS = Factor of Safety
(2) Conversions: 2,000 pounds-force = 1 short ton-force and
  1 short ton-force = 0.90718474 metric ton-force.
(3) Safe Load = Minimum Breaking Strength divided by Factor of Safety.
The appropriate Factor of Safety must be determined by the user. Sequoia Publishing recommends a Factor of Safety of 12. Factors of Safety below 12 should only be used by those with expert knowledge of the conditions and risks of use. The load applied to the rope should never exceed the Safe Load.
(4)Manila rope is made from the fibers of the abaca plant (musa testilus, Manila hemp).
  Nylon rope is made from continuous filiment polyamide (nylon 6 or nylon 6.6).
  Polyester rope is made from continuous filament polyester.
  Polypropylene rope is made from monofilament or film polypropylene.
  Sisal rope is made from the fibers of the sisal hemp plant (agave sisalana, hemp plant).

References: Similar tables may be found in:
Columbian Rope, Guntown, MS (see www.columbianrope.com)
Federal Specification T-R-605B, Rope, Manila and Sisal, General Service Administration, Washington, DC, 1973.
Rope Standards, CIS-1, Cordage Institute, Wayne, PA, 1999 (see www.ropecord.com).
Rope Specifications, Wall Industries, Inc., Granite Quarry, NC, 1988.
Feeney Wire Rope & Rigging, Inc., Oakland, CA, (see www.feeneywire.com)
Handbook Of Rigging, Second Edition, W.E. Rossnagel, McGraw-Hill Book Company, 1957.

Strength and Weight of Wire Rope
6 strand x 19 wire (6x19)

Bright wire, uncoated, fiber core (FC)
Improved plow steel (IPS)

Wire Diameter		Strength				Weight	
		Nominal Strength		Safe Load			
inch	mm	lbf	kN	lbf	kN	lbm/ft	kg/m
1/4	0.25	6.4	5,480	24.4	1,100	4.89	0.11	0.16
5/16	0.31	8	8,520	37.9	1,700	7.56	0.16	0.24
3/8	0.38	9.5	12,200	54.3	2,440	10.9	0.24	0.36
7/16	0.44	11.5	16,540	73.6	3,310	14.7	0.32	0.48
1/2	0.50	13	21,400	95.2	4,280	19.0	0.42	0.63
9/16	0.56	14	27,000	120	5,400	24.0	0.53	0.79
5/8	0.63	16	33,400	149	6,680	29.7	0.66	0.98
3/4	0.75	19	47,600	212	9,520	42.3	0.95	1.41
7/8	0.88	22	64,400	286	12,900	57.4	1.29	1.92
1	1.00	26	83,600	372	16,700	74.3	1.68	2.50
1-1/8	1.13	29	105,200	468	21,000	93.4	2.13	3.17
1-1/4	1.25	32	129,200	575	25,800	115	2.63	3.91
1-3/8	1.38	35	155,400	691	31,100	138	3.18	4.73
1-1/2	1.50	38	184,000	818	36,800	164	3.78	5.63
1-5/8	1.63	42	214,000	952	42,800	190	4.44	6.61
1-3/4	1.75	45	248,000	1,100	49,600	221	5.15	7.66
1-7/8	1.88	48	282,000	1,250	56,400	251	5.91	8.80
2	2.00	52	320,000	1,420	64,000	285	6.72	10.0
2-1/8	2.13	54	358,000	1,590	71,600	318	7.59	11.3
2-1/4	2.25	57	400,000	1,780	80,000	356	8.51	12.7
2-3/8	2.38	60	444,000	1,980	88,800	395	9.48	14.1
2-1/2	2.50	64	488,000	2,170	97,600	434	10.5	15.6
2-5/8	2.63	67	536,000	2,380	107,000	476	11.6	17.3
2-3/4	2.75	70	584,000	2,600	117,000	520	12.7	18.9

Bright Wire, Uncoated, Independent Wire Rope Core (IWRC)
Improved plow steel (IPS)

Wire Diameter		Strength				Weight	
		Nominal Strength		Safe Load			
inch	mm	lbf	kN	lbf	kN	lbm/ft	kg/m
1/4	0.250	6.4	5,880	26.2	1,180	5.25	0.12	0.18
5/16	0.313	8	9,160	40.7	1,830	8.14	0.18	0.27
3/8	0.375	9.5	13,120	58.4	2,620	11.7	0.26	0.39
7/16	0.438	11.5	17,780	79.1	3,560	15.8	0.35	0.52
1/2	0.500	13	23,000	102	4,600	20.5	0.46	0.68
9/16	0.563	14.5	29,000	129	5,800	25.8	0.59	0.88
5/8	0.625	16	35,800	159	7,160	31.8	0.72	1.07
3/4	0.750	19	51,200	228	10,200	45.4	1.04	1.55

Bright Wire, Uncoated, Independent Wire Rope Core (IWRC)
Improved plow steel (IPS) (cont.)

Wire Diameter			Strength				Weight	
			Nominal Strength		Safe Load			
inch		mm	lbf	kN	lbf	kN	lbm/ft	kg/m
7/8	0.875	22	69,200	308	13,800	61.4	1.42	2.11
1	1.000	26	89,800	399	18,000	80.1	1.85	2.75
1-1/8	1.125	29	113,000	503	22,600	101	2.34	3.48
1-1/4	1.250	32	138,800	617	27,800	124	2.89	4.30
1-3/8	1.375	35	167,000	743	33,400	149	3.50	5.21
1-1/2	1.500	38	197,800	880	39,600	176	4.16	6.19
1-5/8	1.625	42	230,000	1,020	46,000	205	4.88	7.26
1-3/4	1.750	45	266,000	1,180	53,200	237	5.67	8.44
1-7/8	1.875	48	304,000	1,350	60,800	270	6.5	9.67
2	2.000	52	344,000	1,530	68,800	306	7.39	11.0
2-1/8	2.125	54	384,000	1,710	76,800	342	8.35	12.4
2-1/4	2.250	57	430,000	1,910	86,000	383	9.36	13.9
2-3/8	2.375	60	478,000	2,130	95,600	425	10.4	15.5
2-1/2	2.500	64	524,000	2,330	105,000	467	11.6	17.3
2-5/8	2.625	67	576,000	2,560	115,000	512	12.8	19.0
2-3/4	2.750	70	628,000	2,790	126,000	560	14.0	20.8
2-7/8	2.875	73	682,000	3,030	136,000	605	15.3	22.8
3	3.000	76	740,000	3,290	148,000	658	16.6	24.7
3-1/8	3.125	79	798,000	3,550	160,000	712	17.8	26.5
3-1/4	3.250	83	858,000	3,820	172,000	765	19.5	29.0
3-3/8	3.375	86	918,000	4,080	184,000	818	21.0	31.3
3-1/2	3.500	89	982,000	4,370	196,000	872	22.7	33.8
3-5/8	3.625	92	1,046,000	4,650	209,000	930	24.3	36.2
3-3/4	3.750	95	1,114,000	4,960	223,000	992	26.0	38.7
3-7/8	3.875	98	1,182,000	5,260	236,000	1,050	27.7	41.2
4	4.000	102	1,254,000	5,580	251,000	1,120	29.6	44.0
4-1/8	4.125	105	1,316,000	5,850	263,000	1,170	31.7	47.2
4-1/4	4.250	108	1,388,000	6,170	278,000	1,240	33.3	49.6
4-3/8	4.375	111	1,468,000	6,530	294,000	1,310	35.4	52.7

Extra-improved plow steel (EIPS)

Wire Diameter			Strength				Weight	
			Nominal Strength		Safe Load			
inch		mm	lbf	kN	lbf	kN	lbm/ft	kg/m
1/4	0.250	6.4	6,800	30.2	1,360	6.05	0.12	0.18
5/16	0.313	8	10,540	46.9	2,110	9.39	0.18	0.27
3/8	0.375	9.5	15,100	67.2	3,020	13.4	0.26	0.39
7/16	0.438	11.5	20,400	90.7	4,080	18.1	0.35	0.52
1/2	0.500	13	26,600	118	5,320	23.7	0.46	0.68
9/16	0.563	14.5	33,600	149	6,720	29.9	0.59	0.88
5/8	0.625	16	41,200	183	8,240	36.7	0.72	1.07
3/4	0.750	19	58,800	262	11,800	52.5	1.04	1.55

Bright Wire, Uncoated, Independent Wire Rope Core (IWRC)
Extra Improved Plow Steel (EIPS)

Wire Diameter			Strength				Weight	
			Nominal Strength		Safe Load			
inch	mm		lbf	kN	lbf	kN	lbm/ft	kg/m
7/8	0.875	22	79,600	354	15,900	70.7	1.42	2.11
1	1.000	26	103,400	460	20,700	92.1	1.85	2.75
1-1/8	1.125	29	130,000	578	26,000	116	2.34	3.48
1-1/4	1.250	32	159,800	711	32,000	142	2.89	4.30
1-3/8	1.375	35	192,000	854	38,400	171	3.50	5.21
1-1/2	1.500	38	228,000	1,010	45,600	203	4.16	6.19
1-5/8	1.625	42	264,000	1,170	52,800	235	4.88	7.26
1-3/4	1.750	45	306,000	1,360	61,200	272	5.67	8.44
1-7/8	1.875	48	348,000	1,550	69,600	310	6.50	9.67
2	2.000	52	396,000	1,760	79,200	352	7.39	11.0
2-1/8	2.125	54	442,000	1,970	88,400	393	8.35	12.4
2-1/4	2.250	57	494,000	2,200	98,800	439	9.36	13.9
2-3/8	2.375	60	548,000	2,440	110,000	489	10.4	15.5
2-1/2	2.500	64	604,000	2,690	121,000	538	11.6	17.3
2-5/8	2.625	67	662,000	2,940	132,000	587	12.8	19.0
2-3/4	2.750	70	722,000	3,210	144,000	641	14.0	20.8
2-7/8	2.875	73	784,000	3,490	157,000	698	15.3	22.8
3	3.000	76	850,000	3,780	170,000	756	16.6	24.7
3-1/8	3.125	79	916,000	4,070	183,000	814	18.0	26.8
3-1/4	3.250	83	984,000	4,380	197,000	876	19.5	29.0
3-3/8	3.375	86	1,058,000	4,710	212,000	943	21.0	31.3
3-1/2	3.500	89	1,128,000	5,020	226,000	1,010	22.7	33.8
3-5/8	3.625	92	1,204,000	5,360	241,000	1,070	24.3	36.2
3-3/4	3.750	95	1,282,000	5,700	256,000	1,140	26.0	38.7
3-7/8	3.875	98	1,360,000	6,050	272,000	1,210	27.7	41.2
4	4.000	102	1,440,000	6,410	288,000	1,280	29.6	44.0
4-1/8	4.125	105	1,514,000	6,730	303,000	1,350	31.7	47.2
4-1/4	4.250	108	1,598,000	7,110	320,000	1,420	33.3	49.6
4-3/8	4.375	111	1,688,000	7,510	338,000	1,500	35.4	52.7

Extra-extra-improved plow steel (EEIPS)

Wire Diameter			Strength				Weight	
			Nominal Strength		Safe Load			
inch	mm		lbf	kN	lbf	kN	lbm/ft	kg/m
3/8	0.375	9.5	16,600	73.8	3,320	14.8	0.26	0.39
7/16	0.438	11.5	22,400	99.6	4,480	19.9	0.35	0.52
1/2	0.500	13	29,200	130	5,840	26.0	0.46	0.68
9/16	0.563	14.5	37,000	165	7,400	32.9	0.59	0.88
5/8	0.625	16	45,400	202	9,080	40.4	0.72	1.07
3/4	0.750	19	64,800	288	13,000	57.8	1.04	1.55
7/8	0.875	22	87,600	390	17,500	77.8	1.42	2.11
1	1.000	26	113,800	506	22,800	101.4	1.85	2.75
1-1/8	1.125	29	143,000	636	28,600	127	2.34	3.48
1-1/4	1.250	32	175,800	782	35,200	157	2.89	4.30
1-3/8	1.375	35	212,000	943	42,400	189	3.50	5.21

Bright Wire, Uncoated, Independent Wire Rope Core (IWRC)
Extra-extra-improved plow steel (EEIPS)

Wire Diameter		Strength				Weight	
		Nominal Strength		Safe Load			
inch	mm	lbf	kN	lbf	kN	lbm/ft	kg/m
1-1/2	1.500	38	250,000	1,110	50,000	222	4.16	6.19
1-5/8	1.625	42	292,000	1,300	58,400	260	4.88	7.26
1-3/4	1.750	45	338,000	1,500	67,600	301	5.67	8.44
1-7/8	1.875	48	384,000	1,710	76,800	342	6.50	9.67
2	2.000	52	434,000	1,930	86,800	386	7.39	11.0
2-1/8	2.125	54	486,000	2,160	97,200	432	8.35	12.4
2-1/4	2.250	57	544,000	2,420	108,800	484	9.36	13.9
2-3/8	2.375	60	602,000	2,680	120,000	534	10.4	15.5
2-1/2	2.500	64	664,000	2,950	133,000	592	11.6	17.3
2-5/8	2.625	66	728,000	3,240	146,000	649	12.8	19.0
2-3/4	2.750	70	794,000	3,530	159,000	707	14.0	20.8
2-7/8	2.875	74	862,000	3,830	172,000	765	15.3	22.8
3	3.000	77	936,000	4,160	187,000	832	16.6	24.7

Compacted Strand Wire Rope
Bright wire, uncoated, fiber core (FC)

Wire Diameter		Strength				Weight	
		Nominal Strength		Safe Load			
inch	mm	lbf	kN	lbf	kN	lbm/ft	kg/m
3/8	0.375	9.5	14,780	65.7	2,960	13.2	0.26	0.39
7/16	0.438	11.5	20,000	89.0	4,000	17.8	0.35	0.52
1/2	0.500	13	26,000	116	5,200	23.1	0.46	0.68
9/16	0.563	14.5	32,800	146	6,560	29.2	0.57	0.85
5/8	0.625	16	40,400	180	8,080	35.9	0.71	1.06
3/4	0.750	19	57,600	256	11,500	51.2	1.03	1.53
7/8	0.875	22	78,000	347	15,600	69.4	1.40	2.08
1	1.000	26	101,400	451	20,300	90.3	1.82	2.71
1-1/8	1.125	29	127,200	566	25,400	113	2.31	3.44
1-1/4	1.250	32	156,400	696	31,300	139	2.85	4.24
1-3/8	1.375	35	188,200	837	37,600	167	3.45	5.13
1-1/2	1.500	38	222,000	988	44,400	198	4.10	6.10
1-5/8	1.625	42	260,000	1,160	52,000	231	4.80	7.14
1-3/4	1.750	45	300,000	1,330	60,000	267	5.56	8.27
1-7/8	1.875	48	342,000	1,520	68,400	304	6.38	9.49
2	2.000	52	386,000	1,720	77,200	343	7.26	10.8

Compacted Strand Wire Rope (cont.)

Bright Wire, Uncoated, Independent Wire Rope Core (IWRC)

Wire Diameter		Strength				Weight	
		Nominal Strength		Safe Load			
inch	mm	lbf	kN	lbf	kN	lbm/ft	kg/m
3/8	0.375	9.5	16,600	73.8	3,320	14.8	0.31	0.46
7/16	0.438	11.5	22,400	99.6	4,480	19.9	0.39	0.58
1/2	0.500	13	29,200	130	5,840	26.0	0.49	0.73
9/16	0.563	14.5	37,000	165	7,400	32.9	0.63	0.94
5/8	0.625	16	45,400	202	9,080	40.4	0.78	1.16
3/4	0.750	19	64,800	288	13,000	57.8	1.13	1.68
7/8	0.875	22	87,600	390	17,500	77.8	1.54	2.29
1	1.000	26	113,800	506	22,800	101	2.00	2.98
1-1/8	1.125	29	143,000	636	28,600	127	2.54	3.78
1-1/4	1.250	32	175,800	782	35,200	157	3.14	4.67
1-3/8	1.375	35	212,000	943	42,400	189	3.80	5.66
1-1/2	1.500	38	250,000	1,110	50,000	222	4.50	6.70
1-5/8	1.625	42	292,000	1,300	58,400	260	5.27	7.84
1-3/4	1.750	45	338,000	1,500	67,600	301	6.12	9.11
1-7/8	1.875	48	384,000	1,710	76,800	342	7.02	10.4
2	2.000	52	434,000	1,930	86,800	386	7.98	11.9

6 Strand x 37 Wire (6 X 37)

Bright wire, uncoated, fiber core (FC)

Improved plow steel (IPS)

Wire Diameter		Strength				Weight	
		Nominal Strength		Safe Load			
inch	mm	lbf	kN	lbf	kN	lbm/ft	kg/m
1/4	0.250	6.5	5,480	24.4	1,100	4.89	0.11	0.16
5/16	0.313	8	8,520	37.9	1,700	7.56	0.16	0.24
3/8	0.375	9.5	12,200	54.3	2,440	10.9	0.24	0.36
7/16	0.438	11.5	16,540	73.6	3,310	14.7	0.32	0.48
1/2	0.500	13	21,400	95.2	4,280	19.0	0.42	0.63
9/16	0.563	14.5	27,000	120	5,400	24.0	0.53	0.79
5/8	0.625	16	33,400	149	6,680	29.7	0.66	0.98
3/4	0.750	19	47,600	212	9,520	42.3	0.95	1.41
7/8	0.875	22	64,400	286	12,900	57.4	1.29	1.92
1	1.000	26	83,600	372	16,700	74.3	1.68	2.50
1-1/8	1.125	29	105,200	468	21,000	93.4	2.13	3.17
1-1/4	1.250	32	129,200	575	25,800	115	2.63	3.91
1-3/8	1.375	35	155,400	691	31,100	138	3.18	4.73
1-1/2	1.500	38	184,000	818	36,800	164	3.78	5.63
1-5/8	1.625	42	214,000	952	42,800	190	4.44	6.61
1-3/4	1.750	45	248,000	1,100	49,600	221	5.15	7.66
1-7/8	1.875	48	282,000	1,250	56,400	251	5.91	8.80
2	2.000	52	320,000	1,420	64,000	285	6.72	10.0
2-1/8	2.125	54	358,000	1,590	71,600	318	7.59	11.3

Improved plow steel (IPS) (cont.)

Wire Diameter			Strength					Weight	
			Nominal Strength		Safe Load				
inch		mm	lbf	kN	lbf	kN		lbm/ft	kg/m
2-1/4	2.250	57	400,000	1,780	80,000	356		8.51	12.7
2-3/8	2.375	60	444,000	1,980	88,800	395		9.48	14.1
2-1/2	2.500	64	488,000	2,170	97,600	434		10.5	15.6
2-5/8	2.625	67	536,000	2,380	107,000	476		11.6	17.3
2-3/4	2.750	70	584,000	2,600	117,000	520		12.7	18.9
2-7/8	2.875	74	634,000	2,820	127,000	565		13.9	20.7
3	3.000	77	688,000	3,060	138,000	614		15.1	22.5
3-1/8	3.125	80	742,000	3,300	148,000	658		16.4	24.4
3-1/4	3.250	83	798,000	3,550	160,000	712		17.7	26.3

Bright wire, Uncoated, Independent Wire Rope Core (IWRC)

Improved plow steel (IPS)

Wire Diameter			Strength				Weight	
			Nominal Strength		Safe Load			
inch		mm	lbf	kN	lbf	kN	lbm/ft	kg/m
1/4	0.250	6.4	5,880	26.2	1,180	5.25	0.12	0.18
5/16	0.313	8	9,160	40.7	1,830	8.14	0.18	0.27
3/8	0.375	9.5	13,120	58.4	2,620	11.7	0.26	0.39
7/16	0.438	11.5	17,780	79.1	3,560	15.8	0.35	0.52
1/2	0.500	13	23,000	102	4,600	20.5	0.46	0.68
9/16	0.563	14.5	29,000	129	5,800	25.8	0.59	0.88
5/8	0.625	16	35,800	159	7,160	31.8	0.72	1.07
3/4	0.750	19	51,200	228	10,200	45.4	1.04	1.55
7/8	0.875	22	69,200	308	13,800	61.4	1.42	2.11
1	1.000	26	89,800	399	18,000	80.1	1.85	2.75
1-1/8	1.125	29	113,000	503	22,600	101	2.34	3.48
1-1/4	1.250	32	138,800	617	27,800	124	2.89	4.30
1-3/8	1.375	35	167,000	743	33,400	149	3.50	5.21
1-1/2	1.500	38	197,800	880	39,600	176	4.16	6.19
1-5/8	1.625	42	230,000	1,020	46,000	205	4.88	7.26
1-3/4	1.750	45	266,000	1,180	53,200	237	5.67	8.44
1-7/8	1.875	48	304,000	1,350	60,800	270	6.50	9.67
2	2.000	52	344,000	1,530	68,800	306	7.39	11.0
2-1/8	2.125	54	384,000	1,710	76,800	342	8.35	12.4
2-1/4	2.250	57	430,000	1,910	86,000	383	9.36	13.9
2-3/8	2.375	60	478,000	2,130	95,600	425	10.4	15.5
2-1/2	2.500	64	524,000	2,330	105,000	467	11.6	17.3
2-5/8	2.625	67	576,000	2,560	115,000	512	12.8	19.0
2-3/4	2.750	70	628,000	2,790	126,000	560	14.0	20.8
2-7/8	2.875	74	682,000	3,030	136,000	605	15.3	22.8
3	3.000	77	740,000	3,290	148,000	658	16.6	24.7
3-1/8	3.125	80	798,000	3,550	160,000	712	18.0	26.8
3-1/4	3.250	83	858,000	3,820	172,000	765	19.5	29.0
3-3/8	3.375	86	918,000	4,080	184,000	818	21.0	31.3
3-1/2	3.500	90	982,000	4,370	196,000	872	22.7	33.8

Improved plow steel (IPS) (cont.)

Wire Diameter		Strength				Weight	
		Nominal Strength		Safe Load			
inch	mm	lbf	kN	lbf	kN	lbm/ft	kg/m
3-5/8	3.625	92	1,046,000	4,650	209,000	930	24.3	36.2
3-3/4	3.750	95	1,114,000	4,960	223,000	992	26.0	38.7
3-7/8	3.875	98	1,182,000	5,260	236,000	1,050	27.7	41.2
4	4.000	102	1,254,000	5,580	251,000	1,120	29.6	44.0
4-1/8	4.125	105	1,316,000	5,850	263,000	1,170	31.7	47.2
4-1/4	4.250	108	1,388,000	6,170	278,000	1,240	33.3	49.6
4-3/8	4.375	111	1,468,000	6,530	294,000	1,310	35.4	52.7

Bright Wire, Uncoated, Independent Wire Rope Core (IWRC)

Extra-improved plow steel (EIPS)

Wire Diameter			Strength					
			Nominal Strength		Safe Load		Weight	
inch		mm	lbf	kN	lbf	kN	lbm/ft	kg/m
1/4	0.250	6.4	6,800	30.2	1,360	6.05	0.12	0.18
5/16	0.313	8	10,540	46.9	2,110	9.39	0.18	0.27
3/8	0.375	9.5	15,100	67.2	3,020	13.4	0.26	0.39
7/16	0.438	11.5	20,400	90.7	4,080	18.1	0.35	0.52
1/2	0.500	13	26,600	118	5,320	23.7	0.46	0.68
9/16	0.563	14.5	33,600	149	6,720	29.9	0.59	0.88
5/8	0.625	16	41,200	183	8,240	36.7	0.72	1.07
3/4	0.750	19	58,800	262	11,800	52.5	1.04	1.55
7/8	0.875	22	79,600	354	15,900	70.7	1.42	2.11
1	1.000	26	103,400	460	20,700	92.1	1.85	2.75
1-1/8	1.125	29	130,000	578	26,000	116	2.34	3.48
1-1/4	1.250	32	159,800	711	32,000	142	2.89	4.30
1-3/8	1.375	35	192,000	854	38,400	171	3.50	5.21
1-1/2	1.500	38	228,000	1,010	45,600	203	4.16	6.19
1-5/8	1.625	42	264,000	1,170	52,800	235	4.88	7.26
1-3/4	1.750	45	306,000	1,360	61,200	272	5.67	8.44
1-7/8	1.875	48	348,000	1,550	69,600	310	6.50	9.67
2	2.000	52	396,000	1,760	79,200	352	7.39	11.0
2-1/8	2.125	54	442,000	1,970	88,400	393	8.35	12.4
2-1/4	2.250	57	494,000	2,200	98,800	439	9.36	13.9
2-3/8	2.375	60	548,000	2,440	110,000	489	10.4	15.5
2-1/2	2.500	64	604,000	2,690	121,000	538	11.6	17.3
2-5/8	2.625	67	662,000	2,940	132,000	587	12.8	19.0
2-3/4	2.750	70	722,000	3,210	144,000	641	14.0	20.8
2-7/8	2.875	74	784,000	3,490	157,000	698	15.3	22.8
3	3.000	77	850,000	3,780	170,000	756	16.6	24.7
3-1/8	3.125	80	916,000	4,070	183,000	814	18.0	26.8
3-1/4	3.250	83	984,000	4,380	197,000	876	19.5	29.0
3-3/8	3.375	86	1,058,000	4,710	212,000	943	21.0	31.3
3-1/2	3.500	90	1,128,000	5,020	226,000	1,010	22.7	33.8
3-5/8	3.625	92	1,204,000	5,360	241,000	1,070	24.3	36.2
3-3/4	3.750	95	1,282,000	5,700	256,000	1,140	26.0	38.7

Extra-improved plow steel (EIPS)

Wire Diameter			Strength				Weight	
			Nominal Strength		Safe Load			
inch		mm	lbf	kN	lbf	kN	lbm/ft	kg/m
3-7/8	3.875	98	1,360,000	6,050	272,000	1,210	27.7	41.2
4	4.000	102	1,440,000	6,410	288,000	1,280	29.6	44.0
4-1/8	4.125	105	1,514,000	6,730	303,000	1,350	31.7	47.2
4-1/4	4.250	108	1,598,000	7,110	320,000	1,420	33.3	49.6
4-3/8	4.375	111	1,688,000	7,510	338,000	1,500	35.4	52.7

Bright Wire, Uncoated, Independent Wire Rope Core (IWRC)
Extra-extra-improved plow steel (EEIPS)

Wire Diameter			Strength				Weight	
			Nominal Strength		Safe Load			
inch		mm	lbf	kN	lbf	kN	lbm/ft	kg/m
3/8	0.375	9.5	16,600	73.8	3,320	14.8	0.26	0.39
7/16	0.438	11.5	22,400	99.6	4,480	19.9	0.35	0.52
1/2	0.500	13	29,200	130	5,840	26.0	0.46	0.68
9/16	0.563	14.5	37,000	165	7,400	32.9	0.59	0.88
5/8	0.625	16	45,400	202	9,080	40.4	0.72	1.07
3/4	0.750	19	64,800	288	13,000	57.8	1.04	1.55
7/8	0.875	22	87,600	390	17,500	77.8	1.42	2.11
1	1.000	26	113,800	506	22,800	101.4	1.85	2.75
1-1/8	1.125	29	143,000	636	28,600	127	2.34	3.48
1-1/4	1.250	32	175,800	782	35,200	157	2.89	4.30
1-3/8	1.375	35	212,000	943	42,400	189	3.50	5.21
1-1/2	1.500	38	250,000	1,110	50,000	222	4.16	6.19
1-5/8	1.625	42	292,000	1,300	58,400	260	4.88	7.26
1-3/4	1.750	45	338,000	1,500	67,600	301	5.67	8.44
1-7/8	1.875	48	384,000	1,710	76,800	342	6.50	9.67
2	2.000	52	434,000	1,930	86,800	386	7.39	11.0
2-1/8	2.125	54	486,000	2,160	97,200	432	8.35	12.4
2-1/4	2.250	57	544,000	2,420	108,800	484	9.36	13.9
2-3/8	2.375	60	602,000	2,680	120,000	534	10.4	15.5
2-1/2	2.500	64	664,000	2,950	133,000	592	11.6	17.3
2-5/8	2.625	67	728,000	3,240	146,000	649	12.8	19.0
2-3/4	2.750	70	794,000	3,530	159,000	707	14.0	20.8
2-7/8	2.875	74	862,000	3,830	172,000	765	15.3	22.8
3	3.000	77	936,000	4,160	187,000	832	16.6	24.7

Compacted Strand Wire Rope

Bright wire, Uncoated, Fiber Core (FC)

Wire Diameter		Strength					Weight	
		Nominal Strength		Safe Load				
inch	mm	lbf	kN	lbf	kN		lbm/ft	kg/m
3/8	0.375	9.5	14,780	65.7	2,960	13.2	0.26	0.39
7/16	0.438	11.5	20,000	89.0	4,000	17.8	0.35	0.52
1/2	0.500	13	26,000	116	5,200	23.1	0.46	0.68
9/16	0.563	14.5	32,800	146	6,560	29.2	0.57	0.85
5/8	0.625	16	40,400	180	8,080	35.9	0.71	1.06
3/4	0.750	19	57,600	256	11,500	51.2	1.03	1.53
7/8	0.875	22	78,000	347	15,600	69.4	1.40	2.08
1	1.000	26	101,400	451	20,300	90.3	1.82	2.71
1-1/8	1.125	29	127,200	566	25,400	113	2.31	3.44
1-1/4	1.250	32	156,400	696	31,300	139	2.85	4.24
1-3/8	1.375	35	188,200	837	37,600	167	3.45	5.13
1-1/2	1.500	38	222,000	988	44,400	198	4.10	6.10
1-5/8	1.625	42	260,000	1,160	52,000	231	4.80	7.14
1-3/4	1.750	45	300,000	1,330	60,000	267	5.56	8.27
1-7/8	1.875	48	342,000	1,520	68,400	304	6.38	9.49
2	2.000	52	386,000	1,720	77,200	343	7.26	10.8

Bright wire, uncoated, independent wire rope core (IWRC)

3/8	0.375	9.5	16,600	73.8	3,320	14.8	0.31	0.46
7/16	0.438	11.5	22,400	99.6	4,480	19.9	0.39	0.58
1/2	0.500	13	29,200	130	5,840	26.0	0.49	0.73
9/16	0.563	14.5	37,000	165	7,400	32.9	0.63	0.94
5/8	0.625	16	45,400	202	9,080	40.4	0.78	1.16
3/4	0.750	19	64,800	288	13,000	57.8	1.13	1.68
7/8	0.875	22	87,600	390	17,500	77.8	1.54	2.29
1	1.000	26	113,800	506	22,800	101	2.00	2.98
1-1/8	1.125	29	143,000	636	28,600	127	2.54	3.78
1-1/4	1.250	32	175,800	782	35,200	157	3.14	4.67
1-3/8	1.375	35	212,000	943	42,400	189	3.80	5.66
1-1/2	1.500	38	250,000	1,110	50,000	222	4.50	6.70
1-5/8	1.625	42	292,000	1,300	58,400	260	5.27	7.84
1-3/4	1.750	45	338,000	1,500	67,600	301	6.12	9.11
1-7/8	1.875	48	384,000	1,710	76,800	342	7.02	10.4
2	2.000	52	434,000	1,930	86,800	386	7.98	11.9

Notes:
(1) Abbreviations used:
 lbf = pound-force, lbm/ft = pound-mass/foot,
 kg/m = kilogram/meter, kN = kilonewton, mm = millimeter
(2) Conversions: 2,000 pounds-force = 1 short ton-force and
 1 short ton-force = 0.90718474 metric ton-force.
(3) Factor of safety = 5; Safe Load = Nominal Strength divided by 5.
(4) References: Similar tables may be found in:

Wire Rope Users Manual, Third Edition, Wire Rope Technical Board, 1993.
Southwest Wire Rope, Houston, TX (see www.southwestwirerope.com)
Wire Rope Corporation of America, Chillicothe, MO (see www.wrca.com)
Standard Handbook For Mechanical Engineers, Tenth Edition, McGraw-Hill, 1996.
Materials Handling Handbook, Second Edition, John Wiley & Sons, 1985.

Screws

Approximate Hole Sizes for Wood Screws..............................576
   Pilot Holes..576
   Shank Clearance Holes..577
   82° Countersink Diameter 577
Sheet Metal Screw Specs 579
Drive Styles 580

Approximate Hole Sizes for Wood Screws

Pilot Holes

Nominal Screw Size	Shank Diameter		Hard Wood Twist Drill Size			
	Nominal	Actual	Inch Series		Numbered Series	
	(inch)	(inch)	(fraction)	(decimal)	Number	(decimal)
# 0	0.060	0.064	3/64	0.047	58	0.042
# 1	0.073	0.077	3/64	0.047	55	0.052
# 2	0.086	0.090	1/16	0.063	53	0.060
# 3	0.099	0.103	1/16	0.063	51	0.067
# 4	0.112	0.116	5/64	0.078	48	0.076
# 5	0.125	0.129	5/64	0.078	44	0.086
# 6	0.138	0.142	3/32	0.094	42	0.094
# 7	0.151	0.155	3/32	0.094	38	0.102
# 8	0.164	0.168	7/64	0.109	35	0.110
# 9	0.177	0.181	1/8	0.125	32	0.116
# 10	0.190	0.194	1/8	0.125	30	0.129
# 11	0.203	0.207	1/8	0.125	29	0.136
# 12	0.216	0.220	9/64	0.141	27	0.144
# 14	0.242	0.246	5/32	0.156	20	0.161
# 16	0.268	0.272	3/16	0.188	16	0.177
# 18	0.294	0.298	3/16	0.188	10	0.194
# 20	0.320	0.324	7/32	0.219	3	0.209
# 24	0.372	0.376	1/4	0.250	D	0.246

Nominal Screw Size	Nominal Shank Diameter	Actual Shank Diameter	Soft Wood Twist Drill Size			
			Inch Series		Numbered Series	
	(inch)	(inch)	(fraction)	(decimal)	Number	(decimal)
# 0	0.060	0.064	1/32	0.031	69	0.029
# 1	0.073	0.077	1/32	0.031	65	0.035
# 2	0.086	0.090	3/64	0.047	59	0.041
# 3	0.099	0.103	3/64	0.047	56	0.047
# 4	0.112	0.116	3/64	0.047	55	0.052
# 5	0.125	0.129	1/16	0.063	53	0.060
# 6	0.138	0.142	1/16	0.063	52	0.064
# 7	0.151	0.155	1/16	0.063	50	0.070
# 8	0.164	0.168	5/64	0.078	48	0.076
# 9	0.177	0.181	5/64	0.078	46	0.081
# 10	0.190	0.194	3/32	0.094	44	0.086
# 11	0.203	0.207	3/32	0.094	43	0.089
# 12	0.216	0.220	3/32	0.094	39	0.100
# 14	0.242	0.246	7/64	0.109	34	0.111
# 16	0.268	0.272	1/8	0.125	31	0.120
# 18	0.294	0.298	9/64	0.141	29	0.136
# 20	0.320	0.324	5/32	0.156	26	0.147
# 24	0.372	0.376	11/64	0.172	18	0.170

Shank Clearance Holes

Nominal Screw Size	Shank Diameter		Hard and Soft Woods Twist Drill Size			
	Nominal	Actual	Fractional Inch Series		Numbered Series	
	(inch)	(inch)	(fraction)	(decimal)	Number	(decimal)
# 0	0.060	0.064	1/16	0.063	52	0.064
# 1	0.073	0.077	5/64	0.078	47	0.079
# 2	0.086	0.090	3/32	0.094	42	0.094
# 3	0.099	0.103	7/64	0.109	37	0.104
# 4	0.112	0.116	7/64	0.109	32	0.116
# 5	0.125	0.129	1/8	0.125	30	0.129
# 6	0.138	0.142	9/64	0.141	27	0.144
# 7	0.151	0.155	5/32	0.156	22	0.157
# 8	0.164	0.168	11/64	0.172	18	0.170
# 9	0.177	0.181	3/16	0.188	14	0.182
# 10	0.190	0.194	3/16	0.188	10	0.194
# 11	0.203	0.207	13/64	0.203	4	0.209
# 12	0.216	0.220	7/32	0.219	2	0.221
# 14	0.242	0.246	1/4	0.250	D	0.246
# 16	0.268	0.272	17/64	0.266	I	0.272
# 18	0.294	0.298	19/64	0.297	N	0.302
# 20	0.320	0.324	21/64	0.328	P	0.323
# 24	0.372	0.376	3/8	0.375	V	0.377

82° Countersink Diameter

Nominal Screw Size	Nominal Shank Diameter	Actual Head Diameter	Countersink Diameter	
	(inch)	(inch)	(fraction)	(decimal)
# 0	0.060	0.119	1/8	0.125
# 1	0.073	0.146	3/16	0.188
# 2	0.086	0.172	3/16	0.188
# 3	0.099	0.199	1/4	0.250
# 4	0.112	0.225	1/4	0.250
# 5	0.125	0.252	1/4	0.250
# 6	0.138	0.279	3/8	0.375
# 7	0.151	0.305	3/8	0.375
# 8	0.164	0.332	3/8	0.375
# 9	0.177	0.358	3/8	0.375
# 10	0.190	0.385	1/2	0.500
# 11	0.203	0.412	1/2	0.500
# 12	0.216	0.438	1/2	0.500
# 14	0.242	0.507	1/2	0.500
# 16	0.268	0.544	5/8	0.625
# 18	0.294	0.635	5/8	0.625
# 20	0.320	0.650	3/4	0.750
# 24	0.372	0.762	3/4	0.750

NOTES:

Pilot hole diameters in the above table are based on thread penetrations of approximately 35% for hard woods and 55% for soft woods. These values were selected as a consensus from drill hole diameters published in various references.

Pilot holes need to be large enough to prevent splitting but small enough to provide adequate holding power.

Pilot holes are strongly recommended for wood screws in hard woods. Pilot holes greatly reduce the possibility of damage to either the wood or the screw.

The total length of the screw should be 1/8 inch shorter than the combined thickness of the two pieces of wood to be joined.

The shank clearance hole should completely pierce the first piece of wood.

The pilot hole should be deep enough into the second piece of wood to accommodate about one half the length of the screw in the second piece of wood.

A countersink is used to make flat or oval head wood screws flush with the wood surface.

SOURCES:

Similar tables have been published in a wide variety of references including:

Woodworker's Pocket Book, Charles H. Hayward, 1957, Evans Brothers Limited, London, England.

Instructions For Selecting And Using Wood Screws and Sheet Metal Screws, A&I Bolt and Nut, Commerce City, CO.

The Visual Handbook of Building And Remodeling, Charlie Wing, 1990, Rodale Press, Emmaus, PA.

Sizes - The Illustrated Encyclopedia, John Lord, 1994, HarperCollins Publishers, Inc, New York, NY.

Benchtop Reference, Fourth Printing, 1986, Popular Science Books, New York, NY.

How To Plan And Build Decks, Fifth Printing, 1983, Sunset Books, Lane Publishing Company, Menlo Park, CA.

WOOD Magazine, www.woodmagazine.com

Pacific Fasteners, www.pacificfasteners.com/catalog/page19.htm

American Fastener, www.americanfastener.com/techref/proper.htm

Bob Vila, www.bobvila.com/screws.htm

Sheet Metal Screw Specs

Screw Diameter # (inch)	Thickness of Metal Gauge #	Diameter of Pierced Hole (inch)	Drilled Hole Size Drill Number
#4 (0.112)	28	0.086	44
	26	0.086	44
	24	0.093	42
	22	0.098	42
	20	0.100	40
#6 (0.138)	28	0.111	39
	26	0.111	39
	24	0.111	39
	22	0.111	38
	20	0.111	36
#7 (0.151)	28	0.121	37
	26	0.121	37
	24	0.121	35
	22	0.121	33
	20	0.121	32
	18	0.121	31
#8 (0.164)	26	0.137	33
	24	0.137	33
	22	0.137	32
	20	0.137	31
	18	....	30
#10 (0.190)	26	0.158	30
	24	0.158	30
	22	0.158	30
	20	0.158	29
	18	0.158	25
#12 (0.216)	24	....	26
	22	0.185	25
	20	0.185	24
	18	0.185	22
#14 (0.242)	24	....	15
	22	0.212	12
	20	0.212	11
	18	0.212	9

Note: The above values are recommended average values only. Variations in materials and local conditions may require significant deviations from the recommended values.

Drive Styles

Torx ©
external
(6-lobe)

Torx ©
internal
(6-lobe)

Torx - internal
Tamper proof
pin (6-lobe)

Frearson

Clutch

Fluted Socket
4 flutes

Fluted Socket
6 flutes

MorTorq ©

Tri-Wing ©

Square
Socket
(Robertson)

Hex Socket
Allen Head
Internal

Hexagon
External

Hexagon
Internal
Tamper proof

Slotted 6
Lobe Combo

Quadrex ©

Phillips ©

Phillips II ©

Phillips/Slot
Combination
(Combo)

Pozi Drive ©
Phillips 1a

Phillips
Square
Supa Drive©

Slotted

Square Slot
Combination

Slotted
Tamper Proof
(One Way)

Spanner
Drilled
Tamper Proof

Spanner
Slotted
Tamper Proof

Phillips ©
Hex Head

5 Node
Security

7 Node
Security

Sheet Metal, Plate and Wire

Weights of Cold Rolled Steel Sheet 582

Weights of Galvanized Steel Sheet 583

Steel Plate Sizes 583

Standard Steel Sheet Gauges 584

Standard Wire Gauges 587

Weights of Cold Rolled Steel Sheet

US Standard Gauge Number	Thickness (inch)	Weight (Mass) per Sheet Area			
		Ounces per square foot	Pounds per square inch	Pounds per square foot	Kilogram per square meter
7/0	0.5000000000	320.0	0.13889	20.000	97.649
6/0	0.4687500000	300.0	0.13021	18.750	91.546
5/0	0.4375000000	280.0	0.12153	17.500	85.442
4/0	0.4062500000	260.0	0.11285	16.250	79.339
3/0	0.3750000000	240.0	0.10417	15.000	73.236
2/0	0.3437500000	220.0	0.09549	13.750	67.133
1/0	0.3125000000	200.0	0.08681	12.500	61.030
1	0.2812500000	180.0	0.07813	11.250	54.927
2	0.2656250000	170.0	0.07378	10.625	51.876
3	0.2500000000	160.0	0.06944	10.000	48.824
4	0.2343750000	150.0	0.06510	9.3750	45.773
5	0.2187500000	140.0	0.06076	8.7500	42.721
6	0.2031250000	130.0	0.05642	8.1250	39.670
7	0.1875000000	120.0	0.05208	7.5000	36.618
8	0.1718750000	110.0	0.04774	6.8750	33.567
9	0.1562500000	100.0	0.04340	6.2500	30.515
10	0.1406250000	90.00	0.03906	5.6250	27.464
11	0.1250000000	80.00	0.03472	5.0000	24.412
12	0.1093750000	70.00	0.03038	4.3750	21.361
13	0.0937500000	60.00	0.02604	3.7500	18.309
14	0.0781250000	50.00	0.02170	3.1250	15.258
15	0.0703125000	45.00	0.01953	2.8125	13.732
16	0.0625000000	40.00	0.01736	2.5000	12.206
17	0.0562500000	36.00	0.01563	2.2500	10.985
18	0.0500000000	32.00	0.01389	2.0000	9.7649
19	0.0437500000	28.00	0.01215	1.7500	8.5442
20	0.0375000000	24.00	0.01042	1.5000	7.3236
21	0.0343750000	22.00	0.00955	1.3750	6.7133
22	0.0312500000	20.00	0.00868	1.2500	6.1030
23	0.0281250000	18.00	0.00781	1.1250	5.4927
24	0.0250000000	16.00	0.00694	1.0000	4.8824
25	0.0218750000	14.00	0.00608	0.87500	4.2721
26	0.0187500000	12.00	0.00521	0.75000	3.6618
27	0.0171875000	11.00	0.00477	0.68750	3.3567
28	0.0156250000	10.00	0.00434	0.62500	3.0515
29	0.0140625000	9.000	0.00391	0.56250	2.7464
30	0.0125000000	8.000	0.00347	0.50000	2.4412
31	0.0109375000	7.000	0.00304	0.43750	2.1361
32	0.0101562500	6.500	0.00282	0.40625	1.9835
33	0.0093750000	6.000	0.00260	0.37500	1.8309
34	0.0085937500	5.500	0.00239	0.34375	1.6783
35	0.0078125000	5.000	0.00217	0.31250	1.5258
36	0.0070312500	4.500	0.00195	0.28125	1.3732
37	0.0066406250	4.250	0.00184	0.26563	1.2969
38	0.0062500000	4.000	0.00174	0.25000	1.2206
39	0.0058593750	3.750	0.00163	0.23438	1.1443
40	0.0054687500	3.500	0.00152	0.21875	1.0680
41	0.0052734375	3.375	0.00146	0.21094	1.0299
42	0.0050781250	3.250	0.00141	0.20313	0.99174
43	0.0048828125	3.125	0.00136	0.19531	0.95360
44	0.0046875000	3.000	0.00130	0.18750	0.91546

Values in the table are based on a density for steel of 480.0 pounds per cubic foot (7,689 kilograms per cubic meter)

Weights of Galvanized Steel Sheet

Galvanized Gauge Number	Thickness inch	Weight (Mass) per Sheet Area			
		Ounces per sq. in.	Pounds per sq. in.	Pounds per sq. ft.	Kilogram per sq. m
8	0.1681	112.5	0.0488	7.031	34.33
9	0.1532	102.5	0.0445	6.406	31.28
10	0.1382	92.5	0.0401	5.781	28.23
11	0.1233	82.5	0.0358	5.156	25.18
12	0.1084	72.5	0.0315	4.531	22.12
13	0.0934	62.5	0.0271	3.906	19.07
14	0.0785	52.5	0.0228	3.281	16.02
15	0.0710	47.5	0.0206	2.969	14.49
16	0.0635	42.5	0.0184	2.656	12.97
17	0.0575	38.5	0.0167	2.406	11.75
18	0.0516	34.5	0.0150	2.156	10.53
19	0.0456	30.5	0.0132	1.906	9.307
20	0.0396	26.5	0.0115	1.656	8.087
21	0.0366	24.5	0.0106	1.531	7.476
22	0.0336	22.5	0.0098	1.406	6.866
23	0.0306	20.5	0.0089	1.281	6.256
24	0.0276	18.5	0.0080	1.156	5.645
25	0.0247	16.5	0.0072	1.031	5.035
26	0.0217	14.5	0.0063	0.906	4.425
27	0.0202	13.5	0.0059	0.844	4.120
28	0.0187	12.5	0.0054	0.781	3.814
29	0.0172	11.5	0.0050	0.719	3.509
30	0.0157	10.5	0.0046	0.656	3.204
31	0.0142	9.5	0.0041	0.594	2.899
32	0.0134	9.0	0.0039	0.563	2.746

Values in the table are based on a density for galvanized steel of 501.9 pounds per cubic foot (8,040 kilograms per cubic meter).

Steel Plate Sizes

Thickness Inches	Weight Lbs/sq foot	Thickness Inches	Weight Lbs/sq foot
3/16	7.65	2–1/8	86.70
1/4	10.20	2–1/4	91.80
5/16	12.75	2–1/2	102.00
3/8	15.30	2–3/4	112.20
7/16	17.85	3	122.40
1/2	20.40	3–1/4	132.60
9/16	22.95	3–1/2	142.80
5/8	25.50	3–3/4	153.00
11/16	28.05	4	163.20
3/4	30.60	4–1/4	173.40
13/16	33.15	4–1/2	183.60
7/8	35.70	5	204.00
1	40.80	5–1/2	224.40
1–1/8	45.90	6	244.80
1–1/4	51.00	6–1/2	265.20
1–3/8	56.10	7	285.60
1–1/2	61.20	7–1/2	306.00
1–5/8	66.30	8	326.40
1–3/4	71.40	9	367.20
1–7/8	76.50	10	408.00
2	81.60		

Standard Steel Sheet Gauges

Number of Sheet Gauge	US Standard Gauge		Manufacturers Standard Gauge		Galvanized Sheet Gauge		Zinc Sheet Gauge	
	Thickness (inch)	(millimeter)	Thickness (inch)	(millimeter)	Thickness (inch)	(millimeter)	Thickness (inch)	(millimeter)
0000000 or 7/0	0.5000	12.7000	- - -	- - -	- - -	- - -	- - -	- - -
000000 or 6/0	0.4688	11.9063	- - -	- - -	- - -	- - -	- - -	- - -
00000 or 5/0	0.4375	11.1125	- - -	- - -	- - -	- - -	- - -	- - -
0000 or 4/0	0.4063	10.3188	- - -	- - -	- - -	- - -	- - -	- - -
000 or 3/0	0.3750	9.5250	- - -	- - -	- - -	- - -	- - -	- - -
00 or 2/0	0.3438	8.7313	- - -	- - -	- - -	- - -	- - -	- - -
0 or 1/0	0.3125	7.9375	- - -	- - -	- - -	- - -	- - -	- - -
1	0.2813	7.1438	- - -	- - -	- - -	- - -	0.002	0.051
2	0.2656	6.7469	- - -	- - -	- - -	- - -	0.004	0.102
3	0.2500	6.3500	0.2391	6.0731	- - -	- - -	0.006	0.152
4	0.2344	5.9531	0.2242	5.6947	- - -	- - -	0.008	0.203
5	0.2188	5.5563	0.2092	5.3137	- - -	- - -	0.010	0.254
6	0.2031	5.1594	0.1943	4.9352	- - -	- - -	0.012	0.305
7	0.1875	4.7625	0.1793	4.5542	- - -	- - -	0.014	0.356
8	0.1719	4.3656	0.1644	4.1758	0.1681	4.270	0.016	0.406
9	0.1563	3.9688	0.1495	3.7973	0.1532	3.891	0.018	0.457
10	0.1406	3.5719	0.1345	3.4163	0.1382	3.510	0.020	0.508
11	0.1250	3.1750	0.1196	3.0378	0.1233	3.132	0.024	0.610
12	0.1094	2.7781	0.1046	2.6568	0.1084	2.753	0.028	0.711

Standard Steel Sheet Gauges

Number of Sheet Gauge	US Standard Gauge		Manufacturers Standard Gauge		Galvanized Sheet Gauge		Zinc Sheet Gauge	
	Thickness (inch)	(millimeter)	Thickness (inch)	(millimeter)	Thickness (inch)	(millimeter)	Thickness (inch)	(millimeter)
13	0.0938	2.3813	0.0897	2.2784	0.0934	2.372	0.032	0.813
14	0.0781	1.9844	0.0747	1.8974	0.0785	1.994	0.036	0.914
15	0.0703	1.7859	0.0673	1.7094	0.0710	1.803	0.040	1.016
16	0.0625	1.5875	0.0598	1.5189	0.0635	1.613	0.045	1.143
17	0.0563	1.4288	0.0538	1.3665	0.0575	1.461	0.050	1.270
18	0.0500	1.2700	0.0478	1.2141	0.0516	1.311	0.055	1.397
19	0.0438	1.1113	0.0418	1.0617	0.0456	1.158	0.060	1.524
20	0.0375	0.9525	0.0359	0.9119	0.0396	1.006	0.070	1.778
21	0.0344	0.8731	0.0329	0.8357	0.0366	0.930	0.080	2.032
22	0.0313	0.7938	0.0299	0.7595	0.0336	0.853	0.090	2.286
23	0.0281	0.7144	0.0269	0.6833	0.0306	0.777	0.100	2.540
24	0.0250	0.6350	0.0239	0.6071	0.0276	0.701	0.125	3.175
25	0.0219	0.5556	0.0209	0.5309	0.0247	0.627	0.250	6.350
26	0.0188	0.4763	0.0179	0.4547	0.0217	0.551	0.375	9.525
27	0.0172	0.4366	0.0164	0.4166	0.0202	0.513	0.500	12.700
28	0.0156	0.3969	0.0149	0.3785	0.0187	0.475	1.000	25.400
29	0.0141	0.3572	0.0135	0.3429	0.0172	0.437	- - -	- - -
30	0.0125	0.3175	0.0120	0.3048	0.0157	0.399	- - -	- - -
31	0.0109	0.2778	0.0105	0.2667	0.0142	0.361	- - -	- - -
32	0.0102	0.2580	0.0097	0.2464	0.0134	0.340	- - -	- - -

Standard Steel Sheet Gauges (cont.)

Number of Sheet Gauge	US Standard Gauge Thickness (inch)	(millimeter)	Manufacturers Standard Gauge Thickness (inch)	(millimeter)	Galvanized Sheet Gauge Thickness (inch)	(millimeter)	Zinc Sheet Gauge Thickness (inch)	(millimeter)
33	0.0094	0.2381	0.0090	0.2286	- - -	- - -	- - -	- - -
34	0.0086	0.2183	0.0082	0.2083	- - -	- - -	- - -	- - -
35	0.0078	0.1984	0.0075	0.1905	- - -	- - -	- - -	- - -
36	0.0070	0.1786	0.0067	0.1702	- - -	- - -	- - -	- - -
37	0.0066	0.1687	0.0064	0.1626	- - -	- - -	- - -	- - -
38	0.0063	0.1588	0.0060	0.1524	- - -	- - -	- - -	- - -
39	0.0059	0.1488	- - -	- - -	- - -	- - -	- - -	- - -
40	0.0055	0.1389	- - -	- - -	- - -	- - -	- - -	- - -
41	0.0053	0.1339	- - -	- - -	- - -	- - -	- - -	- - -
42	0.0051	0.1290	- - -	- - -	- - -	- - -	- - -	- - -
43	0.0049	0.1240	- - -	- - -	- - -	- - -	- - -	- - -
44	0.0047	0.1191	- - -	- - -	- - -	- - -	- - -	- - -

Standard Wire Gauges

Number of Wire Gauge	American Wire Gauge (AWG) or Brown Wire Gauge (BSWG)		British Imperial Standard Wire Gauge (SWG) or British Imperial or Legal Standard or English Imperial Wire Gauge		United States Steel Wire Gauge (USSWG) or Washburn & Moen or American Steel & Wire Co's or Roebling Wire Gauge		Birmingham Wire Gauge or Stubs Iron Wire Gauge		Music Wire Gauge (MWG)	
	Diameter		Diameter		Diameter		Diameter		Diameter	
	(inch)	(mm)	(inch)	(mm)	(inch)	(mm)	(inch)	(mm)	(inch)	(mm)
0000000 or 7/0	0.65136	16.5444	0.50000	12.7000	0.49000	12.4460	-	-	-	-
000000 or 6/0	0.58005	14.7333	0.46400	11.7856	0.46150	11.7221	-	-	0.004	0.102
00000 or 5/0	0.51655	13.1203	0.43200	10.9728	0.43050	10.9347	-	-	0.005	0.127
0000 or 4/0	0.46000	11.6840	0.40000	10.1600	0.39380	10.0025	0.4540	11.532	0.006	0.152
000 or 3/0	0.40964	10.4049	0.37200	9.4488	0.36250	9.2075	0.4250	10.795	0.007	0.178
00 or 2/0	0.36480	9.2658	0.34800	8.8392	0.33100	8.4074	0.3800	9.652	0.008	0.203
0 or 1/0	0.32486	8.2515	0.32400	8.2296	0.30650	7.7851	0.3400	8.636	0.009	0.229
1	0.28930	7.3481	0.30000	7.6200	0.28300	7.1882	0.3000	7.620	0.010	0.254
2	0.25763	6.5437	0.27600	7.0104	0.26250	6.6675	0.2840	7.214	0.011	0.279
3	0.22942	5.8273	0.25200	6.4008	0.24370	6.1900	0.2590	6.579	0.012	0.305
4	0.20431	5.1894	0.23200	5.8928	0.22530	5.7226	0.2380	6.045	0.013	0.330
5	0.18194	4.6213	0.21200	5.3848	0.20700	5.2578	0.2200	5.588	0.014	0.356
6	0.16202	4.1154	0.19200	4.8768	0.19200	4.8768	0.2030	5.156	0.016	0.406
7	0.14429	3.6649	0.17600	4.4704	0.17700	4.4958	0.1800	4.572	0.018	0.457
8	0.12849	3.2636	0.16000	4.0640	0.16200	4.1148	0.1650	4.191	0.020	0.508
9	0.11442	2.9064	0.14400	3.6576	0.14830	3.7668	0.1480	3.759	0.022	0.559
10	0.10190	2.5882	0.12800	3.2512	0.13500	3.4290	0.1340	3.404	0.024	0.610

Standard Wire Gauges (cont.)

Number of Wire Gauge	American Wire Gauge (AWG)or Brown and Sharpe Wire Gauge (BSWG) Diameter		British Imperial Standard Wire Gauge (SWG) or British Imperial Wire Gauge or English Legal Standard or Imperial Wire Gauge Diameter		United States Steel Wire Gauge (USSWG) or Washburn & Moen or Bethlehem Wire Gauge or Roebling Wire Gauge Diameter		Birmingham Wire Gauge or Stubs Iron Wire Gauge Diameter		Music Wire Gauge (MWG) Diameter	
	(inch)	(mm)	(inch)	(mm)	(inch)	(mm)	(inch)	(mm)	(inch)	(mm)
12	0.08081	2.0525	0.10400	2.6416	0.10550	2.6797	0.1090	2.769	0.029	0.737
13	0.07196	1.8278	0.09200	2.3368	0.09150	2.3241	0.0950	2.413	0.031	0.787
14	0.06408	1.6277	0.08000	2.0320	0.08000	2.0320	0.0830	2.108	0.033	0.838
15	0.05707	1.4495	0.07200	1.8288	0.07200	1.8288	0.0720	1.829	0.035	0.889
16	0.05082	1.2908	0.06400	1.6256	0.06250	1.5875	0.0650	1.651	0.037	0.940
17	0.04526	1.1495	0.05600	1.4224	0.05400	1.3716	0.0580	1.473	0.039	0.991
18	0.04030	1.0237	0.04800	1.2192	0.04750	1.2065	0.0490	1.245	0.041	1.041
19	0.03589	0.9116	0.04000	1.0160	0.04100	1.0414	0.0420	1.067	0.043	1.092
20	0.03196	0.8118	0.03600	0.9144	0.03480	0.8839	0.0350	0.889	0.045	1.143
21	0.02846	0.7229	0.03200	0.8128	0.03175	0.8065	0.0320	0.813	0.047	1.194
22	0.02535	0.6438	0.02800	0.7112	0.02860	0.7264	0.0280	0.711	0.049	1.245
23	0.02257	0.5733	0.02400	0.6096	0.02580	0.6553	0.0250	0.635	0.051	1.295
24	0.02010	0.5106	0.02200	0.5588	0.02300	0.5842	0.0220	0.559	0.055	1.397
25	0.01790	0.4547	0.02000	0.5080	0.02040	0.5182	0.0200	0.508	0.059	1.499
26	0.01594	0.4049	0.01800	0.4572	0.01810	0.4597	0.0180	0.457	0.063	1.600
27	0.01420	0.3606	0.01640	0.4166	0.01730	0.4394	0.0160	0.406	0.067	1.702
28	0.01264	0.3211	0.01480	0.3759	0.01620	0.4115	0.0140	0.356	0.071	1.803
29	0.01126	0.2859	0.01360	0.3454	0.01500	0.3810	0.0130	0.330	0.075	1.905

Standard Wire Gauges (cont.)

Number of Wire Gauge	American Wire Gauge (AWG) or Brown and Sharpe Wire Gauge (B&SWG) Diameter		British Imperial Standard Wire Gauge (SWG) or British Imperial Wire Gauge Standard or Imperial Wire Gauge Diameter		United States Steel Wire Gauge (USSWG) or Washburn & Moen or Wethelhem Steel or Roebling Wire Gauge Diameter		Birmingham Wire Gauge or Stubs Iron Wire Gauge Diameter		Music Wire Gauge (MWG) Diameter	
	(inch)	(mm)	(inch)	(mm)	(inch)	(mm)	(inch)	(mm)	(inch)	(mm)
30	0.01003	0.2546	0.01240	0.3150	0.01400	0.3556	0.0120	0.305	0.080	2.032
31	0.00893	0.2268	0.01160	0.2946	0.01320	0.3353	0.0100	0.254	0.085	2.159
32	0.00795	0.2019	0.01080	0.2743	0.01280	0.3251	0.0090	0.229	0.090	2.286
33	0.00708	0.1798	0.01000	0.2540	0.01180	0.2997	0.0080	0.203	0.095	2.413
34	0.00630	0.1601	0.00920	0.2337	0.01040	0.2642	0.0070	0.178	-	-
35	0.00561	0.1426	0.00840	0.2134	0.00950	0.2413	0.0050	0.127	-	-
36	0.00500	0.1270	0.00760	0.1930	0.00900	0.2286	0.0040	0.102	-	-
37	0.00445	0.1131	0.00680	0.1727	0.00850	0.2159	-	-	-	-
38	0.00397	0.1007	-	-	0.00800	0.2032	-	-	-	-
39	0.00353	0.0897	-	-	0.00750	0.1905	-	-	-	-
40	0.00314	0.0799	-	-	0.00700	0.1778	-	-	-	-
41	0.00280	0.0711	-	-	-	-	-	-	-	-
42	0.00249	0.0633	-	-	-	-	-	-	-	-
43	0.00222	0.0564	-	-	-	-	-	-	-	-
44	0.00198	0.0502	-	-	-	-	-	-	-	-
45	0.00176	0.0447	-	-	-	-	-	-	-	-
46	0.00157	0.0398	-	-	-	-	-	-	-	-
47	0.00140	0.0355	-	-	-	-	-	-	-	-

Standard Wire Gauges (cont.)

Number of Wire Gauge	American Wire Gauge (AWG) or Brown and Sharpe Wire Gauge (B&SWG) Diameter		British Imperial Standard Wire Gauge (SWG) or British Imperial Wire Gauge or English Legal Standard Imperial Wire Gauge Diameter		United States Steel Wire Gauge (USSWG) or Washburn & Moen Wire Gauge or Steel Wire Gauge or Roebling Wire Gauge Diameter		Birmingham Wire Gauge or Stubs Iron Wire Gauge Diameter		Music Wire Gauge (MWG) Diameter	
	(inch)	(mm)	(inch)	(mm)	(inch)	(mm)	(inch)	(mm)	(inch)	(mm)
48	0.00124	0.0316	-	-	-	-	-	-	-	-
49	0.00111	0.0281	-	-	-	-	-	-	-	-
50	0.00099	0.0251	-	-	-	-	-	-	-	-
51	0.00088	0.0223	-	-	-	-	-	-	-	-
52	0.00078	0.0199	-	-	-	-	-	-	-	-
53	0.00070	0.0177	-	-	-	-	-	-	-	-
54	0.00062	0.0158	-	-	-	-	-	-	-	-
55	0.00055	0.0140	-	-	-	-	-	-	-	-
56	0.00049	0.0125	-	-	-	-	-	-	-	-

Tools

Tap Drills for INCH Threads 592
Tap Drills for METRIC Threads 599
Drill Sizes & American Wire Gauge 609
Drill and Cutting Lubricants 621
Drill Speed vs. Materials 622
American Standard Taper Pipe 623
American Standard Straight Pipe 623
Fire Extinguishers 624
Sandpaper and Abrasives 625
Saws 627
Drive Styles 630

Tap Drills For INCH Threads (Penetrations Between 70% and 80%)

75% thread penetration is recommended for most applications. 75% to 80% thread penetration is 53% thread penetration will, in most cases, break the bolt before stripping the thread. 75% to 80% thread penetration is recommended for thin stock. 100% thread penetration is recommended for very thin stock. A thread penetration of 100% is only 5% stronger than a thread penetration of 75%, but tapping at 100% thread penetration requires 3 times the power.

All Thread Penetration percentages listed are theoretical.
Reaming is recommended for sizes larger than 1-1/8 inches.
Equation: Percent of Thread = Number of threads per inch x (Nominal Diameter - Tap Drill Diameter)/(0.01299)

Inch Series - Unified National and American National Threads

Bolt or Screw Size (#)	Threads Per Inch	Thread Series	Diameter inch	Tap Drill Diameter Fractional Inch	Tap Drill Diameter Millimeter	Tap Drill Diameter Inch	Drill Number	Thread Penetration
0	80	UNF	0.0600	3/64		0.0465	56	83%
						0.0469		81%
						0.0472		79%
1	64	UNC	0.0730		1.20	0.0571		78%
					1.45	0.0591	53	69%
					1.50	0.0595		67%
1	72	UNF	0.0730		1.50	0.0591	53	77%
						0.0595		75%
2	56	UNC	0.0860			0.0670	51	82%
					1.75	0.0689		74%
						0.0700	50	69%
2	64	UNF	0.0860		1.80	0.0700	50	79%
						0.0709		75%

Tap Drills for INCH Threads - Unified National and American National Threads

Bolt or Screw Size (#) Inch	Threads Per Inch	Thread Series	Diameter Inch	Tap Drill Diameter				Thread Penetration
				Inch	Fractional Inch	Millimeter	Drill Number	
3	48	UNC	0.0990	0.0781	5/64			77%
				0.0785			47	76%
				0.0787		2.00		75%
3	56	UNF	0.0990	0.0807		2.05		79%
				0.0810			46	78%
				0.0820			45	73%
				0.0827		2.10		70%
4	40	UNC	0.1120	0.0860		2.20		80%
				0.0866			44	78%
				0.0886		2.25		72%
4	48	UNF	0.1120	0.0906		2.30		79%
				0.0925		2.35		72%
				0.0935			42	68%
				0.0938	3/32			67%
5	40	UNC	0.1250	0.0995			39	79%
				0.1004		2.55		76%
				0.1015			38	72%
				0.1024		2.60		70%
5	44	UNF	0.1250	0.1015			38	80%
				0.1040			37	71%
				0.1043		2.65		70%
				0.1024		2.60		77%
				0.0890			43	71%

Tap Drills For INCH Threads (Penetrations Between 70% and 80%)(cont.)

Inch Series - Unified National and American National Threads

Bolt or Screw Size (#)	inch	Threads Per Inch	Thread Series	Diameter inch	Tap Drill Diameter			Drill Number	Thread Penetration
					Fractional Inch	Millimeter	Inch		
6	0.1380	32	UNC	0.1380		2.70	0.1063		78%
							0.1065	36	78%
						2.75	0.1083		73%
					7/64		0.1094		71%
							0.1100		69%
6	0.1380	40	UNF	0.1380			0.1110	34	83%
						2.85	0.1122		79%
							0.1130	33	77%
						2.90	0.1142		73%
8	0.1640	32	UNC	0.1640		3.40	0.1339		74%
						3.45	0.1358		69%
							0.1360	29	69%
8	0.1640	36	UNF	0.1640		3.45	0.1358		78%
							0.1360	29	78%
						3.50	0.1378		73%
10	0.1900	24	UNC	0.1900			0.1470	26	79%
							0.1495	25	75%
						3.80	0.1496		75%
10	0.1900	24	UNC	0.1900		3.85	0.1516		71%
							0.1520	24	70%
						3.75	0.1476		78%

Tap Drills for INCH Threads - Unified National and American National Threads (cont.)

Bolt or Screw Size (#) Inch	Threads Per Inch	Thread Series	Diameter Inch	Tap Drill Diameter Inch	Tap Drill Diameter Fractional Inch	Tap Drill Diameter Millimeter	Drill Number	Thread Penetration
10	32	UNF	0.1900	0.1575		4.00	21	80%
				0.1590		4.05		76%
				0.1594			20	75%
				0.1610				71%
				0.1614		4.10		70%
12	24	UNC	0.2160	0.1719	11/64			82%
				0.1732		4.40		79%
				0.1752		4.45		75%
				0.1770			16	72%
				0.1772		4.50		72%
12	28	UNF	0.2160	0.1791		4.55		79%
				0.1800			15	78%
				0.1811		4.60		75%
				0.1820			14	73%
				0.1831		4.65		71%
				0.1730			17	79%
1/4	20	UNC	0.2500	0.1988		5.05		79%
				0.1990			8	79%
				0.2008		5.10		76%
				0.2010			7	75%
				0.2028		5.15		73%
				0.2031	13/64			72%
				0.2040			6	71%
				0.2047		5.20		70%

Tap Drills For INCH Threads (Penetrations Between 70% and 80%)(cont.)

Inch Series - Unified National and American National Threads

Bolt or Screw Size (#) inch	Threads Per Inch	Thread Series	Diameter inch	Tap Drill Diameter Inch	Fractional Inch	Millimeter	Drill Number	Thread Penetration
1/4	28	UNF	0.2500	0.2126		5.40		81%
				0.2130			3	80%
				0.2146		5.45		76%
				0.2165		5.50		72%
5/16	18	UNC	0.3125	0.2559		6.50		78%
				0.2570			F	77%
				0.2598		6.60		73%
				0.2610			G	71%
				0.2638		6.70		68%
5/16	24	UNF	0.3125	0.2717		6.90		75%
				0.2720			I	75%
				0.2756		7.00		68%
3/8	16	UNC	0.3750	0.3110		7.90		79%
				0.3125	5/16			77%
				0.3150		8.00		74%
				0.3160			O	73%
				0.3189		8.10		69%
3/8	24	UNF	0.3750	0.3307		8.40		82%
				0.3320			Q	79%
				0.3346		8.50		75%
7/16	14	UNC	0.4375	0.3642		9.25		79%
				0.3661		9.30		77%

Tap Drills for INCH Threads - Unified National and American National Threads (cont.)

Bolt or Screw Size (#)	Bolt or Screw Size Inch	Threads Per Inch	Thread Series	Diameter Inch	Tap Drill Diameter Inch	Tap Drill Diameter Fractional Inch	Tap Drill Diameter Millimeter	Drill Number	Thread Penetration
7/16	0.4375	14	UNC	0.4375	0.3680			U	75%
					0.3701		9.40		73%
7/16	0.4375	20	UNF	0.4375	0.3858		9.80		80%
					0.3860			W	79%
					0.3898		9.90		73%
					0.3906	25/64			72%
1/2	0.5000	13	UNC	0.5000	0.4213		10.70		79%
					0.4219	27/64			78%
					0.4232		10.75		77%
					0.4252		10.80		75%
					0.4291		10.90		71%
1/2	0.5000	20	UNF	0.5000	0.4488		11.40		79%
					0.4528		11.50		73%
					0.4531	29/64			72%
9/16	0.5625	12	UNC	0.5625	0.4803		12.20		76%
					0.4823		12.25		74%
					0.4844	31/64			72%
					0.4882		12.40		69%
9/16	0.5625	18	UNF	0.5625	0.5039		12.80		81%
					0.5118		13.00		70%
					0.5156	33/64			65%
5/8	0.6250	11	UNC	0.6250	0.5313	17/32			79%
					0.5315		13.50		79%
					0.5413		13.75		71%

Tap Drills For INCH Threads (Penetrations Between 70% and 80%)(cont.)

Unified National and American National Threads for thread penetration between 70% and 80%

Bolt or Screw Size (#)	Inch	Threads Per Inch	Thread Series	Diameter Inch	Inch	Fractional Inch	Millimeter	Drill Number	Thread Penetration
5/8	0.6250	18	UNF	0.6250	0.5709		14.50		75%
					0.5781	37/64			65%
3/4	0.7500	10	UNC	0.7500	0.6496		16.50		77%
					0.6563	21/32			72%
					0.6594		16.75		70%
3/4	0.7500	16	UNF	0.7500	0.6875	11/16			77%
					0.6890		17.50		75%
7/8	0.8750	9	UNC	0.8750	0.7677		19.50		74%
					0.7813	25/32			65%
7/8	0.8750	14	UNF	0.8750	0.7969	51/64			84%
					0.8071		20.50		73%
					0.8125	13/16			67%
1	1.0000	8	UNC	1.0000	0.8661		22.00		82%
					0.8750	7/8			77%
					0.8858		22.50		70%
					0.8906	57/64			67%
1	1.0000	12	UNF	1.0000	0.9219	59/64			72%
					0.9252		23.50		69%
1-1/8	1.1250	7	UNC	1.1250	0.9688	31/32			84%
					0.9843		25.00		76%
					0.9844	63/64			76%
					1.0000	1	25.40		67%
1-1/8	1.1250	12	UNF	1.1250	1.0433		26.50		75%
					1.0469	1-3/64			72%

Tap Drills for METRIC Threads (Penetration Between 70% and 80%)

75% thread penetration is recommended for most applications. 53% thread penetration will, in most cases, break the bolt before stripping the thread. 75% to 80% thread penetration is recommended for thin stock. 100% thread penetration is recommended for very thin stock. A thread penetration of 100% is only 5% stronger than a thread penetration of 75%, but tapping at 100% thread penetration requires 3 times the power.

All Thread Penetration percentages listed are theoretical.

Reaming is recommended for sizes larger than 28 millimeters.
Equation: Percent of Thread = (76.980 / Pitch) x (Nominal Diameter - Tap Drill Diameter)

Metric Threads

Bolt or Screw Size		Pitch	Thread Series	Tap Drill Diameter				Drill Number	Thread Penetration
Millimeter	Inch			Inch	Fractional Inch	Fractional Inch	Millimeter		
1.0	0.0394	0.20	M-Fine	0.03125	1/32		0.7938		79%
				0.03150			0.8000		77%
				0.03200			0.8128	67	72%
1.0	0.0394	0.25	M-Coarse	0.02920			0.7417	69	80%
				0.02953			0.7500		77%
1.1	0.0433	0.20	M-Fine	0.03500			0.8890	65	81%
				0.03543			0.9000		77%
				0.03600			0.9144	64	71%
1.1	0.0433	0.25	M-Coarse	0.03300			0.8382	66	81%
				0.03346			0.8500		77%
1.2	0.0472	0.20	M-Fine	0.03900			0.9906	61	81%
				0.03937			1.0000		77%
				0.04000			1.0160	60	71%
1.2	0.0472	0.25	M-Coarse	0.03700			0.9398	63	80%
				0.03740			0.9500		77%
				0.03800			0.9652	62	72%

Tap Drills For METRIC Threads (Penetrations Between 70% and 80%)(cont.)

Bolt or Screw Size		Pitch	Thread Series	Tap Drill Diameter				Thread Penetration
Millimeter	Inch			Inch	Fractional Inch	Millimeter	Drill Number	
1.4	0.0551	0.20	M-Fine	0.04688	3/64	1.1906		81%
				0.04724		1.2000		77%
1.4	0.0551	0.30	M-Coarse	0.04300		1.0922	57	79%
				0.04331		1.1000		77%
1.6	0.0630	0.20	M-Fine	0.05500		1.3970	54	78%
				0.05512		1.4000		77%
1.6	0.0630	0.35	M-Coarse	0.04921		1.2500		77%
				0.05118		1.3000		66%
1.8	0.0709	0.20	M-Fine	0.06250	1/16	1.5875		82%
				0.06299		1.6000		77%
				0.06350		1.6129		72%
1.8	0.0709	0.35	M-Coarse	0.05709		1.4500	52	77%
				0.05906		1.5000		66%
2.0	0.0787	0.25	M-Fine	0.06890		1.7500		77%
				0.07000		1.7780	50	68%
2.0	0.0787	0.40	M-Coarse	0.06250	1/16	1.5875		79%
				0.06299		1.6000		77%
				0.06350		1.6129	52	74%
2.2	0.0866	0.25	M-Fine	0.07600	5/64	1.9304	48	83%
				0.07677		1.9500		77%
				0.07813		1.9844		66%
2.2	0.0866	0.45	M-Coarse	0.06890		1.7500	50	77%
				0.07000		1.7780		72%
				0.07087		1.8000		68%

Handyman In~Your~Pocket

Tap Drills for METRIC Threads (cont.)

Bolt or Screw Size			Thread Series	Tap Drill Diameter				Thread Penetration
Millimeter	Inch	Pitch		Inch	Fractional Inch	Millimeter	Drill Number	
2.5	0.0984	0.35	M-Fine	0.08465		2.1500	44	77%
				0.08600		2.1844		69%
2.5	0.0984	0.45	M-Coarse	0.08071		2.0500		77%
				0.08100		2.0574	46	76%
				0.08200		2.0828	45	71%
				0.08268		2.1000		68%
3.0	0.1181	0.35	M-Fine	0.10400		2.6416	37	79%
				0.10433		2.6500		77%
3.0	0.1181	0.50	M-Coarse	0.09800		2.4892	40	79%
				0.09843		2.5000		77%
				0.09950		2.5273	39	73%
				0.10039		2.5500		69%
3.5	0.1378	0.35	M-Fine	0.12402		3.1500		77%
				0.12500	1/8	3.1750		71%
				0.12598		3.2000		66%
3.5	0.1378	0.60	M-Coarse	0.11300		2.8702	33	81%
				0.11417		2.9000		77%
				0.11600		2.9464	32	71%
				0.11614		2.9500		71%
4.0	0.1575	0.50	M-Fine	0.13600		3.4544	29	84%
				0.13780		3.5000		77%
				0.13976		3.5500		69%
4.0	0.1575	0.70	M-Coarse	0.12850		3.2639	30	81%
				0.12992		3.3000		77%
				0.13189		3.3500		71%

Tap Drills For METRIC Threads (Penetrations Between 70% and 80%)(cont.)

Bolt or Screw Size		Pitch	Thread Series	Tap Drill Diameter				Thread Penetration
Millimeter	Inch			Inch	Fractional Inch	Millimeter	Drill Number	
4.5	0.1772	0.50	M - Fine	0.15625	5/32	3.9688		82%
				0.15700		3.9878	22	79%
				0.15748		4.0000		77%
				0.15900		4.0386	21	71%
4.5		0.75	M - Coarse	0.14700		3.7338	26	79%
				0.14764		3.7500		77%
				0.14950		3.7973	25	72%
				0.14961		3.8000		72%
5.0	0.1969	0.50	M - Fine	0.17700		4.4958	16	78%
				0.17717		4.5000		77%
				0.17913		4.5500		69%
5.0	0.1969	0.80	M - Coarse	0.16535		4.2000		77%
				0.16600		4.2164	19	75%
				0.16732		4.2500		72%
5.5	0.2165	0.50	M - Fine	0.19600		4.9784	9	80%
				0.19685		5.0000		77%
6.0	0.2362	0.75	M - Fine	0.20550		5.2197	5	80%
				0.20669		5.2500		77%
				0.20866		5.3000		72%
				0.20900		5.3086		71%
6.0	0.2362	1.00	M - Coarse	0.19600		4.9784	9	79%
				0.19685		5.0000		77%
				0.19882		5.0500		73%
				0.19900		5.0546	8	73%

Tap Drills for METRIC Threads (cont.)

Bolt or Screw Size		Pitch	Thread Series	Tap Drill Diameter				Thread Penetration
Millimeter	Inch			Inch	Fractional Inch	Millimeter	Drill Number	
7.0	0.2756	0.75	M	0.24600		6.2484	D	77%
				0.24606		6.2500		77%
				0.24803		6.3000		72%
				0.25000	1/4	6.3500		67%
7.0	0.2756	1.00	M - Coarse	0.23400		5.9436	E	81%
				0.23425		5.9500	A	81%
				0.23438	15/64	5.9531		81%
				0.23622		6.0000		77%
				0.23800		6.0452	B	74%
				0.24016		6.1000		69%
8.0	0.3150	0.75	M - Fine	0.28543		7.2500		77%
				0.28740		7.3000		72%
				0.29000		7.3660	L	65%
8.0	0.3150	1.00	M - Fine	0.27559		7.0000		77%
				0.27700		7.0358	J	74%
				0.27953		7.1000		69%
8.0	0.3150	1.25	M - Coarse	0.26378		6.7000		80%
				0.26563	17/64	6.7469		77%
				0.26575		6.7500		77%
				0.26600		6.7564		77%
				0.26772		6.8000	H	74%
9.0	0.3543	0.75	M - Fine	0.32480		8.2500		77%
				0.32677		8.3000		72%
				0.32813	21/64	8.3344		68%

Tap Drills For METRIC Threads (Penetrations Between 70% and 80%)(cont.)

Bolt or Screw Size		Pitch	Thread Series	Tap Drill Diameter				Thread Penetration
Millimeter	Inch			Inch	Fractional Inch	Millimeter	Drill Number	
9.0	0.3543	1.00	M - Fine	0.31250	5/16	7.9375		82%
				0.31496		8.0000		77%
				0.31600		8.0264		75%
9.0	0.3543	1.25	M - Coarse	0.30200		7.6708	O	82%
				0.30315		7.7000	N	80%
				0.30512		7.7500		77%
				0.30709		7.8000		74%
10.0	0.3937	0.75	M - Fine	0.36417		9.2500		77%
				0.36614		9.3000		72%
				0.36800		9.3472	U	67%
10.0	0.3937	1.00	M - Fine	0.35433		9.0000		77%
				0.35800		9.0932	T	70%
				0.35827		9.1000		69%
10.0	0.3937	1.25	M - Fine	0.34252		8.7000		80%
				0.34375	11/32	8.7313		78%
				0.34449		8.7500		77%
				0.34646		8.8000		74%
				0.34800		8.8392	S	71%
10.0	0.3937	1.50	M - Coarse	0.33200		8.4328	Q	80%
				0.33465		8.5000		77%
				0.33858		8.6000	R	72%
				0.33900		8.6106		71%
11.0	0.4331	0.75	M - Fine	0.40354	13/32	10.2500		77%
				0.40400		10.2616	Y	76%
				0.40551		10.3000		72%
				0.40625		10.3188		70%

Tap Drills for METRIC Threads(cont.)

Bolt or Screw Size Millimeter	Pitch	Thread Series	Inch	Tap Drill Diameter Fractional Inch	Millimeter	Drill Number	Thread Penetration
11.0	1.00	M - Fine	0.39370		10.0000		77%
			0.39700		10.0838	X	71%
			0.39764		10.1000		69%
11.0	1.50	M - Coarse	0.37402	3/8	9.5000		77%
			0.37500		9.5250		76%
			0.37700		9.5758	V	73%
			0.37795		9.6000		72%
12.0	1.00	M - Fine	0.43307		11.0000		77%
			0.43701		11.1000		69%
			0.43750	7/16	11.1125		68%
12.0	1.25	M - Fine	0.42126		10.7000		80%
			0.42188	27/64	10.7156		79%
			0.42323		10.7500		77%
			0.42520		10.8000		74%
12.0	1.50	M - Fine	0.41300		10.4902	Z	77%
			0.41339		10.5000		77%
			0.41732		10.6000		72%
12.0	1.75	M - Coarse	0.40157		10.2000		79%
			0.40354		10.2500		77%
			0.40400		10.2616	Y	76%
			0.40551		10.3000		75%
			0.40625	13/32	10.3188		74%
			0.40945		10.4000		70%
14.0	1.00	M - Fine	0.51181		13.0000		77%
			0.51563	33/64	13.0969		70%

Tap Drills For METRIC Threads (Penetrations Between 70% and 80%)(cont.)

Bolt or Screw Size		Pitch	Thread Series	Tap Drill Diameter				Thread Penetration
Millimeter	Inch			Inch	Fractional Inch	Millimeter	Drill Number	
14.0	0.5512	1.25	M - Fine	0.50000	1/2	12.7000		80%
				0.50197		12.7500		77%
				0.50394		12.8000		74%
14.0	0.5512	1.50	M - Fine	0.49213		12.5000		77%
				0.49606		12.6000		72%
				0.50000	1/2	12.7000		67%
14.0	0.5512	2.00	M - Coarse	0.46850		11.9000		81%
				0.46875	15/32	11.9063		81%
				0.47244		12.0000		77%
15.0	0.5906	1.00	M - Fine	0.55118		14.0000		77%
15.0	0.5906	1.50	M - Fine	0.53125	17/32	13.4938		77%
				0.53150		13.5000		77%
16.0	0.6299	1.00	M - Fine	0.59055		15.0000		77%
				0.59375	19/32	15.0813		71%
16.0	0.6299	1.50	M - Fine	0.57087		14.5000		77%
				0.57813	37/64	14.6844		68%
16.0	0.6299	2.00	M - Coarse	0.54688	35/64	13.8906		81%
				0.55118		14.0000		77%
				0.56102		14.2500		67%
				0.56250	9/16	14.2875		66%
17.0	0.6693	1.00	M - Fine	0.62992		16.0000		77%
17.0	0.6693	1.50	M - Fine	0.60938	39/64	15.4781		78%
				0.61024		15.5000		77%

Tap Drills for METRIC Threads (cont.)

Bolt or Screw Size Millimeter	Inch	Pitch	Thread Series	Tap Drill Diameter Inch	Fractional Inch	Millimeter	Drill Number	Thread Penetration
18.0	0.7087	1.00	M - Fine	0.66929		17.0000		77%
				0.67188	43/64	17.0656		72%
18.0	0.7087	1.50	M - Fine	0.64961		16.5000		77%
				0.65625	21/32	16.6688		68%
18.0	0.7087	2.00	M - Fine	0.62500	5/8	15.8750		82%
				0.62992		16.0000		77%
18.0	0.7087	2.50	M - Coarse	0.60938	39/64	15.4781		78%
20.0	0.7874	1.00	M - Fine	0.74803		19.0000		77%
				0.75000	3/4	19.0500		73%
20.0	0.7874	1.50	M - Fine	0.72835		18.5000		77%
				0.73438	47/64	18.6531		69%
20.0	0.7874	2.00	M - Fine	0.70313	45/64	17.8594		82%
				0.70866		18.0000		77%
20.0	0.7874	2.50	M - Coarse	0.68750	11/16	17.4625		78%
				0.68898		17.5000		77%
22.0	0.8661	1.00	M - Fine	0.82677		21.0000		77%
				0.82813	53/64	21.0344		74%
22.0	0.8661	1.50	M - Fine	0.80709		20.5000		77%
				0.81250	13/16	20.6375		70%
22.0	0.8661	2.00	M - Fine	0.78740		20.0000		77%
				0.79688	51/64	20.2406		68%
22.0	0.8661	2.50	M - Fine	0.76563	49/64	19.4469		79%
				0.76772		19.5000		77%
24.0	0.9449	1.00	M - Fine	0.90551		23.0000		77%
				0.90625	29/32	23.0188		76%

Tap Drills For METRIC Threads (Penetrations Between 70% and 80%)(cont.)

Bolt or Screw Size			Thread Series	Tap Drill Diameter				Thread Penetration
Millimeter	Inch	Pitch		Inch	Fractional Inch	Millimeter	Drill Number	
24.0	0.9449	1.50	M - Fine	0.88583		22.5000		77%
24.0	0.9449	2.00	M - Fine	0.89063	57/64	22.6219		71%
24.0	0.9449	2.00	M - Fine	0.86614		22.0000		77%
24.0	0.9449	3.00	M - Coarse	0.87500	7/8	22.2250		68%
24.0	0.9449	3.00	M - Coarse	0.82677		21.0000		77%
				0.82813	53/64	21.0344		76%
				0.84375	27/32	21.4313		66%
25.0	0.9843	1.00	M - Fine	0.94488		24.0000		77%
25.0	0.9843	1.50	M - Fine	0.92188	59/64	23.4156		81%
25.0	0.9843	1.50	M - Fine	0.92520		23.5000		77%
25.0	0.9843	2.00	M - Fine	0.90551		23.0000		77%
				0.90625	29/32	23.0188		76%

Drill Size and American Wire Gauge

Inch	Millimeter	Fractional Inch	Typical Sizes in Drill Sets inch	mm	Drill Number	Amer. Steel Wire Gauge
			Twist Drill Sizes			
0.0011100	0.0281940					49
0.0012400	0.0314960					48
0.0014000	0.0355600					47
0.0015700	0.0398780					46
0.0017600	0.0447040					45
0.0019800	0.0502920					44
0.0022200	0.0563880					43
0.0024900	0.0632460					42
0.0028000	0.0711200					41
0.0031440	0.0798576					40
0.0035310	0.0896874					39
0.0039650	0.1007110					38
0.0044530	0.1131062					37
0.0050000	0.1270000					36
0.0056150	0.1426210					35
0.0059000	0.1498600				97	
0.0059055	0.1500000			0.15		
0.0062992	0.1600000			0.16		
0.0063000	0.1600200				96	
0.0063050	0.1601470					34
0.0066929	0.1700000			0.17		
0.0067000	0.1701800				95	
0.0070800	0.1798320					33
0.0070866	0.1800000			0.18		
0.0071000	0.1803400				94	
0.0074803	0.1900000			0.19		
0.0075000	0.1905000				93	
0.0078125	0.1984375	1/128				
0.0078740	0.2000000			0.20		
0.0079000	0.2006600				92	
0.0079500	0.2019300					32
0.0082677	0.2100000			0.21		
0.0083000	0.2108200				91	
0.0086614	0.2200000			0.22		
0.0087000	0.2209800				90	
0.0089280	0.2267712					31
0.0090551	0.2300000			0.23		
0.0091000	0.2311400				89	
0.0094488	0.2400000			0.24		
0.0095000	0.2413000				88	
0.0098425	0.2500000			0.25		
0.0100000	0.2540000				87	
0.0100250	0.2546350					30
0.0102362	0.2600000			0.26		
0.0105000	0.2667000				86	

Inch	Millimeter	Fractional Inch	Typical Sizes in Drill Sets		Drill Number	Amer. Steel Wire Gauge
			inch	mm		
0.0106299	0.2700000			0.27		
0.0110000	0.2794000				85	
0.0110236	0.2800000			0.28		
0.0112570	0.2859278					29
0.0114173	0.2900000			0.29		
0.0115000	0.2921000				84	
0.0118110	0.3000000			0.30		
0.0120000	0.3048000				83	
0.0125000	0.3175000				82	
0.0125984	0.3200000			0.32		
0.0126410	0.3210814					28
0.0130000	0.3302000				81	
0.0133858	0.3400000			0.34		
0.0135000	0.3429000				80	
0.0137795	0.3500000			0.35		
0.0141732	0.3600000			0.36		
0.0141950	0.3605530					27
0.0145000	0.3683000				79	
0.0149606	0.3800000			0.38		
0.0156250	0.3968750	1/64	1/64			
0.0157480	0.4000000			0.40		
0.0159410	0.4049014					26
0.0160000	0.4064000				78	
0.0165354	0.4200000			0.42		
0.0173228	0.4400000			0.44		
0.0177165	0.4500000			0.45		
0.0179000	0.4546600					25
0.0180000	0.4572000				77	
0.0181102	0.4600000			0.46		
0.0188976	0.4800000			0.48		
0.0196850	0.5000000			0.50		
0.0200000	0.5080000				76	
0.0201010	0.5105654					24
0.0204724	0.5200000			0.52		
0.0210000	0.5334000				75	
0.0216535	0.5500000			0.55		
0.0225000	0.5715000				74	
0.0225720	0.5733288					23
0.0228346	0.5800000			0.58		
0.0234375	0.5953125	3/128				
0.0236220	0.6000000			0.60		
0.0240000	0.6096000				73	
0.0244094	0.6200000			0.62		
0.0250000	0.6350000				72	
0.0253460	0.6437884					22
0.0255906	0.6500000			0.65		
0.0260000	0.6604000				71	
0.0267717	0.6800000			0.68		

			Twist Drill Sizes			
Inch	Millimeter	Fractional Inch	Typical Sizes in Drill Sets		Drill Number	Amer. Steel Wire Gauge
			inch	mm		
0.0275591	0.7000000			0.70		
0.0280000	0.7112000				70	
0.0283465	0.7200000			0.72		
0.0284620	0.7229348					21
0.0292000	0.7416800				69	
0.0295276	0.7500000			0.75		
0.0307087	0.7800000			0.78		
0.0310000	0.7874000				68	
0.0312500	0.7937500	1/32	1/32			
0.0314961	0.8000000			0.80		
0.0319610	0.8118094					20
0.0320000	0.8128000				67	
0.0322835	0.8200000			0.82		
0.0330000	0.8382000				66	
0.0334646	0.8500000			0.85		
0.0346457	0.8800000			0.88		
0.0350000	0.8890000				65	
0.0354331	0.9000000			0.90		
0.0358900	0.9116060					19
0.0360000	0.9144000				64	
0.0362205	0.9200000			0.92		
0.0370000	0.9398000				63	
0.0374016	0.9500000			0.95		
0.0380000	0.9652000				62	
0.0385827	0.9800000			0.98		
0.0390000	0.9906000				61	
0.0390625	0.9921875	5/128				
0.0393701	1.0000000			1.00		
0.0400000	1.0160000				60	
0.0403030	1.0236962					18
0.0410000	1.0414000				59	
0.0413386	1.0500000			1.05		
0.0420000	1.0668000				58	
0.0430000	1.0922000				57	
0.0433071	1.1000000			1.10		
0.0452570	1.1495278					17
0.0452756	1.1500000			1.15		
0.0465000	1.1811000				56	
0.0468750	1.1906250	3/64	3/64			
0.0472441	1.2000000			1.20		
0.0492126	1.2500000			1.25		
0.0508210	1.2908534					16
0.0511811	1.3000000			1.30		
0.0520000	1.3208000				55	
0.0531496	1.3500000			1.35		
0.0546875	1.3890625	7/128				
0.0550000	1.3970000				54	
0.0551181	1.4000000			1.40		

Inch	Millimeter	Fractional Inch	Twist Drill Sizes		Drill Number	Amer. Steel Wire Gauge
			Typical Sizes in Drill Sets			
			inch	mm		
0.0570680	1.4495272					15
0.0570866	1.4500000			1.45		
0.0590551	1.5000000			1.50		
0.0595000	1.5113000				53	
0.0610236	1.5500000			1.55		
0.0625000	1.5875000	1/16	1/16			
0.0629921	1.6000000			1.60		
0.0635000	1.6129000				52	
0.0640840	1.6277336					14
0.0649606	1.6500000			1.65		
0.0669291	1.7000000			1.70		
0.0670000	1.7018000				51	
0.0688976	1.7500000			1.75		
0.0700000	1.7780000				50	
0.0703125	1.7859375	9/128				
0.0708661	1.8000000			1.80		
0.0719620	1.8278348					13
0.0728346	1.8500000			1.85		
0.0730000	1.8542000				49	
0.0748031	1.9000000			1.90		
0.0760000	1.9304000				48	
0.0767717	1.9500000			1.95		
0.0781250	1.9843750	5/64	5/64			
0.0785000	1.9939000				47	
0.0787402	2.0000000			2.00		
0.0807087	2.0500000			2.05		
0.0808080	2.0525232					12
0.0810000	2.0574000				46	
0.0820000	2.0828000				45	
0.0826772	2.1000000			2.10		
0.0846457	2.1500000			2.15		
0.0859375	2.1828125	11/128				
0.0860000	2.1844000				44	
0.0866142	2.2000000			2.20		
0.0885827	2.2500000			2.25		
0.0890000	2.2606000				43	
0.0905512	2.3000000			2.30		
0.0907420	2.3048468					11
0.0925197	2.3500000			2.35		
0.0935000	2.3749000				42	
0.0937500	2.3812500	3/32	3/32			
0.0944882	2.4000000			2.40		
0.0960000	2.4384000				41	
0.0964567	2.4500000			2.45		
0.0980000	2.4892000				40	
0.0984252	2.5000000			2.50		
0.0995000	2.5273000				39	
0.1003937	2.5500000			2.55		

Inch	Millimeter	Fractional Inch	Typical Sizes in Drill Sets		Drill Number	Amer. Steel Wire Gauge
			inch	mm		
0.1015000	2.5781000				38	
0.1015625	2.5796875	13/128				
0.1018970	2.5881838					10
0.1023622	2.6000000			2.60		
0.1040000	2.6416000				37	
0.1043307	2.6500000			2.65		
0.1062992	2.7000000			2.70		
0.1065000	2.7051000				36	
0.1082677	2.7500000			2.75		
0.1093750	2.7781250	7/64	7/64			
0.1100000	2.7940000				35	
0.1102362	2.8000000			2.80		
0.1110000	2.8194000				34	
0.1122047	2.8500000			2.85		
0.1130000	2.8702000				33	
0.1141732	2.9000000			2.90		
0.1144230	2.9063442					9
0.1160000	2.9464000				32	
0.1161417	2.9500000			2.95		
0.1171875	2.9765625	15/128				
0.1181102	3.0000000			3.00		
0.1200000	3.0480000				31	
0.1200787	3.0500000			3.05		
0.1220472	3.1000000			3.10		
0.1240157	3.1500000			3.15		
0.1250000	3.1750000	1/8	1/8			
0.1259843	3.2000000			3.20		
0.1279528	3.2500000			3.25		
0.1284900	3.2636460					8
0.1285000	3.2639000				30	
0.1299213	3.3000000			3.30		
0.1318898	3.3500000			3.35		
0.1328125	3.3734375	17/128				
0.1338583	3.4000000			3.40		
0.1358268	3.4500000			3.45		
0.1360000	3.4544000				29	
0.1377953	3.5000000			3.50		
0.1397638	3.5500000			3.55		
0.1405000	3.5687000				28	
0.1406250	3.5718750	9/64	9/64			
0.1417323	3.6000000			3.60		
0.1440000	3.6576000				27	
0.1442850	3.6648390					7
0.1456693	3.7000000			3.70		
0.1470000	3.7338000				26	
0.1476378	3.7500000			3.75		
0.1484375	3.7703125	19/128				
0.1495000	3.7973000				25	

Inch	Millimeter	Fractional Inch	Typical Sizes in Drill Sets inch	mm	Drill Number	Amer. Steel Wire Gauge
0.1496063	3.8000000			3.80		
0.1515748	3.8500000			3.85		
0.1520000	3.8608000				24	
0.1535433	3.9000000			3.90		
0.1540000	3.9116000				23	
0.1555118	3.9500000			3.95		
0.1562500	3.9687500	5/32	5/32			
0.1570000	3.9878000				22	
0.1574803	4.0000000			4.00		
0.1590000	4.0386000				21	
0.1594488	4.0500000			4.05		
0.1610000	4.0894000				20	
0.1614173	4.1000000			4.10		
0.1620230	4.1153842					6
0.1633858	4.1500000			4.15		
0.1640625	4.1671875	21/128				
0.1653543	4.2000000			4.20		
0.1660000	4.2164000				19	
0.1673228	4.2500000			4.25		
0.1692913	4.3000000			4.30		
0.1695000	4.3053000				18	
0.1712598	4.3500000			4.35		
0.1718751	4.3656250	11/64	11/64			
0.1730000	4.3942000				17	
0.1732283	4.4000000			4.40		
0.1751969	4.4500000			4.45		
0.1770000	4.4958000				16	
0.1771654	4.5000000			4.50		
0.1791339	4.5500000			4.55		
0.1796875	4.5640625	23/128				
0.1800000	4.5720000				15	
0.1811024	4.6000000			4.60		
0.1819400	4.6212760					5
0.1820000	4.6228000				14	
0.1830709	4.6500000			4.65		
0.1850000	4.6990000				13	
0.1850394	4.7000000			4.70		
0.1870079	4.7500000			4.75		
0.1875000	4.7625000	3/16	3/16			
0.1889764	4.8000000			4.80		
0.1890000	4.8006000				12	
0.1909449	4.8500000			4.85		
0.1910000	4.8514000				11	
0.1929134	4.9000000			4.90		
0.1935000	4.9149000				10	
0.1948819	4.9500000			4.95		
0.1953125	4.9609375	25/128				
0.1960000	4.9784000				9	

			Twist Drill Sizes			
Inch	Millimeter	Fractional Inch	Typical Sizes in Drill Sets		Drill Number	Amer. Steel Wire Gauge
			inch	mm		
0.1968504	5.0000000			5.00		
0.1990000	5.0546000				8	
0.2007874	5.1000000			5.10		
0.2010000	5.1054000				7	
0.2031250	5.1593750	13/64	13/64			
0.2040000	5.1816000				6	
0.2043070	5.1893978					4
0.2047244	5.2000000			5.20		
0.2055000	5.2197000				5	
0.2066929	5.2500000			5.25		
0.2086614	5.3000000			5.30		
0.2090000	5.3086000				4	
0.2109375	5.3578125	27/128				
0.2125984	5.4000000			5.40		
0.2130000	5.4102000				3	
0.2165354	5.5000000			5.50		
0.2187500	5.5562500	7/32	7/32			
0.2204724	5.6000000			5.60		
0.2210000	5.6134000				2	
0.2244094	5.7000000			5.70		
0.2263780	5.7500000			5.75		
0.2265625	5.7546875	29/128				
0.2280000	5.7912000				1	
0.2283465	5.8000000			5.80		
0.2294230	5.8273442					3
0.2322835	5.9000000			5.90		
0.2340000	5.9436000				A	
0.2343750	5.9531250	15/64	15/64			
0.2362205	6.0000000			6.00		
0.2380000	6.0452000				B	
0.2401575	6.1000000			6.10		
0.2420000	6.1468000				C	
0.2421875	6.1515625	31/128				
0.2440945	6.2000000			6.20		
0.2460000	6.2484000				D	
0.2460630	6.2500000			6.25		
0.2480315	6.3000000			6.30		
0.2500000	6.3500000	1/4	1/4		E	
0.2519685	6.4000000			6.40		
0.2559055	6.5000000			6.50		
0.2570000	6.5278000				F	
0.2576270	6.5437258					2
0.2578125	6.5484375	33/128				
0.2598425	6.6000000			6.60		
0.2610000	6.6294000				G	
0.2637795	6.7000000			6.70		
0.2656250	6.7468750	17/64	17/64			
0.2657480	6.7500000			6.75		

			Twist Drill Sizes			
Inch	Millimeter	Fractional Inch	Typical Sizes in Drill Sets		Drill Number	Amer. Steel Wire Gauge
			inch	mm		
0.2660000	6.7564000				H	
0.2677165	6.8000000			6.80		
0.2716535	6.9000000			6.90		
0.2720000	6.9088000				I	
0.2734375	6.9453125	35/128				
0.2755906	7.0000000			7.00		
0.2770000	7.0358000				J	
0.2795276	7.1000000			7.10		
0.2810000	7.1374000				K	
0.2812500	7.1437500	9/32	9/32			
0.2834646	7.2000000			7.20		
0.2854331	7.2500000			7.25		
0.2874016	7.3000000			7.30		
0.2890625	7.3421875	37/128				
0.2892970	7.3481438					1
0.2900000	7.3660000				L	
0.2913386	7.4000000			7.40		
0.2950000	7.4930000				M	
0.2952756	7.5000000			7.50		
0.2968750	7.5406250	19/64	19/64			
0.2992126	7.6000000			7.60		
0.3020000	7.6708000				N	
0.3031496	7.7000000			7.70		
0.3046875	7.7390625	39/128				
0.3051181	7.7500000			7.75		
0.3070866	7.8000000			7.80		
0.3110236	7.9000000			7.90		
0.3125000	7.9375000	5/16	5/16			
0.3149606	8.0000000			8.00		
0.3160000	8.0264000				O	
0.3188976	8.1000000			8.10		
0.3203125	8.1359375	41/128				
0.3228346	8.2000000			8.20		
0.3230000	8.2042000				P	
0.3248031	8.2500000			8.25		
0.3248610	8.2514694					0
0.3267717	8.3000000			8.30		
0.3281250	8.3343750	21/64	21/64			
0.3307087	8.4000000			8.40		
0.3320000	8.4328000				Q	
0.3346457	8.5000000			8.50		
0.3359375	8.5328125	43/128				
0.3385827	8.6000000			8.60		
0.3390000	8.6106000				R	
0.3425197	8.7000000			8.70		
0.3437500	8.7312500	11/32	11/32			
0.3444882	8.7500000			8.75		
0.3464567	8.8000000			8.80		

| Inch | Millimeter | Fractional Inch | Twist Drill Sizes | | Drill Number | Amer. Steel Wire Gauge |
| | | | Typical Sizes in Drill Sets | | | |
			inch	mm		
0.3480000	8.8392000				S	
0.3503937	8.9000000			8.90		
0.3515625	8.9296875	45/128				
0.3543307	9.0000000			9.00		
0.3580000	9.0932000				T	
0.3582677	9.1000000			9.10		
0.3593750	9.1281250	23/64	23/64			
0.3622047	9.2000000			9.20		
0.3641732	9.2500000			9.25		
0.3647960	9.2658184					2/0
0.3661417	9.3000000			9.30		
0.3671875	9.3265625	47/128				
0.3680000	9.3472000				U	
0.3700787	9.4000000			9.40		
0.3740157	9.5000000			9.50		
0.3750000	9.5250000	3/8	3/8			
0.377000	9.5758000				V	
0.3779528	9.6000000			9.60		
0.3818898	9.7000000			9.70		
0.3828125	9.7234375	49/128				
0.3838583	9.7500000			9.75		
0.3858268	9.8000000			9.80		
0.3860000	9.8044000				W	
0.3897638	9.9000000			9.90		
0.3906250	9.9218750	25/64	25/64			
0.3937008	10.0000000			10.00		
0.3970000	10.0838000				X	
0.3976378	10.1000000			10.10		
0.3984375	10.1203125	51/128				
0.4015748	10.2000000			10.20		
0.4035433	10.2500000			10.25		
0.4040000	10.2616000				Y	
0.4055118	10.3000000			10.30		
0.4062500	10.3187500	13/32	13/32			
0.4094488	10.4000000			10.40		
0.4096420	10.4049068					3/0
0.4130000	10.4902000				Z	
0.4133858	10.5000000			10.50		
0.4140625	10.5171875	53/128				
0.4173228	10.6000000			10.60		
0.4212598	10.7000000			10.70		
0.4218750	10.7156250	27/64	27/64			
0.4232283	10.7500000			10.75		
0.4251969	10.8000000			10.80		
0.4291339	10.9000000			10.90		
0.4296875	10.9140625	55/128				
0.4330709	11.0000000			11.00		
0.4370079	11.1000000			11.10		

Inch	Millimeter	Fractional Inch	Typical Sizes in Drill Sets (inch)	(mm)	Drill Number	Amer. Steel Wire Gauge
			Twist Drill Sizes			
0.4375000	11.1125000	7/16	7/16			
0.4409449	11.2000000			11.20		
0.4429134	11.2500000			11.25		
0.4448819	11.3000000			11.30		
0.4453125	11.3109375	57/128				
0.4488189	11.4000000			11.40		
0.4527559	11.5000000			11.50		
0.4531250	11.5093750	29/64	29/64			
0.4566929	11.6000000			11.60		
0.4600000	11.6840000					4/0
0.4606299	11.7000000			11.70		
0.4609375	11.7078125	59/128				
0.4625984	11.7500000			11.75		
0.4645669	11.8000000			11.80		
0.4650000	11.8110000					
0.4685039	11.9000000			11.90		
0.4687500	11.9062500	15/32	15/32			
0.4724409	12.0000000			12.00		
0.4763780	12.1000000			12.10		
0.4765625	12.1046875	61/128				
0.4803150	12.2000000			12.20		
0.4822835	12.2500000			12.25		
0.4842520	12.3000000			12.30		
0.4843750	12.3031250	31/64	31/64			
0.4881890	12.4000000			12.40		
0.4921260	12.5000000			12.50		
0.4921875	12.5015625	63/128				
0.4960630	12.6000000			12.60		
0.5000000	12.7000000	1/2	1/2	12.70		
0.5019685	12.7500000			12.75		
0.5039370	12.8000000			12.80		
0.5078125	12.8984375	65/128				
0.5078740	12.9000000			12.90		
0.5118110	13.0000000			13.00		
0.5156250	13.0968750	33/64	33/64			
0.5157480	13.1000000			13.10		
0.5165000	13.1191000					5/0
0.5196850	13.2000000			13.20		
0.5216535	13.2500000			13.25		
0.5234375	13.2953125	67/128				
0.5236220	13.3000000			13.30		
0.5275591	13.4000000			13.40		
0.5312500	13.4937500	17/32	17/32			
0.5314961	13.5000000			13.50		
0.5354331	13.6000000			13.60		
0.5390625	13.6921875	69/128				
0.5393701	13.7000000			13.70		
0.5413386	13.7500000			13.75		

Inch	Millimeter	Fractional Inch	Twist Drill Sizes		Drill Number	Amer. Steel Wire Gauge
			Typical Sizes in Drill Sets			
			inch	mm		
0.5433071	13.8000000			13.80		
0.5468750	13.8906250	35/64	35/64			
0.5472441	13.9000000			13.90		
0.5511811	14.0000000			14.00		
0.5546875	14.0890625	71/128				
0.5610236	14.2500000			14.25		
0.5625000	14.2875000	9/16	9/16			
0.5703125	14.4859375	73/128				
0.5708661	14.5000000			14.50		
0.5781250	14.6843750	37/64	37/64			
0.5800000	14.7320000					6/0
0.5807087	14.7500000			14.75		
0.5859375	14.8828125	75/128				
0.5905512	15.0000000			15.00		
0.5937500	15.0812500	19/32	19/32			
0.6003937	15.2500000			15.25		
0.6015625	15.2796875	77/128				
0.6093750	15.4781250	39/64	39/64			
0.6102362	15.5000000			15.50		
0.6171875	15.6765625	79/128				
0.6200787	15.7500000			15.75		
0.6250000	15.8750000	5/8	5/8			
0.6299213	16.0000000			16.00		
0.6328125	16.0734375	81/128				
0.6397638	16.2500000			16.25		
0.6406250	16.2718750	41/64	41/64			
0.6484375	16.4703125	83/128				
0.6496063	16.5000000			16.50		
0.6562500	16.6687500	21/32	21/32			
0.6594488	16.7500000			16.75		
0.6640625	16.8671875	85/128				
0.6692913	17.0000000			17.00		
0.6718750	17.0656250	43/64	43/64			
0.6791339	17.2500000			17.25		
0.6796875	17.2640625	87/128				
0.6875000	17.4625000	11/16	11/16			
0.6889764	17.5000000			17.50		
0.6953125	17.6609375	89/128				
0.7031250	17.8593750	45/64	45/64			
0.7086614	18.0000000			18.00		
0.7109375	18.0578125	91/128				
0.7187500	18.2562500	23/32	23/32			
0.7265625	18.4546875	93/128				
0.7283465	18.5000000			18.50		
0.7343750	18.6531250	47/64	47/64			
0.7421875	18.8515625	95/128				
0.7480315	19.0000000			19.00		

Inch	Millimeter	Fractional Inch	Typical Sizes in Drill Sets		Drill Number	Amer. Steel Wire Gauge
			inch	mm		
0.7500000	19.0500000	3/4	3/4			
0.7578125	19.2484375	97/128				
0.7656250	19.4468750	49/64	49/64			
0.7677165	19.5000000			19.50		
0.7734375	19.6453125	99/128				
0.7812500	19.8437500	25/32	25/32			
0.7874016	20.0000000			20.00		
0.7890625	20.0421875	101/128				
0.7968750	20.2406250	51/64	51/64			
0.8046875	20.4390625	103/128				
0.8125000	20.6375000	13/16	13/16			
0.8203125	20.8359375	105/128				
0.8267717	21.0000000			21.00		
0.8281250	21.0343750	53/64	53/64			
0.8359375	21.2328125	107/128				
0.8437500	21.4312500	27/32	27/32			
0.8515625	21.6296875	109/128				
0.8593750	21.8281250	55/64	55/64			
0.8661417	22.0000000			22.00		
0.8671875	22.0265625	111/128				
0.8750000	22.2250000	7/8	7/8			
0.8828125	22.4234375	113/128				
0.8906250	22.6218750	57/64	57/64			
0.8984375	22.8203125	115/128				
0.9055118	23.0000000			23.00		
0.9062500	23.0187500	29/32	29/32			
0.9140625	23.2171875	117/128				
0.9218750	23.4156250	59/64	59/64			
0.9296875	23.6140625	119/128				
0.9375000	23.8125000	15/16	15/16			
0.9448819	24.0000000			24.00		
0.9453125	24.0109375	121/128				
0.9531250	24.2093750	61/64	61/64			
0.9609375	24.4078125	123/128				
0.9687500	24.6062500	31/32	31/32			
0.9765625	24.8046875	125/128				
0.9842520	25.0000000			25.00		
0.9843750	25.0031250	63/64	63/64			
0.9921875	25.2015625	127/128				
1.0000000	25.4000000	1	1			

Drill and Cutting Lubricants

Material to be Worked	Machine Process		
	Drilling	Threading	Lathe
Aluminum	Soluble oil Kerosene Lard oil	Soluble oil, Kerosene, & Lard oil	Soluble oil
Brass	Dry Soluble oil Kerosene Lard Oil	Soluble oil Lard oil	Soluble oil
Bronze	Dry Soluble oil Mineral oil Lard oil	Soluble oil Lard oil	Soluble oil
Cast Iron	Dry Air jet Soluble oil	Dry Sulphurized oil Mineral lard oil	Dry Soluble oil
Copper	Dry Soluble oil Mineral lard oil Kerosene	Soluble oil Lard oil	Soluble
Malleable Iron	Dry Soda water	Lard oil Soda water	Soluble oil Soda water
Monel metal	Soluble oil Lard oil	Lard oil	Soluble oil
Steel alloys	Soluble oil Sulphurized oil Mineral lard oil	Sulphurized oil Lard oil	Soluble oil
Steel, machine	Soluble oil Sulphurized oil Lard oil Mineral lard oil	Soluble oil Mineral lard oil	Soluble oil
Steel, tool	Soluble oil Sulphurized oil Mineral lard oil	Sulphurized oil Lard oil	Soluble oil

The above table of cutting fluids is courtesy of Cincinnati Milacron.

Drill Speeds vs. Materials

Material	Speed rpm	Description
Cast Iron	6000 to 6500	1/16 inch drill
	3500 to 4500	1/8 inch drill
	2500 to 3000	3/16 inch drill
	2000 to 2500	1/4 inch drill
	1500 to 2000	5/16 inch drill
	1500 to 2000	3/8 inch drill
	1000 to 1500	> 7/16 inch drill
Glass	700	Special metal tube drilling
Plastics	6000 to 6500	1/16 inch drill
	5000 to 6000	1/8 inch drill
	3500 to 4000	3/16 inch drill
	3000 to 3500	1/4 inch drill
	2000 to 2500	5/16 inch drill
	1500 to 2000	3/8 inch drill
	500 to 1000	> 7/16 inch drill
Soft Metals	6000 to 6500	1/16 inch drill
(copper)	6000 to 6500	1/8 inch drill
	5000 to 6000	3/16 inch drill
	4500 to 5000	1/4 inch drill
	3500 to 4000	5/16 inch drill
	3000 to 3500	3/8 inch drill
	1500 to 2500	> 7/16 inch drill
Steel	5000 to 6500	1/16 inch drill
	3000 to 4000	1/8 inch drill
	2000 to 2500	3/16 inch drill
	1500 to 2000	1/4 inch drill
	1000 to 1500	5/16 inch drill
	1000 to 1500	3/8 inch drill
	500 to 1000	> 7/16 inch drill
Wood	4000 to 6000	Carving and routing
	3800 to 4000	All woods, 0 to 1/4 inch drills
	3100 to 3800	All woods, 1/4 to 1/2 inch drills
	2300 to 3100	All woods, 1/2 to 3/4 inch drills
	2000 to 2300	All woods, 3/4 to 1 inch drills
	700 to 2000	All woods, >1 inch drills, fly cutters,
	< 700	and multi–spur bits

If in doubt about what speed to use, always select the slower speeds. Speeds for drill sizes not listed above can be estimated by looking at speeds for sizes one step over and one step under.

American Standard Taper Pipe

Pipe Size inch	Threads per inch	Pipe Diameter inch	Tap Drill
1/8	27	0.405	R
1/4	18	0.540	7/16
3/8	18	0.675	37/64
1/2	14	0.840	23/32
3/4	14	1.050	59/64
1	11.5	1.315	1-5/32
1-1/4	11.5	1.660	1-1/2
1-1/2	11.5	1.900	1-47/64
2	11.5	2.375	2-7/32
2-1/2	8	2.875	2-5/8
3	8	3.500	3-1/4
3-1/2	8	4.000	3-3/4
4	8	4.500	4-1/4
4-1/2	8	5.000	4-3/4
5	8	5.563	5-9/32
6	8	6.625	6-11/32
7	8	7.625	...
8	8	8.625	...
9	8	9.625	...
10	8	10.750	...
12	8	12.750	...
>14 OD	8	Same as Col 1	...

American Standard Straight Pipe

Pipe Size inch	Threads per inch	Pipe Diameter inch	Tap Drill
1/8	27	0.405	S
1/4	18	0.540	29/64
3/8	18	0.675	19/32
1/2	14	0.840	47/64
3/4	14	1.050	15/16
1	11.5	1.315	1-3/16
1-1/4	11.5	1.660	1-33/64
1-1/2	11.5	1.900	1-3/4
2	11.5	2.375	2-7/32
2-1/2	8	2.875	2-21/32
3	8	3.500	3-9/32
3-1/2	8	4.000	3-25/32
4	8	4.500	4-9/32
4-1/2	8	5.000	4-25/32
5	8	5.563	5-11/32
6	8	6.625	6-13/32

Fire Extinguishers

Fire extinguishers are an absolute must in any shop, garage, home, automobile, or business. Fire extinguishers are classified by the types of fires they will put out and the size of the fire they will put out. The basic types are as follows:

TYPE A: For wood, cloth, paper, trash and other common materials. These fires are put out by "heat absorbing" water or water based materials or smothered by dry chemicals.

TYPE B: For oil, gasoline, grease, paints & other flammable liquids. These fires are put out by smothering, preventing the release of combustible vapors, or stopping the combustion chain. Use Halon, dry chemicals, carbon dioxide, or foam.

TYPE C: For "live" electrical equipment. These fires are put out by the same process as TYPE B, but the extinguishing material <u>must be electrically non-conductive</u>. Use halon, dry chemicals, or carbon dioxide.

TYPE D: For combustible metals such as magnesium. These fires must be put out by heat absorption and smothering. Obtain specific information on these requirements from the fire department.

Combinations of the above letters indicate the extinguisher will put out more than one type of fire. For example, a Type ABC unit will put out all three types of fires. The "size" of the fire an extinguisher will put out is shown by a number in front of the Type, such as "10B". The base line numbers are as follows:

Class "1A": Will put out a stack of 50 burning sticks that are 20 inches long each.

Class "1B": Will put out an area of burning naptha that is 2.5 square feet in size.

Any number other than the "1" simply indicates the extinguisher will put out a fire that many times larger, for example "10A" will put out a fire 10 times larger than "1A".

Some general recommendations when purchasing a fire extinguisher are as follows:

1. Buy TYPE ABC so that you never have to think about what type of fire you are using it on.

2. For electronic equipment buy an inert gas extinguisher-no equipment damage, less mess. Until 1993, Halon was the gas of choice. Due to EPA regulations, Halon has been replaced with products such as Halotron-I, Inergen, Dupont FE-36, and FM-200. Carbon dioxide can also be used and is less expensive than the other inert gasses.

3. Relative costs of ABC extinguishers are:
   FOAM - very expensive-special use, i.e., aircraft fires
   INERT GAS - very expensive-leaves no mess
   CARBON DIOXIDE- expensive-leaves no mess
   DRY CHEMICAL- inexpensive-leaves a mess.

4. Buy units with metal components and a gauge and are approved by Underwriters Labs or other testing group. Plastic units are generally poorly constructed and break easily; buy good extinguishers - your life and property may depend on it !

5. Buy more than one extinguisher and mount them on the wall near escape routes so that children can reach them.

6. Study the instructions when you get the unit, there may not be time after a fire has started.

Sandpaper and Abrasives

Grit Current System	Grit Old System	Word Description	Use
12	4-1/2	Very Coarse	Very rough work,
16	4	Very Coarse	usually requires
20	3-1/2	Very Coarse	high speed, heavy
24	3	Very Coarse	machines. For
30	2-1/2	Coarse	unplaned woods,
36	2	Coarse	wood floors, rough cut.
40	1-1/2	Coarse	Rough wood work,
50	1	Coarse	#1 is coarsest for
60	1/2	Medium	use with pad sander.
80	1/0	Medium	General wood work,
100	2/0	Medium	plaster patches, 1st
120	3/0	Fine	smooth of old paint.
150	4/0	Fine	Hardwood prep, final for
180	5/0	Fine	softwoods, old paint.
220	6/0	Very Fine	Final sanding or between
240	7/0	Very Fine	coats, won't show sand
280	8/0	Very Fine	marks, dry sanding.
320	9/0	Extra Fine	Polish final coats, between
360		Extra Fine	coats, wet sand paints
400	10/0	Extra Fine	& varnishes, top coats.
500		Super Fine	Sand metal, plastic, &
600		Super Fine	ceramics, wet sanding.

Coating Types

Open coat: Grains cover 50% to 70% of the backing, which leaves a lot of space between each grain. The open space is necessary in applications where the material being sanded has a tendency to clog up or "load" the abrasive surface. The clogging drastically reduces the cutting ability of the abrasive and reduces the life of the abrasive. Less common than Closed coat.

Closed coat: Grains cover all of the backing. This type is much more efficient (removes material faster) than Open coat since there are more abrasion grains per square inch. Closed coat is the preferred coating type as long as grain clogging is not a problem.

Glue Types

Glues are generally restricted to a combination of "Hide" glues and resin based glues, depending on the application. Glues are usually applied as a two part process, the base coat and the top grain holding coat.

Backing Types

Paper: Weights range from "A" through "F". "A" is the most flexible and is used mainly for finishing jobs and with small grain-size abrasives. "A" is primarily used for hand sanding. "C" and "D" weights are stronger, less flexible, and used for both hand sanding and power sanders. "E" is much stronger, very tear resistant and much less flexible than "C" and "D" and is used mainly in belt and disc applications. "F" is the strongest paper and is used mainly for rolls and belts.

Cloth: Weights are "J" (jeans) and "X" (drills). "J" is used for finishing and polishing operations, particularly where contours are involved. "X" is less flexible than "J" but is stronger. "X" is used for heavy belt, disk and drum grinding and polishing.

Fiber: Composed of multiple layers of paper that has been chemically treated. These backings are very tough, heat resistant and used mostly for drum and disc applications, particularly high speed.

Combination: Composed of both paper and cloth or cloth and fiber, producing a very strong, flexible, non-stretching, and tear resistant backing. They are used mostly in high speed, drum sanding applications.

Abrasive Types

Silicon Carbide: The hardest and sharpest of all abrasives, but is more brittle than aluminum oxide. Color is blue–black and it is a manufactured abrasive. Typically used in applications such as finishing of soft metals, glass, ceramics, hard wood floors and plastics. It is very fast cutting and is therefore good for both material removal as well as polishing. This abrasive is very popular for sanding lacquered and enameled surfaces such as car paints. Durite by Norton is a common brand name. Grain sizes normally range from 600 to 12.

Aluminum Oxide: Extremely tough, grit is very sharp and much harder than flint, garnet and emery. Color is red to brown and it is a manufactured abrasive. More expensive than most other types but its toughness results in a longer lasting abrasive so its cost is actually equivalent. Recommended for metals and hard woods and is the preferred choice for power sanding. Norton brand names – Adalox or Metalite. Grain sizes normally range from 500 to 16.

Garnet: Much softer than the synthetic abrasives listed above but harder and sharper than flint. Garnet is a crushed natural mineral, red to brown in color. Used mainly in furniture finishing and woodworking. Yields an excellent wood finish. Grain sizes normally range from 280 to 220.

Flint: Generally poor cutting strength and durability so it is not used in production environments. Used in the leather industry and as a good non–clogging abrasive in paint removal and some woodwork. Flint is gray to white colored natural quartz mineral. Flint is non–conductive and therefore is also useful as an abrasive in the electronics industry. Inexpensive. Grain sizes normally range from 4/0 to 3.

Emery: Good polishing features but poor for material removal. Grains are round and black in color. Poor penetration but good for polishing metals. Poor for wood use. Grain sizes normally range from 3/0 to 3.

Crocus: Soft and short lived. Made of ferrous oxide (red color). Good for polishing, particularly soft metals like gold.

Pumice: Powdered volcanic glass that is commonly used to tone down a glossy finish to a satin, smooth surface. Grades range from 4–F (the finest) through #7 (the coarsest). Frequent inspections of the work surface should be made in order to prevent breaking through the surface.

Cork: Cork is sometimes used as a wet polishing medium.

Rottenstone: Also referred to as diatomaceous earth. It is much softer and finer grained than pumice and is used in combination with water, solvents, or oils to produce a satin finish on woods.

Rubbing Compounds: Sometimes also referred to as "rouge." Normally used as a polish for enamel and lacquer paints. It is not for use on bare woods.

Steel Wool: Although not technically an abrasive, it is commonly used to remove rust or old finishes, and to smooth rough surfaces. Sizes range from 4/0 (the finest) through #5 (the coarsest). With steel wool, it is important to rub the wood in the direction of the grain, not across it, so that the surface is not scratched.

Some of the above abrasive data is courtesy of Norton, Coated Abrasives Division, Troy, New York.

Saws

Chain Saw Classification

Chain saws can be broadly grouped into the following four categories, based on ruggedness and size:

1. Mini-saw: Light weight (6 to 9 pounds), small engine size (1.8 to 2.5 cubic inches or electric), and short bar lengths (8 to 12 inches, 1/4 inch pitch). Good for <3 cords per year.

2. Light-Duty: Light weight (9 to 13 pounds), small engine size (2.5 to 3.8 cubic inches or electric), and medium bar lengths (14 to 16 inches, 3/8 inch pitch). Good for 3 to 6 cords per year.

3. Medium-Duty: Medium weight (13 to 18 pounds), medium engine size (3.5 to 4.8 cubic inches), and medium-long bar lengths (16 to 24 inches, 3/8 to 0.404 inch pitch). Good for 6 to 10 cords per year. If money permits, this class of saw is probably the best choice for the average wood cutter, even if he does not cut the 6 to 10 cords per year. It is heavy duty enough to last a long time under light use. It is heavy duty enough to last a long time under light use.

4. Heavy-Duty: Heavy weight (over 18 pounds), large engine size (over 4.8 cubic inches), and long bar lengths (over 24 inches, 0.404 to 1/2 inch pitch). These heavy duty units are generally for the professional. They are heavy, expensive, and require more strength to use. They can be used continuously.

Depth Capacity of Std Circular Power Handsaws

Blade Diameter	Capacity @ 90°	Capacity @ 45°
4-1/2	1-5/16	1-1/16 to 1-1/14
6-1/2	2-1/16	1-5/8
6-3/4	2-7/32	1-3/4
7-1/4	2-3/8 to 2-7/16	1-7/8 to 1-29/32
7-1/2	2-17/22	2-1/16
8-1/4	2-15/16	2-1/4
10-1/4	3-5/8	2-3/4
12	4-3/8	3-5/16

Circular Powered Handsaws

Abrasive Wheel

Abrasive blade made of aluminum oxide (metal cutting) or silicon carbide (masonry cutting). Comes in standard sizes of 6, 7, and 8 inch diameter and with 1/2 or 5/8 diameter arbor. No teeth. Also called a cut-off wheel.

Combination Blade

Quiet, accurate and leaves a very smooth finish. Designed especially for crosscuts and miters across wood grain. Acceptable for ripping, but it's not as fast as ripping blades. Hollow ground combination blades minimize chipping.

Ripping Blade

These blades have large, set teeth with deep gullets. Designed especially for cutting fast in the direction of the wood grain. Minimum binding of blade. Very rough finish.

Chisel–Tooth Combination Blade

General purpose, settooth blade. Good for both ripping and crosscuts and it cuts fast, but leaves a rough cut. This is the blade most commonly used by contractors. Bevel–ground, carbide–tipped blades of the same basic design are among the most durable of the blades.

Crosscut, Fine–Tooth, and Paneling Blades

All of these blades have a large number of small teeth that are very sharp. Crosscut has the fewest teeth, fine–tooth has more and paneling has the most. Crosscut, as the name implies, was designed for cutting across the wood grain and leaving a smooth edge. It is also good for plywood. Fine–tooth blades are also good for plywood, but are also used on fiber boards (Celotex), veneers, and thin plastics. Paneling blades have many, extra fine teeth. It is particularly useful in cutting paneling and laminates since the cut edge usually does not have to be touched up.

Flattop–Ground Carbide Tipped Blade

A fast cutting, long lasting blade used as a combination blade in construction. Good for ripping, crosscutting and mitering but does not leave a good smooth edge.

Steel Cutting Blade

An unusual blade design that is used to cut ferrous (iron and steel) sheetmetal that is up to 3/32 inch thick. This blade actually "burns" its way through the metal, leaving a clean edge.

Saber Saw Blades

Teeth per inch	Blade Usage
3	Lumber up to 6 inches thick, fast cutting, very rough cut, good ripping blade.
5 or 6	Lumber up to 2 inches thick, fast cutting, rough cut, good ripping blade.
7 or 8	Best general purpose blade, relatively smooth cut. Good for lumber and fiber insulation board.
10	Good general purpose blade, smoother cut than the 7 or 8 blade. Use 10 through 14 for cutting hardwoods under 1/2 inch thick and for plastics, composition board, drywall, and plywood when a smooth edge is needed. If hard, abrasive materials are to be cut, such as laminates, use the metal cutting H.S.S. types. Good for some scrollwork.
12 or 14	Very smooth cutting blade but is also very slow cutting. Good for hardwoods, plywood, fiberglass, plastics, rubber, linoleum, laminates, and plexiglass. As with the 10 tpi blades, if the material is particularly hard or abrasive, use the metal cutting H.S.S. types instead.
Knife	These blades have either a knife edge or a sharp edge with an abrasive grit bonded to the blade. No grit blades are useful for cutting rubber, cork, leather, cardboard, styrofoam, & silicones. Grit blades come in fine, medium and coarse and can be used on fiberglass, epoxies, ceramic tile, stone, clay pipe, brick, steel, & veneer

H.S.S. METAL CUTTING BLADES

6 to 10	Rough cutting for aluminum, brass, copper, laminates, hardwoods and other soft materials. Good up to 1/2 inch thickness.
14	Cuts same materials as 6 to 10 tpi plus mild steels and hardboards. Leaves a much smoother edge. Thickness should be 1/4 to 1/2 inch maximum.
18	Same as 14 tpi but maximum thickness 1/8 inch.
24	Smooth edge cutting for steel and sheet metal. Also good for other hard materials such as plastics, tile, and Bakelite. Maximum thickness should be 1/8 inch.
32	Very fine cuts for steel and thin wall tubing up to 1/16 inch thick.

Drive Styles

Torx ©
external
(6-lobe)

Torx ©
internal
(6-lobe)

Torx - internal
Tamper proof
pin (6-lobe)

Frearson

Clutch

Fluted Socket
4 flutes

Fluted Socket
6 flutes

MorTorq ©

Tri-Wing ©

Square
Socket
(Robertson)

Hex Socket
Allen Head
Internal

Hexagon
External

Hexagon
Internal
Tamper proof

Slotted 6
Lobe Combo

Quadrex ©

Phillips ©

Phillips II ©

Phillips/Slot
Combination
(Combo)

Pozi Drive ©
Phillips 1a

Phillips
Square
Supa Drive©

Slotted

Square Slot
Combination

Slotted
Tamper Proof
(One Way)

Spanner
Drilled
Tamper Proof

Spanner
Slotted
Tamper Proof

Phillips ©
Hex Head

5 Node
Security

7 Node
Security

Water and Air

Air Line Pipe Size Recommendations 632

Compressed Air Requirements for Common Tools
and Equipment 633

Air Discharge from Orifices 641

Hose Tables Introduction 646

Air Discharge through 100 Feet of Hose 647

Pressure Loss Due to Friction in 100 Feet of Air Hose 647

Water Discharge through 100 Feet of hose 649

Pressure Loss Due to Friction in 100 Feet of Water Hose 651

Theoretical Discharge from Nozzles for Water............................653

Water Hardness 657

Water Data and Formulas 658

Boiling Point of Water at Various Altitudes................................659

Vapor Pressure of Water...661

Horizontal Pipe Discharge 669

Vertical Pipe Discharge 670

Weir Discharge Volumes...670

Air Line Pipe, Recommended Sizes

Values in the table are nominal pipe sizes for schedule 40 steel pipe.

Free Air Flow Rate		Length of Pipe, feet							
(cfs)	(cfm)	25	50	75	100	150	200	250	300
0.0833	5	1/2	1/2	1/2	1/2	1/2	1/2	1/2	1/2
0.1667	10	1/2	1/2	1/2	1/2	1/2	1/2	1/2	3/4
0.2500	15	1/2	1/2	1/2	1/2	3/4	3/4	3/4	3/4
0.3333	20	1/2	1/2	3/4	3/4	3/4	3/4	3/4	3/4
0.4167	25	1/2	3/4	3/4	3/4	3/4	3/4	1	1
0.5000	30	1/2	3/4	3/4	3/4	1	1	1	1
0.5833	35	3/4	3/4	3/4	3/4	1	1	1	1
0.6667	40	3/4	3/4	3/4	1	1	1	1	1-1/4
0.7500	45	3/4	3/4	1	1	1	1	1-1/4	1-1/4
0.8333	50	3/4	1	1	1	1	1-1/4	1-1/4	1-1/4
0.9167	55	3/4	1	1	1	1-1/4	1-1/4	1-1/4	1-1/4
1.000	60	3/4	1	1	1	1-1/4	1-1/4	1-1/4	1-1/4
1.083	65	3/4	1	1	1	1-1/4	1-1/4	1-1/4	1-1/4
1.167	70	3/4	1	1	1-1/4	1-1/4	1-1/4	1-1/4	1-1/4
1.250	75	1	1	1	1-1/4	1-1/4	1-1/4	1-1/4	1-1/4
1.333	80	1	1	1-1/4	1-1/4	1-1/4	1-1/4	1-1/4	1-1/4
1.417	85	1	1	1-1/4	1-1/4	1-1/4	1-1/4	1-1/4	1-1/2
1.500	90	1	1	1-1/4	1-1/4	1-1/4	1-1/4	1-1/2	1-1/2
1.583	95	1	1-1/4	1-1/4	1-1/4	1-1/4	1-1/4	1-1/2	1-1/2
1.667	100	1	1-1/4	1-1/4	1-1/4	1-1/4	1-1/2	1-1/2	1-1/2

NOTES:
1. Values in the table are approximations.
2. Values in the table were determined using the Harris Equation for pressure drop in pipe carrying compressed air.

The equation is: $Pf = (k \, L \, q^2)/(r \, d^{5.31})$, where:

Pf is the pressure drop in pounds-force per square inch (psi).

k is an experimental constant which varies from 0.10 to 0.15 depending on pipe diameter. An average value often used is k = 0.1025.

L is the pipe length in feet.

q is the flow rate in cubic feet of free air per second (cfs).

r is the ratio of compression (from free air) at the pipe entrance = [(pressure + 14.7)/ 14.7].

d is the internal pipe diameter in inches.

The following conditions were used to develop the values shown in the table:
- The system is operating at a pressure of 100 psi resulting in a compression ration (r) of 7.803.
- The maximum pressure drop allowed is 1 psi per 100 feet of pipe; for example, in a 50-foot length of pipe, the maximum pressure drop is 0.50 psi.
- A factor of safety of 5 has been applied to the average experimental constant of k = 0.1025.
- The factored constant is k = 0.0205.

3. Similar tables based on the Harris equation have been presented in a variety of different publications some of which include:
   Buying Guide and Technical Handbook, Compressed Air Systems, Hagerstown, MD.
   Fluid Power Data Book, 9th Edition, Womack Educational Publications, Dallas, TX.
   Grainger Catalog, W.W. Grainger, Inc.
Keep in mind that some tables may use factors of safety other than 5.

4. Abbreviations used include:
   cfm = cubic feet per minute
   cfs = cubic feet per second
   psi = pound-force per square inch

Compressed Air Requirements for Common Tools and Equipment

Tool or Equipment	Type	Size	Average Free Air Consumption (cfm)	Range of Air Pressures (psi)
Air arbor			5	80
Air bushing		small or large	20	80 - 90
Air filter cleaner			3	70 - 100
Air hammer		light	4	90 - 100
		heavy	22	70 - 90
Air motor		0.5 hp	16	80
		1 hp	20	80 - 100
		2 hp	38	80 - 100
		3 hp	55	80 - 100
		4 hp	120	80
		5 hp	150	80
		7 hp	175	80
Auger drill	for coal		74	80
Backfill tamper		light, 25 lb and under	25	- - -
		medium, 26 to 35 lb	35	- - -
		heavy, 36 lb and over	80	- - -
Bath enameller			8	80
Bead breaker			12	125 - 150
Blow gun			3	70 - 90
Body polisher			2	70 - 100
Body sander	orbital		5	70 - 100
Brake tester			4	70 - 100
Brick-masonry drill	utility	10 to 25 lb	35	- - -
Brick-masonry drill	plug	10 to 25 lb	30	- - -
Burr machine			18	90
Burring tool		small	4	70 - 100
		large	6	70 - 100

Tool or Equipment	Type	Size	Average Free Air Consumption (cfm)	Range of Air Pressures (psi)
Bus lift		8,000 lb cap.	6	70 - 90
Bushing tool	monu-ment		20	90
Car lift			6	145 - 175
Carving tool	monu-ment		10	70 - 100
Caulking hammer		light	13	80
		medium	15	80
		heavy	22	80
Cement gun		small	100	80
		medium	160	80
Chain saw		lightweight	15	70 - 100
		heavy duty	27	70 - 100
Chipping hammer		light, 2- 4 lb	10	70 - 100
		medium, 10-13 lb	24	70 - 90
		heavy, 13 lb and over	30	70 - 90
Coal cutter	longwall	50 hp	800	80
	percus-sive	2-1/2 in	98	80
		3-1/2 in	144	80
		4 in	180	80
Compression riveter			1	90 - 100
Concrete breaker		30 lb	40	80
		50 lb	50	80
		75-80 lb	70	80
Concrete compactor			8	80
Concrete vibrator		light	35	- - -
		medium	80	- - -
Die grinder		small	5	70 - 100
		medium	6	70 - 100
		large	7	70 - 100
Differential flusher			3	70 - 100
Drifter drill	cradle mount	3 in	155	80
		3-1/2 in	180	80
		4 in	240	80
Drill	piston motor	1/2 to 3/4 in, 13 to 15 lb	45	70 - 90
		7/8 to 1-1/4 in, 25 to 30 lb	78	70 - 90
		1-1/4 to 2 in, 40 to 50 lb	85	70 - 90
		2 to 3 in, 55 to 75 lb	105	70 - 90
	rotary motor	to 1/4 in, 1-1/2 - 4 lb	19	70 - 90
		1/4 to 3/8 in, 6 to 8 lb	30	70 - 90

Tool or Equipment	Type	Size	Average Free Air Consumption (cfm)	Range of Air Pressures (psi)
Drill (cont.)	Rotary Motor	1/2 to 3/4 in, 9 to 14 lb	70	70 - 90
		7/8-1 in, 25 lb	80	70 - 90
		1-1/4 in, 30 lb	95	70 - 90
Drill sharpener		small	50	80
		large	120	80
Drilling machine		1/4 in. holes in steel	13	80
		3/8 in. holes in steel	25	80
		1/2- 3/4 in. holes in steel	30	80
		7/8-1 in. holes in steel	60	80
		1-1/4 in. holes in steel	48	80
		1-1/2 in. holes in steel	90	80
		2 in. holes in steel	100	80
		3 in. holes in steel	115	80
Dusting blow gun			4	70 - 100
Dusting gun			3	90 - 100
Dustless dry drill		3 in.	120	80
		3-1/2 in.	180	80
Fender hammer			15	70 - 100
File machine			18	90
File tool			18	70 - 90
Filing machine		small	3	90 - 100
		large	5	90 - 100
Forging hammer		100 lb	60	80
		300 lb	130	80
		1,000 lb	320	80
		2,000 lb	540	80
Grease gun	high pressure		3	70 - 90
			4	120 - 150
Grinder		1/2 to 3/4 inch	15	80
		2 and 2-1/2 in	19	80 - 90
		4 in.	48	80
		6 in.	58	80
		8 in.	78	80
		W" wheel	50	70 - 90
		Z" wheel	20	70 - 90
		1-1/2 inch and under	10	70 - 90
		2 to 2-1/2 inch	11	70 - 100

Tool or Equipment	Type	Size	Average Free Air Consumption (cfm)	Range of Air Pressures (psi)
Grinder (cont.)	Horizontal	4 inch	12	70 - 100
		6 inch	13	70 - 100
		8 inch	17	70 - 100
	pedestal	8 by 1-1/4 inch	45	80
	vertical	5 inch	10	70 - 100
		7 inch	15	70 - 100
		9 inch	20	70 - 100
		small	22	70 - 90
		medium	30	70 - 90
		large	53	70 - 90
Hand hammer drill		28 lb	50	80
		35 lb	60	80
		45 lb	80	80
		60 lb	150	80
Hoist	air motor	1,000 lb or less	1	70 - 90
		1,001-10,000 lb	5	70 - 90
		10,001 or more	15	70 - 90
Hoist	cylinder		2	90 - 100
Hydraulic floor jack			6	125 - 150
Hydraulic lift		8,000 lb capacity	6	145 - 175
		10,000 lb capacity	7	145 - 175
		12,000 lb capacity	9	145 - 175
		14,000 lb capacity	10	145 - 175
		16,000 lb capacity	11	145 - 175
Impact wrench		1/4 inch	4	70 - 100
		3/8 inch	5	70 - 100
		3/8 inch	8	125 - 150
		1/2 inch	8	70 - 100
		1/2 inch	4	125 - 150
		3/4 inch	9	70 - 100
		3/4 inch	8	125 - 150
		5/8 inch	5	90 - 150
		1 inch	10	90 - 150
		1-1/4 inch	14	70 - 100
		2 to 3 inch	55	70 - 90
		3 to 12 inch	100	70 - 90
Internal vibrator		2-1/2 inch diameter	33	80
		3 inch diameter	68	80
		5 inch diameter	65	80
		5-1/2 inch diameter	85	80
Jackhammer		very light, 28 to 40 lb	62	80
		light, 41 to 54 lb	83	80
		medium, 55 to 64 lb	135	80
		heavy, over 65 lb	160	80

Tool or Equipment	Type	Size	Average Free Air Consumption (cfm)	Range of Air Pressures (psi)
Jigger conveyor engine		11 inch	120	80
		13-1/2 inch	170	80
		15-3/4 inch	250	80
		17-3/4 inch	370	80
Laboratory outlet			1	40 - 70
Nailer			7	70 - 100
Nutsetter		to 5/16 inch, 8 lb	20	90
		1/2-3/4 in., 8 lb	30	90
	angle	to 5/16 in., 8 lb	20	70 - 90
		1/2- 3/4 in., 8 lb	30	70 - 90
Paint scraper			7	80
Panel cutter			4	70 - 100
Paving breaker		very light, 10-25 lb	30	- - -
		light, 26 to 50 lb	35	- - -
		med., 51-70 lb	40	- - -
		heavy, over 70 lb	60	- - -
Pick		light	25	80
		medium	35	80
		heavy	30	80
Plug drill			40	70 - 90
Pneumatic door			2	40 - 90
Pneumatic garage door			3	120 - 150
Power hammer		100 lb	60	80
		300 lb	130	80
		500 lb	190	80
		1,000 lb	320	80
		2,000 lb	540	80
Radiator tester			1	90 - 100
Rammer		small	4	70 - 100
		medium	9	70 - 100
		large	10	70 - 100
	backfill trench type		35	80
	bench type		11	80 - 100
	floor type	light	7	90 - 100
		medium	19	80
		heavy	27	80
Rivet buster		to 7/8 inch	38	70 - 90
Rivet cutter	rapid blow type	to 3/4 inch	35	80
Rivet forge			6	80
Riveter		3/32 to 1 in. rivets	12	70 - 90
		large, 18- 22 lb	35	70 - 90
	copper staybolt	1 inch	33	80

Tool or Equipment	Type	Size	Average Free Air Consumption (cfm)	Range of Air Pressures (psi)
Riveting hammer			8	70 - 100
			15	90 - 100
		3/4 in. hot rivet	24	80
		1 in. hot rivet	26	80
		1-1/4 in. hot rivet	29	80
		1-3/8 in. hot rivet	35	80
		4 in. stroke, 3/8 inch	25	- - -
		5 in. stroke, 3/4 in.	30	- - -
Runner		1/4 to 3/4 inch	18	70 - 90
Sand rammer		1x4 in. cylinder	25	70 - 90
		1-1/4x5 in cylinder	28	70 - 90
		1-1/2x6 in cylinder	39	70 - 90
Sand tamper		1 x 4 in cylinder	25	70 - 90
		1-1/4 x 5 in cylinder	28	70 - 90
		1-1/2 x 6 in cylinder	39	70 - 90
Sander		5 inch pad	10	70 - 100
		7 inch pad	15	70 - 100
		9 inch pad	20	90 - 100
	orbital		9	80
	recipro- cating		9	80
	rotary	7 inch pad	30	90
		9 inch pad	53	90
	vertical	small	22	70 - 90
		medium	30	70 - 90
		large	53	70 - 90
	vertical disc		10	90 - 100
Saw		6 inch	20	80
Sawing machine		small	3	90 - 100
		large	5	90 - 100
Scaling hammer	boiler tubes		3	70 - 90
		light	15	- - -
		large	21	80
	valveless, surface work		7	80
Screwdriver		#2 to #6 screw	5	70 - 100
		#6 - 5/16 inch screw	10	70 - 100

Tool or Equipment	Type	Size	Average Free Air Consumption (cfm)	Range of Air Pressures (psi)
Sheeting driver		light, under 60 lb	100	- - -
		med.,61-125 lb	150	- - -
		heavy, over 126 lb	175	- - -
Shuttering vibrator		7 lb	8	80
		10 lb	13	80
		14 lb	18	80
Sinker drill		3 in.	125	80
		3-1/2 in.	160	80
Sinker hammer		very light, 30 to 40 lb	75	- - -
		light, 41 to 54 lb	85	- - -
		medium, 55 to 64 lb	120	- - -
		heavy, over 65 lb	160	- - -
Spader		light, up to 24 lb	28	80
		med, 25-35 lb	37	80
		heavy, 36-60 lb	60	80
Spark plug cleaner			5	70 - 100
Spark plug tester			1	90 - 100
Spike driver			60	80
Spike puller	per spike		3	80
Spray gun	paint	small	3	70 - 90
		medium	5	50
		large	14	50
		touch-up	4	90 - 100
		production	9	90 - 100
		undercoat	19	90 - 100
Spray gun engine cleaner			5	90 - 100
Spring oiler spray gun			4	90 - 100
Stand riveter		1/2 in. rivet	24	80
		3/4 in. hot rivet	26	80
		1 in. hot rivet	28	80
Stapler			7	70 - 100
Stone tool		lettering and light carving	6	80
		medium dressing	10	80
		roughing and bushing	14	80
Stoping drill		light	70	80
		heavy	125	80
Sump pump		145 gal./min. at 50-ft head	70	70 - 90
		90-250 gal/ min	85	80
Tapper		to 3/8 inch	5	70 - 100
Tie tamper			20	80
Tire changer			1	125 - 150

Tool or Equipment	Type	Size	Average Free Air Consumption (cfm)	Range of Air Pressures (psi)
Tire hammer			12	90 - 100
Tire inflater/gauge			2	70 - 90
Tire inflation line			2	125 - 150
Tire rim stripper			6	125 - 150
Tire spreader			1	125 - 150
Torque wrench	rotary	to 1/4 in	7	80
		to 3/8 in	18	80
		1/2 to 3/4 in	28	80
		7/8 to 1 in	38	80
Transmission flusher			3	70 - 100
Truck lift		8,000 lb cap.	6	70 - 90
Tube cutter		to 2-1/2 in diam	45	80
		2-1/2- 4 in diam	55	80
Tube expander		to 2-1/2 in diam	65	80
		to 3 inch diam	75	80
		to 4 in diam	95	80
Underwater drill			88	80
Vacuum cleaner	shop		7	100 - 150
Valve grinder			2	70 - 90
Wagon drill		3-1/2 in. drifter	175	80
		4 in drifter	210	80
Weld flux chipper			24	80
Wood borer		1 in. diam, 4 lb	40	70 - 90
		2 in diam, 26 lb	80	70 - 90
Wood deck caulker			22	80

NOTES: Values in the table are approximate. Free air comsumption can vary greatly between manufacturers.For more precise information check with the equipment manufacturer.

SOURCES:
Values in the table were extracted and interperted from values published in the following sources:
Buying Guide and Technical Handbook, Compressed Air Systems, Hagerstown, MD.
Compressed Air and Gas Handbook, Fifth Edition, Compressed Air and Gas Institute, Cleveland, OH.
Grainger Catalog, W.W. Grainger, Inc., 1997.
K-A Pocket Wallet Air Estimator, Kellogg-American, Inc., Oakmont, PA.
Pneumatic Handbook, Sixth Edition, Gulf Publishing Company, Houston

Air Discharge from Orifices

Pressure (psi)	Orifice Size fractional inch/Decimal Inch											
	1/64 0.01563	1/32 0.03125	3/64 0.04688	1/16 0.06250	5/64 0.07813	3/32 0.09375	7/64 0.10938	1/8 0.12500	5/32 0.15625	3/16 0.18750	7/32 0.21875	1/4 0.25000
1	0.027	0.108	0.243	0.432	0.675	0.972	1.32	1.73	2.70	3.88	5.28	6.89
2	0.037	0.149	0.335	0.595	0.929	1.34	1.82	2.37	3.71	5.34	7.26	9.48
3	0.047	0.187	0.421	0.749	1.17	1.68	2.29	2.99	4.67	6.72	9.14	11.9
4	0.055	0.220	0.495	0.879	1.37	1.98	2.69	3.51	5.48	7.89	10.7	14.0
5	0.062	0.247	0.556	0.988	1.54	2.22	3.02	3.94	6.16	8.86	12.1	15.7
6	0.068	0.270	0.608	1.08	1.69	2.43	3.30	4.32	6.74	9.70	13.2	17.2
7	0.073	0.291	0.654	1.16	1.81	2.61	3.55	4.64	7.25	10.4	14.2	18.5
8	0.077	0.309	0.695	1.23	1.93	2.78	3.78	4.93	7.70	11.1	15.1	19.7
9	0.081	0.326	0.733	1.30	2.03	2.93	3.98	5.20	8.12	11.7	15.9	20.8
10	0.085	0.342	0.768	1.37	2.13	3.07	4.18	5.45	8.51	12.3	16.7	21.8
11	0.089	0.357	0.802	1.43	2.23	3.20	4.36	5.69	8.89	12.8	17.4	22.7
12	0.093	0.371	0.835	1.48	2.32	3.34	4.54	5.93	9.25	13.3	18.1	23.7
13	0.096	0.386	0.867	1.54	2.41	3.46	4.71	6.15	9.61	13.8	18.8	24.6
14	0.100	0.399	0.899	1.60	2.49	3.59	4.88	6.38	9.96	14.3	19.5	25.5
15	0.103	0.413	0.930	1.65	2.58	3.71	5.05	6.60	10.3	14.8	20.2	26.3
16	0.107	0.427	0.961	1.71	2.67	3.84	5.22	6.82	10.6	15.3	20.8	27.2
17	0.110	0.441	0.991	1.76	2.75	3.96	5.39	7.03	11.0	15.8	21.5	28.1
18	0.113	0.454	1.02	1.82	2.84	4.08	5.56	7.25	11.3	16.3	22.2	29.0
19	0.117	0.468	1.05	1.87	2.92	4.21	5.72	7.47	11.7	16.8	22.8	29.8
20	0.120	0.482	1.08	1.93	3.01	4.33	5.89	7.69	12.0	17.3	23.5	30.7

Air Discharge from Orifices (cont.)

Pressure (psi)	1/64 0.01563	1/32 0.03125	3/64 0.04688	1/16 0.06250	5/64 0.07813	3/32 0.09375	7/64 0.10938	1/8 0.12500	5/32 0.15625	3/16 0.18750	7/32 0.21875	1/4 0.25000
21	0.124	0.495	1.11	1.98	3.09	4.45	6.06	7.91	12.3	17.8	24.2	31.6
22	0.127	0.509	1.15	2.04	3.18	4.58	6.23	8.13	12.7	18.3	24.9	32.4
23	0.131	0.523	1.18	2.09	3.26	4.70	6.39	8.35	13.0	18.8	25.5	33.3
24	0.134	0.537	1.21	2.15	3.35	4.82	6.56	8.57	13.4	19.3	26.2	34.2
25	0.138	0.551	1.24	2.20	3.44	4.95	6.73	8.79	13.7	19.8	26.9	35.1
26	0.141	0.565	1.27	2.26	3.53	5.07	6.90	9.01	14.1	20.3	27.6	36.0
27	0.145	0.579	1.30	2.31	3.61	5.20	7.07	9.24	14.4	20.8	28.2	36.9
28	0.148	0.593	1.33	2.37	3.70	5.33	7.25	9.46	14.8	21.3	28.9	37.8
29	0.152	0.607	1.37	2.43	3.79	5.45	7.42	9.69	15.1	21.8	29.6	38.7
30	0.155	0.621	1.40	2.48	3.88	5.58	7.59	9.91	15.5	22.3	30.3	39.6
31	0.159	0.635	1.43	2.54	3.97	5.71	7.77	10.1	15.8	22.8	31.0	40.5
32	0.162	0.650	1.46	2.60	4.05	5.84	7.94	10.4	16.2	23.3	31.7	41.4
33	0.166	0.664	1.49	2.65	4.14	5.96	8.11	10.6	16.5	23.8	32.4	42.3
34	0.169	0.678	1.53	2.71	4.23	6.09	8.29	10.8	16.9	24.3	33.1	43.2
35	0.173	0.693	1.56	2.77	4.32	6.22	8.47	11.1	17.3	24.8	33.8	44.1
36	0.177	0.707	1.59	2.83	4.41	6.35	8.64	11.3	17.6	25.4	34.5	45.0
37	0.180	0.721	1.62	2.88	4.50	6.48	8.82	11.5	18.0	25.9	35.2	46.0
38	0.184	0.736	1.65	2.94	4.59	6.61	8.99	11.7	18.3	26.4	35.9	46.9
39	0.187	0.750	1.69	3.00	4.68	6.74	9.17	12.0	18.7	26.9	36.6	47.8
40	0.191	0.765	1.72	3.06	4.77	6.87	9.35	12.2	19.1	27.4	37.3	48.7
41	0.195	0.779	1.75	3.11	4.86	7.00	9.53	12.4	19.4	28.0	38.0	49.7
42	0.198	0.794	1.79	3.17	4.96	7.13	9.70	12.7	19.8	28.5	38.7	50.6

Orifice Size Fractional Inch/Decimal Inch

Pressure (psi)	1/64 0.01563	1/32 0.03125	3/64 0.04688	1/16 0.06250	5/64 0.07813	3/32 0.09375	7/64 0.10938	1/8 0.12500	5/32 0.15625	3/16 0.18750	7/32 0.21875	1/4 0.25000
					Orifice Size Fractional Inch/Decimal Inch							
43	0.202	0.808	1.82	3.23	5.05	7.26	9.88	12.9	20.1	29.0	39.4	51.5
44	0.206	0.823	1.85	3.29	5.14	7.39	10.1	13.1	20.5	29.5	40.2	52.4
45	0.209	0.837	1.88	3.35	5.23	7.52	10.2	13.4	20.9	30.0	40.9	53.4
46	0.213	0.852	1.92	3.41	5.32	7.66	10.4	13.6	21.2	30.6	41.6	54.3
47	0.216	0.867	1.95	3.46	5.41	7.79	10.6	13.8	21.6	31.1	42.3	55.2
48	0.220	0.881	1.98	3.52	5.50	7.92	10.8	14.1	22.0	31.6	43.0	56.1
49	0.224	0.896	2.01	3.58	5.59	8.05	11.0	14.3	22.3	32.1	43.7	57.1
50	0.227	0.910	2.05	3.64	5.68	8.18	11.1	14.5	22.7	32.7	44.4	58.0
55	0.246	0.983	2.21	3.93	6.14	8.83	12.0	15.7	24.5	35.3	48.0	62.6
60	0.264	1.06	2.37	4.22	6.59	9.48	12.9	16.8	26.3	37.9	51.5	67.2
65	0.282	1.13	2.54	4.51	7.04	10.1	13.8	18.0	28.1	40.4	55.0	71.8
70	0.299	1.20	2.70	4.79	7.48	10.8	14.7	19.1	29.9	43.0	58.5	76.4
75	0.317	1.27	2.85	5.07	7.92	11.4	15.5	20.3	31.6	45.5	61.9	80.9
80	0.334	1.34	3.01	5.35	8.36	12.0	16.4	21.4	33.4	48.0	65.3	85.3
85	0.352	1.41	3.17	5.63	8.79	12.7	17.2	22.5	35.1	50.5	68.7	89.7
90	0.369	1.48	3.32	5.90	9.22	13.3	18.1	23.6	36.8	53.0	72.1	94.1
95	0.386	1.54	3.47	6.17	9.64	13.9	18.9	24.7	38.5	55.4	75.4	98.4
100	0.403	1.61	3.63	6.44	10.1	14.5	19.7	25.7	40.2	57.8	78.7	103
105	0.419	1.68	3.78	6.71	10.5	15.1	20.5	26.8	41.9	60.2	82.0	107
110	0.436	1.75	3.93	6.98	10.9	15.7	21.3	27.9	43.5	62.6	85.2	111
115	0.453	1.81	4.08	7.25	11.3	16.3	22.2	28.9	45.2	65.0	88.5	116
120	0.469	1.88	4.23	7.51	11.7	16.9	23.0	30.0	46.8	67.4	91.7	120
125	0.486	1.95	4.38	7.78	12.1	17.5	23.8	31.1	48.5	69.8	95.0	124

Air Discharge from Orifices (cont.)

Pressure (psi)	Orifice Size Fractional Inch/Decimal Inch											
	1/64	1/32	3/64	1/16	5/64	3/32	7/64	1/8	5/32	3/16	7/32	1/4
	0.01563	0.03125	0.04688	0.06250	0.07813	0.09375	0.10938	0.12500	0.15625	0.18750	0.21875	0.25000
130	0.503	2.01	4.53	8.05	12.6	18.1	24.6	32.1	50.2	72.2	98.3	128
135	0.520	2.08	4.68	8.32	13.0	18.7	25.4	33.2	51.9	74.6	102	133
140	0.537	2.15	4.83	8.59	13.4	19.3	26.3	34.3	53.5	77.1	105	137
145	0.554	2.22	4.99	8.86	13.8	19.9	27.1	35.4	55.2	79.5	108	141
150	0.571	2.29	5.14	9.13	14.3	20.5	27.9	36.5	57.0	82.0	112	146
160	0.606	2.42	5.45	9.69	15.1	21.8	29.6	38.7	60.4	87.0	118	154
170	0.641	2.57	5.78	10.3	16.0	23.1	31.4	41.0	64.0	92.1	125	164
175	0.660	2.64	5.94	10.6	16.5	23.7	32.3	42.2	65.8	94.8	129	168
180	0.678	2.72	6.11	10.9	17.0	24.4	33.2	43.4	67.7	97.4	133	173
190	0.717	2.87	6.45	11.5	17.9	25.8	35.1	45.8	71.5	103	140	183
200	0.756	3.03	6.81	12.1	18.9	27.2	37.0	48.3	75.4	109	148	193
210	0.797	3.19	7.18	12.8	19.9	28.7	39.0	50.9	79.5	114	156	203
220	0.839	3.36	7.56	13.4	21.0	30.2	41.1	53.6	83.7	121	164	214
225	0.861	3.45	7.75	13.8	21.5	31.0	42.1	55.0	85.9	124	168	220
230	0.883	3.53	7.95	14.1	22.1	31.8	43.2	56.4	88.1	127	173	225
200	0.756	3.03	6.81	12.1	18.9	27.2	37.0	48.3	75.4	109	148	193
210	0.797	3.19	7.18	12.8	19.9	28.7	39.0	50.9	79.5	114	156	203
220	0.839	3.36	7.56	13.4	21.0	30.2	41.1	53.6	83.7	121	164	214
225	0.861	3.45	7.75	13.8	21.5	31.0	42.1	55.0	85.9	124	168	220
230	0.883	3.53	7.95	14.1	22.1	31.8	43.2	56.4	88.1	127	173	225
240	0.928	3.72	8.36	14.9	23.2	33.4	45.4	59.3	92.6	133	181	237

Pressure (psi)	Orifice Size Fractional Inch/Decimal Inch													
	1/64	1/32	3/64	1/16	5/64	3/32	7/64	1/8	5/32	3/16	7/32	1/4		
	0.01563	0.03125	0.04688	0.06250	0.07813	0.09375	0.10938	0.12500	0.15625	0.18750	0.21875	0.25000		
250	0.975	3.90	8.78	15.6	24.4	35.1	47.7	62.3	97.3	140	190	249		
260	1.02	4.10	9.21	16.4	25.6	36.8	50.1	65.4	102	147	200	261		
270	1.07	4.29	9.66	17.2	26.8	38.6	52.5	68.5	107	154	210	274		
275	1.10	4.39	9.88	17.6	27.4	39.5	53.7	70.1	109	158	214	280		
280	1.12	4.49	10.1	18.0	28.1	40.4	54.9	71.7	112	161	219	286		
290	1.17	4.70	10.6	18.8	29.3	42.2	57.4	75.0	117	169	229	299		
300	1.23	4.91	11.0	19.6	30.6	44.1	60.0	78.3	122	176	239	313		

NOTES: Flow is assumed to be air from a reciever or other container, under pressure at 60°F, to the atmosphere at sea level. Values in the table are only correct for orifices with narrow edges. Flow through a pipe of any length will reduce the values shown.

SOURCES: Values in the table were adapted and expanded from data presented in
Pocket Wallet Air Estimator, Bulletin AE-10, Kellogg-American, Inc., Oakmont, PA;
Buying Guide and Technical Handbook, Compressed Air Systems, Hagerstown, MD
Fluid Power Handbook, Anton H. Hehn, Gulf Publishing Co., Houston, TX.

Hose Tables Introduction

Plastic and rubber hoses manufactured in the United States are controlled by standards published by organizations such as the American National Standards Institute (ANSI), the American Society for Testing and Materials (ASTM), and the Rubber Manufactures Association (RMA).

Hose is controlled using the internal diameter. Commonly available diameters are 1/8, 3/16, 1/4, 5/16, 3/8, 7/16, 1/2, 5/8, 3/4, 7/8, 1, 1-1/4, 1-1/2, 2, 2-1/2, 3, 3-1/2, 4, 5, 6, 8, 10, and 12 inches. Other diameters may be available in specialty hoses. Some hose diameters are also specified using a "hose dash size" which is based on the internal diameter of the hose expressed in 16ths of an inch. A hose with an internal diameter of 5/16 inch would have a hose dash number of "-5", 3/8 inch is 6/16 inch for a hose dash number of "-6", and so on.

Modern hose can vary from a simple plastic or rubber tube to a complex, highly-engineered, multi-layer assemblage of rubber and plastic tubes, synthetic cords and fabrics, and steel wires and meshes. The editors at Sequoia Publishing attempted to compile tables of properties for commonly used hose. It quickly became apparent that such tables would provide little useful information. Manufactures are free to use a wide variety of materials in as many layers as necessary to achieve the requirements of the hose design. Wall thicknesses, outside diameters, and weights can vary greatly from one manufacture to another for hoses designed to perform the same function. For instance, we found four manufacturers making thirteen varieties of "chemical transfer hose". All thirteen hoses were designed for a maximum operating pressure of 150 pounds-force per square inch and all have internal diameters (ID) of 2 inches. These thirteen hoses had twelve different outside diameters (OD) which varied from 2-17/32 inches to 2-7/8 inches with thirteen different weights which varied from 1.05 pounds per foot to 1.92 pounds per foot.

The Hose Tables in this book provide flow and pressure loss data for air and water flow in plastic hose.

References

The 1996 Hose Handbook, Sixth Edition, Rubber Manufacturers Association, 1996

ANSI/RMA IP-7, Specifications For Rubber Welding Hose, Sixth Edition, American National Standards Association/Rubber Manufacturers Association, 1982

ANSI/RMA IP-8, Specifications For Rubber Hose For Oil Suction and Dis- charge, Third Edition, American National Standards Association/Rubber Manufacturers Association, 1982

ANSI/RMA IP-14, Specifications For Anhydrous Ammonia Hose, Fifth Edition, American National Standards Association/Rubber Manufacturers Association, 1986

ASTM Designation D 3901-90, Standard Consumer Product Specification for Garden Hose, American Society for Testing and Materials, 1990

ASTM Designation D 3952-87, Standard Specification for Rubber Hose Used in Solar Energy Systems, American Society for Testing and Materials, 1987

Air Discharge through 100 Feet of Hose

Flow rates in cubic feet per minute (cfm)

Pressure at Hose Inlet (psi)	Air hose ID (internal diameter), nominal in inches				
	3/16	1/4	5/16	3/8	1/2
	0.1875	0.2500	0.3125	0.3750	0.5000
30	2.3	4.8	7.1	13	33
35	2.8	5.7	8.6	15	37
40	3.2	6.6	10	18	40
45	3.6	7.5	11	20	44
50	4.0	8.4	13	22	47
55	4.4	9.3	14	25	51
60	4.8	10	16	27	55
65	5.2	11	17	30	58
70	5.6	12	19	32	62
75	6.0	13	20	34	65
80	6.4	14	22	37	69
85	6.9	15	23	39	73
90	7.3	16	25	42	76

* Pressure at the hose inlet is in pound-force per square inch (psi) and the hose outlet is discharging at atmospheric pressure. The values in the table were developed from actual test data. Due to variations air supply source, volume, and pressure the values in the table must be considered approximate.

Pressure Loss Due to Friction in 100 Feet of Air Hose

Pressure loss in pound-force per square inch (psi)

1/2 inch ID (internal diameter) air hose

Gauge Pressure (psi)*	Air Flow - cubic feet per minute (cfm)						
	30	40	50	60	70	80	90
50	9.5	20.2	36.2	-	-	-	-
60	8.1	16.8	29.6	46.8	-	-	-
70	7.0	14.4	25.0	39.2	57.2	-	-
80	4.8	11.9	21.8	34.6	50.4	69.2	-
90	5.0	10.8	18.9	29.8	43.8	61.1	82.0
100	4.7	9.7	16.8	26.4	38.8	54.3	73.3
110	4.2	8.6	15.2	24.0	35.2	49.2	66.6
Gauge Pressure (psi)*	Air Flow - cubic feet per minute (cfm)						
	100	110	120	130	140	150	160
50	-	-	-	-	-	-	-
60	-	-	-	-	-	-	-
70	-	-	-	-	-	-	-
80	-	-	-	-	-	-	-
90	-	-	-	-	-	-	-
100	-	-	-	-	-	-	-
110	89.0	-	-	-	-	-	-

3/4 inch ID (internal diameter) air hose

Gauge Pressure (psi)*	Air Flow - cubic feet per minute (cfm)						
	30	40	50	60	70	80	90
50	1.4	2.6	4.3	6.6	9.5	13.1	17.4
60	1.4	2.5	3.8	5.5	7.7	10.3	13.5
70	0.9	1.8	3.0	4.5	6.4	8.5	11.0
80	0.8	1.6	2.6	3.9	5.5	7.3	9.3
90	0.7	1.3	2.2	3.3	4.6	6.2	8.0
100	0.6	1.2	1.9	2.9	4.0	5.4	7.0
110	0.6	1.1	1.7	2.6	3.6	4.8	6.2

Gauge Pressure (psi)*	Air Flow - cubic feet per minute (cfm)						
	100	110	120	130	140	150	160
50	22.5	28.3	35.0	42.5	-	-	-
60	17.4	22.3	28.2	35.5	44.3	55.2	-
70	14.0	17.6	22.0	27.8	34.8	48.3	-
80	11.7	14.4	17.5	21.2	25.8	31.7	39.7
90	10.0	12.4	15.0	18.0	21.6	25.8	30.9
100	8.8	10.9	13.2	15.8	18.8	22.0	25.7
110	7.9	9.7	11.8	14.2	16.8	19.8	23.1

1 inch ID (internal diameter) air hose

Gauge Pressure (psi)*	Air Flow - cubic feet per minute (cfm)						
	30	40	50	60	70	80	90
50	0.3	0.6	1.0	1.6	2.2	3.0	4.0
60	0.3	0.5	0.8	1.2	1.7	2.3	3.0
70	0.2	0.4	0.7	1.0	1.5	2.0	2.5
80	0.2	0.4	0.6	1.0	1.3	1.8	2.2
90	0.2	0.4	0.6	0.8	1.1	1.5	1.9
100	0.2	0.3	0.5	0.7	0.9	1.3	1.6
110	0.1	0.2	0.4	0.6	0.8	1.1	1.5

Gauge Pressure (psi)*	Air Flow - cubic feet per minute (cfm)						
	100	110	120	130	140	150	160
50	5.2	7.0	9.6	14.0	22.4	42.2	-
60	4.0	5.1	6.6	8.4	10.9	14.4	19.4
70	3.2	4.0	5.0	6.2	7.6	9.4	11.7
80	2.8	3.3	4.0	4.7	5.7	6.9	8.5
90	2.3	2.8	3.4	4.0	4.8	5.6	6.5
100	2.0	2.5	3.0	3.5	4.2	4.8	5.6
110	1.8	2.2	2.6	3.0	3.6	4.2	5.0

* Gauge pressure is in pound-force per square inch (psi).
Values in the table were developed from actual test data.
Due to variations in air supply source, volume, and pressure, the values in the table must be considered approximate.

Test data from *The 1996 Hose Handbook*, Rubber Manufacturers Association, Washington, DC.

Water Discharge through 100 Feet of Hose

Flow rates in gallons (US) per minute (gpm)

Pressure at Hose Inlet (psi)*	Water hose ID (internal diameter), nominal in inches				
	1/8	3/16	1/4	5/16	3/8
	0.1250	0.1875	0.2500	0.3125	0.3750
10	0.075	0.219	0.467	0.839	1.36
20	0.110	0.318	0.679	1.22	1.97
30	0.136	0.396	0.845	1.52	2.45
40	0.159	0.463	0.987	1.77	2.87
50	0.180	0.522	1.11	2.00	3.23
60	0.198	0.576	1.23	2.21	3.57
70	0.216	0.626	1.33	2.40	3.88
75	0.224	0.650	1.39	2.49	4.03
80	0.232	0.673	1.43	2.58	4.17
90	0.247	0.717	1.53	2.75	4.44
100	0.261	0.759	1.62	2.91	4.70
125	0.295	0.857	1.83	3.28	5.30
150	0.325	0.945	2.01	3.62	5.85
200	0.380	1.10	2.35	4.23	6.84

Pressure at Hose Inlet (psi)*	Water hose ID (internal diameter), nominal in inches				
	7/16	1/2	5/8	3/4	7/8
	0.4375	0.5000	0.6250	0.7500	0.8750
10	2.03	2.89	5.20	8.39	12.6
20	2.96	4.20	7.56	12.2	18.3
30	3.68	5.23	9.40	15.2	22.8
40	4.30	6.11	11.0	17.7	26.6
50	4.85	6.89	12.4	20.0	30.0
60	5.35	7.60	13.7	22.1	33.1
70	5.82	8.26	14.9	24.0	36.0
75	6.04	8.58	15.4	24.9	37.4
80	6.25	8.88	16.0	25.8	38.7
90	6.66	9.46	17.0	27.5	41.2
100	7.05	10.0	18.0	29.1	43.7
125	7.95	11.3	20.3	32.8	49.2
150	8.78	12.5	22.4	36.2	54.3
200	10.3	14.6	26.2	42.3	63.5

Water Discharge through 100 Feet of Hose (cont.)

Pressure at Hose Inlet (psi)*	Water hose ID (internal diameter), nominal in inches				
	1	1-1/4	1-1/2	2	2-1/2
	1.00	1.25	1.50	2.00	2.50
10	17.9	32.2	52.0	111	199
20	26.0	46.8	75.5	161	290
30	32.4	58.2	94.0	200	360
40	37.8	68.0	110	234	421
50	42.7	76.7	124	264	475
60	47.1	84.6	137	291	524
70	51.2	92.0	149	317	569
75	53.1	95.5	154	329	591
80	55.0	98.9	160	340	612
90	58.6	105	170	363	652
100	62.0	112	180	384	690
125	70.0	126	203	433	779
150	77.2	139	224	478	859
200	90.2	162	262	558	1,000

Pressure at Hose Inlet (psi)*	Water hose internal diameter, nominal in inches				
	3	3-1/2	4	5	6
	3.0	3.5	4.0	5.0	6.0
10	322	482	685	1,230	1,990
20	468	701	1,000	1,790	2,890
30	582	873	1,240	2,230	3,600
40	680	1,020	1,450	2,610	4,210
50	767	1,150	1,630	2,940	4,750
60	846	1,270	1,800	3,240	5,240
70	920	1,380	1,960	3,530	5,690
75	955	1,430	2,030	3,660	5,910

Pressure at Hose Inlet (psi)*	Water hose internal diameter, nominal in inches				
	3	3-1/2	4	5	6
	3.0	3.5	4.0	5.0	6.0
80	989	1,480	2,110	3,790	6,120
90	1,050	1,580	2,250	4,040	6,520
100	1,120	1,670	2,380	4,270	6,900
125	1,260	1,890	2,680	4,820	7,790
150	1,390	2,080	2,960	5,320	8,590
200	1,620	2,430	3,460	6,210	10,000

* Pressure at the hose inlet is in pound-force per square inch (psi) and the hose outlet is discharging at atmospheric pressure.

Values in table were determined using the Hazen-Williams equation with a coefficient of 140 for clean, smooth plastic.

Pressure Loss Due to Friction in 100 Feet of Water Hose

For ½ inch to 1-1/2 inch Diameter Hose

Pressure loss in pound-force per square inch (psi) for 100 feet of hose

Water Flow (gpm)*	Water hose ID (internal diameter) in inches					
	1/2	5/8	3/4	1	1-1/4	1-1/2
	0.500	0.625	0.750	1.00	1.25	1.50
1	1.41	0.476	0.196	-	-	-
2	5.09	1.72	0.707	0.174	-	-
3	10.8	3.64	1.50	0.369	0.124	-
4	18.4	6.19	2.55	0.628	0.212	0.087
5	27.7	9.35	3.85	0.948	0.320	0.132
10	100	33.7	13.9	3.42	1.15	0.475
15	-	71.4	29.4	7.24	2.44	1.00
20	-	122	50.0	12.3	4.16	1.71
25	-	-	75.6	18.6	6.28	2.59
30	-	-	106	26.1	8.80	3.62
35	-	-	-	34.7	11.7	4.82
40	-	-	-	44.4	15.0	6.17
45	-	-	-	55.2	18.6	7.67
50	-	-	-	67.1	22.6	9.32
55	-	-	-	80.1	27.0	11.1
60	-	-	-	94.1	31.7	13.1
65	-	-	-	109	36.8	15.1
70	-	-	-	-	42.2	17.4
75	-	-	-	-	47.9	19.7
80	-	-	-	-	54.0	22.2
85	-	-	-	-	60.4	24.9
90	-	-	-	-	67.2	27.6
95	-	-	-	-	74.2	30.6
100	-	-	-	-	81.6	33.6
125	-	-	-	-	123	50.8
150	-	-	-	-	-	71.1
175	-	-	-	-	-	94.6
200	-	-	-	-	-	121

Water Flow (gpm)*	Water hose ID (internal diameter) in inches					
	2 2.00	2-1/2 2.50	3 3.0	4 4.0	5 5.0	6 6.0
10	0.117	-	-	-	-	-
15	0.248	0.083	-	-	-	-
20	0.421	0.142	-	-	-	-
25	0.637	0.215	0.088	-	-	-
30	0.892	0.301	0.124	-	-	-
35	1.19	0.400	0.165	-	-	-
40	1.52	0.512	0.211	-	-	-
45	1.89	0.637	0.262	-	-	-
50	2.30	0.774	0.319	0.079	-	-
55	2.74	0.924	0.380	0.094	-	-
60	3.22	1.09	0.447	0.110	-	-
65	3.73	1.26	0.518	0.128	-	-
70	4.28	1.44	0.594	0.146	-	-
75	4.86	1.64	0.675	0.166	-	-
80	5.48	1.85	0.760	0.187	-	-
85	6.13	2.07	0.851	0.210	-	-
90	6.81	2.30	0.945	0.233	0.079	-
95	7.53	2.54	1.04	0.257	0.087	-
100	8.28	2.79	1.15	0.283	0.095	-
125	12.5	4.22	1.74	0.428	0.144	-
150	17.5	5.91	2.43	0.599	0.202	0.083
175	23.3	7.86	3.24	0.797	0.269	0.111
200	29.8	10.1	4.14	1.02	0.344	0.142
225	37.1	12.5	5.15	1.27	0.428	0.176
250	45.1	15.2	6.26	1.54	0.520	0.214
275	53.8	18.1	7.46	1.84	0.620	0.255
300	63.2	21.3	8.77	2.16	0.729	0.300
350	84.0	28.3	11.7	2.87	0.969	0.399
400	108	36.3	14.9	3.68	1.24	0.511
450	-	45.1	18.6	4.57	1.54	0.635
500	-	54.8	22.6	5.56	1.87	0.772
600	-	76.8	31.6	7.79	2.63	1.08
700	-	102	42.0	10.4	3.49	1.44
800	-	-	53.8	13.3	4.47	1.84
900	-	-	66.9	16.5	5.56	2.29
1000	-	-	81.3	20.0	6.76	2.78
1200	-	-	114	28.1	9.47	3.90
1400	-	-	-	37.3	12.6	5.18
1500	-	-	-	42.4	14.3	5.89
1600	-	-	-	47.8	16.1	6.64
1800	-	-	-	59.4	20.0	8.25
2000	-	-	-	72.2	24.4	10.0
2500	-	-	-	109	36.8	15.2
3000	-	-	-	-	51.6	21.2

Pressure Loss due to Friction -2 to 6 inch diameter Water Hose
Pressure Loss in pound-force per square inch (psi) for 100 feet of hose

NOTES: * Water flow is in gallons (US) per minute (gpm). Values in the table were determined using the Hazen-Williams equation with a coefficient of 140 for clean, smooth plastic.

Theoretical Discharge From Nozzles For Water At 60°F

| Head | | Discharge Velocity | Theoretical Discharge in gallons(US) per minute | | | | | | |
| psi | feet | ft/sec | Nozzle Diameter, Fractional Inch/Decimal Inch | | | | | | |
			1/16 0.0625	1/8 0.1250	3/16 0.1875	1/4 0.2500	5/16 0.3125	3/8 0.3750	7/16 0.4375
5	11.5	27.3	0.261	1.04	2.35	4.17	6.52	9.38	12.8
10	23.1	38.5	0.369	1.47	3.32	5.90	9.21	13.3	18.1
15	34.6	47.2	0.451	1.81	4.06	7.22	11.3	16.3	22.1
20	46.2	54.5	0.521	2.09	4.69	8.34	13.0	18.8	25.5
25	57.7	60.9	0.583	2.33	5.25	9.32	14.6	21.0	28.6
30	69.3	66.8	0.638	2.55	5.75	10.2	16.0	23.0	31.3
35	80.8	72.1	0.690	2.76	6.21	11.0	17.2	24.8	33.8
40	92.4	77.1	0.737	2.95	6.63	11.8	18.4	26.5	36.1
45	103.9	81.8	0.782	3.13	7.04	12.5	19.5	28.1	38.3
50	115.4	86.2	0.824	3.30	7.42	13.2	20.6	29.7	40.4
55	127.0	90.4	0.864	3.46	7.78	13.8	21.6	31.1	42.4
60	138.5	94.4	0.903	3.61	8.13	14.4	22.6	32.5	44.2
65	150.1	98.3	0.940	3.76	8.46	15.0	23.5	33.8	46.0
70	161.6	102.0	0.975	3.90	8.78	15.6	24.4	35.1	47.8
75	173.2	105.6	1.01	4.04	9.08	16.2	25.2	36.3	49.5
80	184.7	109.0	1.04	4.17	9.38	16.7	26.1	37.5	51.1
85	196.3	112.4	1.07	4.30	9.67	17.2	26.9	38.7	52.7
90	207.8	115.6	1.11	4.42	9.95	17.7	27.6	39.8	54.2
95	219.3	118.8	1.14	4.54	10.2	18.2	28.4	40.9	55.7
100	230.9	121.9	1.17	4.66	10.5	18.6	29.1	42.0	57.1

Theoretical Discharge From Nozzles For Water At 60°F (cont.)

Head		Discharge Velocity ft/sec	Theoretical Discharge in gallons(US) per minute Nozzle Diameter, Fractional Inch/Decimal Inch						
			1/16	1/8	3/16	1/4	5/16	3/8	7/16
psi	feet		0.0625	0.1250	0.1875	0.2500	0.3125	0.3750	0.4375
105	242.4	124.9	1.19	4.78	10.7	19.1	29.9	43.0	58.5
110	254.0	127.8	1.22	4.89	11.0	19.6	30.6	44.0	59.9
115	265.5	130.7	1.25	5.00	11.2	20.0	31.2	45.0	61.2
120	277.1	133.5	1.28	5.11	11.5	20.4	31.9	46.0	62.6
125	288.6	136.3	1.30	5.21	11.7	20.9	32.6	46.9	63.9
130	300.2	139.0	1.33	5.32	12.0	21.3	33.2	47.8	65.1
140	323.3	144.2	1.38	5.52	12.4	22.1	34.5	49.6	67.6
150	346.3	149.3	1.43	5.71	12.8	22.8	35.7	51.4	69.9
160	369.4	154.2	1.47	5.90	13.3	23.6	36.9	53.1	72.2
170	392.5	158.9	1.52	6.08	13.7	24.3	38.0	54.7	74.5
180	415.6	163.5	1.56	6.26	14.1	25.0	39.1	56.3	76.6
190	438.7	168.0	1.61	6.43	14.5	25.7	40.2	57.8	78.7
200	461.8	172.4	1.65	6.59	14.8	26.4	41.2	59.3	80.8
225	519.5	182.8	1.75	6.99	15.7	28.0	43.7	62.9	85.7
250	577.2	192.7	1.84	7.37	16.6	29.5	46.1	66.3	90.3
275	635.0	202.1	1.93	7.73	17.4	30.9	48.3	69.6	94.7
300	692.7	211.1	2.02	8.08	18.2	32.3	50.5	72.7	98.9

Head		Discharge Velocity	Nozzle Diameter, Fractional Inch/Decimal Inch						
			1/2	5/8	3/4	7/8	1	1-1/8	1-1/4
psi	feet	ft/sec	0.5000	0.6250	0.7500	0.8750	1.0000	1.1250	1.2500
5	11.5	27.3	16.7	26.1	37.5	51.1	66.7	84.4	104
10	23.1	38.5	23.6	36.9	53.1	72.2	94.4	119	147
15	34.6	47.2	28.9	45.1	65.0	88.5	116	146	181
20	46.2	54.5	33.4	52.1	75.1	102	133	169	209
25	57.7	60.9	37.3	58.3	83.9	114	149	189	233
30	69.3	66.8	40.9	63.8	91.9	125	163	207	255
35	80.8	72.1	44.1	69.0	99.3	135	177	223	276
40	92.4	77.1	47.2	73.7	106	144	189	239	295
45	103.9	81.8	50.0	78.2	113	153	200	253	313
50	115.4	86.2	52.7	82.4	119	162	211	267	330
55	127.0	90.4	55.3	86.4	124	169	221	280	346
60	138.5	94.4	57.8	90.3	130	177	231	293	361
65	150.1	98.3	60.1	94.0	135	184	241	304	376
70	161.6	102.0	62.4	97.5	140	191	250	316	390
75	173.2	105.6	64.6	101	145	198	258	327	404
80	184.7	109.0	66.7	104	150	204	267	338	417
85	196.3	112.4	68.8	107	155	211	275	348	430
90	207.8	115.6	70.8	111	159	217	283	358	442
95	219.3	118.8	72.7	114	164	223	291	368	454
100	230.9	121.9	74.6	117	168	228	298	378	466
105	242.4	124.9	76.4	119	172	234	306	387	478
110	254.0	127.8	78.2	122	176	240	313	396	489
115	265.5	130.7	80.0	125	180	245	320	405	500
120	277.1	133.5	81.7	128	184	250	327	414	511
125	288.6	136.3	83.4	130	188	255	334	422	521

Theoretical Discharge from Nozzles for Water at 60°F (cont.)

Head		Discharge Velocity	Nozzle Diameter, Fractional Inch/Decimal Inch						
			1/2	5/8	3/4	7/8	1	1-1/8	1-1/4
		ft/sec	0.5000	0.6250	0.7500	0.8750	1.0000	1.1250	1.2500
psi	feet								
130	300.2	139.0	85.1	133	191	260	340	431	532
140	323.3	144.2	88.3	138	199	270	353	447	552
150	346.3	149.3	91.4	143	206	280	365	463	571
160	369.4	154.2	94.4	147	212	289	377	478	590
170	392.5	158.9	97.3	152	219	298	389	492	608
180	415.6	163.5	100	156	225	307	400	507	626
190	438.7	168.0	103	161	231	315	411	521	643
200	461.8	172.4	105	165	237	323	422	534	659
225	519.5	182.8	112	175	252	343	448	566	699
250	577.2	192.7	118	184	265	361	472	597	737
275	635.0	202.1	124	193	278	379	495	626	773
300	692.7	211.1	129	202	291	396	517	654	808

Notes: Values in the table are based on the following equations and equivalents:

Velocity = (2 gh)$^{0.5}$ where: g = acceleration of gravity = 32.1740486 ft/sec² and h = head in ft.

Flow = 19.63714 C (d₁)² h$^{0.5}$ where: C = discharge coefficient; C = 1.00 for values in table, d₁ = nozzle diameter in inches, h = head in ft, and 19.63714 is a constant to handle conversions. At 60°F: 1 ft of water = 2.310804 psi

Sources:
Cameron Hydraulic Data, 16th Edition, Ingersoll-Rand Company, Phillipsburg, NJ, 1979.
www.pump.net/liquiddata/flowdatanozz.htm
Centrifugal Pumps, Selection, Operation, and Maintenance, Igor J. Karassik and Roy Carter, F.W. Dodge Corporation, New York, 1960.
Water Measurement Manual, 3rd Edition, Bureau of Reclamation, U.S. Department of the Interior, 1997.
Water Well Handbook, 4th Edition, 6th Printing, Keith E. Anderson, Missouri Water Well & Pump Contractors Assn, Inc., 1981.
Flow of Fluids Through Valves, Fittings, and Pipe, Technical Paper No. 410, 13th Printing, Crane Co., New York, NY, 1973.

Water Hardness

Water hardness is a function of the amount of dissolved calcium salts, magnesium salts, iron and aluminum. The salts occur in a variety of forms but are typically calcium and magnesium bicarbonates (referred to as "temporary hardness") and sulphates and chlorides (referred to as "permanent hardness.")

Although the most obvious effect of hard water is in preventing soap from lathering, most people cannot tolerate drinking water that exceeds 300 ppm carbonate, or 1500 ppm chloride, or 2000 ppm sulphate. As shown in the table to the left, >500 ppm sulphate can produce a laxative effect in the body. Livestock can usually tolerate much higher levels of hardness, but total dissolved solids >10,000 ppm will create problems.

The following formula is used to calculate total hardness:

Total Hardness in ppm Carbonate = (ppm Calcium x 2.497)
+ (ppm Magnesium x 4.115) + (ppm Iron x 1.792)
+ (ppm Manganese x 1.822)

Hard water is treated by either a zeolite process (home water softeners) or a lime–soda ash process (large operations).

Hardness is also measured in "grains per gallon" and "degrees". Equivalents are as follows:

1 ppm = 0.058 grains/US gallon
1 ppm = 0.07 Clark degrees
1 ppm = 0.10 French degrees
1 ppm = 0.056 German degrees
1 French degree = 1 hydrometric degree
1 Clark degree = 1 grain / Imperial gallon as calcium carbonate
1 French degree = 1 part / 100,000 calcium carbonate
1 German degree = 1 part / 100,000 calcium oxide
1 grain / US gallon = 17.1 ppm
1 grain / US gallon = 1.20 Clark degrees
1 grain / US gallon = 1.71 French degrees
1 grain / US gallon = 0.958 German degrees

Water Data & Formulas

1 gallon water = 231 cubic inches = 8.333 pounds (@ 65° F)
1 pound of water = 27.72 cubic inches (@ 65° F)
1 cubic foot water = 7.5 gallons = 62.4 pounds (salt water
    weighs approximately 64.3 pounds per cubic foot)
pounds per square inch at bottom of a column of water = height
    of column in feet x 0.434 (@ 39° F)
1 miner's inch = 9 to 12 gallons per minute

Horsepower to Raise Water

$$Horsepower = \frac{gallons\ per\ MINUTE\ x\ Total\ Head\ in\ feet}{3960}$$

(if pumping a liquid other than water, multiply the gallons per
minute above by the liquids specific gravity)
  See page 543 in the Pumps chapter for a table of values.

Gallons Per Minute through a Pipe

$GPM = 0.0408\ x\ Pipe\ Diameter\ inches^2\ x\ Feet\ /\ minute\ water\ velocity$

Weight of Water in a Pipe

$Pounds\ Water = Pipe\ Length\ feet\ x\ Pipe\ diameter\ inches^2\ x\ 0.34$

Gallons per Minute of a Slurry

$$GPM\ Slurry = GPM\ Water + \frac{4\ x\ Tons\ of\ per\ hour\ of\ solids}{Specific\ Gravity\ of\ Solids}$$

Cost to Pump Water – Electric

$$\$\ per\ hour = \frac{gpm\ x\ Head\ in\ feet\ x\ 0.746\ x\ Rate\ per\ KWH}{3960\ x\ Pump\ Efficiency\ x\ Electric\ Motor\ Efficiency}$$

(70% Pump and 90% Motor Efficiency is a good average)

Cost to Pump Water – Gasoline and Diesel

$$\$\ per\ hour = \frac{GPM\ x\ Head\ in\ feet\ x\ K\ x\ \$\ per\ gallon\ fuel}{3960\ x\ Pump\ Efficiency}$$

K = 0.110 for gasoline or 0.065 for diesel
  (K is actually gallons of fuel per horsepower)
(70% Pump Efficiency is a good average value)

Boiling Point of Water at Various Elevations

Elevation Above Sea Level		Boiling Point of Water		Elevation Above Sea Level		Boiling Point of Water	
feet	meters	°F	°C	feet	meters	°F	°C
-1,000	-305	213.9	101.1	14,750	4,496	184.8	84.9
-750	-229	213.5	100.8	15,000	4,572	184.4	84.7
-500	-152	213.0	100.5	15,250	4,648	184.0	84.4
-250	-76	212.5	100.3	15,500	4,724	183.5	84.2
0	0	212.0	100.0	15,750	4,801	183.1	83.9
250	76	211.5	99.7	16,000	4,877	182.7	83.7
500	152	211.0	99.5	16,250	4,953	182.2	83.5
750	229	210.5	99.2	16,500	5,029	181.8	83.2
1,000	305	210.1	98.9	16,750	5,105	181.4	83.0
1,250	381	209.6	98.6	17,000	5,182	180.9	82.7
1,500	457	209.1	98.4	17,250	5,258	180.5	82.5
1,750	533	208.6	98.1	17,500	5,334	180.1	82.3
2,000	610	208.1	97.8	17,750	5,410	179.7	82.0
2,250	686	207.6	97.6	18,000	5,486	179.2	81.8
2,500	762	207.2	97.3	18,250	5,563	178.8	81.6
2,750	838	206.7	97.1	18,500	5,639	178.4	81.3
3,000	914	206.2	96.8	18,750	5,715	178.0	81.1
3,250	991	205.7	96.5	19,000	5,791	177.6	80.9
3,500	1,067	205.3	96.3	19,250	5,867	177.1	80.6
3,750	1,143	204.8	96.0	19,500	5,944	176.7	80.4
4,000	1,219	204.3	95.7	19,750	6,020	176.3	80.2
4,250	1,295	203.8	95.5	20,000	6,096	175.9	79.9
4,500	1,372	203.4	95.2	20,250	6,172	175.5	79.7
4,750	1,448	202.9	94.9	20,500	6,248	175.1	79.5
5,000	1,524	202.4	94.7	20,750	6,325	174.7	79.3
5,250	1,600	202.0	94.4	21,000	6,401	174.2	79.0
5,500	1,676	201.5	94.2	21,250	6,477	173.8	78.8
5,750	1,753	201.0	93.9	21,500	6,553	173.4	78.6
6,000	1,829	200.6	93.6	21,750	6,629	173.0	78.3
6,250	1,905	200.1	93.4	22,000	6,706	172.6	78.1
6,500	1,981	199.6	93.1	22,250	6,782	172.2	77.9
6,750	2,057	199.2	92.9	22,500	6,858	171.8	77.7
7,000	2,134	198.7	92.6	22,750	6,934	171.4	77.4

Boiling Point Of Water At Various Elevations

Elevation Above Sea Level		Boiling Point of Water		Elevation Above Sea Level		Boiling Point of Water	
feet	meters	°F	°C	feet	meters	°F	°C
7,250	2,210	198.2	92.4	23,000	7,010	171.0	77.2
7,500	2,286	197.8	92.1	23,250	7,087	170.6	77.0
7,750	2,362	197.3	91.8	23,500	7,163	170.2	76.8
8,000	2,438	196.9	91.6	23,750	7,239	169.8	76.5
8,250	2,515	196.4	91.3	24,000	7,315	169.4	76.3
8,500	2,591	196.0	91.1	24,250	7,391	169.0	76.1
8,750	2,667	195.5	90.8	24,500	7,468	168.6	75.9
9,000	2,743	195.0	90.6	24,750	7,544	168.2	75.6
9,250	2,819	194.6	90.3	25,000	7,620	167.8	75.4
9,500	2,896	194.1	90.1	25,250	7,696	167.4	75.2
9,750	2,972	193.7	89.8	25,500	7,772	167.0	75.0
10,000	3,048	193.2	89.6	25,750	7,849	166.6	74.8
10,250	3,124	192.8	89.3	26,000	7,925	166.2	74.5
10,500	3,200	192.3	89.1	26,250	8,001	165.8	74.3
10,750	3,277	191.9	88.8	26,500	8,077	165.4	74.1
11,000	3,353	191.4	88.6	26,750	8,153	165.0	73.9
11,250	3,429	191.0	88.3	27,000	8,230	164.6	73.7
11,500	3,505	190.5	88.1	27,250	8,306	164.2	73.5
11,750	3,581	190.1	87.8	27,500	8,382	163.8	73.2
12,000	3,658	189.7	87.6	27,750	8,458	163.4	73.0
12,250	3,734	189.2	87.3	28,000	8,534	163.1	72.8
12,500	3,810	188.8	87.1	28,250	8,611	162.7	72.6
12,750	3,886	188.3	86.8	28,500	8,687	162.3	72.4
13,000	3,962	187.9	86.6	28,750	8,763	161.9	72.2
13,250	4,039	187.4	86.4	29,000	8,839	161.5	72.0
13,500	4,115	187.0	86.1	29,250	8,915	161.1	71.7
13,750	4,191	186.6	85.9	29,500	8,992	160.7	71.5
14,000	4,267	186.1	85.6	29,750	9,068	160.4	71.3
14,250	4,343	185.7	85.4	30,000	9,144	160.0	71.1
14,500	4,420	185.3	85.1	- - -	- - -	- - -	- - -

Values given in the table are approximate since the boiling point of water varies with the atmosphericpressure. The values in the table were computed from data given in Piping Handbook, Reno C. King and Sabin Crocker, 5th Edition, McGraw-Hill Book Co., New York, 1967.

Vapor Pressure of Water

At Temperatures From 32 to 680 °F (0 to 360 °C)

Temperature			Vapor Pressure			
°F	°C	K	kPa	psi	mm of Hg at 0°C	ft of H2O at 4°C
32.00	0.00	273.15	0.61121	0.08865	4.5844	0.20448
34.00	1.11	274.26	0.66236	0.09607	4.9680	0.22159
36.00	2.22	275.37	0.71726	0.10403	5.3798	0.23996
38.00	3.33	276.48	0.77616	0.11257	5.8216	0.25967
40.00	4.44	277.59	0.83929	0.12173	6.2951	0.28079
42.00	5.56	278.71	0.90693	0.13154	6.8024	0.30341
44.00	6.67	279.82	0.97933	0.14204	7.3455	0.32764
46.00	7.78	280.93	1.0568	0.15328	7.9265	0.35355
48.00	8.89	282.04	1.1396	0.16529	8.5478	0.38126
50.00	10.00	283.15	1.2281	0.17812	9.2115	0.41087
52.00	11.11	284.26	1.3226	0.19183	9.9202	0.44248
54.00	12.22	285.37	1.4234	0.20645	10.677	0.47622
56.00	13.33	286.48	1.5310	0.22205	11.483	0.51219
58.00	14.44	287.59	1.6456	0.23867	12.343	0.55054
60.00	15.56	288.71	1.7677	0.25638	13.259	0.59138
62.00	16.67	289.82	1.8976	0.27523	14.233	0.63486
64.00	17.78	290.93	2.0359	0.29529	15.270	0.68112
66.00	18.89	292.04	2.1829	0.31661	16.373	0.73031
68.00	20.00	293.15	2.3392	0.33927	17.545	0.78258
70.00	21.11	294.26	2.5051	0.36334	18.790	0.83810
72.00	22.22	295.37	2.6813	0.38889	20.111	0.89703
74.00	23.33	296.48	2.8682	0.41599	21.513	0.95956
76.00	24.44	297.59	3.0663	0.44473	22.999	1.0259
78.00	25.56	298.71	3.2763	0.47519	24.574	1.0961
80.00	26.67	299.82	3.4988	0.50745	26.243	1.1705
82.00	27.78	300.93	3.7343	0.54161	28.009	1.2493
84.00	28.89	302.04	3.9834	0.57775	29.878	1.3327
86.00	30.00	303.15	4.2469	0.61596	31.854	1.4208
88.00	31.11	304.26	4.5254	0.65636	33.943	1.5140
90.00	32.22	305.37	4.8197	0.69904	36.150	1.6124
92.00	33.33	306.48	5.1304	0.74411	38.481	1.7164
94.00	34.44	307.59	5.4584	0.79167	40.941	1.8261
96.00	35.56	308.71	5.8043	0.84185	43.536	1.9419
98.00	36.67	309.82	6.1691	0.89476	46.272	2.0639
100.00	37.78	310.93	6.5536	0.95052	49.156	2.1925
102.00	38.89	312.04	6.9586	1.0093	52.193	2.3280
104.00	40.00	313.15	7.3851	1.0711	55.392	2.4707
106.00	41.11	314.26	7.8340	1.1362	58.759	2.6209
108.00	42.22	315.37	8.3062	1.2047	62.301	2.7788
110.00	43.33	316.48	8.8027	1.2767	66.025	2.9450
112.00	44.44	317.59	9.3246	1.3524	69.939	3.1196

Vapor Pressure of Water (cont.)

Temperature			Vapor Pressure			
°F	°C	K	kPa	psi	mm of Hg at 0°C	ft of H2O at 4°C
114.00	45.56	318.71	9.8729	1.4319	74.052	3.3030
116.00	46.67	319.82	10.449	1.5154	78.370	3.4956
118.00	47.78	320.93	11.053	1.6031	82.904	3.6978
120.00	48.89	322.04	11.687	1.6951	87.661	3.9100
122.00	50.00	323.15	12.352	1.7916	92.650	4.1326
124.00	51.11	324.26	13.050	1.8927	97.881	4.3659
126.00	52.22	325.37	13.781	1.9987	103.36	4.6104
128.00	53.33	326.48	14.546	2.1098	109.11	4.8665
130.00	54.44	327.59	15.348	2.2260	115.12	5.1347
132.00	55.56	328.71	16.187	2.3478	121.41	5.4155
134.00	56.67	329.82	17.065	2.4751	128.00	5.7092
136.00	57.78	330.93	17.984	2.6083	134.89	6.0165
138.00	58.89	332.04	18.944	2.7476	142.09	6.3377
140.00	60.00	333.15	19.947	2.8931	149.62	6.6734
142.00	61.11	334.26	20.996	3.0452	157.48	7.0242
144.00	62.22	335.37	22.091	3.2040	165.69	7.3905
146.00	63.33	336.48	23.234	3.3698	174.27	7.7730
148.00	64.44	337.59	24.427	3.5428	183.22	8.1721
150.00	65.56	338.71	25.672	3.7234	192.55	8.5885
152.00	66.67	339.82	26.970	3.9116	202.29	9.0227
154.00	67.78	340.93	28.323	4.1079	212.44	9.4755
156.00	68.89	342.04	29.733	4.3124	223.01	9.9473
158.00	70.00	343.15	31.202	4.5255	234.03	10.439
160.00	71.11	344.26	32.732	4.7474	245.51	10.951
162.00	72.22	345.37	34.325	4.9785	257.46	11.484
164.00	73.33	346.48	35.983	5.2189	269.89	12.038
166.00	74.44	347.59	37.708	5.4691	282.83	12.615
168.00	75.56	348.71	39.503	5.7294	296.29	13.216
170.00	76.67	349.82	41.368	6.0000	310.28	13.840
172.00	77.78	350.93	43.307	6.2812	324.83	14.489
174.00	78.89	352.04	45.323	6.5735	339.94	15.163
176.00	80.00	353.15	47.416	6.8771	355.64	15.863
178.00	81.11	354.26	49.590	7.1924	371.95	16.590
180.00	82.22	355.37	51.847	7.5197	388.88	17.345
182.00	83.33	356.48	54.189	7.8594	406.45	18.129
184.00	84.44	357.59	56.619	8.2119	424.67	18.942
186.00	85.56	358.71	59.140	8.5775	443.58	19.785
188.00	86.67	359.82	61.754	8.9567	463.19	20.660
190.00	87.78	360.93	64.464	9.3497	483.52	21.567
192.00	88.89	362.04	67.273	9.7571	504.58	22.506
194.00	90.00	363.15	70.183	10.179	526.41	23.480
196.00	91.11	364.26	73.197	10.616	549.02	24.488
198.00	92.22	365.37	76.318	11.069	572.43	25.532

Vapor Pressure of Water (cont.)

Temperature			Vapor Pressure			
°F	°C	K	kPa	psi	mm of Hg at 0°C	ft of H2O at 4°C
200.00	93.33	366.48	79.549	11.538	596.66	26.613
202.00	94.44	367.59	82.894	12.023	621.75	27.732
204.00	95.56	368.71	86.354	12.525	647.70	28.890
206.00	96.67	369.82	89.933	13.044	674.55	30.087
208.00	97.78	370.93	93.635	13.581	702.31	31.326
210.00	98.89	372.04	97.462	14.136	731.02	32.606
212.00	100.00	373.15	101.42	14.709	760.69	33.930
214.00	101.11	374.26	105.51	15.302	791.35	35.297
216.00	102.22	375.37	109.73	15.915	823.03	36.710
218.00	103.33	376.48	114.09	16.548	855.75	38.170
220.00	104.44	377.59	118.60	17.201	889.53	39.677
222.00	105.56	378.71	123.25	17.875	924.41	41.232
224.00	106.67	379.82	128.05	18.571	960.41	42.838
226.00	107.78	380.93	133.00	19.290	997.56	44.495
228.00	108.89	382.04	138.11	20.031	1,035.9	46.204
230.00	110.00	383.15	143.38	20.795	1,075.4	47.967
232.00	111.11	384.26	148.81	21.583	1,116.2	49.785
234.00	112.22	385.37	154.41	22.396	1,158.2	51.659
236.00	113.33	386.48	160.19	23.233	1,201.5	53.591
238.00	114.44	387.59	166.14	24.096	1,246.1	55.582
240.00	115.56	388.71	172.27	24.985	1,292.1	57.633
242.00	116.67	389.82	178.58	25.901	1,339.5	59.745
244.00	117.78	390.93	185.08	26.844	1,388.2	61.921
246.00	118.89	392.04	191.78	27.815	1,438.5	64.160
248.00	120.00	393.15	198.67	28.815	1,490.1	66.466
250.00	121.11	394.26	205.76	29.844	1,543.3	68.839
252.00	122.22	395.37	213.06	30.902	1,598.1	71.280
254.00	123.33	396.48	220.57	31.991	1,654.4	73.792
256.00	124.44	397.59	228.29	33.111	1,712.3	76.376
258.00	125.56	398.71	236.23	34.263	1,771.9	79.032
260.00	126.67	399.82	244.40	35.447	1,833.1	81.763
262.00	127.78	400.93	252.79	36.664	1,896.0	84.571
264.00	128.89	402.04	261.41	37.915	1,960.7	87.456
266.00	130.00	403.15	270.28	39.200	2,027.2	90.421
268.00	131.11	404.26	279.38	40.521	2,095.5	93.467
270.00	132.22	405.37	288.73	41.877	2,165.6	96.596
272.00	133.33	406.48	298.34	43.270	2,237.7	99.809
274.00	134.44	407.59	308.20	44.700	2,311.6	103.11
276.00	135.56	408.71	318.32	46.168	2,387.6	106.49
278.00	136.67	409.82	328.71	47.675	2,465.5	109.97
280.00	137.78	410.93	339.37	49.222	2,545.5	113.54
282.00	138.89	412.04	350.31	50.808	2,627.5	117.20
284.00	140.00	413.15	361.53	52.436	2,711.7	120.95

Vapor Pressure of Water (cont.)

Temperature			Vapor Pressure			
°F	°C	K	kPa	psi	mm of Hg at 0°C	ft of H2O at 4°C
286.00	141.11	414.26	373.04	54.105	2,798.0	124.80
288.00	142.22	415.37	384.85	55.818	2,886.6	128.75
290.00	143.33	416.48	396.95	57.573	2,977.3	132.80
292.00	144.44	417.59	409.36	59.373	3,070.4	136.95
294.00	145.56	418.71	422.08	61.217	3,165.8	141.21
296.00	146.67	419.82	435.11	63.107	3,263.6	145.57
298.00	147.78	420.93	448.46	65.044	3,363.7	150.03
300.00	148.89	422.04	462.14	67.028	3,466.3	154.61
302.00	150.00	423.15	476.16	69.061	3,571.4	159.30
304.00	151.11	424.26	490.51	71.143	3,679.1	164.10
306.00	152.22	425.37	505.21	73.274	3,789.3	169.02
308.00	153.33	426.48	520.25	75.457	3,902.2	174.05
310.00	154.44	427.59	535.66	77.691	4,017.7	179.21
312.00	155.56	428.71	551.42	79.977	4,136.0	184.48
314.00	156.67	429.82	567.56	82.317	4,257.0	189.88
316.00	157.78	430.93	584.06	84.711	4,380.8	195.40
318.00	158.89	432.04	600.95	87.161	4,507.5	201.05
320.00	160.00	433.15	618.23	89.667	4,637.1	206.83
322.00	161.11	434.26	635.90	92.229	4,769.6	212.74
324.00	162.22	435.37	653.97	94.850	4,905.1	218.79
326.00	163.33	436.48	672.44	97.530	5,043.7	224.97
328.00	164.44	437.59	691.33	100.27	5,185.3	231.29
330.00	165.56	438.71	710.64	103.07	5,330.2	237.75
332.00	166.67	439.82	730.37	105.93	5,478.2	244.35
334.00	167.78	440.93	750.53	108.86	5,629.4	251.09
336.00	168.89	442.04	771.14	111.84	5,783.9	257.99
338.00	170.00	443.15	792.18	114.90	5,941.8	265.03
340.00	171.11	444.26	813.69	118.02	6,103.1	272.22
342.00	172.22	445.37	835.65	121.20	6,267.8	279.57
344.00	173.33	446.48	858.07	124.45	6,436.0	287.07
346.00	174.44	447.59	880.97	127.77	6,607.8	294.73
348.00	175.56	448.71	904.35	131.17	6,783.1	302.55
350.00	176.67	449.82	928.22	134.63	6,962.1	310.54
352.00	177.78	450.93	952.58	138.16	7,144.8	318.69
354.00	178.89	452.04	977.44	141.77	7,331.3	327.01
356.00	180.00	453.15	1,002.8	145.45	7,521.6	335.49
358.00	181.11	454.26	1,028.7	149.20	7,715.8	344.15
360.00	182.22	455.37	1,055.1	153.03	7,913.9	352.99
362.00	183.33	456.48	1,082.0	156.94	8,115.9	362.00
364.00	184.44	457.59	1,109.5	160.92	8,322.0	371.19
366.00	185.56	458.71	1,137.5	164.99	8,532.2	380.57
368.00	186.67	459.82	1,166.1	169.13	8,746.5	390.13
370.00	187.78	460.93	1,195.3	173.36	8,965.1	399.88

Vapor Pressure of Water (cont.)

Temperature			Vapor Pressure			
°F	°C	K	kPa	psi	mm of Hg at 0°C	ft of H2O at 4°C
372.00	188.89	462.04	1,225.0	177.67	9,187.9	409.81
374.00	190.00	463.15	1,255.2	182.06	9,415.0	419.94
376.00	191.11	464.26	1,286.1	186.53	9,646.5	430.27
378.00	192.22	465.37	1,317.6	191.10	9,882.4	440.79
380.00	193.33	466.48	1,349.6	195.74	10,123	451.52
382.00	194.44	467.59	1,382.3	200.48	10,368	462.44
384.00	195.56	468.71	1,415.5	205.31	10,617	473.57
386.00	196.67	469.82	1,449.4	210.22	10,872	484.91
388.00	197.78	470.93	1,484.0	215.23	11,131	496.46
390.00	198.89	472.04	1,519.1	220.33	11,394	508.23
392.00	200.00	473.15	1,554.9	225.52	11,663	520.21
394.00	201.11	474.26	1,591.4	230.81	11,936	532.41
396.00	202.22	475.37	1,628.5	236.20	12,215	544.83
398.00	203.33	476.48	1,666.3	241.68	12,498	557.48
400.00	204.44	477.59	1,704.8	247.26	12,787	570.35
402.00	205.56	478.71	1,744.0	252.94	13,081	583.45
404.00	206.67	479.82	1,783.8	258.72	13,380	596.79
406.00	207.78	480.93	1,824.4	264.61	13,684	610.36
408.00	208.89	482.04	1,865.7	270.60	13,994	624.17
410.00	210.00	483.15	1,907.7	276.69	14,309	638.22
412.00	211.11	484.26	1,950.4	282.89	14,629	652.52
414.00	212.22	485.37	1,993.9	289.19	14,955	667.06
416.00	213.33	486.48	2,038.1	295.60	15,287	681.86
418.00	214.44	487.59	2,083.1	302.13	15,624	696.90
420.00	215.56	488.71	2,128.8	308.76	15,967	712.20
422.00	216.67	489.82	2,175.3	315.51	16,316	727.77
424.00	217.78	490.93	2,222.6	322.37	16,671	743.59
426.00	218.89	492.04	2,270.7	329.34	17,032	759.68
428.00	220.00	493.15	2,319.6	336.43	17,398	776.03
430.00	221.11	494.26	2,369.3	343.63	17,771	792.66
432.00	222.22	495.37	2,419.8	350.97	18,150	809.56
434.00	223.33	496.48	2,471.2	358.41	18,535	826.73
436.00	224.44	497.59	2,523.3	365.98	18,926	844.19
438.00	225.56	498.71	2,576.4	373.67	19,324	861.93
440.00	226.67	499.82	2,630.2	381.49	19,728	879.96
442.00	227.78	500.93	2,685.0	389.43	20,139	898.27
444.00	228.89	502.04	2,740.6	397.49	20,556	916.88
446.00	230.00	503.15	2,797.1	405.69	20,980	935.78
448.00	231.11	504.26	2,854.5	414.01	21,410	954.98
450.00	232.22	505.37	2,912.8	422.47	21,848	974.49
452.00	233.33	506.48	2,972.0	431.05	22,292	994.30
454.00	234.44	507.59	3,032.1	439.78	22,743	1,014.4
456.00	235.56	508.71	3,093.2	448.63	23,201	1,034.8

Vapor Pressure of Water (cont.)

Temperature			Vapor Pressure			
°F	°C	K	kPa	psi	mm of Hg at 0°C	ft of H2O at 4°C
458.00	236.67	509.82	3,155.2	457.62	23,666	1,055.6
460.00	237.78	510.93	3,218.2	466.75	24,138	1,076.6
462.00	238.89	512.04	3,282.1	476.02	24,617	1,098.0
464.00	240.00	513.15	3,347.0	485.43	25,104	1,119.7
466.00	241.11	514.26	3,412.8	494.99	25,598	1,141.8
468.00	242.22	515.37	3,479.7	504.68	26,099	1,164.1
470.00	243.33	516.48	3,547.5	514.52	26,608	1,186.8
472.00	244.44	517.59	3,616.4	524.51	27,125	1,209.9
474.00	245.56	518.71	3,686.3	534.65	27,649	1,233.3
476.00	246.67	519.82	3,757.2	544.93	28,181	1,257.0
478.00	247.78	520.93	3,829.1	555.37	28,721	1,281.0
480.00	248.89	522.04	3,902.1	565.96	29,268	1,305.5
482.00	250.00	523.15	3,976.2	576.70	29,824	1,330.2
484.00	251.11	524.26	4,051.3	587.60	30,387	1,355.4
486.00	252.22	525.37	4,127.6	598.65	30,959	1,380.9
488.00	253.33	526.48	4,204.9	609.87	31,539	1,406.8
490.00	254.44	527.59	4,283.3	621.24	32,127	1,433.0
492.00	255.56	528.71	4,362.8	632.77	32,723	1,459.6
494.00	256.67	529.82	4,443.5	644.47	33,328	1,486.6
496.00	257.78	530.93	4,525.3	656.33	33,942	1,513.9
498.00	258.89	532.04	4,608.2	668.36	34,564	1,541.7
500.00	260.00	533.15	4,692.3	680.56	35,195	1,569.8
502.00	261.11	534.26	4,777.5	692.92	35,834	1,598.3
504.00	262.22	535.37	4,864.0	705.46	36,482	1,627.3
506.00	263.33	536.48	4,951.6	718.17	37,140	1,656.6
508.00	264.44	537.59	5,040.4	731.05	37,806	1,686.3
510.00	265.56	538.71	5,130.5	744.11	38,481	1,716.4
512.00	266.67	539.82	5,221.7	757.35	39,166	1,746.9
514.00	267.78	540.93	5,314.2	770.77	39,860	1,777.9
516.00	268.89	542.04	5,408.0	784.36	40,563	1,809.3
518.00	270.00	543.15	5,503.0	798.14	41,275	1,841.0
520.00	271.11	544.26	5,599.3	812.11	41,998	1,873.3
522.00	272.22	545.37	5,696.8	826.25	42,729	1,905.9
524.00	273.33	546.48	5,795.7	840.59	43,471	1,939.0
526.00	274.44	547.59	5,895.8	855.12	44,222	1,972.5
528.00	275.56	548.71	5,997.3	869.83	44,983	2,006.4
530.00	276.67	549.82	6,100.1	884.74	45,754	2,040.8
532.00	277.78	550.93	6,204.2	899.85	46,535	2,075.6
534.00	278.89	552.04	6,309.7	915.15	47,326	2,110.9
536.00	280.00	553.15	6,416.6	930.65	48,128	2,146.7
538.00	281.11	554.26	6,524.8	946.34	48,940	2,182.9
540.00	282.22	555.37	6,634.4	962.24	49,762	2,219.6
542.00	283.33	556.48	6,745.5	978.35	50,595	2,256.7

Vapor Pressure of Water (cont.)

Temperature			Vapor Pressure			
°F	°C	K	kPa	psi	mm of Hg at 0°C	ft of H2O at 4°C
544.00	284.44	557.59	6,857.9	994.65	51,438	2,294.3
546.00	285.56	558.71	6,971.8	1,011.2	52,292	2,332.4
548.00	286.67	559.82	7,087.1	1,027.9	53,157	2,371.0
550.00	287.78	560.93	7,203.8	1,044.8	54,033	2,410.1
552.00	288.89	562.04	7,322.1	1,062.0	54,919	2,449.6
554.00	290.00	563.15	7,441.8	1,079.3	55,817	2,489.7
556.00	291.11	564.26	7,563.0	1,096.9	56,726	2,530.2
558.00	292.22	565.37	7,685.7	1,114.7	57,646	2,571.3
560.00	293.33	566.48	7,809.9	1,132.7	58,578	2,612.8
562.00	294.44	567.59	7,935.6	1,151.0	59,521	2,654.9
564.00	295.56	568.71	8,062.9	1,169.4	60,476	2,697.5
566.00	296.67	569.82	8,191.8	1,188.1	61,443	2,740.6
568.00	297.78	570.93	8,322.2	1,207.0	62,421	2,784.2
570.00	298.89	572.04	8,454.2	1,226.2	63,411	2,828.4
572.00	300.00	573.15	8,587.9	1,245.6	64,414	2,873.1
574.00	301.11	574.26	8,723.1	1,265.2	65,428	2,918.3
576.00	302.22	575.37	8,860.0	1,285.0	66,455	2,964.1
578.00	303.33	576.48	8,998.5	1,305.1	67,494	3,010.5
580.00	304.44	577.59	9,138.7	1,325.5	68,545	3,057.4
582.00	305.56	578.71	9,280.5	1,346.0	69,609	3,104.8
584.00	306.67	579.82	9,424.1	1,366.8	70,686	3,152.8
586.00	307.78	580.93	9,569.3	1,387.9	71,775	3,201.4
588.00	308.89	582.04	9,716.3	1,409.2	72,877	3,250.6
590.00	310.00	583.15	9,865.0	1,430.8	73,993	3,300.4
592.00	311.11	584.26	10,015	1,452.6	75,121	3,350.7
594.00	312.22	585.37	10,168	1,474.7	76,263	3,401.6
596.00	313.33	586.48	10,322	1,497.0	77,418	3,453.2
598.00	314.44	587.59	10,478	1,519.6	78,587	3,505.3
600.00	315.56	588.71	10,635	1,542.5	79,770	3,558.0
602.00	316.67	589.82	10,795	1,565.6	80,966	3,611.4
604.00	317.78	590.93	10,956	1,589.0	82,176	3,665.4
606.00	318.89	592.04	11,119	1,612.7	83,400	3,720.0
608.00	320.00	593.15	11,284	1,636.6	84,638	3,775.2
610.00	321.11	594.26	11,451	1,660.9	85,891	3,831.1
612.00	322.22	595.37	11,620	1,685.4	87,158	3,887.6
614.00	323.33	596.48	11,791	1,710.1	88,439	3,944.7
616.00	324.44	597.59	11,964	1,735.2	89,735	4,002.5
618.00	325.56	598.71	12,139	1,760.6	91,046	4,061.0
620.00	326.67	599.82	12,315	1,786.2	92,373	4,120.2
622.00	327.78	600.93	12,494	1,812.1	93,714	4,180.0
624.00	328.89	602.04	12,675	1,838.4	95,070	4,240.5
626.00	330.00	603.15	12,858	1,864.9	96,442	4,301.7
628.00	331.11	604.26	13,043	1,891.7	97,830	4,363.6

Vapor Pressure of Water (cont.)

Temperature			Vapor Pressure			
°F	°C	K	kPa	psi	mm of Hg at 0°C	ft of H2O at 4°C
630.00	332.22	605.37	13,230	1,918.9	99,233	4,426.2
632.00	333.33	606.48	13,419	1,946.3	100,650	4,489.5
634.00	334.44	607.59	13,611	1,974.1	102,090	4,553.5
636.00	335.56	608.71	13,804	2,002.2	103,540	4,618.3
638.00	336.67	609.82	14,000	2,030.5	105,010	4,683.8
640.00	337.78	610.93	14,198	2,059.3	106,490	4,750.0
642.00	338.89	612.04	14,398	2,088.3	107,990	4,817.0
644.00	340.00	613.15	14,601	2,117.7	109,510	4,884.7
646.00	341.11	614.26	14,805	2,147.4	111,050	4,953.2
648.00	342.22	615.37	15,013	2,177.4	112,600	5,022.5
650.00	343.33	616.48	15,222	2,207.8	114,170	5,092.5
652.00	344.44	617.59	15,434	2,238.5	115,760	5,163.4
654.00	345.56	618.71	15,648	2,269.5	117,370	5,235.1
656.00	346.67	619.82	15,865	2,301.0	118,990	5,307.5
658.00	347.78	620.93	16,084	2,332.7	120,640	5,380.8
660.00	348.89	622.04	16,305	2,364.9	122,300	5,455.0
662.00	350.00	623.15	16,529	2,397.4	123,980	5,529.9
664.00	351.11	624.26	16,756	2,430.3	125,680	5,605.8
666.00	352.22	625.37	16,985	2,463.5	127,400	5,682.5
668.00	353.33	626.48	17,217	2,497.1	129,140	5,760.0
670.00	354.44	627.59	17,452	2,531.2	130,900	5,838.5
672.00	355.56	628.71	17,689	2,565.6	132,680	5,917.9
674.00	356.67	629.82	17,929	2,600.4	134,480	5,998.2
676.00	357.78	630.93	18,172	2,635.6	136,300	6,079.4
678.00	358.89	632.04	18,417	2,671.2	138,140	6,161.6
680.00	360.00	633.15	18,666	2,707.3	140,000	6,244.8

Source:

Tables of Physical and Chemical Constants, Kaye and Laby, Longman Group Limited, Essex, England, 1995

Abbreviations are as follows:

°F = degree Fahrenheit; °C = degree Celsius; K = kelvin; kPa = kilopascal; psi = pound-force per square inch; mm = millimeter; Hg = mercury; ft = feet; H2O = water

Horizontal Pipe Discharge

L Distance inches	Gallons per Minute Discharge for a given Nominal Pipe Diameter D (Inches)						
	1	1–1/4	1–1/2	2	2–1/2	3	4
4	6	10	13	22	31	48	83
5	7	12	17	27	39	61	104
6	8	15	20	33	47	73	125
7	10	17	23	38	55	85	146
8	11	20	26	44	62	97	166
9	13	22	30	49	70	110	187
10	14	24	33	55	78	122	208
11	16	27	36	60	86	134	229
12	17	29	40	66	94	146	250
13	18	31	43	71	102	158	270
14	20	34	46	77	109	170	292
15	21	36	50	82	117	183	312
16	23	39	53	88	125	196	334
17	...	41	56	93	133	207	355
18	...	...	60	99	144	220	375
19	...	...	...	110	148	232	395
20	...	...	...	...	156	244	415
21	...	...	...	...	...	256	435
22	...	...	...	...	...	...	460

L Distance inches	Gallons per Minute Discharge for a given Nominal Pipe Diameter D (Inches)				
	5	6	8	10	12
5	163	...	...	...	...
6	195	285	...	...	...
7	228	334	580	...	...
8	260	380	665	1060	...
9	293	430	750	1190	1660
10	326	476	830	1330	1850
11	360	525	915	1460	2020
12	390	570	1000	1600	2220
13	425	620	1080	1730	2400
14	456	670	1160	1860	2590
15	490	710	1250	2000	2780
16	520	760	1330	2120	2960
17	550	810	1410	2260	3140
18	590	860	1500	2390	3330
19	620	910	1580	2520	3500
20	650	950	1660	2660	3700
21	685	1000	1750	2800	3890
22	720	1050	1830	2920	4060
23	750	1100	1910	3060	4250
24	...	1140	2000	3200	4440

Vertical Pipe Discharge

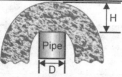

The following formula is an approximation of the output of a vertical pipe.

$$GPM = \sqrt{H} \times K \times D^2 \times 5.68$$

> GPM = gallons per minute
> H = height in inches
> D = diameter of pipe in inches
> K = constant from 0.87 to 0.97 for diameters of 2 to 6 inches and heights (H) up to 24 inches.

Example: K=0.97, 6 inch diameter with 10 inch height ≅ 626 gpm

Weir Discharge Volumes

Height of water flow H

Head Inches	GPM for Width of Weir in Feet			gpm/foot over 5 feet wide
	1	3	5	
1	35	107	179	36
1.5	64	197	329	66
2	98	302	506	102
2.5	136	421	705	142
3	178	552	926	187
4	269	845	1420	288
5	369	1174	1978	402
6	476	1534	2592	529
7	...	1922	3255	667
8	...	2335	3963	814
9	...	2769	4713	972
10	...	3225	5501	1138
12	...	4189	7181	1496

Based on the Francis formula:
Cu ft/sec water = 3.33 (W − 0.2 H) H $^{1.5}$ Where H=height in feet, W=width in feet and distance "A" should be at least 3 H.

Welding

Arc Electrodes – Mild Steel. 672
Electrode Amperages...672
Electrodes – Low Alloy Steel...673
Electrodes – Stainless Steel..673
Electrode Brand Conversion (Steel)..674
Gas Welding Rods 675
Welding Gases 675
Hard and Soft Solder Alloys 676
Solder Flux 676
Tempering Color for Steel 677
Welding Symbols...678

Arc Electrodes - Mild Steel

Electrode #	Description
⇓ This digit indicates the following:	
Exx1z	All positions of welding
Exx2z	Flat and horizontal positions
Exx3z	Flat welding positions only
⇓⇓ These digits indicate the following:	
Exx10	DC, reverse polarity
Exx11	AC or DC, reverse polarity
Exx12	DC, straight polarity or AC
Exx13	AC or DC, straight polarity
Exx14	DC, either polarity or AC, iron powder
Exx15	DC, reverse polarity, low hydrogen
Exx16	AC or DC, reverse polarity, low hydrogen
Exx18	AC or DC, reverse, iron powder, low hydrogen
Exx20	DC, straight polarity, or AC for horizontal fillet welds; and DC either polarity, or AC, for flat position welding
Exx24	DC, either polarity, or AC, iron powder
Exx27	DC, straight polarity, or AC for horizontal fillet welding; and DC, either polarity, or AC, for flat position welding, iron powder
Exx28	AC or DC, reverse polarity, iron powder, low hydrogen

The "xx" shown above is a two digit number indicating the weld metal tensile strength in 1000psi increments. For example, E**70**18 is 70,000 psi weld metal.

Electrode Amperages

	Amperage Per Rod Diameter (inches)				
Type	1/16	5/64	3/32	1/8	5/32
E6010			60-90	80-120	110-160
E6011			50-90	80-130	120-180
E6012			40-90	80-120	120-190
E6013	20-40	25-60	30-80	80-120	120-190
E7010-A1			30-80	70-120	100-160
E7014			80-110	110-150	140-190
E7016			75-105	100-150	140-190
E7018 (& -A1)			70-120	100-150	120-200
E7020-A1					
E7024			90-120	120-150	180-230
E7028					175-250
E8016-B2			60-100	80-120	140-190
E8018-C3			70-120	100-150	120-200
Stainless:					
3xx AC-DC	20-40	30-60	60-90	90-120	120-160
4xx AC-DC	20-40	30-60	60-90	90-120	120-160
5xx AC-DC	20-40	30-60	60-90	90-120	120-160

Amperage Per Rod Diameter (inches)

Type	3/16	7/32	1/4	5/16	3/8
E6010	150-200	175-250	225-300		
E6011	140-220	170-250	225-325		
E6012	140-240	180-315	225-350		
E6013	140-240	225-300	250-350		
E6020	175-250	225-325	250-350	325-450	450-600
E6027	225-300	275-375	350-450		
E7010-A1	130-200				
E7014	180-260	250-325	300-400	400-500	
E7016	190-250	250-300	300-375		
E7018	200-275	275-350			
E7020-A1	250-350				
E7024	250-300	300-350	350-400	400-500	
E7028	175-250	250-325	300-400		
E8016-B2	180-250	300-425			
E8018-C3	200-275				

Stainless:

3xx AC-DC	150-190	225-300			
4xx AC-DC	150-190				
5xx AC-DC	150-190		225-300		

Note: All of the above ratings are estimates and you should always verify amperages with the manufacturer before you start a job.

Electrodes - Low Alloy Steel

Low Alloy Steel Specifications (American Welding Society Specification A 5.5-69) are coded the same as the Mild Steel Specification of two pages ago, except that the specification number is followed by a dash and then a letter-number code indicating the chemical composition of the weld metal. For example, **E8016–C1**

The composition codes are as follows:

–A	Carbon-molybdenum steel
–B	Chromium-molybdenum steel
–C	Nickel steel
–D	Manganese-molybdenum steel
–G	All other Low Alloy Steel Electrodes, with minimums of 0.2% molybdenum, 0.3% chromium, 1% manganese, 0.8% silicon, 0.5% nickel, and 0.1% vanadium.
–M	Military specification

The final digit of the composition code specifies the exact composition of the weld metal.

Electrodes - Stainless Steel

Stainless electrode specifications (AWS A5.4-62T) are coded with the American Iron and Steel Institute alloy type number followed by a dash and two digit number (either 15 or 16) indicating usability or a set of letters (AC, DC, AC–DC or ELC AC–DC) indicating the type of current to be used. For example, **E308–15** or **308 ELC AC–DC.**

Electrode Brand Conversion

Make	E6010	E6011	E6012
Airco	6010	6011,C,LOC	6012,C
Air Products	6010IP	6011,C	6012GP,SF,IP
Arc Products	SW610,AP100	SW14,IMP	SW612,PFA
Gen. Dynamics	610,IP	611,A	612,A
Hobart Bros.	10,IP	335A	12,212A,12A
Lincoln (Fleetweld)	5,5P	35,180,35LS	7
McKay Co	6010,IP	6011,IP	6012
Murex Weld Prod	Speedex 610	Type A,611C	Type N13
Reid Avery (Raco)	6010	6011,IP	6012,IP
Westinghouse	XL610,A	ACP611	FP612,2-612

Make	E6013	E6020	E6027
Airco	6013,C	6020	Easyarc 6027
Air Products	6013GP,SF	6020	6027IP
Arc Products	SW16		DH27
Gen. Dynamics	613,A	620	IP627
Hobart Bros.	13A,447A,413		27
Lincoln (Fleetweld)	37,57		Jetweld 2
McKay Co	6013	6020	
Murex Weld Prod	Type U,U13	Type D,FHP	Speedex 27
Reid Avery Co	6013		
Westinghouse	SW613,2M-613	DH620	ZIP 27

Make	E7014	E7016	E7018
Airco	Easyarc 7014	7016,M	7018MR,C
Air Products	7014IP	7016,A	7018,IP
Arc Products	SW15IP	70LA-2	170LA,SW47
Gen. Dynamics	IP714	716,A	IP718,A
Hobart Bros.	14A	16	LH718
Lincoln (Fleetweld)	47		Jetweld-LH70
McKay Co	7014	Puralloy 70AC	7018
Murex Weld Prod	Speedex U	Type HTS,18,180	HTS,M,718
Reid Avery Co	7014	7016	7018
Westinghouse	ZIP 14	LOH-2-716	WIZ-18

Make	E7024	E7028
Airco	Easyarc 7024	Easyarc 7028
Air Products	7024IP	7028
Arc Products	SW44	DH170
Gen. Dynamics	IP724	IP728
Hobart Bros.	24	
Lincoln	Jetweld 3,1	Jetweld HL3800
McKay Co	7024	
Murex Weld Prod	Speedex 24	Speedex 28
Reid Avery Co		
Westinghouse	ZIP 24	WIZ 28

Gas Welding Rods

Rod Diameter	Rods per Pound (36 inch long)			
	Steel	Brass	Aluminum	Cast Iron
1/16	31	29	91	NA
3/32	14	13	41	NA
1/8	8	7	23	NA
5/32	5	NA	NA	NA
3/16	3-1/2	3	9	5-1/2
1/4	2	2	6	2-1/4
5/16	1-1/3	NA	NA	1/2
3/8	1	1	NA	1/4

Welding Gases

Gas	Tank Sizes Cubic Ft	Comments
Acetylene	300, 100, 75, 40, 10	Formula – C2H2, explosive. Colorless, flammable gas, garlic–like odor, explosion danger if used in welding with gage pressures over 15 psig (30 psig absolute).
Oxygen	244, 122, 80, 40, 20 4500 liquid	Formula – O2, non-explosive Colorless, odorless, tasteless. Supports combustion in welding.
Nitrogen	225, 113, 80, 40, 20	Formula – N2 non-explosive Colorless, odorless, tasteless, inert.
Argon	330, 131, 4754 liquid	Formula – Ar, non-explosive Colorless, odorless, tasteless, inert.
Carbon Dioxide	50 lbs 20 lbs	Formula – CO2 non-explosive Toxic in large quantities Colorless, odorless, tasteless, inert.
Hydrogen	191	Formula – H2, explosive Colorless, odorless, tasteless Lightest gas known.
Helium	221	Formula – He, non-explosive Colorless, odorless, tasteless, inert.

Hard & Soft Solder Alloys

Metal to be Soldered	Alloy Component Percentage				
	Tin	Lead	Zinc	Copper	Other
SOFT SOLDER:					
Aluminum	70		25		Al=3, Pho=2
Bismuth	33	33			Bi=34
Block tin	99	1			
Brass	66	34			
Copper	60	40			
Gold	67	33			
Gun metal	63	37			
Iron & Steel	50	50			
Lead	33	67			
Pewter	25	25			Bi=50
Silver	67	33			
Steel, galvanized	58	42			
Steel, tinned	64	36			
Zinc	55	45			
HARD SOLDER:					
Brass, soft			78	22	
Brass, hard			55	45	
Copper			50	50	
Iron, cast			45	55	
Iron & Steel			36	64	
Gold				22	Ag=11, Au=67
Silver			10	20	Ag=70

FLUX   Metal to be used on

Ammonia Chloride ....Galvanized iron, iron, nickel, tin, zinc, brass, copper, gun metal

Borax ....For hard solders, brass, copper, gold, iron & steel, silver

Cuprous oxide ....Cast iron

Hydrochloric Acid......Galvanized iron and steel, tin, zinc

Organic.....................Lead, pewter

Rosin ....Brass, bronze, cadmium, copper, lead, silver, gun metal, tinned steel

Stainless Steel Flux..Special for stainless steel only

Sterling ....Silver

Tallow ....Lead, pewter

Zinc Chloride ....Bismuth, tin, brass, copper, gold, silver, gun metal, tinned steel

Tempering Color for Steel

Heated Color of Carbon Steel	Temperature F°	Temper Item or Comment
Faint yellow	420	Knives, hammers
Very pale yellow	430	Reamers
Light yellow	440	Lathe tools, scrapers, milling cutters, reamers
Pale straw–yellow	450	Twist drills for hard use
Straw–yellow	460	Dies, punches, bits, reamers
Deep straw–yellow	470	
Dark yellow	480	Twist drills, large taps
	485	Knurls
Yellow–brown	490	
Brown–yellow	500	Axes, wood chisels, drifts, taps 1/2 inch or over, nut taps, thread dies
Spotted red–brown	510	
Brown–purple	520	Taps 1/4 inch and under
Light purple	530	
Full purple	540	Cold chisels, center punches
Dark purple	550	
Full blue	560	Screwdrivers, springs, gears
Dark blue	570	
Medium blue	600	Scrapers, spokeshaves
Light blue	640	
Red-visible at night	750	
Red-visible at twilight	885	
Red-visible in daylight	975	
Red-visible in sunlight	1075	
Dark red	1290	
Dull cherry red	1475	
Cherry red	1650	
Bright cherry red	1830	
Orange–red	2010	
Orange–yellow	2190	
Yellow–white	2370	
White	2550	
Brilliant white	2730	
Blue–white	2900	
Acetylene flame	4080	
Induction furnace	5450	
Electric arc light	7200	

Tempering is commonly a two-step process. Step 1: To harden the tool, heat the tool end to a bright red, quench tool end in cold water until it is cool to the touch, then sharpen or polish tool end. At this point the tool has been hardened but it is now brittle. Step 2: To temper the tool, heat the tool to the temperature indicated by its color in the above table, then quench the tool in water. The amount of temper is a function of what type of work the tool will be doing, so if your tool is not listed above, simply select one of the above tools that does similar work.

Structure of a Welding Symbol

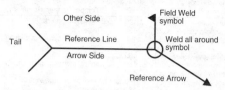

Main Elements:

The **Reference Arrow** connects the reference line to a joint that is to be welded.

The **Reference line** is the core of the weld symbol. The area below it contains information about the weld to be made on the arrow side of the joint. Information above the reference line describes the weld to be made on the side opposite the arrow.

Optional Elements:

The **Field Weld** symbol is included only if the weld is to be done in the field. If no symbol is present, the weld is to be done in the shop.

The **open circle** at the junction of the reference line and arrow is present if the weld is to be made all the way around the joint.

When the Reference Line has a **tail**, it usually contains special instructions.

Joint Types

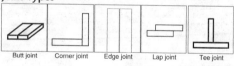

Butt joint   Corner joint   Edge joint   Lap joint   Tee joint

Weld Types

The four main types of welds are

- Fillet welds
- Groove welds
- Plug or slot welds
- Flange welds

Groove Welds

Bevel Groove

Double Bevel   Single Bevel, Full   Partial Bevel   Flare Bevel

May be used on all 5 joint types.

Square Groove

Partial square   Double square

May be used on butt, tee, edge and corner joints

J-Groove

Partial J   Double J   Single J, full

May be used on all 5 joint types

U-Groove

Double U weld   Partial U   Single U, full

Used with butt, edge and corner joints

V-Groove

Double V   Partial V   Single V, Full   Flare V

Used on butt, edge and corner welds

Fillet Welds

Fillet

Fillet, both sides right   Fillet   Fillet, left   Fillet, right

Fillet welds may be used on lap, tee and corner joints.

Plug and Slot Welds

Plug and Slot welds are used on lap joints when one of the pieces has holes in it. Plug welds are round while slot welds are elongated. The symbol is the same for both types.

Plug or slot weld

Flange Welds

Flange Welds are used for joining two rounded objects, such as pipes. Edge Flange welds may be used for butt or edge joints; Corner Flange welds are used for Edge or corner joints.

Edge Flange   Corner Flange

Other types of Welds

Spot or Projection - Used for lap, tee and corner joints

Spot or projection weld

Seam - used for lap, tee, edge and corner joints

Seam Weld

Braze- used for butt, lap, tee and corner joints -

BRAZE

Braze

Weights & Properties of Materials

Weights & Properties of Materials 682
Common Material Dumping Angles............................689
Stockpile Volume and Weight 690

Material	Specific Gravity	Weight lbs per cu foot	Weight lbs per cu yard	Weight kgs per cu meter	Angle of Repose
ABS (acrylonitrile butadiene styrene)	1.05	65.5	1769.8	1050.0	
Acetal	1.58	98.3	2654.8	1575.0	
Acetic acid, 90%	1.06	66.3	1790	1062.0	
Acetone	0.79	49.3	1331.6	790.0	
Acrylic (cast)	1.19	74.0	1997.4	1185.0	
Acrylonitrile	1.15	71.8	1938.4	1150.0	
ADC (Allyl diglycol carbonate,cast sheet)	1.35	84.3	2275.5	1350.0	
ADI fluid	0.90	56.1	1514.8	898.7	
Alcohol, ethyl	0.789	49	1329	788.5	
Alcohol, methyl	0.791	49	1333	790.9	
Alfalfa, ground	0.26	16	432	256.3	+45
Alum, lumpy	0.88	55	1485	881.0	30-45
Alum, pulverized	0.75	47	1269	752.9	30-45
Alumina	0.96	60	1620	961.1	30-45
Aluminum oxide	1.52	95	2565	1521.8	30
Aluminum, solid	2.64	165	4455	2643.1	
Ammonia gas	0.00	0.048	1.29	0.8	
Ammonium sulfate	0.83	52	1404	833.0	
Andesite, solid	2.77	173	4671	2771.2	
Antimony, cast	6.70	418	11286	6695.7	
Apple wood, dry	0.71	44	1188	704.8	
Apples	0.64	40	1080	640.7	
Arsenic	5.67	354	9558	5670.5	
ASA (Acrylate styrene acrylonitrile)	1.06	66.2	1786.7	1060.0	
Asbestos, shredded	0.35	22	594	352.4	30
Asbestos, solid	2.45	153	4131	2450.8	
Ash wood, black, dry	0.54	34	918	544.6	
Ash wood, white, dry	0.67	42	1134	672.8	
Ashes	0.66	41	1107	656.8	
Aspen wood	0.42	26	702	416.5	
Asphalt, crushed	0.72	45	1215	720.8	30-45
Aviation gasoline	0.72	44.9	1213.6	720.0	
Babbitt	7.28	454	12258	7272.4	
Bagasse	0.12	7.5	202	120.1	45
Bakelite, solid	1.36	85	2295	1361.6	
Baking powder	0.72	45	1215	720.8	30-45
Barite, crushed	2.88	180	4860	2883.3	
Barium	3.78	236	6372	3780.4	
Bark, wood refuse	0.24	15	405	240.3	45
Barley	0.61	38	1026	608.7	
Basalt, broken	1.96	122	3294	1954.3	
Basalt, solid	3.01	188	5076	3011.5	
Bauxite, crushed	1.28	80	2160	1281.5	30-45
Beans, castor	0.58	36	972	576.7	
Beans, cocoa	0.59	37	999	592.7	
Beans, navy	0.80	50	1350	800.9	
Beans, soy	0.72	45	1215	720.8	
Beeswax	0.96	60	1620	961.1	
Beets	0.72	45	1215	720.8	
Bentonite	0.59	37	999	592.7	45
Benzene	0.88	54.9	1483.3	880.0	
Bicarbonate of Soda	0.69	43	1161	688.8	42
Birch wood, yellow	0.71	44	1188	704.8	
Bismuth	9.79	611	16497	9787.3	
Bones, pulverized	0.88	55	1485	881.0	
Borax, fine	0.85	53	1431	849.0	30-45
Bran	0.26	16	432	256.3	30-45
Brass, cast	8.56	534	14418	8553.9	
Brass, rolled	8.56	534	14418	8553.9	
Brewers grain	0.43	27	729	432.5	45
Brick, chrome	2.80	175	4725	2803.2	

Material	Specific Gravity	Weight lbs per cu foot	Weight lbs per cu yard	Weight kgs per cu meter	Angle of Repose
Brick, common red	1.92	120	3240	1922.2	
Brick, fire clay	2.40	150	4050	2402.8	
Brick, magnesia	2.56	160	4320	2563.0	
Brick, silica	2.05	128	3456	2050.4	
Bronze	8.16	509	13743	8153.4	
Buckwheat	0.66	41	1107	656.8	
Butter	0.87	54	1458	865.0	
Cadmium	8.65	540	14580	8650.0	
Calcium carbide	1.20	75	2025	1201.4	30-45
Caliche	1.44	90	2430	1441.7	
Carbon dioxide	0.00	0.1234	3.3318	2.0	
Carbon monoxide	0.00	0.0781	2.1087	1.3	
Carbon, powdered	0.08	5	135	80.1	
Carbon, solid	2.15	134	3618	2146.5	
Cardboard	0.69	43	1161	688.8	
Cedar, red	0.38	24	648	384.4	
Cellulose nitrate	1.38	85.8	2317.6	1375.0	
Cement, also see Concrete					
Cement, Portland, mix design only	3.15	197	5309	3150.0	
1 cu. ft. sack	1.51	94	2538	1506	
Cement, slurry	1.44	90	2430	1441.7	45
Chalk, fine	1.12	70	1890	1121.3	45
Chalk, lumpy	1.44	90	2430	1441.7	
Chalk, solid	2.50	156	4212	2498.9	
Charcoal	0.21	13	351	208.2	
Cherry wood, dry	0.56	35	945	560.6	
Chestnut wood, dry	0.48	30	810	480.6	
Chloroform	1.52	95	2565	1521.8	
Chocolate, powder	0.64	40	1080	640.7	
Chromic acid, flake	1.20	75	2025	1201.4	25
Chromium	6.86	428	11556	6855.9	
Chromium ore	2.16	135	3645	2162.5	30-45
Cinders, Coal, ash	0.64	40	1080	640.7	25-40
Cinders, Furnace	0.91	57	1539	913.1	
Clay, compacted	1.75	109	2943	1746.0	
Clay, Dry excavated	1.09	68	1836	1089.3	
Clay, Dry lump	1.07	67	1809	1073.2	25-45
Clay, fire	1.36	85	2295	1361.6	
Clay, Wet excavated	1.83	114	3078	1826.1	
Clay, Wet lump	1.60	100	2700	1601.8	28
Clover seed	0.77	48	1296	768.9	
Coal, Anthracite, broken	1.11	69	1863	1105.3	30-45
Coal, Anthracite, solid	1.51	94	2538	1505.7	
Coal, Bituminous, broken	0.83	52	1404	833.0	30-45
Coal, Bituminous, solid	1.35	84	2268	1345.6	
Cobalt	8.75	546	14742	8746.1	
Coconut, meal	0.51	32	864	512.6	
Coconut, shredded	0.35	22	594	352.4	45
Coffee, fresh beans	0.56	35	945	560.6	35-45
Coffee, roast beans	0.43	27	729	432.5	
Coke	0.42	26	702	416.5	
Concrete, Asphaltic	2.24	140	3780	2242.6	
Concrete, Gravel	2.40	150	4050	2402.8	
Concrete, heavy w/ baryte aggregate	3.20	200	5400	3204	
Concrete, lightweight w/ expanded clay agg.	1.09	68	1836	1089	
Concrete, Limestone agg. w/Portland cement	2.37	148	3996	2370.7	
Copper sulphate, ground	3.60	225	6073	3603.0	
Copper, cast	8.69	542	14634	8682.0	
Copper, rolled	8.91	556	15012	8906.3	

Material	Specific Gravity	Weight lbs per cu foot	Weight lbs per cu yard	Weight kgs per cu meter	Angle of Repose
Copra, expeller					
cake chopped	0.46	29	783	464.5	20
cake ground	0.51	32	864	512.6	30
Copra, meal, ground	0.64	40	1080	640.7	39
Copra, medium size	0.53	33	891	528.6	20
Cork, natural bark	0.24	15	405	240.3	
Cork, ground, commercial	0.08	5	135	80.1	45
Cork, solid, commercial	0.18	11.5	311	184.2	
Corn, grits	0.67	42	1134	672.8	30-45
Corn, on the cob	0.72	45	1215	720.8	
Corn, shelled	0.72	45	1215	720.8	
Cottonseed, cake, lumpy	0.67	42	1134	672.8	30-45
Cottonseed, dry,					
de-linted	0.56	35	945	560.6	30-45
not de-linted	0.32	20	540	320.4	45
Cottonseed, hulls	0.19	12	324	192.2	45
Cottonseed, meal	0.59	37	999	592.7	30-45
Cottonseed, meats	0.64	40	1080	640.7	30-45
Cottonwood	0.42	26	702	416.5	
CPVC (Chlorinated					
polyvinyl chloride)	1.54	95.8	2587.3	1535.0	
Crude oil	0.85	53.1	1432.7	850.0	
Cryolite	1.60	100	2700	1601.8	30-45
Cullet	1.60	100	2700	1601.8	30-45
Culm	0.75	47	1269	752.9	
Cypress wood	0.51	32	864	512.6	
Diesel fuel	0.84	52.1	1407.4	835.0	
Dolomite, lumpy	1.52	95	2565	1521.8	30-45
Dolomite, pulverized	0.74	46	1242	736.9	
Dolomite, solid	2.90	181	4887	2899.3	
Down, goose & duck					
very best	0.002	0.14	3.9	2.3	
good	0.003	0.18	4.9	2.9	
poor	0.006	0.36	9.7	5.8	
Earth, dense	2.00	125	3375	2002.3	30-45
Earth, Fullers, raw	0.67	42	1134	672.8	35
Earth, loam, dry, excavated	1.25	78	2106	1249.4	30-45
Earth, moist, excavated	1.44	90	2430	1441.7	30-45
Earth, packed	1.52	95	2565	1521.8	
Earth, soft loose mud	1.73	108	2916	1730.0	
Earth, wet, excavated	1.60	100	2700	1601.8	30-45
Ebony wood	0.96	60	1620	961.1	
EC (Ethyl cellulose)	1.13	70.5	1904.7	1130.0	
Elm, dry	0.56	35	945	560.6	
Emery	4.01	250	6750	4004.6	
Epoxy	1.26	78.3	2115.4	1255.0	
Ether	0.74	46	1242	736.9	
Ethyl chloride	0.90	56.2	1517.0	900.0	
Ethyl ether	0.71	44.3	1196.7	710.0	
Ethylene glycol	1.11	69.5	1877.7	1114.0	
EVOH (Ethylene vinyl					
alcohol)	1.16	72.4	1955.2	1160.0	
Feathers, goose & duck					
unwashed in bale	0.04	2.5	67.5	40.0	
Feldspar, pulverized	1.23	77	2079	1233.4	45
Feldspar, solid	2.56	160	4320	2563.0	
Fertilizer, acid phosphate	0.96	60	1620	961.1	
Fir, Douglas	0.53	33	891	528.6	
Fish, meal	0.59	37	999	592.7	45
Fish, scrap	0.72	45	1215	720.8	
Flaxseed, whole	0.72	45	1215	720.8	
Flour, wheat	0.59	37	999	592.7	45
Fluorspar, lumps	1.60	100	2700	1601.8	45
Fluorspar, pulverized	1.44	90	2430	1441.7	45

Material	Specific Gravity	Weight lbs per cu foot	Weight lbs per cu yard	Weight kgs per cu meter	Angle of Repose
Fluorspar, solid	3.21	200	5400	3203.7	
Furan	1.75	109.2	2949.7	1750.0	
Garbage	0.48	30	810	480.6	
Gasoline	0.74	45.9	1238.9	735.0	
Glass, window	2.58	161	4347	2579.0	
Glue, animal, flaked	0.56	35	945	560.6	
Glue, vegetable, glue powdered	0.64	40	1080	640.7	
Gluten, meal	0.63	39	1053	624.7	30-45
Glycerin	1.26	78.7	2123.8	1260.0	
Gneiss, bed in place	2.87	179	4833	2867.3	
Gneiss, broken	1.86	116	3132	1858.1	
Gold, pure 24 kt	19.29	1204	32508	19286.3	
Granite, broken	1.65	103	2781	1649.9	
Granite, solid	2.69	168	4536	2691.1	
Graphite, flake	0.64	40	1080	640.7	30-45
Gravel, dry, 1/4 to 2 inch	1.68	105	2835	1681.9	
Gravel, loose, dry	1.52	95	2565	1521.8	30-45
Gravel, w/ sand, natural	1.92	120	3240	1922.2	
Gravel, wet, 1/4 to 2 inch	2.00	125	3375	2002.3	
Gypsum board	0.85	52.8	1425.6	845.8	
Gypsum, broken	1.81	113	3051	1810.1	
Gypsum, crushed	1.60	100	2700	1601.8	
Gypsum, pulverized	1.12	70	1890	1121.3	45
Gypsum, solid	2.79	174	4698	2787.2	
Halite (salt), broken	1.51	94	2538	1505.7	
Halite (salt), solid	2.32	145	3915	2322.7	
Hay, loose	0.08	5	135	80.1	
Hay, pressed	0.38	24	648	384.4	
HDPE (High-density polyethylene)	0.96	59.8	1615.6	958.5	
Hematite, broken	3.22	201	5427	3219.7	
Hematite, solid	4.90	306	8262	4901.7	
Hemlock, dry	0.40	25	675	400.5	
Hickory, dry	0.85	53	1431	849.0	
Hops, moist	0.56	35	945	560.6	45
Hydraulic fluid	0.86	53.9	1454.2	862.7	
Hydrochloric acid 40%	1.20	75	2025	1201.4	
Ice, crushed	0.59	37	999	592.7	
Ice, solid	0.92	57.4	1549.8	919.5	
Ilmenite	2.31	144	3888	2306.7	30-45
Iridium	22.16	1383	37341	22153.6	
Iron oxide pigment	0.40	25	675	400.5	40
Iron, cast	7.21	450	12150	7208.3	
Iron, wrought	7.77	485	13095	7769.0	
Ivory	1.84	115	3105	1842.1	
Jet fuel, JP-4	0.78	48.6	1312.8	778.9	
Kaolin, green crushed	1.03	64	1728	1025.2	35
Kaolin, pulverized	0.35	22	594	352.4	45
Kerosene	0.80	49.9	1348.4	800.0	
LDPE (Low-density polyethylene)	0.92	57.7	1558.3	924.5	
Lead, cast, 20°C (68°F)	11.34	708	19114	11340.0	
Lead, red	3.69	230	6210	3684.3	
Lead, rolled, 20°C (68°F)	11.36	709	19148	11360.0	
Leather	0.95	59	1593	945.1	
Lignite, dry	0.80	50	1350	800.9	30-45
Lignum Vitae, dry	1.28	80	2160	1281.5	
Lime, quick, fine	0.30	18	810	480.6	30-45
Lime, hydrated	0.48	30	2025	1201.4	
Lime, quick, large	1.20	75	1431	849.0	
Lime, stone, large	0.85	53	4536	2691.1	
Lime, stone, lump	2.69	168	2592	1537.8	
Limestone, broken	1.54	96	2619	1553.8	

Material	Specific Gravity	Weight lbs per cu foot	Weight lbs per cu yard	Weight kgs per cu meter	Angle of Repose
Limestone, pulverized	1.39	87	2349	1393.6	45
Limestone, solid	2.61	163	4401	2611.0	
Limonite, broken	2.47	154	4158	2466.8	
Limonite, solid	3.80	237	6399	3796.4	
Linseed, meal	0.51	32	864	512.6	30-45
Linseed, whole	0.75	47	1269	752.9	
Locust, dry	0.71	44	1188	704.8	
Magnesite, solid	3.01	188	5076	3011.5	
Magnesium sulfate, crystal	1.12	70	1890	1121.3	
Magnesium, solid	1.75	109	2943	1746.0	
Magnetite, broken	3.29	205	5535	3283.8	
Magnetite, solid	5.05	315	8505	5045.8	
Mahogany, Honduras,dry	0.54	34	918	544.6	
Mahogany, Spanish, dry	0.85	53	1431	849.0	
Malt	0.34	21	567	336.4	30-45
Manganese oxide	1.92	120	3240	1922.2	
Manganese, solid	7.61	475	12825	7608.8	
Manure	0.40	25	675	400.5	
Maple, dry	0.71	44	1188	704.8	
Marble, broken	1.57	98	2646	1569.8	30-45
Marble, solid	2.56	160	4320	2563.0	
Marl, wet, excavated	2.24	140	3780	2242.6	
Mercury @ 0°C (32°F)	13.61	849	22923	13599.7	
Methyl chloride	0.99	61.8	1668.7	990.0	
Mica, broken	1.60	100	2700	1601.8	30-45
Mica, solid	2.88	180	4860	2883.3	
Milk, powdered	0.45	28	756	448.7	45
Molybdenum	10.19	636	17172	10187.8	
Mortar, sand & cement, set	2.16	135	3645	2162.5	
Mortar, sand & cement, wet	2.40	150	4050	2402.8	
Mud, fluid	1.73	108	2916	1730.0	
Mud, packed	1.91	119	3213	1906.2	
Nickel silver	8.45	527	14229	8441.7	
Nickel, rolled	8.67	541	14607	8666.0	
Nitric acid, 91%	1.51	94	2538	1505.7	
Nitrogen	0.00	0.0784	2.1168	1.3	
Nylon, Type 11	1.04	64.9	1753.0	1040.0	
Nylon, Type 12	1.02	63.7	1719.3	1020.0	
Nylon, Type 6	1.13	70.5	1904.7	1130.0	
Nylon, Type 6/12	1.08	67.4	1820.4	1080.0	
Nylon, Type 6/6	1.14	71.2	1921.5	1140.0	
Nylon, Type 6/9	1.09	68.0	1837.3	1090.0	
Oak, live, dry	0.95	59	1593	945.1	
Oats, red	0.71	44	1188	704.8	
Oats	0.43	27	729	432.5	32
Oats, rolled	0.30	19	513	304.4	30-45
Oil Cake	0.79	49	1323	784.9	
Oil, linseed	0.94	58.8	1587.6	941.9	
Oil, lubricating	0.91	56.8	1533.9	910.0	
Oil, petroleum	0.88	55	1485	881.0	
Oil, transformer	0.88	54.9	1483.3	880.0	
Oxygen	0.00	0.0892	2.4084	1.4	
Oyster shells, ground	0.85	53	1431	849.0	30-45
PAI (Polyamide-imide)	1.42	88.6	2393.5	1420.0	
Paper, standard	1.20	75	2025	1201.4	
Paraffin	0.72	45	1215	720.8	
PAS (Polyarylsulfone)	1.33	83.0	2241.8	1330.0	
PBT (Polybutylene terephthalate)	1.34	83.7	2258.6	1340.0	
PC (Polycarbonate)	1.20	74.9	2022.7	1200.0	
PCTFE (Polychlorotri-fluoroethylene)	2.14	133.6	3607.1	2140.0	
PE-CTFE (Polyethylene-chlorotrifluoroethylene)	1.69	105.5	2848.6	1690.0	
PE-TFE (Polyethylene-					

Material	Specific Gravity	Weight lbs per cu foot	Weight lbs per cu yard	Weight kgs per cu meter	Angle of Repose
polytetrafluoroethylene), modified	1.70	106.1	2865.4	1700.0	
Peanuts, not shelled	0.27	17	459	272.3	30-45
Peanuts, shelled	0.64	40	1080	640.7	30-45
Peat, dry	0.40	25	675	400.5	
Peat, moist	0.80	50	1350	800.9	
Peat, wet	1.12	70	1890	1121.3	
Pecan wood	0.75	47	1269	752.9	
PEEK (Polyetheretherketone)	1.31	81.8	2208.1	1310.0	
PEI (Polyetherimide)	1.27	79.3	2140.7	1270.0	
PES (Polyethersulfone)	1.42	88.3	2385.1	1415.0	
PET (Polyethylene terephthalate)	1.35	84.0	2267.1	1345.0	
PETG (Polyethylene terephthalate glycol)	1.25	78.0	2106.9	1250.0	
Petroleum ethyl	0.66	41.2	1112.5	660.0	
PFA (Perfluoroalkoxy resin)	2.15	133.9	3615.5	2145.0	
Phenolic casting resin	1.28	79.9	2157.5	1280.0	
Phosphate Rock, broken	1.76	110	2970	1762.0	
Phosphorus	2.34	146	3942	2338.7	
PI (Polyimide)	1.40	87.1	2351.4	1395.0	
Pine, White, dry	0.42	26	702	416.5	
Pine, Yellow, Northern, dry	0.54	34	918	544.6	
Pitch	1.15	72	1935.9	1148.5	
Plaster	0.85	53	1431	849.0	
Platinum	21.51	1342	36234	21496.8	
Plywood	0.62	38.4	1036.8	615.1	
PMP (Polymethylpentene)	0.83	52.1	1405.8	834.0	
Polyallomer	0.90	56.0	1512.8	897.5	
Polyaryletherketone	1.30	81.2	2191.2	1300.0	
Polybutadiene	0.97	60.6	1635.0	970.0	
Polybutylene	0.92	57.3	1546.5	917.5	
Polyester, cast	1.25	78.0	2106.9	1250.0	
Polyolefin (High hardness)	0.94	58.7	1584.4	940.0	
Polyolefin (Low hardness)	0.93	58.1	1567.6	930.0	
Polysulfone	1.25	78.0	2106.9	1250.0	
Porcelain	2.40	150	4050	2402.8	
Porphyry, broken	1.65	103	2781	1649.9	
Porphyry, solid	2.55	159	4293	2546.9	
Potash	1.28	80	2160	1281.5	
Potassium chloride	2.00	125	3375	2002.3	30-45
Potatoes, white	0.77	48	1296	768.9	
PP (Polypropylene)	0.91	56.5	1525.4	905.0	
Pine, Yellow, Southern, dry	0.72	45	1215	720.8	
PPS (Polyphenylene sulfide)	1.35	84.3	2275.5	1350.0	
Prop alcohol	0.81	50.9	1373.4	814.8	
PS (Polystyrene)	1.05	65.5	1769.8	1050.0	
Pumice stone	0.64	40	1080	640.7	
PVC (Polyvinyl chloride)	1.30	81.2	2191.2	1300.0	
PVDC (Polyvinylidene chloride)	1.69	105.2	2840.2	1685.0	
PVDF (Polyvinylidene fluoride)	1.78	110.8	2991.9	1775.0	
Quartz sand	1.20	75	2025	1201.4	
Quartz, lump	1.55	97	2619	1553.8	
Quartz, solid	2.64	165	4455	2643.1	
Raps oil	0.91	56.8	1533.9	910.0	
Redwood, Calif, dry	0.45	28	756	448.5	
Resin,synthetic,crshd	0.56	35	945	560.6	
Rice grits	0.69	43	1161	688.8	30-45
Rice, hulled	0.75	47	1269	752.9	
Rice, rough	0.58	36	972	576.7	30-45

Material	Specific Gravity	Weight lbs per cu foot	Weight lbs per cu yard	Weight kgs per cu meter	Angle of Repose
Rip-rap	1.60	100	2700	1601.8	
Rosin	1.07	67	1809	1073.2	
Rubber, caoutchouc	0.95	59	1593	945.1	
Rubber, ground scrap	0.48	30	810	480.6	45
Rubber, mfged	1.52	95	2565	1521.8	
Rye	0.71	44	1188	704.8	
Salt cake	1.44	90	2430	1441.7	30-45
Salt, coarse	0.80	50	1350	800.9	30-45
Salt, fine	1.20	75	2025	1201.4	30-45
Saltpeter	1.20	75	2025	1201.4	30-45
Sand and Gravel, wet	2.00	125	3375	2002.3	
Sand, damp	1.92	120	3240	1922.2	
Sand, dry	1.60	100	2700	1601.8	34
Sand, loose	1.44	90	2430	1441.7	30-45
Sand, rammed	1.68	105	2835	1681.9	
Sand, water filled	1.92	120	3240	1922.2	15-30
Sand, wet	1.92	120	3240	1922.2	45
Sand, wet (2nd source)	2.08	130	3510	2082.4	
Sand, wet packed	2.08	130	3510	2082.4	
Sandstone, broken	1.51	94	2538	1505.7	
Sandstone, solid	2.32	145	3915	2322.7	
Sawdust	0.27	17	459	272.3	
Sewage, sludge	0.72	45	1215	720.8	
Shale, broken	1.59	99	2673	1585.8	30-45
Shale, solid	2.68	167	4509	2675.1	
Silicone epoxy	1.52	94.9	2562.0	1520.0	
Silver	10.46	653	17631	10460.1	
Slag, broken	1.76	110	2970	1762.0	
Slag, crushed 1/4 inch	1.19	74	1998	1185.4	
Slag, furn. granulated	0.96	60	1620	961.1	
Slag, solid	2.12	132	3564	2114.4	
Slate, broken	1.67	104	2808	1665.9	
Slate, pulverized	1.36	85	2295	1361.6	30-45
Slate, solid	2.69	168	4536	2691.1	
Snow, compacted	0.48	30	810	480.6	
Snow, freshly fallen	0.16	10	270	160.2	
Soap, chips	0.16	10	270	160.2	30-45
Soap, flakes	0.16	10	270	160.2	30-45
Soap, powder	0.37	23	621	368.4	30-45
Soap, solid	0.80	50	1350	800.9	
Soda Ash, heavy	0.96	60	1620	961.1	30-45
Soda Ash, light	0.43	27	729	432.5	30-45
Sodium	0.98	61	1647	977.1	
Sodium Aluminate ground	1.15	72	1944	1153.3	
Sodium Nitrate,grnd	1.20	75	2025	1201.4	
Soybeans, whole	0.75	47	1269	752.9	
Spruce, Calif, dry	0.45	28	756	448.5	
Starch, powdered	0.56	35	945	560.6	
Steel, cast	7.85	490	13230	7849.1	
Steel, rolled	7.93	495	13365	7929.2	
Stone, crushed	1.60	100	2700	1601.8	
Sugar, brown	0.72	45	1215	720.8	
Sugar, granulated	0.85	53	1431	849.0	30-45
Sugar, powdered	0.80	50	1350	800.9	
Sugar, raw cane	0.96	60	1620	961.1	45
Sugarbeet pulp, dry	0.21	13	351	208.2	
Sugarbeet pulp, wet	0.56	35	945	560.6	
Sugarcane	0.27	17	459	272.3	45
Sulfur, lump	1.31	82	2214	1313.5	30-45
Sulfur, pulverized	0.96	60	1620	961.1	30-45
Sulfur, solid	2.00	125	3375	2002.3	
Sulfuric acid, 87%	1.79	112	3024	1794.1	
Sycamore, dry	0.59	37	999	592.7	
Taconite	2.80	175	4725	2803.2	

Material	Specific Gravity	Weight lbs per cu foot	Weight lbs per cu yard	Weight kgs per cu meter	Angle of Repose
Talc, broken	1.75	109	2943	1746.0	
Talc, solid	2.69	168	4536	2691.1	
Tanbark, ground	0.88	55	1485	881.0	
Tankage	0.96	60	1620	961.1	
Tar	1.15	72	1935.9	1148.5	
Tin, cast	7.36	459	12393	7352.5	
Tobacco	0.32	20	540	320.4	45
Toluene	0.87	54.3	1466.4	870.0	
Trap rock, broken	1.75	109	2943	1746.0	
Trap rock, solid	2.88	180	4860	2883.3	
Trichloroethylene	1.47	91.8	2477.8	1470.0	
Tungsten	19.62	1224	33048	19606.6	
Turf	0.40	25	675	400.5	
Turpentine	0.87	54	1458	865.0	
Vanadium	5.50	343	9261	5494.3	
Walnut, black, dry	0.61	38	1026	608.7	
Water, pure	1.00	62.4	1684.8	999.6	
Water, sea	1.03	64.08	1730.16	1026.5	
Wheat	0.77	48	1296	768.9	28
Wheat, cracked	0.67	42	1134	672.8	30-45
Willow wood	0.42	26	702	416.5	
Wool	1.31	82	2214	1313.5	
Zinc oxide	0.40	25	675	400.5	45
Zinc, cast	7.05	440	11880	7048.1	

Common Material Dumping Angles

Material	Dumping Angle in Degrees
Ashes, dry	33
Ashes, moist	36
Ashes, wet	30
Asphalt	45
Cinders, dry	33
Cinders, moist	34
Cinders, wet	31
Cinders and Clay	30
Clay	45
Coal, hard	24
Coal, soft	30
Coke	23
Concrete	30
Earth, loose	28
Earth, compact	50
Garbage	30
Gravel	40
Ore, dry	30
Ore, damp	37
Rubble	45
Sand, dry	35
Sand, damp	40
Sand, with crushed stone	27
Stone	30
Stone, broken	27
Stone, crushed	30

Stockpile Volume and Weight

The following formula is used to calculate the volume of a stockpile if the diameter and height are known:

Volume in cubic feet = 0.2618 x D^2 x h
D = Diameter of the base of the cone in feet
h = Height of the cone in feet

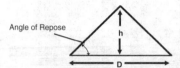

Angle of Repose

In order to calculate the actual weight of material in the stockpile, determine the density or weight/cubic foot (or look up an approximation of the density in the WEIGHTS OF MATERIALS chapter.)

$$\text{Weight (tons)} = \text{Volume (ft}^3) \times \text{Density} \left(\frac{lb}{ft^3}\right) \times \frac{1 \text{ ton}}{2000 \text{ lb}}$$

CONICAL STOCKPILE VOLUMES (37° Angle of Repose)

Diameter in feet	Height in feet	Volume in Cu Yds*	Weight at 100 lbs/cu foot
26.54	10	68	92
39.81	15	230	310
53.08	20	545	740
66.35	25	1065	1440
79.62	30	1845	2490
92.89	35	2930	3955
106.16	40	4370	5900
132.70	50	8540	11525
159.25	60	14755	19920
185.79	70	23430	31630
212.33	80	34970	47210
238.87	90	49790	67220
265.41	100	68300	92210

1 cubic yard = 27 cubic feet
1 cubic foot = 0.037037 cubic yards

Conversion Factors

The tables that follow contain some of the most commonly used conversion factors. If you can not locate the conversion you need (such as "foot" to "inch"), try looking up the reverse conversion ("inch" to "foot") and if it exists, divide that number into 1 to get your conversion. In order to save space, only one direction of conversion is listed in some cases. Additional sources include *Handbook of Chemistry and Physics* and *C.R.C Standard Math Tables* by The Chemical Rubber Publishing Co, *Scientific Tables* by Ciba-Geigy Ltd, *Measure for Measure* by Sequoia Publishing, *Field Geologists Manual* by The Australian Institute of Mining & Metallurgy, *Conversion Factors* by Forney Inc, *Conversions* by Cahn Instruments, and *Technical Reference Handbook* by E.P Rasis.

See page 277 for temperature conversions.

ABBREVIATIONS USED IN CONVERSION TABLES

abs	absolute	in	inch
apoth	apothecary	Int	International
atm	atmosphere	IST	Int Steam Table
avdp	avoirdupois	kg	kilogram
Avogad	Avogadro number	km	kilometer
Btu	Brittish thermal unit	kW	kilowatt
cal	calorie	L	long
cgs	centimeter-gram-second	lb	pound
		lbf	pound-force
chem	chemical	liq	liquid
chg	charge	ln	logarithm (natural)
circ	circular	log	logarithm (common)
cm	centimeter	mech	mechanical
cp	candle power	measure	mesuring
cu	cubic	met	metric
dB	decibel	min	minute
dm	decimeter	mks	meter-kilogram-second
°C	degree Celsius		
°F	degree Fahrenheit	mm	millimeter
K	kelvin	naut	nautical
°R	degree Rankine	oz	ounce
elec	electrical	petro	petroleum
Engl	English	S	short
equiv	equivalent	sec	second
ft	foot	spher	spherical
gal	gallon	sq	square
g	gram	std	standard
Germ	German	thermo	thermochemical
H₂O	water	UK	United Kingdom
Hg	Mercury	US	United States
hr	hour		

Convert From	Into	Multiply By
abampere	ampere	10
	faraday/sec (chem)	1.03638×10^{-4}
	statampere	2.99792×10^{10}
abcoulomb	ampere–hour	0.00278
	coulomb	10
	electronic charge	6.24151×10^{19}
	faraday (chem)	1.03632×10^{-4}
	statcoulomb	2.99792×10^{10}
abfarad	farad	1×10^{9}
	microfarad	1×10^{15}
	statfarad	8.98755×10^{20}
abhenry	henry	1×10^{-9}
abmho	megamho	1000
	mho	1×10^{9}
	statmho	8.98755×10^{20}
abohm	megohm	1×10^{-15}
	microohm	0.001
	ohm	1×10^{-9}
abohmcm	ohmcm	1×10^{-9}
abvolt	microvolt	0.01
	millivolt	1×10^{-5}
	volt	1×10^{-8}
abvolt/cm	volt/cm	1×10^{-8}
	volt/inch	2.54×10^{-8}
acre (Int)	are	40.4686
	hectare or sq. hectometer	0.404686
	sq foot (Int)	43560
	sq foot (US Survey)	43559.826
	sq meter	4046.856
	sq mile (Int)	0.0015625
	sq yard (Int)	4,840
	sq yard	4840
acre (US Survey)	are	40.46873
	hectare or sq. hectometer	0.4046873
	sq foot (Int)	43560.174
	sq foot (US Survey)	43560
	sq mile (US Survey)	0.0015625
acre foot	cu foot	43560
	cu meter	1233.482
	cu yard	1613.33
	gallon (US, liq)	3.259×10^{5}
acre inch	cu foot	3630
	cu meter	102.7901531
	cu yard	134.44
	gallon (US)	27154.286
ampere	abampere	0.1
	ampere (Int)	1.00015
	coulomb/sec	1
	faraday/sec (chem)	1.03638×10^{-5}
	microampere	1×10^{6}
	milliampere	1000
	statampere	2.99792×10^{9}
ampere (Int)	ampere	0.99985
ampere hour	abcoulomb	360
	coulomb	3600
	faraday (chem)	0.03731

Convert From	Into	Multiply By
ampere/meter	amper/inch	0.0254
	oersted	0.012566
	newton/weber	1
ampere/sq cm	amper/sq inch	6.452
	amper/sq meter	1 x 10⁴
ampere/sq inch	amper/sq cm	0.1550
	amper/sq meter	155
ampere/sq meter	amper/sq cm	1 x 10⁻⁴
	amper/sq inch	6.452 x 10⁻⁴
ampere–turn	gilbert	1.25664
ångstrom	centimeter	1 x 10⁻⁸
	inch	3.937 x 10⁻⁹
	meter	1 x 10⁻¹⁰
	micrometer	1 x 10⁻⁴
	micron	0.0001
	millimicron	0.1
are	acre (Int)	0.024711
	sq dekameter	1
	sq foot	1076.39
	sq meter	100
	sq mile (Int)	3.86102 x 10⁻⁵
	sq yard (Int)	119.599
astronomical unit	kilometer	1.496 x 10⁸
atmosphere (std)	bar	1.01325
	cm of Hg @ 0°C	75.9999
	cm of H₂O @ 4°C	1033.228
	dyne/sq cm	1.01325 x 10⁶
	ft of H₂O @ 39.2°F	33.8995
	gram–force/sq cm	1033.23
	in of Hg @ 32°F	29.9213
	kg–force/sq cm	1.0332
	kg–force/sq meter	10332
	kilopascal	101.325
	mm of Hg @ 0°C	759.999
	newton/sq meter	101325
	pascal	101325
	pound–force/sq inch	14.6959
	ton-force(short)/sq inch	0.00735
	ton-force(short)/sq foot	1.05811
	torr	760
barn	sq cm	1 x 10⁻²⁴
barrel (UK)	bag (UK)	1.5
	barrel (US, dry)	1.41541
	barrel (US, liq)	1.37251
	bushel (UK)	4.5
	bushel (US, dry)	4.64426
	cu foot	5.77957
	cu meter	0.16366
	gallon (UK)	36
	liter	163.6592
barrel (US oil)	barrel (US, liq)	1.3333
	cu foot	5.61458
	gallon (US, liq)	42
	liter	158.9873
barrel (US, dry)	barrel (US, liq)	0.969696
	bushel (US, dry)	3.28122

Convert From	Into	Multiply By
	cu foot	4.08333
	cu inch	7056
	cu meter	0.11563
	quart (US, dry)	104.999
barrel (US, liq)	barrel (US, dry)	1.03125
	barrel (US oil)	0.075
	cu foot	4.2109
	cu inch	7276.5
	cu meter	0.11924
	gallon (UK)	26.22924
	gallon (US, liq)	31.5
	liter	119.24
bar	atmosphere (std)	0.98692
	barye (French)	1×10^6
	cm of Hg @ 0°C	75.0062
	dyne/sq cm	1×10^6
	ft of H_2O @ 60°F	33.4883
	gram–force/sq cm	1019.72
	in Hg @ 32°F	29.530
	kg–force/sq cm	1.01972
	millibar	1000
	newton/sq meter	1×10^5
	pascal	1×10^5
	pound–force/sq foot	2088.54
	pound–force/sq inch	14.5038
barye (French)	dyne/sq cm	1.0
	newton/sq meter	0.10
	pascal	0.10
becquerel	curie	2.7027×10^{-11}
	disintegration/sec	1
bel	decibel	10
biot	ampere	10
bit	byte (computers)	0.125
board foot	cu cm	2359.74
	cu foot	0.08333
	cu inch	144
bolt (cloth)	ell	32
	linear foot	120
	meter	36.576
bougie decimale	candle (Int)	0.96
Btu (thermo)	Btu (Int Steam Tab)	0.999331
	Btu (mean)	0.998560
	Btu @ 60°F	0.999687
	calorie (thermo)	251.996
	calorie (Int Steam Tab)	251.827
	calorie (mean)	251.634
	calorie @ 20°C	252.122
	erg	1.0544×10^{10}
	foot–poundal	25020.1
	foot pound–force	777.649
	gram–force cm	1.0751×10^7
	hp–hour	0.000393
	joule	1054.35
	joule (US Int)	1054.16
	kg calorie (thermo)	0.252
	kg force meter	107.514

Convert From	Into	Multiply By
	kilowatthour	0.000292875
	kilowatthour (Int)	0.00029283
	liter atm	10.456
	wattsecond	1054.35
	wattsecond (Int)	1054.18
Btu (IST)	Btu (thermo)	1.00067
	therm	0.0001
Btu (mean)	Btu (thermo)	1.00144
Btu @ 60°F	Btu (thermo)	1.00031
Btu (thermo)/hr	calorie–kg/hr	0.252
	erg/sec	2.92875×10^6
	foot pound–foce/hr	777.649
	calorie/sec	0.07
	horsepower	0.000393
	kilowatt	0.00029
	watt	0.29287
Btu (thermo)/min	foot pound–force/sec	12.97
	horsepower	0.02357
	kilowatt	0.01757
	watt	17.576
Btu (thermo)/lb	calorie (thermo)/gram	0.55518
	foot pound–force/lb	777.649
	joule/gram	2.326
Btu (IST)/sq ft min	watt/sq inch	0.1221
buckets (UK)	cu cm	18184.35
	gallon (UK)	4
bushel (UK)	bag (UK)	0.3333
	bushel (US)	1.03206
	cu cm	36368.7
	cu foot	1.28435
	cu inch	2219.35
	gallon (UK)	8
	liter	36.3687
bushel (US, dry)	barrel (US, dry)	0.30476
	bushel (UK)	0.96894
	cu cm	35239.07
	cu foot	1.24446
	cu inch	2150.42
	cu meter	0.03524
	cu yard	0.04609
	gallon (US, dry)	8
	gallon (US, liq)	9.30918
	liter	35.23907
	ounce (US, liq)	1191.57
	peck (US)	4
	pint (US, dry)	64
	quart (US, dry)	32
	quart (US, liq)	37.23671
butt (UK, liq)	bushel (US)	16.2549
	cu foot	20.2285
	cu meter	0.57281
	gallon (US)	151.3197
byte	bit (computers)	8
cable (UK)	degree latitude	0.00167
	meter	185.37
cable length (US Survey)	fathom (US Survey)	120

Convert From	Into	Multiply By
	foot (US Survey)	720
	meter	219.456
caliber	inch	0.01
	millimeter	0.254
calorie (IST)	Btu (thermo)	0.003971
	Btu (IST)	0.003968
	Btu (mean)	0.003965
	Btu @ 60°F	0.00397
	calorie (thermo)	1.00067
	calorie (mean)	0.99923
	calorie @ 20°C	1.00117
	cu cm atm	41.3205
	cu ft atm	0.00146
	erg	4.187×10^7
	foot poundal	99.3543
	foot pound–force	3.08803
	gram calorie (IST)	1
	gram–force cm	42693.48
	hp hour	1.5596×10^{-6}
	joule	4.18468
	joule (Int)	4.18604
	kg–force meter	0.426935
	kilowatthour	1.163×10^{-6}
	liter atm	0.04129
	watthour	0.001163
	watthour (Int)	0.001162
	wattsecond	4.187
calorie (mean)	Btu (thermo)	0.003974
	calorie (thermo)	1.00144
calorie @ 20°C	Btu (thermo)	0.00397
	calorie (thermo)	0.99949
calorie, kg (thermo)	Btu (thermo)	3.96832
	Btu (IST)	3.96567
	Btu (mean)	3.96261
	Btu @ 60°F	3.96708
	calorie (thermo)	1000
	calorie kg (mean)	0.99856
	calorie kg @ 20°C	1.0005
	cu cm–atm	41292.9
	erg	4.184×10^{10}
	foot–poundal	99288
	foot pound–force	3085.96
	gram–force cm	4.266×10^7
	hp–hour	0.00156
	joule	4184
	kilowatthour	0.00116
	liter atm	41.292
	watthour	1.1622
calorie, kg (mean)	Btu (thermo)	3.974
	calorie, (thermo)	1001.4
calorie/gram	Btu/lb (IST)	1.8
	foot pound–force/lb	1400.7
	joule/gram	4.1868
calorie/hr (IST)	Btu/hr (thermo)	0.00397
	erg/sec	11630
	watt	0.001163

Convert From	Into	Multiply By
calorie, kg/hr (IST)	watt	1.1630
calorie/min (IST)	Btu/min (thermo)	0.00397
	erg/sec	697800
	watt	0.0698
calorie, kg/min (IST)	watt	69.78
calorie/sec (IST)	Btu/sec (thermo)	0.00397
	foot pound–force/sec	3.088
	horsepower	0.0056
	watt	4.186
calorie sec (IST)	Planck constant	6.319×10^{33}
candela	hefner candle (Germ)	1.091
	lumen/steradian	1
candela/sq cm	candela/sq inch	6.4516
	lambert	3.1416
candela/sq ft	candela/sq inch	6.944×10^{-3}
	candela/sq meter	10.7639
	lambert	3.3816×10^{-3}
candela/sq meter	candela/sq foot	0.09290304
	lambert	3.1416×10^{-4}
candle (Engl)	candle (Int)	1.042
candle (Int)	candle (Engl)	0.96
	candle (pentane)	1
	carcel unit	0.104
	hefner candle (Germ)	1.11
candle (Int)	lumen/steradian	1.02
candle/sq cm	candle/sq in	6.452
	candle/sq meter	10000
	foot lambert	2918.6
	lambert	3.1416
candle/sq in	candle/sq cm	0.155
	candle/sq ft	144
	foot lambert	452.39
	lambert	0.4869
candle power	lumen	12.566
carat (metric)	grain	3.0865
	gram	0.2
	milligram	200
carcel unit	candle (Int)	9.61
cental (US)	kilogram	45.359
	pound	100
centiare	are	0.01
	sq foot	10.764
	sq inch	1550
	sq meter	1
	sq yard	1.19599
centigram	grain	0.15432
	gram	0.01
centiliter	cu cm	10
	cu inch	0.610237
	dram (US, liq)	2.705
	liter	0.01
	ounce (US, liq)	0.33814
centimeter	ångstrom	1×10^{8}
	foot	0.03281
	hand (horses)	0.0984
	inch	0.3937

Convert From	Into	Multiply By
	kilometer	1×10^{-5}
	link (Gunter)	0.0497
	link (Ramden)	0.0328
	meter	0.01
	micrometer	10000
	micron	10000
	mile (naut)	5.3996×10^{-6}
	mile (US statute)	6.2137×10^{-6}
	millimeter	10
	millimicron	1×10^{7}
	mil	393.7
	picas (printers)	2.371
	point (printers)	28.4528
	rod (US Survey)	0.00199
	yard	0.01094
cm–dyne	cm gram–force	1.02×10^{-3}
	foot pound–force	7.376×10^{-8}
	meter kg–force	1.02×10^{-8}
cm gram–force	cm–dyne	980.7
	foot pound–force	7.23×10^{-5}
	meter kg–force	1×10^{-5}
cm of Hg 0°C	atmosphere (std)	0.01316
	bar	0.01333
	dyne/sq cm	13332
	ft of H_2O @ 4°C	0.446
	in Hg @ 0°C	0.3937
	kg–force/sq meter	135.95
	newton/sq meter	1333.22
	pascal	1333.22
	pound–force/sq ft	27.845
	pound–force/sq in	0.1934
	torr	10
cm of H_2O 4°C	atmosphere (std)	0.00097
	newton/sq meter	98.0665
	pascal	98.0665
	pound–force/sq in	0.014223
cm/sec	foot/min	1.9685
	foot/sec	0.0328
	km/hr	0.036
	km/min	0.0006
	knots (Int)	0.0194
	meter/min	0.6
	mile/hr	0.02237
	mile/min	0.000373
cm/sec/sec	ft/sec/sec	0.0328
	km/hr/sec	0.036
	meter/sec/sec	0.01
	mile/hr/sec	0.0224
cm/year	inch/year	0.3937
centipoise	gram/cm/sec	0.01
	poise	0.01
	lb/ft/hr	2.4191
	lb/ft/sec	0.00067
centistoke	square inch/hour	5.580 011 2
	square mm/second	1
	stokes	0.01

Convert From	Into	Multiply By
chain (Gunter or US Survey)		
	centimeter	2011.7
	chain-Ramden or engineer	0.66
	foot	66.00013
	foot (US Survey)	66
	Furlong (US Survey)	0.1
	Inch (US Survey)	792
	link (Gunter)	100
	link (Ramden)	66.00013
	meter	20.117
	mile (US statute)	0.0125
	rod (US Survey)	4
	yard (US Survey)	22
chain (Ramden)	chain (Gunter)	1.515152
	foot	100
chaldron (UK, liq)	bushel (UK)	36
cheval vapeur (French)	horsepower	0.98632
circle	degree	360
	grade	400
	minute	21600
	radian	6.2832
	sign	12
circular inch	circular mm	645.16
	sq cm	5.067
	sq inch	0.7854
circular mm	sq cm	0.00785
	sq inch	0.00122
	sq mm	0.7854
circular mil	circular inch	1×10^{-6}
	sq cm	5.06707×10^{-6}
	sq inch	7.85398×10^{-7}
	sq mm	0.000507
	sq mill	0.7854
circumference	degree	360
	radian	6.28318
cord (firewood)	cord foot (timber)	8
	cu foot	128
	cu meter	3.6246
cord foot (timber)	cord (firewood)	0.125
	cu foot	16
coulomb	abcoulomb	0.1
	ampere hour	0.000278
	ampere second	1
	coulomb (Int)	1.00015002
	faraday (chem)	1.0363×10^{-5}
	faraday (phys)	1.0360×10^{-5}
	mks elec chg unit	1
	statcoulomb	2.9979×10^{9}
coulomb/cu meter	abcoulomb/cu cm	1×10^{-7}
	abcoulomb/cu in	1.6387×10^{-6}
	abcoulomb/cu meter	0.1
	coulomb/cu cm	1×10^{-6}
	coulomb/cu in	1.6387×10^{-5}
coulomb/sq cm	coulomb/sq in	6.4516
	coulomb/sq meter	10000
coulomb/sq in	coulomb/sq cm	0.155

Convert From	Into	Multiply By
	coulomb/sq meter	1550
coulomb/sq meter	coulomb/sq cm	1×10^{-4}
	coulomb/sq inch	6.452×10^{-4}
cu centimeter	board foot	0.00042
	bushel (UK)	2.7496×10^{-5}
	bushel (US, dry)	2.8378×10^{-5}
	cu foot	3.5315×10^{-5}
	cu inch	0.06102
	cu meter	1×10^{-6}
	cu yard	1.308×10^{-6}
	drachm (UK, liq)	0.28156
	dram (US, liq)	0.27051
	gallon (UK)	0.000227
	gallon (US, dry)	0.000227
	gallon (US, liq)	0.000264
	gill (UK)	0.00704
	gill (US)	0.00845
	liter	0.001
	ounce (UK, liq)	0.035195
	ounce (US, liq)	0.033814
	pint (US, dry)	0.00182
	pint (US, liq)	0.00211
	quart (UK)	0.00088
	quart (US, dry)	0.00091
	quart (US, liq)	0.00106
cu cm/gram	cu ft/lb	0.01602
cu cm/sec	cu ft/min	0.00212
	gallon (US)/min	0.01585
	gallon (US)/sec	0.00026
cu cm–atm	Btu (thermo)	9.61×10^{-5}
	calorie (thermo)	0.02422
	joule	0.101325
	watthour	2.815×10^{-5}
cu decimeter	cu cm	1000
	cu foot	0.035315
	cu inch	61.0237
	cu meter	0.001
	cu yard	0.00131
	liter	1
cu dekameter	cu decimeter	1×10^{6}
	cu foot	35314.7
	cu inch	6.102×10^{7}
	cu meter	1000
	liter	1×10^{6}
cu foot	acre foot	2.296×10^{-5}
	board foot (timber)	12
	bushel (UK)	0.7786
	bushel (US, dry)	0.8036
	cord (firewood)	0.00781
	cord foot (timber)	0.0625
	cu centimeter	28316.8
	cu inch	1728.0
	cu meter	0.02832
	cu yard	0.03704
	gallon (US, dry)	6.42851
	gallon (US, liq)	7.48052

Convert From	Into	Multiply By
	liter	28.3168
	ounce (UK, liq)	996.614
	ounce (US, liq)	957.506
	pint (US, dry)	51.4281
	pint (US, liq)	59.8442
	quart (US, dry)	25.714
	quart (US, liq)	29.922
cu ft H_2O 60°F	lb of H_2O	62.366
cu ft/hour	acre foot/hr	2.2957×10^{-5}
	cu cm/sec	7.8658
	cu ft/min	0.0167
	gallon (US)/hr	7.4805
	liter/hr	28.317
cu ft/minute	acre foot/hr	0.00138
	acre foot/min	2.2957×10^{-5}
	cu cm/sec	471.95
	cu ft/hr	60
	gallon (US)/min	7.48052
	gallon (US)/sec	0.1247
	liter/sec	0.47195
	pound of H_2O/min (32°F)	62.43
cu ft/pound	cu cm/gram	62.428
	milliliter/gram	62.428
cu ft/sec	acre inch/hr	0.99174
	cu cm/sec	28316.8
	cu meter/sec	0.02832
	cu yard/min	2.2222
	gallon (US)/min	448.83
	liter/min	1699.01
	liter/sec	28.317
	million gallon/day	0.64632
cu ft H_2O/sec	lb H_2O/min	3741.97
cu ft atm	Btu (thermo)	2.7213
	calorie (thermo)	685.76
	foot pound–force	2116.2
	hp hour	0.00107
	joule	2869.205
	kg–force meter	292.58
	kilowatthour	0.000797
	newton meter	2869.205
cu inch	barrel (UK)	0.0001001
	barrel (US, dry)	0.0001417
	board foot	0.00694
	bushel (UK)	0.00045
	bushel (US, dry)	0.00047
	cu cm	16.3871
	cu foot	0.000579
	cu meter	1.639×10^{-5}
	cu yard	2.143×10^{-5}
	dram (US, liq)	4.4329
	gallon (UK)	0.003605
	gallon (US, dry)	0.0037202
	gallon (US, liq)	0.004329
	liter	0.01639
	milliliter	16.3871
	ounce (UK, liq)	0.57674

Convert From	Into	Multiply By
	ounce (US, liq)	0.55411
	Peck (US)	0.00186
	pint (US, dry)	0.02976
	pint (US, liq)	0.03463
	quart (US, dry)	0.01488
	quart (US, liq)	0.01732
cu in H_2O 60°F	lbs of H_2O	0.03609
cu meter	acre foot	0.00081
	barrel (UK)	6.11026
	barrel (US, dry)	8.64849
	barrel (US, liq)	8.38641
	bushel (UK)	27.4962
	bushel (US, dry)	28.3776
	cu cm	1×10^6
	cu foot	35.3147
	cu inch	61023.7
	cu yard	1.30795
	gallon (UK)	219.969
	gallon (US, dry)	227.02
	gallon (US, liq)	264.172
	hogshead (US)	4.1932
	liter	1000
	pint (US, liq)	2113.38
	quart (US, liq)	1056.69
	stere	1
cu meter/kg	liter/kg	1000
	liter/gram	1
	cu foot/lb	16.01846
	cu foot/kg	35.31467
	cu cm/gram	1000
cu meter/min	gallon (UK)/min	219.969
	gallon (US)/min	264.172
	liter/min	1000
cu meter/sec	cu foot/sec	35.315
	gallon (US, liq)/min	15,850.3
cu mm	cu cm	0.001
	cu inch	6.102×10^{-5}
	cu meter	1×10^{-9}
	minim (UK)	0.01689
	minim (US)	0.01623
cu yard	bushel (UK)	21.0223
	bushel (US, dry)	21.6962
	cu cm	764554.9
	cu foot	27
	cu inch	46656
	cu meter	0.76455
	gallon (UK)	168.179
	gallon (US, dry)	173.569
	gallon (US, liq)	201.974
	liter	764.5549
	prospecting dish	112
	quart (UK)	672.714
	quart (US, dry)	694.279
	quart (US, liq)	807.896
cu yard/min	cu ft/sec	0.45
	gallon (US)/sec	3.3662

Convert From	Into	Multiply By
	liter/sec	12.742
cubit	centimeter	45.72
	foot	1.5
	inch	18
cup (US measuring)	cu inch	14.4375
	gallon (US, liq)	0.0625
	gill (US)	2
	liter	0.23659
	pint (US, liq)	0.5
	milliliter	236.588
	ounce (US, liq)	8
	quart (US, liq)	0.25
	tablespoon (US measure)	16
	teaspoon (US measure)	48
cup, metric	milliliter	200
cup, tea	pint	0.25
	milliliter	142.06
dalton	gram	1.66 x 10^{-24}
day (mean solar)	day (sidereal)	1.0027379
	hour (mean solar)	24
	hour (sidereal)	24.06571
	year (calendar)	0.0027397
	year (sidereal)	0.002738
	year (tropical)	0.002738
day (sidereal)	day (mean solar)	0.9972696
	hour (mean solar)	23.93447
	hour (sidereal)	24
	min (mean solar)	1436.068
	min (sidereal)	1440
	second (sidereal)	86400
	year (calendar)	0.002732
	year (sidereal)	0.00273
	year (tropical)	0.00273
decibel	bel	0.1
decigram	gram	0.1
deciliter	liter	0.1
decimeter	centimeter	10
	foot	0.32808
	inch	3.937
	meter	0.1
decistere	cu meter	0.1
degree	circle	0.00278
	minute	60
	quadrant	0.01111
	radian	0.01745
	second	3600
degree/cm	radian/cm	0.01745
degree/foot	radian/cm	0.0005726
degree/inch	radian/cm	0.0068714
degree/min	degree/sec	0.01667
	radian/sec	0.00029
	revolution/sec	4.6296 x 10^{-5}
degree/sec	radian/sec	0.01745
	revolution/min	0.16667
	revolution/sec	0.00278
dekagram	gram	10

Convert From	Into	Multiply By
dekaliter	liter	10
	peck (US)	1.1351
dekaliter	pint (US, dry)	18.162
dekameter	centimeter	1000
	foot	32.8084
	inch	393.7008
	kilometer	0.01
	meter	10
	yard	10.9361
demal	gram–equiv/cu dm	1
denier	kilogram/meter	0.000 000 1
	ounce/foot	0.000 001 2
drachm (UK apoth)	dram (US apoth)	1
	gram	3.8879
	scruple (US apoth)	3
drachm (UK, liq)	cu centimeter	3.55163
	cu inch	0.21673
	minim (UK)	60
	milliliter	3.55163
dram (troy)	dram (avdp)	2.19429
	grain (apoth)	60
	gram	3.8879346
	ounce (troy)	0.125
dram (avdp)	dram (troy)	0.455729
	grain	27.34375
	gram	1.771845
	ounce (troy)	0.056966
	ounce (avdp)	0.0625
	pennyweight (troy)	1.13932
	pound (troy)	0.004747
	pound (avdp)	0.00391
	scruple (apoth)	1.36719
dram (US, liq)	cu cm	3.6967
	cu inch	0.225586
	drachm (UK, liq)	1.04084
	gill (US)	0.03125
	milliliter	3.69669
	minim (US)	60
	ounce (US, liq)	0.125
	pint (US, liq)	0.0078125
dyne	grain–force	0.015737
	gram–force	0.0010197
	joule	1×10^{-7}
	joule/meter	1×10^{-5}
	kilogram–force	1.02×10^{-6}
	newton	0.00001
	poundal	7.233×10^{-5}
	pound–force	2.248×10^{-6}
dyne/cm	erg/sq cm	1
	erg/sq mm	0.01
	gram–force/cm	0.0010197
	poundal/inch	0.0001837
dyne/cu cm	gram–force/cu cm	0.0010197
	poundal/cu inch	0.001185
dyne/sq cm	atmosphere (std)	9.869×10^{-7}
	bar	1×10^{-6}

Convert From	Into	Multiply By
	barye (French)	1
	cm of Hg @ 0°C	7.500616×10^{-5}
	cm of H_2O @ 4°C	0.00101972
	gram–force/sq cm	0.00101972
	in of Hg @ 32°F	2.953×10^{-5}
	in of H_2O @ 4°C	0.0004015
	kg–force/sq meter	0.0101972
	newton/sq meter	0.1
	pascal	0.1
	poundal/sq in	0.0004666
	pound–force/sq in	1.45×10^{-5}
dyne cm	erg	1
	foot poundal	2.373×10^{-6}
	foot pound–force	7.376×10^{-8}
	gram–force cm	0.00102
	inch pound–force	8.8508×10^{-7}
	joule	1×10^{-7}
	kg–force meter	1.0197×10^{-8}
	newton meter	1×10^{-7}
electron volt	erg	1.6021×10^{-12}
	joule	1.602177×10^{-19}
electron charge	abcoulomb	1.6022×10^{-20}
	coulomb	1.6022×10^{-19}
	statcoulomb	4.803×10^{-10}
ell (cloth)	cm	114.3
	inch	45
em (pica–printer)	inch	0.167
	cm	0.42175
erg	Btu (thermo)	9.4845×10^{-11}
	calorie (IST)	2.3885×10^{-8}
	calorie, kg (thermo)	2.3901×10^{-11}
	cu cm atmosphere	9.8692×10^{-7}
	cu ft atmosphere	3.4853×10^{-11}
	cu ft lb–force/sq in	5.122×10^{-10}
	dyne cm	1
	electron volt	6.241×10^{11}
	foot poundal	2.373×10^{-6}
	foot pound–force	7.376×10^{-8}
	gram–force cm	0.0010197
	horsepower hour	3.725×10^{-14}
	joule	1×10^{-7}
	joule (US Int)	9.998×10^{-8}
	kilowatthour	2.778×10^{-14}
	kg–force meter	1.0197×10^{-8}
	liter atmosphere	9.869×10^{-10}
	watthour	0.278×10^{-7}
	wattsecond	1×10^{-7}
erg/sec	Btu/min (thermo)	5.691×10^{-9}
	calorie, kg/minute (IST)	1.43×10^{-9}
	calorie/min (IST)	1.4331×10^{-6}
	dyne–cm/sec	1
	foot pound–force/min	4.425×10^{-6}
	foot pound–force/sec	7.376×10^{-8}
	gram–force cm/sec	0.0010197
	horsepower	1.341×10^{-10}
	joule/sec	1×10^{-7}

Convert From	Into	Multiply By
	kilowatt	1×10^{-10}
	watt	1×10^{-7}
erg/sq cm	dyne/cm	1
	erg/sq mm	0.01
erg/sq mm	dyne/cm	100
	erg/sq cm	100
erg sec	Planck constant	1.5092×10^{26}
faraday (chem)	ampere hour	26.8
	coloumb	9.649×10^{4}
faraday/sec	ampere (absolute)	9.65×10^{4}
farad	abfarad	1×10^{-9}
	farads (Int)	1.00049
	microfarad	1×10^{6}
	statfarad	8.98755×10^{11}
farads (Int)	farad	0.9995
fathom (US Survey)	centimeter	182.88
	foot (US Survey)	6
	furlong (US Survey)	0.0090909
	Inch (US Survey)	72
	meter	1.8288
	mile (naut,Int)	0.00098747
	mile (US statute)	0.0011363
	yard (US Survey)	2
fifth (US, liq)	jigger (US, liq)	17.067
	liter	0.75708
	ounce (US, liq)	25.6
	pint (US, liq)	1.6
	pony (US, liq)	25.6
	quart (US, liq)	0.8
	shot (US, liq)	25.6
firkin (UK)	bushel (UK)	1.125
	cu cm	40914.8
	cu foot	1.44489
	firkin (UK)	1.20095
	gallon (UK)	9
	liter	40.91481
	pint (UK)	72
firkin (US)	barrel (US, dry)	0.294643
	barrel (US, liq)	0.285714
	bushel (US, dry)	0.966788
	cu foot	1.203125
	firkin (UK)	0.832674
	gallon (US, liq)	9
	liter	34.0687
	pint (US, liq)	72
flask of mercury	kilogram	34.473
foot	centimeter	30.48
	chain (Gunter)	0.015151
	fathom (US Survey)	0.166667
	foot (US Survey)	0.999998
	furlong (US Survey)	0.001515
	inch	12
	kilometer	3.048×10^{-4}
	meter	0.3048
	micron	304800
	mile (naut Int)	0.000165

Convert From	Into	Multiply By
	mile (US statute)	0.000189
	millimeter	304.8
	mil	1.2 x 10⁴
	rod (US Survey)	0.060606
	rope (UK)	0.05
	yard	0.333333
foot (US Survey)	centimeter	30.48006
	chain (Gunter)	0.015152
	chain (Ramden)	0.01000002
	foot	1.000002
	inch	12.000024
	link (Gunter)	1.515155
	link (Ramden)	1.000002
	meter	0.304801
	mile (US statute)	0.00018939
	rod (US Survey)	0.06060618
	yard	0.333334
foot of air @ 60°F	atmosphere (std)	3.608 x 10⁻⁵
	ft of Hg @ 32°F	0.0009
	ft of H₂O @ 60°F	0.00122
	in of Hg @ 32°F	0.00108
	pound−force/sq in	0.00053
foot of Hg @ 32°F	cm of Hg @ 0°C	30.48
	ft of H₂O @ 60°F	13.6086
	in of H₂O @ 60°F	163.3
	ounce−force/sq in	94.302
	pound−force/sq in	5.8938
foot of H₂O @ 4°C	atmosphere (std)	0.0295
	cm of Hg @ 0°C	2.24198
	dyne/sq cm	29890.7
	gram−force/sq cm	30.48
	in of Hg @ 32°F	0.882671
	kg−force/sq meter	304.8
	newton/sq meter	2989.07
	pascal	2989.07
	pound−force/sq foot	62.428
	pound−force/sq inch	0.433528
foot/hour	cm/hr	30.48
	cm/minute	0.508
	cm/second	0.008467
	foot/minute	0.016667
	inch/hour	12
	kilometer/hr	0.0003048
	kilometer/min	5.08 x 10⁻⁶
	knots (Int)	0.00016458
	mile/hr	0.0001894
	mile/min	3.15656 x 10⁻⁶
	mile/sec	5.2609 x 10⁻⁸
foot/minute	cm/sec	0.508
	foot/sec	0.016667
	kilometer/hr	0.018288
	meter/min	0.3048
	meter/sec	0.00508
	mile/hr	0.011364
foot/second	cm/sec	30.48
	kilometer/hr	1.09728

Convert From	Into	Multiply By
	kilometer/min	0.01829
foot/second	knot	0.5925
	meter/min	18.288
	mile/hr	0.681818
	mile/min	0.011364
foot/(sec x sec)	cm/(sec x sec)	30.48
	km/(hr x sec)	1.0973
	meter/(sec x sec)	0.3048
	mile/(hr x sec)	0.681818
foot/100 foot	percent grade	1footcandle
lumen/sq ft	foot-candle	1
	lumen/sq meter	10.7639
	lux	10.7639
	milliphot	1.07639
footlambert	candle/sq cm	0.00034
	candle/sq ft	0.31831
	millilambert	1.07639
	lambert	0.0010764
	lumen/sq ft	1
foot poundal	Btu (thermo)	3.9968×10^{-5}
	Btu (IST)	3.9941×10^{-5}
	Btu (mean)	3.991×10^{-5}
	calorie (thermo)	0.010072
	calorie (IST)	0.010065
	calorie (mean)	0.010057
	cu cm atmosphere	0.41589
	cu ft atmosphere	1.4687×10^{-5}
	dyne cm	4.21401×10^{5}
	erg	4.21401×10^{5}
	foot pound–force	0.03108
	hp hour	1.5697×10^{-8}
	joule	0.0421401
	joule (Int)	0.042132
	kg–force meter	0.004297
	kilowatthour	1.1706×10^{-8}
	liter atmosphere	0.0004159
foot pound force	Btu (thermochemical)	0.0012859
	Btu (IST)	0.0012851
	Btu (mean)	0.0012841
	calorie (thermo)	0.3240483
	calorie (IST)	0.3238316
	calorie (mean)	0.3235827
	calorie @ 20°C	0.32421
	calorie, kg (IST)	0.0003238
	cu ft atmosphere	0.0004725
	dyne cm	1.3558179×10^{7}
	erg	1.3558179×10^{7}
	foot poundal	32.174049
	gram–force cm	13825.5
	hp hour	5.0505051×10^{-7}
	joule	1.3558179
	kg–force meter	0.13825495
	kilowatthour	3.766161×10^{-7}
	kilowatthour (Int)	3.765544×10^{-7}
	liter atmosphere	0.01338088
	newton meter	1.3558179

Convert From	Into	Multiply By
	watthour	0.0003766161
foot pound–force/hr	Btu/min (thermo)	2.1432×10^{-5}
	Btu (mean)/min	2.1401×10^{-5}
	calorie/min (thermo)	0.0054
	calorie (mean)/min	0.00539
	erg/min	2.2597×10^{5}
	foot pound–force/min	0.016667
	horsepower	5.0505×10^{-7}
	horsepower (metric)	5.1205×10^{-7}
	kilowatt	3.7662×10^{-7}
	watt	0.00037662
	watt (Int)	0.00037655
foot pound–force/min	Btu/minute (thermo)	1.286×10^{-3}
	Btu/sec (thermo)	2.1433×10^{-5}
	Btu (mean)/sec	2.1401×10^{-5}
	calorie/sec (thermo)	0.0054
	calorie (mean)/sec	0.00539
	calorie, kg(thermo)/min	3.24×10^{-4}
	erg/sec	2.2597×10^{5}
	foot pound–force/sec	0.01667
	horsepower	3.0303×10^{-5}
	horsepower (metric)	3.0723×10^{-5}
	joule/sec	0.0226
	joule (Int)/sec	0.02259
	kilowatt	2.2597×10^{-5}
	watt	0.022597
foot pound–force/lb	Btu/lb (thermo)	0.001285
	Btu (IST)/lb	0.001285
	Btu (mean)/lb	0.001284
	calorie/gram (thermo)	0.00071441
	calorie (IST)/gram	0.00071392
	calorie (mean)/gram	0.00071337
	hp–hr/lb	5.0505×10^{-7}
	joule/gram	0.002989
	kg–force meter/gram	0.0003
	kilowatthour/gram	8.303×10^{-10}
foot pound–force/sec	Btu/hour (IST)	4.6262
	Btu/min (IST)	0.077104
	Btu (mean)/min	0.077045
	Btu/sec (thermo)	0.001286
	Btu (mean)/sec	0.001284
	calorie/sec (thermo)	0.32405
	calorie (mean)/sec	0.32358
	calorie, kg/min	0.019443
	erg/sec	1.3558×10^{7}
	gram–force cm/sec	13825.5
	horsepower	0.001818
	joule/sec	1.3558
	kilowatt	0.001356
	watt	1.3558
	watt (Int)	1.3556
furlong (US Survey)	centimeter	20116.8
	chain (Gunter)	10
	chain (Ramden)	6.6
	foot (US Survey)	660
	inch (US Survey)	7920

Convert From	Into	Multiply By
	meter	201.17
	mile (naut,Int)	0.1086
	mile (US statute)	0.125
	rod (US Survey)	40
	yard (US Survey)	220
gallon (UK)	barrel (UK)	0.02778
	bushel (UK)	0.125
	cu centimeter	4546.09
	cu foot	0.1605
	cu inch	277.419
	drachm (UK, liq)	1280
	firkin (UK)	0.1111
	gallon (US, liq)	1.2009
	gill (UK)	32
	liter	4.546
	minim (UK)	76800
	ounce (UK, liq)	160
	ounce (US, liq)	153.722
	peck (UK)	0.5
	lbs of H₂O @ 62°F	10.0092
gallon (US, dry)	barrel (US, dry)	0.038096
	barrel (US, liq)	0.036941
	bushel (US, dry)	0.125
	cu centimeter	4404.88
	cu foot	0.15556
	cu inch	268.8
	cu meter	0.004405
	gallon (US, liq)	1.163647
	liter	4.4049
gallon (US, liq)	acre foot	3.0689×10^{-6}
	barrel (US, liq)	0.031746
	barrel (US oil)	0.0238095
	bushel (US, dry)	0.10742
	cu centimeter	3785.41
	cu foot	0.13368
	cu inch	231
	cu meter	0.003785
	cu yard	0.00495
	cup (US measuring)	16
	gallon (UK)	0.83267
	gallon (US, dry)	0.85937
	gill (US)	32
	liter	3.7854
	minim (US)	61440
	ounce (US, liq)	128
	pint (US, liq)	8
	quart (US, liq)	4
	Winchester wine gallon	1
gallon (US)H₂O @4°C	lb of H₂O	8.345171
gallon (US)H₂O @60°F	lb of H₂O	8.337172
gallon (US)/day	cu foot/hr	0.00557
gallon (UK)/hour	cu meter/min	7.5768×10^{-5}
gallon (US)/hour	acre foot/hr	3.0689×10^{-6}
	cu foot/hr	0.13368
	cu meter/min	6.309×10^{-5}
	cu yard/min	8.2519×10^{-5}

Convert From	Into	Multiply By
	liter/hr	3.7854
gallon (US)/min	liter/sec	0.06309
	cu foot/sec	2.228×10^{-3}
	cu foot/hour	8.0208
	cu meter/min	0.003786
gallon (UK)/sec	cu cm/sec	4546.09
gallon (US)/sec	cu cm/sec	3785.4
	cu foot/min	8.0208
	cu yard/min	0.29707
	liter/min	227.124
gamma	gauss	1×10^{-5}
	gram	1×10^{-6}
	microgram	1
	tesla	1×10^{-9}
gauss	gauss (Int)	0.9997
	gamma	1×10^{5}
	gilbert/cm	1
	maxwell/sq cm	1
	line/sq cm	1
	line/sq inch	6.4516
	tesla	1×10^{-4}
	weber/sq cm	1×10^{-8}
	weber/sq inch	6.452×10^{-8}
	weber/sq meter	1×10^{-4}
gauss (Int)	gauss	1.00033
geepound	slug	1
	kilogram	14.594
	pound-force sq sec/ft	1
	pound	32.174
gigameter	meter	1×10^{9}
gilbert	abampere turn	0.07958
	ampere turn	0.79577
	gilbert (Int)	1.00016
gilbert (Int)	gilbert	0.99983
gilbert/cm	ampere turn/cm	0.79577
	ampere turn/in	2.02127
	ampere turn/meter	79.58
	oersted	1
	tesla	1×10^{-4}
gilbert/maxwell	ampere turn/weber	7.958×10^{7}
gill (UK)	cu centimeter	142.065
	gallon (UK)	0.03125
	gill (US)	1.20095
	liter	0.142
	ounce (UK, liq)	5
	ounce (US, liq)	4.8038
	pint (UK)	0.25
gill (US)	cu centimeter	118.29
	cu inch	7.2188
	dram (US, liq)	32
	gallon (US, liq)	0.03125
	gill (UK)	0.8327
	liter	0.1183
	minim (US)	1920
	ounce (US, liq)	4
	pint (US, liq)	0.25

Convert From	Into	Multiply By
	quart (US, liq)	0.125
grade	circle	0.0025
	circumference	0.0025
	degree	0.9
	minute	54
	radian	0.01571
	revolution	0.0025
	second	3240
grain	carat (metric)	0.32399
	dram (troy)	0.01667
	dram (avdp)	0.03657
	gram	0.0648
	milligram	64.7989
	ounce (troy)	0.00208
	ounce (avdp)	0.00229
	pennyweight (troy)	0.04167
	pound (troy)	0.00017
	pound (avdp)	0.00014
	scruple (apoth)	0.05
	ton (metric)	6.4799×10^{-8}
grain–force	dyne	63.546
	newton	6.3546×10^{-4}
	poundal	0.0046
grain/cu ft	gram/cu meter	2.28835
grain/gal (US, liq)	part/million (1g/ml)	17.118
	pound/million gal	142.86
grain/gal (UK, liq)	part/million	14.254
gram	carat (metric)	5
	decigram	10
	dekagram	0.1
	dram (troy)	0.2572
	dram (avdp)	0.5644
	grain	15.432
	kilogram	0.001
	microgram	1×10^{6}
	milligram	1000
	myriagram	0.0001
	ounce (troy)	0.03215
	ounce (avdp)	0.03527
	pennyweight (troy)	0.64301
	pound (troy)	0.00268
	pound (avdp)	0.002205
	scruple (apoth)	0.77162
	ton (metric)	1×10^{-6}
gram–force	dyne	980.665
	joule/cm	9.807×10^{-5}
	joule/meter	9.807×10^{-3}
	newton	9.807×10^{-3}
	poundal	0.07093
gram/cm	gram/inch	2.54
	kg/km	100
	kg/meter	0.1
	pound/ft	0.067197
	pound/inch	0.0056
	ton (metric)/km	0.1
gram–force/cm	dyne/cm	980.665

Convert From	Into	Multiply By
	poundal/inch	0.18017
gram/(cm x sec)	poise	1
	lb/(ft x sec)	0.0672
gram/cu cm	grain/milliliter	15.4324
	gram/milliliter	1
	pound/cu foot	62.428
	pound/cu inch	0.0361
	pound/gal (UK)	10.022
	pound/gal (US, dry)	9.7111
	pound/gal (US, liq)	8.3454
gram–force/cu cm	dyne/cu cm	980.665
	poundal/cu cm	1.16236
gram/cu meter	grain/cu ft.	0.437
gram/liter	grain/gallon	58.4178
	part/million (1gm/ml)	1000
	lb/cu foot	0.0624
	lb/1000 gal (US)	8.3454
gram/milliliter	gram/cu cm	1
	pound/cu foot	62.428
	pound/gallon (US)	8.34540
gram–force/sq cm	atmosphere (std)	0.00097
	bar	0.00098
	cm of Hg @ 0°C	0.07356
	dyne/sq cm	980.665
	in of Hg @ 32°F	0.02896
	kg–force/sq meter	10
	mm of Hg @ 0°C	0.73556
	pascal	98.0665
	poundal/sq inch	0.45762
	pound–force/sq inch	0.01422
	pound–force/sq foot	2.0482
gram/ton (long)	milligram/kg	0.9842
gram/ton (short)	milligram/kg	1.1023
gram–calorie	Btu (thermo)	3.968×10^{-3}
	erg	4.1868×10^{7}
	foot/pound–force	3.088
	horsepower hour	1.5596×10^{-6}
	kilowatthour	1.163×10^{-6}
	watthour	1.163×10^{-3}
gram–calorie/sec	Btu/hr (thermo)	14.286
gram–force cm	Btu (thermo)	9.3×10^{-8}
	Btu (IST)	9.295×10^{-8}
	Btu (mean)	9.288×10^{-8}
	calorie	2.344×10^{-5}
	calorie (IST)	2.342×10^{-5}
	calorie (mean)	2.34×10^{-5}
	calorie (15°C)	2.343×10^{-5}
	calorie (20°C)	2.345×10^{-5}
	calorie, kg	2.344×10^{-8}
	calorie, kg (IST)	2.342×10^{-8}
	calorie, kg (mean)	2.34×10^{-8}
	dyne cm	980.665
	erg	980.665
	foot poundal	0.00233
	foot pound–force	7.233×10^{-5}
	hp hour	3.653×10^{-11}

Convert From	Into	Multiply By
	joule	9.807×10^{-5}
	kilowatthour	2.724×10^{-11}
	kilowatthour (Int)	2.724×10^{-11}
	newton meter	9.807×10^{-5}
	watthour	2.724×10^{-8}
gram–force cm/sec	Btu/sec	9.301×10^{-8}
	calorie/sec	2.344×10^{-5}
	erg/sec	980.665
	foot pound–force/sec	7.233×10^{-5}
	horsepower	1.315×10^{-7}
	joule/sec	9.807×10^{-5}
	kilowatt	9.807×10^{-8}
	kilowatt (Int)	9.805×10^{-8}
	watt	9.807×10^{-5}
gram–sq cm	pound sq inch	0.00034
gram–force sec/sq cm	poise	980.665
gravity constant	cm/(sec x sec)	980.665
	ft/(sec x sec)	32.17405
gray	joule/kg	1
	rad	100
	erg/gram	1×10^4
gray/sec	joule/kg sec	1
	rad/sec	100
	erg/gram sec	1×10^4
hand (horses)	centimeter	10.16
	foot	0.3333
	inch	4
hectare	acre	2.471
	are	100
	sq cm	1×10^8
	sq foot	107639.1
	sq meter	10000
	sq mile	0.00386
	sq rod	395.367
hectogram	gram	100
	pound (apoth or troy)	0.26769
	pound (avdp)	0.2205
hectogram–force	poundal	7.0932
hectoliter	bushel (UK)	2.7496
	bushel (US, dry)	2.8378
	cu cm	1×10^5
	cu foot	3.5315
	gallon (US, liq)	26.417
	liter	100
	ounce (US, liq)	3381.4
	peck (US)	11.351
hectometer	centimeter	10000
	decimeter	1000
	dekameter	10
	foot	328.08
	meter	100
	rod (US Survey)	19.88
	yard	109.36
hectowatt	watt	100
hefner candle	candle (UK)	0.864
	candle (Germ)	0.855

Convert From	Into	Multiply By
	candle (Int)	0.901
	10cp pentane candle	0.09
henry	abhenry	1×10^9
	henry (Int)	0.9995
	millihenry	1000
	mks (r or nr) unit	1
	stathenry	1.113×10^{-12}
henry (Int)	henry	1.0005
henry/meter	gauss/oersted	795775
	mks (nr) unit	0.0796
	mks (r) unit	1
hertz	cycle/sec.	1
hogshead (US)	butt (US)	0.5
	cu foot	8.4219
	cu inch	14553
	cu meter	0.238
	gallon (UK)	52.458
	gallon (US, liq)	63
	gallon (wine)	63
	liter	238.47
hogshead (UK)	cu foot	10.11
horsepower (mech)	Btu (mean)/hr	2542.47
	Btu (mean)/min	42.375
	Btu (mean)/sec	0.7062
	calorie/hr (thermo)	6.416×10^5
	calorie (IST)/hr	6.412×10^5
	calorie (mean)/hr	6.4069×10^5
	calorie/min (thermo)	10694
	calorie (IST)/min	10686
	calorie (mean)/min	10678
	calorie, kg/min (IST)	10.686
	erg/sec	7.457×10^9
	foot pound–force/hr	1980000
	foot pound–force/min	33000
	foot pound–force/sec	550
	horsepower (boiler)	0.076
	horsepower (electric)	0.9996
	horsepower (metric)	1.0139
	joule/sec	745.7
	kilowatt	0.7457
	kilowatt (Int)	0.7456
	ton of refrigeration	0.212
	watt	745.7
horsepower (boiler)	Btu (mean)/hr	33445.6
	calorie/min (thermo)	140671.6
	calorie (mean)/min	140469.4
	calorie (20°C)/min	140742.3
	erg/sec	9.8095×10^{10}
	foot pound–force/min	434107
	horsepower (mech)	13.1548
	horsepower (electric)	13.1495
	horsepower (metric)	13.3372
	horsepower (water)	13.1487
	joule/sec	9809.5
	kilowatt	9.8095
horsepower (electric)	Btu/hr (thermo)	2547.16

Convert From	Into	Multiply By
	Btu (IST)/hr	2545.46
	Btu (mean)/hr	2543.49
	calorie/sec (thermo)	178.298
	calorie, kg/hr (thermo)	641.87
	erg/sec	7.46×10^9
	foot pound–force/min	33013
	foot pound–force/sec	550.2
	horsepower (mech)	1.0004
	horsepower (boiler)	0.07605
	horsepower (metric)	1.01428
	horsepower (water)	0.99994
	joule/sec	746
	kilowatt	0.746
	watt	746
horsepower (metric)	Btu/hr (thermo)	2511.3
	Btu (IST)/hr	2509.6
	Btu (mean)/hr	2507.7
	calorie/hr (thermo)	6.328×10^5
	calorie (IST)/hr	6.324×10^5
	calorie (mean)/hr	6.319×10^5
	erg/sec	7.355×10^9
	foot pound–force/min	32548.6
	foot pound–force/sec	542.476
	horsepower (mech)	0.9863
	horsepower (boiler)	0.07498
	horsepower (electric)	0.9859
	horsepower (water)	0.98587
	kg-force meter/sec	75
	kilowatt	0.7355
	watt	735.499
horsepower (water)	foot pound–force/min	33015
	horsepower (mech)	1.00046
	horsepower (boiler)	0.07605
	horsepower (electric)	1.00006
	horsepower (metric)	1.01434
	kilowatt	0.746043
horsepower hour	Btu (thermo)	2546.1
	Btu (IST)	2544.4
	Btu (mean)	2542.5
	calorie (thermo)	641616
	calorie (IST)	641187
	calorie (mean)	640694
	calorie, kg	641.2
	erg	2.685×10^{13}
	foot pound–force	1.98×10^6
	joule	2.685×10^6
	kg-force meter	273745
	kilowatthour	0.7457
	watthour	745.7
horsepower hr/lb	Btu/lb (thermo)	2546
	calorie/gram (thermo)	1414.5
	cu ft (lb/sq in)/lb	13750
	foot pound–force/lb	1980000
	joule/gram	5918.35
hour (mean solar)	day (mean solar)	0.04167
	day (sidereal)	0.04178

Convert From	Into	Multiply By
	hour (sidereal)	1.002738
	minute (mean solar)	60
	minute (sidereal)	60.164
	second (mean solar)	3600
	second (sidereal)	3609.86
	week (mean calendar)	0.00595
hour (sidereal)	day (mean solar)	0.41553
	day (sidereal)	0.04167
	hour (mean solar)	0.99727
	minute (mean solar)	59.836
	minute (sidereal)	60
hundredweight (long)	kilogram	50.802
	pound	112
	quarter (UK)	4
	quarter (US)	4.48
	ton (long)	0.05
hundredweight (short)	kilogram	45.359
	ounce (avdp)	1600
	pound (avdp)	100
	quarter (UK)	3.5714
	quarter (US)	4
	ton (long)	0.04464
	ton (metric)	0.04536
	ton (short)	0.05
inch	ångström	2.54×10^{8}
	centimeter	2.54
	chain (Gunter)	0.001263
	cubit	0.05556
	fathom (US Survey)	0.013889
	foot	0.083333
	foot (US Survey)	0.083332
	link (Gunter)	0.12626
	link (Ramden)	0.08333
	meter	0.0254
	mile	1.578×10^{-5}
	millimeter	25.4
	mil	1000
	picas (printer)	6.0225
	point (printer)	72.27
	yard	0.0278
inch of Hg @ 32°F	atmosphere (std)	0.03342
	bar	0.03386
	dyne/sq cm	33864
	ft of air @ 1atm,60°F	926.27
	ft of H_2O @ 39.2°F	1.13299
	gram–force/sq cm	34.532
	kg–force/sq meter	345.32
	mm of Hg @ 0°C	25.4
	newton/sq meter	3386.389
	ounce–force/sq inch	7.858
	pascal	3386.389
	pound–force/sq ft	70.726
inch of Hg @ 60°F	atmosphere (std)	0.033327
	dyne/sq cm	33768
	gram–force/sq cm	34.434
	mm of Hg @ 60°F	25.4

Convert From	Into	Multiply By
	newton/sq meter	3376.85
	ounce–force/sq inch	7.8363
	pascal	3376.85
	pound–force/sq ft	70.5267
inch of H$_2$O @ 4°C	atmosphere (std)	0.002458
	dyne/sq cm	2490.8
	inch of Hg @ 32°F	0.07355
	kg–force/sq meter	25.4
	ounce–force/sq foot	83.232
	ounce–force/sq inch	0.578037
	pound–force/sq foot	5.202033
	pound–force/sq inch	0.03613
inch pound–force	foot pound–force	0.0833
inch/hour	cm/hour	2.54
	foot/hour	0.0833
	mile/hour	1.5783 x 10^{-5}
inch/minute	cm/hour	152.4
	foot/hour	5
	mile/hour	0.000947
jigger (US, liq)	fifth (US, liq)	0.059
	ounce (US, liq)	1.5
	pint (US, liq)	0.09375
	pony (US, liq)	1.5
	shot (US, liq)	1.5
joule	Btu (thermo)	0.0009485
	Btu (IST)	0.0009478
	Btu (mean)	0.0009471
	calorie (thermo)	0.23901
	calorie (IST)	0.23885
	calorie (mean)	0.23866
	calorie @ 20°C	0.23913
	calorie, kg (mean)	0.000239
	calorie, kg (thermo)	2.390 x 10^{-4}
	cu ft atmosphere	0.0003485
	erg	1 x 10^7
	foot–poundal	23.73
	foot pound–force	0.7376
	gram–force cm	10197.2
	horsepower hour	3.7251 x 10^{-7}
	joule (US Int)	0.9998
	kg–force meter	0.10197
	kilowatthour	2.78 x 10^{-7}
	liter atmosphere	0.009869
	volt coulomb (Int)	0.999935
	watthour	0.0002778
	watthour (Int)	0.0002777
	wattsecond	1
	wattsecond (Int)	0.9998
joule (US Int)	Btu (thermo)	0.000949
	Btu (IST)	0.000948
	Btu (mean)	0.000947
	calorie (thermo)	0.239049
	calorie (IST)	0.238889
	calorie (mean)	0.238706
	cu cm atmosphere	9.87103
	cu ft atmosphere	0.00349

Convert From	Into	Multiply By
	dyne cm	1.000182×10^7
	erg	1.000182×10^7
	foot poundal	23.7347
	foot pound–force	0.7377
	gram–force cm	10199
	joule	1.000182
	kilowatthour	2.778×10^{-7}
	liter atmosphere	0.00987
	volt coulomb	1.000182
	volt coulomb (Int)	1
	wattsecond	1.000182
	wattsecond (Int)	1
joule/ampere hour	joule/abcoulomb	0.00278
	joule/statcoulomb	9.266×10^{-14}
joule/coulomb	joule/abcoulomb	10
	volt	1×10^7
joule/cm	dyne	1×10^7
	gram–force	1.020×10^4
	joule/meter	100
	newton	100
	poundal	723.3
	pound–force	22.48
joule/cu meter	Btu (IST)/cu ft	2.6839×10^{-5}
	dyne/sq cm	10
	foot pound–force/cu ft	0.020885
	watt hr/cu ft	7.86578×10^{-6}
joule/kilogram K	Btu/lb °R	2.38846×10^{-4}
	calorie/gram °C (IST)	2.38846×10^{-4}
	joule/kg °C	1.0
	kilocalorie/kg °C (IST)	2.38846×10^{-4}
	kilojoule/kg °C	1×10^{-3}
joule/second	Btu/hr (thermo)	0.0569
	calorie/min (IST)	14.33
	calorie, kg/min (thermo)	0.01434
	calorie, kg (mean)/min	0.01432
	dyne cm/sec	1×10^7
	erg/sec	1×10^7
	foot pound–force/sec	0.73756
	gram–force cm/sec	10197
	horsepower	0.00134
	watt	1
	watt (Int)	0.9998
joule (US Int)/sec	Btu/min (thermo)	0.05692
	Btu (mean)/min	0.05683
	calorie/min (IST)	14.343
	calorie, kg/min (thermo)	0.01434
	dyne cm/sec	1.000165×10^7
	erg/sec	1.000165×10^7
	foot pound–force/min	44.26
	foot pound–force/sec	0.73768
	gram–force cm/sec	10198.8
	horsepower	0.00134
	watt	1.000165
	watt (Int)	1
karat (gold)	milligram/gram	41.666
kelvin	°C	kelvin-273.15

Convert From	Into	Multiply By
	°F.....................[1.8x(kelvin−273.15)+32]	
kilderkin (UK, liq)	cu cm	81829.6
	cu foot	2.8898
	cu inch	4993.55
	cu meter	0.0818
	gallon (UK)	18
	liter	81.83
kilogram	dram (apoth or troy)	257.21
	dram (avdp)	564.38
	grain	15432.36
	gram	1000
	hundredweight (long)	0.019684
	hundredweight (short)	0.022046
	joule/cm	0.09807
	ounce (apoth or troy)	32.1507
	ounce (avdp)	35.27396
	pennyweight (troy)	643.0149
	pound (apoth or troy)	2.67923
	pound (avdp)	2.20462
	quarter (UK)	0.078736
	quarter (US)	0.088185
	scruple (apoth)	771.6179
	slug	0.06852
	ton (long)	0.000984
	ton (metric)	0.001
	ton (short)	0.001102
kilogram−force	dyne	980665
	joule/meter	9.80665
	newton	9.80665
	poundal	70.9316
	gram−force	1000
	kip	0.002205
	pound−force	2.20462
	sthene	0.009807
kilogram/cu meter	gram/cu cm	0.001
	lb/cu ft	0.0624
	lb/cu inch	3.6127×10^{-5}
	lb/circ mil foot	3.405×10^{-10}
kilogram/meter	pound/ft	0.672
	denier	9,000,000
kilogram−force/sq cm	atmosphere (std)	0.9678
	bar	0.980665
	cm of Hg @ 0°C	73.556
	dyne/sq cm	980665
	ft of H_2O @ 39.2°F	32.8104
	in of Hg @ 32°F	28.959
	newton/sq meter	98066.5
	pascal	98066.5
	pound−force/sq inch	14.223
kilogram−force/sq meter	atmosphere (std)	9.678×10^{-5}
	bar	9.80665×10^{-5}
	dyne/sq cm	98.0665
	ft of H_2O @ 39.2°F	0.00328
	gram−force/sq cm	0.1
	in of Hg @ 32°F	0.0029
	mm of Hg @ 0°C	0.07356

Convert From	Into	Multiply By
	newton/sq meter	9.80665
	pascal	9.80665
kilogram–force/sq meter	pound–force/sq foot	0.20482
	pound–force/sq inch	0.00142
kilogram–force/sq mm	pound–force/sq ft	204816
	pound–force/sq in	1422.3
	ton–force (short)/sq in	0.71117
kilogram sq cm	pound sq ft	0.00237
	pound sq in	0.34172
kilogram–force meter	Btu (mean)	0.00929
	calorie (mean)	2.3405
	calorie, kg (mean)	0.0023405
	cu ft atmosphere	0.003418
	dyne cm	9.807×10^7
	erg	9.807×10^7
	foot–poundal	232.715
	foot pound–force	7.233
	gram–force cm	100000
	horsepower hour	3.653×10^{-6}
	joule	9.80665
	joule (US Int)	9.8049
	kilowatthour	2.724×10^{-6}
	liter atmosphere	0.0968
	newton meter	9.80665
	watthour	0.0027241
	watthour (Int)	0.0027236
kilogram–force m/sec	watt	9.80665
kiloline	maxwell	1000
	weber	1×10^{-5}
kiloliter	cu centimeter	1×10^6
	cu inch	35.315
	cu inch	61023.7
	cu meter	1
	cu yard	1.30795
	gallon (UK)	219.969
	gallon (US, dry)	227.021
	gallon (US, liq)	264.172
	liter	1000
kilometer	astronomical unit	6.685×10^{-9}
	centimeter	100000
	foot	3280.84
	foot (US Survey)	3280.83
	inch	3.937×10^4
	light year	1.057×10^{-13}
	meter	1000
	mile (naut, Int)	0.53996
	mile (US statute)	0.62135
	millimeter	1×10^6
	myriameter	0.1
	rod (US Survey)	198.839
	yard	1093.61
kilometer/hr	cm/sec	27.778
	foot/hr	3280.84
	foot/min	54.6807
	foot/sec	0.91134
	knots (Int)	0.53996

Convert From	Into	Multiply By
	meter/sec	0.2778
	mile (US statute)/hr	0.62137
kilometer/hr/sec	cm/sec/sec	27.78
	ft/sec/sec	0.9113
	meter/sec/sec	0.2778
	mile/hr/sec	0.6214
kilometer/min	cm/sec	1666.67
	foot/min	3280.8
	kilometer/hr	60
	knots (Int)	32.397
	mile/hr	37.2823
	mile/min	0.62137
kilonewton	dyne	1×10^{8}
	pound–force	224.8089
	poundal	7233.014
	ton–force (short)	0.112404
kilopascal	atmosphere (std)	9.8692×10^{-3}
	bar	1×10^{-2}
	pound–force/sq inch	0.1450377
	pound–force/sq ft	20.88542
	pascal	1000
	newton/sq meter	1000
	kilogram–force/sq cm	0.010197
	inch of Hg @ 0°C	0.2953
	inch of H_2O @ 68°F	4.021
kilovolt/cm	abvolt/cm	1×10^{11}
	microvolt/meter	1×10^{11}
	millivolt/meter	1×10^{8}
	statvolt/cm	3.336
	volt/inch	2540
kilowatt	Btu/hr (thermo)	3414.43
	Btu (IST)/hr	3412.14
	Btu (mean)/hr	3409.51
	Btu (mean)/min	56.825
	Btu (mean)/sec	0.9471
	calorie (mean)/hr	859184
	calorie (mean)/min	14319.7
	calorie (mean)/sec	238.66
	calorie, kg (mean)/hr	859.184
	calorie, kg (mean)/min	14.197
	calorie, kg (mean)/sec	0.23866
	cu ft atm/hr	1254.7
	erg/sec	1×10^{10}
	foot poundal/min	1.424×10^{6}
	foot pound–force/hr	2.655×10^{6}
	foot pound–force/min	44253.7
	foot pound–force/sec	737.56
	gram–force cm/sec	1.0197×10^{7}
	horsepower	1.341
	horsepower (boiler)	0.101942
	horsepower (electric)	1.340483
	horsepower (metric)	1.359622
	joule/hr	3.6×10^{6}
	joule (IST)/hr	3.599×10^{6}
	joule/sec	1000
	kg–force meter/hr	3.671×10^{5}

Convert From	Into	Multiply By
	kilowatt (Int)	0.999835
	watt	1000
kilowatt (Int)	Btu/hr (thermo)	3414.99
	Btu (IST)/hr	3412.76
	Btu (mean)/hr	3410.08
	Btu (mean)/min	56.835
	Btu (mean)/sec	0.9472
	calorie (mean)/hr	859326
	calorie (mean)/min	14322
	calorie, kg/hr (thermo)	860.56
	calorie, kg (IST)/hr	860
	calorie, kg (mean)/hr	859.3
	cu cm atm/hr	3.55×10^7
	cu ft atm/hr	1254.9
	erg/sec	1.000165×10^{10}
	foot poundal/min	1.424×10^6
	foot pound–force/min	44261
	foot pound–force/sec	737.68
	gram–force cm/sec	1.0199×10^7
	horsepower	1.341
	horsepower (boiler)	0.102
	horsepower (electric)	1.341
	horsepower (metric)	1.35985
	joule/hr	3.6006×10^6
	joule (Int)/hr	3.6×10^6
	kg–force meter/hr	367158
	kilowatt	1.000165
kilowatthour	Btu (mean)	3409.5
	calorie (IST)	859845
	calorie (mean)	859184
	erg	3.6×10^{13}
	foot pound–force	2.655×10^6
	hp hour	1.341
	joule	3.6×10^6
	kg–force meter	367098
	lb H$_2$O evaporated from and at 212°F	3.51646
	lb H$_2$O raised from 62°F to 212°F	22.764
	watthour	1000
	watthour (Int)	999.8
kilowatthour (Int)	Btu (mean)	3410.1
	calorie (IST)	859986
	calorie (mean)	859325
	cu cm atm	3.5535×10^7
	cu ft atm	1254.9
	foot pound–force	2.656×10^6
	hp hour	1.3412
	joule	3.6006×10^6
	joule (US legal)	3.6×10^6
	kg–force meter	367158
kilowatthour/gram	Btu/lb (thermo)	1.549×10^6
kilowatthour/gram	Btu (IST)/lb	1.548×10^6
	Btu (mean)/lb	1.5465×10^6
	calorie/gram (thermo)	860421
	calorie (mean)/gram	859184

Convert From	Into	Multiply By
	cu cm atm/gram	3.553×10^7
	cu ft atm/gram	1254.703
	hp hr/lb	608.28
	joule/gram	3.6×10^6
kip/sq in	atmosphere (std)	68.045964
	kg-force/sq cm	70.306958
	megapascal	6.8947573
knots (Int)	cm/sec	51.44
	foot/hr	6076.1
	foot/min	101.269
	foot/sec	1.688
	kilometer/hr	1.852
	meter/min	30.867
	meter/sec	0.5144
	mile (naut,Int)/hr	1
	mile/hr	1.1508
	yard/hour	2025.4
lambert	candle/sq cm	0.31831
	candle/sq ft	295.72
	candle/sq inch	2.0536
	foot lambert	929.03
	lumen/sq cm	1
lasts (UK)	liter (dry)	2909.4
lb	see pound	
league (naut, UK)	foot	18240
	kilometer	5.5595
	league (naut, Int)	1.0006
	league (US statute)	1.1515
	mile (US statute)	3.4545
league (naut, Int)	fathom (US Survey)	3038.05
	foot	18228
	kilometer	5.556
	league (US statute)	1.1508
	mile (US statute)	3.4523
league (US statute)	fathom (US Survey)	2640
	foot (US Survey)	15840
	kilometer	4.828
	league (naut, Int)	0.86898
	mile (naut, Int)	2.607
	mile (US statute)	3
light year	astronomical unit	63241.08
	kilometer	9.46073×10^{12}
	mile (US statute)	5.8786×10^{12}
	parsec	0.306601
line	maxwell	1
line (print)	centimeter	0.2117
	inch	0.0833
line/sq cm	gauss	1
	tesla	1×10^{-4}
line/sq inch	gauss	0.155
	tesla	1.55×10^{-5}
	weber/sq cm	1.55×10^{-8}
	weber/sq inch	1×10^{-8}
	weber/sq meter	1.55×10^{-5}
link (Gunter)	chain (Gunter)	0.01
	foot	0.6600013

Convert From	Into	Multiply By
	foot (US Survey)	0.66
	inch (US Survey)	7.92
	meter	0.2012
	mile (US statute)	0.000125
	rod (US Survey)	0.04
link (Ramden)	centimeter	30.48
	chain (Ramden)	0.01
	foot	1
	inch	12
liter	bushel (UK)	0.027496
	bushel (US, dry)	0.028376
	cu cm	1000
	cu foot	0.03531
	cu inch	61.0237
	cu meter	0.001
	cu yard	0.00131
	cup (US measuring)	4.2267
	dram (US, liq)	270.512
	gallon (UK)	0.21997
	gallon (US, dry)	0.22702
	gallon (US, liq)	0.26417
	gill (UK)	7.03902
	gill (US)	8.45351
	hogshead (US)	0.00419
	milliliter	1000
	minim (US)	16230.73
	ounce (UK, liq)	35.1951
	ounce (US, liq)	33.81402
	peck (UK)	0.10998
	peck (US)	0.11351
	pint (UK)	1.7598
	pint (US, dry)	1.8162
	pint (US, liq)	2.1134
	quart (UK)	0.8799
	quart (US, dry)	0.9081
	quart (US, liq)	1.0567
	shot (US, liq)	33.814
	tablespoon (US measure)	67.628
	teaspoon (US measure)	202.88
liter/min	cu ft/min	0.0353
	cu ft/sec	0.0005886
	gal (US, liq)/min	0.26417
	gal (US, liq)/sec	4.403×10^{-3}
liter/sec	cu ft/min	2.1189
	cu ft/sec	0.0353
	cu yard/min	0.07848
	gal (US, liq)/min	15.8503
	gal (US, liq)/sec	0.26417
liter atmosphere	Btu (thermo)	0.0961
	Btu (IST)	0.09604
	Btu (mean)	0.09596
	calorie (thermo)	24.2173
	calorie (IST)	24.2011
	calorie (mean)	24.1825
	cu ft atm	0.0353
	foot poundal	2404.5

Convert From	Into	Multiply By
	foot pound–force	74.733
	hp hour	3.774×10^{-5}
	joule	101.325
	joule (US Int)	101.31
	kg-force meter	10.33
	kilowatthour	2.815×10^{-5}
load (UK)	cu yard of alluvium	1
lumen	candela steradian	1
	candle power (spherical)	0.07958
	watt	0.0015
lumen/sq cm	lambert	1
	lux	1×10^4
	phot	1
lumen/sq ft	foot candle	1
	foot lambert	1
	lumen/sq meter	10.76391
	lux	10.76391
lumen/sq meter	foot candle	0.0929
	lumen/sq ft	0.0929
	phot	0.0001
	lux	1
lux	foot candle	0.0929
	lumen/sq meter	1
	phot	0.0001
magnum	bottle (wine, std)	2
	quart (US, liq)	1.585
maxwell	gauss sq cm	1
	line	1
	maxwell (Int)	0.99967
	volt second	1×10^{-8}
	weber	1×10^{-8}
maxwell (Int)	maxwell	1.00033
maxwell/sq cm	maxwell/sq in	6.4516
maxwell/sq in	maxwell/sq cm	0.155
megabyte	byte (computers)	1048576
meganewton	dyne	1×10^{11}
	pound–force	224808.9
	poundal	7.233014×10^6
	ton–force (short)	112.404
megapascal	atmosphere (std)	9.8692327
	kg-force/sq cm	10.197162
	pound-force/sq in	145.03774
megamho/cm	abmho/cm	0.001
	megamho/inch	2.54
	(microohm cm)⁻¹	1
megmho/inch	megamho/cm	0.3937
megaohm	microohm	1×10^{12}
	ohm	1×10^6
	statohm	1.1126×10^{-6}
meter	ångstrom	1×10^{10}
	centimeter	100
	chain (Gunter)	0.04971
	chain (Ramden)	0.03281
	fathom (US Survey)	0.54681
	foot	3.28084
	foot (US Survey)	3.28083

Convert From	Into	Multiply By
	furlong (US Survey)	0.00497
	inch	39.3701
	kilometer	0.001
	link (Gunter)	4.97096
	link (Ramden)	3.28084
	megameter	1×10^{-6}
	mile (UK, naut)	0.0005396
	mile (Int, naut)	0.00053996
	mile (US statute)	0.0006214
	millimeter	1000
	millimicron	1×10^{9}
	mil	39370.08
	rod (US Survey)	0.1988
	yard	1.0936
meter/hr	foot/hr	3.2808
	foot/min	0.05468
	knots (Int)	0.00054
	mile/hr	0.000621
meter/liter	mile/gal (US liq, Int)	0.00235
meter/min	cm/sec	1.66667
	foot/min	3.2808
	foot/sec	0.05468
	kilometer/hr	0.06
	knot (Int)	0.032397
	mile/hr	0.03728
meter/sec	foot/min	196.85
	foot/sec	3.2808
	kilometer/hr	3.6
	kilometer/min	0.06
	mile/hr	2.2369
	mile/sec	6.2137×10^{-4}
meter/(sec x sec)	cm/(sec x sec)	100
	foot/(sec x sec)	3.281
	kilometer/(hr x sec)	3.6
	mile/(hr x sec)	2.2369
meter candle	lumen/sq meter	1
	lux	1
meter kg–force	cm dyne	9.807×10^{7}
	cm gram–force	1×10^{5}
	foot pound–force	7.233
mho	abmho	1×10^{-9}
	mhos (Int)	1.000495
	mks unit	1
	siemens	1
	statmho	8.9876×10^{11}
mhos (Int)	abmho	9.995×10^{-10}
	mho	0.9995
mhos/meter	abmho/cm	1×10^{-11}
	mhos (Int)/meter	1.000495
	siemens/meter	1
microampere	ampere	1×10^{-6}
	milliampere	0.001
microfarad	abfarad	1×10^{-15}
	farad	1×10^{-6}
	statfarad	8.988×10^{5}
	picofarad	1×10^{6}

Convert From	Into	Multiply By
microgram	gram	1×10^{-6}
	milligram	0.001
microhenry	henry	1×10^{-6}
	stathenry	1.113×10^{-18}
microohm	abohm	1000
	megohm	1×10^{-12}
	ohm	1×10^{-6}
	statohm	1.113×10^{-18}
microohm cm	abohm cm	1000
	circ mil ohms/ft	6.015
	microohm inch	0.3937
	ohm cm	1×10^{-6}
microohm inch	circ mil ohms/ft	15.279
	microohm cm	2.54
micrometer	ångstrom	1×10^{4}
	centimeter	1×10^{-4}
	foot	3.2808×10^{-6}
	inch	3.93701×10^{-5}
	micron	1
	mil	3.93701×10^{-2}
micromicrofarad	farad	1×10^{-12}
micromicron	ångstrom	0.01
	centimeter	1×10^{-10}
	inch	3.937×10^{-11}
	meter	1×10^{-12}
	micrometer	1×10^{-6}
	micron	1×10^{-6}
micron	ångstrom	10000
	centimeter	0.0001
	foot	3.2808×10^{-6}
	inch	3.937×10^{-5}
	meter	1×10^{-6}
	micrometer	1
	millimeter	0.001
	millimicron	1000
mile (US Survey)	chain (Gunter)	8
	foot	5280.0106
	foot (US Survey)	5280
	furlong	8
	mile	1.000002
	mile (US statute)	1
	rod (US Survey)	320
mile (naut,Int)	cable length (US Survey)	8.439
	fathom (US Survey)	1012.68
	foot	6076.12
	foot (US Survey)	6076.10
	kilometer	1852
	league (naut,Int)	0.3333
	meter	1852
	mile (naut,UK)	0.99936
	mile (US statute)	1.15078
mile	centimeter	160934
	chain (Gunter)	79.99984
	chain (Ramden)	52.8
	foot	5280
	foot (US Survey)	5279.9894

Convert From	Into	Multiply By
	furlong (US Survey)	7.999984
	inch	63360
	kilometer	1.609344
	light year	1.701×10^{-13}
	link (Gunter)	7999.984
	meter	1609.344
	mile (US Survey)	0.99998
	mile (naut,Int)	0.86898
	myriameter	0.16093
	parsec	5.21553×10^{-14}
	rod (US Survey)	319.99936
	yard	1760
mile/gallon	meter/liter	425.14
mile/hr	cm/second	44.704
	foot/hour	5280
	foot/minute	88
	foot/second	1.4667
	kilometer/hour	1.6093
	kilometer/min	0.0268
	knots (Int)	0.868976
	meter/min	26.822
	meter/sec	0.44704
	mile/min	0.01667
mile/(hr x min)	cm/(sec x sec)	0.74507
mile/(hr x sec)	cm/(sec x sec)	44.704
	ft/(sec x sec)	1.4667
	kilometer/(hr x sec)	1.6093
	meter/(sec x sec)	0.447
mile/min	cm/second	2682.2
	foot/hr	316800
	foot/sec	88
	kilometer/min	1.6093
	knots (Int)	52.1386
	meter/min	1609.34
	mile/hr	60
milliampere	ampere	0.001
	microampere	1000
millibar	atmosphere (std)	0.000987
	bar	0.001
	barye (French)	1000
	dyne/sq cm	1000
	gram–force/sq cm	1.0197
	in of Hg @ 32°F	0.0295
	newton/sq meter	100
	pascal	100
	pound–force/sq ft	2.0885
	pound–force/sq inch	0.0145
milligram	carat (1877 defn)	0.00487
	carat (metric)	0.005
	dram (troy)	0.000257
	dram (avdp)	0.000564
	grain	0.01543
	gram	0.001
	kilogram	1×10^{-6}
	ounce (troy)	3.215×10^{-5}
	ounce (avdp)	3.527×10^{-5}

Convert From	Into	Multiply By
	pennyweight (troy)	0.000643
	pound (troy)	2.679×10^{-6}
	pound (avdp)	2.205×10^{-6}
	scruple (apoth)	0.000772
milligram/US assay ton	milligram/kg	34.2857
	ounce (troy)/ton (short)	1
milligram/gm	karat	0.024
	gram/ton (short)	907.185
	milligram/US assay ton	29.16667
	ounce (avdp)/ton (long)	35.84
	ounce (avdp)/ton (short)	32
	ounce (troy)/ton (long)	32.66667
	ounce (troy)/ton (short)	29.16667
milligram–force/inch	dyne/cm	0.38609
	dyne/inch	0.980665
	gram–force/cm	0.000394
	gram–force/inch	0.001
	newton/meter	3.8609×10^{-4}
milligram/kg	pound (avdp)/ton (short)	0.002
milligram/liter	grain/gallon	0.05842
	gram/liter	0.001
	part/million	1
	lb/cu ft	6.2428×10^{-5}
milligram/ton (metric)	part/billion	1
milligram–force/mm	dyne/cm	9.80665
millihenry	abhenry	1×10^6
	henry	0.001
	stathenry	1.11265×10^{-15}
millilambert	candle/sq cm	0.000318
	candle/sq inch	0.002054
	footlambert	0.929
	lambert	0.001
	lumen/sq cm	0.001
	lumen/sq ft	0.929
milliliter	cu cm	1
	cu inch	0.06102
	dram (US, liq)	0.27052
	gill (US)	0.00845
	liter	0.001
	minim (US)	16.231
	ounce (UK, liq)	0.035195
	ounce (US, liq)	0.033814
	pInt (UK)	0.00176
	pInt (US, liq)	0.00211
millimeter	ångstrom	1×10^7
	centimeter	0.1
	decimeter	0.01
	dekameter	0.0001
	foot	0.00328
	inch	0.03937
	kilometer	1×10^{-6}
	meter	0.001
	micrometer	1000
	micron	1000
	mil	39.37
	yard	1.094×10^{-3}

Convert From	Into	Multiply By
millimeter Hg @ 0°C	atmosphere (std)	0.001316
	bar	0.00133
	dyne/sq cm	1333.2
	gram–force/sq cm	1.3595
	kg–force/sq meter	13.595
	newton/sq meter	133.3224
	pascal	133.3224
	pound–force/sq ft	2.7845
	pound–force/sq in	0.0193
	torr	1
millimicron	ångstrom	10
	centimeter	1×10^{-7}
	inch	3.937×10^{-8}
	meter	1×10^{-9}
	micrometer	0.001
	micron	0.001
	millimeter	1×10^{-6}
million gal/day	cu ft/sec	1.547
milliphot	footcandle	0.929
	lumen/sq ft	0.929
	lumen/sq meter	10
	lux	10
	phot	0.001
millivolt	statvolt	3.336×10^{-6}
	volt	0.001
mil	centimeter	2.540×10^{-3}
	foot	8.333×10^{-5}
	inch	0.001
	kilometer	2.54×10^{-8}
	millimeter	0.0254
	yard	2.778×10^{-5}
miner's inch (western US)	cu foot/min	1.2 to 1.56
	cu foot/sec	0.02 to 0.026
	liter/sec	0.57 to 0.74
minim (UK)	cu cm	0.0592
	cu inch	0.0036
	milliliter	0.05919
	ounce (UK, liq)	0.002083
	scruple (UK, liq)	0.05
minim (US)	cu cm	0.06161
	cu inch	0.00376
	dram (US, liq)	0.01667
	gallon (US, liq)	1.628×10^{-5}
	gill (US)	0.00052
	liter	6.1612×10^{-5}
	milliliter	0.061612
	ounce (US, liq)	0.002083
	plnt (US, liq)	0.00013
minute (angle)	degree (angle)	0.016667
	quadrant	0.000185
	radian	0.0002909
	second (angle)	60
minute (mean solar)	day (mean solar)	0.000694
	day (sidereal)	0.000696
	hour (mean solar)	0.016667
	hour (sidereal)	0.016712

Convert From	Into	Multiply By
	minute (sidereal)	1.002738
minute (mean sidereal)	day (mean solar)	0.000693
	minute (mean solar)	0.99727
	month (mean calendar)	2.2769 x 10⁻⁵
	second (sidereal)	60
minute(angle)/cm	radian/cm	0.0002909
mole/cu meter	kilomole/cu meter	1 x 10⁻³
	millimole/cu meter	1 x 10³
	mole/liter	1 x 10⁻³
	units/cu meter	6.022137 x 10²³
mole/liter	mole/cu meter	1000
	mole/cu decimeter	1
mole/cu decimeter	mole/liter	1
month (lunar)	day (mean solar)	29.5306
	hour (mean solar)	708.734
	minute (mean solar)	42524.05
	second (mean solar)	2.551 x 10⁶
	week (mean calendar)	4.21866
month (mean calend.)	day (mean solar)	30.4167
	hour (mean solar)	730
	month (lunar)	1.030005
	week (mean calendar)	4.34524
	year (calendar)	0.08333
	year (sidereal)	0.08327
	year (tropical)	0.08328
myriagram	gram	10000
	kilogram	10
	pound (avdp)	22.046
myriawatt	kilowatt	10
neper	decibel	8.686
newton	dyne	100000
	joule/meter	1
	kilogram-force	0.10197
	kilogram-meter/sq sec	1
	poundal	7.233
	pound-force	0.2248089
newton meter	dyne cm	1 x 10⁷
	foot pound-force	0.73756
	gram-force cm	10197
	kg-force meter	0.10197
	pound-force inch	8.8507
newton/sq meter	atmosphere (std)	9.8692 x 10⁻⁶
	bar	1 x 10⁻⁵
	barye (French)	10
	dyne/sq cm	10
	cm of Hg (0°C)	0.0007501
	cm of H₂O (4°C)	0.0101917
	kg-force/sq cm	1.01972 x 10⁻⁵
	kg-force/sq meter	0.101972
	pascal	1
	poundal/sq ft	0.671969
	pound-force/sq foot	0.0208854
	pound-force/sq in	0.00014504
	torr (0°C)	7.50062 x 10⁻³
noggins (UK, liq)	cubic cm	142.065
	gallon (UK)	0.03125

Convert From	Into	Multiply By
	gill (UK)	1
oersted	ampere turn/inch	2.0213
	ampere turn/meter	79.5775
	ampere/meter	79.5775
	gilbert/cm	1
	oersted (Int)	1.000165
oersted (Int)	oersted	0.999835
ohm	abohm	1×10^9
	megohm	1×10^{-6}
	microhm	1×10^6
	ohms (Int)	0.99951
	statohm	1.1126×10^{-12}
ohms (Int)	ohm	1.00049
ohm cm	circ mil ohms/ft	6.015×10^6
	microhm cm	1×10^6
	ohm inch	0.3937
ohm inch	ohm cm	2.54
ohm meter	abohm cm	1×10^{11}
	statohm cm	1.113×10^{-10}
ounce (apoth or troy)	dekagram	3.11035
	dram (apoth or troy)	8
	dram (avdp)	17.554
	grain	480
	gram	31.1035
	milligram	31103.5
	ounce (avdp)	1.0971
	pennyweight (troy)	20
	pound (apoth or troy)	0.0833
	pound (avdp)	0.06857
	scruple (apoth)	24
	ton (short)	3.429×10^{-5}
ounce (avdp)	dram (apoth or troy)	7.2917
	dram (avdp)	16
	grain	437.5
	gram	28.3495
	hundredweight (long)	0.000558
	hundredweight (short)	0.000625
	kilogram	0.02835
	milligram	28.3495
	ounce (apoth or troy)	0.91146
	pennyweight (troy)	18.229
	pound (apoth or troy)	0.07595
	pound (avdp)	0.0625
	scruple (apoth)	21.875
	ton (long)	2.79×10^{-5}
	ton (metric)	2.835×10^{-5}
	ton (short)	3.125×10^{-5}
ounce (UK, liq)	cu cm	28.413
	cu inch	1.7339
	drachm (UK, liq)	8
	dram (US, liq)	7.6861
	gallon (UK)	0.00625
	milliliter	28.413
	minim (UK)	480
	ounce (US, liq)	0.96076
ounce (US, liq)	cu cm	29.5735

Convert From	Into	Multiply By
	cu inch	1.80469
	cup (US measuring)	0.125
	cu meter	2.9574×10^{-5}
	drop (US, liq)	360
	dram (US, liq)	8
	fifth (US, liq)	0.03906
	gallon (US, dry)	0.006714
	gallon (US, liq)	0.007813
	gill (US)	0.25
	jigger (US, liq)	0.66667
	liter	0.02957
	minim (US)	480
	ounce (UK, liq)	1.0408
	pint (US, liq)	0.0625
	pony (US, liq)	1
	quart (US, liq)	0.03125
	shot (US, liq)	1
	teaspoon (US measure)	6
	tablespoon (US measure)	2
ounce–force	newton	0.278
ounce–force/sq inch	dyne/sq cm	4309.2
	gram–force/sq cm	4.39418
	in H2O @ 39.2°F	1.730097
	in H2O @ 60°F	1.73166
	newton/sq meter	430.922
	pascal	430.922
	pound–force/sq foot	9
	pound–force/sq inch	0.0625
ounce (avdp)/ton (long)	milligram/kg	27.9018
ounce (avdp)/ton (short)	milligram/kg	31.25
ounce (troy)/ton (long)	ounce (troy)/ton (met)	0.984
	ounce (troy)/ton (short)	0.8929
	part/million	30.612
ounce (troy)/ton (short)	ounce (troy)/ton (l)	1.12
	ounce (troy)/ton (met)	1.1023
	part/million	34.286
ounce (troy)/ton (met)	ounce (troy)/ton (long)	1.016
	ounce (troy)/ton (short)	0.9072
	part/million	31.103
pace (US Survey)	centimeter	76.2
	chain (Gunter)	0.03788
	chain (Ramden)	0.025
	foot (US Survey)	2.5
	hand (horses)	7.5
	inch (US Survey)	30
	meter	0.762
	rope (UK)	0.125
palm	centimeter	7.62
	chain (Ramden)	0.0025
	cubit	0.16667
	foot	0.25
	hand	0.75
	inch	3
parsec	kilometer	3.08568×10^{13}
	meter	3.08568×10^{16}
	mile	1.9174×10^{13}

Convert From	Into	Multiply By
part/billion	milligram/ton (met)	1
part/million	grain/gal (UK)	0.070157
	grain/gal (US)	0.058418
	gram/liter	0.001
	gram/ton (met)	1
	milligram/liter	1
	ounce (troy)/ton (short)	0.0292
	percent	0.0001
	pound/million gal	8.345
pascal	atmosphere (std)	9.869233×10^{-6}
	atmosphere (technical)	1.01972×10^{-5}
	bar	1×10^{-5}
	barye (French)	10
	dyne/sq cm	10
	foot of water (4°C)	3.34552×10^{-4}
	inch of Hg (0°C)	2.953×10^{-4}
	inch of water (4°C)	4.01463×10^{-3}
	kg-force/sq cm	1.01972×10^{-5}
	kg-force/sq meter	1.01972×10^{-1}
	lbf/sq inch (psi)	0.00014504
	millibar	0.01
	newton/square meter	1
	poundal/sq foot	0.671969
	pound-force/sq in	0.00014504
	pound-force/sq ft	0.0208854
	torr	7.50062×10^{-3}
pascal sec	centipoise	1×10^{3}
	kg-force sec/sq meter	0.102
	newton sec/sq meter	1
	poise	10
peck (UK)	bushel (UK)	0.25
	coombs (UK)	0.0625
	cu cm	9092.18
	cu inch	554.84
	gallon (UK)	2
	gill (UK)	64
	hogshead (UK)	0.031746
	kilderkins (UK, liq)	0.1111
	liter	0.90922
	pint (UK)	16
	quarterns (UK)	4
	quarter (UK)	0.03125
	quart (UK)	8
	quart (US, dry)	8.25645
peck (US)	barrel (US, dry)	0.07619
	bushel (US, dry)	0.25
	cu cm	8809.77
	cu foot	0.31111
	cu inch	537.605
	gallon (US, dry)	2
	gallon (US, liq)	2.3273
	liter	8.8098
	pint (US, dry)	16
	quart (US, dry)	8
pennyweight (troy)	dram (apoth or troy)	0.4
	dram (avdp)	0.87771

Convert From	Into	Multiply By
	grain	24
	gram	1.55517
	ounce (apoth or troy)	0.05
	ounce (avdp)	0.05486
	pound (apoth or troy)	0.00417
	pound (avdp)	0.003429
perch (masonry)	stone 12 in x 18 in x 16.5 foot long	
perche (masonry)	cu foot	24.75
phot	footcandle	929.03
	lumen/sq cm	1
	lumen/sq meter	10000
	lux	10000
picas (printing)	centimeter	0.42175
	inch	0.16604
	point	12
picofarad	farad	1×10^{-12}
	microfarad	1×10^{-6}
pinch	teaspoon (US measure)	less than1/8
pint (UK)	cu cm	568.261
	gallon (UK)	0.125
	gill (UK)	4
	gill (US)	4.8038
	liter	0.56826
	minim (UK)	9600
	ounce (UK, liq)	20
	pint (US, dry)	1.03206
	pint (US, liq)	1.20095
	quart (UK)	0.5
	scruple (US, liq)	480
pint (US, dry)	bushel (US, dry)	0.015625
	cu cm	550.61
	cu inch	33.6003
	gallon (US, dry)	0.125
	gallon (US, liq)	0.14546
	liter	0.5506
	peck (US)	0.625
	pint (US, liq)	1.16365
	quart (US, dry)	0.5
pint (US, liq)	cu cm	473.1765
	cu foot	0.01671
	cu inch	28.875
	cu meter	4.731765×10^{-4}
	cu yard	0.000619
	cup (US measuring)	2
	dram (US, liq)	128
	fifth (US, liq)	0.625
	gallon (US, liq)	0.125
	gill (US)	4
	jigger (US, liq)	10.6667
	liter	0.473176
	milliliter	473.176
	minim (US)	7680
	ounce (US, liq)	16
	pint (UK)	0.8327
	pint (US, dry)	0.85934
	pony (US, liq)	16

Convert From	Into	Multiply By
	quart (US, liq)	0.5
	shot (US, liq)	16
	teaspoon (US measure)	96
	tablespoon(US measure)	32
pipe (UK, liq)	gallon (UK)	108
	liter	490.978
Planck constant	erg second	6.6261×10^{-27}
	joule second	6.6261×10^{-34}
	joule sec/avogad	3.99×10^{-10}
point (printing)	centimeter	0.0351
	inch	0.013837
	pica	0.0833
poise	dyne sec/sq cm	1
	gram/(cm x sec)	1
	newton sec/sq meter	0.1
	pound/foot hour	241.91
poise cu cm/gram	sq cm/sec	1
poise cu ft/lb	sq cm/sec	62.428
poise cu in/gram	sq cm/sec	16.3871
pony (US, liq)	fifth (US, liq)	0.03906
	jigger (US, liq)	0.6667
	ounce, (US, liq)	1
	pint (US, liq)	0.0625
	shot (US, liq)	1
pottle (UK)	gallon (UK)	0.5
	liter	2.273
poundal	dyne	13825.5
	gram–force	14.098
	joule/cm	1.383×10^{-3}
	joule/meter	0.1383
	kilogram–force	0.0141
	newton	0.1383
	pound–force	0.03108
pound (apoth or troy)	dram (apoth or troy)	96
	dram (avdp)	210.65
	grain	5760
	gram	373.24
	kilogram	0.37324
	ounce (apoth or troy)	12
	ounce (avdp)	13.166
	pennyweight (troy)	240
	pound (avdp)	0.82286
	scruple (apoth)	288
	ton (long)	0.000367
	ton (metric)	0.000373
	ton (short)	0.0004114
pound (avdp)	dram (apoth or troy)	116.667
	dram (avdp)	256
	grain	7000
	gram	453.59
	hundredweight (long)	0.008929
	hundredweight (short)	0.01
	kilogram	0.4536
	ounce (apoth or troy)	14.583
	ounce (avdp)	16
	pennyweight (troy)	291.667

Convert From	Into	Multiply By
	pound (apoth or troy)	1.21528
	scruple (apoth)	350
	slug	0.03108
	ton (long)	0.0004464
	ton (metric)	0.0004536
	ton (short)	0.0005
pound–force	dyne	444822.162
	joule/cm	0.04448
	joule/meter	4.44822
	kilogram–force	0.453592
	newton	4.44822
	poundal	32.17405
pound/cu foot	gram/cu cm	0.016018
	kg/cu meter	16.01846
	lb/cu inch	5.787×10^{-4}
	lb/cu yard	27
	lb/circ mil foot	5.45415×10^{-9}
pound/cu inch	gram/cu cm	27.6799
	gram/liter	27679.91
	kg/cu meter	27679.91
	lb/cu foot	1728
	lb/circ mil foot	9.425×10^{-6}
pound/cu yard	lb/cu foot	0.037
pound/foot	kilogram/meter	1.488
pound/gal (UK)	pound/cu ft	6.2288
pound/gal (US, liq)	gram/cu cm	0.11983
	pound/cu ft	7.48052
pound/inch	gram/cm	178.5797
	gram/ft	5443.11
	gram/inch	453.59237
	ounce/cm	6.2992
	ounce/inch	16
	pound/meter	39.37008
pound/circ mil foot	gram/cu cm	2.93693×10^{6}
pound/minute	kilogram/hr	27.2155
	kilogram/min	0.45359
pound–force/sq ft	atmosphere (std)	0.000473
	bar	0.000479
	cm of Hg @ 0°C	0.035913
	dyne/sq cm	478.803
	foot of water (39.2°F)	0.01602
	gram–force/sq cm	0.48824
	in of Hg @ 32°F	0.014139
	in of H_2O @ 39.2°F	0.19223
	kg–force/sq meter	4.88243
	mm of Hg @ 0°C	0.35913
	newton/sq meter	47.8803
	pascal	47.8803
	pound–force/sq inch	0.00694
pound–force/sq in	atmosphere (std)	0.06805
	bar	0.06895
	cm of Hg @ 0°C	5.17149
	cm of H_2O @ 4°C	70.3069
	dyne/sq cm	68947.6
	foot of water (39.2°F)	2.3067
	gram–force/sq cm	70.307

Convert From	Into	Multiply By
	in of Hg @ 32°F	2.036
	in of H₂O @ 39.2°F	27.6799
	kg–force/sq cm	0.07031
	kilopascal	6.89476
	mm of Hg @ 0°C	51.715
	newton/sq meter	6.89476×10^3
	pascal	6.89476×10^3
	pound–force/sq foot	144
pound of water (4°C)	cu foot	0.01602
	cu inch	27.68
	gallon (US, liq)	0.1198
pound of water/min	cu ft/sec	2.67×10^{-4}
pound–force foot	cm dyne	1.356×10^7
	cm gram–force	13825
	joule	1.35582
	meter kg–force	0.1383
	newton meter	1.35582
ppm	see part/million	
prospecting dish	gallon	2
	cu yard	0.008929
puncheons (UK)	cu meter	0.31797
	gallon (UK)	70
	gallon (US)	84
quadrant	degree	90
	minute	5400
	radian	1.5708
quartern (UK, dry)	buckets (UK)	0.125
	bushel (UK)	0.0625
	cu cm	2273.045
	gallon (UK)	0.5
	liter	2.27305
	peck (UK)	0.25
quartern (UK, liq)	cu cm	142.065
	gallon (UK)	0.03125
	liter	0.142065
quarter (US,long)	kilogram	254.0117
	pound (avdp)	560
quarter (US,short)	kilogram	226.796
	pound (avdp)	500
quart (UK)	cu cm	1136.52
	cu inch	69.355
	gallon (UK)	0.25
	gallon (US, liq)	0.30024
	liter	1.1365
	quart (US, dry)	1.0321
	quart (US, liq)	1.2009
quart (US, dry)	bushel (US, dry)	0.03125
	cu cm	1101.2
	cu foot	0.03889
	cu inch	67.2006
	cu meter	0.0011
	gallon (US, dry)	0.25
	gallon (US, liq)	0.29091
	liter	1.10122
	peck (US)	0.125
	pint (US, dry)	2

Convert From	Into	Multiply By
quart (US, liq)	cu cm	946.353
	cu foot	0.0334
	cu inch	57.75
	cu meter	9.464×10^{-4}
	cu yard	1.238×10^{-3}
	dram (US, liq)	256
	fifth (US, liq)	1.25
	gallon (US, dry)	0.2148
	gallon (US, liq)	0.25
	gill (US)	8
	liter	0.94635
	magnum	0.6309
	ounce (US, liq)	32
	pint (US, liq)	2
	quart (UK)	0.83267
	quart (US, dry)	0.859367
	shot (US, liq)	32
quintals (metric)	gram	100000
	hundredweight (long)	1.9684
	kilogram	100
	pound (avdp)	220.462
quintal (US)	kilogram	45.36
	pound	100
quire	ream	0.05
	sheet	24 or 25
radian	circumference	0.15915
	degree	57.29578
	minute	3437.747
	quadrant	0.63662
	revolution	0.15915
	second	206265
radian/cm	degree/cm	57.29578
	degree/ft	1746.37
	degree/in	145.531
	minute/cm	3437.75
radian/sec	degree/sec	57.29578
	revolution/min	9.5493
	revolution/sec	0.15915
radian/(sec x sec)	revolution/(min x min)	572.96
	revolution/(min x sec)	9.549297
	revolution/(sec x sec)	0.15915
ream	quire	20
	sheet	480 or 500
register ton	cu foot	100
	cu meter	2.8317
rem	sievert	0.01
revolution	degree	360
	grade	400
	quadrant	4
	radian	6.2832
revolution/min	degree/sec	6
	radian/sec	0.1047
	revolution/sec	0.01667
revolution/(min x min)	radian/(sec x sec)	1.745×10^{-3}
	revolution/(min x sec)	0.01667
	revolution/(sec x sec)	2.778×10^{-4}

Convert From	Into	Multiply By
revolution/sec	degree/sec	360
	radian/sec	6.283
	revolution/min	60
revolution/(sec x sec)	radian/(sec x sec)	6.283
	revolution/(min x min)	3600
	revolution/(min x sec)	60
reyn (lbf definition)	centipoise	6.8948×10^6
rhe	poise^{-1}	1
	(pascal sec)$^{-1}$	10
rod (US Survey)	centimeter	502.92
	chain (Gunter)	0.25
	chain (Ramden)	0.165
	foot	16.500033
	foot (US Survey)	16.5
	furlong (US Survey)	0.025
	inch	198.0004
	link (Gunter)	25
	link (Ramden)	16.500033
	meter	5.0292
	mile (US statute)	0.003125
	perch (US Survey)	1
	yard (US Survey)	5.5
röntgen	coulomb/kg	2.58×10^{-4}
rope (UK)	foot	20
	meter	6.096
	yard	6.66667
score	unit	20
scruple (apoth)	dram (apoth or troy)	0.3333
	dram (avdp)	0.73143
	grain	20
	gram	1.29598
	ounce (apoth or troy)	0.041667
	ounce (avdp)	0.045714
	pennyweight (troy)	0.8333
	pound (apoth or troy)	0.00347
	pound (avdp)	0.002857
scruple (UK, liq)	minim (UK)	20
sea mile	degree of latitude	0.016667
seam (UK)	bushel (UK)	8
	cu foot	10.275
	liter	290.95
second (angle)	degree	0.000278
	minute	0.016667
	quadrant	3.086×10^{-6}
	radian	4.8481×10^{-6}
second (mean solar)	day (mean solar)	1.1574×10^{-5}
	day (sidereal)	1.1606×10^{-5}
	hour (mean solar)	0.0002778
	hour (sidereal)	0.0002785
	minute (mean solar)	0.0166667
	minute (sidereal)	0.016712
	second (sidereal)	1.002738
second (sidereal)	day (mean solar)	1.1542×10^{-5}
	day (sidereal)	1.1574×10^{-5}
	hour (mean solar)	0.000277
	hour (sidereal)	0.0002778

Convert From	Into	Multiply By
	minute (mean solar)	0.016621
	minute (sidereal)	0.0166667
	second (mean solar)	0.99726957
shot	fifth (US, liq)	0.03906
	jigger (US, liq)	0.6667
	ounce, (US, liq)	1
	pint (US, liq)	0.0625
	pony (US, liq)	1
	quart (US, liq)	0.03125
shot of chain (naut)	foot of chain	90
siemens	abmho	1×10^{-9}
	mho	1
	(ohms)$^{-1}$	1
	statmho	8.988×10^{11}
sievert	curie/kg	21.6
	joule/kg	1
	newton meter/kg	1
	rem	100
	röntgen	8.4 (approx)
skien (cloth)	foot	360
	meter	109.728
slug	geepound	1
	kilogram	14.594
	pound (avdp)	32.174
slugs/cu ft	gram/cu cm	0.51538
span	centimeter	22.86
	hand (horses)	2.25
	foot	0.75
	inch	9
	quarter (cloth)	1
span (Old English)	inch	6
sphere	steradian	12.57
sq centimeter	are	1×10^{-6}
	circ mm	127.324
	circ mil	197352.5
	sq chain (Gunter)	2.471×10^{-7}
	sq chain (Ramden)	1.0764×10^{-7}
	sq decimeter	0.01
	sq foot	0.001076391
	sq foot (US Survey)	0.001076387
	sq inch	0.155
	sq meter	0.0001
	sq mm	100
	sq mile	3.861×10^{-11}
	sq mil	155000
	sq rod (US Survey)	3.9537×10^{-6}
	sq yard	0.0001196
sq chain (Gunter)	acre (US Survey)	0.1
	sq foot (US Survey)	4356
	sq foot	4356.017
	sq inch	627267
	sq link (Gunter)	10000
	sq meter	404.69
	sq mile	0.000156
	sq rod (US Survey)	16
	sq yard	484

Convert From	Into	Multiply By
sq chain (Ramden)	acre	0.22957
	sq foot (US Survey)	10000
	sq foot	10000.04
	sq inch	1.44×10^6
	sq link (Ramden)	10000
	sq meter	929.03
	sq mile	0.000359
	sq rod (US Survey)	36.7309
	sq yard	1111.11
sq decimeter	sq cm	100
	sq inch	15.50003
sq degree	steradian	0.000305
sq dekameter	acre	0.02471
	are	1
	sq meter	100
	sq yard	119.599
sq foot	acre (US Survey)	2.2957×10^{-5}
	are	0.000929
	circular mil	1.833×10^8
	sq cm	929.03
	sq chain (Gunter)	0.0002296
	sq foot (US Survey)	0.999996
	sq inch	144
	sq link (Gunter)	2.2957
	sq meter	0.0929
	sq mile	3.58701×10^{-8}
	sq millimeter	9.29×10^4
	sq rod (US Survey)	0.003673
	sq yard	0.1111
sq foot (US Survey)	acre (US Survey)	2.2957×10^{-5}
	sq centimeter	929.034
	sq chain (Ramden)	0.0001
	sq foot	1.000004
sq hectometer	sq meter	10000
sq inch	circular mil	1273239
	sq cm	6.4516
	sq chain (Gunter)	1.5942×10^{-6}
	sq decimeter	0.064516
	sq foot	0.00694444
	sq ft (US Survey)	0.00694442
	sq link (Gunter)	0.01594
	sq meter	0.000645
	sq mile	2.491×10^{-10}
	sq mm	645.16
	sq mil	1×10^6
	sq yard	0.0008
sq inch/sec	centistokes	645.2
	sq cm/hour	23226
	sq cm/sec	6.4516
	sq meter/sec	6.452×10^{-4}
	sq ft/min	0.41667
	stokes	6.452
sq kilometer	acre	247.1054
	sq centimeter	1×10^{10}
	sq foot	1.07639×10^7
	sq foot (US Survey)	1.076387×10^7

Convert From	Into	Multiply By
	sq inch	1.550003×10^9
	sq meter	1×10^6
	sq mile	0.3861
	sq yard	1.196×10^6
sq link (Gunter)	acre (US Survey)	1×10^{-5}
	sq cm	404.687
	sq chain (Gunter)	0.0001
	sq foot (Gunter)	0.4356017
	sq foot (US Survey)	0.4356
	sq inch	62.727
sq link (Ramden)	acre	2.2957×10^{-5}
	sq foot	1
sq meter	acre	0.000247
	are	0.01
	hectare	0.0001
	sq cm	10000
	sq foot	10.7639
	sq inch	1550.003
	sq kilometer	1×10^{-6}
	sq link (Gunter)	24.71044
	sq link (Ramden)	10.764
	sq mile	3.861×10^{-7}
	sq mm	1×10^6
	sq rod (US Survey)	0.03954
	sq yard	1.19599
sq meter/sec	centistokes	1×10^6
	sq foot/hr	3.875×10^4
	sq in/sec	1550
	stokes	1×10^4
sq mile	acre	640
	hectare	258.999
	sq chain (Gunter)	6399.997
	sq foot	2.78784×10^7
	sq foot (US Survey)	2.78783×10^7
	sq kilometer	2.58999
	sq meter	2589988
	sq rod (US Survey)	102399.59
	sq yard	3.098×10^6
sq millimeter	circular mm	1.2732
	circular mil	1973.5
	sq cm	0.01
	sq foot	1.076×10^{-5}
	sq inch	0.00155
	sq meter	1×10^{-6}
sq mil	circular mil	1.273
	sq cm	6.452×10^{-6}
	sq inch	1×10^{-6}
	sq mm	0.000645
sq rod (US Survey)	acre (US Survey)	0.00625
	are	0.25293
	hectare	0.00253
	sq cm	252929.5
	sq foot	272.25109
	sq foot (US Survey)	272.25
	sq inch	39204.16
	sq link (Gunter)	625

Convert From	Into	Multiply By
	sq link (Ramden)	272.25
	sq meter (US Survey)	25.293
	sq mile (US Survey)	9.7656×10^{-6}
	sq yard (US Survey)	30.25
sq yard	acre	0.000207
	are	0.00836
	hectare	8.3613×10^{-5}
	sq cm	8361.27
	sq chain (Gunter)	0.002066
	sq chain (Ramden)	0.0009
	sq foot	9
	sq foot (US Survey)	8.99996
	sq inch	1296
	sq link (Gunter)	20.661
	sq link (Ramden)	8.99996
	sq meter	0.8361
	sq mile	3.228×10^{-7}
	sq millimeter	8.361×10^{5}
	sq rod (US Survey)	0.03306
statampere	abampere	3.3356×10^{-11}
	ampere	3.3356×10^{-10}
statcoulomb	ampere hour	9.2656×10^{-14}
	coulomb	3.3356×10^{-10}
	electronic charge	2.082×10^{9}
statfarad	farad	1.11265×10^{-12}
	microfarad	1.11265×10^{-6}
stathenry	abhenry	8.9876×10^{20}
	henry	8.9876×10^{11}
	millihenry	8.9876×10^{14}
statohm	abohm	8.9876×10^{20}
	ohm	8.9876×10^{11}
statvolt	abvolt	2.9979×10^{10}
	volt	299.79
statvolt/cm	volt/cm	299.79
	volt/inch	761.47
statvolt/inch	volt/cm	118.028
steradian	hemisphere	0.15915
	solid angle	0.079577
	sphere	0.079577
	spher. right angle	0.63662
	square degree	3282.81
stere	cubic meter	1
	decistere	10
	dekastere	0.1
	liter	1000
stilb	candle/sq cm	1
	candle/sq inch	6.4516
	lambert	3.14159
stokes	sq cm/sec	1
	sq inch/sec	0.1550003
	sq meter/sec	1×10^{-4}
stone	cental (US)	0.14
	pound	14
tablespoon (US measure)	cup (US measure)	0.0625
	drop (US, liq)	180
	gill (US)	0.125

Convert From	Into	Multiply By
	liter	0.0148
	ounce (US, liq)	0.5
	quart (US, liq)	0.015625
	teaspoon (US measure)	3
teaspoon (US measure)	cup (US measure)	0.0208333
	drop (US, liq)	60
	gill (US)	0.04167
	liter	0.0049
	ounce (US, liq)	0.16667
	pinch	3 to 4
	pint (US, liq)	0.01042
	quart (US, liq)	0.00521
	tablespoon (US measure)	0.3333
tesla	gauss	1×10^4
	line/sq inch	6.452×10^4
	weber/sq cm	1×10^{-4}
	weber/sq inch	6.452×10^{-4}
	weber/sq meter	1
therm (US)	Btu (15°C)	100000
tierce	gallon (wine)	42
tonne	kilogram	1000
ton (long)	hundredweight (long)	20
	hundredweight (short)	22.4
	kilogram	1016.05
	ounce (avdp)	35840
	pound (apoth or troy)	2722.2
	pound (avdp)	2240
	ton (metric)	1.01605
	ton (short)	1.12
ton–force (long)	dyne	9.964×10^8
	newton	9964.02
ton (metric)	gram	1×10^6
	hundredweight (short)	22.0462
	kilogram	1000
	ounce (avdp)	35273.96
	pound (apoth or troy)	2679.23
	pound (avdp)	2204.62
	tonne	1
	ton (long)	0.98421
	ton (short)	1.1023
ton–force (metric)	dyne	9.80665×10^8
	newton	9806.65
ton (short)	hundredweight (short)	20
	kilogram	907.185
	ounce (avdp)	32000
	pound (apoth or troy)	2430.55
	pound (avdp)	2000
	ton (long)	0.89286
	ton (metric)	0.90718
ton–force (short)	dyne	8.8964×10^8
	newton	8896.44
ton–force (long)/sq ft	atmosphere (std)	1.0585
	dyne/sq cm	1.0725×10^6
	gram–force/sq cm	1093.66
	newton/sq meter	1.0725×10^5
	pascal	1.0725×10^5

Convert From	Into	Multiply By
	pound–force/sq ft	2240
ton–force (short)/sq ft	atmosphere (std)	0.9451
	dyne/sq cm	957605
	gram–force/sq cm	976.49
	newton/sq meter	9.5761×10^4
	pascal	9.5761×10^4
	pound–force/sq inch	13.889
ton–force (long)/sq in	atmosphere (std)	152.423
	dyne/sq cm	1.544×10^8
	gram–force/sq cm	157488
	newton/sq meter	1.5443×10^7
	pascal	1.5443×10^7
ton-force (short)/sq in	dyne/sq cm	1.37895×10^8
	kg–force/sq mm	1.40614
	newton/sq meter	1.379×10^7
	pascal	1.379×10^7
	pound–force/sq inch	2000
ton of refrigeration	Btu/hr (IST)	12000
ton of water/24 hr	pound of water/hr	83.333
	gallon/min	0.16643
	cu ft/hr	1.3349
torr (0°C)	mm of Hg @ 0°C	0.99999986
	pascal	133.322
township (US Survey)	acre (US Survey)	23040
	section (US Survey)	36
	sq kilometer	93.2399
	sq mile (US Survey)	36
tun (US, liq)	gallon (US, liq)	252
	hogshead (US)	4
	pipe (US, liq)	2
	puncheon	3
volt	abvolt	1×10^8
	statvolt	0.003336
	volt (Int)	0.99966
volt (Int)	volt	1.00033
volt coulomb	joule (Int)	0.9998
volt second	maxwell	1×10^8
	weber	1
volt/meter	abvolt/cm	1×10^6
	kilovolt/cm	1×10^{-5}
	newton/coulomb	1
	statvolt/meter	3.33564×10^{-5}
volt/in	volt/cm	0.393701
	volt/meter	39.3701
	volt/mil	0.001
watt	Btu/hr (IST)	3.41214
	Btu (mean)/hr	3.4095
	Btu (mean)/min	0.056825
	Btu/sec (IST)	0.000948
	Btu (mean)/sec	0.000947
	calorie/hr (thermo)	860.42
	calorie (mean)/hr	859.18
	calorie (@20°C)/hr	860.85
	calorie/min (thermo)	14.34
	calorie (IST)/min	14.331
	calorie (mean)/min	14.3197

Convert From	Into	Multiply By
	calorie, kg/min (thermo)	0.01434
	calorie, kg (IST)/min	0.01433
	calorie, kg (mean)/min	0.01432
	erg/sec	1×10^7
	foot pound–force/min	44.2537
	foot pound–force/sec	0.737562
	horsepower	0.001341
	horsepower (boiler)	0.000102
	horsepower (electric)	0.0013405
	horsepower (metric)	0.0013596
	joule/sec	1
	kilogram–calorie/min(IST)	0.01433
	kilowatt	0.001
	liter atmosphere/hr	35.529
	watt (Int, 1948)	0.99984
watt (Int)	Btu/hr (thermo)	3.41499
	Btu (mean)/hr	3.41007
	Btu/min (thermo)	0.569165
	Btu (mean)/min	0.0568
	calorie/hr (thermo)	860.56
	calorie (mean)/hr	859.326
	calorie, kg/min (thermo)	0.01434
	calorie, kg (IST)/min	0.01433
	calorie, kg (mean)/min	0.01432
	erg/sec	1.000165×10^7
	joule (Int)/sec	1
	watt	1.000165
watt/sq cm	Btu/(hr x sq ft) (thermo)	3172.1
	calorie/(hr x sq cm)	860.421
	foot lbf/(min x sq ft)	41113
watt/sq in	Btu/(hr x sq ft) (thermo)	491.68
	calorie/(hr x sq cm)	133.365
	foot lbf/(min x sq ft)	6372.5
watt/sq meter	foot lbf/hr sq meter	2655.2
	horsepower/sq meter	0.00134
	joule/hr sq meter	3600
	joule/sec sq meter	1
	kilowatt/sq meter	0.001
watt/meter K	Btu/hr foot $^{\circ}$F (IST)	0.5778
	kilocalorie/hr foot $^{\circ}$C	0.26208
watthour	Btu (thermo)	3.4144
	Btu (mean)	3.4095
	calorie (thermo)	860.42
	calorie, kg (mean)	0.85918
	calorie (mean)	859.18
	erg	3.6×10^{10}
	foot pound–force	2655.22
	hp hour	0.00134
	joule	3600
	joule (US legal 1948)	3599.41
	kg-calorie (thermo)	0.8604
	kg–force meter	367.098
	kilowatthour	0.001
	watthour (Int 1948)	0.9998
wattsecond	foot pound–force	0.73756
	gram–force cm	10197.2

Convert From	Into	Multiply By
	joule	1
	liter atmosphere	0.00987
	volt coulomb	1
weber	kiloline	1 x 10⁶
	line	1 x 10⁸
	maxwell	1 x 10⁸
	volt second	1
weber/sq cm	gauss	1 x 10⁸
	line/sq cm	1 x 10⁸
	line/sq in	6.4516 x 10⁸
	tesla	1 x 10⁴
weber/sq in	gauss	1.550003 x 10⁷
	line/sq inch	1 x 10⁸
	weber/sq cm	0.155
	weber/sq meter	1550
	tesla	1.550003 x 10³
weber/sq meter	gauss	1 x 10⁴
	line/sq inch	6.452 x 10⁴
	tesla	1
	weber/sq cm	1 x 10⁻⁴
	weber/sq inch	6.452 x 10⁻⁴
week (mean calendar)	day (mean solar)	7
	day (sidereal)	7.01916
	hour (mean solar)	168
	hour (sidereal)	168.46
	minute (mean solar)	10080
	minute (sidereal)	10107.6
	month (lunar)	0.237042
	month (mean calendar)	0.230137
	year (calendar)	0.019178
	year (sidereal)	0.0191646
	year (tropical)	0.019165
wey (UK)	pound (avdp)	256
yard	centimeter	91.44
	chain (Gunter)	0.454546
	chain (Ramden)	0.03
	cubit	2
	fathom (US Survey)	0.49999
	foot	3
	foot (US Survey)	2.999994
	furlong (US Survey)	0.004545
	inch	36
	kilometer	9.144 x 10⁻⁴
	meter	0.9144
	mile (naut)	4.937 x 10⁻⁴
	mile (US statute)	5.682 x 10⁻⁴
	millimeter	914.4
	pole (US Survey)	0.181818
	quarter (cloth)	4
	rod (US Survey)	0.181818
	span	4
year (calendar)	day (mean solar)	365
	hour (mean solar)	8760
	minute (mean solar)	525600
	month (lunar)	12.360065
	month (mean calendar)	12

Convert From	Into	Multiply By
	second (mean solar)	3.1536×10^7
	week (mean calendar)	52.14286
	year (sidereal)	0.999298
	year (tropical)	0.999337
year (leap)	day (mean solar)	366
year (sidereal)	day (mean solar)	365.2564
	day (sidereal)	366.2564
	year (calendar)	1.000702
	year (tropical)	1.000039
year (tropical)	day (mean solar)	365.242
	day (sidereal)	366.242
	hour (mean solar)	8765.81
	hour (sidereal)	8789.81
	month (mean calendar)	12.00796
	second (mean solar)	3.15569×10^7
	second (sidereal)	3.16433×10^7
	week (mean calendar)	52.17746
	year (calendar)	1.0006635
	year (sidereal)	0.99996

Index

A

ABS pipe 392
absolute pressure 530
admittance formulas, electricity 264
AF transformer color codes 204
affinity laws 529
air 633
    air discharge through 100 feet of hose 647
    air line pipe, recommended sizes 632
    compressed air requirements for common tools and equipment ...633
    discharge from orifices 641
    pressure loss due to friction in 100 feet of air hose 647
aluminum pipe and tube 397
aluminum wire, current carrying capacity 198
American National Threads 592
American Standard
    straight pipe 623
    taper pipe 623
American Wire Gauge (AWG) 587,609
anchors 7
    concrete screws, steel 12
    drop-in bottom plug expansion sleeve stud anchor, steel 21
    drop-in double-acting expansion shield anchor, steel 20
    drop-in long lag shield anchor, zinc alloy 23
    drop-in short lag shield nchor, zinc alloy 22
    drop-in single-acting expansion shield anchor, steel................19
    drop-in tool-set expansion s eeve anchor, steel 18
    epoxy adhesive, in concrete 24
        threaded rod anchors, steel 24
    expansion sleeve anchors, steel 37
    expansion sleeve, steel ....37 - 38
    expansion wedge anchors, carbon steel 34
    for concrete, hollow concrete block and brick 10
    for gypsum wallboard or hollow concrete block 15
    for threaded fasteners in concrete
        for bolts and screws 18
    insert anchors for screws, fluted plastic 14
    insert anchors for screws, plastic 13
    insert-type hollow wall toggle, plastic 16
    low velocity powder actuated fasteners 32
    photo index 8
    pin drive or drive nail expansion anchors, zinc body and steel nail 10
    pre-expanded anchors, steel 14
    self-drilling bottom plug expansion sleeve anchor, steel 21
    self-drilling gypsum wallboard anchors, zinc or plastic 17
    sleeve-type hollow wall anchors, steel 15
    spring wing type toggle bolts, steel 17
    torque controlled, self contained, for concrete 34
    undercut expansion sleeve anchors, steel 39
anchors for gypsum wallboard or hollow concrete block
    sleeve type hollow wall anchors, steel 15
    spring wing type toggle bolts, steel 15
anchors for threaded fasteners in concrete
    for lag screws 18
angle of repose 682,690
angles, convert degrees to
    degrees & minutes 307
    inch rise in 12 inch run 307
    percent grade 307

radians...307
annulus, area of..**339**
arc electrode amperages..**672**
arc electrode brand conversion................................**674**
arc electrodes - low alloy steel..............................**673**
arc electrodes - mild steel....................................**672**
arc electrodes - stainless steel..............................**673**
ASTM standards..**57,59**
atmospheric pressure..**530**
available units/million Btu....................................**273**

B

barometric pressure...**530**
Beaufort wind speed scale.......................................**279**
belt and gear formulas...**42**
   belt length..42
   belt speed...42
   design horsepower..45
   horsepower...45
   speed ratio..45
   transmission formulas..43
      for multiple transmission systems.................*43*
      for single transmission systems....................*43*
belt speeds for pulleys and sheaves..............................**46**
belts, introduction..**42**
belts, pulleys and gears...**41**
   belt and gear formulas...42
   belt speeds for pulleys and sheaves.................................46
   belts, introduction..42
   pulley (sheave) selection tables...................................48
   pulleys: outside diameter vs. pitch diameter.......................47
Bethlehem Steel wire gauge.....................................**587**
bird's mouth cut...**155**
Birmingham wire gauge..**587**
board feet calculations..**92**
boards...**94**
boiling point of water..**659**
bolt torque..**61**
bolts and threads..**55**
   clamping force and bolt torque......................................61
   clearance holes for bolts and screws................................87
      inch series.......................................*87*
      metric series.....................................*88*
   effect of anti-seize compounds, lubricants, platings, coatings, torque
   coefficients, and stress levels on torque for carbon steel bolts.........78
   head styles..90
   screw threads, standard..85
brass pipe and tube...**412**
brick, anchors for...**10**
British Imperial Standard wire gauge (SWG)......................**587**
British Imperial wire gauge.....................................**587**
Brown and Sharpe wire gauge (BSWG)..............................**587**

C

82° countersink diameter..**577**
cable clips for wire rope
   twin-base clips...553
   u-bolt clips...552
capacitance formulas, electricity...............................**266**
capacitors in parallel formulas.................................**265**
capacitors in series formulas...................................**266**

carbon steel bolts
coarse inch-threaded...63
coarse metric-threaded 73
fine inch-threaded..68
torque..63
carpentry and construction
concrete 130
concrete and mortar 132
guide to roofing materials 177
hardwood lumber size & grade...96
insulation value of materials...102
maximum floor joist spans..106
maximum horizontal roof rafter span 159
mortar..133
plywood & panel grading..98
rafter length tables...135
roof pitch rafter seat cut, graphic...154
roof pitch table...155
roofing materials, guide to 177
roofing materials, weight of..183
soft lumber sizes..92
softwood lumber grading...93
softwood lumber sizes..92
strength of wood beams..126
weight of roofing materials...183
wood characteristics...100
wood gluing characteristics 129
wood moisture content vs. strength...97
Centigrade to Fahrenheit conversion 277
centrifugal pumps...520
affinity laws and formulas for..529
brake horsepower..529
flow rate...529
practical lift For 523
total dynamic head 529
chain - strength and weight 554
chain saw classification 627
chisel - tooth saw blade..628
circle segment 342
circles...300
area 341
chord length for dividing the circumference of......................300
circular zone..342
circumference...341
  center angle 300
  dividing into an equal number of segments.......................300
diameter, radius, circumference, and area.............................304
length of arc...341
sector of 342
segment of...342
segments of, for radius = 1 349
circular ring
formulas...347
volume, surface area 347
circular zone 342
Clark degrees of hardness 657
clearance holes for bolts and screws 87
inch series 87
metric series 88
clearance ratio..89
coal vs. other fuels, Btu ....272 - 273
color codes, electric wire 203

compressed air
air discharge from orifices 641
pressure loss due to frictionin 100 feet of air hose...................647
concrete
aggregate 130
air..130
anchors for 10
anchors for threaded fasteners in 18
anchors, torque controlled, self-contained...........................34
coloring...132
epoxy anchors in 24
mixtures by volume...131
portland cement..130
slabs, reommended thickness...131
strength factors...130
types...130
water...130
concrete block, hollow
anchors for 10,15
concrete screws, steel..12
cone, right cone formulas...346
conversion tables..691
copper pipe and tube...433
copper wire
current carrying capacity 200
size vs. voltage drop...214
co-secant...327
cosine...327
co-tangent..327
CPVC pipe..428
crosscut and panel saw blades.....................................628
current adjustment..202
current and voltage formulas..262
current carrying capacity of wire..................................198
cutoff wheel saw blade..628
cylinder volume...545
cylinder, right, formulas...345

D

dam, weir discharge volumes 670
dead load 106
decagon 340
decibel formulas, electricity...265
design horsepower..45
dimension lumber..95
discharge from nozzles..653
dodecagon..340
douglas fir - larch
maximum floor joist spans 106
maximum horizontal roof rafter span tables 159
drafting symbols..185
electrical symbols..186 - 189
heating, ventilation and air conditioning symbols...........190 - 192
household fixtures..195
   plumbing fixtures...196
piping symbols..193
   air conditioning...193
   heating...193
   plumbing..194
drill number 609
drill size...609
drinking water hardness..657

drive styles 630
drop-in tool-set expansion sleeve anchor, steel 18
ductwork, symbols 191
dumping angles...689

E

earthquake scales of magnitude 280
efficiency of any device, formula..265
electric motor
    frame dimensions 257
    horsepower vs. torque vs. rpm 253
    nameplate, how to read 238
    specs..250
    specs, three phase motors..252
electrical 197
    cost to pump water 658
    current adjustment for more than three wires in a cable 202
    current carrying capacity of wire..198
    DC motor wiring specs 256
    electric motor specs...250
    electrical conductors 207
    electrical motor frame dimensions...257
    firewood/fuel comparisons...272 - 273
    formulas for electricity...262
    how to read a motor name plate...238
    maximum number of conductors and fixture wires 215
    motor specs, average 250
    NEMA receptacle configurations..234
    number of conductors in outlet, device, and junction boxes and conduit
    bodies...232
    standard lamp and extension cord current capacities 202
    three-phase electric motor specs 252
    voltage drop vs. wire size..213
    wire classes and insulation...205
    wire color codes, standard...203
    wire size vs. voltage drop..213
electrical conductors 232
    maximum number 215
        in electrical flexible metal tubing or conduit..........................215
        in electrical metal tubing or conduit.......................................222
        in electrical nonmetallic tubing or conduit 227
        outlet, device, and junction boxes and conduit bodies.........232
    physical and electrical properties...207
    volume required per conductor 233
electrical distribution - aerial, symbols...189
electrical distribution - underground, symbols.................................189
electrical symbols...186
electrode amperages, welding...672
electrodes - low alloy steel 673
electrodes - stainless steel 673
electrodes, arc welding, mild steel..672
electronic wire color codes...203
elevation vs. air and water 268
ellipse
    area 344
    perimeter of 344
ellipsoid
    formulas..348
    volume of..348
English legal standard wire gauge 587
epoxy adhesive anchors in concrete
    threaded rod anchors, steel..24

equation..44 - 45,132,304
    area of a regular polygon..321
    area of segment...349
    area, *A*...306
    center angle..304,349
    circumference...306
    diameter of a regular polygon...321
    diameter of circle..304
    distance across hexagons..313
    distance across squares..313
    excess stock...316
    fillet area...316
    flow...656
    flow rate in pipes...533
    friction loss in pipe fittings, steel.......................................518
    Hazen-Williams..387
    head..533
    height above chord...349
    height of a regular polygon...321
    length of arc...349
    length of chord..304,349
    length of wire rope...558
    percent of thread...592
    perimeter..321
    pressure...533
    pressure drop in pipe carrying compressed air.................632
    pressure head..527
    pumps...533
    resistance at new temperature...210
    side of a regular polygon..321
    spheres, surface area & volume of....................................356
    torque...253
    total head..527
    velocity...656
    velocity head..534
    velocity in pipes...534
equivalence tables...691
example
    approximate torque in the bolt..80
    how to size a centrifugal pump...535
    pipe sizing using the pipe tables..387
    to calculate the actual cost of heat....................................273
    to find the approximate area of the roof.............................158
    to find the approximate length of the hip rafter.................158
excess stock...316

F

factors for numbers from 1 to 100.............................319
Fahrenheit to Centigrade conversion........................277
fasteners...32
    driven into concrete...32
    driven into structural steel..33
    low velocity powder actuated..32
feet of wire rope on a drum or reel............................558
fillet area...316,343
finishes and paints...291
fire extinguishers...624
fire rating...182
firewood/fuel comparisons..272
flattop - ground carbide tipped saw blade...............629
floor joist spans, maximum...106
    Douglas Fir - Larch...106

    redwood..122
flow rate, theoretical 392
formulas
    belt and gear...42
    board feet..92
    centrifugal pumps..529
    circular ring..347
    circular zone..342
    clearance ratio..89
    cost to pump water..658
    electrical (ohms, antennas, resistance, etc)......................262
    ellipsoid and spheroid...348
    Francis formula for weir discharge 670
    gallons per minute of a slurry 658
    gallons per minute through a pipe 658
    horizontal tank partial fillage calculation...........................544
    horsepower to raise water 658
    horsepower to torque...255
    mapping scales...276
    oblique triangles..337
    paraboloid..347
    plane figures..338
    prism, right or oblique...345
    regular polygons..320
    right cone...346
    right cylinder..345
    right triangles..336
    segment of circle 342
    solid figures...344
    sound intensity...274
    sphere..347
    stockpile volume/weight...690
    temperature conversions...278
    torque vs. horsepower vs. rpm..255
    transmission, for belt and pulleys or gears 43
    triangle..337
    voltage drop vs. wire length and current............................213
    water general formulas..658
    water total hardness..657
    water, general formulas...658
    weight of water in a pipe..658
    wind chill factor...269
formulas for electricity 262
    admittance: – Y...264
    capacitance of a capacitor...266
    capacitors in parallel...265
    decibels...265
    efficiency..265
    impedance: – Z..264
    multiple capacitors in series..266
    multiple resistors in parallel 263
    Ohm's law (AC current)...263
    Ohm's law (DC current)...262
    power factor...265
    q or figure of merit..265
    quantity of electricity in a capacitor...................................266
    reactance: – X...264
    resistors in series (values...262
    resonance: – f 264
    self inductance...266
    sine wave voltage and current...265
    susceptance: – B...264

two capacitors in series 266
two resistors in parallel 263
French degrees of hardness 657
friction belts 657
friction factor 42
friction factor 61
friction loss
    ABS pipe...392
    aluminum pipe and tube 397
    brass pipe and tube 412
    copper pipe and tube 433
    CPVC pipe 428
    pipe fittings, steel..508
    polybutylene (PB) pipe 451
    polyethylene (PE) pipe 456
    steel pipe and tube 468
fuel oil vs. other fuels, Btu ....272 - 273
    actual cost of heat for each 273
fuel/firewood comparisons 272

G

gallons per minute through a pipe 658
galvanized sheet gauge 584
gas welding rods 675
gases used for welding 675
gases, firewood/fuel comparison 272
gauge pressure 530
gauges
    steel sheet 584
    wire 587
gears 44
general science
    Beaufort wind speed scale 279
    earthquake scales 280
    elevation vs. air and water 268
    firewood/fuel comparisons 272
    heat - humidity factors 271
    mapping scales and areas 275
    Richter earthquake scale 280
    sound intensities..274
    temperature conversions 277
German degrees of hardness 657
glue types and applications 282
glues, paints and solvents 281
    glue hints and general rules 290
    glue types and applications 282
    glues & adhesives, types & applications 282
    paints and finishes ....
    solvents 291
gluing 129
    wood gluing characteristics 129
gpm volume over a weir 670
gpm, from a horizontal discharge pipe 669
gpm, from a vertical pipe discharge 670
grains of hardness 657
gypsum wallboard, anchors for 15

H

hard and soft solder alloys 676
hardness, water 657
hardwood lumber size & grade 96
Hazen-Williams equation 387

head 527
head loss 392
head, pump relationships 527
heat - humidity factors 271
heat conductivity 105
heating and ventilation equipment, symbols 190
heat-power equipment, symbols 192
height above plate 155
hemlock-fir, maximum floor joist spans 110
heptagon 340
hexagons 340
    Corners, d 313
    distance across 313
    Faces, a 313
hollow - ground saw blade 628
hollow circle sector, area 343
horizontal cylinder fillage 544
horizontal pipe discharge 669
horsepower 45
    electric motor average sizes 250
    hp to torque formula 255
    needed to raise water 658
hose tables, introduction 646
house paints and finishes 291
household fixtures symbols 195
household wiring color codes 203
humidity - heat factors 271

I

IF transformer color codes 204
impedance formulas ....263 - 264
impeller velocity 527
impeller velocity, pump relationships 527
imperial wire gauge 587
insert anchors for screws 13
insert-type hollow wall toggle, plastic 16
insulation value of materials 102
insulation, electric wire classes 205
iron wire gauge 587
ISO standards 60

J

joist span maximums
    douglas fir - larch 106
    hemlock-fir 110
    redwood 122
    southern pine 118
    spruce-pine-fir 114

L

lamp and extension cord current capacities, standard 202
lift
    practical, for centrifugal pumps 523
    practical, for reciprocating pumps 525
lighting outlets, symbols 186
load 106
    dead 106
    live 106
lubricants, drill & cutting 621
lumber
    dimension 95

group classification of tree species..99
rough 93
softwood grading 93
strength of wood beams 126
surfaced 93
wood moisture content vs. strength..97
worked 93

M

M.C.M. 252
manufacturers standard gauge 584
mapping scales and areas 275
math
circles: diameter, radius, circumference, and area.....................304
circumference of a circle, chord length for dividing 300
convert angles in degrees...307
convert minutes into decimals of a degree 311
convert seconds into decimals of a degree 312
distance across squares and hexagons 313
excess stock and fillet area 316
factors for numbers from 1 to 100 319
fractions of inches - decimal equivalents....................................322
fractions of inches - millimeter equivalents.................................324
plane figure formulas 338
right triangle trig formulas 335
segments of circles 349
spheres - surface area and volume 354
triangle formulas ....336 - 337
trigonometric functions 327
maximum floor joist spans
hemlock-fir 110
redwood 122
southern pine...118
spruce-pine-fir 114
maximum horizontal roof rafter span tables
hemlock-fir 163
southern pine...168
spruce-pine-fir 172
Mercalli earthquake scale...280
metal tubing or conduit
electrical 221
electrical flexible 215
million Btu/unit 273
minimum breaking strength...560
minimum tensile stress 56
moment magnitude
earthquake scales 280
mortar coloring materials 132
mortar, factors affecting strength 133
mortar, types and mixtures 134
motor
DC, motor wiring specs 256
electric motor frame dimensions 256
how to read a motor nameplate 238
motor, electric, average sizes 250
music wire gauge (MWG) 587

N

nails
basic dimensions...358
box 358

brads...359
casing...360
common..360
concrete..363
double-headed...363
fine...364
finish..364
flooring...365
gypsum wallboard...366
joist hanger..366
masonry..367
masonry drive...367
roofing..368
rubber heel...371
shingle...371
siding...372
underlayment..372
nails, spikes and staples.......................................357
natural gas vs. other fuels, Btu.....................272 - 273
NEMA..234,239 - 240
    design letter...244
    electrical enclosures.....................................240
    electrical motor frame dimensions..................257
    motor efficiency ratings.................................243
nominal strength...567
nonagon...340
nozzles, discharge from..653
nut factor...61

O

octagon..340
Ohm's law...213
    for AC current......................................263 - 264
    for DC current..262
oils, firewood/fuel comparison................................272
OSB (oriented strand board)..................................183

P

paints and finishes...291
    automotive paints...293
    house and industrial paints............................291
    other paints...293
    wood finishes...292
parabola arc length, area.....................................343
paraboloid volume, surface area...........................347
parallelogram
    perimeter...338
parallelogram area, perimeter..............................338
parallelopiped and cube
    surface area...344
    volume...344
pennyweight..358
pentagon..340
pilot holes for wood screws...................................576
pin drive or drive nail expansion anchors.................10
    nylon body and steel nail................................11
    zinc body and steel nail.................................10
pipe discharge
    horizontal..669
    vertical...670
pipe fittings, friction loss in

plastic	508
steel	510
pipes and fittings	**385**
pipe tables, introduction	386
properties and friction loss	392
acrylonitrile-butadiene-styrene (ABS) pipe	*392*
aluminum pipe and tube	*397*
brass pipe and tube	*412*
chlorinated poly (vinyl chloride) (CPVC) pipe	*428*
copper pipe and tube	*433*
friction loss in pipe fittings	*508*
plastic pipe	508
steel pipe	510
poly(vinyl chloride) (PVC) pipe	*443*
polybutylene (PB) pipe	*451*
polyethylene (PE) pipe	*456*
steel pipe and tube	*468*
piping symbols	**193**
heating	193
plumbing	194
pitch diameter	**47**
planks	**94**
plastic pipe	**392,428,451,456**
plumbing fixtures, symbols	**196**
plywood	**183**
plywood & panel grading	**98**
polyethylene (PE) pipe	**456**
polygons, formulas and constants for	**320**
regular polygons	
area, perimeter	*340*
power factor formula, electricity	**265**
power formulas, electricity	**264**
power transformer, color codes	**203**
pressure	**527**
absolute vs gauge	530
pump relationships	527
pressure loss due to friction in 100 feet of water hose	**651**
prime number	**319**
prism	
convex surface area	345
volume	345
proof stress	**56**
pulley (sheave) selection tables	**48**
pulleys	
outside diameter vs. pitch diameter, graphic	47
pump	
cost to pump water, gas and diesel	658
horizontal pipe discharge	669
vertical pipe discharge	670
pump performance curve	**541**
pump relationships	
impeller velocity, specific gravity, head and pressure	527
pumps	**519**
affinity laws and formulas for centrifugal pumps	529
capacities of tanks and cylinders	545
centrifugal pumps	
affinity laws and formulas for	*529*
how to size	*535*
practical lift for	*523*
commonly available pumps	520
equivalents and equations for pipe flow and pumps	531
horizontal cylinder fillage	544

horsepower needed to raise water 542
how to size a centrifugal pump 535
    example *537*
practical lift for centrifugal pumps 523
practical lift for reciprocating pumps 525
pump relationships: impeller velocity, specific gravity, head, and pressure
527
pumps, commonly available **520**
centrifugal 520
reciprocating 522
rotary 521
special purpose 522

Q

Q or figure of merit formula, electricity **265**
quadrilateral, area of **338**
quantity or Q in a capacitor **266**

R

R value **105**
rafter length factor **135**
rafter length tables **135**
intermediate horizontal pan lengths 153
intermediate horizontal span lengths 153
rafter length factor 135
rise in run notation 135
roof pitch 135
roof slope 135
reactance formulas ....**263 - 264**
rebar, standard sizes and weights **132**
receptacle configurations **234**
FSL configurations 237
locking receptacles 235
marine ship to shore 237
midget locking 237
straight blade receptacles 234
travel trailer 237
reciprocating pumps **522**
reciprocating pumps, practical lift for **525**
rectangle
diagonal 338
perimeter 338
redwood, maximum floor joist spans **122**
refrigeration equipment, symbols **192**
regular hip rafter length factor **155**
remote control stations for equipment, symbols **187**
resistance formulas **262**
resistors in parallel formulas **263**
resistors in series formula **262**
resonance formulas, electricity **264**
Richter earthquake scale **280**
right cone
· volume, surface area, lateral area 346
right cylinder
volume, surface area and lateral area 345
right cylinder, frustum of
volume, surface are and lateral area 346
right pyramid
volume, surface area, base perimeter 346
right triangle trig formulas **335**
ripping saw blade **628**

rise in run notation 135,155
Roebling wire gauge 587
Romex, electric wire 205
roof area and gable rafter length factor 155
roof pitch 135,155
roof pitch tables 155
roof rafter span tables 159
roof slope 135,155
roofing materials 177,183
    guide to 177,183
    sheathing material 177
    underlayment material 177
    weight of 177
rope 183
    synthetic and natural fiber 560
        manila 560
        nylon 560
        polyester 561
        polyester/polyolefin 562
        polypropylene 563
        sisal 564
    wire, strength and weight 566
        6 strand x 19 wire 566
        6 strand x 37 wire 570
        compacted strand wire rope 569,574
rope, chain and cable 551
    cable clips for wire rope 552
    chain - strength and weight 554
    load capacity loss due to line angle 559
    strength and weight of wire rope 566
    synthetic and natural fiber rope 560
rotary pumps 521

S

SAE standards 56,58
safe load 56,58
sandpaper and abrasives 560
saw blades 625
    abrasive wheel ....
    chisel–tooth combination blade 628
    combination blade 628
    crosscut, fine–tooth, paneling 628
    depth capacity 627
    flattop–ground carbide tipped 629
    metal cutting 629
    ripping blade 628
    saber 629
    steel cutting 629
saw depth capacity at an angle 627
saws 627
schedule numbers 507
screws ....
    drive styles 580
    sheet metal screw specs 579
    wood, hole sizes for 576
        82° countersink diameter 577
    woood, hole sizes for ....
        shank clearance holes 577
screws, wood 575
seat cut 155
seat cut height 155
secant 327

segment of a circle..342
select and finish materials..94
self inductance formulas, electricity..................................266
self-drilling gypsum wallboard anchors, zinc or plastic 17
shank clearance holes...577
sheathing materials...177,183
sheet metal and wire gauges...581
   galvanized steel sheet, weights of..............................583
   steel plate sizes...583
   steel sheet gauges, standard......................................584
   wire gauges, standard...587
shop and factory lumber 93
signaling systems, symbols
   non-residential..188
   residential..327
sine...188
sine wave voltage and current...265
slabs...131
snow loads..176
softwood lumber
   grading..93
   sizes..92
solder alloys, hard and soft...676
solder fluxes...676
solvents...294
sound intensity..274
   formula...274
southern pine
   maximum floor joist spans..118
   maximum horizontal roof rafter span...........................168
special purpose pumps..522
specific gravity..527
speed of sound..268
speed ratio..45
sphere, volume, surface area..354
   formulas..347
spheroid, volume of...348
spikes
   common..373
   gutter...373
   round..374
spruce-pine-fir
   maximum floor joist spans..114
   maximum roof rafter span tables.................................172
squares...340
   corners, d...313
   distance across...313
   faces, a..313
standard dry torque...63
   coarse inch-threaded carbon steel bolts.......................63
   coarse metric-threaded carbon steel bolts....................73
   coarse-threaded non-ferrous and stainless steel bolts....81
      18-8 stainless steel..83
      316 stainless steel..83
      aluminum...81
      monel..84
      nylon 6/6...81
      silicone bronze..82
      yellow brass..82
   fine inch-threaded carbon steel bolts............................68
staples
   cohered flat top crown..374

electrical 375
fence 376
flat top crown 376
poultry net 382
preformed 384
preformed hoop 382
round or "v" crown 383
steel 583
bolt & screw grades, types & classes 56
cold rolled steel sheet, weight of 582
galvanized steel sheet, weight of 583
standard steel reinforcing bar 132
standard steel sheet gauges ....
steel plate sizes 584
tempering color for 583
steel bolt & screw grades, types & classes 677
inch series - SAE Standards 56
metric series - SAE standards 56
steel cutting saw blade 58
steel pipe and tube 629
stereo - audio channel color codes 468
stockpile volume and weight 203
stress, proof 690
susceptance formulas, electricity 56
switch outlets, symbols 264
synchronous belts 189
....42

T

tangent 327
tank volumes 544
tap drills
inch threads 592
metric threads 599
temperature conversion formulas 278
temperature, Fahrenheit to Centigrade 277
tempering color for steel 677
thread penetration 592
timbers 94
tools 591
american standard taper pipe 623
drill and cutting lubricants 621
drill size and american wire gauge 609
drill speeds vs. materials 622
saber saw blades 629
sandpaper and abrasives 625
saws 627
tap drills
for inch series threads 592
for metric threads 599
torque coefficient 61
torque to horsepower formula 255
torque, approximate required
example 80
trapezium, area, perimeter 339
trapezoid, area, perimeter 338
triangle, equilateral 340
triangle, equilateral, area and perimeter 339
triangle, right triangle trig formulas 335
tubing or conduit, electrical
flexible metal 215
metal 221
nonmetallic 227